RELIGION AND MAN

RELIGION AND MAN AN INTRODUCTION

W. RICHARD COMSTOCK, General Editor
University of California at Santa Barbara

ROBERT D. BAIRD
University of Iowa

ALFRED BLOOM
University of Hawaii

JANET K. O'DEA
University of California at Santa Barbara

THOMAS F. O'DEA
University of California at Santa Barbara

CHARLES J. ADAMS
McGill University

Harper & Row, Publishers
New York, Evanston, San Francisco, London

RELIGION AND MAN: AN INTRODUCTION

Copyright ©1971 by Harper & Row, Publishers, Inc.

Standard Book Number: 06-041337-9

Library of Congress Catalog Card Number: 79-141175

PREFACE

As an *introduction* to the study of religion, this book does not seek to overwhelm the student with an encyclopedic array of information. Rather it is selective and tries to help the student see what is to be studied *first,* as well as indicate the areas for later advanced investigation.

Since the reader we have in mind is a college student with a limited religious background, the first thing he needs to acquire is familiarization with the basic details of religious phenomena as social and historic facts appearing in human culture. We have attempted to provide a survey and sketch of religious systems of symbol and ritual as they have appeared in primitive societies and present-day civilizations.

It is also our conviction that an introduction to the study of religion should emphasize religion as a *discipline of study.* Thus we have been concerned not only with content but also with method. The beginning student of religion often finds it especially difficult to find the proper approach to his study because religion is still to many primarily a personal concern. The instructor therefore has the task of helping the student to develop a set of methodological attitudes that will enable him to study religion in a scholarly manner, whatever his personal feelings about it may be.

We have attempted to encourage the student's awareness of the issues involved in the study of religious phenomena. We seek to instill in him a sense of participation in the methodological problems that have been encountered by scholars in the study of religion and the various solutions that have been proposed. In other words we want the student to learn how to think about religion as well as to amass a number of facts about it.

In this connection no attempt has been made by the various contributors to this volume to achieve complete uniformity on every issue. Thus, for example, slightly different definitions of religion will be found in each section. It is hoped that these divergences will encourage in the reader a sense of the complexity of the issues involved in the study of religion and the way in which diverse approaches can be equally productive if they are pursued with vigor and care. We are anxious to impart to the beginning student the desirability of a scholarly approach to the study of religion and have therefore tried to avoid imposing on him the details of a single orientation as the only viable one. If this volume communicates to the student some sense of the importance of religion as an intellectual discipline and some sense of the problems involved in its pursuit, it has succeeded in its purpose.

The editor and contributors to this volume wish to express their appreciation to the staff of Harper & Row, particularly to Walter Lippincott for his encouragement of this project in all stages of its growth and to Mrs. Leslie Carola and Mrs. Carol Cutler for the patience, energy, and creativity with which they have guided our work to completion.

W. Richard Comstock

A NOTE ON TRANSLITERATION
The simplest English transliterations of Sanskrit, Pali, Chinese, Japanese, and Arabic terms, without diacritical marks, have been used in the text to make reading easier for the student unfamiliar with these languages. The more linguistically correct forms, with diacritics, can be found in the Glossary at the end of the text.

CONTENTS

RELIGION AND MAN

PART ONE

THE STUDY OF RELIGION AND PRIMITIVE RELIGIONS
W. RICHARD COMSTOCK

APPROACHES
TO THE STUDY
OF RELIGION

Religion reveals a fascinating panorama of variegated forms. A tribal man lifts his hands in ecstatic celebration of the sun as the giver of warmth and light; another seeks a spell whereby his wife may be cured of an illness caused by a witch. In India, a holy man sits as he has sat for many years in unmoving contemplation of the Nameless Reality that is his own self; another seeks to use the power of "soul force" to change traditional social patterns that have caused unnecessary misery to his people. In China, a nobleman meditates on the "way" of the universe and seeks to conform to its rhythms in his own being. In Japan, after many years of preparation, an aspirant experiences the moment of Zen enlightenment. In the West, a rabbi meditates on the "law" of God; a congregation gathers on Easter morning to reaffirm the resurrection of its Lord; pilgrims fulfill a vow by making their way to Mecca.

Celebration, despair, ethical vigor, mystic retreat, social activism, monastic quietude, contemplation, animal sacrifice, rituals involving pain and terror, images of hope, symbols of fear, the affirmation of life and the struggle against death, creative growth, unthinking superstition—all these are included in the phenomenon that we call religion. Can such a protean phenomenon be studied according to careful methods that will provide reliable knowledge? At first glance, imposing obstacles seem to stand in the way of such a project.

First, the prospective student may be overwhelmed by the sheer enormity of the subject. The study of religion encompasses a geographical spread that includes Eurasia, Africa, Australia, the South Sea Islands, and the Americas, as well as a temporal spread that begins in the dim paleolithic past and reaches down to the present state of creative flux. Finally, there is a qualitative diversity among the kinds of phenomena that we tend to call religion within a single geographical area at a given segment of time. Religion can refer to subjective experiences like feelings of sacred awe or mystical visions; social facts like the existence of Christian churches and Buddhist congregations called the *sangha;* symbolic systems (communication systems of signs) that include forms like the cross and the swastika as well as beliefs expressed in various theologies and philosophies of religion; ritual acts like a sacred dance or the performance of an ablutionary rite; ethical norms and prescriptions for desired behavior; ideals for a more humane life in this world; techniques for obtaining happiness in another world. The list of religious forms seems almost endless.

Further perplexities are generated by the way that public acts and practices are intertwined with the private emotions, subjective meanings, and personal interpretations of those participating in the acts. Religion seems to mean so many different things to people in different parts of the world. How can we ever hope to capture these meanings in conceptual formulas that will be understandable and acceptable to all concerned?

In the past few centuries scholars from a number of fields—psychology, sociology, anthropology, and history—have studied the phenomena of religion in ways that have led to impressive results. They have produced a body of empirical descriptions of the religions of the world that have increased our knowledge of what the members of the world's religions think and do. Furthermore, these scholars have worked out a number of methods for the study of religion that offer ways of overcoming the difficulties we have noted. In Part 1 of this book we propose to consider ways of studying religion that have been found to be especially rewarding.

The first task in the study of religion is to learn how to ask the right questions. We can only obtain good answers to questions that have been properly formed, because the form of the question determines the kind of answer given. The well-known question "When did you stop beating your wife?" is difficult for some men to answer because the question already prescribes the range of possible answers and prevents the party in question from denying that he has ever beaten his wife at all. In the study of religion one needs to learn how to ask questions that lead to fruitful results and to avoid questions that are unproductive.

The American philosopher George Santayana once observed that those who do not know history are doomed to repeat its errors. This point has its application in the area that we are considering. Scholars who have studied religion in the nineteenth and twentieth centuries have asked a number of questions about religion and have found some of them to be more fruitful than others. Many of these questions will also occur to a student beginning his study of this complex subject. In this connection a preliminary survey of the work that has already been accomplished in this field can be extremely useful. If we see what questions have already been considered and why some of them have proved to be more useful than others, it may save a lot of time and start us on a fruitful course of study.

In the nineteenth and early twentieth centuries great progress was made in the development of sociology and anthropology. Many of the pioneers in these fields devoted a great deal of attention to religion, because they found that religion played a significant role in the various societies that they studied. Without knowledge of the place of religion in human society, any account of how a society was formed and operated proved to be incomplete. During this period the field of psychology also made great strides and a similar situation regarding religion was encountered. Whatever the personal attitudes of the investigator toward religion might be, he found that religious ideas and motives operated in the psychology of the people he studied and had to be included in any full account of the springs of their behavior.

The pioneers in these fields provided accounts of religion that are still useful, though they must be qualified in the light of more recent and exact information. If we summarize in a very general way one common feature of these approaches, we can recognize that they tended to be interested in the question of the "origin" of religion. Although they differed among themselves as to the exact answer, they agreed at the methodological level that this was a proper and rewarding question to ask.

In the nineteenth century many anthropologists, classical scholars, and philologists advocated an approach to religion that was called the nature-myth school. According to this school the great symbols of the world's religions were personifications of natural phenomena: the sun, moon, stars, storms, the seasons of the year. Advocates of this approach argued among themselves about which force of nature was primary in the concerns of early religion. One branch maintained that solar myths were most important and that primitive rituals and myths were primarily concerned with man's relation to the sun. Max Müller (1823–1900), a philologist who did pioneer work in the study of Indo-European languages, advocated this approach. He developed the method of "comparative religion" and tried to show how nature myths operated in both European religions and the religions of India.

One of the great pioneers in the field of anthropology is Edward Tylor (1832–1917). Tylor argued that religion had its origin in the belief in immaterial souls that might inhabit objects like stones, trees, animals, or human bodies, but which also could exist independently of them. He coined the word *animism* (after the Greek word *anima*, "soul") to refer to the belief in the existence of such transempirical souls or spirits. Tylor further argued that the origin of this belief was probably in dreams. For example, a man may dream of a friend who has recently died. In the dream the man seems to continue to exist as a soul independent of his physical body. Through dream experiences, man thus became convinced of the ex-

A shaman's painted leather leggings, probably from the Tshimshian tribe. (Courtesy of the American Museum of Natural History.)

istence of a realm of spirit entities which are the basis of religious beliefs.

The philosopher Herbert Spencer (1820–1903) offered a similar theory with some variations. Spencer found the origin of religion in the respect given to ancestors combined with the belief in ghosts caused by dream experiences. Spencer held that man makes the ghosts of his ancestors into gods. Thus "ancestor-worship is the root of every religion." This theory is sometimes called euhemerism after a fourth century B.C. thinker named Euhemerus who argued that the gods of religion were originally living men of great power and authority who were raised to the status of divine beings.

James Frazer (1854–1941) was a classical scholar who collected a great deal of material on religion and wrote a very influential study in many volumes called *The Golden Bough*. Frazer argued that religion developed out of an original magical stage of human culture. Frazer saw the primitive magician as a person who wants to know how the universe operates and how it can be controlled for human purposes. According to Frazer, the magician mistakes superficial relations between objects for the real underlying causal relations between them discovered by the modern scientist. Nevertheless, the magician is like the modern scientist in his desire to understand how phenomena can be understood and controlled. The magician is simply a primitive scientist who has made mistakes due to insufficient knowledge and techniques. Frazer held that magic and religion are distinct phenomena though related through a process of historical development. The magician believes that phenomena can be controlled through magic spells. The religious man believes in the existence of spirits that must be placated and cajoled by prayers, rather than controlled directly through a magic formula. Nevertheless, the religionist is like the magician in that both seek to explain how the natural world works.

The theories advanced by Tylor, Spencer, and Frazer assume that religion is primarily an attempt to answer questions about the world that are similar in kind to those asked by a modern scientist. The primitive religionist has made a hypothesis on the basis of insufficient evidence. Nevertheless, his beliefs are products of thought though they have reached erroneous conclusions. According to this view, religion has its origin in an intellectual mistake.

These theories stressing an intellectual origin were soon opposed by another group of theories that stressed the emotional aspects of religion. Tylor and Frazer were not unaware of this feature, but other anthropologists insisted more emphatically that it was in the emotions that the origins of religion are to be found. Thus R. R. Marett (1866–1943) argued that religion is not so much an intellectual endeavor as a set of profound emotional responses to various aspects of human existence.

Wilhelm Wundt (1832–1920), a psychologist, argued that in religion emotions like fear "are projected outward into the environment." A philosopher, Rudolf Otto (1869–1937), wrote an influential book called the *Idea of the Holy*. Otto did not mean "idea" in an intellectualist sense. He was rather referring to a form of perception (in the sense meant by Immanuel Kant) which he called the "numinous" and which was characterized by affective tones of the awesome, the mysterious, and the fascinating. Otto did not call the numinous an emotion, but other investigators have adapted his analysis to the thesis that a distinctive emotion conveying a sense of the mysterious, the uncanny, and the sacred is the basis of religion. Others, like William James (1842–1910), have denied that there is a distinctive religious emotion as such, but they have believed that religion has its origins in profound emotional experiences related to beliefs in spirits, gods, and a supernatural world.

These early theories about the origins of religion assumed two forms. At one level, the question of origins dealt with certain structural constants in human psychology that were alleged to be the cause of the rise of religion in human life and culture. The intellectual theories argued that man's mind is such that he inevitably tries out magical or religious hypotheses about the nature of the world and then turns to science when greater knowledge and more sophisticated methods of investigation are finally at his disposal. In similar fashion, emotional theories aver that human psychology is such that certain emotional responses and needs lead to religious practices as expressions of those emotions.

However, at another level, the question about origins is a historical one that looks for the form of religion as it actually appeared in the human past. In the eighteenth century Charles de Brosses

(1709–1777) argued that the first form of religion was fetishism (the worship of inanimate objects like stones, and animate objects like trees and animals). Tylor believed that the first form was animism, or the belief in "souls" distinct from the material objects that the souls might inhabit. Frazer believed that a magic stage preceded the animistic one.

R. R. Marett did a great deal to popularize the view that the stage of animism was preceded by a stage in which primitive man believed in the existence of a general power or force that pervaded both inanimate and animate objects. He was influenced in this point by the work of Robert Henry Codrington (1830–1922), a missionary who had pointed out how the Melanesians referred to "mana" as a kind of power which could produce extraordinary occurrences in nature and also enable man to perform acts beyond his normal capacity. Other primitive tribes have similar conceptions. Among the American Indians, the Sioux refer to "wakenda," the Iroquois to "orenda," and the Algonquin to "manitu" in ways similar to the Melanesian "mana." Marett argued that the belief in mana probably preceded the belief in specific souls that operated at the animistic stage.

A popular evolutionary scheme imposed on these foundations held that religion then developed from the stage of animism (perhaps preceded by a stage of fetishism, magic, or belief in mana) to polytheism, or the belief in souls that have assumed the shape and power of independent gods; this in turn was followed by a henotheistic stage in which one god is held to be more powerful than the others, and finally a monotheistic stage emerges in which one god only is believed to exist and possess absolute power.

On the other hand, Wilhelm Schmidt (1868–1954) and Andrew Lang (1844–1912) argued independently that this scheme distorted the actual facts because it can be shown that belief in a high god or supreme being (the characteristic of monotheism) is by no means a late development. They argued that primitive societies possessing the most simple and rudimentary technology disclose the belief in high gods and often in a supreme God who is the creator of the world. Schmidt thus argued for a scheme of development beginning with a primordial monotheism that later changed (i.e., either developed or degenerated, according to one's point of view) into polytheism, animism, and magic.

Schmidt's view did not gain wide acceptance at the time, but a later generation of investigators has accepted the validity of a great deal of his data about the existence of the belief in high gods in very primitive cultures. Thus Schmidt has shown that an evolutionary scheme based on the supposed existence of some original stage of pure animism, magic, and polytheism is not supported by our present knowledge. No such stage has been found. But neither has a stage of original monotheism been uncovered. All of these evolutionary schemes have remained as speculative hypotheses that can neither be proved or disproved. In any known culture, whether primitive or modern, we find all or most of these elements existing side by side. No method has yet been worked out whereby we can decide on the temporal priority of some of them to others.

We have seen how one group of early theories about religion can be divided between the intellectual and emotional approaches. Another group of theories about the origin of religion can be similarly divided into sociological and psychological approaches.

Emile Durkheim (1858–1917), one of the pioneers in the development of sociology as a scientific discipline, is a representative of the former. In a still useful book entitled *The Elementary Forms of the Religious Life,* Durkheim argued that religious systems of thought and behavior are so pervasive in human culture that it is difficult to believe that they are simply the result of an intellectual mistake or that they deal with purely imaginary concerns. Durkheim believed that, on the contrary, the religions of man deal with a very real empirical object. That object is human society which exists on the concrete plane of human experience as the web of human relations, imposing on each individual man rules of conduct that determine the shape of his social life. Society thus confronts the individual as a force that requires man to behave in ways that often go against his personal inclinations. Nevertheless, since man is a social creature, he finds that he must integrate his personal life into the larger life of the community as a whole. Durkheim argued that religion is one of the ways in which man accomplishes this socialization process. The symbols of religion appear to their users to be about a realm of supernatural powers and forces. They are really about society and its claims on the individual. The laws of a god are really the most crucial laws of a given society.

Durkheim then tied this social theory of religion to a particular theory about the historical origins of religion. Durkheim was intrigued by the phenomenon of totemism, i.e., the practice of taking a particular natural object or animal and making it into the symbol (or totem) of a particular social group called a clan. Durkheim believed that in totemism the social nature of religion as well as its social origin was clearly demonstrated. The totem figures clearly represented social groups and at the same time led to the belief in distinctive gods and spirits ruling over men.

On the other hand, Sigmund Freud (1856–1939) is an influential representative of theories of religion that emphasize psychological factors. Freud argued that the origin of religion can be found in the problems of the child seeking to work out adequate relationships with his parents, particularly his father. At first the child considers his father to be a figure of absolute power. When he learns that his father is human—all too human—with definite limitations to both his benevolence and his power, the youth feels deprived of the psychological support and security he felt as a small child. He therefore projects onto the universe a belief in a cosmic father or god who can continue to give him the support he once had from his human father.

Freud also gave this theory a historical form. He suggested that primitive man originally existed in patriarchal societies where the father-leader kept all desirable females to himself. At some point the sons rebelled, killed the father, and took his women as their own wives. However, this primal act and its ensuing guilt are the psychological cause of belief in a father-god whose wrath has to be placated through sacrifice.

Another equally speculative theory opposing this one was advanced by writers like Johann Bachofen (1815–1887). Bachofen argued that matriarchal societies preceded patriarchal ones and that the first form of religion was worship of mother figures. Father-gods then supplanted the goddesses of primordial antiquity as men wrested the control of society from its matriarchal leaders. Although such a theory is of special interest to literary people, anthropologists have not been able to establish the existence of a primal stage in which only female divinities were worshiped.

It is not necessary here to provide a detailed analysis of the strengths and weaknesses of these various theories. The point for the beginning student of religion to recognize is that all of them remain at the level of speculative hypotheses which have neither been proved nor disproved, since there is no method presently available whereby we can uncover and demonstrate the existence of a stage in human culture where only fetishism, animism, belief in mana, totemism, or a belief in high gods exists. The occurrence of some primal act like Freud's belief in the murder of the father-patriarch has never been demonstrated as a historical fact. What can be studied as social facts are primitive and modern cultures in which religious forms already operate with all or some of these factors in dynamic interaction. It is impossible to say which of them is primary or the origin of the others.

By the same token, no method has yet been devised whereby we can isolate the one factor in the human make-up that can clearly be designated as the single source of man's religious activity. In any existing religious form we can detect elements of thought and feeling, belief and emotion, psychological and social factors, that are inextricably connected. The quest for origins forces us to simplify and distort these very complex phenomena. Each of these theories contains some true insights into how a particular religious form operates. No one of them alone seems to give the basic principle on which all the other aspects of religious activity are based.

For these reasons, the next generation of scholars producing important work in the twentieth century has largely abandoned the quest for the origins of religion. It is not that the questions raised are not interesting or important. On the contrary, much of the material considered by the scholars we have just surveyed remains useful. However, the method of approach has changed. The quest for origins has been superseded by a quest for more adequate description. A different question is now being asked. Instead of asking, "What is the origin of religion?" scholars now tend to ask: "How does religion function?" "What is it like?" "What does it do for the individual or for his society?"

In other words, a more empirical approach to religion is now being adopted. The question as to how religion originated is a speculative question, difficult to answer in a scientific way. But the fact remains that religion does exist as a very concrete factor in human experience and behavior. May it not be more fruitful to accept it as a "given" which it is our task to examine according to the best analytical tools and methods of accurate description that can be devised?

In the twentieth century investigators of religion in a variety of disciplines have turned in the main from the question of the origins of religion to the question of the description of religion. Instead of asking what the ultimate cause of religion is, they now ask what religion as it presently exists is like.

THE QUESTION OF THE DESCRIPTION OF RELIGION

This new question involves the investigator in certain problems of method. What is it that he is studying? We may answer, religious phenomena or facts. But then we must decide what is the proper method for studying a religious fact. Contemporary scholars tend to approach this problem in two related ways. First of all, in studying religion we are studying things that men *do*. In their society and in their personal life they behave in certain ways and make certain things that we characterize as religious. The study of religion has therefore a concrete observable content: specific kinds of human behavior called religious. It is this situation that makes religion susceptible to careful study according to the methods of scholars and scientists. Religion may or may not be about something superempirical that transcends human life. Religion is not itself that superempirical reality. It is a human phenomenon—something that men do—which can be observed and carefully described.

Second, since these acts are human acts, they involve a characteristic that is not present in the realm of inanimate physical objects. This characteristic is the element of symbolism and meaning. Human actions mean something, both to the person performing the action and to those responding to his action. Therefore, in the description of any human action, it is never sufficient to describe the surface details of the action as they appear to sense observation. We must also include a description of what the action means to the one performing it.

For example, suppose that we observe a man stretching his hands out in front of his face. It is not enough to record the physical movements involved. A full account must include the meaning of that act. Perhaps the man is shielding his face from the sun. Perhaps he is warding off some external object, like a shrub or an insect. Perhaps he is invoking a god in a religious rite. Perhaps he is greeting a friend, according to the custom of his particular society. Such considerations of meaning must be included in any complete description of the act in question.

Contemporary scholars of religion have become increasingly aware of these factors. Therefore the question of adequate religious descriptions has taken two dominant forms. One, many psychologists and sociologists ask functional questions. In a given religious act, what is man doing? What does the religious symbol or rite do for him or for his society? What kinds of problems does it solve for him?

Two, many students of human language and culture ask hermeneutical questions. What does a given religious symbol mean? How is a practice to be interpreted? What is its significance in the society where it is used?

Functional and hermeneutical approaches are not mutually exclusive. On the contrary, most scholars at the present time ask questions about religion in which both are involved. Indeed, in the final analysis, they are really two aspects of the same approach. Furthermore, the observation of a fact requires an observer. An observer, in turn, must look at his material from a particular point of observation, which we can call a vantage point or perspective. What we are able to see in any given case depends on the perspective from which we choose to observe it. Functional and hermeneutical approaches must thus face this problem of perspectives.

This leads us to the perplexing problem of cultural perspectives. The observer of a given religious phenomenon is often looking at it from outside of the specific cultural perspective adopted by those performing the particular rite or adopting the particular symbol in question. Some scholars have consequently wondered if the observer can describe the phenomenon in a way that truly captures what it means to the participants. This is a serious problem presently being discussed by philosophers. However, one point should be stressed. The difficulty should not be associated with the perplexing problem of how an observer can appreciate the inner subjective experiences of another person. The student of religion is not studying the subjectivity of other people directly. Rather he is studying their objective acts and symbols which are observable. His task is one of hermeneutics, i.e., how to interpret the meanings that are meant to be conveyed by these acts and symbols. This task is difficult, but not nearly so difficult as somehow getting "inside" the mind of the other. The latter is not necessary. All that is required is that the student make a fair interpretation of the other's meaning as indicated in his overt expressions and acts. This is possible because man's symbolic acts can be interpreted when put into a proper context, just as we can understand what is meant by a handshake if we know something of the cultural context of rules and customs in which it occurs.

Perhaps a story will illustrate the kind of situation meant and the problems that it poses. Two men were having a religious discussion. One man asked: "Do you believe in infant baptism?" The other replied: "Believe in it? I've actually seen it!" The humor in this story depends on a deliberate confusion of perspectives. The second man had adopted the perspective of physical observation. What has he seen? A man applying water to an infant in the presence of some other persons. But the first man asked his question from a different perspective. He assumes knowledge of the physical act, but wants to know if his friend also viewed the fact from a perspective of certain religious meanings, i.e., that this act had included the child in a specific community (the church), that the members of the church believe it to be part of a divine plan ordained by God. The observer does not himself have to believe in the claims made from that perspective. Nevertheless, to describe what has happened, he must be aware of the perspective and include it in his account of the meaning.

So far we have considered in a general way the contemporary approach to religion through a concern with the description of religious acts and meanings. However, such categories—religious acts and meanings—are still too broad in their scope. The student of religion must learn how to adopt a narrower methodological perspective from which specific questions about religion can be asked and answered. At the present time we can distinguish in the voluminous studies of religion by contemporary scholars at least five basic methodological perspectives.

METHODOLOGICAL PERSPECTIVES

First is the *psychological* perspective. Each individual man has personal problems involving the way that he handles his various "drives"—his need for sexual satisfaction, friendship, acceptance by his peers, prestige and power, a sense that his life has importance and value. Psychologists have examined how religious symbols and practices aid or impede the individual in working out these problems.

Within the field of contemporary psychology a number of different schools exist and the approach to religion is partly determined by the psychological presuppositions that are held. Freud interpreted religion primarily as a neurotic solution to feelings of infantile dependency. However, even those disagreeing with Freud on this point find in his work a mine of valuable materials about how religion operates in human attempts to solve problems in the relation of a man to his father, mother, and other authority figures.

Carl Jung (1875–1961) disagreed with Freud's estimation of religion and argued that man had a need to find "meaning" in his life which often assumed a religious form. He also investigated archetypal symbols that appeared in human dreams and which were similar to symbols appearing in the world's religions. Jung believed that these symbols often aided the individual in working out problems concerning the integration of his personality. Other psychologists, from other points of view, have also stressed the role religion plays in finding a meaning for life. Erik Erikson (1902–   ) has done impressive work in showing how the quest for personal identity is often worked out in a religious way.

A second perspective is the *sociological* one. Sociologists have made the basic unit of their study not the individual personality but the network of relations among people binding them together in cohesive groups called societies. They have studied how religion operates at the social level to solve a number of related problems. First, a given religion may itself possess a social structure that must be maintained from generation to generation. Then, too, the religion may operate in the larger structure of some social unit like the tribe or nation and help or impede that society in maintaining its social existence. Finally, a given religion may help or impede the individual in integrating his personal life into the larger life of the society of which he is a part.

Social anthropologists have made important contributions to the study of how religion operates in human society, particularly in primitive (or preliterate) societies. These anthropologists illustrate in an exceptionally striking manner the transition from the quest for religious origins to the quest for religious descriptions that we have noted. The scholars who worked out early theories of origins—men like Tylor and Frazer—depended on reports from missionaries, travelers, and colonial administrators. They did not themselves observe the cultures that they described. Anthropology developed as a scientific discipline by stressing the need for field work and firsthand observations of the cultures being studied. One pioneer in developing adequate techniques of observation and description was Bronislaw Malinowski (1884–1942), whose studies of religious activities (among many other dimensions of human culture) in the Trobriander Islands are still very valuable. A. R. Radcliffe-Brown (1881–1955) has made important contributions to methodological theory. He developed a structural approach (which should be distinguished from the "structuralism" of Claude Lévi-Strauss, considered in a later chapter). Radcliffe-Brown argued that a society should not be considered as a mere aggregate or collection of people who happen to be together. Rather a society exhibits a social structure delineating the way the behavior of people is "connected by a definite set of social relations into an integrated whole." [1] The study of a given society is the study of the totality of its interacting parts, of how family relations, legal forms, political structures, religious practices, artistic expressions, mores, and customs contribute to the successful functioning of social life as a whole. Thus:

> The function of culture as a whole is to unite individual human beings into more or less stable social structures, i.e., stable systems of groups determining and regulating the relation of those individuals to one another, and providing such external adaptation to the physical environment, and such internal adaptation between the component individuals or groups, as to make possible an ordered social life. [2]

This general structural approach leads to a functional method in the study of religion as with all other social forms as well. A functional method does not ask what religion is or what its origins are. It rather asks, what is the function of religion in the social complex of which it is a part? How does religion contribute to social integration? According to this method, one can also ask questions about

1. Quoted in E. E. Evans-Pritchard, *Social Anthropology*, New York, Cohen & West, 1954, p. 54. See bibliography for works on structuralism in sociology.
2. Quoted in ibid., p. 55.

negative function (or dysfunction), i.e., how does religion at times contribute to social disintegration and conflict?

Radcliffe-Brown's theory is one influential approach among many that have been developed by anthropologists and sociologists. Pioneers in the development of sociology like Emile Durkheim and Max Weber (1864–1920) have produced valuable studies of the way religion operates in society. Talcott Parsons (1902–   ) has developed a general scheme of a human action system. According to this scheme, man performs his acts within four subsystems. First is the cultural system of meanings, intentions, norms, and patterns of human behavior; second is the social system, which deals with the patterns of interaction and order among social groups; third is the personality system, which deals with the individual goals of the members of a society; fourth is the organic system directed to the biological needs. Parsons then distinguishes in addition two "environments" in which human action takes place. One is the realm of physical nature; the other is the realm of "ultimate reality." Here Parsons is not making the claim that such a realm necessarily exists; he is rather pointing out that man in society does, in fact, usually fashion his patterns of concrete behavior in such a way that they are validated through reference to ultimate principles that often take a religious form.

According to Parsons, "the cultural system structures commitments vis-à-vis ultimate reality into meaningful orientations toward the rest of the environment and the organismic system similarly adapts itself and the other systems to the physical environment." [3] Religions can then be studied according to the way they operate (or function) in this system of human action.

A third methodological approach to religion is a *historical* one. Psychological and sociological approaches tend to be ahistorical in the sense that they are primarily interested in examining how a religion functions at a given period of time for the human individual or in the society of which he is a part. However, man also exists in a human world that has gone through a series of transformations in time. Historians therefore study the behavior of man through the sequence of events by which various forms of life have come into being and others have passed away. While the historian does not look for ultimate origins, he is interested not only in what presently exists, but in the historical process by which existing forms have assumed their present shape.

It is useful then to consider a given religion as a specific tradition of beliefs and practices that has gone through a complex course of development and transformation. We can apply the methods of historiography to that religion and provide as accurate and thorough an account as is possible of what this historical development has been like.

So far as religion is concerned, this requires the efforts of historians trained in the collection and interpretation of documents that

3. Talcott Parsons, *Societies,* Englewood Cliffs, N.J., Prentice-Hall, 1966, p. 9.

reveal the past history of civilizations. It also involves the work of scholars primarily concerned with languages, classicists and orientalists who can read the documents and artifacts of ancient cultures with facility and understanding. Linguists and philologists make important contributions as do archeologists who interpret cultural artifacts as well as written documents.

It is obvious that the history of religions encompasses a very wide field. Many historians of religion are specialists in a single area, like the history of Indian religions or the religions of Greece and Rome. Others, like Raffaele Pettazzoni (1883–1960), seek to develop a comprehensive knowledge of the entire field. The "History of Religions" school at Chicago, represented by Mircea Eliade (1907–   ) and others, seeks to be faithful to religious phenomena in their full complexity.

The fourth methodological approach to religion is a *form-comparative* one. By a religious form we mean a specific religious phenomenon that reveals a distinctive structure of its own and which is capable of being compared or contrasted with others. This form might be a specific myth, like a certain story of how the world came into being; it might be a specific rite, like a form of animal sacrifice; it might be a specific religious functionary, like a shaman or a priest. The comparative approach first examines this form in one specific religious tradition and then compares it with what appear to be similar forms in other religious traditions. The difficulty in this perspective is how to decide when a similarity of form indicates an important relationship between the forms and when it is a superficial and essentially trivial resemblance. Scholars warn against a simplistic use of the comparative method that will obscure the concrete differences existing between the religion of one culture or historical tradition and another very different one.

Nevertheless, when applied cautiously, the method can be useful. Many scholars interested in comparative matters have been influenced by the philosophy of phenomenology developed by Edmund Husserl (1859–1938). Without accepting this philosophy as a whole, some students of religion have used its techniques to isolate specific "phenomena" of religion according to their essential forms. The "forms" are then studied in a comparative manner as they appear in various cultures. Important work using this approach has been done by Gerardus van der Leeuw (1890–1950) in his *Religion in Essence and Manifestation.* Although he was not a phenomenologist, Rudolf Otto's work is often cited as an example of the approach. For example, Otto's attempt to isolate a distinctive form of consciousness called the numinous is an example of how a specific "phenomenon" can be distinguished and then studied as it "appears" in a variety of cultures.

A fifth perspective is already involved in the other perspectives we have noted. However, it is so important that it merits a separate designation of its own. In a general way, we can characterize it as the hermeneutical or semiological approach. It includes a number of approaches to religion that disagree among themselves but which are united by a common interest in religions as systems of symbols, as kinds of languages that impart meanings which must be interpreted. Here scholars from a number of fields have made distinctive contributions.

For example, psychologists have been impressed by the way that man expresses his dilemmas through symbols. Thus Freud discovered that in his dreams the individual was actually expressing problems of personal and social adjustment through complex dream imagery. Jung developed the theory that dreams revealed archetypal forms (like the great mother or the venerable father) that also appeared in the great religions of the world.

Sociologists and anthropologists have similarly emphasized the importance of studying culture through its expression in symbols. Thus Max Weber approached societies as "systems of meaning" which must be interpreted through a method he called *verstehen*. E. E. Evans-Pritchard (1902–   ) declares that "social anthropology studies societies as moral, or symbolic, systems and not as natural systems . . . it is less interested in process than in design." [4]

Philosophers like Ernst Cassirer (1874–1945) and Susanne Langer (1895–   ) have studied human cultures as the media through which symbolic forms are expressed and which it is the task of the student to interpret. Cassirer was less interested in individual forms, like a specific myth, than in general symbolic structures, like a mythic form of thought, through which particular myths are presented.

In recent years the interest in symbolism has assumed a highly technical form. A French anthropologist, Claude Lévi-Strauss (1908–   ), has expounded the method of structuralism (to be distinguished from Radcliffe-Brown's use of the term). Lévi-Strauss's theory applies to human culture as a whole, but it has particular significance for the study of religion. Lévi-Strauss believes that religious myths and rituals are not the expression of blind emotions and undisciplined imagination. On the contrary, according to him they exhibit patterns and structures that possess logical order and precise relationships among the parts (this theory is dealt with in the discussion of symbolic expression in a later chapter).

These five methodological perspectives—the psychological, sociological, historical, comparative, and hermeneutical—provide useful ways to consider religion. In the following chapters we will consider a number of examples from the religions of tribal societies in which the combinations of these approaches, interacting with one another, help us to understand what is happening in typical religious acts.

4. Evans-Pritchard, op. cit., p. 62.

TOWARD
A DEFINITION
OF RELIGION

In discussing the nature of time, the Christian theologian Augustine once observed: "If you do not ask me what time is, I know; if you ask me I do not know." We may feel in a similar situation concerning the question, "What is religion?"

In the last chapter we considered how scholars have turned from the question of the origins of religion to the question of how it can be described. However, if the task of description does not require an answer to the problem of origins, does it not at least require a definition? Must we not define the kind of subject matter that we are attempting to study, before we can study it?

Max Weber answered this question in the negative. He declared: "To define 'religion,' to say what it *is* is not possible at the start of a presentation. . . . Definition can be attempted, if at all, only at the conclusion of the study." [1] There is some force to his position. How can we provide a comprehensive and conclusive definition of what religion is until we have examined and become familiar with the subject matter in depth and detail? Will not a premature definition based on insufficient evidence cause us to miss certain features of the phenomena that we may not have specified in our original formula? On the other hand, is it not true that we must have some idea of what it is we are studying in order to begin our investigation? Here then is an intriguing dilemma. It seems that we cannot know what religion is until we have studied it, and yet we cannot study it until we know what it is.

Perhaps the source of this dilemma lies in an insufficiently flexi-

---

1. Quoted in Roland Robertson, *The Sociological Interpretation of Religion,* Oxford, Blackwell, 1970, p. 34.

ble approach. It is not the case that we must begin our study knowing either nothing about the subject or knowing everything. On the
contrary, we can begin with a certain common-sense knowledge of
the subject in question and seek to devise scientific tools of con-
ceptualization and investigation that will help us to learn more. Thus
it is instructive to recognize that a physicist can make important
discoveries in his field without defining exactly what "matter" or
"physical reality" is. A biologist deals with living organisms, but
often he is perplexed when asked to define exactly what "life" is.
Certain entities seem to be hybrid forms that have both animate and
inanimate characteristics. Are they living or dead? In a way this is a
semantic question; both physicists and biologists can study these
entities without deciding how the semantic problem should be resolved.

Similarly, the student of religion is often perplexed about how
to classify a given phenomenon. Thus Zen is customarily called a
religion, though many insist it is not a religion but a philosophy of
life. Others want to say that Communism is a religion, though many
people classify it as an economic or political movement. How are
we to decide? In the beginning of our study of religion a certain
flexibility and tentativeness in our answers are desirable. Let us
look at our own customary usage and compare it with past usage
and current usage among scholars in the field. The student of religion can then decide on his own operational definition that can help
point out to him the area that he intends to investigate, even though
he may later change and qualify this initial formula in the light of
further information.

In this connection it will be helpful to glance briefly at the etymology of the word with which we are concerned. Wilfred Cantwell
Smith has provided a very useful history of the word "religion" in
his book *The Meaning and End of Religion.* He points out that the
word is derived from the Latin *religio.* In classical antiquity the Romans performed many rituals in honor of the gods, which were
functions of individual families, larger kinship groups, later of the
state. A sense of obligation that a god must receive "appropriate
honors" (*debitas honores*) was very strong. Smith observes:

> The early phrase religio mihi est *is illuminating. To say that such
> and such a thing was* religio *for me meant that it was mightily in-
> cumbent upon me to do it (alternatively not to do it: both are
> found as is not unusual with "mana," "tabu," the holy, the sa-
> cred). Oaths, family properties, cultic observances and the like
> were each* religio *to a man; or showing the ambivalence, one
> could equally say that to break a solemn oath is* religio, *that is
> tabu—as we might say, sacrilegious.*
>
> *Also the ritual ceremonies themselves were designated reli-
> giones. Throughout Latin usage right to the end of its develop-
> ment, the sense of rite, the outward observance of a particular
> practice, is to be found. This is, perhaps, related to a Roman ten-
> dency to perceive what we would call the divine or holy not so
> much, or not only, in the form of a figure or "god" as in that of a*

series of standardized acts. . . . The religio *of a specified god could then designate the traditional cultic pattern at his shrine.*[2]

In the first century B.C., two Roman authors use the noun *religio* to refer to some phenomenon or quality in human life that is related to earlier usage but now assumes a more universal significance. In his famous poem, *On the Nature of Things,* Lucretius takes a negative attitude toward *religio,* which he blames for "foul impieties" and inhuman acts like the human sacrifice by King Agamemnon of his daughter. Lucretius sees the task of his poem to be the freeing of mankind from the baneful power of religion—personified as a rapacious creature who shows "her head along the region skies, glowering on mortals with her hideous face."

On the other hand, Cicero takes a more positive view in his book *On the Nature of the Gods.* What Lucretius calls religion, Cicero calls superstition (*superstitio*). Cicero urges that man adopt a mean position between atheism (which is failure to honor the gods) and superstition (which is a craven and servile terror before them). Religion rather inculcates piety (*pietas*), the proper and healthy respect for the gods expressed in ritual acts of homage.

The most important event that occurs in the later history of the word in Western culture is the transformation of its meaning from a primary reference to the ritual practices of a specific cult, to a basic reference to a total system of beliefs and practices operating in a given society. The new usage already appears by implication in Patristic writings; by the time of the Reformation, several reformers, notably Calvin, refer to the "Christian religion" as a system of belief and practice which can be compared with other "religions" or systems of belief and practice. The enlightenment thinkers of the eighteenth century develop this usage further and it seems to split into three main types.

The first usage refers not to "religion," but to specific "religions." This usage is still helpful in the study of religion. Religions as specific traditions of belief, symbol, ritual practice, and ethical admonitions exist as concrete cultural forms that can be studied in the light of their historical development. Thus in this book we shall examine the influential traditions of Buddhism, Taoism, Confucianism, Judaism, Christianity, Islam, among others.

A second modern usage should be noted in order to be eschewed, so far as the scholarly study of religion is concerned. According to it there is an ideal essence of "religion" as a set of desirable beliefs and ethical standards which are then contrasted to the superstitions of most or all existing religions. The normative problem of what a good religion ought to be is a problem for philosophers, theologians, religious thinkers; however, the scholarly study of religion is rather concerned with an understanding of how religions have actually operated in human history, not with how they ought to operate according to the particular value scheme of the critic.

2. Wilfred Cantwell Smith, *The Meaning and End of Religion,* New York, Mentor Books, 1964, p. 24.

A third meaning of "religion" refers to the class of all existing religions. This usage remains as a problem and the source of a dilemma. If we refer to "religions," do we not have in mind some notion of the basis for classifying these particular systems and traditions as examples of "religion"? It is here that the question of definition still remains. Let us now consider three definitions of religion that are presently widely used by scholars to answer this question.

First of all, religion is often defined in terms of the distinction made by many "religious" people between an empirical natural order of existence and a superempirical or supernatural order of existence. Thus Roland Robertson, a contemporary sociologist, defines a religious culture as "that set of beliefs and symbols (and values deriving directly therefrom) pertaining to a distinction between an empirical and a superempirical, transcendent reality; the affairs of the empirical being subordinated to the nonempirical." He also defines "religious action" as "action shaped by an acknowledgment of the empirical/superempirical distinction." [3] Probably the majority of anthropologists and sociologists at the present time adopt some form of this position.

THREE DEFINITIONS OF RELIGION

This definition has the advantages of exactness and specificity. It clearly delineates a certain kind of human action and symbolization —that which is oriented toward a realm above the physical natural one—and distinguishes it from other cultural acts and symbols. Furthermore, it has support in our common-sense use of the word "religion." Most of us do use the word "religion" in this way primarily to refer to beliefs in gods, spirits, and other powers who occupy a world beyond the natural one. In many ways Tyler was quite sound in suggesting long ago that the minimal definition of religion was "belief in spirits."

A second possible definition finds the presence of religion in the distinction between the sacred and profane made by most primitive societies and archaic civilizations. This definition has been expressed in classic form by Emile Durkheim in his *Elementary Forms of Religious Life.* He writes:

The real characteristic of religious phenomena is that they always suppose a bipartite division of the whole universe, known and knowable, into two classes which embrace all that exists, but which radically exclude each other. Sacred things are those which the interdictions protect and isolate; profane things, those to which these interdictions are applied and which must remain at a distance from the first. Religious beliefs are the representations which express the nature of sacred things and the relations which they sustain, either with each other or with profane things. [4]

3. Robertson, op. cit., p. 47.

4. Emile Durkheim, *The Elementary Forms of Religious Life,* London, G. Allen, 1915, p. 41.

This definition is often associated with the thesis that the basis for the sacred-profane distinction is to be found in primordial experiences characterized by feelings of awe and sacred wonder. Rudolf Otto has written a study of such experiences entitled *The Idea of the Holy.* In it Otto lists three characteristics of an experience of "the sacred" or "the holy."

First is the sense of the *tremendum* that refers to a feeling of awefulness, and *majestas* or overpowering might that includes the sense of urgency. Second, *mysterium* refers to the uncanniness and mysteriousness that also pervades the experience. Finally, there is an element of *fascinans* as the experience seems to participate in an aspiration toward some ultimate value. The prevailing affective tone thus has an ambivalent texture. The characteristics of *mysterium tremendum* have a negative effect that daunts and repels at the same time that the sense of fascination encourages a positive movement of approach and desire. Otto used the term "numinous" to specify such experiences.

Innumerable examples of the numinous can be cited from religious literature. Here are three:

In Genesis 28:17, Jacob says, "How dreadful is this place! This is none other than the house of Elohim."

In the Bhagavad-Gita, Chapter XI, "Seeing this thy fearful and wonderful form, O great-hearted one, the three-fold world quakes."

In the Kena-Upanishad IV.29, "This is the way It [Brahman] is to be illustrated: What lightnings have been loosed: aaah! When that has made the eyes to be closed—aaah!—So far concerning Deity."

The ambivalence of the numinous experience can be related to two familiar words in anthropological literature. In some primitive societies, *mana* refers to power, which, although dangerous, is also desirable. Thus man moves positively toward it. In touching a sacred object in the right way and at the right time, power may be transferred to him. On the other hand, since the power is superhuman, it can also be overwhelming and destructive to man. Hence the sacred object is also *tabu,* something to be avoided, to be handled circumspectly or not handled at all.

Otto did not call the numinous an emotion, but many anthropologists have, without necessarily depending on Otto, found in intense emotional responses of this kind a definition of what is specifically religious in human culture. Thus R. H. Lowie says that the religious response is "amazement and awe; and its source is in the Supernatural, Extraordinary, Weird, Sacred, Holy, Divine." Paul Radin speaks of "a feeling of exhilaration, exaltation and awe and . . . a complete absorption in internal sensations." Alexander Goldenweiser frequently refers to a "religious thrill." [5]

5. Quoted in E. E. Evans-Pritchard, *Theories of Primitive Religion,* London, Oxford University Press, 1965, pp. 38–39.

On the other hand, it is also possible to consider the sacred as a kind of human behavior or cultural act. As Clifford Geertz observes, "the construction, apprehension, and utilization of symbolic forms are social events like any other; they are as public as marriage and as observable as agriculture." [6] Following this lead we might recognize the sacred in certain ritual acts that men perform. For example, consider this description of the plaiting of sacred mats in Tikopia rituals:

> The women . . . had to turn their bodies to the sea coast, not to the lake. . . . When the actual plaiting began a taboo of silence was imposed: the women might not speak to each other, nor the men to them. . . . All ordinary conversation was barred. Nor might the workers be approached by anyone else. A boy . . . when about to cross the maral (open space used for religious rites) was told to go inland, by the hedge, and not to go near the women.[7]

We see that in this ritual the distinction between sacred and profane reality can be recognized entirely in terms of observations of public behavior, both negative and positive. This definition has several advantages. It allows us to include under the rubric of religion a wide variety of beliefs and practices, so long as they are related to this distinction between the sacred and the ordinary. Furthermore, it can appeal to common-sense usage. Usually, we do tend to call religious any belief that is held with a sense of its sacred importance or any practice that is performed in a manner that conveys a sense of awesome and profound value.

A third definition of religion refers to the distinction between whatever is of ultimate authority and value to man and what is of penultimate or secondary importance. Thus, the theologian and philosopher Paul Tillich declares:

> Religion is the state of being grasped by an ultimate concern, a concern which qualifies all other concerns as preliminary and which itself contains the answer to the question of the meaning of our life. Therefore this concern is unconditionally serious and shows a willingness to sacrifice any finite concern which is in conflict with it.[8]

Many sociologists and anthropologists have found this notion useful and have interpreted it in terms of the society as a whole. Thus, William Lessa and Evan Vogt observe:

> Religion may be described as a system of beliefs and practices directed toward the "ultimate concern" of a society. "Ultimate

6. Clifford Geertz, "Religion as a Cultural System," in M. Banton, ed., *Anthropological Approaches to the Study of Religion,* London, Tavistock Publications, 1966, p. 5.

7. Raymond Firth, *The Work of the Gods in Tikopia,* London, Athlone Press, 1967, pp. 389–390.

8. Paul Tillich, *Christianity and the Encounter with the World Religions,* Chicago, University of Chicago Press, p. 6.

concern," a concept used by Paul Tillich, has two aspects—meaning and power. It has meaning in the sense of ultimate meaning of the central values of a society, and it has power in the sense of ultimate, sacred, or supernatural power which stands behind those values.[9]

This definition has affinities with the second one. What is ultimate and what is sacred to man seem to coalesce. This definition like the others finds support in our common-sense usage. Most societies have found it necessary not only to recommend certain rules for human behavior but to provide for these rules and practices some sort of ultimate justification or validation beyond the pragmatic fact that they are useful or are a matter of custom. The beliefs and symbols by which this ultimate validation is affirmed do tend to be called "religious" in character.

PROBLEMS IN THE
THREE DEFINITIONS

Each of these definitions is useful even though each also contains problems. For example, exceptions that we might want to call religious but which do not fit into one or the other of these definitions can be cited. Thus some phenomena that we commonly call religious do not seem, at least on one possible interpretation, to point to a transcendent or transempirical realm. Some Buddhists cultivate a state of consciousness (satori) characterized by the experience or condition of "nonduality" with this world rather than contact with a higher, transempirical world. Or again, some anthropologists have described religious rites in which a subjective experience of the sacred awe does not seem to be present. Similarly, some beliefs in a particular god or power are not connected with an ultimate justification of the norms of human behavior in that society.

Furthermore, each of these definitions reveals conceptual unclarity. The first has the advantage of definiteness and exclusivity. It specifies exactly what counts as religion (orientation toward the supernatural) and distinguishes it from what does not. For these reasons a great number of anthropologists and sociologists tend to use it as the most useful working definition of religion, preferable for their purposes to references to emotional states of sacred feeling or to ultimate values which can be vague in their application to specific phenomena.

However, the term "supernatural" or "transempirical" has one disadvantage. The word encourages us to interpret all religions according to a Western model that is far from universal. The word "supernatural" suggests a sharp division between two worlds—a natural world of physical objects and human relationships and a supernatural world of gods and supermundane realities. But such a division presupposes the recognition of a natural world that operates by strict causal laws and physical energies, which is then contrasted with a spiritual world of divine powers not subject to these laws. Such a distinction makes sense to people influenced by a sci-

9. William Lessa and Evan Vogt, eds., *A Reader in Comparative Religion*, New York, Harper & Row, 1965, p. 1.

entific culture devoted to the study of lawful regularities of the natural world. However, other cultures do not make the division in quite that way. For example, Lienhardt observes:

I have not found it useful to adopt the distinction between "natural" and "supernatural" beings or events in order to describe the difference between men and Powers, for this distinction implies a conception of the course or laws of Nature quite foreign to Dinka thought. When, for example, the Dinka attribute lightning to a particular ultra-human power, it would falsify their understanding, and indeed exaggerate its difference from our own, to refer to a supernatural Power. The force of lightning is equally ultra-human for ourselves as for the Dinka, though the interpretation we place upon that fact is very different from theirs.[10]

The term "supernatural" seems to make the division between worlds in too radical a manner and to provide too parochial a reflection of Western oppositions between science (nature) and religion (supernatural). The same problem obtains with another proposal—"transempirical." Empirical means experiential; in the West it is closely related to scientific pursuits. Thus, "transempirical" implies a division between an empirical world open to scientific observation and a transempirical world of religion beyond its purview. The distinction has its uses; but in some cultures the gods are considered to be experienced as immediately as are other entities of the natural world.

Perhaps a better term than "supernatural" or "transempirical" to express the kind of division exhibited in many religions is the word "transcendent." This term is helpful, especially if it is used in an operational rather than substantive way. On this view, religion makes a distinction between man and something that transcends him, not substantively in the sense that the religious object is necessarily believed to occupy another world, but functionally in the sense that within his one world of experience the religious man believes that he encounters powers that are impressively greater than (transcendent to) his own.

The definition of religion in terms of the sacred has even greater difficulties. It is very difficult to distinguish a sacred emotion from other emotions of wonder and ordinary respect. Many psychologists, like William James, doubt that a distinct "religious emotion" exists. Furthermore, leading anthropologists find the distinction between sacred and profane a vague one. Thus, E. E. Evans-Pritchard observes:

Surely . . . "sacred" and "profane" are on the same level of experience, and, far from being cut off from one another, they are so closely intermingled as to be inseparable. They cannot, therefore, either for the individual or for social activities, be put in closed departments which negate each other, one of which is left on entering the other. For instance, when some misfortune such

10. Godfrey Lienhardt, *Divinity and Experience,* Oxford, Clarendon Press, 1961, p. 29.

as sickness is believed to be due to some fault, the physical symptoms, the moral state of the sufferer, and the spiritual intervention form a unitary objective experience, and can scarcely be separated in the mind. My test of this sort of formulation is a simple one: whether it can be broken down into problems which permit testing by observation in field research, or can at least aid in a classification of observed facts. I have never found that the dichotomy of sacred and profane was of much use for either purpose.[11]

The notion of ultimacy is similarly infected with a certain vagueness. From one point of view, it could be applied to any and every justification of a behavioral norm without exception. Thus if a naturalist says that one should behave in a certain way because it enhances biological health and another says that one should do so because a god has commanded it, both have offered their own kind of ultimate justification and hence, on this view, are equally religious. But a term with such a broad width of application seems to have lost any determinate meaning.

The perplexity is engendered in part by an ambiguity in the phrase "ultimate concern." Does it refer to the mere facing of ultimate questions; to the state of being concerned about finding an answer? Or does it refer to the actual working out of a certain sort of answer? It would seem that all men and cultures exhibit "ultimate concern" in the sense that the conditions of natural existence force them to face problems about the validation of their values and norms of behavior. However, it would further seem that the solutions can vary greatly and that a distinction between a general class of religious answers and another general class of nonreligious ones ought to be made. In other words, all men probably ask limit (or ultimate) questions. They may or may not find an ultimate or religious answer.

CONCLUSION Although each of the proposed definitions has its difficulties, all of them are useful and have been adopted by influential scholars at the present time. As we have suggested, perhaps they should be treated as enunciations of specific criteria (transcendence, sacredness, ultimacy) that operate in our use of the word "religion." These criteria are not mutually exclusive. Rather they complement one another and together point out an area of human activity and concern which is distinctive and has played an important part in human culture. The definitions are not definitive descriptions of a universal essence but they are "pointers" that designate in a general way a kind of human activity that is recognizable and worth our attention. The task is to use some or all of these criteria to fashion a working definition of religion that helps the student of religion explore aspects of human behavior that he finds worthy of investigation. The more specific definition will usually include other factors in addition

11. Evans-Pritchard, op. cit., p. 65.

to the formal criteria. For example, Clifford Geertz in an important article emphasizes symbolic activity. He defines religion as:

> (1) *a system of symbols which acts to* (2) *establish powerful, pervasive, and long-lasting moods and motivations in men by* (3) *formulating conceptions of a general order of existence and* (4) *clothing these conceptions with such an aura of factuality that* (5) *the moods and motivations seem uniquely realistic.*[12]

Another anthropologist, Anthony Wallace, emphasizes ritual behavior and defines religion as "a set of rituals, rationalized by myth, which mobilizes supernatural powers for the purpose of achieving or preventing transformations of state in man and nature." [13]

The beginning student of religion is thus advised to approach the problem of definition in an open, flexible manner. The question of the definition of religion is not the question of a fact that is either so or not so. It is the question of a choice about how to use a word, and this depends on the purposes and concerns of the prospective user. Shakespeare long ago asked: "What's in a name? That which we call a rose/By any other name would smell as sweet." Humpty Dumpty in Lewis Carroll's *Through the Looking Glass* noted, "When *I* use a word it means just what I choose it to mean—neither more or less." When Alice asked whether you can make words mean so many different things, Humpty Dumpty answered, "The question is which is to be master—that's all."

Let the beginning student consider the criteria that operate in his own usage and compare them with the definitions proposed by leading scholars in the field. He can then decide on an operational definition that seems to be of most use to him at the start of his studies, but which will be held in a tentative manner open to correction and qualification in the light of his increasing familiarization with the field.

12. Geertz, op. cit., p. 4.
13. Anthony Wallace, *Religion: An Anthropological View*, New York, Random House, 1966, p. 107.

RELIGION AS ACTION AND MEANING: RITUAL AND MYTH

In the first chapter we observed that the most useful way to study religion is in terms of actions and meanings, in terms of what people do and how they symbolize what they do. We now turn to some concrete examples of how such study is performed. We shall consider some specific questions that are generated by the methodological perspectives we have noted. In this brief survey we shall not adopt the position of any one school or single investigator but attempt to show how the various perspectives interact with one another to provide a helpful understanding of religious action.

Let us begin by looking at a specific example of religion in action in a primitive society.

TIKOPIA:
THE RITUAL OF
THE "HOT FOOD"

Tikopia is a small island in the British Solomon Islands Protectorate. A sequence of rituals called "the Work of the Gods" was performed there regularly at seasonal intervals until 1956, when the conversion to Christianity of the major chief caused their abandonment. The time of the rites was determined mainly by seasonal changes; one part of the rites was performed roughly in April, when the winds settled down to blow steadily from the southeast or east-southeast and continued thus for about six months. A second part of the series took place around October, when these trade winds were replaced with normally light winds alternating with flat calms.

The series as a whole was elaborate and took weeks to perform. The sequence included a symbolic fire ritual to initiate the cycle; a resacralization of canoes; a reconsecration of temples; a series of planting and harvest rites for the yam; a sacred dance festival; several memorial rites on the sites of vanished temples; and the ritual manufacture of a pigment called tumeric, which is extracted from the root of a plant.

Four clans, politically autonomous and each under its own chief, participated in the rituals in which one chief, the Arika Kafika, occupied a role of special prestige as a kind of *primus inter pares,* i.e., the first among equals.

As an example of the entire sequence, let us consider more closely one of these rites—the ritual of the "hot food"—as it is described by the anthropologist Raymond Firth in *The Work of the Gods in Tikopia.*[1] In preparation for this particular rite, yams are first cooked in the oven house. Shortly before noon, the oven is uncovered, the food is removed and put in a shallow wooden dish of unique shape. The dish is carried to the main building and set in a ritual position in an area devoted to the gods on the seaward side close to the center post.

Meanwhile, the participants in the room prepare for the ceremony by each taking a large leaf in his hand. "An air of tense expectation" grips the crowd and speech is only in whispers. Finally, a basket of yam tubers, smoking hot from the oven, is brought in, and the bearer quickly distributes them to the members. Each man catches his hot yam deftly in his leaf-covered hands and bites it as quickly as he can, while it is still hot. The first person to successfully swallow a mouthful of the scalding food makes a sucking noise with his lips. This man is considered to be specially favored from that time forth. "Ku tu i te Atua," i.e., "He stands in with the god," it is afterward said.

The Arika Kafika, the chief of the most prestigious tribe, then seats himself before the wooden dish of food devoted to the gods. A libation made from the kava plant is served. The chief, without turning his head, takes the cup and, making obeisance by raising it to his forehead, pours it out in front of him. This is done four times in honor of various gods believed to be present. After this, the chief returns to his former seat. The two yams in the special dish are divided, one given away as an ordinary food portion, the other laid in a small basket belonging to the chief.

As soon as the rites are over, the tension relaxes. "The kava of gods is finished," someone says. People begin to talk of their experiences, how their lips burned, how tears came to their eyes, how they made puffing noises in an effort to cool off the burning portions. One who clumsily dropped his yam is laughed at in good-natured fashion by the others. These jovial exchanges are in sharp contrast to the earlier attitudes of respect and restraint exhibited during the ceremony. What is the meaning of this behavior? According to Firth, a kind of "elementary communion feast" has taken place. The feeling of awe is generated by the belief that the highest

1. Raymond Firth, *The Work of the Gods in Tikopia,* New York, Athlone Press, 1967, hereinafter *Work.*

A Tikopia aristocrat. (*From Raymond Firth,* We the Tikopia; *courtesy of George Allen & Unwin, Ltd.*)

god, Atua i Kafika, has been directly present at the ceremony in the person of the chief. Thus the Arika made the following statement to Firth: "I who have sat there am him [the God]; he does not eat since he has left his kava [a libation] to be made by the brethren [the family of principal clan gods]. I there am the God; he has come to me, because I am the chief of importance. From olden times the Arika Kafika has been the chief of prime importance since he has been rendered so by the God." [2]

It is believed that the rite was instituted by the Atua i Kafika when he lived on earth long ago. Since the Atua ate only hot food, he wanted a ceremony to follow his personal habits, and "to this day he himself attends the rite to observe that it is duly carried out."

So much, then, for the rite and the most immediate explanation of its significance. Can anything further be said about its meaning and general import for the life of the Tikopia?

2. *Work,* p. 157.

This account has introduced us to the exceedingly important human behavioral pattern called *ritual*. Ritual is so pervasive and significant in human culture as a whole and in religion in particular that neither can be adequately understood without considering it in some detail. Ritual has been defined as "the formal acting out of a ceremony, usually repeated in exactly the same way on specified occasions." [3] This definition stresses two important features of ritual: the pronounced *formality* of the action and its *repetition* at regular intervals. However, the word "ceremony" must be interpreted in a broad sense to include both elaborate public rites and those simpler gestures that occur between small social units, as when the members of a family regularly bow to each other before eating the evening meal, or two friends shake hands on meeting. Again, we may tend to associate rituals with sacred occasions involving reference to gods and the supernatural world; but we should also recognize that secular, or nonreligious, rituals are possible as when, for example, a culture hero is remembered and celebrated by the community at regular intervals through formal recitations and other symbolic acts.

The question of why men perform ritual acts like those of the Tikopia cycle is a significant one. These rituals involve many behavioral elements that in themselves are not puzzling. In the ritual of the "hot food," men gather together to eat yams. Both the act of eating and the social context in which it is performed are intelligible acts for human beings, who need nourishment and social conviviality. But why the formalization of the actions, the insistence on exact procedural sequences, the air of solemnity, the sense of awe that at times overcomes the participants, the behavioral reference to realities not immediately apparent to the physical senses? Is there any point to such behavior; can we make sense of it and put it into some kind of intelligible pattern that will establish its human appropriateness and reasonableness?

We have already noted how the Tikopia answer this question in terms of a *myth*. According to them, the rite of the "hot food" was set up by Atua i Kafika, the principal deity of Tikopia, while he still lived on earth. Since he ate only hot food, the rite is faithful to his habits.

The word "myth" is derived from the Greek word *mythos,* which literally means "story" and was originally used to refer to the many stories of the gods found in Greek religion. However, in the history of Western culture, many philosophers and theologians have rejected the mythos of Greek religion; the former in the name of rational "logos" or philosophical thought; the latter in the name of the Christian faith. As a result, the word "myth" has become associated in the West with a set of pejorative connotations and is in popular speech almost a synonym for "untrue," "false," or "absurdly fantastic."

However, such judgments prevent a careful description of the

3. Ralph Ross, *Symbols and Civilization,* New York, Harcourt Brace Jovanovich, 1957, p. 182.

data unobscured by premature judgments and emotional denunciations. Investigators of culture find that they still need a word like myth, not to express a negative value judgment about the absurdity or falsity of the material, but to classify a kind of story that appears in a variety of societies with distinctive characteristics worthy of notice. In this book, "myth" is used as a category of *objective* classification of a certain kind of sacred story that can be found in various cultures. No negative valuation of these stories is implied by the term, which should be disinfected of such connotations. Thus Bronislaw Malinowski argues:

> *There exists a special class of stories, regarded as sacred, embodied in ritual, morals, and social organization, and which form an integral and active part of primitive culture. These stories live not by idle interest, not as fictitious or even as true narratives, but are to the natives a statement of a primeval, greater, and more relevant reality, by which the present life, fates, and activities of mankind are determined, the knowledge of which supplies men with the motive for ritual and moral actions, as well as with indications as to how to perform them.*[4]

For example, Malinowski goes on to point out that the Trobrianders make important distinctions between the kinds of stories that they tell. First are folk tales (*kukwanebu*), which are often of a fantastic and grotesque nature, told for pleasure without implication that they are necessarily true, sacred, or important. In this class are stories of hostile snakes slain by young heroes; ogres that afflict villagers; the rivalry existing between various animals and insects. This is the world of fairy tales, personal dreams, wish fulfillment, fantasies, vicarious adventures.

A second group of stories are called *libwogwo*. These stories recount the actual experiences of the teller and are believed to be true; the information they impart is deemed relevant and important to the hearers.

But finally, there is a third class of stories called by the natives *liliu*. These are the sacred tales or myths which are in many respects very different from the others. "If the first class are told for amusement, the second to make a serious statement and satisfy social ambition, the third are regarded, not merely as true, but as venerable and sacred . . . The *myth* comes into play when rite, ceremony, or a social or moral rule demands justification, warrant of antiquity, reality, and sanctity." [5]

In general, myths are stories about events which happened long ago and which provide the normative model, the paradigm or archetypal pattern, for some human condition or custom. Mircea Eliade observes:

> *Speaking for myself, the definition that seems least inadequate because most embracing is this: Myth narrates a sacred history;*

4. Bronislaw Malinowski, *Magic, Science and Religion*, Garden City, N.Y., Doubleday Anchor Books, 1954, p. 108.

5. Ibid., p. 107.

it relates an event that took place in primordial time, the fabled
time of the "beginnings." In other words, myth tells how, through
the deeds of supernatural Beings, a reality came into existence,
be it the whole of reality, the Cosmos, or only a fragment of
reality—an island, a species of plant, a particular kind of human
behavior, an institution. Myth, then, is always an account of a
"creation"; it related how something was produced, began to be.[6]

Myths concerned with "origins" and "beginnings" could then be
appropriately called etiological in function, but the sense in which
this is meant should be carefully distinguished from the etiological
explanations of a modern scientist, who may also be interested in
the "origins" of the solar system or perhaps in the "beginnings" of
life on earth according to evolutionary theory.

Although tribal myths also are concerned with origins and include
stories about how various natural phenomena came into being, it is
a serious confusion to think of them as similar in intention though
inferior in value to our modern scientific explanations. The scientific
cosmologies are interested in determining the exact sequential series of empirical changes leading from a past to a present state of
the natural universe; the tribal myth is, rather, concerned with the
validation of some present human circumstance by relating it to a
primordial sacred event which is both its ultimate cause and its justification.

Even though we may grant that some inevitable overlapping and
confusion may occur between a mythic and a scientific account of
"origins," the fact remains that the profound differences in the
mode of discourse and in the basic categories of relevance and intention render them not so much rival accounts of the same phenomena, as entirely different realms of discourse with very different
concerns and intentions. Myth, properly understood, is not an early
attempt to do what modern science can now do better, any more
than a poem is an early attempt to express what a geometrical
theorem and proof can state more clearly and convincingly.

We will return to this point when we consider more closely the
expressive function of myth. For the moment, let us consider a typical tribal myth of the Trobrianders, as summarized by Malinowski.
According to the natives of the village of Laba'i, people originally
lived very differently from the way they do at present. They lived underground in a more sacred region where they possessed the
power of rejuvenation by sloughing off their old skin, like a snake,
at regular intervals. It is to this region that man presumably returns
after death.

Present-day social life in this particular village of Laba'i began
when representatives of the four main clans emerged to the surface
of the earth, one after another, from a hole in the ground. Following
them came the animals associated with each clan; first the iguana,
then the dog, the pig, and finally the crocodile. Then occurred an
apparently trivial event. The dog and pig ran around, and the dog,

6. Mircea Eliade, *Myth and Reality,* trans. W. Trask, New York, Harper &
Row, 1963, pp. 5—6.

seeing the fruit of the *noku* plant, nosed it, and finally ate it. Said the pig: "Thou eatest *noku,* thou eatest dirt; thou art low-bred, a commoner; the chief, the guya'u, shall be I." Ever since then the chiefs of the Pig clan have been the most important leaders. Malinowski observes:

> To understand this myth, you must have a good knowledge of their sociology, religion, customs, and outlook. Then and only then, can you appreciate what this story means to the natives and how it can live in their life. If you stayed among them and learned the language you would constantly find it active in discussion and squabbles in reference to the relative superiority of the various clans and in the discussions about the various food taboos which frequently raise fine questions of casuistry. Above all, if you were brought into contact with communities where the historical process of the spread of influence of the Malasi clan is still in evolution, you would be brought face to face with this myth as an active force.[7]

THE THEORY
OF THE RITUAL
BASIS OF MYTH

As we have already noted, myths are usually associated with rituals. The precise nature of this "association" has exercised a good deal of attention from scholars. An interesting theory has been advanced that ritual and myth exhibit an essential correlation, so that a sacred myth in a culture will always be found to be the expression or oral interpretation of a ritual. In an extreme form, not usually propounded by its more judicious expositors, the theory suggests that ritual always precedes myth in a causal nexus, so that genuine myths are to be considered as the verbal articulation of certain primal ritual acts of the given culture.

In this extreme form the theory has not found acceptance, for a number of reasons. Significant myths that cannot easily be attached to a ritual are recognizable in many cultures; also, there are notable examples where rituals have been fashioned to conform to a new myth. Furthermore, the thesis in its radical causal form seems to be involved in the unresolvable and unnecessary chicken-egg kind of dilemma. We cannot find an empirically verifiable period in human culture where only ritual existed without myth; we rather discover in all existing cultures the two in dynamic interaction. Why, then, make the unnecessary and unsubstantiated hypothesis that one is the temporal basis of the other? Finally, the theory seems to gain its force from a priori stipulation rather than empirical investigation. By definition, I can declare that only those stories associated with rituals are "genuine or authentic myths." Other impressive stories of a sacred nature not so related are then excluded by fiat from inclusion under this rubric. Yet the stories so summarily dismissed may in all other respects possess the characteristics and functions of myths in that culture. A more judicious statement is provided by Clyde Kluckhohn when he observes:

7. Malinowski, op. cit., p. 113.

The facts do not permit any universal generalizations as to ritual being the "cause" of myth or vice versa. Their relationship is rather that of intricate mutual interdependence, differently structured in different cultures and probably at different times in the same culture.[8]

It is significant that Kluckhohn's careful modification of the ritual-myth theory still retains the sense of an "intricate interdependence" because this is the basic insight which the theory has sought to convey. Too often, ritual has been thought of as purely secondary phenomenon, a kind of symbolic representation of a meaning that is already clear and complete in the ideational form of a belief or dogma. The ritual is then seen as a gratuitious gesture which could be eliminated, if necessary, without serious loss. The insight that must be restored and preserved is that if the myth is an explanation of the ritual, it is also true that the ritual is a kind of explanation or embodiment of the myth, so that the teaching in word and story is only truly fulfilled by its ritual counterpart and base.

Ritual is an element of religion and culture that needs to be emphasized, even at the risk of exaggeration, since the opposite error of underestimating its importance is more serious. Yet ritual is the element most likely to be neglected by Western intellectuals, who naturally are strongly influenced by the ideational elements in culture and life. Thus, in considering a phenomenon like religion, the tendency is first to stress the thought content of religion and to ask questions concerning the "beliefs" of a given people or religious group. Even when a broader set of experiences causes us to enlarge our categories somewhat to include more *concrete* ideational elements like myths and other imagery, we still tend to conceive of a religious stance as the adherence to one or the other of these ideational elements. What myths do they believe? we may still wonder, hoping thereby to determine the essential character of a people's religious approach to existence. The emphasis on ritual helps us to see that action, behavior, operational deeds, are as important, perhaps more important, than solely ideational factors in determining a religious stance.

In this connection, R. R. Marett argues that "savage religion is something not so much thought out as danced out; . . . in other words, it develops under conditions, psychological and sociological, which favor emotional and motor processes, whereas ideation remains relatively in abeyance."[9] Although Marett is usually interpreted as having overstressed the subjectively emotional aspect of religion, it is significant that in this passage he rather emphasizes the "motor" activities of the body itself. The emphasis on ritual is related to this point. The body itself, with its various postures and

An Alaskan "yake," or carved wooden figure, used by a shaman in certain ritual dances. (Courtesy of the American Museum of Natural History.)

8. Clyde Kluckhohn, "Myths and Ritual: A General Theory," in William Lessa and Evan Vogt, eds., *A Reader in Comparative Religion*, New York, Harper & Row, 1965, p. 148.

9. R. R. Marett, *The Threshold of Religion*, London, Methuen, 1909, p. xxi.

stances, is itself a vehicle of symbolic communication. The body conveys meaning as well as words and ideas.

At the very least, then, we can see how ritual action can support and reinforce the ideational meanings of myth and dogma. However, we can go further and observe, as is evidently the intent of those stressing the ritual foundation of religion, and insist that the ritual may bear and convey meanings only partially converted into an ideational form. In other words, it is a serious mistake to think of the ritual as the symbolic dramatic enactment of a meaning already clearly expressed in some kind of ideational mode. On the contrary, the ritual may give a depth of significance and vital power to the religious intention which the accompanying myth itself needs for the full apprehension of its meaning.

Indeed, an emphasis on ritual will also help us to avoid an intellectualistic distortion of our understanding of myth itself. We must remember that myth itself in a tribal society is not a story read in solitude and apprehended by the inner mind. Myth is first of all the product of an oral society where stories are not written and read, but memorized and uttered aloud to a communal group. Myth is therefore itself a ritual act, something that is uttered, an oral event taking place within the environs of a living society. Myth is essentially a social transaction; something is proclaimed and something is heard; the full meaning of the myth includes the tones and overtones in which it is delivered, the total context in which it is listened to.

All this is not to revert to the theory of the ritual basis of myth which we have already rejected in its radical form. But the recognition of the dramatic behavioral, indeed, bodily dimension of religious behavior must not thereby be denied. The religious stance maintains at its center *acts* involving the total person; thought and idea are important only when they participate in the total behavioral situation. Any analysis of religion neglecting or obscuring this important insight does serious violence and distortion to the phenomenon it is purporting to describe. As Anthony Wallace puts it:

> *The primary phenomenon of religion is ritual. Ritual is religion in action; it is the cutting edge of the tool. Belief, although its recitation may be a part of the ritual, or a ritual in its own right, serves to explain, to rationalize, to interpret and direct the energy of the ritual performance. It is not a question of priority in time . . . in observed human behavior the two phenomena go together; few if any rituals are any longer instituted before a mythic base is invented to account for them. The primacy is instrumental: just as the blade of the knife has instrumental priority over the handle, and the barrel of a gun over the stock, so does the ritual have instrumental priority over myth. It is ritual which accomplishes what religion sets out to do.*[10]

10. Anthony Wallace, *Religion: An Anthropological View*, New York, Random House, 1966, p. 102.

In the last section we raised the question why human beings should perform rituals, since rituals do not seem to possess an immediately practical biological purpose in the same sense as an act like hunting or sleeping. Yet men in all cultures overlay practical activities like eating, for example, with ritual patterns of behavior. Why do they do so?

We have already noted that in tribal societies the participants themselves put the answer in mythic terms. Thus, myth justifies for Tikopia the rite of the hot food in the sense that a god is declared to have commanded it. Myth also explains some of the specific elements of the ritual; hot yams are eaten because it is said that the god, long ago when he lived on earth, had such eating habits. If we ask why the Tikopia cycle as a whole was performed, the answer of the Tikopia, as summarized by Firth, is that the ceremonies are the means

> of maintaining contact with powerful spiritual beings and inducing them to look with favor upon Tikopia by the grant of food and health. The spiritual beings were conceived as being in reciprocal relationship with the leaders of particular lineages and clans. . . . Contact with them was to be maintained partly on the same pattern as contact with powerful human beings, that is, by presentation of gifts and conduct of abasement. But they had to be treated with even more deference and even more formality. In particular, they had to be addressed by special titles not necessarily known to ordinary men and in much more elaborate set phraseology.[11]

Such is an interpretation as provided in the forms of thought familiar to the participants themselves. Sociologists and anthropologists have evolved another set of interpretative categories that suggest that rituals may continue to be enacted by a people for reasons other than those explicitly stated in the given mythic explanation. This approach has led to an impressive analysis which has come to be known as *functional theory*. According to it, religious rites and beliefs perform certain positive functions related to social or personal problems that cause the participants to adhere to them, whether or not they are consciously aware of the full effect and importance of these effects.

This suggestion presupposes that human action is complex and ambiguous, and reveals both conscious and unconscious dimensions in which different sets of motivation apply. A person or a social group may perform an action with a certain goal in mind, but really value and reinforce the act for other purposes.

The sociologist Robert Merton has helped clarify the semantic difficulties involved in this point by distinguishing between manifest and latent functions. Manifest functions are the purposes of an act as the actors themselves understand and express them; the latent functions are the results of the act which are unknown to or neglected by the actors but which determine the real value of the act and the need for its repetition. The manifest functions are observed

THE FUNCTIONAL
THEORY OF RITUAL

11. *Work*, p. 6.

by the participants themselves, but the latent ones are more likely to be perceived by objective observers. Thus, while the participants in a primitive ritual may offer a manifestly mythic explanation of their action, the modern sociologist and anthropologist believes he can discern latent functional results of the action of a different sort. We can summarize these latent functional aspects under three headings: social, biological-psychological, and depth-psychological.

THE SOCIAL FUNCTION OF RELIGION

Sufficient examples of how ritual contributes to social integration have already been given and the point is fairly obvious and incontrovertible. A human society is a complex whole made up of many subordinate parts—sexes, age groupings, professional and economic classes, political bodies. In a biological organism, the various parts are integrated into a working, functioning whole according to innate biological patterns automatically establishing and maintaining the very possibility of the life and being of that organism. So much differentiation and relative freedom among the parts of human society is possible that their integration into a common whole seems constantly threatened. One way of overcoming this threat toward disintegration and dissolution of the social bonds is by means of communal rites and rituals.

Ritual-myth complexes accomplish this social integrative function in at least six ways.

1. First is their assistance in the *symbolic articulation* of the social patterns and relationships themselves. Even a cursory examination of primitive myth and ritual must impress the mind with the remarkable congruence of mythic patterns with the specific social patterns of the group in question. Such resemblances are not occasional, but pervasive, perhaps universal, and easy to detect. Often the complex hierarchy of gods and spirits in a given culture will almost exactly correspond to the hierarchy of social segments. In Tikopia, the "religious pyramid of the gods" exactly corresponds to the pyramids of social relation existing among the clans. The chief god, Atua i Kafika, is specially worshiped by the Kafika clan, though the other clans acknowledge him in addition to their own special clan gods. By the same token, the Kafika clan has a very real though legally undefined position of special prestige among the clans. The hierarchy of gods thus provides a perfectly adequate symbolic articulation of this social reality.

Furthermore, in the rituals, the Arika Kafika, head of the most prestigious clan, is given special functions of honor. For example, he declares the beginning of "the Work of the Gods" and has the leading place in the opening rite of the firebrands. On the other hand, he is in no sense an autocrat or absolute monarch over the other tribes. So, in various rituals, each tribe and its chief will in turn occupy a place of special importance and honor. In this manner, the subtle relationships existing between the tribes are expressed in myth and ritual.

2. A second social function is even more important. Something in man's complex social and axiological make-up is not content with

the mere recognition of a social situation as a brute fact, but requires for it some kind of justification. Myth and ritual meet this need in a striking, if obvious, fashion. By relating the human world to a world of divine forces and powers, the social milieu receives a kind of *validation* it does not seem to possess when considered in its own right alone.

3. A third social function is a *performatory* one. It is one thing to state and articulate a certain relationship among the parts of a social group. In the ritual, the relationship is acted out, performed, realized, made to occur. This point may be circular, but it is no less valid for that. Ritual accomplishes social integration by an act of social integration. By coming together in an integral act, the society discovers that it has been maintained, preserved, and reinforced as an integral entity. The family that prays together stays together because in doing their religious thing together they are together.

4. A fourth social function is less obvious but very important. Ritual performs a *heuristic* function. It assists us in concentrating attention and focusing energies in such a way that our human capacities cooperate at their most potent level in the performance of a desired act. As Mary Douglas observes: "an external symbol can mysteriously help the co-ordination of brain and body." Thus:

> The Dinka herdsman hurrying home to supper, knots a bundle of grass at the wayside, a symbol of delay. Thus he expresses outwardly his wish that the cooking may be delayed for his return. The rite holds no magic promise that he will now be in time for supper. He does not then dawdle home thinking that the action will itself be effective. He redoubles his haste. His action has not wasted time, for it has sharpened the focus of his attention on his wish to be in time.[12]

5. Ritual can also provide a directly creative function in solving personal and social dilemmas. It can help man to solve difficulties, release tensions, resolve ambiguities in his social relationships that otherwise might fester and eventually break the social bond.

Too often, functional analysis has presented its thesis in too static a manner, as if a human society were already determined in all its social details and the ritual existed simply to affirm and maintain the already fixed relationship. In point of fact, even the most traditional and unchanging society has dynamic elements within it. Peoples and groups, and the relations among them, are constantly changing. In ritual celebrations, the status of a given leader or clan is either *reaffirmed* or perhaps slightly *modified* according to the slight changes that may be introduced into the ritual each time.

Thus, Firth emphasizes that although the general shape of the Tikopia cycle was fixed, room for innovation and modification was also evident. He concludes:

> In such ways ritual not only represents, describes, and maintains the social order; it may also help in the formation and develop-

12. Mary Douglas, *Purity and Danger*, New York, Praeger, 1966, pp. 63–64.

*ment of the social order. It can have an adaptive and even crea-
tive function. By giving occasion for the public assumption of
roles it also gives occasion for interpreting and modifying them,
and so for re-shaping the social order. But as it does these
things, by the very messages of status-involvement and exercise
of initiative that it conveys it may also be a source of competition
and disunity; one man's ritual asset may become another man's
social affront.*[13]

6. Finally, we can observe in ritual and myth a *mitigative* function
that is subtle but probably of great value in promoting social unity.
It might be wondered why the facts of social relationship cannot be
said in a clear and unequivocal manner without the indirection of
ritual and myth. Such a question indicates no doubt the commenda-
ble honesty of the asker, but also, perhaps, his lack of sensitivity to
human feeling. As Confucius long ago noted, ritual serves as a
buffer protecting the delicate egos of the participants while enabling unpleasant actualities, such as the ascendancy of one man
over another, to be stated in a way that is palatable and acceptable
to both. The blunt edge of the truth is softened by the pleasing
complexity of the ritual. As Firth points out, "statements" can be
made through ritual "in a manner less brusque, more protracted,
more behaviorally involved, than with ordinary language." Thus:

> *One can assume that every individual has emotional dispositions
> and tensions arising from his relation to the external world, in-
> cluding members of his own society. . . . What ritual has done is
> to provide routinization and canalization for such tensions. These
> are not left for random expression, but are assigned their time
> and place for explicit mention and acting-out.*[14]

THE BIOLOGICAL-
PSYCHOLOGICAL
FUNCTION
OF RELIGION

A second major area where the functionality of ritual can be observed is what is here called the psychological-biological. This hy-
phenated term points to the human area where personal and biological problems centering around birth, maturation, and sexual life
are intertwined. These experiences lead to the question of personal
identity. The person must discover who he is in the sense that he
must work out a behavioral style appropriate to his being as a child,
an adult, a boy, a girl, a man, a woman. The question of identity
may also assume a more profound "metaphysical" aspect as he
seeks to determine his "ultimate" nature and destiny in the universe. However, in the interests of analytical clarity, we wish here to
separate this deeper question of identity from the question of identity as a psychological-biological organism which in this section is
our concern.

An intriguing and vivid example of the assistance of myth in this
problem of forming personal identity is to be found in the popular
Trickster stories of the North American Indians. For example, ac-

13. *Work,* p. 23.
14. Ibid., pp. 25, 23.

cording to one story Trickster is butchering a buffalo. He is using a knife with his right hand, when his left arm suddenly grabs the buffalo. The right arm speaks out: "Give that back to me. It is mine!" The left arm releases its hold but shortly afterwards grabs hold of the right arm; a vicious fight between the arms follows and the left arm is wounded.

In another story Trickster treats his anus as if it were an independent agent. After killing some ducks, Trickster tells his anus to keep watch over them while he sleeps. Some foxes then draw near but, much to their surprise, they are startled by the sound of expelled gas. They are frightened by this sound several times, but finally gain courage enough to approach the sleeping Trickster and eat the ducks. When Trickster awakes, he is angry with his anus for doing such a poor job as a guard. He takes a piece of burning wood and burns the mouth of his own anus in punishment. This act causes him to cry out in pain.

What do these strange stories mean? As Mary Douglas points out:

> The trickster starts as an unselfconscious, amorphous being. As the story unfolds he gradually discovers his own identity, gradually recognizes and controls his own anatomical parts; he oscillates between female and male, but eventually fixes his own male sexual role; and finally learns to assess his environment for what it is. . . . Trickster begins, isolated, amoral and unselfconscious, clumsy, ineffectual, an animal-like buffoon. Various episodes prune down and place more correctly his bodily organs so that he ends by looking like a man. At the same time he begins to have a more consistent set of social relations and to learn hard lessons about his physical environment. In one important episode he mistakes a tree for a man and responds to it as he would to a person until eventually he discovers it is a mere inanimate thing. So gradually he learns the functions and limits of his being.[15]

Innumerable myths about young heroes who slay monsters, rescue maidens, find hidden treasures and finally solve fundamental problems for their society no doubt reflect this process of human growth and achievement of personal and social identity. Rituals also participate in this process.

Probably the most significant rituals in any culture are those having to do with rites of initiation, the most important of which mark the transition from youthful existence to that of full participation in all the privileges and responsibilities of the adult members of the community. These rites are both civil and religious in character, since the initiant is usually introduced to the full extent of his social responsibilities and to the deeper meaning of the religious lore of his tribe. Many kinds of initiation rites exist; some are for women,

INITIATION RITUALS

15. Douglas, op. cit., pp. 79–80.

some are for entrance into special societies within the larger society as a whole. However, the most important and extensive ones concern the transition of the male from his state of childhood to full manhood in the tribe.

The following account of an initiation rite, by H. Ian Hogbin, in a New Guinea village conveys some of the qualities of the initiation ceremony in a vivid form. Hogbin tells how the villagers selected two old men to be guardians. A large building was erected in the bush to house the boys. The guardians told the boys that during the next few months they would be tested to see whether they were fit to be presented as a sacrificial meal for the monsters. If they were worthy they would pass through whole and be evacuated. But anyone who failed to measure up to the requirements would remain fast in the monster's belly and never be heard of again. For about three months the boys waited in the house and were subject to beatings, forced to stay awake for long periods, and took only a minimum amount of food and drink.

> At length the day arrived for the summoning of the monsters. Word had been sent out to the villages which had proclaimed the taboo, and a vast concourse of people was by this time in attendance. They remained till the last rite ended, causing severe strain on their hosts' resources.
>
> The pretence was that the monsters lived underground and a hole was accordingly dug from which they could emerge. At first only a faint humming was heard, and the women murmured amongst themselves that the tree roots must be scraping their flanks. Soon afterwards a man covered with earth went along to the village to announce how deep down the monsters had been but that they had at last appeared. The humming now became louder, till in the end the whole countryside rang with the booming of dozens of bullroarers.
>
> The boys had to listen for a few days and were then brought out and shown by their guardians, with much impressive ritual, how the noise was made. A poisonous fish was later flourished in front of their mouths, and they were warned that if a word of what had been disclosed crossed their lips they would perish as assuredly as if they had swallowed a deadly toxin.
>
> This revelation was followed by the incision rite. This time the boys were cut by one or other of the guardians, but on all subsequent occasions each person operated on himself. A long low shed had been built to represent one of the monsters, and inside the two men waited with their obsidian knives. The lads were taken in turn, each one being carried on the back of his sponsor, who also served as a support while the gash was being made. The blood, as the first which they had shed, was especially sacred, and the sponsors gathered it in leaves for use later as face paint.[16]

16. H. Ian Hogbin, "Pagan Religion in a New Guinea Village," in John Middleton, ed., *Gods and Rituals*, New York, Natural History Press, 1967, pp. 57–61.

Afterwards the youths were given a ceremonial bath by their sponsors. This was followed by a great feast where the boys sat while relatives and friends danced and sang songs in their honor.

In his classic account of initiation rites, Arnold Van Gennep characterizes them as "rites of passage" in which, by "crossing a threshold," the initiate feels that he has moved from one world to another. The basic pattern is separation from a previous world, transition, incorporation into the new world.[17] The separation and transition are a period of isolation and danger, as when the New Guinea youth are physically isolated inside the house, tormented by the threat of monsters, and finally wounded by the incision rite, in such a way that the possibility of death becomes very real. Afterward, they are incorporated into a new social reality in the manner indicated. In this example the transition is presented mainly on the social level, but the model is also used to elaborate a more inner rite of passage from a mundane to a sacred mode of spiritual being. Through the dark night of the soul the descent into the belly of the primeval monster, the symbolic death, the resurrection to a new mode of being, the initiate is transformed, re-created, reestablished as a new being.

In the history of religions many examples of this initiation pattern can be recognized; religious art, myths, and theologies constantly exhibit this model, and it is one of the basic and most convincing examples of how ritual provides the structural base for the ideational themes and flights of imagery in a religion's symbolic system.

At the moment, however, we are concerned in particular with how initiation rites provide the means by which the initiate works out the task of forming both his personal and social identity. Various psychological interpretations of initiation patterns overlap and complement rather than contradict one another. For example, circumcision and subincision rites among primitive tribes can be interpreted according to functional theory as the means whereby fear is faced and overcome through the endurance of the frightening act. Anthropologists influenced by Freud will further observe that the perennial hostilities between fathers and sons are also faced and resolved through an act in which a real threat by the "father" is transformed into a symbolic act that resolves tensions and unites the fathers and sons in a common bond.[18] Bruno Bettelheim, on the other hand, argues that in the subincision rite the male discovers a means whereby he works out the problem of his relationship and identity, not in terms of the father and male, but in terms of the mother and the female. The envy of the male for the woman, who possesses a strange power through her menstrual cycle, is mitigated by a rite in which the male also bleeds, thus imitating the woman and finding compensation for his own "inferiority" in this respect.[19]

17. Arnold Van Gennep, *Rites of Passage,* Chicago, The University of Chicago Press, 1960, pp. 20–21.
18. Geza Roheim, *The Eternal Ones of the Dream: A Psychoanalytic Interpretation of Australian Myth and Ritual,* New York, International Universities Press, 1945.
19. Bruno Bettelheim, *Symbolic Wounds,* New York, Collier Books, 1962.

Such practices play an important part in the concerns of the tribal religion. The sexual nature of man is a fact of his life that no philosophy or religion of any scope has ignored. Tribal man has found the means, through ritual and symbol, to resolve tensions and psychic conflicts, restore inner equilibrium, and provide a sense of social, personal, and sexual identity for the developing and maturing person. Indeed, a sophisticated modern who has rejected all myth and ritual as barbaric superstition must still face the task of fashioning a self-image and style with which and by which he can live. Scorning the symbolic tools of a religious culture, the modern often finds himself on a psychologist's couch instead, where he works out a personality transformation (a rite of passage) through myths and symbols (now called dream imagery), in ways similar to those practiced by the primitive religionist on a less deliberate and more traditional level.

THE DEPTH-
PSYCHOLOGICAL
FUNCTION OF
RELIGION

The functions of religion so far noted are interesting and important. However, we only reach the center of functional analysis when we consider how ritual and myth help man face those experiences in life when his ordinary defenses against the dangers of existence are threatened or found to be inadequate. Thomas O'Dea has succinctly summarized these dimensions as contingency (or uncertainty), powerlessness, and scarcity. Often we are uncertain about the course of events that affect our prosperity and good fortune. We are afflicted with the sense of helplessness as we find ourselves impotent to control events according to our own chosen goals. Or, again, nature does not provide with sufficient abundance for our needs.

Such situations lead to frustration and deprivation. Ritual and myth are used to deal with this aspect of human experience in a number of ways. Man may seek to enhance ordinary powers through magical spells. Perhaps he is encouraged to greater effort by rituals that sustain hope and keep confidence alive. Again, he may find in a sacred story consolation and the means to accept that which cannot be changed so that personality disintegration through anxiety and grief is prevented.

Too often this point is made by the modern observer in a curiously detached manner that seems to preclude his own involvement in a human and cosmic situation common to all. Tribal man faces the problem of the "limit-situation" not as the result of his stupidity, superstition, or technological lack. The relation between man and his environment has been such from the dawn of history to the present hour that "contingency, powerlessness, and scarcity" are not expressions of subjective fear only, but appropriate descriptions of the objective relationship of man to nature. Modern man has increased his power through technological efficiency. The fact still remains that he does not know when and if his nation will be destroyed in an atomic war or if national prosperity will continue. The individual man still does not know what accident or illness may suddenly strike him in the midst of an affluent society.

If we once recognize this aspect of our own contemporary situation, we can better appreciate the meaningfulness of the *depth problem* primitive man acknowledges, whether or not we decide to accept his particular solution. John Dewey makes the point with telling accuracy:

> It is an old saying that the gods were born of fear. The saying is only too likely to strengthen a misconception bred by confirmed subjective habits. We first endow man in isolation with an instinct of fear and then we imagine him irrationally ejecting that fear into the environment, scattering broadcast as it were, the fruits of his own purely personal limitations, and thereby creating superstition. But fear, whether an instinct or an acquisition, is a function of the environment. Man fears because he exists in a fearful, an awful world. The world *is* precarious and perilous. It is as easily accessible and striking evidence of this fact that primitive experience is cited. The voice is that of early man; but the hand is that of nature, the nature in which we still live.[20]

Furthermore, we must be careful not to state this situation in too narrowly instrumental a manner. The problem man faces is not simply one of finding a means to gain the power or method that can overcome or subvert the effects of the humanly frustrating aspects of nature, though this personal instrumental need is certainly important. More significant, however, is the problem, indeed the *crisis*, generated in man by the occurrence of tragic events which he cannot satisfactorily integrate into his system of beliefs and values.

This is the *problem of meaning* which existential philosophers argue still perplexes modern man. It is true that many modern thinkers rather insist that it is "the question of meaning" itself that is "meaningless." It is not necessary for us to engage here in this philosophical dispute, but it is important to see that whatever may be our decision about the logical viability of the problem according to present-day norms of intelligibility, descriptive accuracy forces us to recognize the problem as a real one in the tribal patterns we are examining. We would add that it also afflicts modern man as well, whether or not this discloses a logical confusion on his part.

Fundamentally, the problem is an existential one concerning the fate of the individual within the wider nexus of natural events. When disease or disaster strikes a person, he may be initiated into a confused and disintegrated state of personal being in which the question of "Why?" or even more directly "Why me?" is an inevitable response. What does such a question mean? The person may have a very clear notion of the causal chain of events that led to tragedy. This does not prevent him from experiencing shock, confusion, alienation.

Evidently the shock is generated by a sense of inner dislocation, a felt incongruity between man and outer world taking place on an emotional and valuational level rather than a strictly logical or common-sense one. When the events of nature and his own desires coalesce in a set of successful goal-directed actions, man feels a

20. John Dewey, *Experience and Nature,* New York, Dover, 1958, p. 42.

sense of harmonious relation between himself and his world. Failure and frustration generate an inner sense of disharmony. One still perceives the external structure of the natural pattern, but he no longer feels that he either understands or appreciates it. He is emotionally and axiologically alienated from his world and its underlying significance. The question "Why?" is the expression of his alienation.

We can see the structure of the problem in the classic study of Azande witchcraft by Evans-Pritchard; he points out that it is a serious error to deem the Azande, an African tribe, to be ignorant or oblivious to a nexus of ordinary or natural causation among events. For example, if a granary collapses and injures people who were sitting under it to avail themselves of its shade, the Azande clearly understand the common-sense series of causes that led to the catastrophe. Termites had undermined the supports, a fact the Azande know and acknowledge. The motives that led the people to be sitting there are also obvious and understandable. The fact still remains that the Azande feel the need to add a further explanation—witchcraft—to explain, not why such events occur in general, but why this happened at that particular time and place to those particular people. Evans-Pritchard insists that the witchcraft explanation is not an alternative to ordinary common-sense explanations, but a supplement needed to meet the existential factor of the event as it afflicts a specific individual. Thus, "Fire is hot, but it is not hot owing to witchcraft, for that is its nature. It is a universal quality of fire to burn, but it is not a universal quality of fire to burn *you*. This may never happen; or once in a lifetime, and then only if you have been bewitched." [21]

We need not here decide whether tribal patterns finally "answer" this question. Since, as we have noted, its basic components are emotional and axiological rather than intellectual, the question is answered well enough on one level through rituals and myths that enable the person to overcome his emotional alienation and reestablish some kind of behavioral harmony with his world. As Clifford Geertz observes:

As a religious problem, the problem of suffering is, paradoxically, not how to avoid suffering but how to suffer, how to make of physical pain, personal loss, worldly defeat, or the helpless contemplation of others' agony something bearable, supportable— something, as we say, sufferable. . . . As religion on one side anchors the power of our symbolic resources for formulating analytic ideas in an authoritative conception of the overall shape of reality, so on another side it anchors the power of our, also symbolic, resources for expressing emotions—moods, sentiments, passions, affections, feelings—in a similar conception of its pervasive tenor, its inherent tone and temper. For those able to embrace them, and for so long as they are able to embrace them,

21. E. E. Evans-Pritchard, *Witchcraft, Oracles and Magic Among the Azande*, London, Oxford, 1940, p. 69.

*religious symbols provide a cosmic guarantee not only for their
ability to comprehend the world, but also, comprehending it, to
give a precision to their feeling, a definition to their emotions
which enables them, morosely or joyfully, grimly or cavalierly, to
endure it.*[22]

How do religious rites and myths accomplish this purpose? A full
explanation is beyond the scope of this introductory survey and has
probably not yet been formulated. Furthermore, we must leave open
the possibility that religion does not fully accomplish its purpose but
merely makes a valiant attempt to do so.

However, a provisional explanation that fits a great deal of the
material and is in harmony with the emphasis of many contemporary historians of religion might call attention to the way in which
rite and myth enable the sufferer to feel that he is participating in a
cosmic drama transcending his private existence and in which his
personal pain is seen as a significant part of this larger meaningful
whole.

It is not suffering that is the problem so much as meaningless
suffering. Man can endure pain but not chaos. Says Geertz, quoting
Salvador de Madariaga, the minimal definition of religion might be
"the relatively modest dogma that God is not mad." [23] Through ritual and myth, man is able to correlate the inexplicable and unacceptable elements of his life from the threat of this final incoher-
ence. His pain may still be terrible and heart-rending. It is not finally
unendurable.

Lévi-Strauss offers a fascinating account of how ritual and myth
accomplish this feat in his summary of the song sung by a Cuna
shaman (a tribal holy man possessing unusual powers) over a
woman suffering from a difficult childbirth. According to the song,
the shaman sets out for the house of Muu who is a spirit responsible for the fetus. She is not a fundamentally evil power, but a force
gone awry who destroyed the bodily health by disturbing the powers
belonging to various parts of the body and destroying the natural
harmony of that body. The shaman goes on a hazardous journey, a
descent into the depths where Muu is and which reminds us of the
initiation patterns of separation, descent, return, which we have already noted. In this case, what is so fascinating is that the encounter with various mythical powers can be seen to clearly correspond
to various parts of the woman's body, so that her suffering and
physical problems are rendered in the song as a part of a larger
cosmic drama. She faces on the conscious level the details of her
suffering through the mythical language of the song. In doing so,
she does not escape the pain, but it is rendered more bearable
through its participation in struggle with Muu, who is both a mythic
power and the vagina and womb of the pregnant woman.

Lévi-Strauss points out that such practices do effect cures. As the

22. Clifford Geertz, "Religion as a Cultural System," in M. Banton, ed.,
Anthropological Approaches to the Study of Religion, New York, Praeger,
1966, p. 19.

23. Ibid., p. 13.

shaman conquers Muu and returns from her stronghold, the woman may have successful birth. What has happened?

> *The cure would consist, therefore, in making explicit a situation originally existing on the emotional level and in rendering accept-able to the mind pains which the body refuses to tolerate . . . the tutelary spirits and malevolent spirits, the supernatural monsters and magical animals, are all part of a coherent system on which the native conception of the universe is founded. The sick woman accepts these mythical beings, or, more accurately, she has never questioned their existence. What she does not accept are the in-coherent and arbitrary pains, which are an alien element in her system but which the shaman, calling upon the myth, will re-inte-grate within a whole where everything is meaningful.*[24]

Lévi-Strauss continues:

> *The shaman provides the sick woman with a* language, *by means of which unexpressed, and otherwise, inexpressible, psychic states can be immediately expressed. And it is the transition to this verbal expression—at the same time making it possible to undergo in an ordered and intelligible form a real experience that would otherwise be chaotic and inexpressible—which induces the release of the physiological process, that is, the reorganization, in a favorable direction, of the process to which the sick woman is subjected.*[25]

Even when a ritual does not purport to specifically cure an ill, it may in a general way perform the kind of function Lévi-Strauss de-scribes. It is significant that most myths contain accounts of strug-gle and loss; rituals contain elements of pain and sacrifice. Through participation in these forms, the participant prepares himself for the encounter with tragedy; he does not escape his ordeal nor does he pretend to; but the total devastation of the pain is mitigated by its incorporation in a larger cosmic pattern. The alienation from an in-tractable world is overcome. Suffering man still belongs.

In this light we may appreciate Susanne Langer's apt observation:

> *Myth . . . at least at its best is a recognition of natural conflicts, of human desire frustrated by non-human powers, hostile oppres-sion, or contrary desires; it is a story of the birth, passion, and defeat by death which is man's common fate. Its ultimate end is not wishful distortion of the world, but serious envisagement of its fundamental truths; moral orientation, not escape.*[26]

THE EXPRESSIVE
FUNCTION OF
RITUAL AND MYTH

The obvious facts of the social functionality of ritual and myth can-not be denied. Yet something seems to be missing from the ac-count. Many sociologists and philosophers have opened up a fresh

24. Claude Lévi-Strauss, *Structural Anthropology*, Garden City, N.Y., Doubleday Anchor, 1967, pp. 192–193.

25. Ibid., p. 193.

26. Susanne Langer, *Philosophy in a New Key*, New York, Mentor Books, 1964, p. 153.

avenue of approach by stressing another aspect of ritual and myth that functional analysis tended to neglect. The problem is that a functional approach encourages us to look at all human behavior in a purely practical and manipulative way. Functionality tends to be identified with instrumentality, so that each activity is considered as a *means* by which we accomplish some other goal external to the action itself. Activity is thought of as goal-oriented, and each specific action is the instrument or tool by which we hope to achieve a given aim.

However, we may begin to wonder, are all activities instrumental in this sense? If so, do we never reach our goals? Are we always on the way, and never arriving? Are there no activities which are not means to ends, but rather ends in themselves?

Two dimensions of human activity in particular accentuate these questions: play and art. What is the functionality of play? In answering this question, the perplexing issues that have plagued us in the preceding discussion are brought into sharper focus. We might want to argue that a child's play has obvious biological and psychological value. It can exercise bodily muscles, relax tensions, provide welcome interludes between tiring periods of study or work. Perhaps it generates learning under the guise of pleasure. Many parents cognizant of these possibilities encourage their children to play, convinced of the basic "usefulness" of such behavior. Yet if the child himself entered into his play activity with those goals in mind, the event would cease to be play. The deliberate attempt to activate bodily functions is called exercise, not play. Deliberate relaxation is called rest. The development of skills, even when enjoyable, is called learning. The distinguishing character of play is that it is spontaneous, unmotivated, an activity pursued exuberantly for its own sake. We can either say it has no goal (when defined as an aim external to the action itself) or that its goal is inherent in the action itself. The purpose of the behavior is in the behavior. It is not the means to some other end, but an end in itself.

Similarly, art may serve all kinds of subsidiary purposes. It may be used for instruction, an aid in psychological integration, or diversion of the mind from some unpleasant truth. However, the artist who produces the work is not primarily concerned with these kinds of instrumental goals. He delights in making the art product as an aesthetic entity, an end in itself. So we make a house to protect ourselves from the elements; but the artistic decorations of that house do not serve the same kind of practical purpose. Yet they are valued, appreciated, and make living in the house a rich human experience, not a matter of brute necessity alone.

We are not necessarily insisting that this observation comprises a fully adequate aesthetic theory. It is sufficient for our purposes to observe that the cultural activities of man reveal aspects in which play and aesthetic expression are as important, sometimes more important, than strictly instrumental and practical considerations. John Dewey makes this point:

Human experience in the large, its course and conspicuous features, has for one of its most striking features preoccupation with direct enjoyment, feasting and festivities, ornamentation, dance, song, dramatic pantomime, telling yarns and enacting stories. In comparison with intellectual and moral endeavor, this trait of experience has hardly received the attention from philosophers that it demands. Even philosophers who have conceived that pleasure is the sole motive of man and the attainment of happiness his whole aim, have given a curiously sober, drab account of the working of pleasure and the search for happiness. Consider the utilitarians, how they toiled, spun, and wove, but who never saw man arrayed in joy as the lilies of the field. Happiness was to them a matter of calculation and effort, guided by mathematical book-keeping. The history of man shows however that man takes his enjoyment neat, and at as short range as possible. . . . The body is decked before it is clothed. While homes are still hovels, temples and palaces are embellished. Luxuries prevail over necessities except when necessities can be festally celebrated. Men make a game of their fishing and hunting. . . . Useful labor is, whenever possible, transformed by ceremonial and ritual accompaniments, subordinated to art that yields immediate enjoyment.[27]

When Dewey says that the play element has not received the attention from philosophers that it deserves, there are notable exceptions like John Huizinga and Susanne Langer. John Huizinga has written a classic on the play element in culture called *Homo Ludens.* He defines play as

voluntary activity or occupation executed within fixed limits of time and place, according to rules freely accepted but absolutely binding, having its aim in itself and accompanied by a feeling of tension, joy and the consciousness that it is "different" from "ordinary life." [28]

This point of the "difference" generated by play is important. Huizinga argues that an intriguing similarity between play and religious ritual is to be found in the way that both set apart a sort of area—the "play-ground" or the "holy place"—where their respective actions are pursued. "Formally speaking, there is no distinction whatever between marking out a space for a sacred purpose and marking it out for purposes of sheer play. The turf, the tennis-court, the chess board and pavement-hopscotch cannot formally be distinguished from the temple or the magic circle." [29]

Another point of similarity between play and ritual lies in the "play-acting" quality exhibited in both. Play quickly assumes the form of drama (which we commonly call "a play") where the actors assume identities different from their everyday personalities and simulate actions different from those performed in their practical

27. Dewey, op. cit., pp. 78–79.
28. John Huizinga, *Homo Ludens,* Boston, Beacon Press, 1950, p. 28.
29. Ibid., p. 20.

life. The participants in a ritual also often assume a special garb—ceremonial robes, for example—and roles different from their ordinary selves. We have seen how the Tikopia chief, for example, claimed to be the god during the time of ritual. This claim can be explained in various ways. Here we want to stress that the chief's action is analogous to that of an actor who assumes a role for the duration of the play.

There is in both play and ritual the sense of generating or creating "another world" where the action, separated from everyday concerns, is integrated into a "make-believe," "imaginary," or "magic" realm. The performers of a ritual introduce us to "another world" different from that of everyday practical life. We have already witnessed many examples in the preceding discussion where ritual and myth assume the form of play. In the ceremony of the hot food, the solemnity of a feast with the high god is interwoven with a kind of game (who can eat his hot yam first). The solemnities finish with laughing and humorous exchanges. In the initiation of the New Guinea youths, we have seen how the youths are frightened by stories of the monsters. Finally they discover that the monsters are really their fathers. They do not respond with anger at the "deception," but enjoy their participation in the dramatic play.

Certain semantic difficulties beset the analysis of play and art. Shall we say such activities are "goal-less" or rather that the "goal" is inherent in the action itself? Even if a person performs an action for no purpose external to the action itself, do we not still want to say that he has a "purpose" or "reason" for performing it? The philosopher Immanuel Kant characterized aesthetic experience as "purposiveness without purpose." Some decisions as to basic usage of these words is required. Perhaps we can say that all behavior without exception has a "function." It does something and when we have adequately determined what is being done, we discern its functionality. We then can observe that many functions are "instrumental," i.e., they are means to an end external to the behavior itself. Other functions are "expressive," i.e., their performance has a self-justifying quality absent from purely instrumental activities. We may also observe that acts can be both instrumental and expressive at the same time.

Insight into the play element of culture is a key that will probably unlock many doors to a more profound understanding of religion. Nevertheless, the point must not be exaggerated. Play is intimately related to ritual, but probably not identical with it. For example, the solemnity of many rituals and the rigidity with which some of their sequential patterns are followed seem different from the spirit of spontaneous play. Furthermore, play complements but does not exclude the instrumental aspect of life. Religion seems to operate in both realms and it is the intricate way in which practical purposes and expressive celebration are intertwined that make it so difficult to interpret in a single formula.

In this connection the relation between magic and religion that is often discussed in anthropological literature is significant.

MAGIC
AND RELIGION

Although many of the ideas of James Frazer about archaic religions have been rejected by later scholars, his description of magic is still illuminating. According to Frazer, primitive magic is based on two principles. One is that homeopathic magic is based on the principle of similarity. In this view, a picture of an object can be used to affect the condition of the object that it resembles. For example, if you stick pins into a doll the person whom the doll resembles will be hurt. A second principle of magic that Frazer notes is the law of contagion, whereby magical influences are based on physical contiguity. Thus a sorcerer can injure another person if he can obtain a bit of his hair, a nail clipping, a shred of his clothes, even the dust he has trodden. In these instances it seems as if the separate identities of things have been lost. A thing like another seems to become in some sense the other. The part (a bit of hair) becomes the whole (the person). What is done to the part affects the whole.

According to Frazer, magic in its pure state is completely unrelated to religion defined as an orientation toward spirits, gods, or other beings transcending the natural order of the physical cosmos. The magician "supplicates no higher power: he sues the favour of no fickle and wayward being: he abases himself before no awful deity. Yet his power, great as he believes it to be, is by no means arbitrary and unlimited. He can wield it only as he strictly conforms to the rules of his art, or to what may be called the laws of nature as conceived by him." [30] Frazer argued that the magician had greater affinities to the scientist than to the religionist. Both magician and scientist assume the succession of events to be "perfectly regular and certain, being determined by immutable laws, the operation of which can be foreseen and calculated precisely; the elements of caprice, of chance, and of accident are banished from the course of nature." [31]

The only difference between the two is that the magician employs a "total misconception of the nature of the particular laws which govern that sequence," since similarity and contiguity are not the basis of real causality in nature.

Malinowski accepted this distinction in the main, but with some interesting qualifications. He adds to Frazer's analysis the point that magic is individualistic while religion is predominantly social. Thus Malinowski argues that religion is expressed in myths and rituals that have a social import and in which the whole tribe participates, while magic is usually an affair in which a private individual seeks out the sorcerer in order to accomplish some specific personal goal, like the death of an enemy, the realization of love from a desired man or woman, cure for disease, the achievement of prosperity or victory in war.

According to this distinction, it seems that magic aspires to attain an essentially manipulative relation with the forces of nature. It wants to control them for personal ends. Religion, on the other

30. James Frazer, *The Golden Bough,* Vol. I, abridged edition, New York, Macmillan, 1958, p. 56.
31. Ibid., p. 56.

hand, seeks to enter into a *communal* relation with spiritual beings (the gods) who are more than impersonal forces. Religion may seek help from the gods, but it can only beseech, never command. We might expand this distinction by use of the famous categories "I-it" and "I-thou" propounded by Martin Buber. Magic in its pure form establishes a manipulative, I-it relation with nature; religion aspires to an I-thou relationship of personal meeting in which man seeks to serve and adore his god as much as he seeks to be served by him. Or again, using the terminology developed in the second chapter, magic is essentially concerned with the instrumental dimension of life, while religion emphasizes the expressive. Thus Malinowski points out that magic uses its techniques as means to external ends, while religion usually develops a social ritual that is an end in itself. He portrays "magic as a practical art consisting of acts which are only means to a definite end expected to follow later on; religion as a body of self-contained acts being themselves the fulfillment of their purpose." [32]

Although this distinction is useful for certain purposes, it encourages a wide separation of human practices that cannot be meaningfully maintained. We seldom, if ever, find in a human society the instance of magic as oblivious to the realm of personal spirits and gods as Frazer described. The magical element is not as purely manipulative nor the religious as nonmanipulative as is here suggested. Also, religion can be individualistic, and some magical ceremonies have a communal and social form to their enactment. Thus Raymond Firth, for example, observed:

> The Arika Kafika, in praying for rain to fertilize the crops, did not pour water on the ground or make motions to imitate clouds. He spoke of rain and clouds by way of appeal, and where he symbolized them he did so in verbal imagery and not by crude signs. So also in other respects the Tikopia pagan priest was much more allusive, much more "poetic" in his rite and formula than is the public functionary presented to us by Frazer.[33]

The fact is that we rarely, if ever, find in human culture an example of "pure" manipulative magic devoid of communal elements, or a pure religion that stresses only the I-thou relation with no thought of personal needs and goals at all. On the contrary, we find the instrumental and the expressive, the manipulative and the communal, in dynamic interaction.

This point has led William Goode to suggest that magic and religion should be conceived as polar variables rather than exclusive alternatives. In this view magic and religion should be conceived as existing along a single continuum, magic representing one extreme limit of total manipulation and religion the other extreme limit of communal expressiveness. Most examples fall somewhere in between and represent a magico-religious complex in which both poles may be in equilibrium or one or the other may predominate.

32. Malinowski, op. cit., p. 88.
33. *Work*, pp. 17–18.

Thomas O'Dea has admirably summarized the relation between magic and religion:

Religion has been defined in terms of functional theory as the manipulation of non-empirical or supraempirical means for non-empirical or supraempirical ends; magic as the manipulation of non-empirical or supraempirical means for empirical ends. But the use of the term "manipulation" in the definition of religion is inaccurate and fails to describe adequately the religious attitude. Religion offers what is felt to be a way of entering into a relationship with the supraempirical aspects of reality, be they conceived as God, gods, or otherwise. Magic differs from religion in that it is manipulative in essence; yet magical manipulation too is conducted in an atmosphere of fear and respect, marvel and wonder, similar to that which characterizes the religious relationship.[34]

An analogy of religion with ordinary human social relationships is here helpful. When we engage in a meaningful relation with another person, what is our motive? Is it the purely manipulative one of "getting something" from him. We can describe the relation in these terms, because even altruistic impulses like love can be converted into the form of a "need for love" which is satisfied by a relation with the other.

However, such language distorts the full complexity of what is taking place. It would be too unrealistic to say that a friend can never be of "use" to us; but neither is it accurate to say that we do not value the friendship for its own sake; it is a fact that we want to give to as well as get from the relationship, so that practical and communal concerns are intimately intertwined. In the same manner, the religious relationship probably contains within it both magical and communal elements in varying degrees of interaction.

One problem in the use of this distinction is that it seems to assume that religion, by definition, is a benign phenomenon contrasted with dehumanizing magic. It would seem more useful as an objective categorical tool to refer to manipulative and communal poles both of which participate in the phenomenon we call religion. Religion can assume a manipulative form when the gods are cajoled, begged, tricked, or forced into serving some limited human end. It can also have the more expansive, altruistic dimensions we have noted. By the same token, magic has in it elements that are more noninstrumental and expressive than is often recognized. Thus Langer argues that

whatever purpose magical practice may serve, its direct motivation is the desire to symbolize great conceptions. It is the overt action in which a rich and savage imagination automatically ends. Its origin is probably not practical at all, but ritualistic; its central aim is to symbolize a Presence, to aid in the formulation

34. Thomas O'Dea, *The Sociology of Religion*, Englewood Cliffs, N.J., Prentice-Hall, 1966, p. 7.

of a religious universe. . . . Magic is never employed in a commonplace mood, like ordinary causal agency; this fact belies the widely accepted belief that the "method of magic" rests on a mistaken view of causality. After all, a savage who beats a tom-tom to drive off his brother's malaria would never make such a practical mistake as to shoot his arrow blunt end forward or bait his fishline with flowers. It is not ignorance of causal relations, but the supervention of an interest stronger than his practical interest, that holds him to magical rites. This stronger interest concerns the expressive *value of such mystic acts.*

Magic, then, is not a method, but a language; it is part and parcel of that greater phenomenon, ritual, *which is the language of religion. Ritual is a symbolic transformation of experiences that no other medium can adequately express. Because it springs from a primary human need, it is a spontaneous activity—that is to say, it arises without intention, without adaptation to a conscious purpose; its growth is undesigned, its pattern purely natural, however intricate it may be. It was never "imposed" on people; they acted thus quite of themselves, exactly as bees swarmed and birds built nests, squirrels hoarded food, and cats washed their faces. No one made up ritual, any more than anyone made up Hebrew or Sanskrit or Latin. The forms of expressive acts—speech and gesture, song and sacrifice—are the symbolic transformations which minds of certain species, at certain stages of their development and communion, naturally produce.*[35]

We conclude that a proper account of religious phenomena must include recognition of both instrumental and expressive elements. In the end, the distinction between them should not be made in a sharp and exclusive manner. Actually, instrumental symbols have an expressive element and expressive symbols are functional and even instrumental in some sense. The recognition of the expressive character of religious symbols will keep us from approaching them with a heavy, hyperserious frame of mind that misses their exuberant, creative, often playful character. Many religious acts and symbols are both means to an end and an end in themselves.

35. Langer, op. cit., p. 52.

RELIGION AS SYMBOLIC EXPRESSION: THE INTERPRETATION OF MYTH

THE HERMENEUTICAL APPROACH TO RELIGION

In the preceding chapter we considered how ritual actions perform various functions for human beings in their personal and social lives. In the course of this examination we have seen how doing and meaning are inextricably connected. Ritual acts are themselves highly symbolic. Furthermore, myths, emblems, and other symbolic devices are often used in conjunction with ritual to convey complex meanings. In this chapter we want to look at religious phenomena primarily as modes of symbolic expression.

At the present time great interest exists among scholars from a variety of fields in the phenomenon of human symbolism. Psychologists study the symbols man forms in his dreams. Archeologists look for the significance of human artifacts from ancient civilizations. Mathematicians and logicians have made great advances in understanding how systems of very abstract signs operate. Linguists, philologists, and semanticists have investigated the function of meaning in human language. Some contemporary philosophies have turned to a consideration of problems generated by the "uses" of language. Susanne Langer therefore argues in *Philosophy in a New Key* that the emphasis on symbolization is the "key" to contemporary thought taken as a whole. The focus of attention has turned from what a man says to the symbolic modes by which he says it, though the two aspects are, of course, intricately related.

It is this entire approach that we here call the hermeneutical perspective. We might with equal appropriateness call it the semiological approach, but this term has come to be associated with one specific school within the entire spectrum of studies of symbolism. "Hermeneutics" is also used in a narrower sense to refer to the techniques by which scholars interpret the meanings of written documents. For example, in the study of Judaism and Christianity the interpretation of the biblical writings is called hermeneutics. However, for want of a better word we use the term here in a broader sense to include all attempts to interpret the meanings of any kind of symbol whatsoever. As Mircea Eliade puts it:

> *By means of a competent hermeneutics, history of religions ceases to be a museum of fossils, ruins, and obsolete mirabilia and becomes what it should have been from the beginning for any investigator: a series of "messages" waiting to be deciphered and understood.*[1]

The approach to the study of man through the act of symbolization thus has important implications for the study of religion. Let us look at some of the presuppositions of this approach.

Man has been defined in different ways. For example, he has been called the rational animal, the religious animal, the tool-making animal. According to the emphasis of contemporary thought, he is frequently defined as the symbol-making animal. Symbols should be distinguished from signals or "triggers." Animals, for example, can respond to various sounds or smells that trigger certain actions. Thus an animal hunting another animal finds that the smell of that animal is a "trigger" that directs his movements toward the one hunted.

THE
SYMBOL-MAKING
ANIMAL

Human beings also respond to signals. But in addition, human beings are able to distinguish between the sign and the thing signified by it and to perceive the symbolic relation between them. For example, language is an obvious illustration of the human symbolic capacity. Combinations of sounds are used as symbolic counters to mean various aspects of human experience. Yet the sounds have no intrinsic connection with what they mean; the relation between the two is a symbolic one established by man's capacity to distinguish between sign and the thing signified.

Man uses many other kinds of phenomena besides sounds as symbolic devices. For example, facial expressions are symbolic, as the phrase implies. A smile means pleasure or approval; a frown indicates displeasure or disapproval. A hunter marks a tree or puts a twig on the ground pointing a certain way; a man who later reaches this place interprets the symbolic vehicles as meaning that the hunter has gone ahead in a given direction. A man may paint his body or put on certain kinds of clothing which indicate the status or role that he has assumed in a given society.

1. Mircea Eliade, *The Quest*, Chicago, The University of Chicago Press, 1969, preface.

Religion provides a striking and extremely widespread example of man's symbolic activity. Religions throughout the world have made use of various phenomena of nature and human culture to serve as symbolic devices through which complex meanings are conveyed. For example:

1. *Sounds.* Certain exclamations and sacred cries are used in tribal religious rites. In the Upanishads of Hinduism we learn of a sacred sound or word, *om.*

2. *Myths expressed in language.* As we have seen, sacred stories are often told that convey complex meanings.

3. *Beliefs expressed in language.* Many religions contain a set of statements about man, the world, and the gods that are orally transmitted or set down in writing.

4. *Rituals.* As we saw in the last chapter, ceremonial actions are used to convey religious meanings.

5. *Colors.* Colors or combinations of colors can be used as symbols. Green has been taken to mean fertility, red sacrifice, and so forth.

6. *Emblems.* Distinctive forms like a cross, a swastika, the yin-yang circle, are used to convey complex meanings.

7. *Natural objects.* Stones, trees, rivers, mountains, have been used in various religions as symbols with sacred significance.

8. *Buildings.* Religious edifices often have symbolic intentions as well as functional utility. For example, some Christian churches deliberately take the form of a cross. Islamic mosques face Mecca, and so forth.

This brief list is in no sense exhaustive of the symbolic possibilities in religion. There is no phenomenon of nature or human thought that cannot be used as a religious sign.

Many helpful studies of religious symbols have been made by modern scholars. One difficulty for the beginning student is caused by the fact that there is no common agreement in the voluminous literature on how words like "sign" and "symbol" are to be used. The student must learn how such terms are defined by a given writer and recognize the fact that another writer may define them differently.

Some common religious symbols. Top to bottom: chi-rho; swastika; yin-yang; mandala.

Often the terms "sign" and "symbol" are used as synonyms to refer to the entire range of devices that can be used to convey meanings. Sometimes a distinction is made between a sign which has one direct meaning and a symbol which is more complex and conveys many meanings through a single vehicle. For example, Susanne Langer describes presentational symbols that combine a number of meanings into a single comprehensive and unitary form. Thus an animal might respond to a drop of splashing water as the natural signal of a river nearby. A human being may, in addition, use the word "water" as a linguistic sign of that same river. Or again, he may paint a picture of that river which now functions as a presentational symbol. What does the symbol mean? The significations are complex and multiform. Perhaps it still refers to the physical river, but in addition conveys memories of the refreshing quality of water in general and its value for human life. Perhaps the painting is put in a religious temple and is interpreted in connection with a need for the spiritual water of eternal life or the need of ritual cleansing from moral defilement. The notion of the physical river is now subordinated to the idea of moral cleansing and that which quenches a "spiritual" thirst. Many religions use the symbol of water in these complex ways.

Paul Tillich makes a distinction between sign and symbol that is similar but not identical with that of Langer. To Tillich the former points to a single object in an external and largely instrumental manner. A symbol, as Tillich sees it, not only points to its referent, but in some sense, seems to the user of the symbol to participate in it. For example, the phrase "United States" is a "sign" referring to a certain country. The American flag is a "symbol" that somehow shares in the reality that it represents. Consequently, respect shown the flag is respect for the country itself. Symbol and symbolized are integrally connected.

It is obvious that the religions of the world display many such symbols like the Buddhist lotus flower, the yin-yang symbol of the Chinese, the Jewish star of David, the Christian cross. An adequate interpretation of any religion must include an engagement with its most fundamental symbols. Emblems and icons, architectural shapes, colors, natural objects like stones or mountains, can assume such a symbolic significance according to the religious context in which they are placed.

An awareness of the symbolic texture of religion can help us avoid interpretations of religious forms that are simplistic or reductionist. Too often we treat a religious expression as if it conveyed one single meaning that can easily be understood on some literal level of significance restricted to the external apprehension of the physical world.

However, we have already seen evidence that rituals and myths have the capacity for symbolic condensation whereby a number of interacting meanings are conveyed simultaneously. It is this insight that helps us to see that the various interpretations of ritual we have so far considered are complementary meanings rather than exclusive alternatives. The Tikopia rite, for example, can refer to social relations, personal problems, depth meanings concerning limit questions, and the realm of the gods simultaneously through their amazing symbolic capacity to compress the manifold dimensions of existence into unifying symbolic forms.

A typical totempole of the Northwest Coast Indians. (Courtesy of the American Museum of Natural History.)

Recently a number of scholars have sought to develop a new science called semiology which is distinct from though related to linguistics. Linguistics is the study of the structures of language. Important work has been done in this field by such figures as R. Jakobson, M. Halle, N. Chomsky, among others. Ferdinand de Saussure was a pioneer in the study of linguistics who considered the possibility of a more comprehensive study of symbolism that would include other systems of meaning beside language. Thus one of his disciples, Roland Barthes, defines semiology as the study of

THE SEMIOLOGICAL APPROACH TO RELIGION

any system of signs, whatever their substance and limits; images, gestures, musical sounds, objects, and the complex associations of all these, which form the content of ritual, convention, or public entertainment: these constitute, if not languages, *at least systems of signification.*[2]

This last phrase is important. We are all aware that a language is not a mere collection of sounds. To be a language, the sounds must be patterned into words according to the laws of phonetics. Then the words must be arranged according to the rules of syntax. For example, in Indo-European languages certain words called nouns are connected with other words called verbs according to very specific rules of how they can be related. It is clear that a language is a system of sounds arranged in a certain way. The student of a language does not merely study each individual sound or word made up of a combination of sounds. He also studies the structure or system whereby the words are arranged into meaningful patterns.

Now it is the thesis of the semiologists that other symbolic entities besides sounds are also arranged together according to definite structural laws. By analogy we could call them "languages" composed of their own kinds of symbolic counters. In the interest of clarity, Barthes suggests that they should rather be called "systems of signification" which are like languages in that they follow structural laws similar to those that operate in languages.

To make clear how sets of symbolic devices can exhibit structures similar to a language, let us look at some simple examples. Consider a system of traffic lights as it operates in many Western societies. Green means go, red means stop, yellow means caution. Here a relation among three colors is used to signify a relation among three possible actions. Red is to green is to yellow as stopping is to moving is to a cautionary pause between stopping and going. It is important here to see that the structure is more important than the surface qualities of the symbols used. Any other three colors, or these three colors applied differently, would do as well. What is important is that the person perceive the structural relation among the three colors and its congruence with a structural relation among three actions that are possible for him to perform.

Another more complicated example that might be used is the way that foods are structured in a given society. In a restaurant a menu provides a pattern in which the various items of food are organized. The hors d'oeuvres are distinguished from the main courses and these are distinguished from the desserts. Furthermore, the way foods are arranged has many symbolic functions. Thus, as a person chooses a certain wine to go with a certain kind of meat or fish, he often thereby indicates the class in society that he occupies. In preliterate societies, foods are also arranged according to how they are cooked, boiled, roasted, etc., and various meanings are attached to these arrangements.

Similarly clothes can be shown to form a system of signification.

2. Roland Barthes, *Elements of Semiology,* London, Cape, 1967, p. 9.

The world of fashion indicates the way individual items—the hat which goes with certain dresses and shoes only—are arranged into a pattern with definite meaning. By one's system of clothes arrangement he shows whether he is a businessman, a student, an industrious person, a "swinger," and so forth. In preliterate societies the arrangement of clothing and color has an even more obvious function of symbolizing various roles played in the society in question.

These then are examples of how individual items from the world of nature or human culture can be combined into a "system of signification." Semiological theory offers a very technical account of how this is done. To understand the theory in detail, the student will have to master important distinctions between language and speech, signified and signifier, syntagm and system, denotation and connotation. Very precise definitions are given to terms like sign, symbol, system, structure, and so on. We have attempted here simply to impart to the student a very general idea of what is meant by "system of signification" and "structure." The interested student is referred to works cited in the bibliography that can help him proceed further with this kind of analysis.

Claude Lévi-Strauss is an influential anthropologist in France who has been strongly influenced by semiological theory. He has sought to apply semiological principles to the study of man in preliterate societies. His methods and those of others moving in the same direction are often called "structuralism." Since this movement is presently very influential and has important implications for the study of religious phenomena, it will be useful here to consider further some aspects of its approach to religious symbolism. Let us look at one specific kind of religious symbol—myth—and see how a structuralist examines it.

Lévi-Strauss has devoted a great deal of attention to the study of myths and many examples of his approach are to be found in his monumental three volume work, *Mythologiques.* However, for the beginning student, the clearest and most accessible example of how he applies structural principles to the study of myth can be found in his essay "The Story of Asdiwal." [3]

THE STORY OF ASDIWAL

The story of Asdiwal is to be found in the culture of the Tsimshian Indians who live in British Columbia, immediately south of Alaska, in a region which embraces the basins of the Nass and Skeena rivers and is on the northwest Pacific coast. The anthropologist Franz Boaz has recorded several versions of the story which are examined by Lévi-Strauss. The following is a highly condensed summary of the story:

> *Two women, a mother and daughter, lived in the Skeena valley. The mother lived down-river in the west with her husband and the daughter lived up-river in the east with hers. Both husbands died*

3. Claude Lévi-Strauss, "The Story of Asdiwal," in G. Leach, ed., *The Structural Study of Myth and Totemism,* London, Tavistock Publications, 1967, pp. 1—48.

of hunger. Winter came and a famine occurred. Both women simultaneously desired to be reunited. They traveled on the frozen
bed of the Skeena River, one traveling eastward and the other
westward. They met half-way and pitched camp. During the night
a stranger named Hatsenas (meaning bird of good omen) visited
them and took the daughter as his wife. From their union was
born Asdiwal. The father gave him various magic objects: a bow
and arrow which never missed, a quiver, a lance, a basket, snowshoes, a bark raincoat, and a hat which rendered the wearer invisible. With these tools, Asdiwal provided an inexhaustible supply of food for the group.

Hatsenas disappeared and the elder of the two women died.
Asdiwal and his mother then traveled westward to the mother's
native village. One day Asdiwal saw a white she-bear and followed her as she climbed a vertical ladder into the sky. At the top
was a heavenly prairie covered with grass and flowers. The bear
revealed herself as a beautiful woman named Evening Star who
was the daughter of the Sun. Asdiwal went through a series of
tests arranged by the Sun after which he was allowed to marry
Evening Star.

Asdiwal began to pine for his mother. He and his wife were allowed to return to earth with food for the mother and her kinsmen who were starving. Asdiwal then had relations with a woman
of the village. Evening Star, offended, returned to her home on
high. Asdiwal followed but half-way up was struck dead by a
look from his wife. He was then brought back to life by his celes-
tial father-in-law and for a time lived with his wife on high.

Again he pined for earth. His wife accompanied him to earth
and then bade him a final farewell. Asdiwal then discovered that
his mother had died. He traveled downstream to another village
where he married the daughter of a local chief. His relations with
the four brothers of his wife were marked by rivalry and strife.
Asdiwal showed his superiority to the brothers in hunting bears
in the mountains. Humiliated and enraged, the brothers took their
sister and abandoned Asdiwal.

Asdiwal met another group of four brothers and again married
their sister. Their union gave birth to a son. Again there was rivalry. This time Asdiwal demonstrated his superiority in hunting
sea lions. In the process this time Asdiwal killed the hostile brothers with the help of his wife.

Again Asdiwal felt a desire to visit the scenes of his childhood.
He left his wife and returned to the Skeena valley where he was
joined by his son to whom he gave his magic bow and arrows.

When winter came Asdiwal went off to the mountains to hunt,
but forgot his snowshoes. Without them, he could go neither up
or down. He was turned to stone and can still be seen in that
form at the peak of the great mountain.[4]

How is this myth to be interpreted? In order to see more clearly
what is distinctive about a structural answer to this question, let us
first consider other useful ways the story can be approached.

4. This account is my condensation of ibid., pp. 4–7.

A Tshimshian tribesman in full regalia. (Courtesy of the American Museum of Natural History.)

First of all, a Freudian might be interested in the recognition of a common oedipal situation expressed in the myth. According to Freud, all males go through a childhood process whereby they are strongly attracted toward their mother and view their father as a rival. Later they learn to identify themselves with their father and to free themselves from their early emotional attachment to the mother. The Greek myth of Oedipus reveals the situation in which this process of identification with the father is not successfully completed. Through a set of tragic mistakes, Oedipus killed his father and married his mother. The result was that he was blinded, i.e., prevented from maturing into a confident adult.

A follower of Freud would probably see in the story of Asdiwal traces of this problem. Asdiwal leaves his mother and goes to live with a father figure, the Sun, who lives in a world on high. However, atavistic longings to return to the mother overwhelm him and lead to a series of difficulties.

A follower of Jung might accept this interpretation but add other features as well. Jung believed that many symbols appearing in myths and dreams are archetypal forms that are part of the collective unconsciousness of mankind. According to Jung, these archetypal forms represent common patterns of events and psychological forces in which all human beings are involved. Thus a follower of Jung would probably see Asdiwal as the archetypal hero who overcomes various obstacles in order to achieve self-integration and bring gifts of healing and order to human society. When Asdiwal hunts the bear, later transformed into a beautiful woman, we have echoes of archetypal myths in which the hero subdues various monsters as a prelude to his assumption of power and authority. Asdiwal's meeting with the Sun is another archetypal situation as is his later death and resurrection.

Mircea Eliade, on the other hand, sees myths as sacred exemplary tales told in preliterate societies and archaic civilizations to express the conviction of a fundamental relationship between the profane world of human life and the sacred world of the primordial gods. Thus,

> in such societies the myth is thought to express the absolute truth, because it narrates a sacred history; that is, a transhuman revelation which took place at the dawn of the Great Time, in the holy time of the beginnings (in illo tempore). Being real and sacred, the myth becomes exemplary, and consequently repeatable, for it serves as a model, and by the same token as a justification, for all human actions. In other words, a myth is a true history of what came to pass at the beginning of Time, and one which provides the pattern for human behaviour. In imitating the exemplary acts of a god or of a mythic hero, or simply by recounting their adventures, the man of an archaic society detaches himself from profane time and magically re-enters the Great Time, the sacred time.[5]

Now an interpretation of the story of Asdiwal following this approach would no doubt stress the way that a sacred world on high is connected with the world of man and nature by a ladder. In many myths throughout the world one can find references to a ladder, rope, or pole connecting heaven and earth. The story of Asdiwal can be interpreted as one example of stories of how a primal hero brings the gifts of culture to man after he has made contact with the sacred world of the mythic gods.

Now Lévi-Strauss has provided us with a structural analysis of this story. The first point to see is that his approach does not differ from the others on matters of detail about what this figure or the other means (e.g., the ladder, the bear, the sun, the hero). Lévi-Strauss rather argues that the first step is to perceive how the various parts or elements of the myth are related together. In other words, he is less interested in the meanings of the specific elements of the myth than he is in the pattern of relationships by which they

5. Mircea Eliade, *Myths, Dreams and Mysteries,* New York, Collins, 1968, p. 23.

are bound together. To put it another way, he is less interested in the individual signs than he is in the "system of signification" by which they are put together into a meaningful whole.

In this connection, Lévi-Strauss offers another interesting analogy. In French society a *bricoleur* is a kind of handyman who collects miscellaneous objects like pieces of discarded machinery which he then uses in unconventional ways. He may, for example, improvise a new tool out of discarded items to perform a specific task like cleaning a chimney. Lévi-Strauss calls the myth-maker a kind of *bricoleur* who takes various images and symbols from his culture and combines them in unexpected ways to convey his meanings. Lévi-Strauss's point is that we should not look at the individual parts of the myth in isolation. It is the way they are combined together into a "system of signification" that is important.

For example, consider again our traffic light systems. We might wonder why red is chosen to mean stop and green to mean go. Is there some psychological reason why red is taken for the negative and green for the positive? Is red associated with blood and death; is green associated with fertility of plant life? Perhaps so. But a structuralist is more interested in the arrangement or structure of the colors in this particular system. Any other three colors would do as well. In fact, colors are not necessary. We might use dots. One dot is to two dots is to three dots as stop is to go is to caution. It is the structural arrangement of the parts, not the parts themselves, that is important. Similarly, in a given myth, it is more important to perceive the arrangement among the parts than to look at the meaning of each part in isolation from the others.

To see how this is done in practice, let us consider how Lévi-Strauss approaches the story of Asdiwal. He distinguishes a number of schema implicit in the story. First is a geographical schema. The figures in the story move in various directions throughout the story which may be schematized as follows:

Second there is a cosmological schema:

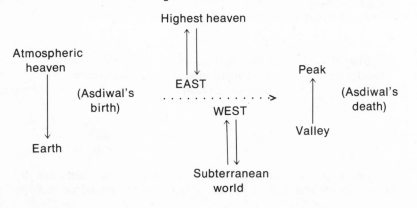

These schema in turn reflect a very general pattern of binary oppositions and integrations. For example:

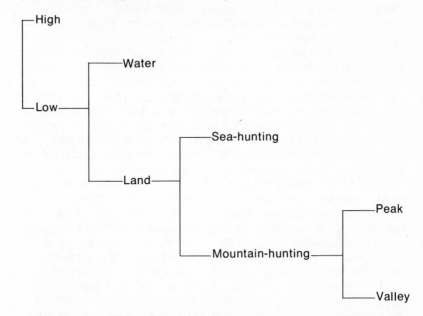

According to Lévi-Strauss these schema and others interact with one another to form a complex whole. Here a musical analogy is helpful. A musical score contains a set of relationships between sounds on a horizontal level that is called the melody. It also contains a set of vertical relations among notes that is called the harmony. Some forms of music involve counterpoint in which one melody moves horizontally at the same time that it interacts vertically with another melody as well. In the same way, according to Lévi-Strauss, a myth is like a musical score in that vertical and horizontal structures interact and convey a number of complex meanings simultaneously.

To make this clear, let us look at another schema Lévi-Strauss discovers in the story of Asdiwal. This is a sociological schema:

(mother, daughter
without husband)

Patrilocal
residence

matrilocal residence
(husband, wife,⎯⎯⎯⎯⎯→
brothers-in-law)

Patrilocal
residence

(father, son
without wife)

What does this schema mean? In their actual existence, the Tsimshian Indians have a system of social order based on matrilineal filiation and patrilocal residence. This means that when a man and woman marry, they go to live in the husband's village. Nevertheless, the children are considered to belong to the mother's clan and not the father's. Now such a system might be expected to generate various kinds of practical tensions among the generations, since the children are living among one group of people in the father's village but continue to have a cultural identification with the mother's clan.

In the story of Asdiwal this tension is explored through the structural arrangement of the sociological schema. In the beginning the deaths of their husbands lead the women to reject their patrilocal residence and return to a matrilocal one. Hatsenas marries Asdiwal's mother and lives with her (matrilocal residence). Asdiwal marries Evening Star and lives with her father (matrilocal residence). Asdiwal's second and third marriages are also matrilocal ones in which he lives with his wives' brothers. However, the situation is rife with tension. Finally, Lévi-Strauss points out,

> *patrilocality triumphs when Asdiwal abandons his wife* (*whereas, in the previous marriages, it had been his wife who had abandoned him*) *and returns to the Skeena where he was born, and where his son comes alone to join him. Thus having begun with the story of the* reunion of a mother and her daughter, *freed from their affines or* paternal kin, *the myth ends with the story of the* reunion of a father and his son, *freed from their affines or* maternal kin.[6]

According to Lévi-Strauss, the story of Asdiwal does not provide a solution to the sociological tensions experienced by the Tsimshian Indians. It rather explores and expresses the tension through the structural arrangement we have considered. In the end the immobility of Asdiwal (turned into stone) indicates that a completely satisfactory solution to the tension between patrilocal and matrilineal practices has not been found.

Other tensions are also exhibited in the structure of the story. For example, the alternatives between plenty and famine reflect the way the Tsimshians would collect a store of smoked fish and dried meat during the summer when they fished and hunted bears and goats in the mountains. At the end of winter their store of food was often exhausted and they endured periods of severe famine until they were able to fish again in the spring. Also, the Tsimshians moved according to the seasons between their winter villages and their summer fishing places. These structures are reflected in the geographical movements of Asdiwal in the story.

Lévi-Strauss goes into many details of these various schema that we cannot reproduce here. Enough has been presented to show how a structural analysis proceeds. To return to our musical analogy, we have seen how Lévi-Strauss argues that a myth proceeds through an intersection of patterns, like harmony and melody, or two melodies in counterpoint, to indicate the complexities of Tsimshian existence.

6. Lévi-Strauss, op. cit., pp. 12–13.

It is important to see that Lévi-Strauss's structural analysis is not an alternative to the other approaches to myth that we have indicated. Myths are about psychological, sociological, cosmological, and transcendent themes. All these are clearly in the story of Asdiwal. The structural analysis simply shows that these materials are organized into schemata or structures that help to elucidate the meaning. Although the structuralist emphasizes the structure as against the parts of which the structure is composed, he is still interested in what the structure means. As Lévi-Strauss put it in his discussion of the story of Asdiwal: "Having separated out the codes, we have analysed the structure of the message. It now remains to decipher the meaning." We have already considered examples of how this is done.

THE PROBLEM OF THE "PRELOGICAL" MIND

The structural approach that we have outlined here has important light to shed on the nature of religious symbolization taken as a whole. Often the forms of expression used in preliterate myths appear to the modern observer unfamiliar with them as devoid of precise meaning and intellectual order. For example, at first glance the story of Asdiwal seems to be a chaotic succession of events that have no central point. Indeed, our brief summary of the story left out a host of details that contribute even more to the general impression that it is a formless story that is the product more of a kind of mindless reverie than of thought.

Furthermore, mythic expressions seem to be oblivious to important distinctions. In the preceding chapter we saw how the Arika chief declared that he is the god Arika Kafika even while he is a human being. Again the Cuna shaman went on a journey both to the realm of the gods and into the sick woman's body at one and the same time.

Such usages are more than accidental in primitive cultures. They occur in all kinds of situations and seem to deny basic differentiations between separate things and between levels of reality. This aspect of primitive expressions has caused some scholars to speculate on the possibility that the "primitive mind" may operate according to principles or categories of thought that are in some ways different from those of civilized man. Thus Lucien Levy-Bruhl characterized native thought as determined by what he called the law of participation. According to this way of thinking,

> objects, beings, phenomena can be, though in a way incomprehensible to us, both themselves and something other than themselves. In a fashion no less incomprehensible, they give forth and they receive mystic powers, virtues, qualities, influences, which make themselves felt outside, without ceasing to remain where they are.[7]

7. Lucien Levy-Bruhl, *How Natives Think,* New York, Washington Square Press, 1966, p. 61.

In many books Levy-Bruhl called this kind of thinking "prelogical," by which he meant a kind of thought that

does not bind itself down, as our thought does, to avoiding contradiction. It obeys the law of participation first and foremost. Thus oriented, it does not expressly delight in what is contradictory (which would make it merely absurd in our eyes), but neither does it take pains to avoid it. It is often wholly indifferent to it, and that makes it so hard to follow.[8]

The philosopher Ernst Cassirer was also influenced by this notion. Cassirer argued that preliterate man not only composed specific myths, but organized his world according to a mythic form of organization. According to the rules of this mythic form of thought, the sense of the separate identity of different entities is not present. On the contrary, in mythic thought one object can easily be transformed into another, and to put the matter more strongly yet, can be both itself and the other at the same time. Thus in the story of Asdiwal we encounter a bear who is also a beautiful woman. No surprise that this transformation takes place because, Cassirer would argue, according to the laws of mythic thought such transformations are quite natural. Similarly, the woman's father seems to be both the physical sun seen in the sky *and* some kind of primordial father figure living in the heavenly prairie.

Levy-Bruhl later expressed doubts about his own notion of a "prelogical" mentality and most contemporary anthropologists have rejected it. The problem with this notion is that it implies a radical difference between the cognitive processes of primitive and civilized man. Western man adheres to a tradition of logic exemplified by Aristotle's presentation. In his works are found the three traditional canons of logic: the law of identity ($A = A$), the law of the excluded middle (A is either A or not A—there is no other possibility), and the law of noncontradiction (A cannot be both A and not A at the same time and in the same sense). Are we to believe that primitive man is oblivious to such distinctions? Data provided by anthropologists show us that, in fact, primitive peoples are capable of careful distinctions and differentiations.

We might well wonder if a being could survive if unable to make and hold on to distinctions between, for example, hot and cold, friend and enemy, food and poison. Here survival seems to depend on the ability to perceive such differences. Furthermore, there is no marked difference in the physiology, the nervous system, the brain structure, of primitives and civilized peoples. It is hardly likely, then, that primitives perceive their world at the level of the physical senses in a markedly different way than do civilized persons.

Specific anthropological studies support these suppositions. Primitive man may not make the same distinctions as do members of a civilization. Nevertheless, he has a sharp eye for detail and distinguishes carefully between phenomena according to his own pur-

8. Ibid., p. 63.

poses and interests. For example, the Hanunóo of the Philippines classify all forms of the local avifauna into seventy-five categories; they distinguish about a dozen kinds of snakes, sixty-odd types of fish, more than a dozen types of fresh and salt water crustaceans; every child of the Ryukyu archipelago can look at a tiny wood fragment and, by considering its bark, smell, hardness, make an identification according to his categories of classification. Such examples can be multiplied almost ad infinitum.

Furthermore, many primitive cultures, when examined carefully, can be shown to exhibit more subtlety and sophistication in expression than may at first be acknowledged. For example, we are aware of distinctions between literal assertions (the king is the ruler of the land; metonyms (the land is subject to the crown); similes (the king is like a lion); metaphors (the king is a lion). Primitive language often reveals similar forms which are not taken by the user with a greater degree of literalness than we do ourselves.

Thus, Evans-Pritchard insists that among native societies like the Nuer, the verb "to be" should not be interpreted as always meaning identity, any more than it is with us. For example, the Nuer say that in certain circumstances a cucumber is an ox and that it can therefore be substituted for an ox in a ritual sacrifice (see the following chapter). Nevertheless, the Nuer have not lost sight of the difference between an ox and a cucumber. Thus they never make the relation a symmetrical one, i.e., they never say that an ox is a cucumber. What is meant is that in certain circumstances (for example, where an ox is not available, probably because of the penury of the officiant) a cucumber may be treated *like* an ox.

Levy-Bruhl's notion of a "prelogical" mind is wrong in so far as it implies that preliterate men express themselves without regard to principles of structure and order. Nevertheless, it is also important to recognize that the structures and relations of preliterate societies involve metaphors and metonyms that are "poetic" rather than "scientific" without violating the laws of formal logic. As John Beattie puts it:

> Even though he overstated his case, Levy-Bruhl was right in emphasizing the poetical, analogical character of much "primitive" thinking. The predominantly scientific orientation of modern thought has much obscured the fact that peoples who are less concerned than Western Europeans are with scientific experimentation and logical method think about the world they live in in terms which are often symbolic and "literary" rather than scientific. This is no less true of European peasant cultures than it is of remote African or Oceanic tribes. We do the grossest injustice to the subtle allusive and evocative power of language if we require all meaningful verbal expression to conform to the rules of syllogism and inductive inference. Coherent thinking can be symbolic as well as scientific, and if we are sensible we do not subject the language of poetry to the same kind of examination that we apply to a scientific hypothesis.[9]

9. John Beattie, *Other Cultures,* New York, Free Press, 1964, pp. 68–69.

Furthermore, many preliterate rituals and myths express a sense of relationship between man and the world that is "participational" rather than "manipulative." For example, the sharp separation between animate beings and inanimate objects, common among people influenced by modern science, is profoundly minimized in primitive cultures. The attitude of primitive man in this connection is difficult to describe and further investigation is needed. It seems clear that primitive man behaves toward many objects we call inanimate—stones, for example—as though they were alive; the realm of natural objects as a whole seems to be animated and energetic.

However, the stance of primitive man should not be oversimplified in this respect. It is not the case that every object that he encounters is endowed with a personal soul exactly like his own. A. Irving Hallowell, for example, suggests that the Ojibwa (an American Indian tribe) exhibit a thought pattern in which "personhood" is a "cultural constituted cognitive set" that can include stones. "Whereas we should never expect a stone to manifest animate properties of any kind under any circumstances, the Ojibwa recognize, a priori, potentialities for animation in certain classes of objects under certain circumstances." [10] Thus, when Hallowell asked an old man whether all stones are alive, he answered, "No! But some are." He told of the experience of his father who during a sacred ceremony had seen a big round stone follow him around as he moved.

According to Hallowell, the Ojibwa thus recognize the possibility of personal dynamic properties in what people from a scientific culture would call inanimate objects. Nevertheless, such beliefs are *not* evidence of an illogical disordered "mind." On the contrary, as Hallowell argues, the belief can be shown to be part of a specific structural "cognitive set."

Such attitudes lead to a strong sense of communal relation between man and nature in preliterate societies. Dorothy Lee observes:

> All economic activities, such as hunting, gathering fuel, cultivating the land, storing food, assume a relatedness to the encompassing universe, and, with many cultures, this is a religious relationship. In such cultures, men recognize a certain spiritual worth and dignity in the universe. They do not set out to control, or master, or exploit. Their ceremonials are periods of intensified communion, even social affairs, in a broad sense, if the term may be extended to include the forces of the universe. They are not placating or bribing or even thanking; they are rather in a formal period of concentrated enjoyable association. [11]

10. A. Irving Hallowell, "Ojibwa Ontology, Behavior, and World View," in S. Diamond, ed., *Culture in History*, New York, Columbia, 1960, pp. 24–25.

11. Dorothy Lee, "Anthropology," in Hoxie N. Fairchild, et al., *Religious Perspectives in College Teaching*, New York, Ronald Press, 1952, pp. 340–341.

An old Wintu woman told Lee:

> *The white people never cared for the land or deer or bear. When we Indians kill meat, we eat it all up. . . . We shake down acorns and pinenuts. We don't cut down trees. We only use dead wood. But the white people plow up the ground, pull up the trees, kill everything. The tree says, "Don't, I am sore. Don't hurt me." But they chop it down and cut it up. The spirit of the land hates them. . . . How can the spirit of the land like the white man? Everywhere the white man has touched it, it is sore.*[12]

It is important here to see that there is no conflict between a recognition of such participational attitudes between man and nature and a structural analysis of myth and ritual. Structuralists like Lévi-Strauss acknowledge that preliterate men often organize their understanding of their world according to different principles of organization than do men in modern technological societies. The point that they stress is simply the fact that preliterate people do *organize* and *structure* their beliefs and in that sense exhibit logical and rational thought, even though their structures may be very different from our own.

We conclude then that the work of structuralists like Lévi-Strauss has provided important support for the thesis that all men, whether preliterate or modern, religious or secular, use their symbolic media according to patterns that exhibit order and a precise sense of relationship between clearly distinguished parts. We have seen how an apparently irrational sequence of events like the story of Asdiwal reveals on closer scrutiny a complex set of very exact structures in intricate relation with one another. We should never assume in advance that any set of religious forms is the expression of blind emotion or a vague imagination oblivious to logic and order.

It is true that many problems remain which cannot be considered at this introductory level. In places Lévi-Strauss asserts that all men reveal a common and universal mental structure that is revealed in each of their symbolic expressions. For our purposes this question can be left open as a matter for further study. It is sufficient here if we adopt the methodical maxim that in examining any piece of religious symbolism we will look for underlying patterns of meaning. If we adopt this heuristic principle, we will be constantly surprised to find that ideas, images, and tales, which at first glance appear to be quite fantastic, often disclose underlying meanings that are important to the culture concerned and often have relevance to our own as well.

12. Ibid.

PRIMITIVE RELIGIOUS SYSTEMS: THE NUER AND THE DINKA

The poet William Wordsworth once observed that "we murder to dissect." In the preceding two chapters we have looked in a piecemeal fashion at various rituals, myths, and symbols. In doing so, we have made useful discoveries about how religion functions in concrete circumstances. At the same time, we have not yet considered the manner in which these parts interact with one another to form a unified whole. In this chapter we shall look at an example of how a religious system operates as a totality in the life of a given society. We shall take our example from among the many primitive societies still in existence.

THE NATURE OF PRIMITIVE SOCIETIES

However, we must first define what we mean by a "primitive society." The term refers to a specific kind of social structure with distinctive characteristics. Primitive societies are small and originally isolated from larger civilizations. Kinship structures are usually a dominant factor in their social organization.

Furthermore, there is relative absence of social *differentiation.* As Marshall Sahlins puts it:

> The tribal structure is generalized; in this lies its primitiveness. It lacks an independent economic sector or a separate religious organization, let alone a special political mechanism. In a tribe, these are not so much different institutions as they are different functions *of the same institutions: different things a lineage, for instance, may do. Holding an estate in land, the lineage appears as an economic entity; feuding it is a political group; sacrificing to the ancestors, a ritual congregation.*[1]

1. Marshall Sahlins, *Tribesmen*, Englewood Cliffs, N. J., Prentice-Hall, 1968, p. 15.

Other characteristics of primitive societies are the prominence of religion in the structure as a whole; the lack of "advanced" technology, especially the skill of writing; the absence of cities. Such societies have existed since Neolithic times and before; they continue to survive in North and South America, Africa, the Andaman Islands, Australia, and the islands of the Pacific, but seem to be fast dying out under impact with the larger, technically advanced, socially differentiated civilizations.

Recently many anthropologists have warned against the negative connotations of the term "primitive" which seem to suggest inferiority.[2] This is an important point and involves a question of attitude as much as the use of a specific term. The first representatives of "civilization" (explorers, traders, and missionaries) looked down on the "primitive" societies they invaded. Since then, we have come to appreciate the cultural achievement of peoples who have worked out impressive ways of living with one another that are different, but not inferior, to those of civilization. If we believe this, we will use the word "primitive" with no sense of devaluation. If we do not, then any alternative term we substitute will soon become infected with the same negative feeling. For example, many have suggested using the descriptive term "preliterate" for the societies we have described. But if we have a bias in favor of writing and a disdain for the "ignorance" of those without that skill, then this term will soon possess the same difficulties as "primitive." The solution is not to change the word, but to enlarge our sympathetic understanding of cultures different from our own.

NUERLAND AND DINKALAND: EXAMPLES OF RELIGIOUS BELIEF SYSTEMS

There is a danger that reference to "primitive society" as a collective noun may obscure the diversity and heterogeneity existing among primitive societies in different parts of the world. Just as it is more accurate to say that we are studying religions, rather than religion, so we must learn how to study the *religions* of primitive societies, not a single homogeneous entity called "primitive religion." The religious forms of tribal societies differ in various parts of the world.

We propose to sketch briefly the religious beliefs of two geographically contiguous societies: the Nuer and the Dinka. These two cultures are not "typical" of African tribal societies as a whole. On the contrary, their social forms and religious practices have features peculiar to themselves. However, they will serve our purpose here, which is to look at a particular primitive religious system *in concreto*.

The Nuer are a cattle-herding people dwelling in the swamps and savannah of the southern Egyptian Sudan. Dinkaland is to the south and west of Nuerland in the swamps of the central Nile Basin. We are fortunate to have detailed accounts of the religions of these societies by trained and highly gifted anthropologists. E. E. Evans-

2. Ashley Montague, ed., *The Concept of the Primitive,* New York, Free Press, 1968.

Pritchard has provided us with a penetrating study of the Nuer, and Godfrey Lienhardt has done the same for the Dinka.[3] In this chapter we will follow their accounts closely and reproduce their descriptions of certain beliefs, rites, and myths in detail. This is because we now want to obtain a three-dimensional picture of what religious actions are like in their concrete manifestations. The reader is asked to attend closely to the details. It is in them that the life and vitality of what we mean by religion is present.

We will seek to examine the religious systems of these people in both synthetic and analytical terms. On the one hand, we want to see the system as a dynamic whole (synthesis); at the same time we want to become more self-consciously aware of its many interacting parts (analysis). Thus the various *elements* of religious systems— beliefs, rituals, sacred forms and objects, religious functionaries, ethos or life-style, basic thought forms—will all be considered through concrete examples.

Nuer religion refers to spirits (*kuth*), the plural of the word for spirit (*kwoth*). These spirits fall into two main categories, spirits of the above (*kuth nhial*) and spirits of the below or of the earth (*kuth piny*). The spirits of the above include powerful beings of the air such as Deng, Teny, and Wiu. These spirit beings may on occasion attach themselves to a certain family or individual. It is believed that they can enter into a person and possess his mind either temporarily or permanently.

A RELIGIOUS BELIEF SYSTEM

The spirits of the earth include totemic spirits, nature spirits, and fetishes. A totem is an animal, plant, or physical object which is identified with a particular clan. Nuer believe that various spirits are associated with these totemic figures. Nature spirits called *bieli* are inferior powers connected with natural phenomena like a meteorite, a river, or fire. Fetish spirits are associated with particular physical substances like a piece of wood. The word "fetish" has been used by some observers to refer to a physical object which primitive people supposedly venerate in itself as an ultimate object of worship. In the case of the Nuer, certain substances are called "medicine which talks," but it turns out that Nuer believe that a fetish spirit of the earth is in the material, and it is this which they respect, not the substance alone.

We have not yet touched on the heart of Nuer belief. To do this, we must look again at the crucial word *spirit*. The Nuer use this word as a singular proper noun (*Kwoth*) to refer to the Spirit who has created the world and determines the occurrence of all events. Evans-Pritchard translates the word as "God." To avoid a too hasty identification with the Western biblical use of that name, we may prefer to consider it here as Spirit.

Spirit is closely associated with the sky and although believed to be everywhere, he is also located in a special way in the heav-

3. E. E. Evans-Pritchard, *Nuer Religion*, Oxford, Clarendon Press, 1956. Godfrey Lienhardt, *Divinity and Experience*, Oxford, Clarendon Press, 1961.

ens. Nuer say he is in this respect "like wind" and "like air." He is often called *Kwoth Neahl* (Spirit of the Sky) or *Kwoth a nhial* (Spirit who is in the Sky). Spirit is a living person (*ran*) and is addressed as "grandfather," "ancestor," or as "Spirit who created my ancestor." He sees and hears all that happens, can be angry and can love; however, he is not anthropomorphic in the sense of possessing a human body; says Evans-Pritchard, "I have never heard Nuer suggest that he has human form." On the other hand Lienhardt records an instance where a Dinka claimed to have seen his corresponding deity who looked to him like "an old man, with a red and blue pied body and a white head." [4]

Spirit upholds what might be called the moral order of the world. Nuer are aware that good conduct is not necessarily followed immediately by happy situations, nor wicked acts by retribution. In the long run, however, they believe that Spirit sees to it that a kind of correlation between goodness and happiness and the obverse does take place. No man can avoid all misfortunes, for some are a part of the natural situation, to be accepted as the will of Spirit. But special misfortunes come to a man as the result of a "fault" (*duer*), as when he breaks a divinely sanctioned interdiction, wrongs another, or fails in his obligations to spiritual beings and the ghosts of his kith and kin. If a man remains in the right, i.e., avoids "fault," Spirit will probably protect him from dire troubles and woes. However, Spirit cannot be controlled or compelled by any particular ritual or action. The final decisions about a man's destiny belong to Spirit, who in the end is always in the right.

The Dinka use different semantic terms for their spirits but exhibit an almost identical pattern with the Nuer. According to Lienhardt, "the word which any inquirer into Dinka religion will first and most frequently hear is *nhialic*." This is the Dinka word for sky; in Dinka religion it becomes the name of the mighty being who is addressed as "creator" (*aciek*) and "my father" (*wa*) and to whom prayers and sacrifice are offered.

Lienhardt suggests translating *nhialic* when used this way as *Divinity*, a word with more flexibility for shades of nuance than the word "God." Divinity is *jok*, a word which can be translated "spirit" but which Lienhardt calls "power." According to the Dinka, there are many powers and *yeeth* is a collective name for "powers which are related to people." They can be called divinities. Lienhardt notes two major kinds of divinities among the Dinka: clan divinities, which are connected specifically with particular lineage groups, and free divinities, which sometimes appear to individuals irrespective of their clan affiliations.

We may ask a similar question of both Dinka religion and Nuer religion concerning the relation between the Nuer Spirit and the spirits and between the Dinka Divinity and the many powers. In both cases we are provided with a religious pattern that in some respects seems to be monotheistic, i.e., oriented

4. *Divinity and Experience,* p. 46.

toward a single god. In other respects the patterns seem to be polytheistic, i.e., oriented around belief in many gods; there are also suggestions of *pantheistic* conceptions, i.e., beliefs that divine reality is an animating power interpenetrating and infusing all beings and entities of the natural world.

As an example of this ambiguity, Leinhardt tells us, "All Dinka assert that Divinity is one, *nhialic ee tok.*" Nevertheless, it is also possible to say of each special divinity, "it is Divinity" (*ee nhialic*). Lienhardt declares: "This unity and multiplicity of Divinity causes no difficulty in the context of Dinka language and life, but it is impossible entirely to avoid the logical and semantic problems which arise when Dinka statements bearing upon it are translated together into English." [5] The same ambiguity is present in Nuer expressions. On the one hand, we have here a clear example of a polytheistic hierarchy of divine spirits. Spirit is the father of the greater spirits of the air, and the lesser of them are said to be children of his sons, of his lineage. The totemic spirits are children of his daughters, a lower order on the hierarchical scale. The fetishes are lower yet, children of the daughters of the air spirit *Denq*.[6]

However, Evans-Pritchard insists that the Nuer takes these schemes in a metaphoric sense. The actual relation between Spirit and the spirits is more complex. Evans-Pritchard approaches the question largely through attention to the linguistic pattern involved, which is curious. *Kwoth* is not a proper name, but the word is used to refer to the creator of the world who has no name but is simply the "Spirit in the sky." The same word is then used to refer to the other spirits of the air and earth. Yet the "Spirit in the sky" does not belong to a class in common with the other spirits. Nuer either speak collectively of "the spirits" or singularly of the Spirit in the sky, but the latter is not included as one member of the former. In other words, Spirit is not one of the spirits, but rather the spirits are special forms or "refractions" of Spirit. This might be called pantheism, but Evans-Pritchard finally decides that the term "modalism" is more useful at this point. He writes:

It follows from the conception of God as Spirit that though he is figured in many diverse figures he can be thought of both as each and as all alike and one. But if we say that in spite of the many different spirits Spirit is one and that Nuer religion is in this sense monotheistic we have to add that it is also modalistic. Spirit, though one, is differently thought of with regard to different effects and relations.[7]

Since God is Kwoth *in the sense of Spirit, the other spirits, whilst distinct with regard to one another, are all, being also* Kwoth, *thought of as being of the same nature as God. Each of them,*

5. Ibid., p. 56.
6. *Nuer Religion,* p. 119.
7. Ibid., p. 316.

that is to say, is God regarded in a particular way; and it may help us if we think of the particular spirits as figures or representations or refractions of God in relation to particular activities, events, persons, and groups.[8]

The Nuer thus believe that an encounter with a specific spirit in a religious rite is in the end an encounter with Spirit. There is a distinction between Spirit and spirits but there is also a fundamental unity. The Nuer do not claim to be able to define what Spirit is, but they believe that it is the ultimate power inhabiting the world "above" and that all creatures, whether spirits or human beings, depend on him for their existence in the world.

SOULS, GHOSTS, AND LIFE AFTER DEATH

The Nuer have a number of different words to specify various aspects of the human being. *Ring* is the word for flesh, the corporal body. *Yiegh* means life or breath. It is the animating principle which on death returns to Spirit. *Ran* is the person, primarily in his social setting as determined by kinship relationship. To make this clear, we might note that identical twins have a common or single *ran*. Finally, the word *tie* is best translated as "soul." It embraces the intellectual and moral faculties and often refers to a man's "cleverness" or "wisdom." It is the center of his personality both as an individual and social entity.

Care should be taken not to force on these conceptions a greater sense of division than is actually meant. To judge that the Nuer has separated the person into a number of distinct entities—*tie, joagh, ran, tiep*—is as misleading as to judge that modern Westerners have divided the person up into distinct entities called self, personality, ego, intellect, life, soul, spirit, mind, and consciousness. These terms are used by us in different ways to refer to various functions of the human being, according to the context specified. The same is true of the Nuer, who have words to express wholeness as well as distinction: *Pwong* is the whole creature, the total organism; *ran* is the total personality.

Nuer believe that at death the physical flesh goes into the ground, but a part of the person, the ghost (*joagh*), continues to exist. The Nuer have not worked out the details of their beliefs about the final state of human existence after death into a unified system. Two different sets of statements are often made. One is that when people die, "they have become ghosts." The other is that the dead person "has joined Spirit" and "His soul has gone above, [only] his flesh was buried." The distinction operating in the Nuer mind seems to be between souls that still retain the possibility of returning to the living as ghosts in dreams or haunting them in other ways and souls that are completely cut off from the living, since they have returned to Spirit as their final destination.

In this connection an unusual and dramatic incident is recorded by Evans-Pritchard. In western Nuerland he met "an unhappy-looking man of unkempt appearance." This man had gone on a journey

8. Ibid., p. 107.

years before and after a long time the villagers received news of his death and a mortuary ceremony was held for him. The news proved to be false; the man returned, but he was declared by the villagers to be a "living ghost." It was affirmed that "his soul was cut off. His soul went with the soul of the (sacrificed) ox together. His flesh alone remains standing." In other words, he was believed to still possess body and life, but to be without soul. This meant he had lost his social role and was forbidden to participate in sacrificial rituals. One native explained: "He lives in our village . . . but we do not count him a member of it because he is dead. The mortuary ceremony has been held for him." [9]

An important point to realize about the religion of the Nuer is that although they definitely believe in the continued existence of the soul after death, the focus of their concern is with the ongoing life of the community and with the existence of the dead insofar as it affects the living. Many rituals, for example, have as their purpose the assurance that ghosts will continue on the way to their final destination and not return to haunt or otherwise afflict the living. At a mortuary ceremony the ghost is addressed: "Turn away! Turn thy face away into the bush! Do not look at us again! We have given thee thine own things, but then leave us alone!" [10] Thus Raymond Firth observes "primitive communities have no great *concern* about the fate of their own souls." He goes on to note: "It is rather as a framework for activity in *this* world and for positive experience in *life* that concepts about the continuity and fate of the soul are developed rather than as protection against death . . . the concern for freedom of action of the living is most marked." [11]

This judgment is true of the Nuer. As Evans-Pritchard puts it: "They are not interested in the survival of the individual as a ghost, but in the survival of the social personality in the name." Their desire is to participate in a lineage having roots in the distant past and which will continue on earth after the person's death. Hence, if a man has died without children, it is the duty of his next of kin to marry a woman in the dead man's name before he takes a wife in his own. In theory, every man must have at least one son to form a link in the chain of genealogical descent. Souls after death continue the lineage patterns of the living and their relations among themselves as dead are similar to those that pertained while alive. The living and the dead thus comprise a single cosmic pattern of social existence.

RITUAL SACRIFICE

In an earlier chapter we stressed the importance of ritual in understanding religion. In the case of the Nuer and the Dinka, the texture and tone of their beliefs only come truly alive when we consider them in relation to their central rituals—in both cases acts of animal sacrifice.

9. Ibid., p. 153.
10. Ibid., p. 149.
11. Raymond Firth, "The Fate of the Soul," *Tikopia Ritual and Belief,* London, G. Allen, 1967, p. 334.

A Nuer sacrifice: final invocation over slain victim. (From E. E. Evans-Pritchard, Nuer Religion; *courtesy of the Clarendon Press, Oxford.*)

Animals such as goats and ewes, or grain products like maize and millet, are offered in Nuer sacrifices. However, the principal sacrificial object is the bull or ox. Almost all sacrifices follow a common sequence. The first act is the *pivot,* driving a stake into the ground and tethering the animal to it. Then takes place the *buk,* the rubbing of ashes on the animal as an act of consecration. This is followed by the *lam,* or invocation. The officiant, holding his spear in his right hand, speaks to Spirit over the consecrated victim. Finally is the *kam yang,* the giving or offering of the animal. The ox is speared on the right side so expertly it usually falls to the right side as intended a few seconds after the thrust. Afterward the meat of the animal is divided up and eaten by the community.

Sacrifices occur on two sets of occasions. Often they are attempts to prevent or alleviate some misfortune that may befall a person, usually as the result of fault. These can be called piacular sacrifices. Second, a sacrifice may accompany a rite of passage like an initiation or wedding. These can be called confirmatory sacrifices, since they have the effect of validating and celebrating the particular act in question.

These two kinds of sacrificial acts reveal a striking example of an ambivalence common in many religious forms. Confirmatory sacrifices invoke the presence of Spirit and are, in that sense, a desire for communion. At the same time, piacular sacrifices have the idea of ridding man of Spirit's presence, which is disturbing and dangerous. If man has done wrong, Spirit is manifested in some affliction that has beset him. The sacrifice causes Spirit to depart and leave man to his ordinary course of life.

We cannot appreciate the full significance of this sacrificial act until we understand the importance of cattle to Nuer and Dinka. The relation between Nuer and cattle is personal, intimate, profound. First of all, these people are dependent on the milk of their herds for life itself. The land in which they live exhibits a harsh environment and is poor in natural resources. In this situation a condition of mutual dependence exists between man and cattle, since it is not likely that either would long survive without the other.

Furthermore, a man's social identity is determined through cattle. The Dinka words for basic social groupings refer equally to groupings of men and to groupings of cattle. Each clan has an ox name. In many sacrifices the meat of the animal is divided according to lineage groupings. The owning of a herd or possessing rights to a herd determines social status, prestige, and power in the community.

Personal identity is also related to cattle. Upon passing through the rite of passage from boy to man, the initiate is given an ox name and an ox from the herd, which becomes his own. The man is identified with his ox and it becomes his friend and companion. Dinka explicitly conceive their own lives and the lives of cattle in some ways on the same model. Men imitate cattle. "A characteristic sight in western Dinkaland is that of a young man with his arms curved above his head, posturing either at a dance or for his own enjoyment when he is alone with his little herd." [12]

It is also important to realize that cattle are never killed and eaten for any other purpose than sacrifice, except in times of great distress as when famine and drought are threatening the community.

Nuer explain the meaning of sacrifice in a number of different ways. They often call a sacrifice a *kok,* which contains the notion of a debt, a ransom, a price paid. The image behind this idea suggests a commercial transaction. On the other hand, the word *lor* is also used to describe sacrifice; it literally means "to go to meet" and has the idea of honoring the person concerned. Another word, *kier,* conveys the sense of an act of expiation, whereby the anger of Spirit, aroused by some human "fault," has been appeased. The word *col,* in this connection, has the notion of reparation, whereby an injury done another is paid for or indemnified.

Evans-Pritchard judges that the basic idea operating in Nuer sacrifice is substitution, *vita pro vita.* The life of the ox is given to Spirit. But the life of the ox is a substitute for the life of the owner of the ox. The Nuer has so identified his own life with the ox that one can serve as the substitute for the other. In the sacrificial rite, the man has given Spirit his own self in the form of the ox. In return, Spirit may confirm the validity of a certain ceremony, forgive a transgression, according to the request accompanying the act. Through sacrifice the human life of the Nuer and Dinka achieves a strong sense of identification with the ultimate reality of Spirit or Divinity. The ritual of sacrifice is thus an act through which Dinka

12. *Divinity and Experience,* p. 16.

and Nuer understand the meaning of their world and their own place within it. It is the central focus of their life as a whole.

THE SACRED SPEAR

A religious system makes use of a variety of symbolic tools. Not only myths and rituals, but symbolic objects play an important role in expressing religious meaning. Among the Nuer the spear assumes a place of special importance.

The spear is to the Nuer both a tool and a weapon which he keeps constantly with him and never tires of sharpening and polishing. It is treated almost like an animate object for "it is an extension and external symbol of the right hand, which stands for the strength, vitality, and virtue of the person." It is a projection of the self, so when a man hurls his spear he cries out either "my right hand" or the name of the ox with which he is identified. The spear plays a great role in religious rituals. At initiation, the boy is invested with a special fighting spear as well as an ox so that the two are deeply connected with his own adult identity. In sacrifice, a spear is brandished in the right hand as the officiant walks up and down past the victim.

Evans-Pritchard points out that the spear names and actual existing spears in the tribe assume an essential symbolic function.

> The virtue is in the idea of "the spear of our fathers," not in any material clan relic. Consequently, in invocations any spear will serve the purpose of the rite and represent that of the ancestor of the clan and hence symbolize the clan as a whole. Any spear will do, but . . . there must be a spear; and when Nuer sitting in my tent recounted to me what is said in invocations they gestured with their right hands as though they had spears in them, for they found it difficult to speak the words without the gestures, just as in recounting what is said in prayers (pal) they found it difficult to do so without moving outstretched hands up and down.[13]

In the Nuer relationship with the spear we see another example of the function of the expressive symbol to the Nuer. The spear combines aspects of personal and social life with a feeling for ancestral ties and a sense of transcendent power on which human life depends. It is a single compelling form in which idea and gesture have become one.

RELIGIOUS FUNCTIONARIES

A religious system is not a constellation of beliefs and rituals floating around in an abstract and ethereal realm of ideas. A religion is enacted by concrete men. Hence the religious functionary—the personage who assumes a given religious role within a certain community—becomes important. One meaningful way of studying a

13. *Nuer Religion*, pp. 240–241.

religious system is through the kinds of religious figures who maintain the practices in the midst of the community.

Evans-Pritchard designates two religious functionaries as having special importance in Nuer religion. The first is the *Kuaar,* which can be translated as "priest." Many sacrifices are performed by the head of a given clan or kinship group; but for sacrifices involving the breaking of some divine interdiction, it is considered desirable to seek the services of a *Kuaar twac,* "priest of the leopard skin." For example, if one man has slain another, to avoid being slain by the dead man's kin he may stay for a time in the home of the priest, who is considered sacred, and whose environs are consequently considered a sanctuary where violence cannot take place. The priest will help the guilty man make his compensation to the aggrieved relatives and also officiate in a sacrificial ritual whereby the guilty man can come to terms with Spirit who is offended by the act.

Another kind of religious functionary in Nuer society is the *Gwan Kwoth,* the "possessor of spirit." Evans-Pritchard translates this term by the word "prophet." It is believed that the "possessor of spirit" has been seized by Spirit and has literally become Spirit's mouthpiece. He enters into ecstatic states of consciousness in which he leaps about and makes utterances that represent messages from Spirit. Ordinary people may on occasion have such an experience, but it is only when the soul of man has become permanently seized and transformed by Spirit that he is called a prophet. Among the Dinka such a person is called *ran nhialic,* "man of divinity." Because of the possession, they are believed to have unusual powers. The prophets offer divine instructions to assist in warfare; they perform healings and the exorcism of bad spirits. They also predict the future and can offer advice helpful to the asker in working out his personal problem.

The prophet is evidently a much later development in Dinka religion than is the priest. People feel ambivalent toward him because Spirit is believed to be directly present in him; although Spirit can help man, his presence is also dangerous, so the prophet is one who is both sought out and avoided.

These two figures in Dinka and Nuer religion represent two religious roles found in many forms of religion. They appear in Old Testament religion and Max Weber has used the terms to indicate two ideal types of religious figures. Evans-Pritchard sketches their differences in terms of Nuer religion as follows:

The priest is a traditional functionary of Nuer society; the prophet is a recent development; the priest has an appointed sacrificial role in certain situations of the social life, particularly in homicide and blood-feud; the prophet's functions are indeterminate. The priest's powers are transmitted by descent from the first priest—a social heritage; the prophet's powers are charismatic—an individual inspiration. The virtue of the priest resides in his office; that of the prophet in himself. . . . But the most outstanding con-

ceptual difference is that whereas in the priest man speaks to God, in the prophet God, in one or other of his hypostases, speaks to man. The priest stands on the earth and looks to the sky. Heavenly beings descend from the sky and fill the prophets.[14]

Considered as ideal types, the priest has an essentially conservative role in maintaining the rituals of the cult and the harmonious life of the community, whereas the prophet can be more revolutionary and innovative; the words Spirit speaks through him may generate changes in the patterns of social order or at least introduce some notion to the person that is relevant to him individually without being part of an already existing communal lore. Both priest and prophet have played an important role in the history of religion.

MYTH AND
LIFE-STYLE

We have already noted the important part that myth plays in primitive religions. Among the Dinka is an interesting myth about the origin of the present human world.

A myth tells how Divinity (and the sky) and men (and the earth) were originally contiguous; the sky then lay just above the earth. They were connected by a rope, stretched parallel to the earth and at the reach of a man's outstretched arm above it. By means of this rope men could clamber at will to Divinity. At this time there was no death. Divinity granted one grain of millet a day to the first man and woman, and this satisfied their needs. They were forbidden to grow or pound more. Divinity here clearly emerges as a person, with the attributes of father and creator, and conceptually distinct from the observable sky; in this context we can thus refer to Divinity with the personal pronoun, as "he."

The first human beings, usually called Garang and Abuk, living on earth had to take care when they were doing their little planting or pounding, lest a hoe or a pestle should strike Divinity, but one day the woman "because she was greedy" (in this context any Dinka would view her "greed" indulgently) decided to plant (or pound) more than the permitted grain of millet. In order to do so she took one of the long-handled hoes (or pestles) which the Dinka now use. In raising this pole to pound or cultivate, she struck Divinity who withdrew, offended, to his present great distance from the earth, and sent a small blue bird (the colour of the sky) called atoc to sever the rope which had previously given men access to the sky and to him. Since that time the country has been "spoilt," for men have to labour for the food they need, and are often hungry. They can no longer as before freely reach Divinity, and they suffer sickness and death, which thus accompany their abrupt separation from Divinity.[15]

This myth reveals a theme found in numerous creation stories in the religions of tribal societies and archaic civilizations. In the

14. Ibid., p. 304.
15. *Divinity and Experience*, pp. 33–34.

Dinka story a rope unites heaven and earth. In other stories it is a ladder ("The Story of Asdiwal" in the preceding chapter), a pole, a sacred tree. These sacred stories reveal a common pattern that describes a primordial condition in which heaven and earth are originally connected (sometimes intermingled) before a radical separation of them brings about the present human condition.

Another Dinka myth of some importance explains the origin of the priestly clan of the spear masters. The myth tells of Aiwel who was born of a union between a mortal woman and a Power of the river named Malengdit. On reaching maturity, he returned one day from the river with an ox of every known color, but predominantly the color of rain clouds. Aiwel took the ox's name—Longar—as his own.

The central action of the myth deals with a curious set of circumstances that is described with variations in different forms of the myth. The basic situation finds Longar on one side of a river and the people attempting to cross the river and join him. Longar stands at the side of the river and spears each person who attempts to mount the banks on his side.

Lienhardt points out that Longar is "an essentially mysterious figure to the Dinka themselves." They have no real answer as to the reason for his hostility, other than it is as much a part of his nature to do so, as is his subsequent kindness. When disaster strikes, the Dinka say *"acie nhialic,"* i.e., "is it not Divinity?" From this point of view Longar is as motiveless as nature itself.

In a sense Longar seems to represent the point of contact between man and the mysterious Power on whom his existence depends. As one Dinka observed: "Longar was like a Power (*jok*) and he was like a man. It was he who was the first of all to be created. He had just come from Divinity's hand. He was at the head (source) of all life. He wanted to try everything, to test everything." [16] Through Longar, Divinity and man meet and the nature of man is tested, formed, developed. The present condition of man grows out of this primordial encounter.

Various forms of the myth then explain slightly different ways in which Longar is changed from an enemy into a friend of the different clans of the spear masters. One interesting version is as follows:

> Longar called the people, and called upon them all in turn to repeat his invocations (gam lung de); as soon as they did so, they died. And there was a man called Adheou, the youngest son created in the river, who said he would try to repeat the invocations of Longar. Ajiek tried to dissuade him, telling him that he would surely die, but Adheou began to repeat the invocations and did not die.

Longar was baffled and he thought of several other trials. Always Adheou prevailed. Finally Longar said:

16. Ibid., p. 182.

A Dinka spear master's shrine and spears. (*From Godfrey Lienhardt,* Divinity and Experience; *courtesy of the Clarendon Press, Oxford.*)

"Adheou, you have exhausted me. You shall be the foremost of the people to whom I have given my flesh, and even though I invoke against you myself, I shall not prevail." The people stayed thus. The land was good and well-ordered. It was so. It was great Longar; he divided (shared out) the fishing-spears, and he shared out the flesh.[17]

The myth of Longar and Adheou provides an important expression of the ethos or life style of the Dinka and the Nuer. Clifford Geertz defines ethos of a people as "the tone, character, and quality of their life, its moral and aesthetic style and mood; it is the underlying attitude toward themselves and their world that life reflects."[18]

The two myths of the Dinka which we have considered express a life style in which humble acceptance and self-assertion are combined. On the one hand, the Dinka live in a world which is largely beyond their control. At the same time it is only by acts of self-assertion combined with underlying respect before the mysterious power of Divinity that a human society can be achieved.

17. Ibid., pp. 180–181.
18. Clifford Geertz, "Ethos, World-View and the Analysis of Sacred Symbols," *Antioch Review* (Winter 1957–1958), p. 421.

Both Nuer and Dinka stress the basic right of Spirit or Divinity to direct all events of life as he chooses. Thus the Nuer stress humility before Spirit and the virtue of accepting his will without complaint. They say, "we, all of us, have the nature of ants in that we are very tiny in respect to Spirit." However, it would be a serious mistake to conclude that this humility leads to a kind of servility and general passivity before the course of nature. On the contrary, Evans-Pritchard tells us that the Nuer display a proud, almost provocative, and towards strangers even insulting, bearing to men." [19]

The sense of human self-assertion comes out most strongly in the myth of Longar which we have also considered. As Lienhardt points out:

> We see that what appears in all the versions given is original opposition between leaders of the Dinka, in which some wrest strength from an original master of the fishing-spear, who is at the same time a human being and a Power, and receive a mandate from him. The man who causes him to share his powers is one who acts intelligently to outwit and oppose him, and finally propitiates him. The themes of human initiative, and propitiation, appear similarly in the effective regulation of human relations with the free-divinities. The men who in these myths eventually save their people from the human power, Longar, are those who act, with force and intelligence but, finally, with respect.[20]

In this last sentence is stated the two poles of the Nuer and Dinka life-style. On the one hand human "force" is approved; man must strive to maintain himself in a universe in which the benign and the dangerous elements are intermixed. At the same time he must inculcate a proper "respect" for the ultimate power on which he depends. The Nuer call this attitude *theok*, or, in its verbal form, *thek*. *Thek* conveys the attitude of "deference, constraint, modesty or shyness" with which one should approach a totemic object, treat certain humans, like a wife's parents, or treat divine interdictions and ritual acts.[21] Lienhardt defines *thek* (the same word is used by both Dinka and Nuer) as "a compound of behavior which shows inaggressiveness and deference to its object, and of behavior which shows esteem for it." [22] Respect is shown to clan divinities during the sacrifices in their honor. Sacrificial oxen are treated with respect and are declared to be *mac*, i.e., dedicated for sacrifice to a particular divinity. "Teasing, joking, and horseplay, which are not inappropriate between those who regard themselves as familiar equals and perhaps in some sense rivals, are improper between those who practise *thek*." [23] The attitude of respect is clearly related to what other scholars call the sense of the sacred.

We may summarize the life-style of the Nuer and Dinka by ob-

19. *Nuer Religion*, p. 12.
20. *Divinity and Experience*, pp. 184–185.
21. *Nuer Religion*, p. 180.
22. *Divinity and Experience*, p. 126.
23. Ibid., p. 125.

serving that it seeks to combine the vitality of human assertiveness with the sense of respect for the power and mystery exhibited in the universe. A man who does not show respect for the divine interdictions and rules is "crazy" (*yong*) because he loses both support of his kin and the favor of Spirit. Human pride and respect, then, are not mutually exclusive, but complementary poles that together enable man to make his way in a baffling but also wondrous world.

CONCLUSION   We have now considered a number of ways in which religion can be studied. We have considered the task of adequate *description* and its relation to the task of *interpretation*. Can anything more be said? Can we offer any further *explanation* of what happens in the religious activity of mankind?

An explanation involves the relating of the questioned phenomenon to some wider context of meaning which for us seems to be satisfactorily understood, and, at least for the moment, not itself demanding an explanation. For example, if a person drops to his knees, I might ask "why?" i.e., request an explanation. A curt "why not?" will not satisfy me; I feel that this behavior is not understandable and acceptable in itself, because a man usually stands, sits, or lies down, rather than rests on his knees. I may then be told that he has dropped a coin and is looking for it (economic explanation), is playing a game (social explanation), is looking at a pattern in the rug (aesthetic explanation), or is praying (religious explanation). Whichever of these proves to be correct may serve as an explanation since it has integrated a puzzling fact into a wider context that is for me understandable. However, if that wider context is itself puzzling, then the offered explanation requires a still wider context of meaning into which it can be placed. Thus the fact the man is praying explains why he is on his knees, but now I ask in turn, "why is he praying?"

How are we to answer this question? The beginning student is urged to keep in mind the complexity of religious symbolism and to avoid premature reductionism and oversimplification. As Mircea Eliade observes:

> There is no such thing as a "pure" religious fact. Such a fact is always also a historical, sociological, cultural, and psychological fact, to name only the most important contexts. If the historian of religions does not always insist on this multiplicity of meanings, it is mainly because he is supposed to concentrate on the religious signification of his documents. The confusion starts when only one aspect of religious life is accepted as primary and meaningful, and the other aspects or functions are regarded as secondary or even illusory.[24]

But if we do not reduce religion to a concern with some natural, psychological, or social dimension of life, what categories remain in

24. Mircea Eliade, *The Quest,* Chicago, The University of Chicago Press, 1969, p. 19.

which to specify its own autonomous focus? Mircea Eliade suggests that the notion of sacred existence as distinct from the ordinary and mundane form of life may be useful. Religious symbols seem to evoke a sense of sacred reality in some form. The participant feels that he is in the presence of that which is awesome, mysterious, of overwhelming value. How are we to describe this experience of *hierophany,* i.e., the manifestation of sacred presence? We can speak of a sacred *world* to which religious symbols relate the user as a higher *realm* or *being* in which the perplexities and distortions of this life are finally resolved. Or we can speak of a sacred *modality* in which religious symbols provide the religious man with a special way or mode of *being in this world* through sacred rite. On this view religious myths and rituals help men to achieve a sacred style and stance in which his life finds ultimate equilibrium and meaning.

If we ask the Nuer and Dinka themselves for an explanation of what they are doing in their religious practices, they are inclined to be cautious and circumspect. Many Western observers attribute to the primitive religious mind a greater cognitive pride and presumption than it actually possesses.

Evans-Pritchard writes:

> *If we seek for . . . a statement of what Spirit is thought to be like in itself, we seek of course in vain. Nuer do not claim to know. They say that they are merely* doar, *simple people, and how can simple people know about such matters? What happens in the world is determined by Spirit and Spirit can be influenced by prayer and sacrifice. This much they know, but no more; and they say, very sensibly, that since the European is so clever perhaps he can tell them the answer to the question he asks.*[25]

This polite request of the Nuer can be, and has been, answered in many ways. A Christian theologian may be impressed by the similarity between Nuer patterns and the Old Testament. He may then offer a theological explanation: *Kwoth* is a reflection of the Old Testament God in the hearts of primitive man and an indication of a natural revelation. On this view Nuer religion has been *explained* by relating it to the context of a religion more familiar to the theologian. Again, a Vedanta philosopher from India may say that, on the contrary, *Kwoth,* with its many forms and modalistic refractions, more clearly indicates an awareness of the eternal invisible Reality called Brahman, of whom all forms of the visible world are manifestations.

On the other hand, secular philosophers may rather put the Nuer religion into some more familiar natural context. A follower of Freud might argue that while Nuer religion purports to be about "Spirit," it is really explained as the human projection of infantile needs for security and a protecting father into images of supportive divine beings. A follower of Durkheim may rather feel that the evidence has clearly shown that Nuer religion is about "society," which is symbolized by the relationships among divine beings.

25. *Nuer Religion,* pp. 315–316.

Evans-Pritchard ends his study of Nuer religion by letting the religious phenomenon itself have, so to say, the last word. He writes in conclusion:

> We can, therefore, say no more than that Spirit is an intuitive apprehension, something experienced in response to certain situations but known directly only to the imagination and not to the senses. Nuer religious conceptions are properly speaking not concepts but imaginative constructions. If we regard only what happens in sacrifice before the eyes it may seem to be a succession of senseless, and even cruel and repulsive, acts, but when we reflect on their meaning we perceive that they are a dramatic representation of a spiritual experience. What this experience is the anthropologist cannot for certain say. Experiences of this kind are not easily communicated even when people are ready to communicate them and have a sophisticated vocabulary in which to do so. Though prayer and sacrifice are exterior actions, Nuer religion is ultimately an interior state. This state is externalized in rites which we can observe, but their meaning depends finally on an awareness of God and that men are dependent on him and must be resigned to his will.[26]

Whatever may be our personal conclusions about the final impact of religious phenomena, we must take care to avoid simplifications. Religion is a human phenomenon that is complex, intimate, important. It can be studied in an objective manner by human scientific skills that will provide ever more accurate *descriptions* and ever more sensitive *interpretations* of what is occurring. We have argued that agreement among careful investigations is possible at these levels of discourse. However, it is more difficult to agree on final *explanations*. The final explanation of the import and meaning of religious phenomena depends on complex decisions about man and his relation to his world. Each student must decide what best helps him to understand the role that religion finally plays in the drama of human existence.

26. Ibid., pp. 321–322.

THE HISTORICAL FORMS OF RELIGION

In the preceding chapters we have examined examples of religious phenomena primarily from psychological, sociological, and hermeneutical perspectives. However, most comparative questions concerning the relation between a religious form in one tradition and that in another have been deliberately avoided since they become involved in complicated and difficult problems best dealt with in a subsequent course.

The most glaring omission in our account so far has been the lack of a historical approach. The reason is that we have begun our study with a consideration of tribal or preliterate societies. These societies tend to be ahistorical in the sense that they are not oriented toward an interest in the sequences of changes in the life of the society that comprise its history.

Modern Western societies have become acutely aware of the fact that both the worlds of nature and human society are in a continual process of change. We realize that even tribal societies have not existed forever in a static and immutable form, but have gone through various processes of transformation and development. Nevertheless, in a tribal society these changes have been more gradual than in modern societies. Tribal societies tend to orient themselves through symbol and ritual practice toward a view of the world in which change is minimized and the existing society is viewed as a constant form repeating patterns learned in the distant past. As Lévi-Strauss puts it:

Each of these societies considers that its essential and ultimate aim is to persevere in its existing form and carry on as it was es-

tablished by its ancestors, and for the sole reason that it was so fashioned by its ancestors. There is no need for any further justification; "that is how we have always done it" is the reply we receive without fail whenever we ask an informant the reason for a particular custom or institution. The fact that it exists is its only justification. It is legitimate because it has endured.[1]

It is in this sense that we can say that tribal societies are ahistorical and that modern Western societies are historical ones. Lévi-Strauss argues, ". . . whereas so called primitive societies are surrounded by the substance of history and try to remain impervious to it, modern societies interiorize history, as it were, and turn it into the motive power of their development."[2]

In the remainder of this book the approach is primarily historical, though, needless to say, such an approach will also utilize materials gained from psychological, sociological, formal, and hermeneutical perspectives. In this chapter we will take a "bird's-eye" look at the historical panorama as a whole. We will then proceed to examine in more detail the historical development of the great religious systems that are still vital forces in the modern world.

STONE AGE RELIGION
AND THE HUNTERS

According to conservative estimates, man in some form has been present on the earth for at least one million years. About 98 percent of this time consists of an immense period which geologists call the Pleistocene Age and most of which coincides with what archeologists call the Paleolithic (old stone age) period. During this time great glaciers moved south covering great portions of Eurasia and North America, only to recede each time, leaving interglacial interludes in which life adapted to warmer climates could flourish.

The first great cultural event—the use of fire—is lost in the obscurity of the Pleistocene Age. Probably Sinanthropus, or Peking man, had learned how to make use of fire gained from forest conflagrations some 360,000 years ago. We know nothing about his religion, or if he had any. Sometime during the last interglacial period, about 200,000 B.C. or earlier, Neanderthal man appeared in northern Europe.

There are indications that Neanderthal man was concerned with ritual burial of the dead. In one cave, situated in southern France, the remains of two Neanderthal adults and two children have been found. One of the adults, evidently a woman, had been placed in a crouched or flexed position, legs pressed against her body and arms folded upon her breast. In another cave, an adolescent has been buried in a sleeping posture, with his head pillowed on a neat pile of flint fragments. Such arrangements give the impression of ceremonial respect for the dead.

The art of Cro-Magnon man, 30,000–25,000 to 10,000 B.C. has been discovered in a number of caves in southern France and north-

1. G. Charbonnier, *Conversations with Claude Lévi-Strauss*, London, Cape, 1969, pp. 49–50.
2. Ibid., p. 39.

The "Sorcerer" from the cave of Les Trois Frères, France. (Courtesy of the American Museum of Natural History.)

ern Spain. Drawings and paintings were made with ochre on the walls. The fact that some of these representations are placed in interior, not easily accessible, parts of the caves suggests that the enclosures may have been places for religious or magic rites.

In one cave in the Pyrenees is the famous "Sorcerer of Trois Frères." To reach it one has to crawl on his belly through a narrow tube forty or fifty yards long. The figure is two and a half feet high, painted in black, and surrounded by numerous animals. It might represent a controlling god or spirit, or, at the very least, a human sorcerer who has donned ceremonial masks and animal garments.

Scholars continue to debate the meaning of these mysterious paintings. While some have argued that they have a purely decorative function, others argue that they reveal a sense of profound participation between man and the forces of nature, particularly animal life. Some kind of magic or religious relation between men and animals seems to be affirmed.

In general we may assume that paleolithic man probably lived in hunting societies, where the basic means of livelihood is the capturing and killing of wild game. Many primitive hunting societies, like

the Eskimos, Indian tribes of North and South America, Bushmen and pygmies in Africa, etc., are still in existence. Now, it is clearly a dangerous and methodologically unsound practice to infer that the beliefs and practices among living primitive groups were necessarily adhered to by man in prehistoric times. Contemporary primitive societies are the product of much change and transformation. Nevertheless, some continuity between paleolithic hunting societies and modern ones probably exists.

An important figure in hunting societies is the shaman who has the capacity to fall into a trance and receive insight and power that confer on him the role of religious leader in the community. A shaman must go through a terrifying psychological ordeal that accomplishes his initiation into a mode of being and power transcending the everyday life of his fellow tribesmen. Usually, the initiation is described as a long journey during which the shaman fights monsters, descends into nether regions, is "killed" and dismembered. Then the gods restore him to life, sometimes with magic substances placed in his body in lieu of ordinary organs. Finally the shaman goes up to the sky and learns secrets from gods and heroes. All this has occurred in a trance. The shaman is adept in the technique of ecstasy. He returns to the world of his people with powers of healing and the ability to assist them in performing successful hunts.

The religions of hunting societies express a close relationship between the hunters and the animals that they must kill. The killing is a necessity, but the act is done not with hostility or cold mechanical skill; man and animal belong to a common world of dynamic existence and each shares in the being of the other. The killing is then done with reverence and ritual.

The religions of such societies usually contain reference to a high god or some cultic ancestor with great powers. The totem—an animal or other entity with which a clan identifies—is often present. The basic concern is to establish and reinforce a basic connection between man and the animal world through ritual and myth. The religious symbols tend to be theriomorphic, i.e., the gods are represented or symbolized in animal form. There is no doubt that hunter images and insights have provided symbolic materials used in different ways in later religions. One of the roots of religious phenomena is found in the world of the hunters.

Two paleolithic bas-reliefs: above, a woman with a drinking horn; below, a spearthrower. (Courtesy of the American Museum of Natural History.)

NEOLITHIC RELIGION:
PASTORALISTS
AND PLANTERS

The paleolithic culture, covering an epoch of approximately a million years, is followed by a period of mesolithic culture that leads into the important Neolithic time—the new stone age. It should be remembered that we are referring here to periods of culture which have not appeared uniformly and simultaneously throughout the world. In the Near East, the Neolithic period emerges into full flower around 5000 B.C. and lasts until the ensuing iron age civilization, around 3000 B.C. In Denmark, on the other hand, the Neolithic period covers the time 2500 to 1500 B.C., and among the Australian aborigines, neolithic culture never emerged at all.

The Neolithic period is important because it marks the most important change in human culture since the discovery of fire: the transition from food-gathering and hunter societies to food-producing societies. Food-gathering societies are dependent on wild life for their own existence; they either gather plants, insects, and small animals or hunt for game. In the Neolithic period the skills of domesticating animals, cultivating farmland, weaving cloth, and making pottery were developed. This led to the emergence of two new kinds of societies: pastoral and agricultural ones.

Religions of pastoral societies tend to be "Uranian," i.e., the prime religious symbol is the sky, which is the abode of the gods. We have already considered in some detail examples of pastoral societies in the Nuer and Dinka. These societies tend to view the power of their deities in the sky, sun, thunder, and storm, which are the forces with which herders are much concerned. Such societies and their gods are usually patriarchal. This religious pattern has been transmitted to many early civilizations. The Greek Zeus and Roman Jupiter, the Semitic Jehovah, Indra and Varuna of the Aryans, Thor of the Scandinavians are examples of "High Gods" of the sky related to pastoral religion.

On the other hand, agricultural or planter religions tend to stress the recurring cycles of springtime and harvest, of the regenerative and reproductive powers of nature. The prime symbol is the earth rather than the sky, the feminine rather than the masculine. The basic concern is with birth, fertility, growth, and maturation. Here, a goddess often assumes preeminence over a god. In various ways agricultural religions have oriented themselves toward symbols of a great goddess—"Mother of the Wheat" or "Mother of the Maize." In later religions the "Great Mother" appears as the Greek Diana, Demeter, Hecate, and Persephone, the Roman Cybele, the Indian Kali. She is Inanna to the Sumerians, Ishtar to the Assyrians and Babylonians, Isis to the Egyptians.

A modern poet, Robert Graves, has written the following poem in her honor:

THE WHITE GODDESS

All saints revile her, and all sober men
Ruled by the God Apollo's golden mean—
In scorn of which we sailed to find her
In distant regions likeliest to hold her
Whom we desired above all things to know,
Sister of the mirage and echo.

It was a virtue not to stay,
To go our headstrong and heroic way
Seeking her out at the volcano's head
Among pack ice, or where the track had faded
Beyond the cavern of the seven sleepers:
Whose broad high brow was white as any leper's,
Whose eyes were blue, with rowan-berry lips,
With hair curled honey-coloured to white hips.

Egyptian bird deity, c. 4000 B.C., depicting the female form with uplifted arms and the head of a bird. (Courtesy of the Brooklyn Museum.)

The paleolithic "Venus" of Willendorf, Austria, an obvious fertility figure. (Courtesy of the American Museum of Natural History.)

Green sap of Spring in the young wood a-stir
Will celebrate the Mountain Mother,
And every song-bird shout awhile for her;
But we are gifted, even in November
Rawest of seasons, with so huge a sense
Of her nakedly worn magnificence
We forget cruelty and past betrayal,
Heedless of where the next bright bolt may fall.[3]

A key image of agricultural religion is the seed which dies in the earth, only to come to life again as a burgeoning crop: The pattern of death and rebirth in endless alternation, just as the life of summer always follows the death of winter, is celebrated in myth and ritual.

Human and animal sacrifice played a significant role at times in agricultural religion. In order to influence, encourage, and participate in life processes that are fecund and bounteous, agricultural communities sometimes made ritual offerings of human beings, whose death was believed to release the powers of life and fertility in the community. The patterns of planter religion later merged with those of archaic civilizations.

In ancient times tribes of war-like peoples wandered throughout Europe and Asia, frequently conquering local inhabitants and establishing their own culture and religion. Their influence plays an important part in the religious history of India as well as in northern Europe. The Celts, the Teutons, and the Slavs are tribes whose religious practices made a strong impression on the development of later religions in Europe. The mythology of the Teutons has, along with that of the Greeks, become part of the literary lore of Western man.

ANCIENT RELIGIONS OF NORTHERN EUROPE

The Celts migrated to Germany, France, Spain, Italy, Greece and England. Their priests were called Druids who cultivated religious practices establishing close relations between man and natural objects, particularly trees. At one period they evidently practiced human sacrifice.

The Teutons have provided Western man with an exciting mythology contained in two works, the *Poetic Edda* and the *Prose Edda.* Here we learn of one of the oldest of the gods, Ziu, who is related to the Greek Zeus, the Roman Jupiter, and the Dyaus Pitar of the Vedic gods. Thor is the god of thunder, Wodan or Odin is the god of war who welcomes warriors who have fallen in battle to Valhalla where heroes lived after death in a great hall in the sky. Freyr is the god of summer and fertility, Freyja is his sister and wife.

Teutonic myths contain an account of the creation of the world and of the end of the world. The world began when an original state of cold, heat, lime and slush generated a cosmic giant named Ymir. Another giant, Buri, who had been frozen in the ice, was freed by the cosmic cow Andumla. Buri's offspring slew Ymir and made the parts of the world from the parts of his body; earth from his flesh, the sea from his blood and so forth. The first man and woman Askr and Embla were made from two trees.

The world order now consisted of Utgard where the frost giants lived, Askgard where the gods lived, Nidgard where man lived, and Hel, the abode of the dead, except for heroes who went to Valhalla. However, the time would come when this order was expected to disintegrate; a final holocaust would take place in which the gods would be defeated by forces of chaos—giants and other creatures from Hel and regions at the end of the world. Man would be extinguished in a general conflagration that marked the Götterdammerung, or the death of the gods.

Afterwards, a new earth would emerge out of the chaos and two survivors of the holocaust would be the origin of a new race of man that would establish a more benign social order.

The Slavs possessed a religious orientation toward nature and the virtues of a warrior society similar to that of the Celts and Teu-

Sakkara Pyramid, Egypt. (Photo by Fritz Henle, from Monkmeyer Press Photo Service.)

tons. Christianity later became the dominant religion of these Indo-European tribes, but traces of the earlier religious practices and beliefs remain to this day as part of the heritage of Western man.

THE RELIGIONS
OF THE ARCHAIC
CIVILIZATIONS

As used in this book, the word "civilization" is not a synonym for culture. A culture is the totality of learned, socially transmitted behavior present in a human society. By definition, every society without exception has "a culture." "Civilization," however, refers to a certain kind of social and cultural organization that emerged in the Near East around 3000 B.C. Two basic characteristics of civilizations are the use of writing and the greater differentiation of the parts of the social complex when compared to a primitive society. The development of cities, urbanization, is also a mark of civilization. Finally, the development of metallurgy in the Bronze Age beginning around 3000 B.C. and the Iron Age beginning around 2000 B.C. coincides with the rise of civilization.

During this period from 3000 to 536 B.C. there emerged in the Tigris-Euphrates valley a succession of great archaic civilizations —the Sumerian, the Babylonian, the Assyrian, and the Chaldean. In the region of the Nile during the same period, the Egyptian civilization dominated from 3000 B.C. until it succumbed to the Persians in 525 B.C. These civilizations exhibit a common religious form in which the political structure and the divine structure of the cosmos are considered as congruent parts of an external sacred pattern and process. The human political world is viewed as a microcosm of the divine macrocosm.

The religions of these Near Eastern civilizations represent a fusion of religious forms operative in agricultural societies with forms concerned with the political life of the community centered in the great cities. The city and the surrounding areas devoted to farming were parts of an integrated social system. In Mesopotamia many of the townspeople worked their own fields and "the life of all was regulated by a calendar which harmonized society's progress through the year with the succession of the seasons." [4]

The Sumerians worshiped a pantheon of gods that included An, a sky god; Enlil, a god of the atmosphere who conferred on the king his authority; Enki, sovereign of the fields. Dumuzi is a hero who later assumes the role of a fertility god, representing the dying and reviving vegetation. According to myth, he is the consort of Inanna, the love goddess, who sends him to the region of the dead to abide there in her place. With the Assyrians and Babylonians, Inanna is called Ishtar or Astarte, and Dumuzi is Tammuz, for whom the Bible notes that "there sat women weeping" (Ezek. 8:14).

A famous document has been preserved from Babylonian times called the *Enuma Elish,* the epic of creation. It tells how the gods emerge from the primeval waters of Apsu and Tiamat. Tiamat later assumes the role of a monster whom the gods ask Marduk to destroy. He finally does so, and from Tiamat's body he makes the world and also creates man. As the controller of the destiny of the world, he founds Babylon and its temple and becomes its national god.

The creation myth is connected with certain ritual ceremonies in which agricultural and political myths are combined. Thus, the Babylonian king begins his reign on New Year's day in the month of Nisan at the time of the spring rains. Each year at this time, the Akitu festival was usually performed. It apparently included ceremonies where the king was divested of his crown, ring, and scepter, only to be reinvested with them after he declared his innocence of wrongdoing before Marduk. This ceremony is correlated with other symbolic acts acknowledging the threat of chaos. The *Enuma Elish* was read and ritual enactment of Marduk's victory over Tiamat was performed. Evidently at the end of this sacred festival, the king and queen engaged in ritual intercourse symbolizing the union of Ishtar and Tammuz, which ensured the continued fertility of the earth.

The religions of the archaic civilizations of the Near East were centered in the idea of kingship. The king was the mediating point that joined the world of the gods and the world of human society into a single dynamic interacting process. Through the agency of the king, human society functioned according to the norms and patterns decreed by the gods and which the gods also exemplified in their relations to one another. Thus the political patterns in human society reflected the pattern of authority that also operated among the gods themselves.

Henri Frankfort, a renowned scholar in this area, points to an important difference between the idea of kingship in the Mesopotamian civilizations and in Egypt.[5] In Mesopotamia, the king was the

4. Henri Frankfort, *The Birth of Civilization in the Near East,* London, Williams and Norgate, 1951, p. 58.

5. Henri Frankfort, *Kingship and the Gods,* Chicago, The University of Chicago Press, 1948.

agent of the gods and ruled in their name. But he himself was regarded as human and subject to death. For example, in a famous
Babylonian document we learn the story of Gilgamesh, a great king,
part divine and part mortal, who performs various heroic feats and,
when his friend dies, sets out on a search for eternal life. He finally
finds the plant of eternal life, but before he can partake of it, a
snake snatches it away. In this myth both the greatness and essential finitude of man are expressed. Through the king the will of the
gods is imposed on the government of the city-state. Nevertheless,
an essential difference between divinity and mankind, including the
king, is also declared. Only the gods are immortal. The human king,
representing his people, must die.

In Egypt, on the other hand, the pharaoh himself was regarded as
one of the gods who had descended among men. In the civilizations
of the Near East some distance between the divine and human
worlds is maintained. In the Egyptian scheme, the social order,
through the authority of the divine pharaoh, has itself been divinized. The Egyptian pantheon of gods included Horus, depicted in
human shape with a falcon's head. He was the god of political authority, and the pharaoh was sometimes regarded as the kingly
incarnation of Horus on earth. The development of the cult of Isis
and Osiris is of special interest. According to the myth, Osiris is
killed by his brother Seth. Isis, his wife, mourns over him and
through magic spells gets herself impregnated by her dead husband. She gives birth to Horus, to whom the gods give the rights
and dignity originally belonging to his father. Osiris is then restored
to life and made sovereign over the realm of the dead. It seems
likely that the cult was directed toward the kingship motif, in which
the dying pharaoh assumes the role of Osiris and his successor that
of Horus.

One fascinating interlude in Egyptian religion concerns the attempt of the Egyptian Pharaoh Amenhotep IV (Akhenaten) to institute a monotheistic cult centered around the worship of the sun disc
under the name of Aton. The cult was short-lived and was destroyed
by the Egyptian priests on the death of Akhenaten.

A similar cultural stage was also reached in Central and South
America at a later period. By 2000 B.C. the inhabitants had made
the transition from hunting to agricultural patterns and thereby entered the Neolithic stage of culture. From this culture emerged
three great civilizations: the Aztec of Mexico, the Mayan of Guate-
mala and the Yucatan peninsula, and the Inca of Peru. Let us briefly
consider one of them—the Aztec.

The Aztecs reigned from about 1325 until their defeat by the
Spaniards in 1521. Their pantheon included Ometecuhtli, the supreme god; Tezcatlipoca, originally a tribal god who also assumed
the form of the war god Huitzilopochtli; Xiuhtecuhtli, the lord of
fire; and Tlazolteotl, a "great goddess" figure similar to Ishtar
and Inanna. The most interesting god to moderns is Quetzalcoatl,
the "plumed serpent." According to myth, Quetzalcoatl was a culture hero who brought the arts of civilization to the Mexican tribes.
Later, during the time of the Aztecs, he became the god of the wind

and of heaven at night. Finally, he left his people as an old man and wandered to the east, where he cremated himself and became the morning star. However, he had promised to return in the form of a man. The Aztecs made the crucial mistake of believing that the prophecy had been fulfilled in the coming of the Spanish conquistador Cortez; for this error they paid dearly.

The Aztecs are especially remembered for the intensity with which they performed human sacrifices. Here the motifs and memories, which in the other archaic civilizations pointed to ancient practices largely sublimated into symbolic images, erupted with literal ferocity. It is alleged, for example, that twelve thousand prisoners were killed at one time during the reign of Montezuma II. It was believed that through these sacrifices the intimate relationship among human life in the city, the forces of nature, and the realm of the gods was maintained.

The religious forms exhibited by the archaic civilizations of Mesopotamia, Egypt, and the Americas are an impressive achievement. They provide an important historical bridge between the religions of tribal societies—hunters, pastoralists, and agriculturalists—and the religions of the succeeding civilizations which still exist today as living cultural forces.

GREEK RELIGION

As we turn from the religions of the archaic civilizations, Greek religion deserves special notice. The Greeks produced a remarkable culture that has influenced Western civilization far in excess of the actual material power it exerted during its period of ascendancy. Indeed, in an important sense, it is responsible for the ideal of civilization as a social form cultivating a reasonable and humane life. As Toynbee notes: "Interpreted literally, the word 'civilization' ought to mean an attempt to attain the kind of culture that had been attained by citizens of a Graeco-Roman . . . city state." [6]

Greek religion is the product of a fusion of the cults of a native population, the Pelasgians, with those of northern invaders. Behind the pantheon of gods with which most Western students are familiar are rituals and practices tied in with tribal patterns of thought and behavior. Homer, the author of the two great epic poems, *The Iliad* and *The Odyssey,* seems to be responsible for the formalization of various ritual beliefs into a systematic pantheon of gods in which each divinity possesses a distinctive individuality.

The pantheon of gods that emerged into view during the classical period included Zeus, the god of the sky, and Hera his wife; Ares, god of war; Hephaestus, the god of fire and of the smithy; Pallas Athena, goddess of wisdom who was the guiding power of Athens; Apollo, the sun god who presided over music and is the exemplar of calm, clear reason, and light.

The Olympian gods comprise the Uranian element in Greek religion which, during its classical period, is the dominant one. However, the other elements are also important. First are cults directed

6. Arnold Toynbee, *Reconsiderations,* New York, Oxford, 1961, p. 273.

The Temple of Apollo at Delphi, Greece, the seat of the famous Delphic oracle.

toward the Chthonoi, spirits who live in the dark recesses of the earth. They are connected with fertility and death, since the earth is the matrix of living things but also the place in which the bodies of men are buried. The chthonian spirits thus have the qualities of demons, hobgoblins, gods of the night, darkness, terror, and death. These beings are not necessarily evil in any absolute sense, but they represent the darker passions and fears of man contrasted with his aspiration after light, clarity, and freedom. We thus can speak of Uranian and chthonian elements in religion. The Greeks acknowledged both, as when Pindar writes: "O ye gods above and reverend Chthonoi who dwell in tombs."

The other non-Olympian element in Greek religion is the presence of various "mystery religions." We do not know if any or all of these cults are indigenous to Greece, or foreign intrusions, perhaps from Asia Minor. Three of them are of special importance: Orphism, the Dionysian cult, and the Eleusinian mysteries.

The Eleusinian mysteries celebrate the well-known story of Demeter and her daughter Kore, who was abducted by Hades, god of the dead, and taken to his nether realm. Demeter, one form of the Great Mother of fertility, mourned and did not allow the agricultural realm to rejuvenate itself. Zeus prevailed on Hades to give Kore up, but because she had eaten a pomegranate seed while below, she was forced to return to Hades each year. Winter and summer were the seasons of her descent and return. The rites of this mystery cult enabled the members to feel that they were participating in the divine events proclaimed in the myth. Thus, *on the evening of their arrival at Eleusis, the initiates broke off their dances and rejoicings when they were told that Kore had been carried away. Torch in hand, crying and lamenting, they wandered everywhere, searching for Kore. Suddenly a herald announced that Helios had revealed where Kore was; and again all was gaiety, music, dancing. The myth of Demeter and Kore became contemporary once more; the rape of Kore, Demeter's laments, take place* here and now, *and it is by virtue of this nearness of the Goddesses, and finally of their* presence, *that the initiate* (mystes) *will have the unforgettable experience of initiation.*[7]

The cult of Dionysus cultivated frenzied and orgiastic emotions and dances and is often contrasted with the calm and clarity of Apollo. According to one myth associated with this cult, Dionysus was a son of Zeus, born from his father's body when his mother died before giving him birth. Another myth tells how Zagreus (an early form of Dionysus) was torn apart and devoured by divine beings called Titans. The Orphic cult has a similar story to tell about Orpheus.

These mystery cults apparently promised the initiate access to a kind of immortality not available to the outsider. Other cults that influenced Mediterranean cultures include the mysteries of the Phrygian Cybele and Attis and the Egyptian Isis and Osiris; and later, in the second century A.D., the cult of the Persian light-god Mithras. One important feature of these cults is that they reveal a growing independence from their original cultural matrix. Most of the mystery cults are not tied to a specific tribe, or nation, but form universal societies composed of members from a variety of places.

RELIGIONS OF ROMAN CIVILIZATION

The religious traditions of Rome are of importance because Roman civilization formed the soil out of which the Western societies of the modern world have emerged. The religious practices of the ancient Romans were centered around the family and civic life. Through symbol and rite a respect was paid to the numinous powers and forces believed to be present in natural phenomena and in hearth and home. Rudolf Otto coined the term "numinous" to characterize the feeling of religious awe on the basis of this Roman usage (see p. 22).

Later the numina, which at first were felt as vague forces in archaic symbols and rituals, took on more specific forms in the familiar pantheon of Roman gods which were in many instances patterned after Greek models. Thus Jupiter is the sky god: Juno, his consort; Diana, the moon goddess; Neptune, the sea god; Mars, the war god.

The Roman approach to religion was profoundly affected by the emergence of the empire in the first century B.C. As the Romans

7. Mircea Eliade, *Rites and Symbols of Initiation*, New York, Harper Torchbooks, 1965, p. 110.

conquered surrounding territories, contact with alien cultural patterns led to a cosmopolitan approach to religion. Indeed, it is interesting to observe that the root word for religion is of Roman derivation (see pp. 19–20). Use of the noun form to refer to a phenomenon called "religio" became prominent during this period when Rome was making contact through conquest with many different cultures. This led to some interest in comparative problems, as philosophers noted similarities between the gods of different religions and cultures.

Among the educated Romans two attitudes are particularly noteworthy. One is skepticism about the truth of any religious system. References to the gods are thus treated by many Romans of the period as poetical expressions and not as matters of conviction. Also present among some philosophers is a syncretist attempt to compose a comprehensive religious system in which gods from a number of different cultures are included. The Emperor Julian attempted without success to impose such a system as the official religion of the empire as a whole.

One Roman philosopher, Varo, summarized the various forms of Roman religion under three headings: mythological religion, represented by the gods referred to in the writings of poets and sometimes worshiped by numerous groups of the populace; civic religion, represented by those rites that maintained loyalty to the Roman state; natural religion, represented by the speculations of philosophers like the Platonists and the Stoics.

The emergence of the empire created for the Romans the problem of developing a sense of loyalty to Roman authority as the controlling center of its far-flung political structure. Rites of obeisance to the emperor as a divine personage were instituted as a supplement to other existing religious practices. These rites seem to have been the result of a pragmatic desire to achieve a form of political unity rather than of the deeply felt convictions among large numbers of people.

In the fourth century A.D. the Roman Empire attempted to solve its problems of finding a uniting center by adopting Christianity, first as simply one among many acceptable religions, and then as the official religion of the empire. The Roman genius for order on both the political and intellectual level provided patterns of systematic thought which are part of the heritage bequeathed to the modern Western world. In many ways the modern concern with the problem of "religion" has its roots in the Roman experience.

HISTORIC RELIGIONS OF LATER CIVILIZATIONS

We are now ready to consider the religions that are our primary concern in this book. The word "historic" is used for want of a better word to designate religions that have appeared fairly recently so far as the total span of man's existence on this planet is concerned, and which continue to exert a significant influence on contemporary affairs. These religions are grouped according to the three geographical areas in which each of them originated or is presently active: Jainism, Hinduism, and Buddhism as religions in India;

Confucianism, Hinduism, Mahayana Buddhism, and Shinto in the Far East; Judaism, Christianity, and Islam in the Near East, Europe, and the Americas.

These are the so-called "living" religions that continue to be vital factors in contemporary societies. These religions have been selected for study in this book partially on the basis of their influence in terms of numbers of adherents. Numerous contemporary cults with small memberships are also worthy of detailed study, but we suggest this be deferred until the patterns of the larger religious complexes are mastered. This book attempts to assist the reader in this introductory purpose.

These religions have been selected for study because they are significant constituents of societies that command attention in the international scene. Religion is more than its social form; yet, as we have seen, it is deeply involved in a social matrix and we must admit that the criterion by which we identify a given religion is often its social manifestation.

However, the historic religions reveal a high degree of autonomy and cultural differentiation; this means that the structures of the historic religions can be examined apart from their social matrix as well as in connection with it. The point may seem obvious, but we hope that the preceding account has shown that this feature of the historic religions is a new and distinctive one. By contrast, the tribal religions of primitive societies are integral parts of the social nexus that is the tribe. The religion is almost literally nonexistent when considered apart from its tribe. For example, one could hardly today become a follower of Dinka religion without becoming a full member of a Dinka tribe. The same situation is true of the religions of the archaic civilizations, which were profoundly connected with the political order and perished with the dissolution of that order.

In many ways the historic religions perpetuate features we have observed in the archaic religions. However, they also focus more sharply on individual goals (like salvation of the soul, release from the wheel of time, etc.) that can be differentiated from social concerns.

Behind this growth in autonomy and independence from the political order is a breakthrough in thought and insight which took place in the first millennium before Christ. The philosopher Karl Jaspers calls attention to the fact that the cultural foundation of basic norms, models, insights, and visions which still influence contemporary man appeared during a period of time that he calls the axial period. He writes: "In the years centering around 500 B.C.—from 800 to 200—the spiritual foundations of humanity were laid, simultaneously and independently, in China, India, Persia, Palestine, and Greece. And these are the foundations upon which humanity still subsists today." [8] In the following chart we have enlarged Jaspers' time boundaries to include the following religious and philosophical figures.

8. Karl Jaspers, *The Origin and Goal of History*, London, Routledge, 1953, p. 1.

THE AXIAL PERIOD

Unknown authors of the Vedas	before 1000 B.C.
Moses	1250 B.C.
Unknown authors of the Upanishads	800–600 B.C.
The Hebrew Prophets	800–400 B.C.
Confucius	551–479 B.C.
Zoroaster	c. 660 B.C.
Lao-Tze	c. 604–517 B.C.
Mahavira	599–527 B.C.
Gautama Buddha	560–480 B.C.
Socrates	470–399 B.C.
Plato	428–348 B.C.
Jesus	4 B.C.–29 A.D.
Mani	216–277 A.D.
Mohammed	570–632 A.D.

While building on past religious forms from primitive and archaic societies, these emerging religions and philosophies have developed a new understanding of themselves and their relation to society in which we as moderns are still participating.

Some observations by Arnold Toynbee are important at this point. He acknowledges that when he began his monumental study of civilizations, he thought of religion as one of the cultural forms through which a given civilization could be studied. However, as certain religions—Christianity, Mahayana Buddhism, for example—were found to persist as autonomous entities after their germinating civilization had died or been abandoned, he revised his judgment. He now argues that the historic religions "catch a new vision of the spiritual presences, higher than man, in which these presences are no longer seen through the medium of human economic and political needs and activities but are seen as direct powers that are not implicated *ex officio* in their local worshippers' human concerns." Thus he concludes:

> The higher religions have made their epiphany in the course of the age of the civilizations; and if we take them at their adherents' valuation of them we shall find in them alternative fields of study that will be more illuminating than civilizations because, in the higher religions, we shall be studying man's most important activity.[9]

Since the term "higher" religions conveys an unfortunate suggestion of superiority, we prefer here to call them "historic" religions which have been important in the development of the civilizations of China, India, Europe, and the Americas. We are now ready to embark on an exploration of the growth and development of these religions in the course of historical time. It is a story full of important insights for a proper understanding of how man has in the recent historical past interpreted his world. Let us begin.

9. Toynbee, op. cit., pp. 83, 218.

For a survey of theories about religion see:

de Vries, Jan, *The Study of Religion,* Kees W. Bolle, trans., New York, Harcourt Brace Jovanovich, paperback ed., 1967.

Evans-Pritchard, E. E., *Theories of Primitive Religion,* New York, Oxford University Press, 1965.

For a history of anthropological schools see:

Lowie, Robert, *The History of Ethnological Theory,* London, Harrap, 1937.

For a popular survey of anthropological studies see:

Hays, H. R., *From Ape to Angel,* New York, Capricorn Books, paperback ed., 1964.

For representative examples of 19th-century studies of religion that are still useful see:

Frazer, James, *The Golden Bough,* 13 vols., New York, St. Martin's, 1890–1936. Cf. Edmund Leach, "Frazer and Malinowski," *Encounter, 25,* no. 5 (November, 1965), 24–36.

Marett, R. R., *The Threshold of Religion,* London, Methuen, 1909.

Tylor, Edward B., *Religion in Primitive Culture,* New York, Harper & Row, paperback ed., 1958 (originally published in 1871).

For the presence of "high gods" in primitive cultures see:

Eliade, Mircea, "Australian Religions: An Introduction: Part I," *History of Religions,* Vol. 6, Chicago, The University of Chicago Press, pp. 108–134.

Lang, Andrew, "God (Primitive and Savage)," in J. Hastings, ed., *Encyclopedia of Religion and Ethics,* New York, Scribner, 1908–1927.

Pettazzoni, R., "The Supreme Being: Phenomenological Structure and Historical Development," in M. Eliade and J. Kitagawa, eds., *The History of Religions: Essays in Methodology,* Chicago, The University of Chicago Press, 1959.

For the contemporary emphasis on description see:

Beattie, John, *Other Cultures,* New York, Free Press, paperback ed., 1964.

Eliade, Mircea, "The History of Religions in Retrospect: 1912 and After," *The Quest,* Chicago, The University of Chicago Press, 1969, pp. 12–36.

———, "The Quest for the 'Origins of Religion'," *History of Religions,* Vol. 4, Chicago, The University of Chicago Press, pp. 154–169.

Evans-Pritchard, E. E., *Social Anthropology,* London, Cohen & West, 1951.

For discussions of the study of religion see:

Eliade, Mircea, and Joseph Kitagawa, eds., *The History of Religions: Essays in Methodology,* Chicago, The University of Chicago Press, 1959.

Kitagawa, Joseph, ed., *The History of Religions: Essays in the Problem of Understanding,* Chicago, The University of Chicago Press, 1967.

For the psychological approach to religion see:

Allport, Gordon, *The Individual and His Religion,* New York, Macmillan, paperback ed., 1960.

BIBLIOGRAPHY
Approaches to the
Study of Religion

Erikson, Erik, *Identity: Youth & Crises,* London, Faber, 1968.

Freud, Sigmund, *Civilization and Its Discontents; Future of an Illusion; Totem and Taboo;* many editions. See, for example, *Standard Edition of the Complete Psychological Works of Sigmund Freud,* London, Hogarth, 1961.

Jung, Carl, *Modern Man in Search of a Soul,* London, Routledge, 1958.

Jung, Carl, and C. Kerenyi, *Introduction to a Science of Mythology,* London, Routledge, 1951.

Neumann, Eric, *The Origins and the History of Consciousness,* 2 vols., New York, Harper & Row, paperback ed., 1962.

For the sociological approach see:

Firth, Raymond, *Essays on Social Organization and Values,* London, Athlone Press, 1964.

O'Dea, Thomas, *The Sociology of Religion,* Englewood Cliffs, N.J., Prentice-Hall, paperback ed., 1966.

Parsons, Talcott, *Theories of Society,* New York, Free Press, 1965.

Robertson, Roland, *The Sociological Interpretation of Religion,* Oxford, Blackwell, 1970.

Weber, Max, "The Social Psychology of the World Religions," in H. H. Gerth and C. Wright Mills, eds., *From Max Weber,* New York, Oxford University Press, 1946.

——, *The Sociology of Religion,* Boston, Beacon Press, paperback ed., 1963.

For the historical approach to religion see:

Volumes of *History of Religions,* Chicago, The University of Chicago Press.

For the comparative approach to religion see:

Eliade, Mircea, *Patterns in Comparative Religion,* New York, Sheed, 1958.

——, *Shamanism,* New York, Bollingen, 1964.

Kristensen, W. Brede, *The Meaning of Religion,* Hague, Martinus Nijhoff, 1960.

Littleton, C. Scott, *The New Comparative Mythology: An Anthropological Assessment of the Theories of Georges Dumezal,* Berkeley, Calif., University of California Press, 1966.

Van Der Leeuw, Gerardus, *Religion in Essence and Manifestation,* London, G. Allen, 1938.

Wach, Joachim, *Types of Religious Experience,* Chicago, University of Chicago Press, 1957.

For the hermeneutical approach to religion see the bibliography for "Religion as Action and Meaning," below.

For the problem of cultural perspectives see:

Macintyre, Alasdair, "Is Understanding Religion Compatible with Believing?" in John Hick, ed., *Faith and the Philosophers,* New York, St. Martin's, 1966, pp. 115–155.

Toward a Definition of Religion

For the problems of definition in general see:

Robinson, Richard, *Definition,* New York, Oxford University Press, 1954.

For definitions of religion with good bibliographies see:

Geertz, Clifford, "Religion as a Cultural System," in Michael Banton, ed., *Anthropological Approaches to the Study of Religion,* London, Tavistock Publications, 1966, pp. 1–46.

Spiro, Melford E., "Religion: Problems of Definition and Explanation," in Michael Banton, ed., *Anthropological Approaches to the Study of Religion,* London, Tavistock Publications, 1966, pp. 85–126.

Baird, Robert, "Interpretive Categories and the History of Religions," *History and Theory, 8* (1968), 17–30.

For the definition of religion as a reference to the superempirical see:

Glock, Charles Y., and Rodney N. Stark, *Religion and Society in Tension,* Chicago, University of Chicago Press, 1965.

For the definition of religion as a reference to the sacred see:

Caillois, Roger, *Man and the Sacred,* New York, Free Press, 1959.

Durkheim, Emile, *The Elementary Forms of the Religious Life,* New York, Free Press, paperback ed., 1965.

Eliade, Mircea, *The Sacred and the Profane,* New York, Harper & Row, paperback ed., 1961.

Nisbet, Robert, "The Sacred," *The Sociological Tradition,* London, Heinemann, 1966, pp. 221–263.

For the definition of religion as a reference to ultimacy see:

Luckmann, Thomas, *The Invisible Religion,* New York, Macmillan, 1967.

Parsons, Talcott, "Religion in a Modern Pluralistic Society," *Review of Religious Research, 7* (Spring, 1966), 125–146.

Tillich, Paul, *Christianity and the Encounter of the World Religions,* Chicago, University of Chicago Press, 1960.

Religion as
Action and Meaning

For the study of ritual see:

Bettelheim, Bruno, *Symbolic Wounds,* New York, Collier, paperback ed., 1962.

Emmet, Dorothy, "Religion and the Social Anthropology of Religion: II," *Theoria to Theory, 3* (January, 1969), 33–44.

Firth, R., *Tikopia: Ritual and Belief,* London, G. Allen, 1967.

————, *The Work of the Gods in Tikopia,* London, Athlone Press, 1967.

Goody, J., "Religion and Ritual: The Definition Problem," *British Journal of Sociology, 12,* 143–164.

Middleton, John, ed., *Gods and Rituals,* New York, Natural History Press, 1967.

Turner, Victor, *The Ritual Process,* London, Routledge, 1969.

For a survey of the ritual myth school see:

Fontenrose, J. E., *The Ritual Theory of Myth,* Berkeley, Calif., University of California Press, 1966.

For discussions of functional theory see:

Emmet, Dorothy, *Function, Purpose and Powers,* New York, Macmillan, 1958.

Merton, Robert K., *On Theoretical Sociology,* New York, Free Press, paperback ed., 1967.

Radcliffe-Brown, A. R., *Structure and Function in Primitive Society,* New York, Free Press, paperback ed., 1952.

For discussions of expressive symbolism and "play" theory see:

Beattie, John, *Other Cultures,* New York, Free Press, paperback ed., 1964, chap. 12.

Huizinga, John, *Homo Ludens,* Boston, Beacon Press, paperback ed., 1950.

Langer, Susanne, *Philosophy in a New Key,* New York, New American Library, paperback ed., 1964.

Pieper, Josef, *Leisure, the Basis of Culture,* London, Faber, 1952.

For discussions of "mana" see:

Firth, R., "The Analysis of Mana: An Empirical Approach," *Tikopia: Ritual and Belief,* London, G. Allen, 1967, pp. 174–194.

For discussions of primitive views of "soul" see:

Firth, R., "The Fate of the Soul," *Tikopia: Ritual and Belief,* London, G. Allen, 1967, pp. 330–353.

For discussions of Totemism see:

Lévi-Strauss, Claude, *Totemism,* Boston, Beacon Press, 1963.

Worsley, Peter, "Groote Eylandt Totémism and Le Totemisme aujourd'hui," in E. Leach, ed., *The Structural Study of Myth and Totemism,* London, Tavistock Publications, 1967, pp. 141–160.

For discussions of magic see:

Beattie, John, *Other Cultures,* New York, Free Press, 1964.

Douglas, Mary, *Purity and Danger,* London, Routledge, 1966.

Evans-Pritchard, E. E., *Witchcraft, Oracles and Magic among the Azande,* New York, Oxford University Press, 1940.

Goode, William, *Religion Among the Primitives,* New York, Free Press, paperback ed., 1951.

Malinowski, B., *Magic, Science and Religion,* New York, Doubleday, paperback ed., 1954.

Nadel, S., "Malinowski on Magic and Religion," in R. Firth, ed., *Man and Culture,* London, Routledge, 1957, pp. 189–208.

Religion as Symbolic Expression

For the study of symbolism see:

Cassirer, Ernst, *The Philosophy of Symbolic Forms,* 3 vols., New Haven, Conn., Yale, 1954–1957.

Geertz, Clifford, "Religion as a Cultural System," in Michael Banton, ed., *Anthropological Approaches to the Study of Religion,* London, Tavistock Publications, 1966, pp. 1–46.

Langer, Susanne, *Philosophy in a New Key,* New York, New American Library, paperback ed., 1954.

For discussions of myth see:

Eliade, Mircea, *Myth and Reality,* New York, Harper & Row, paperback ed., 1963.

————, *Myths, Dreams and Mysteries,* New York, Collins, paperback ed., 1968.

Emmet, Dorothy, "Religion and the Social Anthropology of Religion: III," *Theoria to Theory, 3* (April, 1969), 42–55.

Long, Charles, "Religion and Mythology: A Critical Review of Some Recent Discussions," in *History of Religions,* Vol. 1, Chicago, University of Chicago Press, pp. 322–331.

Malinowski, B., *Myth in Primitive Society,* New York, Norton, 1926.

Middleton, John, ed., *Myth and Cosmos,* New York, Natural History Press, 1967.

Studies by Lévi-Strauss on structuralism:

Lévi-Strauss, Claude, *The Savage Mind,* London, Weidenfeld & Nicholson, 1967.

———, *The Scope of Anthropology,* London, Cape, 1967.

———, "The Story of Asdiwal," in E. Leach, ed., *The Structural Study of Myth and Totemism,* London, Tavistock Publications, 1967, pp. 1–47.

———, *Structural Anthropology,* New York, Basic Books, 1963.

Introductions to the study of structuralism:

Barthes, Roland, *Elements of Semiology,* London, Cape, 1967.

Charbonnier, C., *Conversations with Claude Lévi-Strauss,* London, Cape, 1969.

Lane, Michael, ed., *Structuralism: A Reader,* London, Cape, 1970.

Leach, Edmund, *Lévi-Strauss,* New York, Collins, 1970.

Primitive Religious Systems

For a discussion of Nuer society see:

Evans-Pritchard, E. E., *Nuer,* New York, Oxford University Press, 1940.

———, *Nuer Religion,* New York, Oxford University Press, 1956.

For a discussion of Dinka society see:

Lienhardt, Godfrey, *Divinity and Experience,* New York, Oxford University Press, 1961.

For the study of preliterate religion in general see:

Birket-Smith, Kaj, *Primitive Man and His Ways,* New York, New American Library, paperback ed., 1963.

Goode, William, *Religion Among the Primitives,* New York, Free Press, paperback ed., 1951.

Lessa, William, and Evan Vogt, eds., *A Reader in Comparative Religion,* New York, Harper & Row, 1965.

Lowie, Robert, *Primitive Religion,* New York, Liveright, 1924.

Radin, P., *Primitive Religion,* New York, Dover, paperback ed., 1957.

Wallace, Anthony, *Religion: An Anthropological View,* New York, Random House, 1966.

For a study of over-view and ethos see:

Geertz, Clifford, "Ethos, World-View and the Analysis of Sacred Symbols," *Antioch Review* (Winter, 1957–1958), 421–437.

For the concept of "primitive" see:

Montague, A., ed., *The Concept of Primitive,* New York, Free Press, paperback ed., 1968.

For discussions of the problem of the preliterate "mind," in addition to those by Lévi-Strauss, see:

Boas, Franz, *The Mind of Primitive Man,* New York, Free Press, paperback ed., 1965.

Durkheim, E., and Marcel Maas, *Primitive Classification,* Chicago, University of Chicago Press, 1967.

Levy-Bruhl, Lucien, *How Natives Think,* New York, Washington Square Press, Pocket Books, paperback ed., 1966.

———, *Primitive Mentality,* Boston, Beacon Press, paperback ed., 1966.

Radin, Paul, *Primitive Man as Philosopher,* New York, Dover, paperback ed., 1957.

————, *The World of Primitive Man,* New York, Grove Press, 1960.

The Historical Forms of Religion

For prehistoric religions and cultures see:

James, E. O., *Prehistoric Religion,* New York, Barnes & Noble, 1961.

Maringer, J., *The Gods of Prehistoric Man,* New York, Knopf, 1960.

Ucko, P. J., and A. Rosenfeld, *Paleolithic Cave Art,* New York, paperback ed., McGraw-Hill, 1967.

For religions of hunters, pastoralists, and agriculturalists see:

Eliade, Mircea, "Mother Earth and the Cosmic Hierogamies," *Myths, Dreams and Mysteries,* New York, Collins, 1968, pp. 156–192.

Sahlins, Marshall, *Tribesmen,* Englewood Cliffs, N.J., Prentice-Hall, paperback ed., 1968.

Service, Elman, *The Hunters,* Englewood Cliffs, N.J., Prentice-Hall, paperback ed., 1966.

Wolf, Eric, *Peasants,* Englewood Cliffs, N.J., Prentice-Hall, paperback ed., 1966.

For religions of archaic civilizations see:

Frankfort, Henri, John Wilson, and Thorkill Jacobson, *The Intellectual Adventure of Ancient Man,* Chicago, University of Chicago Press, 1946. Reprinted in paperback as *Before Philosophy,* Baltimore, Penguin, 1949.

Frankfort, Henri, *Kingship and the Gods,* Chicago, University of Chicago Press, 1948.

Kramer, S. N., *Sumerian Mythology,* New York, Harper & Row, paperback ed., 1960.

Wilson, John, *The Burden that Was Egypt,* Chicago, University of Chicago Press, 1951.

For religions of ancient Greece and Rome see:

Guthrie, W. K. C., *The Greeks and Their Gods,* Boston, Beacon Press, 1950.

Moore, C. H., *The Religious Thought of the Greeks,* Cambridge, Mass., Harvard, 1916.

Rose, H. J., *Religion in Greece and Rome,* New York, Harper & Row, paperback ed., 1961.

For the relationship between religions of primitive cultures and the religions of archaic and historic civilizations see:

Bellah, Robert, ed., *Religion and Progress in Modern Asia,* New York, Free Press, 1965.

Parsons, Talcott, *Societies,* Englewood Cliffs, N.J., Prentice-Hall, paperback ed., 1966.

Redfield, Robert, *The Primitive World and Its Transformations.* Ithaca, N.Y., Cornell, 1965.

Toynbee, Arnold, *Reconsiderations,* New York, Oxford University Press, 1961.

PART TWO

INDIAN RELIGIOUS TRADITIONS

ROBERT D. BAIRD

If the study of religion is characterized as the study of what is ultimately important to persons and communities, then the study of Indian religious traditions is the study of what has been and is of ultimate importance to Indians. One could begin such a discussion with a series of generalizations about "Hinduism," "Buddhism," "Jainism," or the "Indian Mind." By the end of our study, most if not all such generalizations would have been proven false. Instead, we will approach the study of religion in India with the openness that is necessary if one is to grasp the rich variety of religious expressions. We will find an interesting combination including imports from other lands as well as indigenous developments. Hence, we are not suggesting that what we will consider is "typically" or "essentially" Indian. Even the possibility of sifting an "essence" from the variety here presented is questionable.

RELIGION
IN THE
VEDIC PERIOD

About one thousand years before the Aryans (see pp. 116 ff.) entered India through the northwest mountain passes, twenty-five hundred years before the Christian era, there existed a highly developed civilization now known as the Indus Valley Civilization. Excavations in the area centering around the once large cities of Mohenjo-Daro on the Indus river and Harappa on the Ravi river give evidence of an awareness of city planning and the existence of comfortable and spacious domestic dwellings.

While no written documents have been uncovered, archeological remains in the form of figurines, seals, and other objects have raised the question of the relationship between the religion of these early inhabitants and religious expressions found in later periods. It has been tempting to see more in the remains than the evidence clearly warrants. Nevertheless, certain finds are remarkable because they emphasize aspects of religious expression that came to be important in later India, but which were apparently of little significance in the Vedic literature (see pp. 117 ff.), the assumed source of most later Indian religious expressions.

No building has been found that can be clearly identified as a temple. In the Vedic period sacrifices took place in open fields, not in temples. Unlike the Vedic period, though, which gives no clear evidence of having made anthropomorphic images of the deities worshiped, the Indus Valley has yielded figurines which seem to have had religious significance.

Although some may simply be toys with no religious meaning, numerous female figurines appear to be representations of the mother goddess. Laden with ornaments, with protruding breasts and ample hips, they seem to connote fertility, and suggest the existence of a fertility cult. Others, either pregnant or with children in their

Horned deity surrounded by animals. (Courtesy of the New Delhi Museum.)

arms, may be ex-voto offerings or examples of sympathetic magic. The generally accepted view, however, is that they represent the Great Mother Goddess who is still worshiped in India. The abundance of female figurines is particularly significant when one couples the present prevalence of the Mother Goddess in India with the slight attention given to female deities in the *Rigveda* (see p. 118). Perhaps the historical antecedents of the worship of the Mother in India are pre-Aryan and pre-Vedic.

In one of the seals there is a seated figure which has been designated a "proto-type of Shiva." [1] According to the most common interpretation, the seal contains a human form with three visible faces seated in a yogic posture. The figure is surrounded by an elephant, a tiger, a rhinoceros, and a buffalo. A pair of horns resembling the trident of Shiva crowns his head. A striking coincidence occurs here since the later Shiva is three-faced, is called the lord of beasts (*pashupati*), and the great ascetic (*mahayogi*). The relationship must be considered a problematic one that has not been substantiated. [2]

The worship of animals and trees has also been inferred from some of the finds. The pipal tree (since honored because under it the Buddha is held to have achieved enlightenment) was apparently sacred in the Indus Valley Civilization as evidenced by its association with the figures of deities on seals. Although not all the animals represented on the seals may be sacred, some seem to be. The rhinoceros, tiger, and bison are frequently depicted as feeding from troughs. These are not simply feeding troughs, but food offerings to appease wild animals, since oxen, which are presumed to have been domesticated, are never shown feeding from them. On one seal a god in a yogic position has a canopy of snakes over him, anticipating the *nagas* (serpent deities) of later Indian mythology. (Vishnu, as well as other later deities—indeed, even the Buddha—is often pictured with snake hoods extending over his head.)

Numerous cone-shaped objects have been found which seem to be *lingas* and point to the possible worship of the phallus. Whether other ring-shaped stones are *yonis* is a matter of debate. Since the worship of the linga is later connected with Shiva, and since such worship is absent from the *Rigveda,* the idea of a historical connection is tempting, even if only a possibility.

Several finds have indicated presence of the swastika symbol, although the meaning of it for the Indus Valley Civilization is not definitely known. It is also commonly found in later Indian temple structures.

COMING OF THE ARYANS

In the area from Poland to Central Asia there were large numbers of seminomadic peoples who in the early part of the second millennium B.C. migrated eastward and southward. Some stayed in what is now Iran and others moved as far as India, entering the land

1. Sir John Marshall, ed., *Mohenjo-Daro and the Indus Civilization,* London, Arthur Probsthain, 1931, vol. 1, p. 52.
2. For a critique of this interpretation and a counterproposal, see Herbert P. Sullivan, "A Re-examination of the Religion of the Indus Civilization," in *History of Religions,* vol. 4, no. 1, 1964, pp. 115–125.

through the Kyber Pass in the northwest mountains. They were not accustomed to urban living as were many of the inhabitants of the Indus Valley Civilization, but they were not barbarians. These invaders, who reached India about 1500 B.C., called themselves Aryas (a term that has since been Anglicized as Aryans). That this name also survived in Iran will surprise no one who is familiar with the numerous parallels between the religion of the *Rigveda* and the ancient Iranian religion.

Sir Mortimer Wheeler, who excavated in the Indus Valley, believes that the invading Aryans overthrew Harappa.[3] Although nomadic, the Aryans were militarily advanced. They first took the surrounding villages, and refugees apparently fled to the cities for protection. The cities then became overcrowded causing the previously existing order and planning to collapse. The cities, particularly Harappa, were walled as a defense from the attacks. When the cities were finally seized, most of the inhabitants of Mohenjo-Daro fled, but skeletons found on the steps of a well and in other unexpected places indicate that some may have been overtaken and killed in flight.

The Aryans arrived with a patrilinear system of tribal organization and a rather well-defined priesthood. They had developed a poetic technique in the composition of hymns in praise of their gods which were chanted at sacrifices. For some time these hymns were remembered by families of priests, and a sacredness was attached to them. Even minor alterations were not permitted and they were passed on with remarkable accuracy. This collection of hymns was later committed to writing and it gives us the first substantial body of Indian texts for religious interpretation. At this point archeological evidence is slight compared with that available for the Indus Valley Civilization, but written evidence of the religion of the Indo-Aryan people of the Vedic age is quite full. With the Brahmanas, Aranyakas, and Upanishads (see pp. 120 ff.), it is possible to construct with a certain degree of accuracy the beliefs and cult practice of the Vedic period.

Two words of caution are in order. The first is that the texts which have come to us are quite clearly the work of a priestly class and hence may or may not reflect what the people actually believed and practiced. At least we can say that the texts reflect the priestly ideal which was held before the people (we will see that the *Atharvaveda* is one possible exception). A second point is that due to the lack of historical allusions in the texts themselves, it is difficult, if not impossible, to date specific texts with any degree of accuracy. The best that can be given is a relative chronology placed within centuries.

The term *veda* means knowledge, and, in the present context, it bears the special connotation of sacred knowledge. The ancient Vedas contain the priestly tradition which the Aryans brought into

RELIGIOUS LITERATURE IN THE VEDIC PERIOD

3. Sir Mortimer Wheeler, *The Indus Civilization,* 3rd ed., London, Cambridge University Press, 1968.

India and developed in the course of centuries on Indian soil. The Vedas have been and still are considered *shruti* ("that which is heard," and hence not of human origin) by many Indians. They are revelation, not in the sense that they contain truths revealed by a Supreme Being, but in that they are eternal truth "seen" or "apprehended" by the *rishis* or seers. The Vedas are to be distinguished from another class of sacred writings often designated as *smriti* ("that which is remembered," and hence of human origin). *Smriti,* then, is human commentary on *shruti,* and generally includes all non-Vedic literature.

The Vedic texts include Samhitas or collections of basic verses; the Brahmanas, which are theological and ritual commentaries on the Samhitas, written in prose; the Aranyakas ("forest texts") and Upanishads which follow the Brahmanas and are commentaries of a mystical and philosophical nature.

In the course of time there developed four distinct collections (Samhitas) for specific purposes. The *Rigveda* (*Riksamhita*) is the oldest and is basic to the others. Consisting of 1028 hymns, it has a total of 10,462 verses divided into ten books. Most of the hymns of the *Rigveda* are addressed to specific deities and are basically poetic in form like the following one addressed to Agni the fire god:

> Agni I praise, the household priest,
> God, minister of sacrifice,
> Invoker, best bestowing wealth.
>
> Agni is worthy to be praised,
> By present as by seers of old:
> May he to us conduct the gods.
>
> Through Agni may we riches gain,
> And day by day prosperity
> Replete with fame and manly sons.
>
> The worship and the sacrifice,
> Guarded by thee on every side,
> Go straight, O Agni, to the gods.
>
> May Agni, the invoker, wise
> And true, of most resplendent fame,
> The god, come hither with the gods.
>
> Whatever good thou wilt bestow,
> O Agni, on the pious man,
> That gift comes true, O Angiras.
>
> To thee, O Agni, day by day,
> O thou illuminer of gloom,
> With thought we, bearing homage, come:
>
> To thee the lord of sacrifice,
> The radiant guardian of the Law,
> That growest in thine own abode.

So, like a father to his son,
Be easy of reproach to us;
Agni, for weal abide with us.[4]

The second Veda is a collection of sacrificial formulae (*yajus*) called the *Yajurveda* (*Yajuhsamhita*). Since this Samhita contains verses from the *Rigveda*, it must have been composed later than the *Rigveda*. Contained in this collection are instructions regarding the times and materials for sacrifice, the construction of the fire altar, and formulae for the soma sacrifice (see p. 127).

The third Veda contains melodies (*samans*) and is therefore called the *Samaveda* (*Samasamhita*). These are largely verses taken from the *Rigveda*, some 1810 of them, and are set to music. As the *Yajurveda* was composed for ritual purposes, these verses were meant to be chanted at the soma sacrifice.

The fourth Veda is the *Atharvaveda* (*Atharvasamhita*)—a collection of magical formulae (*atharvan*). Sometimes mention is made of the three Vedas, excluding the *Atharvaveda* collected at a later date. It is probably not accurate, however, to restrict the materials of the *Atharvaveda* to a single period, since the magic and charms more likely existed side by side with the high cult as is the case today. This collection contains prayers for long life and prayers to cure sickness and demonic possession. There are curses upon demons, sorcerers, enemies, as well as charms to secure love. As a collection of magical charms, the *Atharvaveda* was probably more the possession of the laity. The following is a charm for perfect health.

From thy eyes, thy nostrils, ears, and chin—the disease which is seated in thy head—from thy brain and tongue I do tear it out.

From thy neck, nape of thy neck, ribs, and spine—the disease which is seated in thy fore-arm—from thy shoulders and arms do I tear it out.

From thy heart, thy lungs, viscera, and sides; from thy kidneys, spleen, and liver do we tear out the disease.

From thy entrails, canals, rectum, and abdomen; from thy belly, guts, and navel do I tear out the disease.

From thy thighs, knees, heels, and the tips of thy feet—from thy hips I do tear out the disease seated in thy buttocks, from thy bottom the disease seated in thy buttocks.

From thy bones, marrow, sinews and arteries; from thy hands, fingers, and nails I do tear out the disease.

The disease that is in thy every limb, thy every hair, thy every joint; that which is seated in thy skin, with Kasyapa's charm, that tears out, to either side do we tear it out.[5]

4. *Rigveda* I.1, from A. A. Macdonell, *Hymns of the Rigveda,* London, Oxford University Press, n.d., pp. 72–73.
5. *Atharvaveda* II.23, from Maurice Bloomfield, trans., *Hymns of the Atharvaveda,* Delhi, Motilal Banarsidass, 1964 (first published 1897), pp. 44–45.

Collections of accepted interpretations (*brahmanas*) by the Brahmans or priests developed. They were collections of theological statements arising from scholastic controversy, some of which relate to the stanzas of the Samhitas while others describe and explain the rites. Following the divisions of the priestly cult, the Brahmanas are classified according to the Veda to which they refer and out of which they grew, and are related to the growing specialization of the priesthood. The Brahmanas connected with the *Rigveda* are intended for the *hotri* ("pourer" of oblation—reciter of the verses of the *Rigveda*); those attached to the *Yajurveda* are for the *adhvaryu,* who is responsible for the manual operations of the sacrifice. The Brahmanas attached to the *Samaveda* are for the *udgatri,* who sings the hymns at the soma sacrifice. Since all the other Samhitas had Brahmanas attached to them, it was not long before one was also attached to the *Atharvaveda.* The Brahmanas began as liturgical appendices to the Samhitas, but later became independent. Most important is the *Shatapatha Brahmana,* the "Brahmana of the hundred ways," consisting of one hundred lectures. It is more elaborate than most of the other Brahmanas, dealing in detail with the nature of vegetable offerings, the soma sacrifice, fire offerings, rites connected with the king, and the elaborate horse sacrifice.

The Aranyakas are "texts of the forest." They are secret and perhaps dangerous because of their magical power, and therefore must be kept from the public and read in forests.[6] Concerned neither with the performance nor the explanation of sacrifice, the Aranyakas explicate its mystical meaning and symbolism. As such they form a natural transition to the Upanishads, the oldest of which are included in or appended to the Aranyakas, and the line of demarkation is not always easily determined.

The Brahmanas emphasized ritualism. The Aranyakas are an admission that the exceedingly detailed and complex sacrificial rituals could not be expected of all; they emphasize meditation rather than ritual performance. The Aranyakas helped to bridge the apparent gap between *karmamarga* (the way through works, i.e., through sacrifice) and *jnanamarga* (the way through knowledge, i.e., through meditation), by showing the mystical, symbolic, and meditative meaning of the sacrifices.

The most ancient Upanishads are closely connected with the Aranyakas. Continuing the mystical tendency, they discuss the symbolism of melodies and words, expound the theory of breathing, and move into cosmological theories of the Atman-Brahman theme. It is commonly accepted that *upanishad* is derived from *sad,* "to sit," *upa,* "nearby," and *ni,* "devotedly." In the Upanishads themselves the term is usually synonymous with "secret" (*rahasya*). Hence the term which etymologically means "to sit nearby" (as a teacher and student for instruction) came to refer to the secret instructions imparted at such private meetings. The texts probably began in the

6. Louis Renou, *Vedic India,* Calcutta, Susil Gupta (India), Private Limited, 1957, trans. from French by Phillip Spratt (1st French ed. 1947), pp. 32–33.

form of short philosophical statements. These statements were communicated from teacher to pupil, the communication being preceded and followed by expository discourses. In time the discourses assumed a definite shape and when committed to writing, resulted in the Upanishads as we now know them. The heterogeneity of thought in the Upanishads suggests that they contain the views of a series of teachers, old and new ideas mingled in a single Upanishad. When the texts were finally brought together and arranged, the Upanishads were appended to the Brahmanas. Standing thus at the end of the Vedas, they came to be known as *vedanta* (*veda,* "knowledge" + *anta,* "end"), and later the term which first indicated position came to imply aim or fulfillment much as the English term "end" serves both meanings. Although the number of Upanishads exceeds two hundred there are about ten principle ones.

It is repeatedly stated in the Upanishads that the teachings contained therein are a mystery and that much care should be taken to keep them from the unworthy lest they become misused and misunderstood. In the *Prashna Upanishad,* six pupils go to a great teacher seeking instruction in the highest reality. He asks them to live with him for a year, apparently with the purpose of watching them to ascertain their fitness to receive the teaching. In the *Katha Upanishad,* when Naciketas wants to know whether or not the soul survives after death, Yama (god of the dead) does not reply until he has tested the sincerity and strength of the mind of the young inquirer. Even in the earlier Upanishads, such a point of view is assumed. "Verily, a father may teach this Brahma to his eldest son or to a worthy pupil, (but) to no one else." [7]

The following chart of Vedic literature may be useful in summarizing the relationship of the various texts to each other, particularly in seeing which Brahmanas and Upanishads are attached to which Samhitas.[8]

Samhitas	Brahmanas	Aranyakas	Upanishads
Rigveda	*Aitareya*	*Aitareya*	*Aitareya*
	Kaushitaki	*Kaushitaki*	*Kaushitaki*
Yajurveda	*Taittiriya*	*Taittiriya*	*Taittiriya*
			Mahanarayana
			Kathaka
			Maitrayaniya
			Shvetashvatara
	Shatapatha	*Brihad*	*Brihadaranyaka*
			Isha
Samaveda	*Pancavimsha*		
	Chandogya		*Chandogya*
	Talavakara		*Kena*
Atharvaveda	*Gopatha*		*Mundaka*
			Prashna
			Mandukya

7. R. C. Zaehner, *Hindu Scriptures,* New York, Dutton, 1966, p. 86. *Chandogya* III.11.4.

8. R. De Smet and J. Neuner, eds., *Religious Hinduism,* Allahabad, St. Paul Publications, 1964, p. 32.

The date of the texts can be affixed in terms of a relative chronology. *Rigveda* is older than any of the other Samhitas, since the others presuppose it. Nevertheless, the question of dating is complicated when one distinguishes the compilation of the *Rigveda,* which may have taken place about the time of the Brahmanas, from its composition, which took place earlier. Vedic writers considered the matters being explicated as timeless and independent of historical events and chronology. Nevertheless, the Vedic literature was probably composed as a whole after the entry of the Aryans into India (c. 1500 B.C.), and before the arrival of the Buddha (563–483 B.C.), since some of the geographical locations, animals, etc., mentioned in the *Rigveda* are Indian.

It is difficult to date the Brahmanas, but they must come after the Samhitas. The somewhat modern grammar used in them would date them after the *Rigveda,* perhaps 1000 to 800 B.C. One might well follow the dating scheme of J. A. B. Van Buitenen.

Rigveda—1400 B.C.

Yajurveda—1400–1000 B.C.

Samaveda—1400–1000 B.C.

Atharvaveda—1200 B.C.

Brahmanas—1000–800 B.C.

Aranyakas—800–600 B.C.

Oldest Upanishads (*Brihadaranyaka, Chandogya, Taittiriya*)—600–500 B.C.

Early metrical Upanishads (*Shvetashvatara, Katha*)—500–300 B.C.

Other Upanishads rarely older than 300 B.C.[9]

GODS OF
THE RIGVEDA

Consisting primarily of hymns addressed to various deities in vogue, the *Rigveda* offers considerable information on how the gods were viewed. But due to the lack of any probable chronology, it is impossible to trace their historical development with any degree of accuracy. Nor should one expect a consistently developed mythology in which certain gods are assigned certain areas of sovereignty. Rather, it is a collection of hymns addressed to gods whose functions and characteristics overlap. Max Müller, trying to avoid calling the religion of the *Rigveda* either monotheism or polytheism, used the term "henotheism" for the tendency to ascribe all power to the specific deity that was uppermost in the mind of the worshiper at a given time. There is in the *Rigveda* a tendency, found in later Indian mythology, to ascribe attributes of other gods to the particular deity being addressed.

Although many of the deities reflect an early worship of the powers inherent in nature, the deities of the *Rigveda* do not represent mere nature worship. While there is no strong evidence for the use of images at this time, many of the nature powers are described in anthropomorphic terms. Sky and sun gods are particularly prevalent.

9. J. A. B. Van Buitenen, "Vedic Literature," in *Civilization of India Syllabus,* Madison, Wis., University of Wisconsin Press, 1965.

In spite of the fact that the hymns of the *Rigveda* are a priestly work produced chiefly for use with the sacrifices, not all hymns reveal a clear sacrificial orientation. Since the hymns represent a considerable period of development prior to their present written state, one should not be surprised to find some hymns which carefully reflect a particular sacrificial situation and others which portray a more general type of outpouring. There is hardly a god in the *Rigveda* who is so insignificant that he does not receive homage from the other deities.

Taking into account that one cannot decide which deities were important by the number of hymns addressed to them or the frequency with which they are mentioned, it is perhaps significant that Indra is addressed alone in some 250 hymns (approximately one-fourth of the hymns of the *Rigveda*) and is addressed jointly with other deities in some fifty more.

Although there is reason to suppose that Indra had storm-god connections and hence had a basis in one of the forces of nature as did many of the other Vedic deities, he is frequently described anthropomorphically. He has a body, hands, legs, lips, jaws, and even a beard. His exploits are superb and began when at birth he emerged from the womb through his mother's side—a motif later added to the birth of the Buddha. As protector of the warrior class, he is considered somewhat dangerous and unpredictable. His overindulgence in soma makes him all the more able to engage in mighty exploits, including those of the lover.

Indra's connection with the warrior class is supported by his superlative exploits. He carries a thunderbolt (*vajra*) and through drinking soma amasses power and energy to slay Vritra the serpent and to release the pent-up waters. The serpent may be a reference to the demon of drought who is pierced by the lightning accompanying a thunder storm. Both Indra and Vritra are furnished with *maya*, a term signifying occult, superhuman power. *Maya* later came to mean trick, magic, or illusion and was used to express the cosmic illusion of the phenomenal world in Advaita philosophy (see p. 188). Indra as the war god of the Vedic Indians humbled the Dasyas, their Dravidian foes, and gave the Dasyas' possessions to his own worshipers.

Sometimes found in association with Indra are the Maruts. They travel through the sky in golden chariots drawn by horses. Clothed in rain, they direct and create the storm. Although they recognize Indra as their superior and help him in his wars, they are terrifying and sometimes malevolent. Later, in the Brahmanas, they abandon him and become hostile.

Although mentioned in only a few Vedic hymns, Rudra is of interest because of the possible connection with the later deity Shiva. Armed with bows and arrows, he is a deity to be feared. Yet he redresses wrongs, dwells in the forest, and has dominion over animals. He is sometimes described as fierce and as destructive as a wild beast, one to whom the title *shiva* ("auspicious") was attached, perhaps euphemistically.

Of high cultic significance, Agni the fire god is addressed in some two hundred hymns. Indeed, all but two of the books of the *Rigveda* begin with an Agni hymn. Because of his connection with the sacrificial fire, Agni dwells in the fire pit (*vedi*) where he is kindled every morning. This pit is the "navel of the earth." Because of the use of *ghee* (clarified butter) in the sacrifices, Agni is called butter-backed and butter-haired, and since ghee, as a drink of the gods, is poured into the sacrificial fire with a spoon, Agni is labeled "one whose mouth is a spoon." The elaborate sacrificial rituals of Vedic times required several priests who specialized in certain aspects of the ritual. Knowing and performing the functions of each, Agni is the archetypal priest, the divine counterpart of the earthly priesthood. Agni is also called lord of the house (*grihapati*), an aspect reflecting an earlier setting in which he was more the center of domestic life than of sacrificial cult. As a dispeller of darkness he repels enemies who might attack at night. He banishes illness and puts demons to flight. Agni is all-seeing, taking account of the wicked deeds of men. He is sometimes besought for forgiveness.

Of comparable importance among the cult deities is Soma. Some 120 hymns are addressed to Soma, and the ninth book of the *Rigveda* seems to be a collection of some hymns which were brought together from their previous places in other books. It is necessary to distinguish between soma the plant, soma the exhilarating juice that is prepared with pressings from the plant, and soma the heavenly nectar of which the plant juices are the embodiment. Soma is seen as a protector from accident, illness, or trouble and as the giver of joy, comfort, riches, and long life. One who fears an enemy in battle can gain strength and help by drinking soma. Its preparation involved pressing the stalks of the soma plant and straining the liquid through a sieve of woolen cloth. Hymns were composed to praise the tawny color as well as the movement and sound of the liquid. Indra sometimes drank pure soma, but most of the deities, as well as men participating in the sacrifice, drank it mixed with milk, curd, or grain. Although all the gods had a share in the soma offering, Indra and Vayu seem to have received a much larger portion. In both the *Avesta* and the *Rigveda* soma (hoama in the *Avesta*) is important enough to suggest it was part of the pre-Indian Aryan heritage.

In the *Rigveda*, solar deities and sky gods dominate the scene. Most clearly related to the sun is Surya, also a name for the sun. An all-seeing god, he beholds the good and evil deeds of men. He rides in a car drawn by steeds who are unyoked at sunset. Since Surya appears after dawn, he is described as the child of Dawn (Ushas). The lack of a consistent mythology is brought to the fore by the fact that Surya is also described as a young man who follows the maiden "Dawn." In the *Rigveda*, Ushas is one of the few female deities and she is consistently portrayed as a delightful and beautiful maiden. Sometimes Ushas is depicted as the wife of Surya. Indeed, they are also considered brother and sister, since in some hymns both are regarded as the children of Dyaus (sky deity, counterpart to the Greek deity Zeus).

Also sons of Dyaus are the Ashvins ("possessors of horses").

These sons are twins who make their home in the heavens where they journey in a golden chariot drawn by birds or horses. In ritual they are worshiped in the morning because of their connection with the rising sun. When they yoke their car in the morning, Ushas (Dawn) is born.

A most famous verse, named "Gayatri" because of its poetic form, is addressed to Savitri and is repeated from memory by devout Brahmans every day:

> May we attain that excellent
> Glory of Savitri the god,
> That he may stimulate our thoughts.
>
> Rigveda III.62.10

A solar deity, Savitri is the golden deity, possessed of golden arms and equipped with a golden car and golden yoke pins. At evening he impels all creatures to go to sleep and in the morning he stirs them to awaken for a working day. Some of his functions overlap with those of Surya in the morning and with those of Ratri (night) in the night, a fact which again reinforces the view that the Rigveda contains no completely consistent mythology.

There are several other deities connected with the sun, but one more should be isolated because of his later significance rather than for his relative importance in the Rigveda. Vishnu was later included as the preserver in the so-called triad of gods which also include Brahma (the creator) and Shiva (the destroyer) (see p. 173). One of Vishnu's chief characteristics was his "three steps," which probably referred either to the three stations of the sun (sunrise, zenith, sunset) or to his encompassing of the three regions (earth, middle air, heaven).

Varuna, the sovereign of the cosmic order, creates and rules through rita (cosmic and ethical order, the later extension of which is dharma). As sovereign of the universe, he controls the appearance and movement of the heavenly bodies. Rain falls from the sky at his command. Varuna is omniscient, knowing the flight of the birds in the sky. No creature winks without his knowledge. His sovereignty and knowledge extend to the ethical realm. It is this ethical dimension which distinguishes him from the other Vedic deities and has led some to point out his affinity with the Hebrew Yahweh. As the support of rita (cosmic and ethical order), all decrees and statutes proceed from his holy will. Varuna knows the secret violations of that will, which are caused by thoughtlessness, weakness of the will, bad example, dice, anger, or wine. Specific prohibitions exist against deception and gambling, or, if one cannot keep from the latter, against cheating at dice.

Sin against the moral precepts laid down by Varuna might result in disease or even in falling out of fellowship with Varuna. In each of the hymns addressed to him, Varuna is entreated to release the sinner from the penalty of his faults.

In the Rigveda deification extended to rivers, mountains, and even to the sacrificial implements. An example of this is Sarasvati, a goddess of the river who is another of the few female deities of the *Rigveda* and one who would later become the goddess of learning.

While there was in general a positive attitude toward the deities, some were feared for their malicious deeds. The *rakshas* were demons who walked by night, assumed many forms, and interfered with sacrifices by eating meat and drinking milk set aside for the sacrifice. There were *gandharvas,* spirits of the clouds and waters who guarded the Soma and sometimes monopolized it. The *apsaras* or water nymphs were the *gandharvas'* wives; they wielded magical powers and symbolized fecundity.

In the pre-Vedic Iranian period *Asuras* were a class of deities alongside the *devas*. In Iran the *Asuras* won an ascendancy (cf. the prime deity Ahura Mazda) while the *devas* became known as demons. In India the reverse occurred. The *devas* were the deities, and since the *asuras* were their enemies, they became demons. In the earlier part of the Vedas, *asuras* are favorable and the term is applied to Varuna. Later in the *Yajurveda* and the *Atharvaveda* they become enemies of the gods and are lowered to the level of demons.

CULT PRACTICE   Sacrifice was central to the cult. As early as the *Rigveda,* there probably were both domestic sacrifices performed by the head of the house around a domestic fire as well as more elaborate sacrifices performed in public often sponsored by a king or some other official. The latter rites are elaborately detailed in the Brahmanas, while for the former we are dependent on the *Grihya Sutras,* a body of texts which were not composed until the post-Vedic period (500–200 B.C.).

The sacrifices of the Vedic cult did not take place in temples, but in the house of the sacrificer or on altars on a level spot of ground covered with grass. The dimensions of the altars and the methods of construction were prescribed in great detail. The offering consisted in what men themselves enjoyed eating: milk, ghee, and cakes of barley or rice. The ancient Vedic worshipers do not appear to have been vegetarians or to have held to the later doctrine of *ahimsa* (noninjury) which would have excluded animal sacrifice. In addition to animal sacrifices there is some evidence of human sacrifice, which was considered the most efficacious of all.

While some of the less complicated sacrifices required only one priest, there was a development which led to various priests performing different parts of the sacrifice. The growing complexity of the sacrifice itself seemed to have required such specialization. The most important priest was the Hotri, whose chief duty came to be the recitation of stanzas of the *Rigveda*. The Adhvaryu was responsible for the manual operation of the sacrifice; he tended the fires, prepared the altar, utilized the utensils, and cooked the oblations. The Brahman came to be the overseer of the cult; he ordered the various performances and was aware of the expiation to be performed in case of error in the sacrifice. In addition there was the

Udgatri, or singer of those portions of the *Samaveda* used during the soma sacrifice.

At first the sacrifices were primarily means whereby the favor of the gods could be obtained. As time passed and as the sacrifices became more elaborate, the sacrifice became more a powerful mystery. Through the sacrifice the priest created the world anew and men came to believe that the order of nature ultimately rested on the perfect performance of the sacrifice. The result was that the gods themselves became dependent on the sacrifice, and, since the sacrifice depended upon the accuracy of the priestly class, the Brahmans became more powerful than any earthly king or even any god. Special honoraria always accompanied the sacrifices and were given to the priests in the form of cows, gold, clothes, a horse, or other valuable objects. The Vedic sacrifice presents itself in the form of a drama with the priests as actors, and with portions of the sacrifice set to music with interludes and climaxes.

The soma sacrifice (*agnishtoma*) is named in praise of Agni, perhaps because the last of the hymns used on that day is addressed to Agni. This sacrifice was performed each spring and involved certain preliminary operations, such as the consecration of the area and the participants. The soma was ceremoniously purchased, altars were built, and preparations for the sacrifice were made for three days. The sacrifice proper was accomplished in one day. It consisted of three pressings of the soma: morning, noon, and evening, of which the noon pressing was the climax of the sacrifice. In addition to vegetable and animal sacrifices, the pressing of the soma from the soma plant, and the drinking of it by the officiant, the noon pressing was also the time when the honoraria were distributed. The sacrificer might give up to one thousand cows or even all of his wealth—sometimes even his daughter who might marry one of the priests. The worshipers, having drunk the invigorating soma, saw visions of the gods and experienced sensations of power. They even identified themselves with the gods.

Among the Vedic rituals, most impressive was the horse sacrifice (*ashvamedha*). It was a demonstration of triumph indulged in by a king, thereby manifesting his royal authority. Although the sacrifice itself lasted for three days, the preparatory ceremonies extended for a year or even two. After preparatory oblations, a prize horse was left to run at large for a year while further preparatory activities took place. During this time the king and his army followed the horse, claiming all territory through which it passed. At the end of the year the horse returned, and, while there were numerous animal and soma sacrifices, the horse was finally sacrificed by strangulation. The horse sacrifice was, among other things, a popular festival to obtain prosperity for the kingdom and for the subjects.[10]

In addition to the public rites, there were domestic ones. For the most part, domestic rites consisted of a series of small sacrifices with simple ceremonies involving offerings of a vegetable nature,

10. Benjamin Walker, *Hindu World: An Encyclopedic Survey of Hinduism,* London, G. Allen, 1968, vol. I, p. 458.

and only rarely involving animals. It was the master of the house who normally performed these rites and it was his responsibility, along with his family and his pupil, to maintain the fire.

There were also sacred events (*samskaras*) which followed members of the three upper classes from conception to death. Each transitory phase of life was fraught with danger, which made it essential to perform special rites to counteract evil influences. The number of such threshold rites was at one time quite large.

> *Nearly every formal observance was referred to as a samskara and was attended by fire and water rituals, prayers and sacrifices, oblations, lustrations and other ceremonies, regulated by ancient taboos. Stress was laid on proper orientation,* mantras, *auspicious times and so on, many details of which were preserved in the later samskaras. The number of samskaras was gradually reduced from over 300 to about 40, then to 18 or even 10.*[11]

In terms of the life cycle, the first ceremony had to do with conception, and was followed, in the third month of pregnancy, with a ceremony to ensure the birth of a male offspring. Between the fourth and eighth month of the first pregnancy the husband would stand behind the wife, and, in the "parting of the hair" ceremony, would part the hair of the wife, starting at the front of the head and moving backward. Tying green fruit from the *udambara* twig around the wife's neck was intended to ensure fertility to her and exuberance and heroism in the child. Another ceremony was performed immediately after birth. The father would smear the child's tongue with a mixture of butter, curds, and honey taken from a golden spoon, and the navel cord was cut. Other rites were intended to endow the child with wealth and intelligence. Ten days after birth came the naming ceremony, and usually in the third year (for the Brahman), fifth year (for the Kshatriya), or seventh year (for the Vaishya), the tangled hair was moistened and the rite of tonsure took place.

Of prime importance was the initiation rite (*upanayana*). According to class, this was to take place in the eighth (Brahman), eleventh (Kshatriya), or twelfth (Vaishya) year. While the three upper classes all had such a rite, it became much more significant for the Brahman. Prior to the initiation he was classless. In the *upanayana* rite, the young male was endowed with the sacred thread and was taught the famous "Gayatri" stanza from the *Rigveda*. A period of studentship was thus initiated, during which time the youth lived with his teacher and served him. In exchange for his instruction, the young man begged for food and brought fuel for the sacred fire. Not until he had gone through the *upanayana* rite was the boy permitted to study the Vedas. This ceremony, which involved the shaving of the head, bathing, and being clothed in a new garment, is still practiced today, although it is modified because of the availability of education in public schools. When the boy returned to the world after his period as a student, he participated in a rite of return, the main feature of which was a ceremonial bath.

11. Ibid., p. 315.

Upanayana rite as performed in Bombay in 1965. (Photo by Robert D. Baird.)

A series of ceremonies in honor of the male ancestors also formed an important part of Vedic ritual. Offerings were made to the *pretas,* spirits who had lately departed, and also to the *pitris,* who were distant and more mythical ancestors. The continuing homage to the dead from generation to generation depended on the continuation of the family line and emphasized the importance of male offspring.

When death occurred, the hair and nails of the person were cut off and the body was washed, annointed, and clothed in a new garment. It was placed on the funeral pyre and the wife of the deceased was made to accompany her husband's body on the pyre. During this period, the wife would arise and leave the pyre before the conflagration (*Rigveda* IX.18.8). The practice of *sati* (see p. 238), or the immolation of the widow with her husband, does not seem to have been practiced in Rigvedic times. After the burning of the corpse, the mourners bathe and offer libations of water. Certain Rigvedic verses indicate that the fire conducts the *pretas* to the company of the *pitris.* Later a ceremony was developed for this purpose and took place on the twelfth day after death, or at the end of a year from death. When the dead was added to the group of *pitris,* his great-grandfather was dropped, since the number of *pitris* honored always remained at three. Offerings to the *pitris* are made at regular monthly intervals.

Renunciation was not a popular ideal in the *Rigveda.* The hymns of the *Rigveda* include prayers for sons, wealth, or military victory. In the period of the *Rigveda* men were generally not dissatisfied with life as they experienced it. The ideal of four stages in life (*ashra-mas*) did not develop until the period of the Upanishads, when the path of renunciation became popular. Some of the earlier Upani-shads stress the conflict between the family life and the idea of as-ceticism and renunciation of the world which came to be the means for religious realization. The later development of the doctrine of *ashramas* is an attempt to combine within one orthodoxy these two opposing positions, making place for the contemplative life and the secular life in one system. The division came to involve, succes-sively, life as a student (*brahmacarin*) which began at the time of initiation, the life of the householder (*grihastha*), and the life of the recluse or forest dweller (*vanaprasthya*). There was added the fourth stage of the *atyashramin,* or "he who is beyond the *ashra-mas.*" Such persons were later called *sannyasins,* although the term is not used in the Vedic literature.

The religious convictions expressed in the designation of four *ash-ramas* were also revealed in the recognition of four broad social groups. As early as the purusha hymn of the *Rigveda* the division of society into classes was given religious sanction. In the Vedic pe-riod there were two main groups in society, the Aryas and the Das-yus or Dasas. The former were sacrificers and worshipers of the fire, were fair, and probably corresponded to the invaders. The Dasas were dark-skinned and were criticized because they wor-shiped the phallus. This, coupled with the fact that the term for class (*varna*) means color, indicates a certain class distinction on the basis of color. The *Rigveda* narrates how Indra killed the Das-yus and protected the Arya color, and how he trampled down the caves of the Dasa color (*Rigveda* III.34.9; II.12.4). In time the Aryas came to have Dasa wives or mistresses.

As early as the *Rigveda,* a threefold division existed among the Aryas. Although the terminology varies, these divisions correspond to the classes of the Brahman, Kshatriya, and Vaishya. They do not seem at this time to have developed into rigid castes (*jati*) with pro-scription against intermarriage and interdining. These three classes were somewhat occupationally determined along the lines of intel-lectual progress, military might, and cattle prosperity, and in that order of social status. These professions do not seem to have been hereditary although there must have been the natural tendency to follow in the path of one's father. These classes continued to be fluid in the periods of the Brahmanas and Upanishads. The view of later periods that the teaching and study of the Vedas was the ex-clusive privilege of the Brahmans was a Brahman point of view which was not universally held in the Vedic age. Some of the au-thors of the Vedic hymns were Kshatriyas, and in the Upanishads, heredity received more emphasis, but was not rigidly followed. There seems to have been intermarriage, particularly among the three Aryan classes, and occasionally between them and the Shu-dras, which was the name given to the Dasas. Interdining took place but there was a proscription against using food cooked by a Shudra for the sacrifice.

While there are exceptions in which women were held to have had the knowledge of Brahman,[12] in general women had a low social position, perhaps equivalent to that of the Shudra. A woman did not have inheritance rights, and there was no initiation (*upanayana*), for women did not study the sacred texts. Society was male-oriented and a male child was more important than a female one because of the necessity of carrying on the family line and continuing the religious ceremonies for one's ancestors.

By the end of the Rigvedic period there was a growing tendency to seek for some unifying principle in the *Rigveda*. This tendency is already present in the henotheistic tendencies of the *Rigveda,* but the last book contains hymns that move toward a theistic interpretation. The title *Prajapati* (Lord of Beings), which originally was a title for other deities, came to refer to a separate deity who was above all, and responsible for the creation and governing of the universe (*Rigveda* X.121). Similar characteristics are attributed to *Vishvakarman* (All Creator) (*Rigveda* X.82.3). This does not represent a monolithic development, but illustrates varied attempts to find an explanation of the universe. That these efforts were still far from unified is clearly indicated in one hymn which ends its speculation about the origins of the universe with an expression of profound uncertainty.

DEVELOPMENT OF RELIGIOUS THOUGHT

> *Then neither Being nor Not-being was,*
> *Nor atmosphere, nor firmament, nor what is beyond.*
> *What did it encompass? Where? In whose protection?*
> *What was water, the deep, unfathomable?*
>
> *Neither death nor immortality was there then,*
> *No sign of night or day.*
> *That One breathed, windless, by its own energy:*
> *Nought else existed then.*
>
> *In the beginning was darkness swathed in darkness;*
> *All this was but unmanifested water.*
> *Whatever was, that One, coming into being,*
> *Hidden by the Void,*
> *Was generated by the power of heat.*
>
> *In the beginning this (One) evolved,*
> *Became desire, first seed of mind,*
> *Wise seers, searching within their hearts,*
> *Found the bond of Being in Not-being.*

12. It is necessary to distinguish several words which look somewhat alike. In this text, *Brahma* (Brahmā) is the creator god, *Brahman* (Brahman) is the principle of Ultimate Reality so basic to Shankara and found in many earlier texts (i.e., Upanishads), *Brahman* (Brāhmaṇ) is the priestly class. When the diacritical marks are removed the last two (Ultimate Reality or priestly class) must be distinguished by context. There are also the *Brahmanas* (Brāhmaṇas) which are a body of vedic texts. In some books members of the priestly class are referred to as *Brahmins*.

Their cord was extended athwart:
Was there a below? Was there an above?
Casters of seed there were, and powers;
Beneath was energy, above was impulse.

Who knows truly? Who can here declare it?
Whence it was born, when is this emanation.
By the emanation of this the gods
   Only later (came to be),
Who then knows whence it has risen?

Whence this emanation hath arisen,
Whether (God) disposed it, or whether he did not—
Only he who is its overseer in the highest heaven knows,
(He only knows), or perhaps he does not know! [13]

Most of these more speculative hymns are found in the tenth book of the *Rigveda,* which is admittedly later than the rest. In one of these hymns the high place of sacrifice is assumed and the creation of the world is depicted in terms of a sacrifice of primal man (X.90). There is little to suggest that the doctrines of rebirth and karma were known at this time or that the later notions of Atman and Brahman were part of the religious views (see p. 189).

By the time of the Brahmanas, sacrifice became more important than the gods themselves who were frequently presented as the exemplary performers of the sacrificial rituals. It was commonly assumed that sacrifice was eternal like the Vedas. Not only was the world created by an original sacrifice, but the natural laws of the physical world were maintained by the proper enactment of sacrifices. Although it may not be possible to trace historical dependence, the concept of *rita* in the *Rigveda* and the absolute dependableness of the sacrifices in the Brahmanas paved the way for the development of the doctrine of karma, which assumed a dependable causal connection within the spiritual order.

The conception of Brahman, which in later Vedanta and in some strains of the Upanishads is the only Real, was earlier connected with sacrifices. Das Gupta (an Indian scholar) indicates that some of the earlier meanings of the term are food for the food offering, the chant of the sama singer, a magical formula or text, duly completed ceremonies, and simply "great." [14] By the time of the *Shatapatha Brahmana,* Brahman is declared to be the moving force behind everything.

There is a debate among scholars regarding the point of continuity or discontinuity between the Samhitas and the Brahmanas and Upanishads. Undoubtedly there is considerable religious difference. But the question of whether those responsible for the Upanishads rejected sacrifices in favor of meditation is unanswerable in those

13. *Rigveda* X.129. R. C. Zaehner, *Hindu Scriptures,* New York, Dutton, 1966, Everyman's Library, pp. 11–13.

14. Surendranath Das Gupta, *A History of Indian Philosophy,* London, Cambridge, 1963 (first published in 1922), vol. I, p. 20.

terms, since several attitudes exist in the Upanishads themselves. While the later Indian philosophical systems have committed themselves to a unified interpretation of the Upanishads, such unanimity did not exist in the upanishadic period, for religious speculation was still quite fluid. In some passages there is strong rejection of sacrificial methods, while in others there is an attempt to make the transition to meditative internalization less abrupt. The *Brihadaranyaka Upanishad* which was attached to the *Shatapatha Brahmana* proceeds by transforming the horse sacrifice, elaborately described in the *Shatapatha Brahmana,* into a mediational device. Hence it is implicitly admitted that it is either impossible or undesirable to perform the sacrifice itself, but that the same result can be assured by meditating on the correspondences between various portions of the horse and the various parts of the universe. Such a revaluation of this ancient sacrifice makes the transition easier than if the sacrifice were simply rejected. That many of the existing Upanishads were originally embedded as literary documents in the Brahmanas indicates that there was no sudden break but rather a gradual reinterpretation which took place while the sacrifices continued to exert their influence.

As interest moved from the sacrifice to the forms of meditation, an understanding of particular correspondences between the sacrifice and aspects of the human body or the universe considered as Brahman became indispensable. In the important Upanishads the search for this basic reality, Brahman, was intensified. One encounters sages who move from place to place in search of a competent teacher to instruct them in the nature of Brahman. While the *Rigveda* seemed to move in the direction of a supreme being outside of man or the universe as the explanation of the world, the upanishadic seers looked within man and found there a substance or essence of the universe (Brahman). But this point was not reached without considerable effort. Many visible objects such as the sun, or even the wind, were considered for this honor and found to be inadequate. The search continued for that which was unchangeable. Brahman was identified as *prana* (vital breath in man) and various passages labor to show that *prana* was superior to other physical organs and therefore that meditation on *prana* led to the best results.

Dissatisfaction with any identification of Brahman with the elements of the physical world led some to conclude that positive definitions of Brahman were impossible. By whatever means they tried to give form to the Ultimate Reality, they failed. Some therefore concluded that all positive attributions were erroneous and that only negative statements could be made. In the *Brihadaranyaka Upanishad* (IV.15.5) Yajnavalkya says that "He the atman is not this, not this (neti . . . neti). He is inconceivable, for he is not changed, untouched, for nothing changes him." In the *Katha Upanishad* (III.15) it is stated: "That which is inaudible, intangible, invisible, indestructible, which cannot be tasted, nor smelt, eternal, without beginning or end, greater than the great, the fixed. He who knows it is released from the jaws of death." The implication to be drawn from this line of thought in a later period was that ultimate realization is best explained by remaining silent.

In the *Rigveda* and somewhat in the Brahmanas the ideal aimed at is length of days on earth, and life in heaven in companionship with the gods. In the Brahmanas one begins to hear more about "re-death" (*punarmrityu*), which was feared because it would end that enjoyable life after death.[15] Hence means were sought to avoid this "re-death" by religious and magical means. In the early Upanishads, such a concern is absent, for life after death is not regarded as somehow different from the present earthly life. In the course of Indian history, this notion was transformed into the well-known belief in reincarnation or the transmigration of souls from one body to another. It was believed that a person lived a series of lives in the condition of man, an animal, or even as a *deva* (god) in one of the numerous heavens.

The condition of each succeeding rebirth was determined by the relative balance of good and bad deeds in previous existences. This points to an early belief in the doctrine of karma by which man's relation to morality (*dharma*) determines his destiny. "The two went away and deliberated. What they said was *karma* (action). What they praised was *karma*. Verily, one becomes good by good action, bad by bad action." [16] While such a belief could logically offer the reassurance that one's situation is never hopeless and that, being based on one's previous deeds one's predicament is surely just, in fact the opposite was not infrequently the case. Disease, suffering, and bondage to the continual course of migration was man's lot.

Continued existence in successive states of reincarnated life came to be thought of as an unfortunate entanglement in the endless wheel of time. The goal for which man longed was no longer reincarnation in a more blissful state of existence, but release from the entire web of endless births and rebirths.

> *He, however, who has no understanding,*
> *Who is unmindful and ever impure,*
> *Reaches not the goal,*
> *But goes on to reincarnation* (samsara).[17]

Although in the Upanishads man longed for release from *samsara*, it was recognized that release was not easy. It was only possible for a few and then only after considerable study and discipline. One did not treat the truth lightly, but only instructed those who were clearly worthy. Worthiness often implied the willingness to detach oneself from otherwise normal life patterns. Existence as a householder was both distracting and transitory.

Thus arose the ideal norm of the wandering monk (samnyasin, bhiksu, muni), *the homeless ascetic, living on alms, cut off from*

15. Franklin Edgerton, *The Beginnings of Indian Philosophy,* London, G. Allen, 1965, p. 29.

16. *Brihadaranyaka Upanishad* III.2.13. Robert Ernest Hume, *The Thirteen Principal Upanishads,* Madras, Oxford University Press, 1949, p. 110.

17. *Katha Upanishad* VI.7. Hume, op. cit., p. 352.

family ties, possessions, and all worldly life. He stood outside of everything, even of caste; a member of any caste, or of none, might become a truth-seeking mendicant.[18]

Even ascetic practices (*tapas*) were sometimes utilized, although it would be left to the Jainas (see p. 153) to emphasize that as a primary method.

Nevertheless, liberation is the ideal in the Upanishads; emancipation or *moksha* is the state of infinity that is attained when one comes to know the identity of Atman and Brahman. The ceaseless course of transmigration is only for those who do not know their true nature. *Moksha* is the elimination of all duality. Hence it is not that *we know,* for such a statement sustains a distinction between the knower and the object known. Instead, we are pure knowledge itself. Such emancipation is not a new acquisition, nor the result of some action, but always exists as the truth of our nature. The meditative practices are only methods used by people in a state of ignorance whereby they uncover their true selves. Yet even this type of language, indeed all language, is inadequate, since it is structured in terms of subject and object. The state is therefore inexpressible.

We are all emancipated already, but just "as he who does not know the place of a hidden treasure fails to find it, though he passes over it constantly, so all these creatures fail to find the world of Brahman, though they daily (in deep sleep) enter into it; for by unreality are they turned aside" (*Chandogya Upanishad,* VIII.3.2). In this enlightened state all desire, hope, and fear are obliterated. The loss of individuality involves the loss of suffering and pain. Likewise, all works no longer have any effect. Such knowledge is a matter of immediate intuition and hence cannot be doubted—it is self-authenticating. And, this awareness eliminates rebirth which is merely part of the world of ignorance.

18. Edgerton, op. cit., p. 32.

RELIGION
IN THE
POST-VEDIC
PERIOD

The sixth century B.C. was a time of religious change. Even in the Upanishads the emphasis on sacrifice was questioned either through outright rejection or through reinterpretation. In general the Upanishads represent the Brahmanical attempt at adjusting to the mounting criticism of the sacrificial system and the growing rigidity of the caste system.

The Brahmanical religious system was challenged by numerous sects which arose and lapsed, never to be heard from again. Teachers appeared, propounding doctrinal theories accompanied by certain methods for the realization of their ideal. Such men were often ascetics, or homeless wanderers who accumulated a group of followers bound together in a search for the Real. They wore the yellow robe of the ascetic and, in contrast with the earliest forest dweller who probably lived on wild fruit and roots, were dependent on the householders for their daily food.

These homeless ones were called various names such as *shramanas* (ascetics) or *bhikshus* (almsmen). The followers of the Buddha preferred the latter, while other groups chose other terms. Of all the teachers who accumulated groups of disciples, two have had lasting importance in India or throughout Asia. One was Gotama (Pali form of Sanskrit Gautama), who, as the Buddha, became an object of faith, or the teacher of the path to the elimination of suffering. After his doctrine and appeal died out in India, it continued to be the faith of millions throughout Southeast Asia, Tibet, China, and Japan. The other teacher was Mahavira, from whom the present Jain community received inspiration.

Sometime in the sixth century B.C. within the present boundary of
Nepal, an individual was born who was to have an influence
throughout India, Asia, and, as of the twentieth century, throughout
the world. Known commonly by his title Buddha ("Enlightened
One"), Siddhattha Gotama would live, according to all traditions, a
full life of eighty years. His dates are variously given, but can be
taken as 563–483 B.C.

Not only is the date of the Buddha somewhat uncertain, but one's
ability to write a historically reliable life of the Buddha, or to describe the original teachings of the Buddha himself, is hampered by
the nature of the available documents. The Buddha wrote nothing
himself, and the various texts which have come to us all date a few
hundred years after the death of the Buddha and are the result of
the work of certain schools or sects and hence bear their doctrinal
marks.

The texts themselves indicate that shortly after the death of the
Buddha there existed numerous schools which differed on matters
of practice and doctrine. While the standard number is eighteen, we
know of some thirty-five sects by name alone. The Pali Canon,
which is the scriptural corpus of the so-called Theravada Buddhists
of Ceylon and Southeast Asia, is the preserved canon of one of
these schools.

In order to understand better what these documents can reveal
and how far back toward the Buddha they can take us, we must indicate the contents of the Pali Canon and other important works
which are acceptable within this tradition. The following canon was
preserved in Pali, a language akin to Sanskrit. It is held sacred even
today by that community called Hinayana, or "little vehicle," by
their Mahayana competitors, or self-named Theravada, or the "way
of the elders." This canon, called the *Tipitaka* (Sanskrit *Tripitaka*),
or "three baskets," contains the following:

A. *Vinaya-Pitaka.* A basket of discipline which contains the rules
   for the monastic order, the Sangha.
   1. *Sutta-vibhanga,* or "principles" within which is the *Patimokkha*
      (Sanskrit *Pratimoksha*), some 252 rules which are recited
      at fortnightly confessions by the monks.
   2. *Mahavagga* (major division) contains rules for entry into order,
      and regulations for the behavior of the monks. It also enu-
      merates rules for the rainy season and gives a short account
      of the Buddha's life.
   3. *Cullavagga* (minor division) includes further information about
      life in the Sangha, reasons for exclusion, manner of ordina-
      tion for nuns, and accounts of the first two councils.
B. *Sutta-Pitaka* (Sanskrit *sutra*). The word *sutta* means thread, and
   while it refers to aphoristic statements in the Brahmanical
   sutras, it here consists of five collections (*nikayas*) of dialogues
   supposed to have been uttered by the Buddha and arranged according to length.
   1. *Digha-nikaya* contains thirty-four "long *suttas*" including the

important *Mahaparinibbanasutta* which gives account of the death of the Buddha.

2. *Majjhima-nikaya* includes 152 *suttas* of "medium length" which tell of the Buddha's austerities, enlightenment, and early teachings.

3. *Samyutta-nikaya* (kindred sayings) includes 2889 *suttas* in fifty-six groups among which are the Deer Park Sermon and discourses on the chain of causation and other doctrinal matters. These are arranged in a further fivefold classification.

4. *Anguttara-nikaya* (gradual sayings) includes 2308 *suttas* in eleven sections which are arranged according to number from discourses dealing with one thing up to lists of eleven things.

5. *Khuddaka-nikaya* (minor discourses) are fifteen books of short discourses among which are the *Jataka,* or stories of the previous births of the Buddha, and the *Dhammapada,* the "Path of Truth."

C. *Abhidhamma-Pitaka* includes seven books which deal with further doctrinal refinements of a rather technical nature. This includes the *Kathavatthu* (points of controversy) in which Theravada doctrine is expounded over against other "false" views.

Later texts highly honored in the Southern School are the *Milindapanha* ("Questions of King Milinda," c. A.D. 100), in which King Menander has his questions satisfactorily answered by the monk Nagasena and is finally converted; the *Dipavamsa* (c. fourth century A.D.), a history of the island (Ceylon); the *Mahavamsa* (c. fifth century), or great chronicle of Ceylon; and the *Visuddhimagga* ("The Path of Purity"), an exposition of the Buddha's doctrine by Buddhaghosha in the fourth century A.D.

In addition to the Pali texts, there are numerous Sanskrit texts which are more relevant for understanding Mahayana interpretations of the Buddha's doctrine. The Pali Canon is generally dated earlier than the Sanskrit manuscripts. Even the Pali Canon, however, was not reduced to written form until some time after the Buddha. At the time of King Ashoka (274–236 B.C.) it seems that the *Abhidhamma* was not yet committed to writing, since only the *Dhamma* (i.e., *Sutta-Pitaka*) and the *Vinaya* are mentioned. It also seems that the *Vinaya* developed gradually, perhaps the *Patimokkha* being composed within fifty years of the Buddha. The sections which deal with the Buddha's life could not have been written for one to two hundred years after the time of the Buddha. Further, the canon represents only one school of thought. The best procedure one can follow is to describe the tradition and use it to reach the beliefs and practices of the early followers of the Buddha. While such followers may be accurately describing the life and teachings of the Buddha, there is little chance at present to verify this historically. By examination of layers of tradition within the Pali Canon, and by comparisons with other canons, one can project partial traditions into the oral period prior to the dated manuscripts, but this can only point to a possible (not even probable) account of the life and teachings of the Buddha.

It is the tradition of the Theravada community that the entire *Tipitaka* was recited at the First Council, which reportedly took place at Rajagaha right after the death of the Buddha, and that the entire *Tipitaka* was transmitted by memory until it was written down early in the sixth century after the Buddha (c. 25 B.C.) in Ceylon.[1] It appears, however, that certain portions were written down prior to that time. Nevertheless, if one is to accept the *Tipitaka* as straightforward accounts of the life and teachings of the Buddha, one must accept the reliability of the oral tradition. There is considerable evidence that the cult and imagination of the devotees was at work in the formulation of the canonical materials.[2]

TRADITION ON THE LIFE OF THE BUDDHA

It is fruitless to try to empty the accounts of the Buddha of the miraculous or unusual. Even in the relatively early *Mahaparinibbanasutta* the miraculous occurs, and in the earliest texts the devotion of the Buddha's followers has left its mark on the accounts of his life. While the miraculous element increases in time, even the Theravada community presents the Buddha in a remarkable light.

As seen in the *Tipitaka,* the life of the Buddha has an end, but no appropriate beginning. Since the very term "Buddha" means "enlightened one," there can be many Buddhas but only one Siddhattha Gotama. It was eons ago, through the existence of an ascetic named Sumedha and in the presence of a previous Buddha Dipankara, that the Buddha who now concerns us took the vows of a Bodhisattva (a Buddha to be) and thereby initiated the discipline that would eventually lead him to Buddhahood. In the Tushita heaven from which he was reborn as Shakyamuni, he himself determined the time and place of his birth. It was in the Shakya clan and into the family of the king that he was born. In a dream, King Shuddhodhana's first wife, Maya, received Gotama into her body in the form of a white elephant (symbol of perfect wisdom and royal power). He was born in Lumbini in the foothills of the Himalayas, within the present boundary of Nepal.

When the child was born, the trees of Lumbini Park burst into bloom. Gods and men worshiped him with scented garlands. After birth the child was taken to the palace where his horoscope was told. It was determined that he would become either a "universal monarch," or a *tathagata* (one who has thus come) or *arhat* (one who is worthy to be honored). Yashodhara, his future wife, thousands of other personages of noble and servant birth, and even Kanthaka, the Bodhisattva's future steed, were born at the same time as the Buddha.

1. Bhikkhu J. Kashyap, "Origin and Expansion of Buddhism," in Kenneth W. Morgan, ed., *The Path of the Buddha,* New York, Ronald, 1956, p. 38.
2. Sukumar Dutt, *The Buddha and Five After-Centuries,* London, Luzac & Company Limited, 1957.

Gotama was cared for by thirty-two nurses and was provided with three palaces (one each for the hot, cool, and rainy seasons), and four pleasure parks at each of the cardinal points at the edge of the city. Every conceivable gratification was provided, including fragrant flowers, luxurious couches, women, dancing, singing, and instrumental and orchestral music. Numerous guards were provided for his protection.

One might well wonder why the young prince, surrounded by luxury and married to a lovely wife who had just given birth to his son Rahula (bond), would leave this for the life of a monk. The religious community explained this with the legend of the four passing sights through which Gotama, who had been shielded from all unpleasantness throughout his youth, saw successively an old man wrinkled, toothless, and bent over a stick; a diseased man with fever; and a corpse wrapped in cloth being carried in procession to the funeral pyre. Finally he saw a monk, serenely begging with bowl in hand. It was this conjunction of experiences which caused Gotama to search for the means whereby a man could maintain serenity in face of the greatest evils of existence—old age, sickness, and death.

Gotama began his search with what is called in the tradition the great renunciation. As the household slept, he took a final look at his sleeping wife and child and left for the courtyard where his groom and horse were waiting. A large retinue of gods and men assisted him, even to keeping the hoofs of Kanthaka from pounding the ground. They assisted him until he stopped at daybreak. Then he dismissed the numerous gods, tore off his princely garments which he exchanged for the clothes of a huntsman, and cut off his hair with a sword. No longer the prince, he was now a wandering seeker after enlightenment, one in a long tradition extending before and after him in India to the present day.

Transformed thus from a layman to a mendicant, the Buddha put aside his resplendent jewelry, including the heavy earrings which left his ears distended because of their heavy weight. This deformity was captured by later sculpture and interpreted by the Chinese and Tibetans as a sign of wisdom. Although he is reported to have cut his hair, artists continued to present the Buddha with his hair tightly curled, one of the thirty-two traditional marks of a great man. His dismissal of the gods is also significant for the Theravada community, because they believed that salvation could be achieved only by personal effort without the help of men or gods.

Gotama studied under Alara Kalama, but the lessons were not to his taste. The biographers present the Buddha as omniscient; he knew all the answers before they were given to him. Having practiced yoga, he tried ascetic austerities. Even with his foreknowledge that this was not the way, he engaged in such austerities in order to lead blind humanity through the authority of experience. His meditational practices and dietary abstentions were so severe that his body wasted away until it was unable to bear his spirit.

Like dried canes now became my arms and legs, withered through this extremely scanty diet; like the foot of a camel be-

came my buttock; like a string of beads became my spinal col-
umn with the vertebrae protruding. Just as the roof-beams of an
old house sharply protrude, so protruded my ribs; just as in a
deep well the little water-stars far beneath are scarcely seen, so
now in my eye-balls the sunken pupils were hardly seen; just as a
gourd freshly cut becomes empty and withered in the hot sun, so
now became the skin of my head empty and withered. When I
wished to touch my belly, I reached to the back of my spine, and
when I wished to touch my spine, I again reached to the belly,—
thus near had come my belly to my spinal column. To reinforce
this body, I chafed the limbs with the hand and the badly rooted
hair fell from the skin. So strangely was the pure color of my skin
affected by the scanty diet that some said, "The ascetic Gotama
is black," while others said, "The ascetic Gotama is yellow."
Then this thought came to me: This is the uttermost; beyond this
one cannot go.[3]

In addition to limiting his diet, he practiced complete immobility,
seeking neither shade nor sunshine, nor shelter from wind or rain.
He did not move as much as a finger to protect himself from horse-
flies, mosquitos, or reptiles. Realizing that his body and mind were
impoverished, he ceased his fast in an effort to restore his strength,
an act which resulted in the break with the five ascetics who had
thus far accompanied him and who now thought he was going back
on his intentions. These five would later hear his first sermon near
Benares and become his disciples.

Taking some strands of kusha grass for a seat, he sat facing the
west and resolved: "Upon this seat, though my body dry up and my
skin, my bones and my flesh be dissolved—without having reached
enlightenment, no matter how long and difficult to reach, I shall not
stir from this seat." A. Foucher comments:

He did not have to go to such lengths. His studies, quickly ended,
took a year; his fruitless austerities cost him six years; his com-
plete success was to come in twenty-four hours. The following
day the rising sun would shine, not upon one ascetic among oth-
ers, but upon a unique Being without equal anywhere in the
world; for it is one of the dogmas of Buddhism that in a given
time and universe there can exist only one Buddha.[4]

His later followers described the struggle that was his that night
in terms of a conflict between himself and Mara, the tempter. A
theme for the artist, Mara's assault launched an army of repulsive
monsters, ghosts, devils, and other hideous figures. The attack was,
of course, brushed aside by the Buddha. He reached his right hand
downward toward the earth in the earthwitnessing *mudra* (symbolic
position of the hands). The response of earth to his victory is contained in the words: "It is true, O great man, it is true; it is as you
say and I am the eyewitness." At the sight of this miraculous appa-

3. Sukumar Dutt, op. cit., p. 39.
4. A. Foucher, *The Life of the Buddha, According to the Ancient Texts
and Monuments of India,* Middletown, Conn., Wesleyan University Press,
1963, abridged translation by Simone Brangier Boas., p. 107.

rition, Mara's army scattered in flight. Next ensued the three watches of the night, a process in which Gotama came to know the twelve-fold chain of causation and its meaning (see p. 145).

Gotama achieved enlightenment as dawn broke. Mara tempted the Buddha to go immediately into *Parinibbana* (see p. 149), but he resisted the temptation. His struggle with Mara symbolizes the conflict between existence in the world and the Nibbanic experience which takes one out of the world. A similar struggle was experienced by the monastic order that produced the Pali Canon.

The Buddha's hesitation to preach the *Dhamma,* or truth, to others was based upon the fact that it was difficult to understand and that it took moral effort beyond the grasp of the average man. However, Gotama's concern for humanity overcame the more selfish motive, which suggested that he simply enter *Parinibbana.*

Gotama traveled to what is now Sarnath, four miles north of Benares and about 130 miles west of Gaya, the spot of his enlightenment. The five ascetics who had left him previously saw him approaching from a distance and vowed not to rise or offer him a seat, food, or respect. In spite of their resolve, the manner of his personal presence caused them to do precisely what they vowed not to do. After his sermon, which is referred to as the turning of the wheel of the *Dhamma,* they became his first converts. This encounter shows that Gotama was not immediately successful, since he had already traveled some 130 miles from Gaya and had encountered a number of persons along the way. His Deer Park Sermon contained the four noble truths and the noble eightfold path. The following is the content in skeletal form.

1. Life is suffering (*dukkha*).
2. The cause of this suffering is grasping or desire (*tanha*).
3. Suffering can be eliminated when desire is extinguished.
4. Desire can be eliminated through the eightfold path, consisting of
    a. Right understanding;
    b. Right aspiration;
    c. Right speech;
    d. Right conduct;
    e. Right vocation;
    f. Right effort;
    g. Right mindfulness;
    h. Right concentration.

After considerable success at winning converts, some seven years after enlightenment he returned to his native city where he conferred ordination on his son Rahula, his half-brother Nanda, and numerous other candidates. His death was the result of a meal of dried boar's flesh (or perhaps some kind of roots) which, according to tradition, resulted in a frequently recurring case of dysentery. Of course, a Buddha cannot simply die. During the night he went through a series of mystical states of trance prior to entering *Parinibbana* and complete bliss.

While the Pali tradition was only one of several stemming from the Buddha, it exerted considerable influence and still dominates Southeast Asia. The Theravada community attributes this system of thought to the Buddha, and it is for that reason that they profess it as their own.

The Pali Canon consistently portrays the Buddha as uninterested in purely metaphysical or philosophical questions. He is portrayed as an intensely practical person whose ultimate concern is the alleviation of suffering and rebirth. He who will not tend to the problem of suffering until he has had his metaphysical questions adequately answered is like a man who has been wounded by a poisoned arrow and refuses to allow its removal until he knows what kind of arrow it is, the caste, height, name, color, and other details about the one who shot it, and the type of bow and bowstring that was used. In this futile concern with irrelevant questions, he dies.

All of the theoretical analysis which follows should be interpreted in the light of this dominant emphasis on the practical function of truth. The acquisition of right views about ourselves and the world has as its purpose the elimination of suffering through the experiential realization of the truth of these views.

As one surveys man and the world, there are three characteristics of all existence.[5] This is set forth in the *Anguttara-Nikaya* III.134 as follows:

Three Marks (Lakkhana) of Existence

Whether Buddhas arise, O priests, or whether Buddhas do not arise, it remains a fact, and the fixed and necessary constitution of being that (1) All its constituents are transitory. (2) All its constituents are misery. (3) All its elements are lacking in an Ego. This fact a Buddha discovers and masters, and when he has discovered and mastered it, he announces, teaches, publishes, proclaims, discloses, minutely explains, and makes it clear, that all the constituents of being are transitory, are misery, and are lacking in an Ego.

One mark of all existence, then, is *anicca* (Sanskrit *anitya*), or impermanence. Everything, according to the *Tipitaka*, is transitory. In the Upanishads the search was for Being, and Brahman or Atman was considered the only thing that abides. The emphasis of the *Tipitaka* is on the phenomenal world and its constant flux.

We are deceived if we allow ourselves to believe that there is ever a pause in the flow of becoming, a resting place where positive existence is attained for even the briefest duration of time. It is only by shutting our eyes to the succession of events that we come to speak of things rather than of processes. The quickness or slowness of the process does not affect the generalization.[6]

5. Edward Conze, *Buddhist Thought in India,* London, G. Allen, 1962, pp. 34 ff.
6. Ananda Coomaraswany, *Buddha and the Gospel of Buddhism,* New York, Harper & Row, 1964, first published in 1916, p. 95.

A second mark of all existence is *anatta* (Sanskrit *anatman*). It is not unrelated to the doctrine of impermanence, for if impermanence is the rule, then it follows that there can be no permanent self or Atman. One of the false notions under which we labor is that there is an abiding "I." Instead of thinking of the self as a distinct and continuing entity, we are instructed that the empirical self is compounded and temporary. It is at any moment merely the conjunction of five *khandhas* (Sanskrit *skhandhas*), or groups which are continually restructured according to the law of *kamma*. There is one physical *khandha* and four of a mental nature:

1. *Rupa* (form) is the material or physical aspect of the empirical being. *Rupa* is capable of refinements, and in higher beings is so subtle that it approaches the immaterial.

2. *Vedana* (sensations) are the result of the contact of senses with the external world. This includes both physical and psychical sensibilities and they can be classified as pleasant, unpleasant, or neutral.

3. *Sanna* (Sanskrit *sanjna*) is the power which produces conceptions of physical objects within the human psyche. There are six, which correspond to the six sense organs (five ordinary sense organs plus the *citta,* or mind, which receives impressions from the other senses).

4. *Sankara* (Sanskrit *samskara*), or impulses, refer to all active dispositions, tendencies, impulses, volitions, strivings, emotions whether conscious or repressed.

5. *Vinnana* (Sanskrit *vijnana*) or consciousness is the most important since the others depend on it. This is the psychic power of discrimination and hence is more akin to intelligence than mere consciousness.

All the facts of experience involving ourselves or objects in relation to us can be understood in terms of the *khandhas.* There is no self existing independently of the *khandhas.* In the *Milindapanha,* Nagasena illustrates this doctrine by indicating that the term "chariot" is merely a convention for referring to the pole, axle, wheels, chariot body, and banner staff in a certain conjunction. Neither one of these components is the chariot, nor is the chariot something else outside of them. Likewise, the use of the term "self" is only a convention and has no more reality than the chariot conceived as an entity distinct from its physical parts.

A third mark of existence is *dukkha* (suffering). Life is characterized by suffering or "ill," that is, it is out of joint. One can begin with the rather obvious point that sickness, old age, death, and separation from what one loves are causes of suffering. But the point of this doctrine is that all of life is suffering. Those who have come to a high level of realization through meditation will sense this more clearly than others. Existence is suffering because we cling to things which are transitory and confuse the impermanent *khandhas* with a permanent self which is, as we have learned, nonexistent. The full realization of this characteristic of existence is reserved for the Arhat. Because only holy men are sure of it, it is sometimes called a "holy truth."

The Arhat is so much more sensitive than we are, makes so much greater demands than we do. No one minds feeling an eye-lash on the palm of his hand, but everyone is irritated when it drops into his eye; just so the ordinary person is insensitive to the ills of the conditioned, whereas they torment the sage. Saints suffer more intensely in the highest heaven than fools in the most terrible hells.[7]

The doctrine of *paticcasamuppada* (Sanskrit *pratityasamutpada*), or dependent origination, was thought basic to the doctrine of the Buddha by the Theravada community. It is also called the wheel of causation, or the doctrine of causation, and is mentioned either in terms of the complete twelve causes (*nidanas*) or in partial form in no less than ninety-six suttas. The importance of the twelve causes is that they are an expansion of the last two noble truths of the Buddha's Deer Park Sermon—namely the cause of suffering and the method for the elimination of suffering. The causes are not always listed as twelve, but the following came to be accepted as standard.

Dependent Origination (Paticcasamuppada)

1. Ignorance (*avijja*) is the first link and the primary root of all evil and suffering. It is ignorance of the true doctrine as found in the four noble truths and the three marks of existence that cause all of man's sorrow and suffering.

2. Volitional activities (*sankara*) include all moral and immoral actions of body, mind, and speech. Both moral and immoral actions are included, for all such distinctions are part of our state of ignorance which true insight eliminates. Ignorance is the cause of these activities.

3. Consciousness (*vinnana*) is consciousness which is linked with another existence, and this is caused by the moral and immoral activities of a being and hence leads to rebirth.

4. Name and form, or mind and matter (*nama-rupa*), are the kamma-determined results of mental and physical phenomena, and are the result of relinking consciousness.

5. Sense fields (*salayatana*) refer to the six senses together with their objects. These sense fields of operation arise as the result of the existence of mind and matter.

6. Contact (*phassa*) refers to the sensory and mental impressions which result from the contact between the senses and objects of sense.

7. Feeling (*vedana*) comes through sensory and mental impressions, and can be classified as favorable, unfavorable, or neutral.

8. Craving or desire (*tanha*) arises as the result of pleasant sounds, tastes, smells, sights, objects of touch, or thought.

9. Attachment (*upadana*) is the result of grasping or craving. The four types of attachment are to sensuality, to false views, to wrong rites and ceremonies, and to self-deception.

10. Becoming (*bhava*) is the process which stems from attachment and results in another rebirth.

7. Edward Conze, op. cit., p. 36.

11. Rebirth (*jati*) is the result of the process of becoming which stems from attachment.

12. Old age and death (*jaramarana*) result from the fact of being born, for without rebirth there would be no old age, sickness, or death.

Not infrequently the Buddha indicates that the list can be reversed, a fact that emphasizes its intensely practical purpose: without rebirth there would be no death, without becoming there would be no rebirth, and so on until without ignorance there would be no moral or immoral activities.

The doctrine of the twelve causes is an attempt to show that there is no first cause, that everything, including our suffering and rebirth, is dependent on something else, which, if eliminated, will also eliminate the problem. Ignorance is more of a logical starting point than a chronological one. If ignorance were eliminated, so would all suffering and rebirth be eliminated.

> For the Blessed One in his discourses on the round of rebirth was accustomed to choose from Dependent Origination two of the factors of being as his starting points: either, on the one hand, ignorance, as when he says, "As I have told you, O priests, the first beginning of ignorance cannot be discerned, nor can one say, 'Before a given point of time there was no ignorance, it came into being afterwards.' Nevertheless, O priests, it can be discerned that ignorance possesses a definite independence": or, on the other hand, desire for existence, as when he says, "As I have told you, O priests, the first beginning of desire for existence cannot be discerned, nor can one say, 'Before a given point of time there was no desire for existence, it came into being afterwards.' Nevertheless, O priests, it can be discerned that desire for existence possesses a definite dependence." [8]

Kamma and Rebirth

Kamma (Sanskrit *karma*) is what governs the changing processes of the phenomenal world, particularly the continuously regrouping *khandhas*. *Kamma* refers to a deed, but also to its result. According to the *Samyutta-Nikaya*, the result is inevitable.

> According to the seed that's sown,
>   So is the fruit ye reap therefrom.
> Doer of good will gather good,
>   Doer of evil, evil reaps.
> Sown is the seed, and thou shalt taste
>   The fruit therof.

Kamma operates in an impersonal and impartial manner, characterized by neither love nor hate. Not only is *kamma* operative in the moral realm in that one becomes what he does, but there is a connection between the moral and the physical so that good or evil

8. Quoted in Henry Clarke Warren, *Buddhism in Translations*, New York, Atheneum Publishers, 1963, reprint, p. 171.

deeds have a certain physical effect as well. This is portrayed in the *Milindapanha.*

> *Why is it Nagasena, that all men are not alike, but some are short-lived, some are long-lived, some sickly and some healthy, some ugly and some beautiful, some without influence and some of great power, some poor and some wealthy, some lowborn and some highborn, some stupid and some wise?* [9]

Nagasena replied that just as different vegetables are produced by different seeds,

> *Just so . . . are differences you have mentioned among men to be explained. For it has been said by the Blessed One: Beings, O Brahmin, have each their own karma, are inheritors of karma, belong to the tribe of their karma, are relatives by karma, have each their own karma as their own protecting overlord. It is karma that divides into high and low and the like divisions.* [10]

The abode of one's birth is determined by one's *kamma* as well. This can best be illustrated with a quote from the *Majjhima-Nikaya* I.389.

> *(1) If a man produces injurious aggregations of body, speech, and mind, he is reborn in an injurious world. There he is affected by injurious impressions, and feels injurious feelings extremely painful, such as do those who are beings in Hell. Thus the rebirth of a creature is due to the creature. It is through what he does that he is reborn. Thus beings are the heirs of their karma.*
>
> *(2) If a man produces a non-injurious aggregation of body, speech, and mind, he is reborn in a non-injurious world. There he is affected by non-injurious impressions, and feels non-injurious feelings extremely pleasant, such as do the wholly-bright gods.*
>
> *(3) If a man produces an injurious and non-injurious aggregation of body, speech, and mind, he is reborn in a world both injurious and non-injurious. He is affected by both kinds of impressions and feelings, such as human beings, some gods, and some beings in states of punishment.*
>
> *(4) When the intention is directed to the abandonment of black karma with black ripening, or white karma with white ripening, and of black-white karma with black-white ripening, this is called neither black nor white, producing neither black nor white karma. It tends to the destruction of karma.* [11]

One can be born in various heavens and hells as well as in human form, and one's *kamma* in a previous existence determines the locus of the birth. Not all *kamma* produces its effect in the same life in which the deed is done. Some ripens in the same life, some

9. T. W. Rhys Davids, trans., *The Questions of King Milinda,* New York, Dover, 1963 (first pub. as vol. XXXV of S. B. E.), vol. I, p. 100.

10. Ibid., p. 101.

11. Quoted in Edward J. Thomas, *The History of Buddhist Thought,* London, Routledge, 1933, pp. 112–113.

in the next, and some in successive births. Furthermore, some *kamma* is more weighty and takes precedence over other *kamma*. Examples of this are matricide, patricide, murder of an Arhat, wounding a Buddha, or causing a schism in the Sangha.

What one does at the moment of death determines the future birth, since one cannot at that time act out of character but must act in terms of the habitual *kamma* which has been developing a certain character throughout life. While the Buddha's doctrine of *kamma* has at times led to fatalism, it can also be an incentive for the future, knowing that what one will be is presently being determined by acts.

The Pali tradition also affirmed belief in rebirth, although it rejected the concept of transmigration because of its rejection of permanence. The latter seemed to imply that there was something that transmigrates. The Buddha, having rejected the concept of Atman held by the Upanishadic seers, posed a problem that was dealt with by such later thinkers as the author of the *Milindapanha*. If there is nothing permanent, and if there is no permanent entity which is reborn, how can one still hold to the doctrine of rebirth? The *Milindapanha* uses analogies to explain that just as there is a causal connection within a life as the *khandhas* continuously regroup from one moment to another, so there is a causal connection from one life to the next. Just as one is neither identically the same person from one moment to another, nor for that matter an entirely different one, but is at any moment whatever the kammic force makes him be, so is the same principle applied to the transition from one life to another.

> Said the king: "Bhante Nāgasena, does rebirth take place without anything transmigrating (passing over)?"
>
> "Yes, your majesty. Rebirth takes place without anything transmigrating."
>
> "How, bhante Nāgasena, does rebirth take place without anything transmigrating? Give an illustration."
>
> "Suppose, your majesty, a man were to light a light from another light; pray, would the one light have passed over (transmigrated) to the other light?"
>
> "Nay, verily, bhante."
>
> "In exactly the same way, your majesty, does rebirth take place without anything transmigrating."
>
> "Give another illustration."
>
> "Do you remember, your majesty, having learnt, when you were a boy, some verse or other from your professor of poetry?"
>
> "Yes, bhante."
>
> "Pray, your majesty, did the verse pass over (transmigrate) to you from your teacher?"
>
> "Nay, verily, bhante."
>
> "In exactly the same way, your majesty, does rebirth take place without anything transmigrating."
>
> "You are an able man, bhante Nāgasena."
>
> (*Milindapanha* LXXI.16)

It is the view of the Pali Canon that through meditation one can develop a memory of one's past lives. That is what the Buddha himself came to see when he achieved enlightenment. The Buddha saw first one life, then two, and so on up to a hundred thousand and more. The *Jataka* tales refer to these previous births.

The Buddha is depicted as rejecting the concept of caste, the authority of the Vedas, and the efficacy of the sacrifices. However, although the Buddha's doctrine of *anatta* was in tension with the popular beliefs in *kamma* and the rebirth of the soul, they were evidently so much a part of the Indian thought patterns at that time that the Buddha maneuvered and transformed part of them rather than overtly rejecting them as a whole. His own solution was to reject the notion of the transmigration of a substantial soul, but to retain the belief in *kamma* and rebirth in the ways indicated above. This fact illustrates how commonly held the doctrines of *kamma,* rebirth, and transmigration of the soul must have been at that time.

Nibbana

The suffering that is inherent in existence is only eliminated when one achieves the state of *Nibbana* (Sanskrit *Nirvana*).[12] *Nibbana* cannot be accurately described since it transcends all the distinctions which are inherent in language. *Nibbana* means the absence of craving and involves the extinction of hatred, lust, or ignorance. In *Nibbana* there is no birth, old age, sickness, death, or defilement. It is a state utterly incomparable with any state in phenomenal existence. It is for this reason that most statements about *Nibbana* are negative ones. This is not to be taken to imply that *Nibbana* is negative or annihilating. The *Tipitaka* refers to it as Highest Refuge, Safety, Unique, Absolute Purity, Supramundane, Security, Emancipation, Peace. The Sanskrit term *Nirvana* means "the blowing out." But this is not annihilation or the blowing out of all existence, but the blowing out of suffering and desire.

Nibbana is achievable in this life. It is a condition in which passion is destroyed, but the *khandhas* remain. The person in this state of realization while living is an Arhat, the ideal of the Pali Canon. When an Arhat dies he reaches the state of *Parinibbana,* a state in which the *khandhas* do not remain. In the *Suttas* the Buddha is sometimes asked whether or not the Buddha or an Arhat exists after death. In such cases the Buddha held that such speculative questions are unprofitable in contributing to the alleviation of suffering. Furthermore, as the question is framed, it is impossible to answer. It is like asking where the fire goes when it goes out.

Nibbana is called the "Uncompounded Element" in the *Abhidhamma,* and in the *Milindapanha* it is one of two things that are causeless (the other being space).

While the *Tipitaka* makes such attainment the goal, and the Arhat the one who has so realized it, there is also the idea that the struggle to realize *Nibbana* is long and extends over several births. This

12. Since this is a discussion of the Pali tradition, we are using the Pali term *Nibbana* instead of the Sanskrit *Nirvana.*

route is described as breaking the ten fetters.[13] Special names were affixed to those who had made progress in breaking the fetters and who were therefore closer to *Nibbana* by degrees. The *Sotapanno* is one who has entered the stream and is on his way to *Nibbana,* having broken the first three fetters. He will be reborn on earth or in heaven not more than seven times before he achieves *Nibbana.* The *Sakadagamin* is the once returner who will be born once more in this world and then attain *Nibbana.* He has broken the first three fetters, and has reduced four and five (lust and anger) to a minimum. The *Anagamin* is one who will not return, having freed himself from the first five fetters. He will not be reborn in this world or in a sensuous heaven, but will be reborn in a Brahma world only once. Finally, the *Arhat* has eliminated all evil and impurity, has attained *Nibbana,* and will not be reborn.

LIFE IN THE SANGHA   It was common for those seeking wisdom and release to group themselves around a teacher. Numerous disciples followed the Buddha, and in his own lifetime the beginnings of the *Sangha,* or Order, appeared. At first the *bhikkhus* appear to have spent nine months of the year as wanderers, living in a community only during the rainy season. After Buddha's death there was no central authority to bind together the various communities that existed in scattered places. Sites first used as rain retreats were donated by lay followers as places for monastic dwelling.

The early laws of the Sangha were probably the *Patimokkha,* recited at the fortnightly confessions of the *Uposatha* service. According to the *Tipitaka,* the Buddha determined all the laws of the *Vinaya* during his lifetime, but it is more likely that some of the minor rules in the *Patimokkha* were framed and added in the course of time. The three refuges, I take refuge in the Buddha, the Dhamma, and the Sangha, seem to have originated after the Buddha's death, since it is improbable that anyone would have thought of taking refuge in the Sangha so long as the Buddha was living. The *Vinaya* that we have is from the school responsible for the Pali Canon, but there are many other versions belonging to different schools. Since there was no central authority, even the decisions supposed to have been made at the First Council at Rajagaha could not command universal acceptance—each community accepted as much or as little as it chose.

Actually, the Sangha was a body of *bhikkhus* who formed a common life free from the cares of food and clothing so that they could concentrate on Arhatship.

Two ceremonies were part of the admission. The preparatory ordination (*Pabbajja,* or outgoing) represented going forth from the world and was symbolized when the novice had his head shaven, was robed in yellow, and recited the three refuges and the ten pre-

13. These are: belief in the existence of the self, doubt, trust in ceremonies of good works, lust, anger, desire for rebirth in worlds of form, desire for rebirth in formless worlds, pride, self-righteousness, ignorance.

Ajanta caves. Inhabited by Buddhist monks from the second century B.C. to the seventh century A.D. (Photo by Robert D. Baird.)

cepts.[14] Full membership in the circle of the *bhikkhus* came with the *Upasampada* (the arrival). For this the candidate had to be at least twenty years old, and was introduced to the chapter by a learned and competent monk who asked those in favor of his admission to signify such by their silence. This request was repeated three times and if there were no objections the *Upasampada* was complete. The newly admitted *bhikkhu* had a preceptor who instructed him and upon whom he waited.

As an individual the *bhikkhu* may possess three robes, a girdle for the loins, an alms bowl, a razor, a needle, and a water strainer so as not to injure unnecessarily any forms of life in the water that he might drink. As a group the Sangha could have other possessions and property which expanded in quantity as the laity fulfilled their obligations of giving.

There were four offenses (*parajikas*) which could mean the expulsion of a *bhikkhu* from the Sangha, but only on his confession of an offense, which he was morally obliged to offer. These offences were sexual intercourse, theft, knowingly depriving a creature of life, and boasting of some superhuman perfection.

An order of nuns (*bhikkhunis,* Sanskrit *bhikshunis*) was formed, but only after considerable hesitation on the part of the Buddha. There seems to have been some fear that the *bhikkhunis* would try to usurp the power of ruling the order, and so they were subordinated to the *Bhikkhu-Sangha.* The *bhikkhuni* was required to bow reverently before every *bhikkhu* even if he had only been ordained for a day, and she for many years. She could never scold or revile a *bhikkhu,* nor ever accuse a *bhikkhu,* although a *bhikkhu* might scold, revile, or accuse a *bhikkhuni.*

While the Sangha was the heart of this community it could only be sustained by the existence of lay devotees, men (*upasakas*) and women (*upasikas*). The *upasaka* could take the threefold refuge, al-

14. The ten precepts are to abstain from destroying life, stealing, impurity, lying, intoxicants, eating at forbidden times (*bhikkhus* eat one main meal before noon), dancing, music and theaters, garlands, perfumes and ornaments, high or large beds, accepting gold or silver.

though this did not imply living the life of a *bhikkhu*. He might not even be exclusively devoted to the teaching of the Buddha. The *upasaka* would keep the first five, or sometimes eight (especially at certain times), of the precepts. On full-moon days he took the vow of eight precepts and stayed at the temple because of the difficulty of fulfilling such vows at home. While it might be possible for a devout *upasaka* to achieve *Nibbana* at death, his more normal goal was to accumulate merit for a better birth through living a moral life and through giving alms to the *bhikkhus*. The *bhikkhus* do not beg for their own sake, but offer the *upasakas* and *upasikas* the opportunity to give, and hence increase their merit.

MORAL PRECEPTS
Since *Nibbana* is the goal, and is characterized by nonattachment, it is natural that actions which come closest to this goal are desirable. In the good life one moves from various degrees of attachment to detachment. Hence *sila* (morality), while part of the relative distinctions which are ultimately erroneous, plays an important role for one on the road to *Nibbana*. *Sila* is represented by the ten precepts that are followed by the *bhikkhus,* and the five or eight that are accepted by the *upasakas* and *upasikas.*

There seem to be three broad steps in the path to perfection: *sila, samadhi* (concentration), and *panna* (Sanskrit *prajna*—insight or wisdom). *Sila* is the first step toward the goal. However, the mental attitude is more important than the deed itself. The *Abhidhamma,* for example, spends considerable time on the analysis of mental states, but practically none on social problems. In the proscription against killing, the consummation of the act is less significant than the intent to do so. Anger and greed are wrong because they indicate attachment.

In addition to the ten precepts there is also *dana-sila* (giving), the merit of which is increased by the closeness of the gift to *Nibbana.* Hence the Sangha is a rich field of merit.

The so-called four immeasurables (*apramanani*), however, come closer to the heart of Theravada morality. They are called this because of their desirable universal extension. (1) *Metta* (loving kindness) is a benevolent harmlessness which begins with one's own feelings and is radiated to others until it is extended to the whole world. Even if one does not enter directly into action to cure the ills of the world, he can have an effect by radiating *metta*. Such activity can turn aside the rush of a wild elephant or stop the bite of a venomous serpent. It can be practiced by both *bhikkhu* and *upasaka*. The more one approximates *Nibbana,* the more he turns from direct action to the radiation of universal good will. (2) *Karuna* (compassion) involves pity or helpful sympathy without the emotional factor which would imply attachment. The mere extension of emotion is sentimental. *Karuna,* however, does not distinguish between one's own suffering and another's; it involves a compassion for others who are caught in the same rounds of birth and rebirth as oneself. (3) *Mudita* (sympathetic joy) is the counterpart of *karuna,* for one has the capacity for joy in the success of another. (4) *Upekha* (equanimity) is the closest to *Nibbana*. The others seem to have an element of attachment involved in them, but the closer they come to *Nibbana,* the more they approximate equanimity or the quality of neutrality and nonattachment. The "perfect deed" is characterized by *upekha.* While the basis for an active social ethic is slight in the Pali Canon, Buddhists in Southeast Asia today are busy reinterpreting their tradition to give basis for a "Buddhist" approach to economics, politics, or world peace. Such a concern is part of their attempt to emerge from domination by the colonial powers and show that one can deal with contemporary problems in terms of one's indigenous tradition.

There is evidence that the Jain religious community is at least as old as the Buddha, but it would be historically safer to say that the Jainas existed as contemporaries of the followers of the Buddha.

MAHAVIRA AND THE JAINAS

Vardhamana, as Gotama, was a Kshatriya (see p. 130) and is reported to have been born near Vaishali. Some of the details of his life are similar to those of Gotama and this has led some scholars to claim that we are dealing with a single individual. Such a view is no longer held. Vardhamana is better known by his epithet *Mahavira* (great hero) just as Gotama has come to be remembered as the Buddha. Jainas are followers of the *Jina,* which means victor or conqueror and is an appellation given to one who has attained *moksha,* or enlightenment. Mahavira was raised in luxury, and did not enter a state of homelessness until his parents died of voluntary starvation, an accepted manner of death for those who had completed prescribed austerities. After twelve years of austerities, similar to those which proved unsatisfactory for the Buddha, Vardhamana became the *Jina,* or conqueror. After thirty years of teaching and organizing he was finally liberated by death at the age of seventy-two. At that time his *jiva* (in this system a term referring to the "soul") went to the top of the universe where it is no longer touched by prayers or requests. The Jainas hold that *moksha* is a matter of personal effort and in this they agree with the Pali Canon.

According to the Jainas, however, their religion is eternal and Mahavira is not the founder, but the last in a long line of *Tirthankaras* ("fordfinders" who have achieved Nirvana at death). The twenty-third *Tirthankara* was Parshva, who is said to have lived about two hundred and fifty years before Mahavira and is generally accepted as a historical figure. It is the position of the Jainas that Mahavira did not found a new religion, but merely revived one that existed from eternity. As one goes back toward the first *Tirthankara* *Rshabha,* however, the time spans between *Tirthankaras* become unbelievably long and the physical dimensions of the *Tirthankaras* and their life spans become increasingly immense. Although all of the *Tirthankaras* have been released from the world and have no attachment to nor influence over worldly cares, the Jainas have made them objects of worship. The *Tirthankaras* are regarded as gods, as indeed, are all people potentially, and all liberated souls actually. They are worshiped in image form and in elaborate temples. All of the *Tirthankaras* were Kshatriyas according to the tradition, but the first twenty-two *Tirthankaras* are generally not believed to have any historical base.[15]

Doctrinal Summary

While the Upanishads were moving toward the affirmation that Being was One in the Atman-Brahman doctrine, and the Buddhists of the Pali tradition were denying any reality to permanence in favor of a view characterized by becoming and change, the Jainas proposed a view that rejected both as absolute systems and affirmed them as partial truths. The Jainas have come to be known for their doctrine of *syadvada,* or the doctrine of maybe. In terms of a seven-fold formula, they supported their view that every proposition is only conditional and no proposition can be either absolutely affirmed, or absolutely negated. In each case the assertion is prefaced with "maybe," "somehow," or "in a certain sense."

1. Maybe (somehow) a thing exists.
2. Maybe (somehow) a thing does not exist.
3. Maybe (somehow) a thing both exists and does not exist.
4. Maybe (somehow) a thing is indescribable.
5. Maybe (somehow) a thing exists and is indescribable.
6. Maybe (somehow) a thing does not exist and is indescribable.
7. Maybe (somehow) a thing both exists and does not exist and is indescribable.

In the first assertion we choose to make a statement of affirmation about a pot (or some other thing) according to its "substance, place, time, and nature." [16] But since the pot does not exist in the form of another substance, place, time, or nature, the second negating statement can also be made. Since the existence and nonexistence of the pot are intimately bound together, the third assertion becomes possible. But, if one wants to emphasize both existence and nonexistence as primary modifications and do this simultaneously, one is affirming the indescribability of the pot. But the pot is not indescribable in every way, for total inexpressibility would deny us the right to even describe it with the word "inexpressible." The last three assertions are merely the combination of indescribability (the fourth) with the first three.

The doctrine of *syadvada* has been criticized because it supposedly makes it possible to offer contradictory statements about the same object. But the Jainas reply that only according to this doctrine are contradictions avoided, since all statements are made only from a point of view and not absolutely.

Jaina logic admits that contradictory statements cannot be made about the same thing in the same sense at the same time and place, but stresses the fact that contradiction can be avoided only

15. For a list of the twenty-four *Tirthankaras* with their ages, sizes, and other details, see Jack Finegan, *The Archeology of World Religions,* Princeton, N.J., Princeton University Press, paperback edition, 1965, vol. I, p. 190.

16. *Syadvadamanjari,* quoted in S. Radhakrishnan and Charles A. Moore, *A Source Book in Indian Philosophy,* Princeton, N.J., Princeton University Press, 1957, p. 264.

by their own doctrine of syādvāda, *in which every statement is made only from a particular point of view. The charge of contradiction lies, if at all, at the door of the absolutist, who affirms or denies a statement about a thing from no point of view, as it were, which, according to the Jaina logician is impossible.*[17]

According to the Jainas, the entire universe can be explained in terms of two categories: *jiva* and *ajiva.* The *jiva* refers to the conscious and the *ajiva* to the unconscious. The *jiva* means the living principle, but in this system it seems equivalent to the soul or permanent spiritual aspect of man. In man the *jiva* is joined with matter or *ajiva,* which obscures the infinite intelligence and power which characterize the *jiva* as such. These characteristics are obscured during *samsara* (successive states of rebirth) but are not destroyed. The *jiva* acts and is acted upon. It is, curiously enough, capable of changing its size to fit the physical object it inhabits, thus illuminating the whole of the space. Hence the unalterable nature of the *Atman* which is affirmed in the Upanishads is denied by the Jainas in the doctrine of the *jiva.* Also, there are an infinite number of *jivas* which are eternal (as is matter) and although in their liberated state they are identical with one another (although sometimes they vary in size), they are not reduced to One as is the case with the Atman-Brahman doctrine of the Upanishads. The goal is to subdue the material element of one's being and hence eliminate its unhappy influence so that *jiva* may rise unfettered in its purity and excellence to the top of the universe.

The category of *ajiva* is distinguished from *jiva* in that *ajiva* lacks life and consciousness. *Ajiva* includes space, time, and matter (also *dharma* and *adharma,* which indicates the ability to rest and move). Matter is eternal and consists of atoms which are not visible to the senses except in combinations which form our objects of sense. The Jainas hold, however, that in addition to animals and plants, also the smallest particles of the elements such as earth, fire, water, and wind, are endowed with *jivas.* Matter is equally real with the spiritual order, but impedes the brilliance of the latter.

Knowledge constitutes the very essence of the *jiva.* It is capable of knowing anything unaided and with precision, and it is only through the interference of karma that omniscience is not actually operative. Instead of explaining lack of knowledge as the result of ignorance (*avidya*), as does the Pali Canon and some passages of the Upanishads, the Jainas explain this lack of knowledge as the result of karma. Karma is elaborately classified in types by the Jainas, but is invariably conceived as a subtle matter which permeates the *jivas* and hence weights them down. If, through the appropriate means, the influx of karma is stopped and the permeating karma is worked out, the individual becomes a *kevalin* (omniscient one), as did Mahavira while he was still living. At death the *jiva* is released from the bondage of the body and rises until it reaches beyond the *lokakasha* (place of space) to the top of the universe, where it rests in eternal bliss. In that state the knowledge of the *jiva* is not ham-

17. Radhakrishnan and Moore, op. cit., p. 262.

pered, it is void of cares for worldly affairs, and the only influence it continues to exert is the one of example. The *jiva* is able to exist between enlightenment and the attainment of godhead (all *jivas* are gods although there is no supreme Creator God) without any fresh influx of karma. He is at this time called an Arhat (as in the Pali Canon) and this corresponds to the *jivan-mukti* (one liberated while living) of Shankara (see p. 188) or the attainment of *Nibbana* as distinct from *Parinibbana* in the Pali Canon.

Laity and the Order

Like the division among the followers of the Buddha of the *bhikkhus* (and *bhikkhunis*) and the *upasakas* (and *upasikas*), so among the Jainas the highest calling is to the order of *yatis* (strivers) while the lower calling is less demanding for the *shravakas* (hearers, referring to laity). For both *yatis* and *shravakas* one reaches the state of liberation by the three jewels, a phrase common to the Pali Canon. The three jewels are right faith (in Mahavira and his teaching), right knowledge (in terms of correct doctrine), and right conduct.

Right conduct was similar in principle for *yatis* and *shravakas,* but the former pursued the rules more intensely. For the *yatis* there are five vows. The first was the vow of *ahimsa* (noninjury), which avoided injury to any form of life. Since there were *jivas* in even the smallest particles of matter, the *yati* went to every possible precaution to avoid injury. He would strain his water, he would cover his mouth with a cloth when speaking, so as not to risk injury to the air, and he would look six feet ahead of him when walking, to avoid stepping on any form of life. He had a soft broom which he used to brush the place before sitting or before laying an object down. He would engage in no swift movements and would often hesitate to scratch an itch for fear of causing injury to an unseen guest. The householder tried to take every precaution to avoid such injury, but he seldom went to the length of the *yatis.*

The Jainas have avoided agriculture because of the possibility of injury to worms or other sentient beings living in the soil. They also avoided butchering and fishing. To escape from such occupations many of them moved into commerce and banking, where they are a prosperous and respected community today. They have also maintained hospitals for sick and feeble animals and birds, and have placed numerous bird feeders in the streets and in various other places throughout communities where the Jainas exist in substantial numbers. Such expressions of *ahimsa* still exist today.

The doctrine of *ahimsa* is interpreted as extending not only to physical injury, but also to psychological or emotional injury by thought, word, or deed. In the twentieth century the Jainas feel that if the doctrine of *ahimsa* were heeded, the world could be saved from self-destruction.

A second vow is not to speak untruths, even in jest. This also means not to cause others so to speak, nor to consent to the lies of others. A third vow is against greed and is a promise to take nothing that is not given. Again, this vow implies that one will not cause others to be avaricious, nor will one be a party to others who do so. A fourth vow is to observe chastity. For the *yatis* this means re-

Puja scene inside Jain Temple, Ahmedabad. (Photo by Robert D. Baird.)

nouncing all sexual pleasures, while for the householder, it is taken
to mean fidelity in marriage. The fifth vow is the most radical in
that it involves the renouncement of all attachments. This renunciation extends to all sensual pleasures, such as gratifying sounds,
sights, textures, odors, and flavors. Nonattachment means that one
would neither love nor hate any object. Nonattachment was also a
significant part of Pali Buddhist morality. For the householder this
vow involved checking greed through placing a limit on one's
wealth and giving away the excess.

Actually, the householder had twelve vows. These included the
above five in their modified form, and the following: (6) to avoid
temptation by refraining from unnecessary travel, (7) to limit the
number of things in daily use, (8) to be on guard against evils that
can be avoided, (9) to keep specific times for meditation, (10) to impose special periods of self-denial, (11) to spend occasional days as
monks, and (12) to give alms in support of the *yatis.*

For one who has gone through the various forms of self-denial,
who has undertaken penance for twelve years and is ripe for Nirvana, death by starvation might be the culmination. But this was
never to be used as a means of circumventing the need for a long
period of austerities. Extreme self-imposed austerities were repudiated by the Buddha, but were considered by Mahavira and the
Jainas to be the most successful means of stopping the influx of
karma, expelling karma that adheres to the *jiva,* and attaining release. Jaina saints who attain release are distinguished by names
which were also common among the followers of the Buddha, such
as Buddha, Kevalin, Tathagata, Arhat, and Jina. But while the followers of the Buddha tended to use the terms Buddha, Arhat, and
Tathagata, the Jainas favored the term Jina (conqueror). The idea
that *Tirthankaras* appear periodically in history is a form of the view

Inside scene of Dilwara Temple, Mt. Abu. (Photo by Robert D. Baird.)

which is also expressed in the concept of the appearances of numerous Buddhas, or the descents of Vishnu or Krishna in the *Bhagavad Gita*.

Sectarianism It seems that shortly after the death of Mahavira, the community split into several sects. Numerous divisions exist today. In broad terms there are two important sects, the *Digambaras* ("clothed in space") and the *Shvetambaras* ("white-clothed"). The *Digambaras* contend that perfection could not be reached by anyone who wore clothing. Nudity was part of several sects in this period and was practiced by Mahavira, but was condemned by the Buddha. The *Digambaras* also deny that sanctity can be attained by women and hold that perfected saints, such as *Tirthankaras,* live without food.

The *Shvetambaras* hold that one can attain Nirvana even though clad. They also allow women to enter the monastic order under the assumption that they have a possibility of attaining Nirvana. Another sect, the *Sthanakavasis,* are opposed to the use of images. Since they have no temples, they worship anywhere, principally through acts of meditation.

Jaina Temples Images of the *Tirthankaras* are housed in imposing temples. The images so resemble each other that it is difficult to see any differences from one *Tirthankara* to another. The *Digambara* images are always without ornamental glass eyes and are unclothed. The *Shve-tambara* images are more elaborately decorated and often clothed. Since there is no priesthood to care for the worship of the images, this service is performed by *Shravakas* or sometimes even by Brahmans who are hired by the Jainas to tend to the temple duties. The *Tirthankaras* receive the same kind of worship as do the other popular deities of the *bhakti* movement: Vishnu, Krishna, Shiva, and the Buddha (see pp. 160 ff.).

The carvings in the temples on Mt. Abu in Gujarat, on Mt. Girnar, or the temple on Mt. Satrunjaya near Palitana, are outstanding. The Jainas are still numerous in Gujarat, and there are a few in the south of India. They number about one and one-half million. At Sravanabelgola there is a fifty-six-foot image of a naked saint, exposed to the elements of the heat or rain. With vines growing up his arms, he stands in utter detachment to the world. Pilgrims come to this site frequently and a large festival is held every twelve years.

BHAKTI MOVEMENTS

As early as 500 B.C. there were tendencies which later developed into what is known as the *bhakti* movement. *Bhakti,* often translated "devotion," includes faith, love, surrender, and devotional attachment. *Bhakti* is a religious orientation which is common in association with theism. As devotion to a personal deity, it is expressed in *puja,* which means adoration or worship on the theoretical level. Concrete expressions of *puja* include the offering of fruit or flowers to the deity and circumambulating the temple. In both terms, *puja* and *bhakti,* a personal relationship and an attitude of reverential dependence is implied. Devotees can be seen in the temples bowing or prostrate before the image enshrined there. While the supreme object of *bhakti* and *puja* is the deity itself, parents or elders, spiritual teachers and holy men, and even the motherland, have been objects of devotion to some extent.

Perhaps the most concise and systematic accounts of *bhakti* theology are to be found in the *Narada Bhakti Sutras* and the *Shandilya Sutras.* While these are not much older than the twelfth century A.D., they articulate a religious orientation which is approximated in various degrees by other movements in India. For these sutras, *bhakti* is neither knowledge, nor the following of ritual acts, nor belief in a system. It is affection and submission to a person. *Bhakti* is not preliminary to something else, but is an end in itself. It is surrender (*prapatti*) to no earthly object but to God only. *Bhakti* can be directed not only to the Adorable One (*Bhagavan*), but to any of his incarnations (*avataras*) which are the result of his pure compassion. *Bhakti* is higher than external observances and activities and higher than philosophical meditition. Since it involves submission on man's part, it also implies divine grace.

Bhakti is classified as lower or imperfect when it is motivated by worldly concerns such as sickness, danger, or the desire for some favor such as the birth of a male child. Even this, however, is to be cultivated by listening to and singing the praises of the Lord, through offerings of flowers and food to the image, and through prostration before and circumambulation of the image. One is counseled to worship the Lord in the form of one's friend or master. Later works divide imperfect *bhakti* into eighty-one degrees.

In addition to imperfect or lower *bhakti,* there is higher *bhakti.* This is completely selfless and involves single-hearted attachment to God, all other affections having been destroyed. Higher *bhakti* is not the result of human striving, but of pure grace. Such *bhakti* is not the means to liberation; it is liberation.

Some scholars would like to find the roots of *bhakti* as early as the *Rigveda.* But, with few exceptions, the attitude of the Vedic man to his deities was not one of devotional attachment. Likewise, there are *bhakti* tendencies in some of the Upanishads, such as the *Shvetashvatara.* But this view does not dominate the Upanishads and is more commonly found in the later ones than in the early ones.

In the *Bhagavad Gita,* the doctrine of *bhakti* is taught. But the *Gita* is a transitional document not always consistent with itself. It begins with an emphasis on disciplined action (*karmayoga*), and ends with the superiority of devotion (*bhakti*) to *Krishna.* Though the *Gita* contains references in which *bhakti* is seen as the means to knowledge, subordinating it to *jnanayoga,* or the way to God through knowledge, its more characteristic emphasis is that *bhakti* itself is liberation.

In its fully developed form, *bhakti* is a highly articulate theological system which can be used to justify the tendency of many to express ultimacy in terms of intense love or devotion to a personal god.

One need not argue whether *bhakti* began within the Buddhist fold or whether it was pre-Buddhist. Regardless of when the system began, one can detect a devotion to the Buddha which developed almost immediately after his death and which reached its logical fulfillment in the Mahayana systems of grace and the attainment of salvation by faith in Amitabha Buddha.

BUDDHA BHAKTI

There were no temples during the lifetime of the Buddha. After his death his remains were distributed to various places and enclosed in *stupas*—originally funerary mounds that later became more elaborate and central to worship and devotion. Artists capitalized on *stupas* and created elaborately sculptured gateways which depicted certain scenes and episodes from the traditional life of the Buddha.

At first the Buddha's presence was depicted with a wheel to symbolize turning the wheel of the law, or a tree (the Bodhi tree), or a footprint of the Buddha. Later the sculptor became bolder in his representation of the Buddha and created images of him either meditating or teaching in seated or standing posture.

Devotees would come from some distance to offer flowers and walk around the *stupa.* At some of the more important sites, the path of circumambulation was enclosed with a stone railing at-

Great Stupa, Sanchi. In existence at the time of Ashoka. (Photo by Robert D. Baird.)

tached to the lofty gates which were erected at each of the cardinal points. Wood or stone umbrellas were placed above the *stupa,* and if its relics were of the Buddha or some other important person, several umbrellas appeared above each other. The *stupa* at Sanchi has three umbrellas while a *stupa* nearby, supposedly containing the relics of two important disciples, has only one umbrella.

The growing *bhakti* attitude toward the Buddha can be seen not only in the increasing elaborateness of the artistic forms, but also in the type of literary productions stemming from the Mahayana groups. The lives of the Buddha become more elaborate and supernatural. The *Mahavastu* (second century B.C.) tells us little that is new about the life of the Buddha, but a different emphasis is apparent. Here the Buddha not only decides to be born in India, and determines the other details of his birth, but he is pictured as a superman superior to the world. He is a great magician who can touch the sun or moon with his hand. *Bhakti* comes to the fore when adoration of the Buddha produces enough merit to achieve Nirvana. An offering of flowers or circumambulation of the *stupa* earns for the devotee an infinite reward. Later portions of the *Mahavastu* contain references to images of the Buddha with a halo, such as appears in Indo-Greek art in the first century A.D. The role of the Bodhisattva, or Buddha-to-be, is elaborated with devoted concern in terms of ten stages (*bhumis*) through which the Buddha-to-be must go in order to reach the brink of Nirvana.

The *Lalitavistara,* another late life of the Buddha, also glorifies his nature. Here Buddha's life on earth is described as the diversion or sport (*lalita*) of a supernatural being. As a Bodhisattva in the Tushita heaven, all the gods, including Brahma, do homage to him. In Vaishnava works the same picture is painted, with the single exception that Vishnu replaces Buddha. And, when the boy Bodhisattva was brought to the temple by his foster mother, all the images of the gods fell down before him.

Another sutra of considerable importance for Mahayana which reflects the *bhakti* attitude to the Buddha is the *Lotus of the True Law* (*Saddharmapundarika*). In the process of trying to bring the followers of the Pali tradition over to the new way of looking at the Buddha and his doctrine, the Buddha appears as an eternal personage. The tradition of his earthly life and the attainment of Nirvana is conceded, but is seen as a device (*upaya,* or skill in means) to lead people to the higher doctrine (*Mahayana*). The doctrine of Nirvana which the Buddha taught in the Pali Canon was only a means of attracting those weary with suffering. All the beliefs of the Pali Canon are admittedly true, but only as appearance and not as reality. As the sutra opens, the Buddha is surrounded by twelve hundred Arhats, eighty thousand Bodhisattvas, numerous gods led by Shakra (Indra) and Brahma, and various other beings numbering in the millions. The Buddhas are mentioned and are portrayed in such a way that they rival other Indian gods who are also objects of *bhakti.* In some chapters the Bodhisattvas are given such prominence and worship that even the Buddhas recede into the background. Mention is made throughout the sutra of the adoration of relics and the worship of images which are found at *stupas* and in magnificent temples or monasteries.

Buddha *bhakti* perhaps reaches its peak in the *Sukhavativyuha,* or description of the land of bliss. There had developed a belief in numerous Buddhas, and the worlds over which they exerted influence. Amitabha, sometimes called Amitayus (Infinite Life), ruler of the Western Paradise, became particularly popular. The *Sukhavativyuha* exists in a longer form and in a later condensed form. The longer one was translated into Chinese about A.D. 170, but the date of its original composition is unknown. These books contain a description of the land of bliss where all sorts of pleasures abound. If anything deemed necessary is missing, one can have it merely by wishing. Furthermore, the element of *bhakti* reaches its peak when one learns that entrance can be gained into this perfect land by prayer to Amitabha. Even a single thought or repetition of the name Amitabha will suffice. Such were the happy results of a transfer of merit from Amitabha. Having practiced virtues and sacrifice through innumerable lives, Amitabha had acquired a store of merit which he could transfer to devotees in compensation for their demerits.

The flowering of Buddha *bhakti* thus involved a modification in the traditional view of karma held by the Theravada camp, the followers of the Pali tradition. They held that the Buddha taught that one could only save himself through self-effort since the Buddha had entered *Parinibbana*. This emphasis on self-effort was now replaced by a doctrine of grace which included the notion that merit could be transferred from the Buddha to the follower who adopts the way of love and devotion.

KRISHNA BHAKTI

Certainty about the origin of the devotion to Krishna is not possible. Krishna is mentioned only a few times prior to the *Mahabharata,* an epic which was in the process of being written and edited from 400 B.C. to A.D. 400. In the *Mahabharata,* Krishna appears substantially as a human hero. The *Bhagavad Gita,* which forms only a small portion of that epic (which is three and one-half times the length of the Christian Bible), presents Krishna as the Supreme God, who, if made the object of devotion, will save men. In this work Krishna is sometimes seen as having all the features that Brahman had in the Upanishads, but with the theistic flavor which permeates the *Gita.*

The *Gita* begins on the battlefield, and in places teaches that disciplined action, that is, action done in a nonattached manner, without concern for the fruits of the action, is the most adequate path to liberation. Nevertheless, the climax of the *Gita* is chapter 11 where the devotee Arjuna is given a mystical vision of Lord Krishna. All of the emphases of *bhakti* are present. The key is devotion and faith toward the Lord (*Bhagavan*). The vision is seen as given to those who are devoted to him and it is given out of Krishna's free grace. The interpretation of karma which emphasizes self-effort is somewhat set aside. Although the *Gita* teaches that action is inevitable and that bad karma is the result of attached action, it is stated elsewhere in this work that one who is devoted to Krishna will not be reborn.

While some interpreters hold that in the *Gita* Krishna is an incarnation (*avatara*) of the god Vishnu, this is hardly the impression conveyed by a careful reading of the text. Krisha appears in the *Gita* as the Supreme God. Vishnu is mentioned in only two passages and there, merely as a title applied to Krishna, perhaps in the way that various Vedic gods were given the qualities of other deities when they became the object of praise.

The tales of Krishna are more fully developed in the fourth-century addition to the *Mahabharata,* the *Harivamsa,* and in the medieval *Bhagavata Purana.* No longer the teacher of the *Gita,* now Krishna's exploits as a child, or as a lover, are portrayed. Tradition says he was born at Mathura, where an edifice marks his birthplace today. His father was Vasudeva, a name by which Krishna was also known. Krishna performed miracles as a child, killing demons and sheltering the *gopis* (cowherd lasses) by holding Mount Govardhana over their heads with his finger. He also stole butter and sweets in childhood. He is pictured in adolescence as a lover who had numerous love affairs with the cowherd lasses. On one occasion he hid the clothes of the *gopis* while they bathed in the river at a spot that is pointed out by temple priests today (it must be said that different priests point to different spots). While he had amorous affairs with numerous *gopis,* his favorite came to be Radha. They are often pictured together, Krishna playing his flute with Radha by his side in a moonlit garden.

In Mathura, the cruel king Kamsa issued an order to kill all the children of Devaki (Krishna's mother), since it was prophesied that her eighth child would kill him. Krishna's father saved his son from

Seventeenth-century miniature, probably from Jaipur, depicting Krishna and the gopis. (Courtesy of the Museum of Fine Arts, Boston.)

such a fate, and as he carried him across the Jumna river the water gradually subsided so that it never touched the child.

From the sixth to the ninth centuries there was a series of twelve poet-saints who significantly influenced South Indian religious life. They were called the *Alvars*, or those who are immersed in God. More devotional than theological, they sang about the lives of Krishna and Rama throughout South India. *Bhakti* lauds various types of love toward the deity, such as that between father and child, mutual friendship, and that between the lover and the beloved. The *Alvars* expressed their basic devotion to God in terms of friendly love (*sakhya*), a servant's devotion to his master (*dasya*), a mother's affection for her son (*vatsalya*), a son's respect for his father (*pitribhakti*), and also a woman's love for her beloved (*madhurya*). The *Alvars* were followed by a series of theologians called *Acharyas* who provided a philosophical basis for *bhakti* and theism. Ramanuja was one in this succession.

Surrender to God, or *prapatti,* is an aspect which is emphasized in the hymns of the *Alvars. Prapatti* involves a sense of absolute humility and the willingness to give up anything that is against God's will. It also involves faith that God will protect his devotees.

In South India during the twelfth or fourteenth centuries, Nimbarka identified Krishna with Brahman, the essence of the universe. Other *bhakti* philosophers in the south (Ramanuja and Madhva) had been devoted to Krishna, but had placed little emphasis on the cowherd element and had ignored Radha. For Nimbarka, Radha was the eternal consort of Krishna and was incarnate like him at Vrindavan. Nimbarka was emphatic in his worship of Krishna and his consort Radha, even to the exclusion of other gods. His sect became popular in the north as well, and the success of the *bhakti* movement there is dependent on him to a large degree.

In the fifteenth century, Vallabha founded a school which emphasized the grace of god coming through devotion as a cause of liberation. Vallabha and descendants of his who headed this community were considered as incarnations of Krishna. Vallabha ultimately settled in Benares where he wrote a commentary on the *Bhagavata Purana.*

After the death of Vallabha his seven sons wandered throughout India gaining proselytes. Their sect attached itself to the adolescent Krishna, whose amorous sport with the *gopis* is the theme of the tenth chapter of the *Bhagavata Purana.* The *guru* of this sect was considered to be the manifestation of Krishna. Imitation of Krishna's amorous deeds was taken quite seriously, and union with Krishna was sought through intercourse with the *guru.* Husbands accepted this role for their wives and daughters. The male worshiper would sometimes drink water wrung from the wet garments of the *guru,* eat portions of his food, or chew again the betel spit from his mouth.[1] This is not the first time that union with the God was to be attempted through sexual union.

The worship of Krishna has been strong in Bengal, appearing in literary form as early as the twelfth century with the *Gitagovinda* of Jayadeva. A movement which stems from Chaitanya (1486–1533) places considerable emphasis on the cowherd manifestation of Krishna and on the *gopi* Radha. Although not the originator of the movement, Chaitanya's personality was so forceful that even within his lifetime he was considered an incarnation of Krishna by some, while others thought of him as Krishna himself. Still others saw him

1. The leaf of the betel vine is covered with lime, sprinkled with areca nut, folded over, and fastened with a clove. This is chewed, and the saliva and mouth become a brilliant red in the process.

as the ultimate form of the divine—Radha and Krishna in a single body.

While Chaitanya was no theologian, he sensed the importance of his movement and sent theologians to Vrindavan to establish an *ashram* (monastery) to shape the formal doctrine of the sect. These theologians were anxious to show that Krishna was not merely an *avatara* of Vishnu, as held by some, but the Supreme God himself.

One of the questions considered was the question of the nature of the love of the *gopis,* who were married women, for Krishna. One interpretation was that since the *gopis* were married and belonged to another, their love for Krishna was all the more pure and ideal. If they were his own, the relationship might have resulted in self-centered desire. But it is precisely because it is love for one who belongs to another that the love is so intense and yet so unselfish. The pain of separation from their beloved draws the *gopis'* interest away from worldly concerns and leads them to meditation on Krishna which is the heart of *bhakti.*

One can still walk along the Jumna and visit temples in Vrindavan and Mathura which are dedicated to Krishna and Radha. The images here may be plain or elaborate. Sometimes they are placed in a swing so that devotees can rock them. Special festivals are held in their honor.

RAMA BHAKTI

There are two Indian epics, the *Mahabharata* and the *Ramayana.* The *Ramayana* was substantially complete as early as the fourth century B.C. It contains seven chapters but it is generally agreed that the first and the last are later additions. Apart from a few editorial editions, Rama is presented in chapters 2 through 6 as a great hero, but still a man. Most of the Vedic gods are mentioned and Vishnu and Shiva hold positions of prime importance. In chapters 1 and 7, however, Rama becomes an incarnation of Vishnu just as Krishna came to be. It was perhaps some time in the second century B.C. that this divine Rama became embodied in the written tradition.

The *Ramayana* centers around Rama who won the hand of Sita in an archery contest. Rama and Sita were banished to a life in the forest because of a favor promised to Dasharatha's second queen. Disguised as an ascetic, the demon king Ravana came to their hermitage and carried Sita away in his aerial car to his island kingdom of Lanka (Ceylon). Rama and his brother Lakshmana sought for her, but were unsuccessful until aided by Hanuman, brave leader of the monkeys. Leaping over the straits and building a causeway of stones to Ceylon, they slew Ravana and rescued Sita. Although Sita lived a chaste life in the palace of her abductor, her purity was questioned and she went through several ordeals to prove her innocence. As a final proof she called on her mother Earth to swallow her. The earth opened and she disappeared. This epic has so endeared itself to the hearts of numerous Indians that they not only worship Rama, but see Rama and Sita as the ideal divine couple. Indians have even built shrines to Lakshmana and Hanuman.

Street temple to Hanuman, Agra. (Photo by Robert D. Baird.)

Shrines, particularly to Hanuman, abound in the north today. He is usually painted orange and given a muscular physique. So popular is Rama that friends often greet each other in his name.

Ramananda lived in the fifteenth century and exerted considerable influence on the course of religious history in the north. Ramananda worshiped Rama and Sita alone. He also disregarded caste to an extent beyond some of the other *bhaktas*. It is common in *bhakti* to hold that a man can achieve release through devotion to God regardless of his caste. But Ramananda went so far as to include among his disciples a woman, a Muslim, and an outcaste. His concern to speak to the common people led him to speak and write in the vernacular rather than in Sanskrit. A sect stemming from him is called the *Ramanandis* or sometimes the *Ramawats*. United in their faith in the one personal God whom they call Rama, they hold that *bhakti* consists in perfect love toward God and that all men are brothers.

Ramananda had reportedly broken with his teacher because of staunch regulations about abstentions and because of proscriptions about eating with persons of other castes. The worship of Rama was free of the erotic tendencies that one finds in Krishna worship. Through Ramananda and his disciples the worship of Rama was spread throughout northern and central India.

Kabir, one of the important figures in Ramananda's school, objected to ceremonies and rejected caste. Holding that Rama is a spirit, Kabir concluded that he could not be worshiped in images but only through prayer. Furthermore, God is not the exclusive right of Hindus or Muslims. Kabir was of importance to the Sikh community (see p. 211) which attempted to bring together some of the chief tenets in the Hindu and Muslim creeds and hence eliminate some of the tension between the two communities.

Perhaps no one has been more influential in spreading the worship of Rama than the poet Tulsi Das (1532–1623). Tulsi married and lived a householder's life, later to become a sannyasin, to go on pilgrimages throughout India, and finally to settle in Benares. Although he wrote more than twenty formal works, his most famous and influential was his *Ramacharitmanas* ("The Lake of Rama's Deeds"). Based on the standard *Ramayana,* it was written in Hindi and has probably had the popular appeal in supporting devotion to Rama that the *Gita* or the *Bhagavata Purana* has had for Krishna. The poet exhibits deep feeling in his tender description of Rama's character. Tulsi lays great stress on the repetition of the name of *Rama* for the cultivation of *bhakti.* He urges the control of the senses and dedication of all actions to God.

In Tulsi the grace of Rama reigns supreme. Tulsi leaves the door open to approach God through various ways. Once man has begun the search, God will mercifully do the rest. Even the demon king Ravana is ultimately saved, emphasizing the compassion and mercy of God. Rama meets the Brahman Valmiki in the forest and inquires as to a suitable place to build a dwelling where he may live with his wife Sita and his brother Lakshmana. The following reply of Valmiki captures the spirit of Tulsi's devotion:

> Listen, O Rāma, now I shall tell you
> Where you should live with Sītā and Lakṣmaṇa:
> Those whose ears, like unto the sea,
> By the stories of your life, like unto various rivers,
> Are always being filled, but are never satisfied;
> Their hearts are your home.
>
> Those whose eyes, being like the cātaka bird;
> Are ever longing for the rain-cloud of the vision of God,
> O giver of joy, O Lord of the Raghus,
> Live in their hearts with your brother and Sītā.
>
> Your good name, being like the Mānasa lake,
> Those whose tongues, like the swans,
> Pick up the pearls of your divine qualities,
> Live in their hearts, O Rāma.
>
> He who can smell only the fragrant offering to God,
> He who offers his food to you before eating it,
> He whose very clothes and jewels are consecrated to the Lord,
> He whose head bows down to Brāhmaṇas, gods, and guru,
> With love and great humility,
> Whose hands daily worship the feet of Rāma,
> Who depends in his heart on Rāma and looks to no one else,
> Whose feet ever walk to the holy places of pilgrimage,
> O Rāma, live in their hearts.
>
> Those who desire only devotion to God as the fruit of all their
>   good deeds in the world,

*Live in the temple of their hearts, O Sītā, and you two sons of
Raghu.*
*Those who have neither desire nor anger, nor pride, nor deceit,
nor delusion,*
*Who neither covet nor lament, and are without attachment or
aversion,*
Who have neither hypocrisy, arrogance, nor deceit,
O Rāma, live in their hearts.

Those who are loved by all and are well-wishers of all,
Who are the same in sorrow and happiness, praise and blame,
Who speak sweet words of truth, having pondered well on them,
Who, sleeping or awake, seek refuge in thee,
Who look upon the wives of others as their own mothers,
And on the wealth of others as the worst poison,
*Who rejoice to see the prosperity of others, and grieve greatly in
their diversity,*
They who love you more than life,
Their hearts are auspicious places for you to live in.

Those who look upon you as master, friend, father,
Mother, and teacher, to whom you are all in all,
Dwell in the temple of their hearts,
Both ye brothers with Sītā.
Those who never wish for anything,
Who love you quite naturally,
Live in their hearts forever,
There is your home.[2]

VISHNU BHAKTI   Krishna-Vasudeva was the founder of the Bhagavata religion and
was eventually deified himself. In the course of time this deity was
identified with Vishnu, a solar deity who was of minimal significance
in the *Rigveda* but who came into more prominence in the Brahmanas, during which time the cult of Vishnu became known. By the
fourth century B.C., it appears that the two most popular deities
were Vishnu and Shiva. By the period of the *Puranas* (A.D.
300–1200), Vishnu had expanded his scope and dominance, chiefly
by reason of the doctrine of *avataras.*

Theistic trends were commonly found to grow outside the influence of the Brahmans. When a local deity became sufficiently prominent, the Brahmans would attempt to bring such worship into their
orbit of influence, either by indicating that the local deity was really
Vishnu under a different name, or that he was an *avatara* (incarnation or descent) of Vishnu. This process has been called Brahmani-
zation because it was a means of bringing the deities under Brah-
manic control. This can also be called Sanskritization, since it was

2. *Ayodhyakanda*, 127.2–131. Quoted in H. Bhattacharyya, ed., *The Cultural Heritage of India*, Calcutta, The Ramakrishna Mission Institute of Culture, 1956, vol. IV, pp. 404–405.

a process whereby local deities were brought into the orbit of a widely accepted notion of orthodoxy.[3]

In the *Puranas,* Vishnu came to have numerous *avataras.* Although the traditional list contains ten, some list over twenty. These incarnate deities not only extended the worship of Vishnu, but also expanded his nature as well. The traditional list of ten *avataras* includes both human and animal forms.

1. The Fish (*Matsya*). In the form of a fish Vishnu saved Manu (the progenitor of the human race) from a destructive flood. Recognizing the divinity of a fish that had grown so large that only the ocean could contain it, Manu worshiped the fish and was told of the coming flood. Manu boarded a ship that he had built for his family. Vishnu appeared in the sea as a fish with a huge horn to which the ship was tied until the waters subsided. Vishnu is also said to have saved the Vedas from the flood by assuming this form.

2. The Tortoise (*Kurma*). Vishnu appeared in this form to retrieve some things that were lost in the deluge. Placing himself (as a tortoise) at the bottom of the sea of milk, he served as a base for Mount Mandara. Twisting the serpent Vasuki around the mountain as a rope, the gods then pulled the serpent, thus churning the sea and recovering the desired objects. These included Amrita (water of life which renewed the gods), Lakshmi the goddess of wealth, and other deities and valuable objects.

3. The Boar (*Varaha*). When the earth was dragged to the bottom of the sea by the demon Hiranyaksha, Vishnu as the Boar killed the demon and raised the earth to its former position. This *avatara* may stem from a divine boar which was originally a tribal totem.

4. The Man-Lion (*Narasimha*). A demon had become invulnerable. He could not be killed by day or by night, by man or by beast, inside or outside of the temple. When this demon sought to kill his own son because he worshiped Vishnu, his destruction was sealed. Vishnu took the form of a Man-Lion (neither man nor beast) and came forth from a pillar of the temple (neither inside nor outside of the temple) at sunset (neither day nor night). Thus was the demon destroyed.

5. The Dwarf (*Vamana*). Through countless devotions and austerities a demon named Bali had gained dominion over the three worlds. In order to restore such power to the gods from whom it had been taken, Vishnu appeared in the form of a dwarf. He asked Bali to grant him as much land as he could traverse in three steps. Once the request was granted, Vishnu assumed gigantic form and in two strides restored heaven and earth. He graciously left Bali in control of the infernal regions.

6. Rama with the Ax (*Parashurama*). Here Vishnu took the form of a Brahman who destroyed the Kshatriyas because of their arrogant

3. "Sanskritization, then, refers to a process in the Indian Civilization in which a person or a group consciously related himself or itself to an accepted notion of true and ancient ideology and conduct." J. A. B. Van Buitenen, "On the Archaism of the *Bhagavata Purana,*" in Milton Singer, ed., *Krishna: Rites, Myths, and Rituals,* Honolulu, East-West Center Press, 1966, p. 35.

dominance. This *avatara* is not to be confused with the Rama of the *Ramayana.*

7. Rama. This is the Rama whose story is the theme of the *Ramayana.* Vishnu took this form in order to destroy the demon Ravana.

8. Krishna. Vishnu took the form of Krishna in order to kill the demon Kamsa.

9. Buddha. Vishnu took this form to destroy the wicked who rejected the Vedas. By so doing he established the authority of those sacred writings.

10. Kalki. This *avatara* is future. At the end of the present Kali age, Kalkin will come, mounted on a white horse. He will judge the wicked, reward the good, and set up a new age.

Since Krishna was one of the most popular deities, it was only a matter of time before he would also be identified as an *avatara* of Vishnu. As we have seen in our discussion of Krishna, there are explicit cases where the identification of Krishna as an *avatara* of Vishnu is resisted and Krishna is proclaimed as the Supreme Being. Likewise Rama was destined to be drawn into orbit, although not until considerably later. There were also those such as Tulsi Das who proposed the worship of Rama and Sita to the exclusion of the other *avataras* of Vishnu.

Even the Buddha, who rejected the authority of the Vedas, the Brahmanical authority, and the efficacy of the sacrifices, was taken into the fold as an *avatara.* In this way the Brahmans could admit his religious significance in the light of his strong following, and at the same time denounce his teachings. The Brahmans held that Vishnu became the Buddha in order to delude the wicked by leading them to deny the Vedas and the efficacy of the sacrifices, thereby assuring their damnation. In this way the destruction of the wicked would be an example to others. Until recently the temple of the Buddha at Budhgaya was run by Brahmans and the Buddha was the object of *puja* just as any other deity might be—much to the chagrin of contemporary Buddhists.

The difficulty with most discussions of Vishnu is that they take the interpretative position of the Vaishnava (i.e., devotees of Vishnu), and fail to recognize that not infrequently the effort to incorporate other religious expressions in this manner was resisted. Although it is usually stated that Vaishnavas comprise the largest group of Indian devotees, it must quickly be added that by far the largest number of such Vaishnavas are devotees of Krishna or Rama.

Vishnu is usually pictured with his vehicle the bird Garuda or with his wife Lakshmi or Shri, the goddess of wealth. While in the *Puranas* a triad of gods is mentioned, Brahma the creator, Vishnu the preserver, and Shiva the destroyer, those who are devoted to Vishnu commonly set this triad aside and focus on Vishnu as the Lord of creation, preservation, and destruction.

Today Vishnu is worshiped at Puri in Orissa as Lord Jagannath, whose car festival is well known. In it Lord Jagannath is carried in a huge car from the temple to his summer palace, and is later returned. In Maharashtra he is worshiped as Vithoba, where a sect has grown into significant proportions. In the south he is worshiped on a mountain near Tirupati. There a seven-foot, four-armed image is enshrined in a large temple. This is a common place for devotees to go on a pilgrimage, and is so sacred to them that non-Hindus are not permitted to enter the temple. Such is also the case at the Jagannath temple in Puri.

Shiva, meaning "auspicious," was a euphemistic epithet given to the Rigvedic Rudra. As Rudra, Shiva inspires more fear than love. He is conceived as the destroyer when in the company of Brahma and Vishnu. As the great ascetic, Shiva is often depicted with a garland of skulls and surrounded with ghosts and demons.

> On the high slopes of the Himālayan Mount Kailāsa, Śiva, the great yogī, sits on a tiger skin, deep in meditation and through his meditation the world is maintained. He is depicted thus as wearing his long matted hair (jaṭā) in a topknot, in which the crescent moon is fixed, and from which flows the sacred river Ganges. In the middle of his forehead is a third eye, emblem of his superior wisdom and insight. His neck is black, scarred by a deadly poison which was the last of the objects churned from the cosmic ocean, and which he drank to save the other gods from destruction. Snakes, of which he is the lord, encircle his neck and arms. His body is covered with ashes, a favorite ascetic practice. Beside him is his weapon, the trident, while near him are his beautiful wife Pārvatī and his mount, the bull Nandi.[4]

Shiva is also the lord of animals and the lord of dance. As Nataraja, his dance supports the rhythm of the universe. Powerful and creative, he is worshiped most commonly in the form of the linga (i.e., a representation of the male sexual organ). In the innermost heart of the Shaiva temple is the linga. Nandi the bull stands outside the inner sanctum, his eyes fixed on this most sacred symbol, the linga, which is even more commonly used than anthropomorphic representations of the deity.

In the *Shvetashvatara Upanishad, bhakti* is enjoined to Shiva. The final verse of this Upanishad states that the truths contained therein are to be told to a "high-minded man who feels the highest devotion (*bhakti*) for God and for his *guru* as for God." As early as the second century B.C., the grammarian Patanjali mentions a Shiva-bhagavata sect. In their attempts to spread the influence of Shiva, the devotees identified him with local deities as the followers of Vishnu had done. Shiva is even given *avataras* in imitation of the doctrine held by Vaishnavas, but they never played the significant role which they did for Vishnu. In the case of Vishnu, the *avataras,* particularly Krishna and Rama, were more prominent than Vishnu himself. Such is not the case for Shiva.

While followers of Shiva have had a greater tendency toward ad-

---

4. A. L. Basham, *The Wonder That Was India,* New York, Grove Press, Inc., 1959 (first published 1954), p. 307.

Sixteenth-century southern Indian copper figure of Shiva as Nataraja. (Courtesy of the Museum of Fine Arts, Boston.)

vaitin views (see p. 188) than the *bhaktas* previously considered, there have still been those whose message was devotional and emotional rather than meditative. The Vaishnava Alvars have their counterparts in the Shaiva Nayanars. Some sixty-three of them produced hymns of a devotional nature. Some of these hymns form the *Devaram*, the first of twelve canonical books called *Tirumurai* which are considered by some Shaivites (Shaiva Siddhanta) as *shruti* (see p. 118). This shows that sometimes in theory and often in practice the Vedas are not the supreme authority. These hymns are not an attempt at a systematic theology but an account of a vivid experience. Optimism reigns as God's mercy and grace are pro-

Shaiva priest in Poona. Nandi is facing the inner shrine where there is a Shiva Linga. (Photo by Robert D. Baird.)

claimed. Devotion to Shiva is useful for all. Shiva exists everywhere and appears even to the illiterate if, as a true *bhakta,* his mind is intent on Shiva's love and service.

The prominence given to grace cannot be ignored. When man realizes his condition, the freely given grace of God seems even more wonderful.

> *Thou gav'st thyself, thou gainest me;*
> *which did the better bargain derive?*
> *Bliss found I in infinity;*
> *but what didst thou from me derive?*

In South India there developed a theological tradition called Shaiva Siddhanta. The first systematic attempt to state the beliefs of Tamil Shaivism is the *Shiva-jnana-bodham* of Meykandar in the first half of the thirteenth century. Meykandar's position is realistic and theistic. Shiva is the *guru* par excellence whose grace illuminates the intellect when one submits to the teachings of the human *gurus.* Shiva, the soul of man, and the bonds of ignorance are all considered real. Karma and *maya* are not evils, but agencies used by Shiva for the purification of the soul from ignorance. The three paths of service, worship, and meditation are proposed, but all are to be animated by *bhakti.* This makes the soul open to Shiva's grace, by which union with him is possible. Shiva imparts divine knowledge (*patijnana*) by way of intuition to highly advanced souls. To those less advanced, he works through a human *guru,* which explains the concern of the *bhakta* to meet a *guru* through whom Shiva can give divine knowledge. Liberation is union with Shiva, but not a complete cessation of separateness. Shiva is bliss itself, while

Shaiva priests in Srirangam Shiva Temple, southern India. (Photo by Robert D. Baird.)

the soul can only enjoy bliss. Hence in this emphatically *bhakti* system theism is maintained.

The Kashmir brand of Shaivism is quite different. It appears just before the ninth century. Here Shiva is merely a form for presenting *advaita* philosophy (see p. 188). Shiva is the underlying reality of the universe, the world being an emanation from him. While the world is quite real inasmuch as it has the reality it appears to possess, it is illusory in the sense that Shiva, the prime reality, remains unaffected by change in the sensible world. In its true nature the soul is identified with Shiva, but by reason of its ignorance it considers itself finite and imperfect. The awakened soul realizes its true nature as Shiva through *bhakti* worship and devotion.

SHAKTI BHAKTI Shakti worship is worship of the deity's power in the form of his consort. This has taken various forms, from simply representing the deity with his consort to singling her out as the chief object of worship. Although erotic practices might well be expected, not all Shaktism is erotic, and some forms are highly philosophical. Rites and rituals of a sacramental and magical nature accompanied with diagrams and gestures comprise a wide-ranging practice which has not been sufficiently studied for us to get an overview or a very penetrating understanding. The texts which describe the elaborate rites and theories connected with Shaktism are called *Tantras*.

Although the Mother Goddess seems to have been venerated in the Indus Valley Civilization, little place is given to goddesses in the Vedic literature. Female deities were probably worshiped to some extent on the popular level from earliest times, but in the fourth century they came to be worshiped in special temples, and from the sixth to the tenth centuries the cult association with Shakti worship became elaborately developed. Worship of the Mother Goddess grew in importance until early in the Muslim period.

While devotion of a sort was directed to Sarasvati, the wife of Brahma, and to Lakshmi, the wife of Vishnu, Shakti is most commonly worshiped as the wife of Shiva. Since the name Shakti has been used to identify a number of local goddesses, the name of Shiva's consort varies in different locales. Her most common names are Durga, Kali, Parvati, and Uma.

The concept underlying worship of Shakti is that since the eternal Shiva is inactive while his wife is Shakti or pure activity, the creation of the world and the work of grace and liberation are her functions. Hence Shakti becomes more important than Shiva himself, who is static and ineffective without his wife.

The Shaktas (devotees of Shakti) made use of adoration *mantras,* which were brief expressions of reverence for the goddess. The Shaktas also made use of diagrams of mystic import (*mandalas*), ritual gestures with the fingers (*mudras*), and ritual movements of the hands (*nyasa*) for bringing the goddess into the body.

The worship of Shakti became particularly significant from A.D. 550 to 900, when an elaborate cult developed. Some of it was closer to *bhakti* principles than were other parts. It was the view of the Shaktas that in the *kali* (black) age in which we now exist, their methods were the only adequate ways to liberation. One of the means was the public worship of the goddess in temples. Offerings to the goddess were vegetable, animal, or human. Tradition indicates that Hsüan tsang, a Chinese pilgrim, was almost sacrificed to Durga. Human sacrifice was abolished by the British, and even animal sacrifice has since been made illegal by the State of Madras. While the vegetable offerings were laid before the image, animals were sacrificed in the temple courtyard some distance from the image.

A second method was circle worship (*cakra-puja*), sometimes called left-handed tantra. An equal number of men and women meet secretly at night and sit in a circle. The goddess is represented in the center of the circle by a yoni (i.e., a mystical sign representing the female sexual organ.) In addition to the repetition of *mantras,* the participants partake of the five *tattvas* (sometimes called the five M's, since each begins with that letter in Sanskrit): wine, meat, fish, parched grain, and sexual intercourse.

A third method was meditative exercises or discipline (*sadhana*), intended to bring the participant to perfection. Finally, there was the use of sorcery and spells. As with other sects, the Shaktas advised those who wanted to make real spiritual progress to select a *guru* and undertake initiation.

The worship of the goddess was also found among the followers of the Buddha. These same principles were implied in the tantric texts which appeared in the sixth and seventh centuries. The Buddhas and Bodhisattvas came to be seen as inert while their wives were active and wide-awake. Hence, in addition to the three traditional bodies of the Buddha (see pp. 184 ff.), tantrism taught that there was a fourth body, the *vajrasattva,* whereby the Buddha embraced his Shakti, *Tara* or *Bhagavati.*

Perhaps the best known goddess in India today is Kali, the Shakti of Shiva, who is worshiped in her own right. In Bengal, particularly in the Kalighat Temple in Calcutta, devotees fall before her image on their bellies, often with sighs and groans of devotion. Goats are sacrificed to her in the courtyard. The image of Kali is similar to the description in the *Kali Tantra*.

> *Most fearful, her laughter shows her dreadful teeth. She stands upon a corpse. She has four arms. Her hands hold a sword and a head and show the gestures of removing fear and granting boons. She is the auspicious divinity of sleep, the consort of Śiva.*
>
> *Naked, clad only in space, the goddess is resplendent. Her tongue hangs out. She wears a garland of heads. Such is the form worthy of meditation of the Power of Time, Kālī, who dwells near the funeral pyres.[5]*

Thus portrayed, Kali manifests both the powers of destruction and grace. All the pleasures of the world are transient, while only Kali is permanent and can grant happiness. Why is she black? Because she is the ultimate energy. Colors are distinctions, while in Kali all colors dissolve into shapelessness and darkness.

ATTEMPTS
AT SYNTHESIS

While it was common to place other deities in a hierarchy beneath one's chief deity, and sometimes to even move toward monotheism, there were also attempts to synthesize the deities without placing one above another. Such an attempt at synthesis can be illustrated on three levels.

There is the attempt to combine male and female. Not only can one find images that are half male and half female, but Shiva and Shakti are sometimes portrayed in this manner. As common as the worship of Shiva in the form of a linga is the worship of Shakti in the form of a yoni. Sometimes one finds the linga and yoni as part of a single representation. In this way the male and female aspects of the universe are united in one artistic representation. This was also seen in the unification of Krishna and Radha in a single person.

The two most popular deities by far are Vishnu and Shiva. Therefore, it should not be surprising that there would be an effort to combine the two of them. This was done in the form of the deity Harihara (or Shankara-Narayana), that is, Vishnu and Shiva combined. A hymn is addressed to him and is contained in the *Harivamsa*. There is evidence that he was rather widely worshiped in the Deccan and in South India. Various local village deities have been assimilated with him.

Another form of synthesis is to combine gods into groups. Some temples are dedicated to the five deities Shiva, Vishnu, Durga, Ganesha, and Surya. The *trimurti* of Brahma, Vishnu, and Shiva is another example of such grouping. This triad is not nearly as important for Indian devotion as has sometimes been suggested.

5. Quoted in Alain Danielou, *Hindu Polytheism*, London, Routledge, 1964, p. 496.

Nevertheless, it is another manifestation of the attempt at synthesis. In this context Brahma is the Creator, Vishnu the Preserver, and Shiva the Destroyer. These are dominant characteristics in the deities considered individually; but as separate objects of devotion, each one assumes all three characteristics. As a matter of fact, Brahma never had a large cult or following of his own, but did find his place in various pantheons.

RELIGIOUS
SYSTEMS

The discussion of Indian religious or philosophical systems often includes a description of the six "orthodox" systems: the Nyaya, Vaisheshika, Sankhya, Yoga, Purvamimamsa, and Uttaramimamsa (or Vedanta). These systems are called "orthodox" because they each rely, at least in word, on the authority of the *Vedas*. The systems of the Jainas, the Pali Canon, and the Carvakas (materialists) are then considered "heterodox," because they reject Vedic authority.

The historian of religions, however, cannot present his material as either "orthodox" or "heterodox," regardless of how strong or prominent the majority party happens to be. His goal is not to interpret material according to some standard of "orthodoxy," however arrived at, but to seek to understand the religions of as many persons and groups as possible.

The Indian philosophical tradition is exceedingly complex and varied. Some of the systems exist today while others exerted their main influence in past ages. We will discuss several attempts at religious systematization. In each case the system is religious because it is a systematic articulation of what someone believes ought to be ultimately important for man. The first two systems to be considered (Madhyamika and Yogacara) are variations of what is usually called "Mahayana Buddhism" in distinction from the "Theravada Buddhism" represented in the Pali Canon.

MADHYAMIKA   Some time in the middle or toward the end of the second century A.D., there lived a South Indian Brahman named Nagarjuna, whose religious system was called Madhyamika because it was the "middle way" between realism and nihilism, the views, respectively, that phenomena are real and that nothing exists.[1] Having been raised in

1. For a fuller exposition of Madhyamika, cf. T. R. V. Murti, *The Central Philosophy of Buddhism,* London, G. Allen, 1955; K. Venkata Ramanan, *Na-*

a Brahman family, Nagarjuna received thorough religious instruction. According to legendary accounts, he was renowned for his learning and his superhuman powers by the time he reached manhood. He and three companions studied magic and learned to make themselves invisible. They used this knowledge to enter the palace where they seduced women. Their escapades were discovered and Nagarjuna's companions were slain. Nagarjuna concluded that the root of suffering was lust. He went to a mountain *stupa* and took the rites of going forth (*pabbajja*). It is reported that in ninety days he mastered the *Tipitaka* and then turned to the Mahayana scriptures. He is remembered as an avid debater who always won his debates.

The *Vajracchedika* or Diamond Cutter Sutra, and the *Ashtasahasrika Prajnaparamita Sutra*, were systematized by the Madhyamika school of thought. The former argues for the negation of all phenomenal distinctions, while the latter emphasizes the perfection of nondual wisdom. Nagarjuna's system is a commentary on such and other *prajnaparamita* sutras.

Although the Madhyamika was intended to be an authentic understanding of the thought of the Buddha, it differs from the doctrine of the Pali Canon which also proposes to present the teachings of the Buddha. Nagarjuna's system is not an ontological system, but a system of dialectic intended as a means to realization.

Important for understanding Nagarjuna is his understanding of the silence of the Buddha. As early as the Pali Canon there are accounts which indicate that the Buddha would not answer certain types of questions. These came to be called the fourteen Inexpressibles, and are as follows:

1. Whether the world is eternal, or not, or both, or neither;
2. Whether the world is finite (in space), or infinite, or both, or neither;
3. Whether the Tathagata exists after death, or does not, or both, or neither;
4. Whether the soul is identical with the body or different from it.

There is no reason why the last statement could not also contain four alternatives, but in the dialogues of the Buddha it usually does not. In refusing to answer such questions, was the Buddha agnostic to, or innocent of, metaphysics?

According to Nagarjuna, the Buddha's silence was much more sophisticated than any of the above-proposed answers. For the Buddha, the Real actually transcended all thought and rational categories. He was convinced that any view about the Real that was presented could be shown to be logically absurd, since such categories of thought, while applicable to the phenomenal world, are not applicable to the Real.

Considering all such metaphysical speculations as dogmatism

garjuna's Philosophy as Presented in the Maha-Prajnaparamitasastra, Tokyo & Rutland, Vt., Charles E. Tuttle Co., 1966; Richard H. Robinson, *Early Madhyamika in India and China,* Madison, Wis., University of Wisconsin Press, 1967; Frederick J. Streng, *Emptiness: A Study in Religious Meaning,* New York and Nashville, Abingdon, 1967.

(*dhitthi-vada*), the Buddha consistently avoided falling into the same net by refusing to answer such questions. Any answer that might be given in response to such inquiries would be inadequate. Hence the Buddha rejected all views, and by not offering in their place an alternative view, raised the more basic question of the relation of Reality to all viewpoints. The silence of the Buddha implies the recognition that the Unconditioned Reality is indescribable.

Madhyamika is a system, not in offering an articulate ontology but in the sense that it offers a critique of all other systems of ontology. This critique goes deeper than a mere refutation of alternatives, for it tends thereby to show that when it comes to a question of Reality, the conflict is in reason itself. Madhyamika utilizes the *reductio ad absurdum* to show the logical absurdity of all metaphysical statements. But, by refuting other points of view Madhyamika does not propose its own point of view in terms of reason and logic. On the other hand, it is not, simply by reason of its refutation of all other views, nihilism. Madhyamika's criticism of all views might be called *upaya,* or the means to a spiritual end. If Reality transcends all language and reason, then only by the repudiation of all such views can Reality appear.

By the time of Nagarjuna, the upanishadic view that the Real was the Atman was well developed. This view attempted to solve the problem of suffering by arguing that only the permanent is Real, that the changing things to which we cling are not Real. On the other hand, the Pali Canon solved the problem of suffering in the reverse manner by denying any permanence and affirming a world of constant flux. Hence there was no Atman and no Brahman. All of the human experiences could be accounted for without positing a permanent entity within. But the Pali Canon did not question the reality of the *khandhas* which it used to account for human experience. It also broke things down into *ayatanas* (sense organs and sense data) and *dhatus* (ultimate elements of existence), of which there were six (earth, fire, water, air, space, and consciousness).

The Madhyamikas question the doctrine of the *khandhas.* How can one, on the basis of the *khandhas* alone, explain the grouping of the *khandhas,* since this is not an inherent feature of the *khandhas* themselves? Furthermore, the constant regrouping of the *khandhas* from one moment to another involves one in all the problems associated with the doctrine of causation (see p. 183). The *dhatus* were taken as radical elements which were irreducible. But to be a basic element distinguishable from other such basic elements, each must have a specific character which distinguishes it from others. In the *Abhidhamma,* such *dhatus* are given characteristics which distinguish them. The earth is characterized by hardness, for example. The Madhyamika philosopher asks if there is anything which differentiates hardness from earth. If the answer is no, then it is not possible to distinguish one *dhatu* from another. If there is a distinction between the *dhatu* earth and its hardness, then it is asked if the earth could exist prior to its hardness. If the answer is affirmative, then the *dhatu* could exist without its distinctive property and hence would itself be nondescript, and a nondescript entity is a nonentity. Hence we end with no distinctions to apply. Without a nature of their own, the *dhatus* are nothing in themselves. And, the same argument applies to the *khandhas*.

If the view contained in the Pali Canon is contradictory, so is the substance view of the Upanishads. If the Atman were identical with the states of existence, it would have to be subject to birth and death. The Pali view that all we have are changing *khandas* offends the moral sense by having the deeds of one "person" become results which affect another "person," hence putting the responsibility of a deed on one who did not commit it. If, however, one says that the Atman as an eternal substance exists independently of the changing states, then it should be perceivable apart from those states, but this is not so. The only conclusion, according to Nagarjuna, is that the self is neither different from nor identical with the states of existence. Furthermore, there is no self apart from the states, nor can one say it is nonexistent.

The doctrine of causation (*paticcasamupada*) is basic to an understanding of Pali Buddhist thought. The doctrine is used to show that nothing is independent of everything else, but that everything has a cause and thus arises from another. But Nagarjuna argued that by maintaining that there is essential difference between cause and effect, one is arguing that the effect is totally different from the cause. The implication is that anything should be able to produce anything, hence enabling anything to arise anywhere and at any time. To insist on the essential difference between cause and effect means to give up the notion of causation.

To hold to the identity of cause and effect by arguing that things are produced out of themselves, as does the Sankhya philosophy,[2] would avert the problem but would introduce another, namely the loss of a meaningful distinction between cause and effect if they are identical. Hence this view is also self-contradictory, since one cannot retain the notion of cause without introducing the differences.

When the Jainas try to combine the two views by maintaining the continuous and emergent aspects, they fall into still greater problems, since the Real must then have two different aspects. If we admit that we are unable to explain the relationship between these two aspects, then we have admitted what the Madhyamika position is trying to say—that it is beyond reason.

The alternative of the skeptics and materialists is quickly disposed of by Nagarjuna. Theirs is the view that things appear by chance. He merely asks for the reason for the assertion that things arise at random. If an answer is given, it refutes itself by admitting that the conclusion is arrived at causally. If no answer is given, the statement is ignored since it is merely dogmatically stated.

According to Nagarjuna, the meaning of the doctrine of causation is that things depend on each other and have no reality of their own. Hence it teaches that they are *shunya* (empty). If there is any

2. A philosophical position that is realistic and dualistic, holding that both spirit and matter are eternal and real.

term used for Reality, it is *Shunyata* (void or emptiness) which is the disavowal of all views about Reality.

The foregoing is not mere idle argumentation, but has relationship to a religious goal. For Nagarjuna, the Real is not produced, but is known by being uncovered. The refutation of views performs this service. After negating all views, the intellect becomes so pure that it is indistinguishable from the Real. Madhyamika seems to have a preference for speaking of the Ultimate in epistemological rather than in metaphysical terms. Hence Madhyamika refers to *Prajna* which is nondual intuition of the Real or *Prajnaparamita,* the perfection of wisdom.

Prajna, however, is a particular knowledge which does not participate in the dualistically conceived knowledge of our phenomenal existence. In this lower knowledge there is always a distinction between the subject and the object known. *Prajna* is immediate, intuitive, nondual, and contentless. When it arises, after all dualistic views are eliminated through criticism, there is no change ontologically, but only in terms of our apprehension. The mind is free of all impediments, all suffering and pain. This *Prajna* is the same as *Shunyata.* The one indicates that it is perfect nondual wisdom, while the other indicates that it is void of all views. *Tathata* is another term applied to the Real, which means "thatness" or "suchness" and indicates that the Real is the way it is without distinctions.

We have previously noted the growing emphasis on the Buddha as an object of worship and devotion (*bhakti*). The Buddha had also been called *Tathagata,* or "one who has thus come." In time *Tathagata* came to be more than merely a term for an enlightened being. *Tathagata* came to be closer to a Perfect Being or God. This is taken into the Madhyamika system as a personalized aspect of *Shunyata.* This is also part of the element of grace and mercy which seems so foreign to the Pali Canon, but which came to be a feature of later interpretations of the Buddha's teaching. Hence the *Tathagata* can be spoken of in personal terms. *Tathagata* engages in various activities for the salvation of men and assumes forms out of his infinite compassion to save all beings out of his free grace. There is no limit to the number of *Tathagatas* or to the forms they may assume. The number of Buddhas is numerous and the idea that they may arise according to human needs is a doctrine that is paralleled in the *Bhagavad Gita* with reference to Krishna. Nevertheless, in all of this, Nagarjuna remains firm in his position that the Real is indescribable and best expressed in silence. Hence, although in one sense *Prajnaparamita* is equated with *Tathagata,* this would only be from the relative point of view, for *Prajna* is silence and cannot be said to be born or to assume forms or to be compassionate.

Even Madhyamika, which emphasized the emptiness of all views, incorporated the doctrine of the three bodies of the Buddha. This *Trikaya* doctrine became a way of organizing the images under which the Buddha had come to be conceived. Buddhology had developed to such an extent that the Gautama of history was of less concern than other Buddhas.

The first body, or *Dharmakaya,* is the cosmic body, the essential nature of the Buddha and one with the Absolute. Although the *Dharmakaya* is closest to *Shunyata*, it is still personal, with innumerable merits and powers, and is indeed an object of devotion. The arising of the *Dharmakaya* from *Shunyata* is inexplicable, for ultimately *Shunyata* is void of all views or dualistic conceptions. The second body, *Sambhogakaya*, is the "body of bliss." A reflection of the *Dharmakaya* in the material world, it is the form in which the Buddha appears at the beginning of the Mahayana *sutras* with innumerable rays shooting from his body and accompanied by innumerable spiritual beings and Bodhisattvas. He is endowed with thirty-two primary and eighty secondary marks of beauty and excellence. The *Nirmanakaya* is an apparitional body which the Buddha assumed in order to save beings from misery. The *Nirmanakaya* is a manifestation of *Sambhogakaya* in the world and corresponds to the historical Gautama and other Buddhas of history. Buddhas and Bodhisattvas are forms chosen by *Tathagata* to help men. They are deliberate descents of Divinity. But all of this is a concession to ignorance.

The *Trikaya* doctrine is more than mere speculation. It was a functional way of uniting various aspects of thought and devotion that had developed around the memory of the Buddha, though Theravadins were inclined to minimize such forms of devotion. The Madhyamikas, however, held to the view that *all* is void, and hence could not propose that such practices and developments were inferior forms of expression. Such a proposal would impute to them a qualified reality, and to other views a higher degree of reality. But since *all* views are void, they could accept such devotional expressions as part of the skill in means (*upaya*) which was possessed by Buddhas and Bodhisattvas. In the *Diamond Sutra* it is stated that once one recognizes that there is no Bodhisattva, no dharmas, no Nirvana, and no beings to be led to Nirvana, then one can speak of them. Once it is recognized that all such designations are empty, then they can be used as "skill in means" (*upaya*). One example of such argumentation is the following:

> The Lord asked: What do you think Subhuti, is the Tathagata to be seen through his possession of marks?—Subhuti replied: No indeed, O Lord. And why? This possession of marks, O Lord, which has been taught by the Tathagata, as a no-possession of no-marks this has been taught by the Tathagata. Therefore, *it is called "possession of marks."* [3]

According to Nagarjuna, one does not distinguish the phenomena from *Shunyata* since *Shunyata* is actually the real nature of the phenomena. *Shunyata* is known through the appearances which are *upaya* (means or devices) for reaching the Absolute. There is no fall and recovery, since Nirvana does not cease. All that is necessary for the apprehension of the Real is the dissolution of false views. This is why Madhyamika is not nihilism, for if there were nothing, no

3. Edward Conze, *Buddhist Wisdom Books*, London, G. Allen, 1958, pp. 60–61 (emphasis added).

views would be false. Views are false only because they falsify the Real.

If the Real is *Shunyata,* then the appearances are due to *avidya,* or ignorance. It might be asked if *avidya* is real or unreal. One view is to say that if *avidya* is really the cause of the unreal, it must itself be real for the unreal cannot be a cause. Nagarjuna argues that *avidya* is unreal, otherwise its products would have to be real. Furthermore, *avidya* has no beginning, but it does have an end in *Prajna.*

There are three movements on the route to realization. The first is dogmatism (*drishti*), the second is criticism of all views, and the third is *Prajna,* or intuitive knowledge. The dogmatism of views is necessary as a means, for one would never see the conflict without at least two views. As a result of this conflict one comes to an awareness of the fact that the Absolute is *Shunyata,* void of all views, transcending reason and thought. Hence the criticism culminates in *Prajna.*

YOGACARA This school of thought existed from the second century A.D. After its chief fourth-century systematizers, Asanga and Vasubandhu, it came to be the dominant school of thought, eclipsing Madhyamika among the professed followers of the Buddha. Born into a North Indian Brahman family, Asanga was one of three brothers, all of whom were originally known by the name of Vasubandhu. The oldest later acquired the name of Asanga. The youngest is not part of this study since no doctrinal importance attaches to him. All of the brothers were converted to the Sarvastivadin school,[4] but Asanga was the first to move over to a Mahayana position. As a Sarvastivadin, the second brother, Vasubandhu, is credited with several works of significance. Asanga exerted considerable effort and subtlety to convert him to Mahayana. Toward the latter part of his life, Vasubandhu also came to believe in Amitabha and looked forward to rebirth in his Western Paradise.

In addition to the designation of Yogacara, this school is called *Vijnanavada,* or the viewpoint that only consciousness is Real. It is because of this basic doctrine that the school has been characterized as subjective idealism. The independent existence of objects is rejected in favor of pure thought. The denial of the independent existence of external objects is not just part of an abstract philosophical system, but becomes a new way of stating man's problem and attempting a solution. Man's problem is that he projects objects independent of thought, and he will not be liberated as long as he conceives of a subject and an object. Liberation for the Pali Canon and the Madhyamika also was an experience of nonduality and hence eliminated the distinction of subject and object. But this time there exists an ontology which emphasizes mind and attempts a solution not by seeing that there is no ego and that all is flux, or as

4. This school held to the reality of the past, present, and future and developed a canon (not presently available to us) that seems to have been somewhat parallel to the Pali Canon.

Madhyamika did by seeing the inherent contradictions in all views and thereby transcending this dualism in *Prajna,* but rather by withdrawal of the senses from supposed external objects until there is thought only.

The Yogacarins used several arguments to defend their idealistic point of view, but the most significant for their entire viewpoint were those which were based on experience. Their appeal was not to common sense experience which would seem to belie a view that rejects the reality of external objects, but the experience of the Buddhas and those who have not achieved complete awareness, however, could approximate it through various steps and levels of meditation. This meditative process was designed to make the practitioner perceive that in realization there is nothing apart from thought.

The Yogacarins are called so because of the emphasis they place on meditative and yogic practices. They represent a reaction against what they consider an overemphasis on the logical process by the Madhyamika dialectic which had little concern for the practice of meditation and the various states of trance which result therefrom. The Yogacarins did not reject the notion of the void, but called it thought. Once one comes to realize that all is thought, all external objects are dissolved. Of course, the implication of Madhyamika is accepted that thought is "really no thought." This is the case since it is the pure subject free from all objects.

By talking of the Absolute as Nirvana (blowing out), or *Shunyata,* transcendence is preserved by reverting to negative designations. The Yogacarins, however, wanted to emphasize the locus of this transcending experience. One cannot achieve this nondual experience through introspection, since as soon as we thus turn in toward the subject, it becomes the object of thought. But by "ruthless withdrawal from each and every object, in the introversion of trance, one could hope to move toward such a result." [5] In this way the problem of grasping is also solved, since there is no grasping when there is nothing to be grasped. Instead of removing the object of desire through analyzing away both subject and object in terms of a world of flux, or by showing the utter irrationality of all views, this school removed the object of desire by withdrawing from it in meditation.

Everything, then, is only mind and our illusion consists in projecting real external objects. This is not merely abstract speculation any more than was the analysis found in the Pali Canon. It is true that these texts can appear to be involved in barren intellectual hairsplitting, but here, as in previous interpretations of the Buddha's teachings, the practical result of liberation is the goal.

The highest insight is reached when everything appears as sheer hallucination. The Yogācārins based this conviction not merely on a number of logical arguments which proved the impossibility of

---

5. Edward Conze, *Buddhism: Its Essence and Development,* New York, Harper Torchbooks, 1959, pp. 166–167.

an external object, but on the living experience of ecstatic meditation.[6]

The Yogacarins are also noted for their doctrine of the "store consciousness" (*alaya-vijnana*). Interpreters of the teachings of the Buddha had been plagued with the opposition of common sense observation to the doctrine of *anatta*. Although the Pali Canon and most later interpreters disavowed permanence or the existence of the person as a sustained entity, certain doctrines crept in which appear to compromise the radical nature of impermanence as a universal characteristic of existence. One early school, the *Pudgalavadins* (those who believe in a person), spoke of a principle called the *pudgala,* or person, which was neither different nor not-different from the *khandhas*. Hence they brought in the notion of a person, while simultaneously affirming the Pali analysis of man. The Yogacarins' concept of the "store consciousness" serves a similar function in attempting to account for the awareness that some of our past experiences are stored up for a time, only to come to fruition in a later life. This consciousness is the basis of all of our acts of thought, and accounts for deeds which do not reach immediate fruition. Once this doctrine was conceived, however, it led to considerable metaphysical speculation regarding the relation of the physical world to the store consciousness in terms of emanations. While the Yogacarins did emphasize liberation in their yogic concerns, they also interpret the Buddha and his teachings considerably differently than does the Pali Canon. The Pali tradition as well as Madhyamika had disavowed metaphysical questions. The Yogacarins developed a full ontological system. Along with the Madhyamikas, they elaborated the *Trikaya* doctrine. The *Lankavatara Sutra* comes closest to embodying their doctrinal position.

ADVAITA VEDANTA This position is called *Vedanta* because it is based on the Upanishads which come at the end of the *Veda,* and *Advaita* because it is a nondual (*a + dvaita*) system. Shankara (788–820), with whom this system is commonly associated, was the son of a *Shivaguru* and was born in the Malabar country of the Deccan. He was considered an *avatara* of Shiva, and accounts of his life contain references to miraculous deeds. At the age of eight he became an ascetic, and he is said to have written his commentary on the *Brahma Sutras* at the age of twelve. He traveled throughout India, engaging his opponents in debate, and established four monasteries (*maths*) which still exist today: Badarinath in the Himalayas; Dwaraka on the west coast; Puri on the east coast; and Shringeri in Mysore State.

Since Shankara believed himself to be interpreting *Shruti,* most of his position is found in his commentaries, which include digressions in which he attempts a refutation of all opposing positions. His main commentary is on the *Brahma Sutras*. Of considerable importance also are his commentaries on ten Upanishads, particularly the

6. Ibid., p. 168.

Chandogya and the *Brihadaranyaka,* a commentary on the *Gita,* and a more systematic treatise called *Upadeshasahasri* ("A Thousand Teachings"). The various philosophical schools based on *Vedanta* all regarded the *Brahma Sutras* as condensations of the teachings of the Upanishads, and the differences of opinion arose about the *meaning* of the sutras and the upanishadic texts to which they refer.

Shankara did not originate the *advaita* position which was already rather well worked out by his teacher's teacher Gaudapada. Gaudapada, however, was explicitly dependent on the Madhyamika and Vijnanavada systems of the Buddhists, while Shankara harshly rejects such formulations even though he was accused of being a "crypto-Buddhist." *Advaita* continued to develop after Shankara, his followers splitting philosophical hairs in an attempt to perfect his system.

The basic question to be considered here has to do with the nature of Brahman. Brahman, or Ultimate Reality, is pure consciousness devoid of all attributes (*nirguna*) and devoid of all categories of the intellect (*nirvishesha*). There is no distinction between Atman and Brahman. Brahman is nondual (*advaita*), transcending the distinctions between knower, knowledge, and known. And since there is ultimately no duality, Brahman alone is ultimately Real. Transcending all categories, Brahman can best be described in negative terms. Positively the best one can do is to say that Brahman is pure consciousness, pure existence, and pure bliss. By stating the matter this way, one is denying that Brahman is a substance that has such qualities in favor of the position that existence and consciousness and bliss are one. In Brahman all intellectual distinctions end.

Associated with Brahman is its potency, or *maya,* which allows Brahman to appear as qualified Lord (*Ishvara*) who is the creator, preserver, and destroyer of the world, which is his appearance. In this state one often refers to *Saguna Brahman,* or Brahman with qualities as distinct from *Nirguna Brahman,* without qualities. *Nirguna Brahman* is ultimately a designation which describes a state of immediate experience of the plenitude of Being rather than being a mere concept.

In much Indian thought one must get used to thinking in terms of levels of being rather than in terms of whether something is real or unreal. Some entities are more real than others, and this is ultimately determined by their degree of participation in Brahman, Brahman alone being ultimately Real. Shankara's system can be understood in terms of three such levels.

1. Reality (*sat paramarthika*). The whole truth and the sole Reality.
2. Appearance (*vivarta*). Illusory and characterized by change.
    a. Phenomenally real (*vyavaharika*). Ordinary waking experience. Religiously speaking it is the theistic religious experience.

Metaphysical Questions

   b. Illusory existent (*pratibhasika*). The illusion of dreams and
   other illusory experience.
3. Unreality (*asat*). The level of logical contradictions.

These levels are to be understood in terms of the principle of devaluation (*badha,* or contradiction). This is the process whereby we
devalue a previously approved object in light of new experience. In
this scheme the levels of appearance are not unreal (*asat*), since
they do not consist in logical contradictions, but neither are they
Real, since they can be devalued by experience of the Real. They
have the level of appearance or phenomenal "reality" but ultimately
they can be devalued. The level of appearance does not *in fact* have
an objective counterpart, but the level of *asat* cannot *in principle*
have a counterpart.

The world is appearance (*vyavaharika*). It has a practical reality,
but does not qualify for the designation "Real" since it can be devalued. It is real only so long as we are in a state of ignorance and
so long as knowledge does not dawn. In describing the relationship
of the world to Brahman, several terms are used which are almost
identical in meaning. It is *maya* in that it is not what it appears to
be, *avidya* in that it is based on ignorance, *adhyasa,* in that it is a
superimposition such as when one mistakes a rope for a snake at
dusk, and *vivarta* in that it is merely appearance. In his ignorance,
man takes the world for what it is not—the Real.

Ultimately the doctrine of *maya* is inexplicable. *Maya* itself is not
Real, for it exists on the level of appearance and has no existence
apart from Brahman. On the other hand, one cannot say it is unreal,
since it projects the world of appearance. Such conflicts led Nagarjuna to ultimate silence and the rejection of all logic. Shankara, by
holding that *maya* has only a phenomenal and relative character, is
saying nearly the same thing, and the similarity led to the accusa-
tion of his being a "crypto-Buddhist." When right knowledge appears, ignorance and *maya* are removed.

Shankara held to the view that the cause alone was real and that
the effects were false (*satkaryavada*). This is the view of causation
which states that the effect (*karya*) is existent (*sat*) in the material
cause and is not a novel thing. The process of the imaginary attribution of something where it does not exist is *adhyasa* (superimposition). As Nagarjuna, Shankara rejected the view that things arise by
chance. But since Brahman alone is Real, he was forced to take the
view that there is no change in substance and hence no change in
Reality. Change belongs to the level of appearance. While we must,
on this level, live as though things change, when knowledge dawns,
we will see that such views are due to our ignorance.

Psychological The levels of the phenomenal and the Real are equally relevant for
Questions an examination of human nature. To begin with, there is the supreme Atman (*Paramatman*). Atman fits into the level of the Real,
and hence is pure, undifferentiated, self-shining consciousness.
Atman transcends all such distinctions as subject and object, time,
space, or thought. Atman cannot be an object knowable by the mind

or perceivable by the senses, since thought functions only through forms and multiplicity. Thought is a process, while Atman is a state. Atman is not different from Brahman, which means that in the depth of man's being, he is not different from Reality.

On the phenomenal level is the *jiva* which represents the individual human person, the phenomenal self which is a combination of reality and appearance. *Jiva* is reality to the extent that Atman is its ground, but it is appearance since it is finite, conditioned, and relative. Hence the individual self is empirically real for it is part of our experience, but it is transcendentally unreal for the only Real is the Atman which is not different from Brahman. Unlike the Pali tradition, man's problem is not that he holds to permanence when all is change, but that he identifies the change, of which the *jiva* is a part, with the Real. The consciousness of human limitation is grounded in ignorance. The Atman is essentially unlimited and Real.

Reason does not occupy a primary place in the system of Shankara. The value of reason is that it is a necessary tool for assisting us to understand *Shruti*. The ultimate truth cannot be known by reason alone since it transcends reason which is part of the realm of appearance. What one debater shows to be reasonable can be shown by a more expert debater to be false. The ultimate truth is found in *Shruti*.

Epistemological Questions

This means that Shankara was not compelled to show that his metaphysical system was completely and compellingly rational. Its truth depended on *Shruti*. If his position could be shown to be faithful to *Shruti* and if its apparent contradictions could be explained away without flying in the face of experience, there was little more for him to do. In the final analysis, his position would only be convincing to those who had achieved realization. As one moves up the levels of being and has the corresponding experiences, thus devaluing lower levels of existence, he becomes more convinced of the truth of the formulation. Absolute certainty comes only at that point at which the request for certainty is meaningless. In the final analysis, it is realization which clinches the matter. But, one must hasten to add, when that occurs, Shankara's entire system is devalued and seen for what it actually is—part of the level of appearance.

Perfection is possible in this life. When one comes to the realization that he is Brahman, he is a *Jivanmukta,* one who is liberated while living. Although living, the *Jivanmukta* does not identify himself with the body, which he realizes is only appearance. The world still appears for him, but he is not deceived by it. He is not affected by the world's misery and has no desire for the world's objects.

Liberation and Ethics

The reason why one can be liberated and still continue a bodily existence is explained by distinguishing three kinds of karma. There is karma that has brought forth its effects, karma that still lies accumulated, and karma that is gathered in this life. Knowledge of Reality (*Jnana*) destroys accumulated karma and makes it impossible to gather more karma in this life. But the karma that has already borne its effects in having produced the body must run its natural course.

This karma ceases when its force is exhausted just as the turning wheel of the potter comes to a full stop only when its momentum is spent. When the body perishes, the *Jivanmukta* is said to attain the disembodied state of liberation called *videhamukti*.

The role of ethics must also be placed in terms of the levels of being. If Brahman is beyond all distinctions, this includes ethical distinctions as well. The *Jivanmukta* is above all distinctions of good and evil. He is not susceptible to moral judgments. While he would probably not involve himself in the world of moral distinctions since he is not touched by sorrow or desire, neither would he be inclined to commit murder or other acts which would seem to presume egoism.

On the lower level of the phenomenal world, moral distinctions are necessary for ordering existence. In general one might say that those actions which lead to the highest good, or *moksha,* and tend to minimize ego involvement are good. On the other hand, those acts which lead to ego involvement are bad. All the acts of the *jiva* are to some extent involved in selfish desire, a fact which makes ethical virtues desirable on the lower level. Shankara generally accepts the *Dharmashastras* for ordering the phenomenal world. Yet it must be admitted that in terms of the Real, all such distinctions could be devalued.

VISHISHTADVAITA

From the time of the *Gita,* and even before, one can see evidence of the growth of the *bhakti* movement. Alongside the *bhakti* movement was the development of an articulate *advaita* position based on the Upanishads and culminating in the thought of Shankara. Shankara systematized his position prior to the composition of the *Bhagavata Purana* which systematized the *bhakti* of that time. With arguments which convinced many, Shankara relegated *bhakti* to the lower level of appearance. His view continues to dominate philosophy departments in India today. Nevertheless, *bhakti* was not easily relegated as merely preliminary to a nondual system. Many *bhaktas* did not find such a preliminary role for *Bhagavan* (the personal God and object of devotion) acceptable. The reaction against Shankara reached its peak in the writings of Ramanuja (1017–1137). Intending to remain loyal to the theism of the *bhakti* sects, Ramanuja attempted to offer a sound philosophical basis, which claimed the Upanishads and *Brahma Sutras* for its authority.

Ramanuja's position was furthered by the formation of a sect called *Shri-Vaishnavism* or *Shri Sampradaya.* This sect carried on many of Ramanuja's emphases. They developed the doctrine of *prapatti,* or submission to God, and opened Vedic knowledge even to Shudras (members of the lowest caste). Although in traditional fashion Shankara denied Vedic knowledge to those who were not of the twice born, Ramanuja admitted Jainas, Buddhists, Shudras, and even untouchables into his fold. Ramanuja also placed some emphasis on the use of images and included in his texts elaborate directions for the construction of temples and the various rituals associated with image worship.

Ramanuja rejected Shankara's doctrine of levels of reality. This rejection carried implications which made his view of Ultimate Reality, man, and liberation somewhat different from Shankara's. Ramanuja's view of Ultimate Reality is called *Vishishtadvaita,* or qualified nondualism. For him the Absolute is not distinctionless, but is qualified by diversity. It is a whole which consists of interdependent and interrelated elements. There is no undifferentiated pure consciousness. All knowledge involves distinctions. When the Upanishads speak of Brahman as devoid of qualities, they only mean that Brahman has no bad qualities and not that he has no qualities whatever.

Having rejected Shankara's distinction of levels of reality, it follows that he would also reject the distinction Shankara made between Brahman and Ishvara. For Ramanuja, Brahman is no formless entity, but a Supreme Person qualified by matter and souls, which are sometimes called his body. Ramanuja considers three things as ultimate and real: matter (*achit*), soul (*chit*), and God (*Ishvara*). While all three are real, the first two are dependent on God. Ishvara is Brahman. God manifests himself in various forms for his devotees: as the immanent soul of the universe; as the transcendent personal Lord; as creator, preserver, or destroyer; as *avatara* in human or animal form; as images enshrined in temples so that his devotees can see him physically.

Shankara's interpretation of *avidya* and *maya* is also rejected. *Maya* is the real power of God whereby he creates the world. There is no illusion involved since the world is also real. This position leaves open to Ramanuja a view of causation in which the effect is as real as the cause. For him, change is not apparent but real, being contained in the cause. Just as curd is a real transformation of milk, so an effect is as real as a cause.

Ramanuja spends considerable energy arguing against Shankara's view of *maya.* He asks, for example, where *maya* resides if it indeed exists? It cannot exist in Brahman without nondualism breaking down, nor in the individual self, which is mere appearance. Ramanuja concludes it is a pseudo-concept which exists in the mind of the *advaitin.* Furthermore, when Shankara maintains that *maya* is neither real nor unreal, he is merely engaging in intellectual gymnastics. Real and unreal are exhaustive and exclusive. A thing is either one or the other; no further alternative exists without the violation of well-established canons of logic.

Ignorance (*avidya*) is the cause of bondage, which means that the *jiva* wrongly identifies its reality with material objects such as the body. And, immediate intuitive knowledge is liberation. Souls are bound because of their ignorance and karma. While meditation is useful, it is subordinate to *bhakti* and is obtained by throwing oneself on the mercy of God. The highest *bhakti* only dawns by the grace (*prasada*) of God.

Liberation is not the realization that ultimately there is no distinction between Brahman and Atman, but the intuitive realization on the part of the soul that it is a mode of God. The liberated soul never becomes identical with Brahman. It is always finite while God remains infinite, and the soul does not share God's power as creator, preserver, and destroyer of the universe. For Ramanuja there is no possibility of liberation while one lives (*Jivanmukta*). As long as the soul remains associated with the body, it is clear that karmas persist and the soul cannot become pure.

Two centuries after Ramanuja, his followers divided into two schools. The Vadagalai, or northern school, held that one had to purify himself in order to receive divine grace. It maintained the need for man's cooperation with God in salvation and came to be known as the monkey school. Just as the monkey clings to the mother, so the devotee clings to God. While man casts himself entirely upon God, he does have to exert an effort to cling to him. The Tengalai, or southern school, magnified the importance of divine grace in liberation, and held that no individual effort was necessary for divine grace to dawn. This position came to be known as the cat view. As the mother cat lifts its kitten and carries it to a safe place without any effort from the kitten, so does God bestow his grace on man.

DVAITA

Madhva lived during the thirteenth century and developed a system called *dvaita,* or dualism. He was born in a village near Udipi in South Kanara and died there as the head of a new order founded by him, called Brahma Sampradaya. As a young Sannyasin, he had been trained in Shankara's *advaita* but broke away to develop his own system, later converting his teacher. In order to propound his view, he relied on the whole *shruti* and *smriti*. While not neglecting the Upanishads, he utilized the Vedas and Brahmanas more than his predecessors and made heavy use of the Puranic literature, especially the *Bhagavata Purana* and *Vishnu Purana*. Being a strict Vaishnava, he held that Shaiva literature should be interpreted in the light of the conclusions of Vaishava literature.

Like Ramanuja, Madhva was devoted to Vishnu, but more particularly to his son Vayu, the wind god. In the present age Madhva held that liberation could only be acquired through Vayu, which meant through Madhva, since he was considered the god's incarnation. In the interest of *bhakti*, Ramanuja had proposed a qualified nondualism. Thus he was able to give some place to the prominent position of Shankara and the upanishadic passages which emphasized unity. On the other hand, Ramanuja preserved a place for *bhakti* by maintaining that the ultimate unity is a unity with distinctions. Madhva did not grant so much to unity. In his encounters with *advaitins,* particularly with the head of the Shankara monastery at Shringeri, the battle was fierce and they parted as enemies. Madhva called *advaitins* "deceitful demons." They reciprocated with a period of persecution in an attempt to destroy the movement.

While he was outspoken against the *advaitins,* Madhva did not speak against the followers of Ramanuja, even though his position differed from theirs. Madhva accused Shankara of being a "cryptoBuddhist" and actually teaching *Shunyavada* Buddhism (Madhyamika). Like Ramanuja, Madhva holds to three realities: God, souls, and matter. Hence the world is real and Shankara's doctrine of *maya* is rejected with many of the same arguments that were given by Ramanuja.

Madhva's view is *dvaita,* or dualism. He has no interest in holding things together in a unity, but stresses duality. For him there are five basic distinctions:

1. God is distinct from individual souls.
2. God is distinct from nonliving matter.
3. One individual soul is distinct from another.
4. Individual souls are distinct from matter.
5. When matter is divided, its parts are distinct from one another.

In each of the above cases Madhva goes somewhat further than Ramanuja and rejects Shankara altogether. Ramanuja held to the reality of God and the individual souls, but saw the latter as dependent on the former. While for Ramanuja, God is distinct from matter, the world was seen as the body which God animates. While individual souls were distinct for Ramanuja, they were identical when liberated. Madhva holds so strongly to the notion of distinctness that souls are not only numberless and atomic in size, but each is unique. Furthermore, while Ramanuja held that the liberated soul was like God except that it was finite and did not participate in the creation, preservation, and destruction of the world, Madhva stressed the difference between God and the liberated soul.

While believing that souls are unique, Madhva also classified them into three groups: those who are devoted to God alone and are destined to attain liberation; those who will never attain liberation and are destined to perpetual rebirth; and those who revile Vishnu and his devotees and are subject to damnation. In the whole history of Indian philosophy, this doctrine of damnation is peculiar to Madhva and the Jainas. It is more common to find the view that hells are temporary abodes where bad karma is allowed to spend itself, after which the soul progresses upward again.

Madhva's preference for difference also leads him to hold to degrees in the possession of knowledge and even in the enjoyment of bliss in liberated souls. No such doctrine is possible in Ramanuja since all liberated souls are identical, nor in Shankara since liberation is the elimination of all distinctions.

Worship of Vishnu takes place in three forms. It may involve putting on one's body the symbolic marks for Vishnu. The use of such *tilak* marks is practiced also by Shaivites who use ashes or paint to mark their foreheads and even their bodies and arms with horizontal marks. Vaishavas, on the other hand, are identified with vertical marks on their foreheads. But Madhva emphasized this somewhat more than others. He extended it to monks and laity. The marking involves two perpendicular lines meeting at the bridge of the nose, with a straight black line in the middle. Madhva also advocated naming one's sons after Vishnu, and worshiping him in word, thought, and deed.

YOGA   The classical presentation of Yoga [7] is found in the *Yoga Sutras* of Patanjali. This sutra contains four parts which deal respectively with the nature and aim of concentration, the means for attaining realization, the supranormal powers which are by-products of this discipline, and the nature of liberation and the reality of the transcendent self (*purusha*).

The Yoga system has been closely connected with the Sankhya system since it accepts, with minor modifications, the epistemology and metaphysics of Sankhya. It is basically a dualistic system which distinguishes between *purusha* and *prakriti*. *Purusha* is the eternal self which is pure consciousness. It is changeless and omniscient. *Prakriti* is the principle which accounts for everything that is physical, including matter and force. *Prakriti* is characterized by change. Because of the reflection of the *purusha* in the changing states of the mind (*citta*), one is led, however erroneously, to believe that it is the Self (*purusha*) which is subject to change and rebirth. It is the *citta*, or mind, which is responsible for performing the functions that we often attribute to the Self (*purusha*). Essentially, the *citta* is not conscious, but is merely a transformation of *prakriti* which is attributed with consciousness because of the reflection of the *purusha*.

> *Chitta, therefore, is the physical medium for the manifestation of the spirit. Just as in a red-hot iron ball, formless fire appears spherical and cold iron appears hot, similarly on account of its reflection in the Chitta, Puruṣa appears changing and Chitta appears conscious. Just as the moon appears as moving when seen reflected in the moving waves, and waves appear as luminous, similarly Puruṣa appears as undergoing modifications and Chitta appears as conscious due to Puruṣa's reflection in it.*[8]

Unlike *Advaita*, the world of change and matter is real. The *purusha* is also real. Liberation (*moksha*) comes when one ceases to confuse the activities of the *citta* with the uncharging *purusha*. It is not the *purusha* which suffers and undergoes rebirth, but the phenomenal self or *jiva* which is the *purusha* as reflected in the *citta*.

Liberation is effected through a carefully worked out discipline for which Yoga philosophy is most commonly remembered. But the word "yoga" has numerous meanings. Sometimes it simply means "method." On other occasions, as in *advaita*, it refers to the spiritual union of Atman and Brahman. "In Patanjali, Yoga does not mean union, but only effort, or, as Bhoja says, separation (viyoga) between puruṣa and prakṛti."[9] The goal of yoga is the cessation of mental modifications after which one will no longer identify the *purusha* with the modifications of the *citta*. The eight steps of this discipline are enumerated in Patanjali's *Yoga Sutras*.

1. *Yama* (restraint). One cannot hope for spiritual success if his

7. For an excellent treatment of Yoga, see Mircea Eliade, *Yoga: Immortality and Freedom,* New York, Pantheon, 1958.

8. Chandradhar Sharma, *Indian Philosophy: A Critical Review,* New York, Barnes & Noble, 1962, p. 158.

9. S. Radhakrishnan, *Indian Philosophy,* London, G. Allen, 1923, vol. II, p. 337.

mind is tainted with impurities. For this reason yoga presupposes restraint in the form of abstaining from any injury to living creatures (*ahimsa*), truthfulness in word and thought (*satya*), not taking what is not given (*asteya*), control of passions and sexuality (*brahmacarya*), and not accepting unnecessary gifts which might lead to greed (*aparigraha*).

2. *Niyama* (observances). While *yama* is negative, *niyama* is positive, and involves purification of the body through ritual washing and through eating foods not likely to increase the passions. There is also purification of the mind by cultivating friendliness and other good sentiments. *Niyama* also includes developing contentment with what one has (*santosha*), austerities including exposure to heat and cold (*tapas*), study of religious texts (*svadhyaya*), and devotion to God (*Ishvarapranidhana*). Although Sankhya denied the existence of *Ishvara* (Supreme Lord), Yoga included such a belief.

3. *Asana* (posture). One can make little progress toward the spiritual goal if he is uncomfortable. Numerous positions are described which will enable one to remain comfortably in one position for a period of time. One of the most common *asanas* is the full lotus position in which one sits cross-legged, with each instep over the opposite thigh. Such a posture, when developed, can be maintained effortlessly for hours at a time. This eliminates the possible distractions which might otherwise interrupt meditation by reason of bodily discomfort.

4. *Pranayama* (breath control). Since irregular breathing can also disrupt the meditative process, one must learn to control the breath through "suspension of the breathing processes either after exhalation (recaka), or inhalation (puraka), or simply by retention of the vital breath (kumbhaka)."[10] Since the mind tends to fluctuate when one is inhaling or exhaling, the yogin learns to suspend breathing for a long time. This enables him to prolong his concentration accordingly. Such practices are considered dangerous without expert guidance from a qualified *guru* because of the possibility of bad aftereffects.

5. *Pratyahara* (control of senses). Having controlled the breathing process and the body, one must learn to master the senses so that they will not be easily distracted. Difficult to attain, this state requires a resolute will and long practice. It is the withdrawal of the senses from external stimuli.

6. *Dharana* (attention). This is accomplished through fixing the mind on an object of meditation. The object of meditation may be the tip of the nose, the moon, or an image of a deity among others. Through practice one's ability to hold his mind undistracted on the object can be increased.

7. *Dhyana* (meditation). This is the steady contemplation of the object without interruption from either internal or external sources. Continued *dhyana* will reveal to the mind the reality of the object contemplated.

10. Satichandra Chatterjee and Dhirendramohan Datta, *An Introduction to Indian Philosophy,* Calcutta, University of Calcutta Press, 1960, p. 304.

8. *Samadhi* (concentration). Here the mind is so deeply absorbed in the object of contemplation that it loses the distinction between the subject and the object. While in *dhyana* meditation is intent, one is still conscious of a distinction between the object of meditation and the meditator. There is *conscious samadhi* (*samprajnata*) in which one is still conscious of the object of meditation even though the subject and object are fused together. In *unconscious samadhi* (*asamprajnata*), the fusion is so complete that consciousness of both subject and object is gone. "It is the highest means to realize the cessation of mental modifications which is the end. It is the ecstatic state in which the connection with the external world is broken and through which one has to pass before obtaining liberation." [11]

Up to the point of *samadhi,* one is engaged in a negative process of distinguishing the *purusha* from *prakriti,* but in the final state of realization, the positive nature of the eternal *purusha* manifests itself untainted by *prakriti.*

Each step toward *samadhi* is attended by supranormal powers. Yogins are said to be able to tame the most ferocious wild beast, see through solid objects, and pass through them as well. They can appear and disappear at will. They can know the past, present, and future immediately. It is tempting to be sidetracked by such "rewards" for one's diligence, but the texts continually warn that these are really hindrances to ultimate realization, since they have the power to become ends in themselves. Delight in such powers will prevent the yogin from reaching the goal. "They are by-products of the higher life. They are the flowers which we chance to pick on the road, though the true seeker does not set out on his travels to gather them. Only through the disregard of these perfections can freedom be gained." [12]

CARVAKA One group that has been placed without the pale by those who accept the authority of the Vedas is called Carvaka. "The Cārvāka school has been the butt of ridicule for long. The very designations of its followers—cārvāka and lokāyata—have acquired a disparaging sense, much as the term 'sophist' did in ancient Greece, and have become bye-names for the infidel and the epicure." [13] The significance of the name Carvaka is uncertain, but another common name for the school, *lokayata,* has a meaning that is more clear. *Lokayata* indicates that this school holds that only this world (*loka*) exists and that there is no beyond.

There is reference to a sutra ascribed to Brihaspati who is described as a heretical teacher in the *Maitri Upanishad* (VII.9). However, that sutra is lost and fragments of its contents are found in the form of quotations in works that use them as a basis for the

11. Sharma, op. cit., p. 160.
12. Radhakrishnan, op. cit., p. 367.
13. M. Hiriyanna, *Outlines of Indian Philosophy,* London, G. Allen, 1932, p. 188.

refutation of the Carvaka system. Nevertheless, the view of this school can be described in broad outline.

For the Carvaka, the only valid source of knowledge is perception. They reject inference since it is based on universal connections which cannot be perceptually verified. Likewise, intuition, as well as the testimony of the Vedas, is rejected. It is this rejection of the Vedas that leads many to classify this school as "heterodox."

Since only perception is a valid source of knowledge, it follows that all "entities" which are not empirically verifiable are not real. There is no karma or rebirth, no supreme Ishvara, no divine providence or purpose in the world. The Vedic sacrifices are merely ways of keeping a priesthood employed, since there is nothing gained by such religious contortions. This view is described in the *Sarvadarshanasamgraha:*

If you object that, if there be no such thing as happiness in a future world, then how should men of experienced wisdom engage in the Agnihotra *and other sacrifices, which can only be performed with great expenditure of money and bodily fatigue, your objection cannot be accepted as any proof to the contrary, since the* Agnihotra, *&c., are only useful as means of livelihood, for the Veda is tainted by the three faults of untruth, self-contradiction, and tautology; then again the impostors who call themselves Vaidic (for Vedic) pandits are mutually destructive. . . . And to this effect runs the popular saying—*

The Agnihotra, *the three Vedas, the ascetics three staves, and smearing oneself with ashes,—*

Bṛhaspati says these are but means of livelihood for those who have no manliness or sense.[14]

The entire universe is accounted for in terms of four basic elements: earth, water, fire, and air. Space (*akasha*), which is held to be an element by other schools, is rejected, since it is based on inference rather than perception.

There is no Atman or principle of permanence in man. What we experience as consciousness is simply the result of a certain conjunction of the four basic elements. Consciousness is always associated with the body and when the body disintegrates, consciousness disappears as well. Just as when someone chews a combination of betel leaf, areca nut, and lime, a red color appears in the mouth even though none of the ingredients possess the red color, so the combination of elements produces consciousness even though they do not separately possess it.

With the rejection of all of these supposedly religious doctrines and practices, what could be ultimately important for the Carvaka? What would characterize his life stance? If only the senses offer valid knowledge, and if the material world is all that exists, one should enjoy life to the fullest while it lasts. The Carvaka knows of no future rewards or punishments. His is an individual enjoyment of

14. S. Radhakrishnan and Charles A. Moore, *A Source Book in Indian Philosophy,* Princeton, N.J., Princeton University Press, 1957, pp. 229–230.

pleasure more than a concern for the most pleasure for the most people. The only real end for man is sensual enjoyment, the accumulation of wealth being a means to such an end. This is captured in a refrain.

> While life is yours, live joyously;
> None can escape Death's searching eye:
> When once this frame of ours they burn,
> How shall it e'er again return? [15]

Unlike most Indian religious systems, the Carvaka does not seek freedom from suffering. Pain is an inevitable characteristic of existence. But the possibility of future pain is no reason for denying ourselves pleasure.

> The pleasure which arises to men from contact with sensible objects,
> Is to be relinquished as accompanied by pain,—such is the reasoning of fools;
> The berries of paddy, rich with the finest white grains,
> What man, seeking his true interest, would fling away because covered by husk and dust? [16]

While the Carvaka orientation never gained wide and enduring philosophical acceptance, aspects of its viewpoint appear throughout Indian religious thought.[17] And, whatever the "orthodox" might have thought of it, it was a way of ordering life for some thinkers.

15. Ibid., p. 228.
16. Ibid., p. 229.
17. Cf. Dale Riepe, The Naturalistic Tradition in Indian Thought, Delhi, Motilal Bararsidass, 1961.

MEDIEVAL
ARRIVALS

While the *bhakti* movement continued to spread, and articulate religious systems took on new completeness, several other religious traditions appeared which were to make their presence felt on Indian soil. Christians were present in India prior to the medieval period, but had no firm base until the arrival of Jesuit missions in the sixteenth century.

It is a mistake to call some of these religions non-Indian, since after centuries on the Indian subcontinent, they have been or are presently making an effort to share in Indian culture and national goals. Nor is it significant to point out that some of them came from outside the Indian borders, since that can be said for the religion of the Vedic Aryans. The Sikh tradition was formulated in India and the others were influenced in various ways by their new environment.

If the tradition about Saint Thomas is reliable, Christian presence in India preceded its spread throughout Europe. Tradition states that about A.D. 52 Thomas landed in Cranganore, preached the Christian message, and established several churches on the Malabar coast. There is stronger historical evidence that in the fourth century, Christians migrated from Persia and Mesopotamia. By the sixth century, a church with clergy existed in Ceylon, Malabar, and in the Bombay area where bishops had been installed. The Christians on the Malabar coast were called "Christians of Saint Thomas" although they are now often spoken of as Syriac Christians because of their connection with Syriac-speaking churches in the East.

CHRISTIANS
AND JEWS

The largest portion of Indian Christians are Roman Catholics, who became influential because of the rise of Portuguese power in the early sixteenth century. Jesuit missions grew with such notable missionaries as Francis Xavier (1506–1552) and Robert de Nobili (1577–1656) who was successful in presenting the Christian message to the Indian intelligentsia. Colleges and seminaries were established, and a college bearing de Nobili's name still exists outside of Poona. While Jesuit missions declined in importance with the loss of Portuguese political influence, missions sponsored by other orders such as the Franciscans, Dominicans, Augustinians, and Carmelites followed. Catholics exist as a large minority force in the state of Kerala today.

In the seventeenth century and following, Protestant missions also contributed to the growing Christian presence. This development was given impetus in the north by the arrival of William Carey in 1793, and spread all over India with the support of foreign mission societies.

Christians, Protestant and Catholic alike, placed a high premium on education. Colleges and lower-level schools developed in number and quality.

> *In 1954, there were, under the auspices of the National Christian Council, 46 colleges, 448 high schools, 553 middle schools, and 103 teacher-training institutions in the whole of India. In 1951, the Roman Catholics had 42 colleges, 474 high schools, and 4,362 primary schools.*[1]

Medical missions also played an important role in spreading the Christian message. Considerable emphasis was placed on the care of those afflicted by leprosy and tuberculosis. As of 1956, there were over five hundred Christian-sponsored hospitals and dispensaries throughout India and Pakistan.

Christians also exerted considerable energy in work with outcasts and tribals. Many Hindus have interpreted this concern, and the mass conversions which sometimes resulted, as dishonest and not in the best national interest.

In South India the Church was fragmentized by reason of its associations with numerous foreign denominations. In 1947 India had some 150 missionary societies, with many of them at work in the south. Most of these missionary societies and the greater number of Protestant denominations merged in 1947 in the formation of the Church of South India. South Indian Christians have thus become a symbol of ecumenism for other Christians throughout the world.

Jews also settled in Malabar. The earliest reference to this community was in the tenth century, although tradition indicates a settlement of Jews at Cochin in the first century A.D. One group has, through intermarriage, taken on characteristic Indian features, while another has attempted to retain racial distinctiveness.

PARSIS   In the beginning of the eighth century A.D., a community settled in western India and has remained there until the present. To under-

1. C. A. Abraham, "The Rise and Growth of Christianity in India," in *The Cultural Heritage of India,* Calcutta, The Ramakrishna Mission Institute of Culture, 1956, vol. IV, p. 565.

stant these people and the faith which they brought with them from Iran, it is necessary to go back to the seventh century B.C. and even earlier. These people are called Parsis because they migrated from Persia, or Zoroastrians because they trace their teachings back to Zoroaster. In the Bombay area the Parsis number about 100,000. There are about 20,000 in Iran, 6,550 in Pakistan, nearly 4,000 in Europe, a small group in Canada, and about 1,000 in the United States, Africa, and the Far East combined.

While some Parsis date Zoroaster as early as 6000 or 7000 B.C., thus making theirs a religion of great antiquity, most Western scholars would tend toward a seventh century B.C. date. Apart from the centuries between 331 B.C. when Alexander of Macedon defeated the last Achaemenian king and A.D. 220 which marks the beginning of the Sassanian dynasty, the Zoroastrian faith went through various changes but grew in influence because of the support of its kings. In A.D. 637 when the Arabs took Persia, the long Sassanian dynasty fell, and Zoroastrian faith ceased to be a favored religion.

During their long history in Persia, the followers of Zoroaster had developed a complicated system of ritual and scholastic distinctions which were more concerned with ritual purity than with ethical purity. The system of ritual taboos had become so complicated that only the priesthood was able to interpret it correctly.

Having lost their royal support, the Iranians found themselves at the mercy of the Arab Muslims. Persecution by them was one of the factors that led them to flee their homeland. Some went to China or westward, but a goodly number migrated to India where a permanent settlement was established at Sanjan in 716. There were migrations as early as 636, however, and the Parsis did not arrive in a single wave. Over the years they settled around Bombay and have been a highly successful business community.

The sacred writings of the Parsis are called the *Avesta,* or sometimes the *Zend-Avesta.* The word *zend* means "interpretation." Hence the *Zend-Avesta* refers to the *Avesta* plus certain commentaries or interpretations which have been added as time progressed. The meaning of the term *avesta* is either "knowledge" or "original text." The *Zend-Avesta* is a collection of diverse materials without any clear cohesion. The *Avesta* proper contains the *Yasna,* which is a liturgical book from which Parsi priests read while celebrating rituals that honor all the many deities of later Zoroastrians.

Zoroaster himself proclaimed a monotheistic faith in protest of the popular Iranian polytheism. The materials that are thought to go back to Zoroaster himself are called the *Gathas,* which are chapters 28–34 and 43–53 of the *Yasna.* These hymns are concerned with praising Mazda, Zoroaster's one deity, and they set forth the nature of the universal struggle between good and evil. Another part of the *Avesta* is the *Vispered* ("All the Lords"), a liturgical appendix to the *Yasna* which is addressed to numerous heavenly beings. It is a short liturgy and contains little that is not already in the *Yasna.* A third part of the *Avesta* is the *Vendidad,* a priestly code of ritual purification and taboos. The *Vendidad* is chronologically later than the

Gathas, which explains the strong emphasis on ritual purity. Also important for Parsi theology are the *Pahlavi* books written in a Persian variant called Pahlavi. These books were probably written in the ninth century A.D. and reflect the theology which developed in the last century of Sassanian rule.

Prior to the appearance of Zoroaster, the Iranians worshiped *daevas* (Sanskrit *devas*), or shining ones. Zoroaster considered *daevas* to be demons, but the people before him did not. The *daevas* were a class of beings closely resembling the early Vedic deities by reason of their common Aryan ancestry. In the *Rigveda* two classes of deities are distinguished: *asuras* and *devas.* In India the *asuras* came to be thought of as demons, while in Iran, because of Zoroaster, the *daevas* were considered demonic. Part of the elevation of the *asuras* was the place given to Ahura Mazda; he was elevated to the position of Supreme God by Zoroaster.

Besides the worship of ancestors as guardian spirits, the Iranians worshiped fire from antiquity. While Zoroaster himself prohibited the worship of fire, he retained it as a symbol of the deity. Parsis today keep fires burning continually in their temples, and five times daily the fire is ceremonially replenished with incense and sandalwood.

The counterpart of the Indian *Rita* is seen in the Iranian concept of truth or justice (*asha*), the basis of order in nature and in the society of men and gods.

The stories that cluster around the life of Zoroaster illustrate the faith of his followers. Demons tried to prevent the birth of Zoroaster and later attempted to injure his health. After birth the infant Zoroaster laughed instead of cried because the Lie Demon had been confounded. According to tradition, Zoroaster assumed the sacred thread (*kusti*) at the age of fifteen. At twenty he left his family in search for the meaning of life and at thirty he had a series of miraculous visions. The Archangel Vohu Manah (Good Thought) appeared to him as a figure nine times as large as a man. Vohu Manah ushered him into the presence of Ahura Mazda, who instructed him in the principles of the True Religion. Ten years later he won his first convert, but his most crucial convert was a prince Vishtaspa, who favored Zoroaster's faith.

In the *Gathas* one finds an ethical dualism in the form of an opposition between Truth (*Asha*) and the Lie (*Druj*). This conflict between truth and wickedness is portrayed without the possibility of compromise. Not being a philosophical work, the *Gathas* reflect the practical situation of their Persian setting—a pastoral community engaged in tilling the soil and cattle raising that was habitually threatened by a nomadic tribal society which destroyed men as well as cattle. This violence was merely part of a cosmic battle between good and evil, and those who followed the truth cultivated the soil and pulled the weeds.

The moral dualism between Asha *and* Druj, *Truth and the Lie, Righteousness and Unrighteousness, which is so characteristic of the Gāthās can be seen as a universalization of a concrete political and social situation in which a peaceful, pastoral and cattle-*

breeding population was constantly threatened by the inroads of
fierce nomadic tribes.[2]

Zaehner is even convinced that an actual state of war existed between the two parties.

Zoroaster saw no hope of compromising with evil. The enemy was
to be either converted or defeated. To love one's enemy implied
aligning oneself with him. As long as people are on the side of the
Lie, they should be shown no mercy. Men are free to choose to be
followers of either *Druj* or *Asha,* but so long as one follows *Druj* he
is to be opposed. Nevertheless, the possibility of conversion is always present. Freedom is not philosophically defended but merely
assumed.

Zoroaster also spoke out against a growing ritualism and against
the slaughter of cattle for sacrificial purposes. The sacrifice seems
to have been accompanied by drinking Homa juice (Indian Soma)
resulting in ritual intoxication. Some of his opponents, therefore,
were the priests who presided at these rituals. Zoroaster was firmly
convinced that both cosmically and tactically, there were only two
sides: Good and Evil. He was equally convinced that one had the
freedom to choose on which side he would serve, that he had chosen the Good and that those who opposed him had chosen the Evil.

The greater cosmic conflict was between Ahura Mazda and Angra
Mainyu, who was the chief personification of the Lie. In later
thought, Ahura Mazda became assimilated with Spenta Mainyu
(Holy or Bounteous Spirit), who was the protagonist against evil.
Still later a metaphysical dualism developed to replace what was
previously only an ethical dualism. There is some ambiguity within
the early texts and even in the descriptions in the later tradition
about the origin of evil. If one says that ultimately there is only one
supreme deity, Ahura Mazda, then the question arises as to whether
or not he is responsible for evil. On the other hand, if one proposes
two eternal spirits such as Ahura Mazda and Angra Mainyu, he offers a metaphysical dualism which explains the problem of evil but
offers no hope for its ultimate defeat.

In the *Gathas,* consideration is given to the Amesha Spentas, six
divine abstractions which later came to be thought of as beings in
their own right. For Zoroaster, they were aspects of God which man
could share if he lived according to the truth. While the Amesha
Spentas had no independent existence apart from God, his operations took place through them. One contemporary Parsi characterizes them as divine abstractions and lists them as follows:

1. *Vohu Manah,* The Good Mind;
2. *Asha Vahishta,* The Best Order, or Righteousness;
3. *Khshathra Vairya,* The Absolute Power;
4. *Armaiti,* High Thought, or Devotion;
5. *Haurvatat,* Perfection;
6. *Ameretat,* Immortality.

2. R. C. Zaehner, *The Dawn and Twilight of Zoroastrianism,* New York,
Putnam, 1961, p. 34.

Zoroaster was convinced of the truth and finality of his teaching, having received it from Ahura Mazda himself. He was equally confident that Ahura Mazda would ultimately triumph over evil. He was eschatologically optimistic. In later theological thought, a well-worked-out eschatology developed. At the end of time, Saoshyans (savior) will renew all existence. The spirits of the dead will be raised, united with their bodies, and a mighty conflagration will take place. All men will wade through a stream of molten metal which will be as soothing as warm milk for the just, but will be a burning experience for the wicked. Sins will be purged and all creation will return to its maker. There is also an individual judgment which takes place at death, when the individual is judged at the Chinvat Bridge. In one account, the righteous soul is guided across the bridge by a beautiful maiden who is in reality his own good conscience. The wicked soul is met by an ugly hag who embraces him so that they fall into hell together (she is his own bad conscience). One's deeds, therefore, determine one's destiny. The question of the destiny of one whose good and evil deeds balanced inevitably arose, and it was said that they go to *Hamestakan*—an abode between earth and the stars.

Parsi fire temples have few external characteristics which distinguish them as temples. In Bombay they are identified by the symbol of Ahura Mazda on the outside. Inside the fire temple is an urn in the center of the room. The presiding priests wear a cloth covering their faces so that they will not breathe impurities into the fire, nor are they to cough or sneeze near the fire. Worshipers come at any time and after having washed the uncovered parts of their bodies, they give offerings of money and sandalwood to the priest. He in turn offers them some ashes from the sacred fire which they apply to their forehead. The worshiper bows and offers prayers toward the fire. I. J. S. Taraporewala indicates that the prophet chose fire as the chief symbol since it is the purest of God's creations. In the opinion of this contemporary Parsi, there are two other characteristics of fire which make the symbol meaningful: (1) fire has "the power of immediately transmuting everything it touches into a likeness of itself"; and (2) "the flames of fire always tend *upwards,* and thus aptly symbolize our yearning for the Higher Life." [3]

Fire is not to be contaminated by burning a dead body. If this does happen, the fire must be ceremonially purified, after which it becomes particularly sacred. The concern not to contaminate the sacred fire is also a reason why Parsis are not permitted to smoke. To draw impure air or breathe through the sacred fire would be a matter of disrespect. This does not mean that the community universally follows the precept.

Some fires are more holy than others; hence the temple in which they are housed becomes more important, as does the priest in charge of that temple. There are only eight first-grade temples in India, four of them being in Bombay. A first-grade temple requires

3. I. J. S. Taraporewala, *The Religion of Zarathushtra,* Bombay, Taraporewala, 1965, p. 41.

that the fire be filtered and brought together from seventeen sources. This includes fire from a thunderbolt igniting dry wood. Certain religious rituals are performed before the varying levels of fires.

The Parsis dispose of their dead by placing them in *dakmas,* or "towers of silence." There are scriptural prohibitions against cremation or burial in order not to pollute the fire or earth. Furthermore, it is considered a sin to waste the earth for cemeteries when it could be used to produce food. Although towers of silence are a curiousity to Westerners, they pose no embarrassment to Parsis.

The *dakma* itself is to be constructed on a hill, if possible, in an isolated locality where vultures may be attracted. The tower is constructed with three rows of niches, or *pavis.* The top circle is large and designed for men. The second row is smaller and for women, while the third is smaller still and intended for children. Each niche is separated by a passage where the bearers may walk. Large towers have some 450 niches. In the center is a pit which has a concrete or stone floor. When the bones are dried, they are thrown into the central pit where the action of sun and water pulverizes them. Burial of bones is permitted since they are not thought to be unclean, but no tomb is ever erected. The tower has an intricate drainage system whereby the water is filtered through four deep subterranean wells. When the body is taken into the towers, no one enters except the bearers and they must be purified. At a certain point in the cermony, non-Zoroastrians are no longer permitted to remain. The non-Parsi might break some of the detailed prescriptions for ceremonial purity since he is not familiar with them.

A leading Bombay priest, Dastur Dabu, justifies this method of disposing of the dead thus:

1. *It is charitable. A Parsi's last act on earth is the donation of his dead body to hungry birds, nature's appointed scavengers.*
2. *It is the speediest method of disposal. In about twenty minutes all flesh is devoured leaving only the bones exposed to the rays of the sun.*
3. *It is economical. Other methods require the purchase of ground, construction and maintenance of tombs, expanding cemeteries, and the purchase of fuel for cremation. The Parsi method is free. The same tower can accommodate hundreds of corpses and a small plot of ground is sufficient.*
4. *Rich and poor, humble and great are placed on the same platform without distinction. The garment and funeral procession are the same for all. There are no costly funerals or mourners. When the bones are dried up and begin to crumble under the rain and heat, they are put into the central pit where they are again mixed without distinction.*
5. *This is the most hygienic system. The corpse has no contact with residential surroundings; whatever water enters due to rain is diverted to four underground wells. There is no contamination of watermains nor is there any odor from burning flesh. "The towers of Bombay, having existed for centuries in the*

*most fashionable locality, have never created any nuisance.
Even during epidemics the towers receive sterilizing Sun's rays
and are quite innocuous and safe."*

6. *There is no false sentimentality. Death should be treated as
the inevitable phenomenon that it is. Monuments that proclaim
the deep sorrow of survivors are based on unnecessary sentimentality. The Parsi treats death in a sensible manner without
a great deal of unnecessary fuss.*[4]

Initiation ceremonies in the Parsi community are called the *Naojote* ceremony and extend to girls as well as boys. The word *naojote*
is composed of two words: *nao,* or new, and *zote,* or one who offers
prayers. The ceremony is so named because after its performance
the Parsi child is said to be responsible for offering prayers and observing religious customs and rites as a Zoroastrian.

After the ceremony the individual who is a Parsi by birth becomes
a Zoroastrian by choice. The initiate is vested with a sacred shirt
(*sudrah*), and the sacred thread (*kusti*). A Parsi without the sacred
thread after the age of fifteen is out of the fold and considered
likely to fall into evil ways. He is therefore initiated between the
ages of seven and fifteen.

Toward the beginning of the twentieth century, Parsis were agi-
tated over the question of admitting aliens into the community.
Could one marry into the Parsi community? In 1905 the community
at Bombay expressed its disapproval of admitting converts into the
community. The law courts upheld this stand as follows.

*The Parsi community consists of Parsis who are descended from
the original Persian immigrants and who are born of both
Zoroastrian parents and who profess Zoroastrian religion, the
Iranis from Persia professing the Zoroastrian religion, who come to
India either temporarily or permanently, and the children of Parsi
fathers by alien mothers who have been duly and properly admitted into the religion.*[5]

One section of the community was even opposed to admitting children of Parsi fathers and alien mothers. There was also a minority
favoring the possibility of admitting persons who desired to join.
That minority concedes, however, that such a provision is not likely
to be permitted in the very near future, if at all.

MUSLIMS   While some Muslim contact with India resulted from small peaceful
settlements, the main source of Muslim influence in India was the
result of a series of invasions which culminated in 1526, a date
which marks the beginning of the rule of the Mughals over North
India. Mughal rule lasted until the death of Aurangzeb in 1707, after

---

4. Dastus Khurshed S. Dabu, *Message of Zarathushtra*, Bombay, The New
Book Co. Private Ltd., 1959, pp. 120–121 *passim.*
5. *Dinsha Petit* v. *Jamsetji Jijibhai* (1909) 33 Bombay, as quoted in P. P.
Balsara, *Highlights of Parsi History*, Bombay, 1966, p. 72.

which it slowly declined until the British gained control of India in 1858.

The first Muslim invasion occurred in the early eighth century when Muhummad Ibn Qasim marched into Sind. A limited Arab rule was extended until 1005 when the Arabs were overthrown by Mahmud of Ghazna, the ruler of a small Turkish kingdom in Afghanistan. Prior to the establishment of the Mughal regime, the kings who settled in Delhi did not always honor the judgments of their religious leaders, nor did they follow with great care the regulations of Islamic law.

The Mughals were more influenced by Persian than by Turkish culture which became the vehicle for their artistic expression. But since Muslims who had invaded India at various times were once Arabs, then Turks, and finally Persians, and since they did not come in one great invasion, they not only exerted influence on the Indians they found, but were influenced in return. The invaders were monotheistic and theoretically submitters to Allah. Their invasions and reign was marked by persecution, razing temples and images, offering of benefits to converts, and the imposition of burdens on non-Muslims.

All non-Muslims were required to pay a poll tax, which was lifted for converts. Idolators who opposed the Muslim armies were slaughtered and Brahmans were not infrequently massacred. One should neither underestimate the brutality which existed under monotheistic guise in order to tell a complimentary story, nor should one universalize the brutality so that the impression is left that Muslims never got along with their neighbors. In the reign of two Mughal rulers we have the two extremes typified.

While brutality was common during the reign of Akbar from 1556 to 1605, there were aspects of his rule which also indicated a spirit of tolerance. Akbar placed men of various religious persuasions in high government positions, after he had solidified his relations with his Hindu neighbors by marriage. He abolished the deeply resented poll tax even though it meant considerable loss of income.

Due to a spiritual crisis in 1578 (he had Sufi-type mystical experiences when a boy), Akbar built a hall in which religious debates were held. These debates began as Muslim theological discussions, but Akbar soon invited Brahmans, Jainas, and Parsis as well. He came to see that there were many men deserving of respect even though their religious allegiances varied. In addition to his religious motivation, there was probably the political desire to find a creed on which he could unite the diverse traditions of his kingdom. In 1579 he drew up an Infallibility Decree which made him the final arbiter in all matters of religious dispute. Later he promulgated a new creed which he called Divine Faith (*Din Ilahi*) which was an attempt to bring together what Akbar considered good in various religions. It was intended as a sort of religious fraternity within Akbar's court. This creed, however, died with its author.

At times Akbar showed hostility toward Islam, a tendency that made him less than popular with many Muslims. He had Sanskrit books translated into Persian, and incorporated many Parsi and

Taj Mahal, Agra. (Photo by Robert D. Baird.)

sectarian religious customs. Akbar worshiped the Sun and the Sacred Fire, forbade the slaughter of animals, wore sectarian marks on his forehead, and proclaimed religious toleration.

At one point Akbar sent to Goa for Catholic priests whom he engaged in debate. These priests were permitted to build a temple where Akbar attended Mass. The Mughal ruler admired the teachings and person of Jesus, but found the doctrines of the Incarnation and the Trinity unacceptable.

Akbar was followed by Jahangir (1605–1628) and then by Shah Jahan (1628–1659) who built the beautiful Taj Mahal as his wife's mausoleum.

Aurangzeb, the last of the powerful Mughal emperors, took the throne at the death of Shah Jahan. If Akbar illustrates the more pacificatory religious type, Aurangzeb typifies the more brutal features. Aurangzeb pledged himself to purge the land of "heretics" and "idolators." He curbed the extravagences of the Court, and suppressed many practices that he considered to be vices. Here is a description by a contemporary Muslim:

The Emperor, a great worshipper of God by temperament, is noted for his rigid attachment to religion. In his great piety he passes whole nights in the palace mosque and keeps the company of devout men. In privacy he never sits on a throne. Before his accession he gave in alms part of his food and clothing and still devotes to alms the income of some villages near Delhi and of some salt tracts assigned to his privy purse. He keeps fast throughout Ramazān and reads the holy Koran in the assembly of religious men with whom he sits for six or even nine hours of the night. From his youth he abstained from forbidden food and practices, and from his great holiness does nothing that is not pure and lawful. Though at the beginning of his reign he used to hear the exquisite voices of ravishing singers and brilliant instrumental performances, and himself understands music well, yet now for several years past, in his great restraint and self-denial, he entirely abstains from this joyous entertainment. He never wears clothes prohibited by religion, nor uses vessels of silver and gold. No unseemly talk, no word of backbiting or falsehood, is permitted at his Court. He appears twice or thrice daily in his audience chamber with a mild and pleasing countenance, to dispense justice to petitioners, who come in numbers without hindrance and obtain redress. If any of them talks too much or acts improperly he is not displeased and never knits his brows. By hearing their words and watching their gestures he says that he acquires a habit of forbearance and toleration. Under the dictates of anger and passion he never passes sentence of death.[6]

Aurangzeb demolished the schools and temples of the "infidels" and attempted to wipe out their teachings, which he considered destructive. He razed temples and had mosques erected in their places. One great temple, erected at the cost of over one million dollars, was destroyed, and jewels from the images were taken to Agra where they became part of the threshold of a mosque to be walked on by the true believers. Many Hindus were relieved of their government posts and the poll tax was imposed again. An appeal was made to Aurangzeb to soften his harsh actions as Akbar had done, but the plea went unheeded. Later in the seventeenth century in Maratha State, a Hindu state was set up through the military leadership of Sivaji. To this day he continues to be a Hindu hero because of his courageous leadership.

Muslims today engage in pilgrimages not only to Mecca, but also to the tombs and shrines of saints and heroes. Sometimes annual celebrations accompanied by fairs are held at the tombs of saints. Wreaths are laid, candles are burned, and costly drapes are placed over the tombs. Some pilgrims pray to the dead to help them in supplying their mundane needs, though such practice is opposed by the orthodox to little avail. Hindus visit the same tombs and offer the same reverence. Common religious practices in India have thus influenced the popular expression of Muslim faith.

In addition to this, there were more deliberate attempts to bring Muslims and Hindus together. One such effort grew into the religious tradition of the Sikhs.

Nanak (1469–1539), the first Sikh *guru,* was born some forty miles from Lahore in the Punjab area. Here the conflict between Hindus and Muslims had resulted in fighting and killing for centuries. Nanak was born into a *kshatriya* family. His father was rather low on the economic scale, being in the employ of a Muslim ruler. As a boy,   SIKHS

---

6. Quoted in H. G. Rawlinson, *India, A Short Cultural History,* New York, Praeger, 1952, first published in 1937, p. 343.

Nanak had meditative tendencies, and although he was married at the age of twelve, his religious tendencies were not abated. He left his wife and two children with his parents while he took a position in the district capital, but even there he could not keep his mind on his employment. He spent considerable time in the evenings singing hymns with a Muslim minstrel, Mardana.

One morning, while bathing in the river, he had a vision of God's presence. He was offered a cup of nectar which he accepted, and God said to him:

> I am with thee. I have made thee happy, and also those who shall take thy name. Go and repeat Mine, and cause others to do likewise. Abide uncontaminated by the world. Practice the repetition of My name, charity, ablutions, worship, and meditation. I have given thee this cup of nectar, a pledge of My regard.[7]

Tradition has it that Nanak responded with the words that introduce the *Japji,* which is repeated by devout Sikhs as a morning devotional prayer:

> There is but one God whose name is True, the Creator, devoid of fear and enmity, immortal, unborn, self-existent, great and bountiful. The True One was in the beginning, the True One was in the primal age. The True One is, was, O Nanak, and the True One also shall be.[8]

Tradition states that, after a full day's silence, Nanak uttered this pronouncement: "There is no Hindu and no Mussalman." Nanak then set out on an extended tour of northern and western India. To emphasize the basic unity of Muslim and Hindu teaching and practices, he even wore a unique garb which combined a Muslim headpiece and an Indian sectarian mark on his forehead, among other things.

In the *Adi Granth,* holy book of the Sikh community, are Nanak's teachings which attempt to combine, as did his garments, the faith of Hindus and Muslims. Nanak's belief in a single Creator God came from the Muslim side. In an attempt not to limit God to any one community, he avoided such names as Allah, Rama, Shiva, or Vishnu, simply calling God the True Name. Nanak's Creator God ordained that man be served by the lower forms of life in the creation, a notion which eliminated the need for vegetarianism.

Nanak also held to the doctrine of *maya,* in common with his Brahman neighbors. But although he retained the doctrine of *maya,* he did not follow its advaitin implications. The world, however, was ultimately unreal, God having created matter by drawing a veil over himself. In addition to this concept, Nanak believed in the law of karma, the doctrine of rebirth, and held that men prolonged the rounds of rebirth by living apart from God, thereby accumulating bad karma.

7. M. A. MacAuliffe, *The Sikh Religion: Its Gurus, Sacred Writings and Authors,* New Delhi, S. Chand & Co., 1963 reprint, vol. I, pp. 33–34.
8. Ibid., p. 35.

There was in Nanak a strong *bhakti* strain which comes through Kabir who preceded him, and Ramananda who preceded Kabir. Although simple repetition of the True Name is more efficacious than going on pilgrimages, bathing images, or bathing in sacred rivers, salvation was seen in terms of absorption into God, the True Name. The strong *bhakti* emphasis in Nanak would not allow him to espouse an ultimate elimination of individuality.

Nanak took a strong stand against both ritualism and asceticism. Since he was not a philosopher, he did not attempt to reconcile the apparent conflict between theism and *advaita*. *Bhakti* theologians solved this problem to their satisfaction by identifying Brahman with the Supreme Deity. By so doing they had to deny Shankara's doctrine of the levels of being as well as his view of *maya*. Shankara, on the other hand, solved the problem by relegating *bhakti* and the Supreme Deity to the preliminary level of the phenomenal world. Nanak was a mystic who felt his religion, not a theologian who made an intense effort to eliminate all logical conflicts.

The significant role of the *guru* was emphasized by Nanak and the community which followed him. The guidance of a *guru* was both necessary and sufficient to lead men to God. Those men who committed themselves to Nanak's teachings and became his followers were known as Sikhs, or disciples.

There was a succession of ten *gurus*, beginning with Nanak. Prior to his death, Nanak appointed one of his disciples as his successor. Angad, the second *guru*, devised a new script called *Gurmukhi*, in which he wrote the literature of his faith, and also began the compilation of the Sikh scriptures. At this stage these scriptures, which were later to be the *Adi Granth*, were mostly composed of the hymns of Nanak. Nanak's practice of operating a public kitchen where guests and friends could eat regardless of caste or religion was enlarged by Angad. Operating free kitchens in the Sikh gurdwaras (temples, literally, "gate of the *guru*") continues even today. Travelers who are hungry or weary can share a meal and obtain a place to lodge for the night.

Guru Angad selected as his successor Guru Amar Das (1479–1574), who prohibited the veiling and seclusion of women (*purdah*) as commonly practiced by Muslims. He also opposed the practice of widows throwing themselves on the funeral pyres of their husbands (*sati*). Amar Das continued the free kitchen and visitors accepted the hospitality of the *guru* by eating with the disciples. One of his visitors during this period was the Emperor Akbar.

The fourth *guru* was Guru Ram Das (1574–1581), who is remembered for having started the famous Golden Temple at Amritsar which remains today the center of the Sikh community. The temple is beautifully reflected in the artificial lake which surrounds it.

The fifth *guru*, Guru Arjan (1581–1606), completed the Golden Temple and installed in it the *Adi Granth* which he collated. The Muslim emperor Akbar, having been told by his advisers that the *Adi Granth* was a heretical book, examined it and found nothing that offended him. But Akbar died during the time that Arjan was *guru*, and his son Jahangir proved to be more cruel and fanatical.

Golden Temple, Amritsar. (Courtesy of the Government of India Tourist Office.)

Guru Arjan was tortured to death, but before he died he instructed the sixth *guru,* Guru Har Govind (1606–1646), to "sit fully armed on his throne and maintain an army to the best of his ability."

When Har Govind became *guru,* he wore two swords but would not wear the turban and necklace which had been symbolic of pacifying tendencies. He organized an army and drew to his side thousands of Sikhs who were willing to engage in battle. Hostility between Sikhs and Muslims continued to grow as the Muslims interpreted the Sikh presence as a political threat and a religious error. The Sikh movement, which began in an attempt to bring Muslim and Hindu together, was becoming a source of provocation for

Muslim hostility. Har Govind increased the missionary outreach of the Sikh community and was an able administrator as well.

The growing hostility continued during the period of the seventh *guru*, Har Rai (1630–1661), the eighth *guru*, Har K'ishan (1656–1664), and the ninth *guru*, Tegh Bahadur (1621–1675). Tegh Bahadur became a martyr for his faith as a victim of the fanaticism of Aurangzeb.

The tenth and final *guru*, Govind Singh (1666–1708), played a formative role in the military tendency of the Sikh community in the face of Muslim opposition. Convinced of his own divine authority, in 1699 he instituted the *Khalsa,* the Community of the Pure. Members were formally initiated with a baptism in which the initiates were required to drink and be sprinkled with sweetened water which had been stirred with a sharp sword. This nectar, *amrit,* was supposed to confer ceremonial purity and immunity in battle. Members of the casteless *Khalsa* changed their name to Singh ("Lion") and they repeated the battle cry of the Sikhs: "The pure are of God and the victory is to God." Their marks of identification were the five K's:

1. *Kesh,* or long hair, a sign of saintliness;
2. *Kangh,* a comb for keeping the hair tidy;
3. *Kach,* short drawers, insuring quick movement in battle;
4. *Kara,* a steel bracelet, signifying sternness and restraint;
5. *Kirpan,* or sword for defense.

Four further rules were prescribed for all members. They were not to cut any hair from the body; not to smoke, chew tobacco, or drink alcohol; not to eat the meat of any animal slaughtered by the Muslim method of bleeding to death; not to molest Muslim women, but to live a life of marital fidelity. The Sikhs were fearless fighting men, and their battles with Muslims were often brutal. Even after the Muslim threat had passed, the Sikhs continued their military prowess as honored members of the British army, and later, after Independence, in the Indian army.

Guru Govind Singh taught that after his death his followers were to regard the *Granth* as their *guru* and that there would be no further need for a human *guru.* Since that time there has been no human *guru* in the Sikh community, but the *Granth* has been worshiped as their one divine authority. In the Golden Temple and also in other gurdwaras as well, the *Sri Guru Granth Sahib* is enshrined with honor. On special occasions its words are read continuously day and night, and it is treated with all the care and reverence that a Vaishava might offer to an image of Vishnu. In the course of development from Guru Nanak through Guru Govind Singh, the community has undergone a transformation from pacifism to military emphasis.

Although Guru Nanak intended to bring together both Muslim and Hindu, it is almost prophetic that Muslims and Hindus quarreled over the disposal of his body at the time of death. Prior to his demise, the Muslims had proposed to bury him while the Hindus wanted to cremate him, but Nanak told the Hindus to place flowers on his right and the Muslims to place flowers on his left. Those whose flow-

Priest reading Adi Granth, Golden Temple, Amritsar. (Photo by Paul E. Pfuetze.)

ers remained fresh in the morning would have their way. On the morning following his death, they raised the sheet that had covered him to find the body gone. The flowers on both sides were fresh.

The story is intended to emphasize the unification of the two hostile religious groups, but it seems that their original hostility was more prophetic. By the reign of Guru Arjan, the *distinctiveness* of the Sikh community was emphatically stated. Guru Arjan is quoted as saying,

> *I have broken with the Hindu and the Muslim,*
> *I will not worship with the Hindu nor like the Muslim go to Mecca.*
> *I shall serve Him and no other.*
> *I will not pray to idols nor say the Muslim prayer.*
> *I shall put my heart at the feet of the one Supreme Being,*
> *For we are neither Hindus nor Mussalmans.*[9]

There has been a tendency for the Sikh community to absorb the practices of the Hindu community around them. Many of the youth have abandoned the distinctive symbols (five K's), and others have modified them by replacing the dagger with a small symbolic dagger on the wooden comb or by trimming the beard to improve its appearance. As the external symbols of the community are given up, there remains less to distinguish a Sikh from his Vaishvana neighbor. Hence many of the older generation place an emphasis on these externals as means of preserving their identity. One can find considerable literature emphasizing the glories of the Sikh tradition, the struggles with which it developed in the face of Muslim opposition, or the health value of long hair. One pamphlet, the result of research at a Human Hair Research Institute, emphasizes that on scientific grounds it can be shown that health depends upon

9. Khushwant Singh, *The Sikhs*, London, G. Allen, 1953, p. 27.

the solar rays of energy taken into the body through the hair. Hence, although the most healthy existence would be to live without clothing, without cutting the hair, and without washing the natural oils from the hair and skin too frequently, given the necessity of common decency, the Sikh alternative is the best.

There has been agitation for a Punjabi sabha, a political state with borders determined by the dominant use of Punjabi. The intent is to maintain a distinctive Sikh community; though it was the cause of bitter Hindu-Sikh communal controversy, a Punjabi sabha has been granted.

While the most famous gurdwara is the Golden Temple at Amritsar, there are numerous Sikh temples throughout India, particularly in the north. There the *Granth* is read, and each worshiper receives in his outstretched, cupped hands a portion of pudding which is eaten. Equal portions are given to all, symbolizing equality in the community. On holidays a mass meal may be eaten at the *langer,* or kitchen, of the gurdwara. Pilgrimages are important and devotees flock to important sites in Sikh history. The Sikhs are a hardworking people who have taken part in every level of Indian life. Nevertheless, the increasing inroads of secularism, a growing emphasis on externals of the faith, and the preservation of a distinctive identity make it difficult not to conclude that a significant religious shift has taken place. Whereas for Nanak, the ultimate matter was devotion to the True Name, for the present community, self-preservation appears to be somewhat more important. Nevertheless, there remain those who share Nanak's devotion to the transcendent ideal.

THE MODERN PERIOD

By 1818 the power of the British in India had spread from the Himalayas in the north to Cape Comorin in the south. After the Mutiny of 1857, the government was transferred from the East India Company to the British Crown. Peace was restored in 1858 and a unified system of administration was put into operation. The British were to continue in control until 1947 when political independence was achieved.

Although the British were in India primarily for economic reasons, their presence resulted in an Indian encounter with the West. It was originally the British policy to remain neutral on religious and cultural matters, but over the years a challenge to traditional values took both direct and indirect courses. During the eighteenth and nineteenth centuries grants were given by the British government through certain officials for the support of temples and mosques while under others missionary work was encouraged. In 1813 Parliament established a legal connection between the government of India and the Church of England.

One source of encounter was the challenge to various traditional practices by Christian missionaries. These missionaries spoke out against the practice of *sati* and were concerned about the fate of widows who were not permitted to remarry. They were disturbed also by the situation of children's marriage before the age of puberty, where the death of the boy would add to the number of young widows.

Western education also introduced Indians to new value systems. The scientific spirit drew Indians to the West, although attacks on polytheism and certain social practices were part of the encounter as well. In the early nineteenth century Indians were willing to look to the West for guidance and to accept its superiority; only later would they go through the stages of rejection, and then synthesis. Application of scientific knowledge to technological advance was also to be seen in marked contrast with predominantly village India.

The response to this encounter took the form of either vigorous reform or staunch defense, or various degrees between these two extremes.

One of those organizations which has tended to favor more radical change is the Brahma Samaj. The term *Brahma* is an adjective formed from *Brahman* of the Upanishads, and *Samaj* means a society. In its varied history the Brahma Samaj has been strongly theistic; it has rejected polytheism, the worship of images, and sacrifice of animals; it has advocated the abolition of *sati,* child marriage, and polygamy. Still the very title of this organization indicates its intention of remaining firmly attached to its Indian past.

Ram Mohun Roy (1772–1833), who founded the Brahma Samaj in 1828, was born in a Bengali village and was married three times while still a child. At the age of twelve he left home, studied Persian and Arabic at Patna, engaged in Islamic studies, and then went to Benares where he studied Sanskrit. His first book, written in 1802 in Persian with an Arabic introduction, was a defense of monotheism. He studied Vaishnava, Tantric, Jain, and Buddhist positions, and was not content until he learned Hebrew, Latin, and Greek and had launched on a serious study of Christian literature.

In 1816 Ram Mohun published *Vedanta-sara* which attempted to find monotheism in the Vedanta point of view. Somewhat of a Unitarian, his contact with Christian missionaries led to some of his books, such as *The Precepts of Jesus, Appeal to the Christian Public,* and *The Ideal Humanity of Jesus.*

The Trust Deed for the Samaj temple indicates that the building was to be used for the worship and adoration of God without respect to the castes of worshipers. No images, pictures, or likenesses were to be permitted in the building. Sacrifices were also forbidden on the premises. Only sermons, hymns, and prayers that would strengthen the bonds of union among men of all religious creeds were to be used. Further, the Trust Deed warned against a contemptuous attitude toward the modes of worship of alien groups regardless of how illegitimate they might seem. The organization of the Samaj thus shows a social as well as a theistic orientation.

Ram Mohun contemplated a universal religion which he thought might some day have universal acceptance. This universal religion would include all that is common to all religions, with divisive elements omitted. Having found the Upanishads to teach monotheism, he was convinced that the notion of the one true God would be part of this common faith. This emphasis on the fundamental unity of all religions was also to be stressed by Ramakrishna, Vivekananda, Tagore, and Radhakrishnan, even though the nature and extent of that unity is diverse.

Devendranath Tagore (1817–1905), the father of the famous Bengali poet Rabindranath Tagore, succeeded Ram Mohun as head of the Brahma Samaj. He continued to support the Samaj opposition to idolatry. He also exerted caution to avoid undue Christian influence which might compromise the transcendence of God through incarnation, or *advaita* influence which might dissolve the difference be-

GROWTH OF MOVEMENTS AND ORGANIZATIONS

Brahma Samaj

tween the worshiper and the Worshiped. Also, monotheism was strengthened by publishing an anthology of Upanishadic texts which he felt supported monotheism (*Brahma-Dharma*).

Since the Samaj had been little more than a weekly meeting, Devendranath saw the need, in 1843, for a structural organization and drew up a list of vows called the Brahma Covenant which was to be affirmed by members of the society. The main promises were to avoid idolatry and to worship God with love and obedience. Prayer and devotional exercises were introduced into the services of the Samaj and the direct communication of man with the Divine Being was stressed. Devendranath was less rationalistic than Ram Mohun.

Since the Vedas were considered the sole authority for the Samaj, the question of their infallibility was raised. A controversy arose which led to the sending of four individuals to Banaras to study and copy the Vedas and to report their findings. The result was the repudiation of the doctrine of the Vedas' infallibility and a new emphasis was placed on intuition.

Keshab Chandra Sen (1838–1884) joined the Samaj in 1857. Keshab held that the Brahma religion could be summed up in the two concepts of the fatherhood of God and the brotherhood of man. He was less concerned with theological controversy than with actual life. More than previous leaders, Keshab was enamored with Christ. He had to face mounting opposition from members who were anti-Hindu or anti-Christian. Such remarks as the following did not help to heal the rift: "Who rules India? Not politics or democracy, but Christ. None but Jesus ever deserved this bright, precious diadem—India. And Jesus shall have it!" [1]

Keshab even called himself a "servant of Jesus." Yet he emphasized religious unity and even Asian unity. Christianity was founded by Asians and the idea of a universal religion is a Christian idea. In 1869 the differences between the older members and the younger faction led by Keshab came to a head and resulted in the formation of the Brahma Samaj of India under Keshab. The older organization took the title Adi Brahma Samaj (original Brahma Samaj).

Keshab introduced a more devotional form of worship which included the singing of Vaishnava *bhajans*. Keshab himself became an object of devotion and was taken to task by the Adi Brahma Samaj. When Keshab failed to interfere with the devotion of his followers in his behalf, the cleavage between the two parties increased. Since he had previously opposed Hindu marriages because of their idolatrous connections, Keshab's integrity became suspect when he consented to the Hindu marriage of his daughter to the prince of Bihar. This led to a further split in the Samaj in 1878 when the dissenters organized the Sadharan Brahma Samaj, depreciated the cult of personalities, and reaffirmed their stand against idolatry. Social reform remained in the foreground in these concerns.

Keshab did not form the Brahma Samaj of India without a certain amount of sorrow, since it meant a break with his close friend De-

1. Quoted in V. S. Naravane, *Modern Indian Thought,* Bombay, Asia Publishing House, 1964, p. 43.

vendranath who became the leader of the Adi Brahma Samaj. Keshab was the last dynamic leader of the Brahma Samaj, which movement had pretty well spent its force by the time Keshab died. It exerted a powerful force for social reform in its day and based its social concerns on a faith in one Supreme Being. Frequently it gave evidence of concern for devotional life. While more radical than most movements in nineteenth-century India, the Brahma Samaj not only embraced the West or Christianity, but maintained a connection with its previous Indian tradition, however tenuous that connection became at times.

Mula Shanker (1824–1883) was dissatisfied with image worship in his early years and left his family to live the life of a wandering monk. Initiated into the Saraswati order of Sannyasins, he took the name by which he is commonly known, Dayananda Saraswati. In 1875 he founded the Arya Samaj as a universal religion open to anyone, regardless of caste or nationality. Dayananda held to the infallibility of the *Vedas* and used the slogan "back to the *Vedas.*" He rejected the polytheism and idolatry of the texts of the later Indian tradition such as the *Puranas,* holding they were immoral. In accepting the authority of the Vedas, many Indians included the Brahmanas and Upanishads. Dayananda limited his authority to the Vedic *samhitas.* He opposed the ritual of the Brahmanas and the *advaitin* tendencies of the Upanishads.

> Arya Samaj

It was Dayananda's view that the Vedic hymns taught that there was only one God, who was to be worshiped spiritually and not by means of images. The various Vedic deities were interpreted merely as so many names for the one God rather than as reference to a variety of deities. Dayananda held to the doctrines of karma and rebirth and contended that they were also taught in the Vedas.

For Dayananda, the Vedas are the eternal utterances of God and hence contain no historical or temporary references. Those made to particular places or times are only apparent. The Vedas contain complete knowledge. Although the European has come upon the scene with impressive technological achievements brought about by science, this is much less impressive when one realizes that such accomplishments were already foreseen in the ancient Vedas.

> *To him not only was everything contained in the Vedas perfect truth, but he went a step further, and by the most incredible interpretations succeeded in persuading himself and others that everything worth knowing, even the most recent inventions of modern science, were alluded to in the Vedas. Steam-engines, railways, and steamboats, were all shown to have been known, at least in their germs, to the poets of the Vedas.*[2]

To become a member of the Arya Samaj one had to subscribe to ten fundamental principles.

2. Quoted in J. N. Farquhar, *Modern Religious Movements in India,* New York, Macmillan, 1919, p. 116.

1. *God is the primary cause of all true knowledge, and every-thing known by its name.*
2. *God is All-Truth, All-Knowledge, All-Beatitude, Incorporeal, Almighty, Just, Merciful, Unbegotten, Infinite, Unchangeable, without a beginning, Incomparable, the Support of the Lord of All, All-Pervading, Omniscient, Imperishable, Immortal, Exempt from fear, Eternal, Holy, and the Cause of the Universe. To Him alone is worship due.*
3. *The Vedas are the books of true knowledge, and it is the par-amount duty of every Ārya to read or hear them read, to teach and preach them to others.*
4. *One should always be ready to accept truth and renounce un-truth.*
5. *All actions ought to be done conformably to virtue, i.e. after a thorough consideration of right or wrong.*
6. *The primary object of the Samaj is to do good to the world by improving the physical, spiritual, and social conditions of mankind.*
7. *All ought to be treated with love, justice, and due regard to their merits.*
8. *Ignorance ought to be dispelled and knowledge diffused.*
9. *No one ought to be contented with his own good alone, but everyone ought to regard his prosperity as included in that of others.*
10. *In matters which affect the general social well-being of the whole society, one ought to discard all differences and not allow one's individuality to interfere, but in strictly personal matters everyone may act with freedom.*[3]

Their Sunday morning service had more affinity with a Protestant service with the singing of hymns, prayer, and a sermon, than it had with Vedic sacrificial worship. While certain of the laws of Manu were enjoined, child marriage was prohibited, although virgin widows and widowers were permitted to marry.

The Arya Samaj was strongly organized, and developed an anti-foreign policy which led to the institution of the ceremony of *Shud-dhi* for reclaiming those who left Hinduism and were later reconverted and purified. The Arya Samaj has been militantly anti-Christian. It felt that having withstood the Muslims for hundreds of years, it could also withstand the Christian attack on their ancient religion.

Ramakrishna
Movement

While the Ramakrishna movement established a tradition of social work and education, the man chiefly responsible for it was more of a contemplative than an activist. Gadadhar Chatterji (1836–1886) is known by the name he took as a sannyasin, Ramakrishna, or some-times by his title Paramahamsa, which means "the highest swan." Unable to read or write, he could not be considered a scholar even though he showed considerable grasp of certain aspects of Indian philosophy and tradition. His only sayings have been collected and

3. Ibid., p. 120.

Dakshineshwar Temple. (Photo by Robert D. Baird.)

published by a follower in the volume *The Gospel of Sri Rama-krishna.* Ramakrishna was not responsible for the formation of the Ramakrishna Mission or the Order instituted by his successor Vive-kananda.

To try to synthesize the thought of Ramakrishna would not only be difficult, but would also miss the real thrust of his life. He placed more stock in intuition than in intellect. Those who emphasize the latter are like men who go to an orchard and, instead of eating the mangoes, speculate about the number of branches on each tree and the number of leaves on each branch.

As early as the age of six, Ramakrishna was prone to mystic visions. At the age of seventeen he went to live with his brother who was the priest at the new temple at Dakshineshwar, north of Calcutta. Upon the death of his brother he became the priest, and spent considerable time in loving devotion to the goddess Kali. Ramakrishna is said to have been examined by a physician while in a trance, and no trace of pulse or heartbeat could be discerned.

Ramakrishna seems to have had a passion for as wide a variety of religious experiences as possible. He submitted to the disciplines of Tantra, and practiced *bhakti* by approaching God as parent, master, friend, child, and sweetheart. He devoted himself to Rama by playing the part of Hanuman even to the extent of climbing a tree, and, according to his devoted followers, growing the stub of a tail. Ramakrishna was initiated into *advaita* by Totapura, and in a surprisingly short time is said to have achieved *Nirvikalpa Samadhi,* the highest *advaita* experience.

Having practiced Muslim rites for a short time he also had visions of Jesus, and a picture of the Madonna with child once sent him into ecstacy. These experiences led him and his followers to conclude that they had ample proof of the basic unity of all religions.

Since Ramakrishna had all these mystical experiences, he was able to testify that they were not essentially different. Various religions and opinions are just so many streams which eventually merge into the same ocean. Ramakrishna used imagery and analogy to express himself rather than technical philosophical terminology. He did not see any point in making a great distinction between transpersonal Brahman and the personal God. No ultimate difference exists—any more than can be found between a diamond and its luster. If one has an instrument with seven holes, why should he always play a monotone? The entire throng of worshipers, whether Christians, Vaishnavas, Muslims, or Shaktas, are seeking the same God through different ways. As Ramakrishna put it, "You may eat your cake with icing either straight or sideways, it will taste sweet either way." [4]

In spite of the fact that some of Ramakrishna's actions might be considered irregular, those who came to know him were usually impressed. In his early years his family was concerned about his stability and encouraged his marriage in the hope that he might come down to earth from his mystic flights. Later Ramakrishna's wife joined him in a common spiritual quest, but they did not live together as husband and wife.

It was left to his disciple Narendranath Datta (1862–1902) to proclaim Ramakrishna's message literally around the world, to organize the movement, and to attach the social dimension by which the movement has been identified. Known as Vivekananda, Narendranath Datta was educated at Presidency College where he was exposed to Western education. At the time he met Ramakrishna, he was passing through an acute crisis of skepticism. He had read approvingly the works of J. S. Mill, Hume, and Herbert Spencer. He was impressed with Ramakrishna, and his own crisis coupled with poverty and the death of his father led him to attach himself to the Master.

After the teacher's death, Vivekananda gathered some disciples into a brotherhood in Banaras. Becoming a sannyasin, he wandered throughout India. In 1893 he came to Chicago for the World Parliament of Religions. His address there attracted much attention and he was heralded in the American and Indian press. Returning to India in 1897, he was enthusiastically received as he landed in Ceylon and traveled up the eastern coast of India. In 1897 he organized the Ramakrishna Mission and, one year later, the Belur Math where the Ramakrishna monks still reside.

While the Arya Samaj and the Brahma Samaj have dwindled in influence, the Ramakrishna Mission continues to contribute significantly to Indian life. The headquarters of the Mission are at Belur, north of Calcutta, and in other Indian cities there are Missions which have an organizational tie to the central headquarters. The movement has a press and publishes numerous books on Indian religion and culture.

4. Swami Nikhilananda, trans., *The Gospel of Sri Ramakrishna,* 4th ed., Madras, Sri Ramakrishna Math, 1964, p. 590.

Vivekananda considered himself an *advaitin*, but attempted to make his position understandable beyond academic circles. He preceded Radhakrishnan in arguing that to say that the world is *maya* is not an outright rejection of the universe nor is it equivalent to saying that the world does not exist. To designate the world as *maya* is not to say that it is illusion, but merely to indicate its relative reality. *Maya* indicates that the world is full of contradictions and, to that extent, can be considered unreal or illusory. But it is through *maya* that we come to the realization of Reality. Hence *advaita* does not imply inactivity or an attempt to escape from the world, but proposes to use the world as a means of transcending it.

Once it is emphasized that *maya* does not mean that the world is nonexistent, the qualified reality of the world is in turn emphasized in order to make room for social concern and activity. "The man who says that he will work when the world has become all good and then he will enjoy bliss, is as likely to succeed as the man who sits beside the Ganga and says, 'I will ford the river when all the water has run into the ocean.' " [5]

While he held a place for *jnanayoga* (the way of knowledge), and although this experience transcended reason, Vivekananda also held that no genuine inspiration contradicts reason. Inspiration sees things in flashes and is higher than reason, yet one must be on guard to distinguish inspiration from mere intellect or even deception. Vivekananda was particularly cautious with regard to occultism and mysticism, but he had no doubts about the authenticity of Ramakrishna.

Like many of those thinkers who have been characterized as "neo-advaitin," Vivekananda put considerable stock in science. Although he spoke out against Western materialism, he read in the sciences and not infrequently used scientific analogies to clarify and add weight to *advaita*. Vivekananda nevertheless did maintain the distinction to be taken up by Radhakrishnan, that India's role had been to stress the spirit while the West had concentrated on unraveling the forces of nature. He felt that nationalistic expressions of his day which attempted to lay the blame for India's ills at the door of religion were misplaced. India could not survive without religion since it had always been integrated with her destiny.

While an ardent defender of Vedanta, Vivekananda was not beyond attacking certain practices that he held were irrational or sentimental. He felt that it was sometimes necessary to abandon custom. There were certain ideas about food that he ridiculed. As for bathing ritual, if its merits were to be accepted we should expect a fish to reach Heaven before anyone else, since it bathes all the time.[6]

Vivekananda's *advaita* did not lead to inactive meditation, but was a call to action. He did not see knowledge, devotion, or action as three paths leading in different directions but as complements rein-

5. *Selections from Swami Vivekananda*, Calcutta, Advaita Ashrama, 1963, p. 146.

6. Cf. Naravane, op. cit., p. 101.

forcing each other. He placed stress on practical work, for liberation was never an escape from the world. The critics of *advaita* had contended that by declaring Brahman to be the sole Reality, a devaluation of human life had resulted. On the contrary, Vivekananda held that if man is identical with God he should seek to abolish the indignities of the world. "Religion is the manifestation of the Divinity already in man." [7]

Using Shankara's ultimate level in support of action on the relative level poses a difficulty, since ultimately such distinctions as "the world" do not exist. But a shift in emphasis has taken place coupled with a reinterpretation of the *advaitin* position. Vivekananda has attempted to make room for social concern and the dignity of the individual which is so commonly affirmed in the twentieth century.

Theosophical Society

The Theosophical Society was organized in New York in 1875 by Madame Blavatsky and Colonel Olcott. The latter was elected the first president and the former the corresponding secretary. In 1907, at the death of Colonel Olcott, Annie Besant became president.

In 1879 the founders moved their society to India, reportedly on orders from their Masters in Tibet, from which source Madame Blavatsky claimed to have received her first religious instructions. The Society was active in counteracting the work of Christian missionaries by emphasizing the long and valuable heritage of Indian culture and religion. In 1882 the headquarters were moved from Bombay to Adyar just outside Madras, where a spacious center is maintained today.

The Theosophical Society was consistently involved with the occult and miraculous. Followers believe that their leaders possess miraculous powers including the ability to produce material objects out of nothing. Attempts to expose these claims have been made, and while outsiders feel the exposition reasonably sure, devotees remain unconvinced.

Although Annie Besant was of English descent, she endeared herself to the Indians by proclaiming that India was her true land, because she lived a previous existence there. Mrs. Besant assumed Indian dress, sat cross-legged on the floor, and ate with the right hand in Indian style rather than with a knife and fork. She stirred Indians to maintain their Hinduism, and at the time when Hinduism was under attack from many sources, such encouragement from a Westerner was impressive to Indian ears.

Make no mistake. Without Hinduism India has no future. Hinduism is the soil into which India's roots are struck, and torn out of that she will inevitably wither, as a tree torn out of its place. Many are the religions and many are the races which are flourishing in India, but none of them stretches back into the far dawn of her past, nor is necessary for her endurance as a nation. Every one

7. *The Complete Works of Swami Vivekananda,* Calcutta, Advaita Ashrama, 1962, 8th ed., vol. IV, p. 358.

might pass away as they came, and India would still remain. But let Hinduism vanish, and what is she? A "geographical expression" of the past, a dim memory of her perished glory. Her history, her literature, her art, her monuments, all have Hinduism written across them. Zoroastrianism came for refuge and her sons have found asylum and welcome in India; but Zoroastrianism might pass, and India would remain. Buddhism was founded here, but Buddhism has disappeared and India remains. Islam came, a wave of conquest, and the Mussalmans form a part of the Indian people, and will share in the making of the future; yet Islam might pass, and India would remain. Christianity has come, and Christians rule the land and influence its steps; yet Christianity might pass and India would remain. India lived before their coming; India could live after their passing. But let Hinduism go, Hinduism that was India's cradle, and in that passing would be India's grave. Then would India with India's religion be but a memory, as are Egypt and Egypt's religion now. India would remain then as a subject for the antiquarian, the archaeologist, a corpse for dissection, but no longer an object of patriotism, no longer a Nation.[8]

Mrs. Besant started Central Hindu College which later became the nucleus of the present Banaras Hindu University. Although her political activities and her increased emphasis on the occult and clairvoyance lowered her esteem in Indian eyes, she is more remembered for her positive work in what D. S. Sarma has called the "renaissance of Hinduism." In 1943 a statue of Mrs. Besant was unveiled in the Madras Marina.

According to Theosophy, the Absolute emanates souls from within Itself. These souls or monads are of the same divine nature as the Absolute and therefore partake of *sat* (being), *cit* (intelligence), and *ananda* (bliss). In their present state the souls are dormant and unaware of their own potential and true nature. But they descend into matter (mineral, vegetable, and finally animal) and through a series of rebirths gain experience of themselves whereby they come to the level of "individualization." After individuation, at which point conscious evolution begins, the soul is no longer born into animal states since "no experience useful for the growth of the soul can be obtained through the small and primitive brains of animals."[9]

At the point of individuation, karma is operative. Karma means that when one does what is good and right, conditions result which aid in the soul's progressive realization and unfolding. Actions contrary to the divine will create conditions which thwart such progress. Karma is never punishment, but merely a means of learning what we are capable of becoming.

The purpose of rebirth is to provide the soul with all the experi-

8. "Address to Students at Central Hindu College," quoted in D. S. Sarma, *Hinduism Through the Ages,* Bombay, Bharatiya Vidya Bhavan, 1967, pp. 113–114.

9. C. Jinarajadasa, "What Theosophists Believe," in H. Bhattacharya, ed., *The Cultural Heritage of India,* Calcutta, The Ramakrishna Mission Institute of Culture, 1956, vol. IV, p. 642.

ences which will enable it to unfold its true nature. Once individuation is reached, one is born as male and female, and into various races and cultures. As one commits blunders by testing the Divine Law the soul gains illumination.

The goal of liberation (*moksha, Nirvana,* salvation) is not an escape from suffering nor is it the end of individual existence. In liberation, however, the soul is freed from all ignorance which surrounds it. Then rebirth is no longer necessary, but the soul continues to grow as it "becomes a larger embodiment of the wonders of Divinity." [10] Such beings participate in what is called "The Divine Plan."

Theosophy believes that there are *adepts* who are agents of the evolutionary process and who work under divine guidance for the benefit of man. The adepts are perfected men and they work together to assist in bringing about the divine evolutionary process ("The Divine Plan") in which souls progressively come to realize their true natures. The adepts are part of an organization called the "Great Hierarchy."

> *They form an organization called the Great Hierarchy or the Great White Brotherhood. They are not all of equal capacity, because some achieved liberation ages ago and others but recently, and therefore the former have a longer record of work and experience. But all of them are united by one will, which is to serve the plan of God for men. They are the flowers of the evolutionary process, since their consciousness is all the time in intimate communion with that of the Divinity.*[11]

These beings supervise all the processes of nature which we have become accustomed to call laws. They guide the origin and migration of races and provide men with great religious founders when it seems most beneficial. The universe, then, is in a process of unfolding the potential of the souls of men. Things are moving in a generally favorable direction. Life takes on an optimistic hue.

All religions are considered of value because they are derived from one source. Each religion thus fulfills a role in providing the transmigrating soul with a fullness of experience. Religiously, *bhakti,* yogic meditation, the example of Jesus, and the words of Muhammad are all divinely ordained means for the soul's progress to freedom.

The Theosophical Society headquarters has on its grounds a Catholic chapel as well as a Buddhist temple. People of all faiths are welcome and their library contains books from all religious traditions. With walled plaques symbolizing Christianity, Islam, Buddhism, Hinduism, and Judaism, the movement presents itself as taking the best of all faiths.

MODERN INDIAN THINKERS

In the nineteenth and twentieth centuries there emerged certain important Indian religious thinkers who cannot be dealt with in terms

10. Ibid., p. 644.
11. Ibid., p. 645.

of any particular institutional expression of religion. These thinkers represent an attempt to bridge the gap between technical philosophy and actual life and to place more emphasis on the relevance of religion for affirming the present existence rather than as a method for escaping from it.

A Bengali by birth, Rabindranath was raised in a home that was steeped in the Upanishads and the Vaishnava tradition. His father was Devendranath, whose Brahma Samaj attempted to reform Indian religion. While holding membership in the Adi Brahma Samaj and being an honorary member of the Sadharan Samaj, Rabindranath could not be contained in such organizations.

Rabindranath Tagore (1861–1941)

He was first a poet, the recipient of a Nobel Prize, and had an artistic view of the universe. Without degrading reason, he was more interested in apprehending the overarching harmony of a fluid universe.

> *My religion is essentially a poet's religion. Its touch comes to me through the same unseen and trackless channels as does the inspiration of my music. My religious life has followed the same mysterious lines of growth as my poetic life. Somehow they are wedded to each other.*[12]

Since he believed that truth lies primarily in relatedness, in seeing the harmony of apparently contrary forces, Tagore did not see the necessity of constructing a logically coherent philosophical system.

Tagore liked to see himself in the role of a reconciler of East and West. The historical influences upon him make this intention easily understandable. He often quotes from the Upanishads which had so deeply impressed his father. While the Upanishads were influential in Tagore's thought, he was inclined to interpret them theistically. Moreover, he felt there was in the Upanishads a positive element which enabled him to hold a decidedly affirmative view of life. Tagore's theistic leanings were probably due more to his Vaishnava upbringing than to any contact with Christians. His artistic nature made him more amenable to the *bhakti* ideal of devotion to God than to the *advaita* ideal of *Nirvikalpa Samadhi*. Since he held a complementary view of the world, he never felt compelled to reject Shankara's *advaita*. The influence of the Buddha as a force for cultural unity in Asia impressed him, but the Mahayana ideal of compassion touched him more than the less active ideal proposed in the Pali Canon.

Tagore was influenced by such Western thinkers as Benedetto Croce, Henri Bergson, Bertrand Russell, Albert Schweitzer, and John Dewey. As with other modern Indian thinkers, Tagore felt that science was Europe's greatest gift to humanity. He also emphasized that Christianity was originally an Asiatic religion. His thought was formed in an India where religious, cultural, and social changes

12. "The Religion of an Artist," in S. Radhakrishnan and J. H. Muirhead, eds., *Contemporary Indian Philosophy*, London, Allen & Unwin, 1936, p. 32.

were in process. His birth and privileged position enabled him to keep abreast of all such changes.

Tagore saw the universe through a universal principle of harmony and balance. God was a primary fact of experience and not a Being whose existence had to be proved. While Tagore's statements vacillated between theism and *advaita,* he seems to have emphasized the personalistic dimension. A personal God was not finite, nor did such a designation bring God down to man's level. While it did not exhaust the nature of God to speak of him as personal, it was the highest thing one could say about him.

Man is as real as God. Unwilling to side either with the *advaitins* or pluralists, Tagore held that the many are real without the organic unity of the whole being destroyed. While the one and the many are both real, it is impossible to explain how they are related. The doctrine of *maya* does not mean that the world is nonexistent, but points to the false belief that the world is independently real. Man, God, and the world find their reality in the harmonious interrelatedness of the three.

Tagore's joy came not by withdrawal from the world but in the discovery of the divine in nature and man. The universe was a symphony. The conviction that the universe was a creation of joy reinforced his certainty that God is love. Tagore could not accept the ideal of renunciation that had been so influential in India. For him escape from the world meant escape from God. He held that all work should be dedicated to God but the homeless mendicant was a denial of the God who created the world. "Deliverance is not for me in renunciation. . . . I will never shut the doors of my senses. The delights of sight and hearing and touch will bear thy delight." [13] Freedom does not come into being as the result of the cessation of action, but is achieved in action, just as joy is expressed through law.

Even death was seen affirmatively as God's messenger and the friend of man.

> Just as a child cries out when taken by its mother from her right breast but is immediately consoled when she puts it to her left breast, so death is nothing but a change in the arms of God.[14]

Tagore's stance might well be an aesthetic type of religion.

Mohandas Karamchand Gandhi (1869–1948)

Born into a Vaishya Vaishnava family in Kathiawad, Gandhi was married at the age of thirteen. He was permitted to sail across the sea to study law in England only after promising his mother than he would abstain from wine, meat, and women during his stay abroad. He returned to India in 1891 and then sailed to South Africa in 1893 where he struggled for the rights of Indians who were serving as indentured servants. In 1914 Gandhi entered the Indian political arena under Gokhale. At Gokhale's death, Gandhi was thrust into positions of leadership which culminated in the independence of India in Au-

13. Quoted in A. C. Underwood, *Contemporary Thought of India,* New York, Knopf, 1931, p. 173.
14. Ibid., p. 175.

gust 1947, and his assassination at the hand of a Hindu fanatic in January 1948.

Having grown to despise Western materialism, Gandhi wanted more than self-rule (swaraj). He wanted a revision of the social order so that the technological advances which crushed the spirituality of Europe would not do so to India. Gandhi feared that the victory of mechanized civilization would mean the death of spiritual values.

> All modern machinery is of the devil. It enslaves those who use it. All India requires is her plough and spinning-wheel (charka), for on them her ancient prosperity was founded. It is curious to notice that Western medical science comes under the Mahatma's condemnation. It is materialistic, whereas according to Mr. Gandhi "disease is the result of our thoughts as much as our acts." [15]

Gandhi retained a belief in transmigration and karma, placed an emphasis on the ascetic ideal, permitted worship of images as a means of religious concentration, taught sexual abstinence as a means to spiritual perfection, visited Hindu temples, taught the sanctity of the cow, and recognized the caste system. Through these beliefs Gandhi made contact with the Indian masses. Wavering at one time between Christianity and Hinduism, he came to consider himself a Hindu. Nevertheless, the Sermon on the Mount exerted considerable influence on him as did the Bhagavad Gita.

Ahimsa was a doctrine which led the Jainas to practice vegetarianism, among other things. While the term means noninjury, Gandhi gave it an additional meaning. He saw it not merely as a state of harmlessness, but as a positive state of love in which one did good even to the evildoer.

> Literally speaking, ahimsā means non-killing. But to me it has a world of meaning and takes me into realms much higher, infinitely higher, than the realm to which I would go, if I merely understood by ahimsā, non-killing. Ahimsā really means that you may not offend anybody, you may not harbour an uncharitable thought even in connection with one who may consider himself to be your enemy. If we return blow for blow, we depart from the doctrine of ahimsā. But I go further. If we resent a friend's action or so-called enemy's action, we still fall short of this doctrine. But when I say, we should not resent, I do not say that we should acquiesce: but by resenting I mean wishing that some harm should be done to the enemy, or that he should be put out of our way, not even by any action of ours, but by the action of someone else, or say, Divine Agency. If we harbour even this thought we depart from the doctrine of ahimsā.[16]

The term satyagraha (holding on to truth) was used by Gandhi in his South African campaign to describe the nonviolent agitation he was pursuing. While he could use this method for all nonviolent ac-

15. Ibid., p. 180.
16. "Address to the Y.M.C.A.," quoted in J. Neuner, ed., Religious Hinduism, Allahabad, St. Paul Publications, 1964, p. 298.

tion, it came to be associated with struggle in the political realm. Hence *satyagraha* stood for the struggle against what was considered an unjust law or regime through noncooperation and civil disobedience. Noncooperation meant the refusal to participate in the working of an unjust system and might involve boycott of schools, colleges, or government jobs. It implied for Gandhi, however, a "readiness to cooperate on the slightest pretext with the worst of one's opponents." [17] Civil disobedience is the breaking of an unjust law remaining ready to suffer the consequences. It involved going to jail, and Gandhi served some eight terms there himself.

The violation of law, however, is not to become contempt for law. Fasting was the ultimate weapon and was not to be used lightly. A fast should proceed in a religious spirit, never against an enemy, but against a "loved one." The object of such action is not to extract rights but to reform the individual or individuals involved. *Satyagraha* is not for the weak but for the strong. Resistance it is, but it must be nonviolent since the goal is dissolution of antagonisms, not antagonists. Nevertheless, if the choice were between violence and cowardice, Gandhi would choose violence. *Satyagraha,* if fully nonviolent, however, will infallibly be effective. While it may be difficult and even result in the loss of lives, no oppressors, regardless of their violence and ruthlessness, are beyond the reach of suffering love. The value of such suffering love Gandhi learned from Tolstoi.

Gandhi formed an Ashram near Ahmedabad and those who joined took eleven vows. Among these was the vow of *Brahmacarya*. Gandhi held that marriage was a barrier to the practice of *satyagraha* since husband and wife lavish on each other the love that they should devote to the world. Gandhi himself practiced married *brahmacarya,* or restraint in the married life. He insisted that the only legitimate means of birth control was self-control. He also held that man should work on a progressive reduction of his needs. To save what is not immediately needed is paramount to theft in the light of the starvation of others. In his diary he wrote: "Not to accumulate things not necessary for the day." He also taught the principle of *swadesi* by which only things produced in the immediate neighborhood would be used, thus explaining his use of homespun *khadar.*

Although he wore a political guise, Gandhi held that he was a religious man at heart. Hence the ultimate goal of *satyagraha* was *moksha.* But the immediate goal was *swaraj* (self-rule), which meant a complete social revolution. It meant political and economic decentralization whereby the state would give way to an enlightened anarchy in which everyone would be his own ruler. Being realistic enough to see the difficulty in this state, Gandhi held that the best government was the one which governed least. He envisaged a series of self-governing, self-sufficient villages, supported by cottage industries.

While he did not argue for the abolition of caste, he fought for the elimination of untouchability, calling such people *Harijans* (People of God). He identified with them, and also with widows whose plight he tried to alleviate.

17. Quoted in Neuner, op. cit., p. 299.

Aurobindo was born into a Calcutta Brahman family much enamored with English education. To assure a minimum of contact with Indians, Aurobindo was sent to a convent school in Darjeeling at the age of five and to England at the age of seven. His education there included English literature and the Western languages, classical and modern. Fourteen years later, in 1893, he returned to India. There he served as a revenue officer, and as a professor and later Vice Principal of Baroda College until 1906. During this time, Aurobindo acquired a knowledge of Sanskrit, Indian culture, and the religious classics. He was influential in the nationalist movement, preaching nonviolence as an expedient. In 1908 while in prison as a consequence of his political activism, he received a vision of Krishna which led him, in 1910, to found an ashram at Pondicherry where he lived until his death on December 5, 1950. The ashram continues under the leadership of Mira Richard. Aurobindo's prison vision was described as follows.

> I looked at the jail that secluded me from men and it was no longer by its high walls that I was imprisoned; no, it was Vasudeva who surrounded me. I walked under the branches of the tree in front of my cell but it was not the tree, I know it was Vasudeva, it was Sri Krishna whom I saw standing there and holding over me his shade. I looked at the bars of my cell, the very grating that did duty for a door and again I saw Vasudeva. It was Narayana who was guarding and standing sentry over me. Or I lay on the coarse blankets that were given me for a couch and felt the arms of Sri Krishna around me, the arms of my Friend and Lover. . . . I looked at the prisoners in the hall, the thieves, the murderers, the swindlers, and as I looked at them I saw Vasudeva, it was Narayana whom I found in these darkened souls and misused bodies.[18]

Aurobindo's publications were voluminous and he also started a weekly magazine called *Arya* which aimed at "a systematic study of the highest problems of existence, and the formulation of a vast synthesis of knowledge, harmonizing the diverse religious traditions of humanity, occidental as well as oriental." [19] After 1926 Aurobindo was in seclusion and his contact with the outer world was through the Mother who virtually ran the Ashram.

His most widely known work, *The Life Divine,* contains a rather lengthy account of his philosophy. His thought is a reinterpretation of certain traditional themes in the light of modern thought (Western and Eastern). A coherence is supplied by the joint concepts of "involution" and "evolution." While Aurobindo is most interested in evolution and in the possible developments for humanity in the future, he believes that no evolution is possible without previous involution. Involution refers to the divine descent even to the world of matter. The utterly transcendent Eternal Spirit is beyond all description but it nevertheless descends into the lower realms of being

Sri Aurobindo Ghose
(1872–1950)

18. Quoted in Herbert Jai Singh, *Sri Aurobindo: His Life and Religious Thought,* Bangalore, Christian Institute for the Study of Religion and Society, 1962, p. 4.
19. Ibid., p. 5.

and then by evolution ascends until it returns to its source. In this descent the "Supermind" is the transition from the original unity to the multiplicity of the phenomenal world. The "Supermind" stands between the Supreme where there are no distinctions and the human Mind which is responsible for all the distinctions and mutations in existence.

Matter, the lowest level of being, is virtually devoid of consciousness, yet it is not merely what it appears to be, but is a low form of the Supreme. The characteristic stage of evolution reached by humans is Mind, which is preparatory to "Supermind." The Mind, however, interprets the truth of universal existence for practical purposes and since it is a fall from the Supermind, its salvation lies in returning to its original state.

The doctrine of karma points to the means whereby the soul grows through rebirth and the evolutionary process, rather than a series of rebirths where penalties from previous existences are experienced. The determining factor in the spiritual evolutionary process is not the law of karma, but the Spirit, which uses karma for its progressive upward development.

The doctrine of the resurrection of the body is rejected since death implies, in the evolutionary scheme, that the soul has outgrown the present body. Such a view is a divination of the present life rather than an escape from it. For Aurobindo the doctrine of *maya* does not teach that the world is illusion, but refers to the power of differentiation which gives form and shape to all phenomenal existence as it arises out of the indivisible unity of Brahman. Through the agency of *maya,* the world of the One becomes the world of the many. Hence the phenomena are not unreal, but the substantial form of Truth.

The practice of yoga is a method for awakening the potentiality for self-perfection which is latent in man. Yoga is not occult, but merely the intensification of Nature's ways for the perfection of man. The Yogi need not renounce the world. Hathayoga may perfect the body, but neglects the social sphere. Rajayoga aims at perfecting the senses, emotions, the mind, but puts too much emphasis on abnormal trances. The purpose of yoga should be to make the "spiritual life and its experiences fully active and fully utilizable in the waking state and even in the normal use of the functions." [20] Integral Yoga is the synthesis of all other yogas and aims at the divinization of the total life of man. This involves three steps: (1) surrendering oneself completely into God's hands; (2) watching with detachment the working of the divine in one's life—that is, the recognition that one's progress is not due to personal efforts, but to the Shakti working within; and (3) seeing the divine vision of the personal deity in everything. God's power manifests itself in the human life and man realizes that a "great power, not of our own, is thinking for us, feeling for us, acting for us, and that our heart and mind are being moved and motivated by it rather than ourselves." [21]

20. Ibid., p. 30.
21. Ibid., p. 32.

Historically, evolution proceeded from matter up to the present state of Mind. But a thin veil separates Mind from Supermind, and when that veil is removed, through the descent of the one the ascent of the other is achieved. Thus a higher level of humanity is attained whereby a newly constituted gnostic being is created who will be involved in action but indifferent to its fruits. The life of such a one is not governed by external laws but by the Divine Life within. This higher level of humanity will begin when groups of gnostic beings grow in different parts of the world. The number of such gnostic communities will gradually increase until humanity itself reaches a new level of human existence. The ashram at Pondicherry is a place where men and women of differing cultures live together to achieve that gnostic experience which Aurobindo envisaged.

While Aurobindo passed from a politically active life to the seclusion of the ashram at Pondicherry, Radhakrishnan moved from a position as professor of philosophy to President of India. A professional philosopher, and a defender of Hinduism, he was also concerned with showing that the Hinduism he defended was relevant to social and international problems. Radhakrishnan left his imprint upon the social, educational, and cultural development of his country. While holding that all religions are merely manifestations of *Sanatana Dharma* or eternal religion, he nevertheless leveled cogent attacks on phenomenal Christianity in the formulation of his staunch defense of Hinduism.

Sarvepalli
Radhakrishnan
(1888–   )

Born into a Telegu Brahman family, his traditional manner of life was challenged by the education he received in Christian missionary institutions such as Madras Christian College from which he graduated. Radhakrishnan has attempted to go back to the sources of his tradition (he has published books on the principal Upanishads, the *Bhagavad Gita,* and the *Brahma Sutra*) and to construct on such interpretations a Hinduism that will be relevant in a period that evidences pressing social and political problems. That he held a post at Oxford University and is the subject of one volume of the Library of Living Philosophers gives evidence that his intellectual stature has been recognized outside his native land.

Radhakrishnan has been sensitive to criticisms of Vedanta which characterize it as an attitude of world and life negation. Albert Schweitzer developed such an interpretation in his *Indian Thought and Its Development.* Radhakrishnan argues that such an oversimplification does not do justice to the complexity of Indian thought and practice.

Radhakrishnan's defense of "Hinduism" is closely connected with his interpretation and defense of Shankara. He argues that for Shankara, the doctrine of *maya* is not to be construed as illusionism nor is it to mean that the world is unreal. Ultimate Reality, or Brahman, is unitary to be sure, but Shankara accords the world and the phenomenal self a relative reality. The world is not independently real, but it is derived being. To point to the temporal character of the world is not to say it is unreal or that it has no meaning or significance.

Part of the concern to give meaning to the world and human activity is seen in Radhakrishnan's understanding of karma. Karma should not be interpreted pessimistically or deterministically. Karma has a past and a future. The past cannot be changed and while it affects man's present possibilities, it does not determine the future. Man remains free to act within the limits imposed by the past.

Life is like a game of bridge. The cards in the game are given to us. We do not select them. They are traced to past karma *but we are free to make any call as we think fit and lead any suit. Only we are limited by the rules of the game.*[22]

In addition to the interpretation of karma and *maya*, Radhakrishnan is able to emphasize certain other aspects of Indian thought and practice that give emphasis to meaningful activity in the world. There are the four aims of life: *artha* (material well-being), *kama* (normal use of the appetites and desires of man), *dharma* (duty of performing one's appointed place in the nature of things), and *moksha* (final liberation). Furthermore, there are four traditional stages in life through which one should go, which are an ever-present ideal even if not universally followed. The stage of the student is a time when one acquires the discipline of spiritual wisdom under the tutelage of a teacher. As a householder, a man is responsible for the continuity of the family. Radhakrishnan argues that the unmarried life was not an Indian ideal. The third stage of the forest dweller involves retiring from active life for meditation, but only after one's children are settled and one's social responsibilities are fulfilled. The sannyasin is the final stage where one has renounced all. But a sannyasin, says Radhakrishnan, is in the world and remains there without attachment. Thus we see that the four stages include a social orientation and concern for this world. Only at the end of life, after fulfilling all social obligations, does one retreat to the forest for spiritual realization.

The social system that Hinduism has devised also emphasizes its concern for the world. The caste system has been criticized by Westerners and Indians alike. Radhakrishnan rejects the numerous subcastes, and the rigid proscriptions against intermarriage and interdining, and the definition of caste by birth. He does this by distinguishing between class and caste. The caste spirit must go and mobility between classes must be allowed. The organization of society into four main classes of people according to their qualities (*gunas*) rather than according to birth is desirable. This social order is not only valid for Indians but has universal significance, because mankind is, in fact, divided by nature into four types. There are men of learning and wisdom (Brahmans), men of administrative ability (Kshatriyas) with heroic determination to carry out in the political realm the principles of the thinkers, men who engage in commerce and trade (Vaishyas) without whom society would collapse, and men whose contribution to society is manual labor and service (Shu-

22. S. Radhakrishnan, *An Idealist View of Life,* London, G. Allen, 1961, first pub. 1932, p. 279.

dras). Radhakrishnan sees no justification for the existence of out-castes. His system, however, is a spiritual democracy which enables men of equal capacities to work side by side rather than to be matched with unequals. The purpose of this arrangement is not to guarantee rights, but to clarify responsibilities and opportunities.

Radhakrishnan would stress unity rather than diversity. He speaks of Hindu unity, or Indian unity, sometimes of Asian unity, but most often of religious unity. He aligns himself with Ramakrishna and Vivekananda in holding that the different religions are only aspects of one eternal religion, *Sanatana Dharma*. But *Sanatana Dharma* turns out to be something closely related to Vedanta, even though it is thought to be the religion underlying all religions.

Pakistan, a state which was created in 1947 by the partition of India, later proclaimed itself an Islamic state, and in its 1956 Constitution required the head of the state to be a Muslim and required that laws enacted not be repugnant to the *Qur'an*. Burma, which was a province of India until 1937, declared itself a Buddhist state in 1961. India, however, has proclaimed herself a secular state, which has had implications for the religion of its citizens. Nevertheless, in spite of the avowed separation of religion from governmental control, the secular state has enacted laws which have had an effect on religious change. Some of the changes preceded India's independence in 1947, but instances of laws effecting religious change have increased since that time.

LAW AND
RELIGIOUS REFORM

The ease with which Indians committed to a secular state depend on legislation to settle religious questions can be traced to several factors. First, it has been part of the past tradition in India for the king to promote religion by building pagodas or temples, and by maintaining the clerical class. This was true of the so-called Hindu kings, Buddhist monarchs, or Muslim rulers. Hence such state involvement is in keeping with traditional Indian conceptions and practices. In terms of the four classes, the Kshatriyas were to rule in keeping with the spiritual principles enunciated by the Brahmans.

Second, Indian religions have not had rigid ecclesiastical organizations. This is particularly true of the conglomeration of temples, orders, rites, and rituals that are sometimes classified as Hindu. Since the organizational structure for effective reform and ordered change do not exist as part of the religious entity, it is necessary for the state to step in and fill the void. Not infrequently this is welcomed by those involved. Buddhist monarchs were often responsible for the reform of the Sangha.

Third, there is the secularization of law. In the traditional sense, Hinduism and Islam saw personal law and social structure as an extension of religion, or better still, the distinction between religion and these dimensions is itself the result of secularization. Today, not only is there no unified personal Hindu law, but different laws for Muslims exist as well. Hence, Hindus, Buddhists, Christians, and Muslims are governed by different legal standards regarding marriage and divorce. One of the present goals is to arrive at a unified personal law for all Indians. But such an achievement means the secularization of law and the restriction of religion to the more personal sphere. This amounts to a redefinition of religion and is also a factor in the relationship of law to religious change.

Cases will now be considered where legislation has resulted in the suppression of practices previously considered religious, cases where legislation has regulated religious practices, and finally cases where legislation has directly engaged in reforming religion.

Suppression of Religious Practices

The suppression of certain religious practices deemed undesirable by ruling powers was effected before independence. One of the first cases of this type was the rendering illegal of the practice of *sati* in Bengal presidency in 1829 and in Bombay and Madras in 1830. *Sati,* a word which originally referred to a virtuous and chaste woman, came to refer to the self-immolation of a widow on the funeral pyre of her husband. While the ancient lawgivers considered this a virtuous act, it was not obligatory. In the early nineteenth century, however, there were strong social pressures upon widows to make such a sacrifice. *Sati* was more prevalent in Bengal than elsewhere, and in the early nineteenth century about five hundred cases of *sati* were reported in the Calcutta area each year. The reformer, Ram Mohun Roy, led an attack on the practice of *sati* which gained Indian support. The practice became illegal under Governor General William Bentinck.

Another practice which came under attack was that of sacrificing children to the river Ganges. In fulfillment of religious vows, a child would be cast into the Ganges if a previously barren woman were granted more than one child. In 1802 such acts, though religiously motivated, were declared acts of murder and punishable as such.

Organized bands of *thags* (from which we get "thugs"), in devotion to the goddess Kali, traveled in disguise and murdered their victims by strangulation. Their sanction came from the myth of the great battle between Kali and the all-devouring demon. From every drop of blood that fell, another demon was born, so Kali finally resorted to giving a cloth to two men to strangle the demons. The command to go forth and overcome men by the same method became a religious sanction for these bands of *thags* who terrorized train travel in certain parts of India. During the years 1831–1837, more than three thousand *thags* were apprehended and the organized bands were suppressed at the direction of the Governor General William Bentinck.

In 1950 an act was made in the state of Madras to prohibit the sacrifice of animals in Hindu temples. This piece of legislation is only regional, since the sacrifice of goats is still part of the worship of Kali in Bengal. Animal sacrifice was an integral part of the Vedic religion, but has continued into the modern period mainly with reference to Kali. Other deities are adored through elaborate *puja* ceremonies. Sensitivities were sharpened by the image such sacrifices were creating in the minds of Westerners. In addition, there was ground for dissatisfaction in the doctrine of *ahimsa* which was responsible for spreading the practice of vegetarianism. The debate in the Madras Assembly was over the reason for prohibiting such slaughter rather than the prohibition itself.

In many temples it was the practice to dedicate young girls to the deity and to the service of the temple. They were called *devadasis* (servants of God). These girls danced in the temples and engaged in sacred prostitution. The state of Mysore abolished such dedicatory practices as early as 1909, and Madras followed in 1927. The Madras Act 31 of 1947 goes so far as to eliminate certain practices commonly associated with the *devadasis,* such as dancing in the temple.

> *Dancing by a woman, with or without* kumbhaharathy (*the ceremony of* devadasi *dedication*) *in the precincts of any temple or other religious institution, or in any procession of a Hindu deity, idol or object of worship . . . or at any festival or ceremony . . . is hereby declared unlawful.*[23]

Where governmental legislation has stepped into the religious picture and effected change, it has not always acted to prohibit practice. Frequently the government has regulated religious practices in the interests of the people at large. The Indian Constitution guarantees the freedom to profess, practice, and propagate religion "subject to public order, morality, and health." [24] It is these last qualifications that permit the government to intervene in religious matters when they seem detrimental to the public good.

For both Hindus and Muslims, festivals and processions are important religious expressions. Pilgrimages and festivals attract huge crowds of devotees. In order to minimize the possibility of disease, epidemic, and injury, the government has regulated such events. Every twelve years at the confluence of the Ganges and Jumna rivers in Allahabad, there is a festival which attracts millions of pilgrims. The government has set up officers in charge of this Khumbha Mela with appointed subofficials. In 1954 the police force totaled 2,882 in addition to 250 watchmen. Some 550 additional policemen were attached to the cholera inoculation barriers. Eight hospitals and eight first-aid posts were staffed with seventeen medical officers, three women doctors, twenty nurses, and a host of ward boys, cooks, and stretcher bearers. Sanitary arrangements were covered by forty medical officers of health, nine chief sanitary inspectors, thirty-three sanitary inspectors, and nine hundred and twenty-six provincial armed constabulary men. More than six thousand sweepers were employed. In all, the government spent over 1,700,000 rupees ($360,000). A pilgrim tax was used to defray expenses, and this tax has been extended to other pilgrimage sites as well.

An important part of Muslim faith is the pilgrimage to Mecca which each Muslim should take at least once in a lifetime. Some fifteen thousand Indians make the trek each year. The Indian govern-

Regulation of Religious Practices

23. Quoted in Donald Eugene Smith, *India as a Secular State,* Princeton, N.J., Princeton University Press, 1963, p. 239.

24. Ibid., p. 216.

Bathing at the Ghats, Benaras. (Courtesy of the Government of India Tourist Office.)

ment has taken certain precautions for their protection on this trip. Medical teams are sent by the government to Saudi Arabia to give medical assistance to Indian pilgrims. Pilgrim passes make the obtaining of international passports unnecessary and income tax clearance certificates have become unnecessary for deck class Haj pilgrims. Given the difficulty in getting permission for foreign travel and the care taken in regulating foreign exchange, these concessions are quite significant.

With the crowds and the emotional pitch common at processions in which the deity is carried through the streets of the town, the possibility of riots or injury is always present. If a Hindu procession plays music as it passes a Mosque, or if Muslims include the slaughter of cows, the possibility of violence is further heightened. Donald Eugene Smith relates an interesting incident of this nature and how it was diplomatically resolved.

*A Muslim procession at Benares during the Muharram festival had
to pass under a peepal tree which belonged to a nearby Hindu
temple. A low branch of the tree obstructed the passing of the tazias (wood and paper representations of the tombs of the martyrs
Hasan and Hussain) borne by the procession. Because the peepal
tree is regarded by Hindus as holy, the Muslims were not permitted to cut down the projecting bough. The Hindus accused the
leaders of the procession of having built the tazias bigger than
usual. As the Muslims refused to take the tazias through in a
slanting position, the procession was held up for three hours and
the discussion became heated. With a communal clash imminent,
a resourceful police officer ordered the road under the tree to be
dug to the depth of one foot so that the tazias could pass in an
upright position.*[25]

Indian law has required the licensing of processions which demands an account of the extract course of the procession and the
provision for police accompaniment.

One of the areas in which legislation has effected religious change
through direct reform is in the administration of temples. Many
Hindu temples had accumulated vast wealth in the form of money,
jewels, or land holdings which had been bequeathed by kings or
wealthy devotees. The administration of such temples had been seen
as a function of the state, but in the middle of the nineteenth century the British abandoned such religious involvement. Without governmental supervision, the misappropriation of funds was not un-
common. In the state of Madras, several attempts at legislation led
to the Madras Hindu Religious and Charitable Endowments Act of
1951. This provided for an executive department under a cabinet
minister, and the appointment of three deputy commissioners who
were assigned territorial jurisdictions. Part of the Act reads,

Reform of Religion

> *Subject to the provisions of this act, the administration of all reli-
> gious endowments shall be subject to the general superintend-
> ence and control of the commissioner; . . . the power to pass any
> orders which may be deemed necessary to ensure that endow-
> ments are properly administered and that their income is duly
> appropriated for the purpose for which they were founded or
> exist.*[26]

The commissioners had power to enter the premises of the temples, to dismiss trustees, and even to appoint others in their places.
If convinced that the temple or math was mismanaged, commissioners could take it over completely and appoint their own officer over
it. These commissioners were required to be Hindus. Smith points
out,

> *It is no exaggeration to assert that the commissioner for Hindu
> religious endowments, a public servant of the secular state, today*

25. Ibid., p. 222.
26. Ibid., pp. 245–246.

exercises far greater authority over Hindu religion in Madras state than the archbishop of Canterbury does over the Church of England.[27]

In 1959 an act exempted maths from such control. Sometimes commissioners have directed funds away from religious purposes to more social ends, such as orphanages, hospitals, schools, and even universities. The *Hindu,* a Madras daily, in 1961 wrote:

Existing state legislation governing Hindu endowments has erred on the side of stretching the doctrine of cy pres *to such an extent that surplus resources of temples could be diverted to a variety of purposes, far removed from the intentions of the original donors. Such diversion could have little justification when, as against a few religious institutions with a surplus, there are thousands of others that have not the wherewithal for even the conduct of the daily* pujas, *or still worse, stand desolate or in ruins.*[28]

The central government has also appointed a commission to examine the administration of religious endowments and recommend measures for its improvement. In May 1962 the commission submitted its report which suggested regional legislation in states where such was lacking and reported that it saw no problem in enacting uniform legislation which would cover the administration of religious endowments all over India within all religious communities. The commission also recommended the creation of four Hindu theological colleges where the study of religion and the humanities could be pursued and the level of the Hindu "clergy" could be raised.

Legislation has also reformed religion in the area of caste. This is partially a direct reform, partially a suppression of certain practices and regulation of others, and partially due to the increasing tendency to limit religion to the personal dimension, thereby making the social order the concern of the state.

The discussion of caste usually includes the question of whether caste is inextricably bound up with religion or whether it can be treated as a social matter which would be under the rightful control of a secular state. Much of this discussion is not well-placed if one is asking the role of legislation in the modification of religious practices and beliefs. While reformers might want to separate caste from religion so that they can modify or eliminate aspects of the caste system while claiming they have not touched a religious matter, the fact remains that traditionally, and for many Indians today, religion is understood in terms of caste responsibilities.

It is commonly held that the more than three thousand castes (*jati*) existent in India today are merely subdivisions of the four ancient classes (*varnas*), and that they are predominantly the result of intermarriage among the classes. This "confusion of class" led to the thousands of "subcastes." We do not know exactly how the modern caste system developed, but "it did not develop out of the

27. Ibid., p. 246.
28. Ibid., p. 251.

four Aryan varnas, and the two systems have never been thoroughly harmonized." [29]

The term "caste" is derived from the word *castas* which the Portuguese applied to the social divisions they found when they came to India in the sixteenth century. However, castes developed religious responsibilities and these were perhaps more important than the responsibilities deliniated for the traditional four *varnas.*

> *To the present day the life of the lower orders is much more affected by caste than by varna—it is not being a vaiśya or a śūdra, but being an ahīr, a kayāsth, or a sonār which matters, and corporate feeling is centered around this caste group, whether based on region, race, profession or religion.*[30]

It is well to remember that even the "untouchables" or "scheduled castes" have a complicated hierarchy of divisions. Most such groups believe that there are other "scheduled castes" that are lower than they are on the social scale.

By holding that the numerous castes are only developments from the original four classes (*varnas*), the religious sanction for the *varnas* was used to attribute religious sanction for the thousands of castes as well. In the *Purusha* hymn of the *Rigveda,* the creation of the world was seen as an original sacrifice in which the four "castes" came from the mouth, arms, thighs, and feet of the Creator. In the *Bhagavad Gita,* Lord Krishna is interpreted as assuming responsibility for the "caste" system. The *Laws of Manu,* which are taken as of divine origin, relate laws to the fourfold distinction of the classes. This also was taken as religious sanction for caste. In Manu penalties are determined not only by who commits the crime (for Brahmans the penalty is often less), but also by noting against whom the crime is committed (more serious against a Brahman than a Shudra).

Today many village Indians make no distinction between their caste duties and religious responsibility. Hence the latter extends even to the avoidance of untouchables. As one Harijan puts it,

> *Much of the propaganda against untouchability is wasted. . . . The voice of reason doesn't carry because most Hindus still feel that it is their religious duty to shun the Harijan. For generations this teaching has been drilled into them by mothers and grandmothers.*[31]

Because of this religious sanction, legislation which modifies one's caste duty must be seen as religious reform. The Indian Constitution guarantees equal protection before the law for all citizens. Article 17 abolished untouchability and forbade its practice. Not only does this include a pledge on the part of the government, but it makes untouchability an offense punishable by law even in the case

29. A. L. Basham, *The Wonder That Was India,* New York, Grove Press, Inc., 1959, pp. 149–150.
30. Ibid., p. 149.
31. Quoted in Smith, op. cit., p. 308.

of discriminatory acts of individuals against individuals. There are cases where *dhobis* (washermen) were prosecuted for not washing the clothes of Harijans, and where a barber was prosecuted for refusing to cut the hair of leather workers.

The Untouchability Act of 1955 provides penalties for preventing an individual's access to roads, wells, shops, hotels, hospitals (public), educational institutions, or employment on the grounds of untouchability. Legislation permitting intercaste marriage runs counter to the ancient *Shastras,* and permitting Harijans to enter certain temples violates certain *Agamas.* But the legislation has nevertheless been made, and it has been enforced with varying degrees of consistency. However one evaluates such events—whether from the point of view of the Hindu who feels his religion has been attacked, or from a modern human rights perspective—the fact remains that such legislation has been, is, and will continue to be a means of effecting religious change.

THE GROWTH OF HINDU CONSCIOUSNESS

The terms "Hinduism" and "Hindu," terms which we commonly associate with a system of thought and practice, come from the Sanskrit *sindhu* which means "river" and was applied particularly to the Indus river which, since the partition of India and Pakistan, empties into the Arabian Sea through West Pakistan. The Persian form of the Sanskrit was *hindu* and the Greeks, using forms based on the Persian, omitted the *h* and came up with India. The term India was used for the whole country even though the full geographical expanse was unknown.[32]

Logically, then, the term "Hindu" refers to India, and "Hinduism" could only mean the religion or religions found there. When the term was first used for *a religion,* it was not realized how diverse the religions to be found in India were.

> The term "Hindu" as a religious designation was developed by the Muslims after they had invaded the country in the second millennium A.D. For the Muslims it served to designate these aliens whom they conquered and whose not being Muslim was of course now for the first time significant. It retained for some time its geographical reference: "Indian," "indigenous, local," virtually "native." And the indigenous groups themselves and their traditional ways from these invading Muslim foreigners. It covered all such groups: those whom we now call Hindus, but also Jains, Buddhists, and all the others.[33]

In addition to the influence of the Muslims, Christian missionaries and the presence of the British helped to engender a growing "Hindu" consciousness. Not only do such contemporary thinkers as Radhakrishnan or Vivekananda defend "Hinduism" against any attack, but there is a new concern to indicate the overarching unity among all "Hindus."

32. Cf. Wilfred Cantwell Smith, *The Meaning and End of Religion,* New York, Macmillan, 1962.
33. Ibid., p. 64.

The difficulty of this should be apparent to anyone who is familiar with the vast variety in Indian religions. Nevertheless, the search for an "essence" of Hinduism symbolizes the stance of some modern believers.

D. S. Sarma, former president of Vivekananda College in Madras, discusses at some length the theme "Unity in Diversity." [34] His position is that the soul of "Hinduism" is ever the same, although its embodiments differ according to time and place. But all Hindus share common scriptures, common deities, common ideals, common beliefs, and common practices.

Prior to the Muslim period, there would have been no purpose for such an inquiry. Not only did religious diversity exist, but the diverse regional languages and political allegiances made the very concept of Indian nationalism impossible. And, if the various states were not in any sense a unity, it would hardly do to suggest that the people of "Hindustan" were religiously united. Today, however, there exists a "Hindu" consciousness which has at times supported "Hindu" political movements.

A survey of religion in India should reveal that one cannot with accuracy speak of an "Indian Mind." Religious expression in India is as varied as religious expression could possibly be. Theists and Advaitins, materialists and skeptics, secularists and nationalists, all live side by side in the subcontinent. Sometimes they exist together peacefully, on other occasions they do not. That is the condition of men.

BIBLIOGRAPHY
Religion in the Vedic Period

Works on Indian religious traditions in general:
For an examination of various aspects of Indian culture prior to the Muslim rule see:
  Basham, A. L., *The Wonder That Was India,* New York, Grove Press, paperback ed., 1959.
For an historical examination of Sanskrit literature see:
  Macdonell, A. A., *History of Sanskrit Literature,* New York, Appleton-Century-Crofts, 1900.
For numerous notes on terms and for articles on specific topics see:
  Hastings, James, ed., *Encyclopedia of Religion and Ethics,* New York, Scribner, 1908–1927.
  Walker, Benjamin, *Hindu World,* 2 vols., London, G. Allen, New York, Praeger, 1968.
For an examination of Indian philosophical themes, see the following three works (listed in order of increasing difficulty):
  Hiriyanna, M., *The Essentials of Indian Philosophy,* London, G. Allen, 1949.
  Radhakrishnan, S., *Indian Philosophy,* 2 vols., New York, Macmillan, 1927.
  Dasgupta, Sarendranath, *A History of Indian Philosophy,* 5 vols., New York, Cambridge, 1922–1955.

34. Kenneth W. Morgan, ed., *The Religion of the Hindus,* New York, Ronald, 1953.

For an examination of Indian artistic traditions see:

Zimmer, H., *Myth and Symbol in Indian Art and Civilization,* New York, Harper & Row, paperback ed., 1962.

Coomaraswamy, Ananda K., *History of Indian and Indonesian Art,* New York, Dover, paperback ed., 1965.

Kramrisch, Stella, *The Hindu Temple,* 2 vols., Calcutta, University of Calcutta, 1946.

For further bibliographical suggestions see:

Adams, Charles J., *A Reader's Guide to the Great Religions,* New York, Free Press, 1965.

Mahar, J. Michael, *India: A Critical Bibliography,* Tucson, Ariz., University of Arizona Press, 1964.

Works specifically on the Vedic and Pre-Vedic periods.

For some of the more important texts of this period see:

Griffith, R. T. H., *Hymns of the Rigveda,* 2 vols., Banaras, E. J. Lazarus, 1920–1936.

Hume, R. E., trans., *The Thirteen Principal Upanishads,* New York, Oxford University Press, 1962.

Zaehner, R. C., trans., *Hindu Scriptures,* New York, Dutton, paperback ed., 1966.

For an understanding of the Pre-Vedic Period see:

Allchin, Bridget, and Raymond Allchin, *The Birth of Indian Civilization,* Baltimore, Penguin, paperback ed., 1968.

Wheeler, Sir Mortimer, *The Indus Civilization,* New York, Cambridge, paperback ed., 1968.

For an authoritative study of Vedic religion, with considerable emphasis on the cultic dimension, see:

Keith, A. B., *The Religion and Philosophy of the Veda and Upanishads,* Harvard Oriental Series, Vols. 31, 32, Cambridge, Mass., Harvard, 1925.

For a systematic treatment of the thought of the Upanishads see:

Duessen, Paul, *The Philosophy of the Upanishads,* New York, Dover, paperback ed., 1966.

For summaries by a modern authority see:

Louis, Renou, *Religions of Ancient India,* New York, Schocken, paperback ed., 1968.

————, *Vedic India,* Calcutta, Susil Gupta Private Ltd., 1957.

Religion in the Post-Vedic Period

For selections of texts in the Pali tradition see:

Cowell, Edward B., *The Jataka: or Stories of the Buddha's Former Births,* London, Luzac, 1957.

Davids, T. W. Rhys, trans., *The Questions of King Milinda,* 2 vols., New York, Dover, paperback ed., 1963.

Warren, H. C., trans., *Buddhism in Translations,* New York, Atheneum, paperback ed., 1963.

For selections of Jain texts see:

Ghoshal, Sarat C., ed., *The Sacred Books of the Jainas,* Central Jaina Publishing House, 1917–1937.

Jacobi, H. B., trans., *Jaina Sutras,* Sacred Books of the East, Vols. 22, 45, New York, Dover, paperback ed.

For an account of the life of the Buddha see:

Foucher, A., *The Life of the Buddha*, Middletown, Conn., Wesleyan University Press, 1963.

Thomas, Edward J., *The Life of the Buddha as Legend and History*, New York, Barnes & Noble, 1952.

For an account of the development of the Buddhist monastic tradition see:

Dutt, Sukumar, *The Buddha and Five After Centuries*, London, Luzac, 1957.

————, *Early Buddhist Monachism*, Bombay, Asia Publishing House, 1960.

————, *Buddhist Monks and Monasteries of India*, London, G. Allen, 1962.

For accounts of the history and thought following the life of the Buddha see:

Bapat, P. V., ed., *2500 Years of Buddhism*, Delhi Publications Division, Ministry of Information and Broadcasting, Government of India, 1956.

Conze, Edward, *Buddhism: Its Essence and Development*, New York, Harper & Row, paperback ed., 1959.

————, *Buddhist Thought in India*, London, G. Allen, 1962.

Guenther, Herbert V., *Philosophy and Psychology in the Abhidhamma*, Lucknow, Pioneer Press, Ltd., 1957.

Jayatilleke, K. N., *Early Buddhist Theory of Knowledge*, London, G. Allen, 1963.

Keith, A. B., *Buddhist Philosophy in India and Ceylon*, Oxford, Clarendon Press, 1923.

Thomas, Edward J., *History of Buddhist Thought*, London, Routledge, 1951.

For studies of the Jaina community see:

Jaini, J. L., *Outlines of Jainism*, New York, Cambridge, 1940.

Sangrove, Vilas A., *Jaina Community: A Social Survey*, Bombay, Popular Book Depot, 1959.

Schubring, Walther, *The Doctrine of the Jainas*, Delhi, Motilal Banarasidass, 1962.

Stevenson, Margaret Sinclair, *The Heart of Jainism*, New York, Oxford University Press, 1915.

Bhakti Movements

For important *bhakti* texts see:

Deutsch, Eliot, trans., *The Bhagavad Gītā*, New York, Holt, Rinehart and Winston, 1968.

Dutt, M. N., *A Prose Translation of the Mahabharata*, 18 vols., Calcutta, H. C. Dass, 1895–1905.

Hill, W. D. P., *The Holy Lake of the Acts of Rāma*, New York, Oxford University Press, 1952.

Hooper, J. S. M., trans., *Hymns of the Alvars*, Calcutta, Association Press, 1929.

Kern, H., trans., *The Saddharma-Pundarika*, New York, Dover, paperback ed., 1963.

Mueller, Max F., ed., *Buddhist Mahayana Texts*, E. B. Colwell, trans., New York, Dover, paperback ed., 1967.

Sanyal, J. M., trans., *The Śrīmad-Bhāgavatam* (5 vols.), Calcutta, Oriental Publishing Company, 1952–1954.

Sastri, H. P., trans., *Nārada Sūtras,* London, S. Sadan, 1963.

Wilson, H. H., trans., *The Viṣṇu Purāṇa,* Calcutta, Punthi Pustak, 1961.

For a discussion of *bhakti* movements in India see:

Bhandarkar, R. G., *Vaisnavism, Śaivism and Minor Religious Systems,* London, Routledge, 1913.

Carpenter, Joseph E., *Theism in Medieval India,* London, Benn, 1921.

Macnicol, Nicol, *Indian Theism from the Vedic to the Muhammadan Period,* New York, Oxford University Press, 1915.

Majumdar, A. K., *Bhakti Renaissance,* Bombay, Bharatiya Vidya Bhavan, 1965.

For specific considerations of Krishna worship see:

Archer, W. G., *The Loves of Krishna in Indian Painting and Poetry,* New York, Grove Press, paperback ed., 1960.

De, S. K., *Early History of the Vaishnava Faith and Movement in Bengal,* Calcutta, K. L. Mukhopadhyay, 1942.

Dimock, Edward C., *The Place of the Hidden Moon,* Chicago, University of Chicago Press, 1966.

Singer, Milton, ed., *Krishna: Myths, Rites and Attitudes,* Honolulu, East-West Center Press, 1966.

Religious Systems

For an examination of texts contributing to the Madhyamika position and for expositions of that position see:

Conze, Edward, *Aṣṭasāhasrikā Prajñāpāramitā,* Calcutta, The Asiatic Society, 1958.

———, *Buddhist Wisdom Books,* London, G. Allen, 1958.

———, *The Prajñāpāramitā Literature,* the Hague, Mouten & Co., 1960.

Murti, T. R. V., *The Central Philosophy of Buddhism: A Study of the Mādhyamika System,* London, G. Allen, 1955.

Streng, Frederick J., *Emptiness: A Study in Religious Meaning,* Nashville, Tenn., Abingdon, 1967.

For an examination of texts contributing to the Yogacara position and for expositions of that position see:

Chatterjee, Ashok K., *The Yogācāra Idealism,* Banaras, Banaras Hindu University Press, 1961.

Suzuki, D. T., *The Laṅkāvatāra Sūtra,* London, Routledge, 1932.

———, *Studies in the Laṅkāvatāra Sūtra,* London, Routledge, 1930.

For an examination of texts contributing to the Advaita position and for expositions of that position see:

Deussen, Paul, *The System of the Vedanta,* La Salle, Ill., Open Court, 1912.

Jagadananda, Swami, trans., *A Thousand Teachings,* Madras, Ramakrishna Math, 1941.

Mahadevan, T. M. P., *The Philosophy of Advaita,* Madras, Ganesh, 1957.

Thibaut, George, trans., *The Vedānta-Sūtras with the Commentary of Śaṅkarākārya,* New York, Dover, paperback ed., 1962.
For an examination of texts and an exposition of Vishishtadvaita see:
Kumarappa, Bharatan, *The Hindu Conception of Deity as Culminating in Rāmānjua,* London, Luzac, 1934.
Thibaut, George, trans., *The Vedānta-Sūtras with the Commentary of Rāmānuja,* New York, Dover, paperback ed., 1963.
For an examination of texts and an exposition of Dvaita see:
Narain, N., *An Outline of Madhva Philosophy,* Allahabad, Udayana Publications, 1962.
Rau, S. Subba, trans., *The Vedanta-Sutras with the Commentary by Shri Madhwacharya,* Madras, 1904.
Sharma, B. N. K., *Philosophy of Śrī Madhvācarya,* Bombay, Bharatiya Vida Bhavan, 1962.
For a discussion of Yoga in Indian thought see:
Eliade, Mircea, *Yoga: Immortality and Freedom,* Willard R. Trask, trans., Bollingen Series, Vol. 56, Princeton, N.J., Princeton University Press, 1958.
For a discussion of materialism in Indian thought see:
Riepe, Dale, *The Naturalistic Tradition in Indian Thought,* Delhi, Motilal Banarasidass, 1964.

For a discussion of Christian presence in India see:
Thomas Paul, *Christians and Christianity in India and Pakistan,* London, G. Allen, 1954.
For the history, thought, and practices of the Parsis see:
Dalla, M., *History of Zoroastrianism,* New York, Oxford University Press, 1928.
Masani, Sir Rustrom, *Zoroastrianism: The Religion of the Good Life,* New York, Collier, paperback ed., 1962.
Modi, J. J., *Religious Ceremonies and Customs of the Parsis,* London, Luzac, 1954.
Taraporewala, I. J. S., *The Religion of Zarathustra,* Bombay, Taraporewala, 1965.
Zaehner, R. C., *The Dawn and Twilight of Zoroastrianism,* New York, Putnam, 1961.
For an understanding of Islam in India see:
Arberry, Arthur J., *The Koran Interpreted,* New York, Macmillan, 1955.
Chand, Tara, *Influence of Islam on Indian Culture,* Allahabad, Indian Press, 1954.
Iqbal, Sir Muhammad, *Reconstruction of Philosophy in Islam,* London, Oxford University Press, 1934.
Smith, Wilfred Cantwell, *Modern Islam in India: A Social Analysis,* London, Gollancz, 1946.
For the history and tradition of the Sikhs see:
Macauliffe, Max A., *The Sikh Religion: Its Gurus, Sacred Writings and Authors,* 6 vols., New Delhi, S. Chand & Co., 1963.
McLoed, W. H., *Guru Nanak and the Sikh Religion,* Oxford, Clarendon Press, 1968.

Medieval Arrivals

Singh, Khushwant, *History of the Sikhs, 1469–1839,* Princeton, N.J., Princeton University Press, 1963.

Archer, John Clark, *The Sikhs,* Princeton, N.J., Princeton University Press, 1946.

The Modern Period   For a survey of modern Indian religion and thought see:

Farquhar, J. N., *Modern Religious Movements in India,* New York, Macmillan, 1915.

Naravane, V. S., *Modern Indian Thought,* Bombay, Asia Publishing House, 1964.

Sarma, D. S., *The Renaissance of Hinduism,* Banaras, Banaras Hindu University Press, 1944.

For an understanding of specific modern Indian thinkers see:

Chaudhuri, Haridas, and Frederick Spiegelberg, eds., *The Integral Philosophy of Sri Aurobindo,* London, G. Allen, 1960.

The Complete Works of Swami Vivekananda, Calcutta, Advaita Ashrama, 1940–1946.

Isherwood, Christopher, *Ramakrishna and His Disciples,* Calcutta, Advaita Ashrama, 1965.

Tagore, Rabindranath, *The Religion of Man,* Boston, Beacon Press, paperback ed., 1961.

Gandhi, M. K., *An Autobiography: Or the Story of My Experiments With Truth,* Boston, Beacon Press, paperback ed., 1959.

Ghose, Aurobindo, *The Life Divine,* New York, Greystone, 1949.

Nag, K., and D. Burman, eds., *The English Works of Raja Rammohun Roy,* 3 vols., Sadharan Brahmo Samaj, 1945–1951.

Radhakrishnan, S., *Eastern Religions and Western Thought,* Oxford, Clarendon Press, 1939.

———, *The Hindu View of Life,* New York, Macmillan, n.d.

———, *An Idealist View of Life,* London, G. Allen, 1932.

Radhakrishnan, S., *The Philosophy of Rabindranath Tagore,* New York, Macmillan, 1918.

For a discussion of Indian law and its relationship to religious change see:

Derrett, J. Duncan M., *Hindu Law, Past and Present,* A. Mukherjee, 1957.

Heimsath, Charles N., *Indian Nationalism and Hindu Social Reform,* Princeton, N.J., Princeton University Press, 1964.

Smith, Donald Eugene, *India as a Secular State,* Princeton, N.J., Princeton University Press, 1963.

———, *South Asian Politics and Religion,* Princeton, N.J., Princeton University Press, 1966.

PART THREE

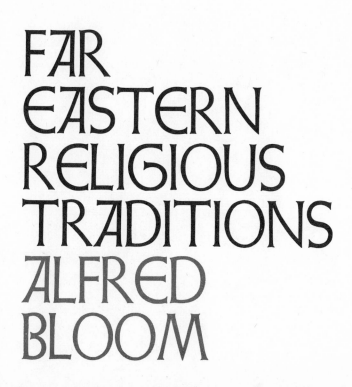

FAR EASTERN RELIGIOUS TRADITIONS

ALFRED BLOOM

SECTION ONE

CHINA: THE QUEST FOR ULTIMATE HARMONY AND THE GREAT TRANQUILLITY

INTRODUCTION: RELIGION IN CHINA

THE CONCEPTS
OF HARMONY
AND TRANQUILLITY

Chinese religio-philosophical traditions are dominated by a desire to achieve and maintain harmony with the forces of the cosmos. They reveal a central concern for the proper, the fitting, the appropriate, in all areas of life. In the midst of social struggle and tensions throughout their history, the Chinese have sought the foundations of ultimate harmony.

In the earliest periods this quest was directed toward the natural forces which impinged directly on the lives of the people in their agricultural existence. Harmony was sought through very concrete ritual means in sacrifice and divination.

As society became more complex and conflicts more intense, Confucius and his successors saw that ultimate harmony rested on the character of human relations. Harmony was not merely a matter of complying with natural forces, but of finding ways to bring lives of varying stations and capacities together for the good of the whole.

The Taoists quickly perceived that placing emphasis on external human relations merely gave rise to new conflicts and competitions. They claimed that one must find harmony at the deepest level in Nature—the source of existence. Conforming one's life to cosmic principle was the only way to harmony between man and Nature and between man and man.

Buddhism, imported from India, challenged men to achieve the highest harmony by cutting through the delusions of the ego to an understanding of the nature of things. The perception of the Real aimed at transforming human personality by reducing attachments to the world. Buddhism pointed the way for later Neo-Confucianism in finding the root of harmony beyond the world of appearances.

The quest for harmony still proceeds in China, though on a political level. It is still a problem to unite the Chinese people with a common sense of destiny and meaning.

China occupies a large portion of the globe and has one of the largest concentrations of population. Since the Chinese have developed one of the most durable societies, their varied systems of thought and value possess great historical significance. To aid the student in assessing the importance of Chinese tradition, we shall analyze its various strands of religio-philosophical thought represented by Confucianism, Taoism, and Buddhism, focusing upon the dominant interests and insights that have given Chinese culture its distinctive character.

PERSPECTIVES ON
CHINESE RELIGION

Religion has been a strong force in China as man's response to elements in his environment over which he had no direct control. On both the societal and individual levels the unpredictable elements stimulated activities designed to prevent or alleviate disasters. From ancient times traditional rites existed to care for such matters. Chinese theories of government and morality drew upon religious sources for their authority.

We cannot enforce on Chinese tradition a Western standard which strictly divides the sacred and profane elements of life. The Chinese, generally, have not considered religion as something apart from life, an independent activity possessing its own intrinsic value. Except perhaps for Buddhism, Chinese religio-philosophic thought and experience does not manifest any of the "tension toward the world" which characterizes Western religious perspectives. The Chinese would not share the sentiment that it is the whole duty of man to glorify God, making religion an end in itself. The instrumental nature of Chinese religion has deep roots in ancient fertility rites designed to stimulate food production and preserve the community. This background helps to explain the anthropocentric, practical, magical, and generally tolerant features of Chinese religion. It is the basis for the organic view of Nature controlling Chinese thought and the social ideal of harmony governing moral and social existence.

Religion for the Chinese is primarily a social function for the good of society as a whole. Those elements which we call religious in the sense of orientation toward the supernatural assume importance for the Chinese only when they function to strengthen social existence. The organic view of Nature includes society, so that harmony with Heaven through religious rites guarantees social existence. Religion was employed as a sanctioning force for the political and social order. Specific, institutional forms of religion were constantly controlled by the government because they were potentially independent centers of faith and allegiance which could threaten the traditional order.

Buddhists in China argued that monasticism and religious practices such as donations to the order benefited the individual but were not merely an individualistic concern. They maintained that society also profited from the aid offered to ancestors in their progress to a higher destiny and through the believer's good citizenship inspired by Buddhist piety. Further, they claimed that Buddhism augmented the magical and spiritual resources of Chinese religion through the use of Buddhist spells and incantations and through belief in numerous Indian gods which had been absorbed into Buddhism as well as the multitude of mythical Buddhas and Bodhisattvas depicted in Mahayana, Buddhist mythology.

The awareness of varying levels of understanding within Chinese society contributes to more accurate assessment of Chinese religiosity. As we shall see, the basic cleavage in the Chinese religious world has not been between the clergy and the laity, but rather between the scholar-bureaucrat (ordinarily the Confucian elite or literati) and the generally uneducated, illiterate masses of people. While the larger mass of people remained unsophisticated concerning their religious beliefs and practices, the intellectual elite became more critical and philosophical. The two levels of perception were mainly distinguished by the depth of reflection and insight achieved by individuals within their life situation.

The scholar-bureaucrats rationalized religion and opposed excesses of superstition and magic. In order to foster their outlook on the masses, they transformed the ancient myths and traditions into didactic, moralistic stories in which the gods served as anthropomorphic models of virtue to be imitated by men. They were aware, however, of the sanction and support religion gave to political and social authority, and therefore made no attempt to abolish popular cults. When such cults were kept within proper limits, they helped to maintain order through cultivating belief in the supernatural basis of events as the will of Heaven and disposing people to be more acquiescent to the demands made by society on their lives.

While China did not develop a special class of religious personnel who tended primarily to religious matters, the scholar-bureaucrats ensured cosmic and social order and harmony through teaching moral norms and performing rituals. They criticized the contemporary order when it appeared to depart from its basic function of realizing harmony and enforcing values, and they criticized religious activities when they seemed inimical to social goals and ideals. In no case did they present for the individual a way of salvation as an alternative to life in this world and society.

Confucianism, Taoism, and Buddhism have so fused that the average person may not be aware of the source of his beliefs or practices. Even the scholars and monks who were consciously committed to a specific system would not explicitly reject other systems. Confucianism and Taoism long coexisted and mutually influenced each other; in the first stages of its introduction into China, Buddhism was confused with Taoism. As the various traditions came to be better understood, they appeared more complementary than opposing. Confucianism gave guidance for the moral life; Taoism provided techniques of magic to secure longevity, to deal with spirits, and to gain benefits from alchemy. Buddhism came to be related primarily to the afterlife in the Pure Land or Heaven. Through the ceremonies of Buddhism one fulfilled filial piety for his deceased loved ones. This fusion was expressed in the popular morality text, *T'ai-shang Kan-ying P'ien*, in which a Taoist priest discoursed on religion and destiny:

> "The soul," he said, "is Tao, and Tao is soul. The soul and the Tao are not different in essence. If the Tao is separated from the soul, you will transmigrate through the six domains and keep on the three paths, but if the soul and the Tao are united, you will finally reach paradise and the land of immortals. Hell and heaven are in your own heart. Unless heaven reside within you, the mere reading or reciting of sacred books profiteth nothing." [1]

In this passage the reference to Tao and the land of immortals points to Taoism, while the concept of transmigration and the six domains and three paths is clearly Buddhist. The virtues stressed throughout the volume reflect Confucian interest.

The merging of religious traditions can be observed in the diversity of divinities to whom people appeal to fulfill their desires and needs. Of the major deities, some have a Taoist background, some a Buddhist, and one the divinized Confucius. While most of the hundreds of deities relating to every facet of human existence and nature may be located within Taoist religion, Buddhist figures such as Kuan-yin (Avalokitesvara), Ti-tsang-wang (Kshitigarbha), and Yen-lo-wang (Yama) are important in dealing with affairs of this life or the afterlife. On the practical level, the Chinese outlook on the unity of the three teachings has been succinctly stated by Francis Hsu:

> The Chinese may go to a Buddhist monastery to pray for a male heir, but he may proceed from there to a Taoist shrine where he beseeches a god to cure him of malaria. Ask any number of Chinese what their religion is and the answer of the majority will be that they have no particular religion, or that since all religions benefit man in one way or another, they are equally good. [2]

Recent historical and archeological sources have pushed back the boundaries of myth and legend to reveal ancient organized life and culture. The once legendary Shang people have been found to be historical and in possession of a highly developed culture.

The Shang (ca. 1500–1100 B.C.) had already developed advanced techniques of bronze-casting, sericulture, weaving, and most significant for Chinese culture—writing. Despite their sophistication in comparison with surrounding peoples, they were unable to defend themselves from invasions and finally fell before the onslaught of the hardier Chou tribes of Northwest China.

THE HISTORICAL CONTEXT OF CHINESE RELIGION

1. Teitaro Suzuki, Paul Carus, trans., *T'ai-shang Kan-ying P'ien*, LaSalle, Ill., The Open Court Pub. Co., 1944, p. 84.

2. Francis L. K. Hsu, *Americans and Chinese: Two Ways of Life*, p. 237, quoted in Derk Bodde, *China's Cultural Tradition*, New York, Holt, Rinehart and Winston, 1963, p. 21.

The Chou dynasty (1100–221 B.C.) witnessed the establishment and eventual decline of feudalism. The gradual dissolution of the political power of the Chou forms the background for the most creative era in Chinese thought.

Generally, the Chou era divides into three periods. The initial period of the flourishing Chou hegemony extended from the conquest of the Shang in about 1100 to 722 B.C. when the ruler was driven from his capital in Hao to Loyang in Honan. The second period was termed the time of *Ch'un-ch'iu* (Spring and Autum—722–481 B.C.). This phase was the title of a historical chronicle of the kingdom of Lu, traditionally ascribed to Confucius. During this time, numerous petty rulers attempted to extend their authority as the royal house declined. The final period, from 481 to 221 B.C., was one of constant conflict known as the age of Warring States. The continual strife among principalities ended finally when the Chou and other states came under the despotic rule of the founder of the Ch'in dynasty, Shih Huang-ti (First Emperor).

The period of the breakdown of the Chou dynasty and Warring States was one of the most intellectually creative periods that China has experienced. According to tradition, the age witnessed the flowering of a hundred schools, representing the most diverse viewpoints. From among the host of contenders six became traditionally significant. The Confucian school was represented by Confucius (K'ung Fu-tzu, 551–479 B.C.), Mencius (Meng-tzu, 371–289 B.C.), and Hsun-tzu (298–238 B.C.). Derived from the class of literati, this school supported aristocratic morality. In contrast, the Mo-ist school, founded by Mo-ti (479–439 B.C.), appeared to represent a lower-class perspective with a doctrine of universal love and egalitarianism. A different approach to morality was furnished by the Taoist philosophy of Lao-tzu (sixth–fourth century B.C.) and Chuang-tzu (c. 399–295 B.C.). Other significant philosophical schools were the School of Names, composed of men skilled in logic and debate similar to ancient Greek sophists, the Yin-yang school and the Five Elements school,[3] which together explained phenomena in more materialistic or naturalistic terms, and the Legalist school of Han Fei-tzu (d. 233 B.C.), followed by professional politicians. Confucianism and Taoism overshadowed all other schools in shaping Chinese outlook and providing significant insight into the pressing problem of establishing and maintaining a durable society and way of life.

The period of creativity came to an end with the enforced unification under the short-lived Ch'in dynasty (221–206 B.C.). Ch'in despotism, symbolized by the persecution of scholars and destruction of classical texts, was almost immediately replaced by the great Han dynasty which lasted for some four hundred years from 206 B.C. to A.D. 220. Under the Han, Confucianism became the orthodox

---

3. *Yin-yang* refers to the contrasting cosmic forces which act to produce the world of experience, while the Five Elements, which include metal, water, earth, fire, and wood, are the basic constituents from which all things are formed.

ideology of the state and the basis of education and competitive examinations for official positions. As a result of the practical supremacy of Confucianism, study of other schools of thought waned.

The next major period of intellectual ferment attended the breakdown of the Han age and the ensuing period of disunity (A.D. 221–589). Confucianism also fell into disrepute and a mystical tendency developed as a response to the disruption and anxiety of the age. In this background Neo-Taoist philosophy emerged, and Buddhism, imported from India, spread easily through Chinese society, benefiting from initial confusion with Taoist philosophy and religion.

The spread of Buddhism through Chinese society enabled it to provide the unifying element in the establishment of the Sui dynasty (A.D. 589–618). During the succeeding T'ang dynasty (A.D. 618–907) Buddhism reached the zenith of its power and prestige. This prestige ended in the great persecution of 845, and during the Sung dynasty (A.D. 960–1127) a revived Confucianism absorbing elements from Taoism and Buddhism displaced Buddhist intellectual leadership.

From the time of the Sung until the establishment of the Republic in 1912, Confucianism was the dominant intellectual force and basis of education. The Neo-Confucian philosophies taught by Chu Hsi (A.D. 1130–1200) and Wang Yang-ming (A.D. 1472–1529) were comprehensive in promoting traditional Confucian morality as well as metaphysical and mystical elements which answered needs formerly met by Taoism and Buddhism. Throughout this long period no radically new approach in the realm of thought or religion appeared except for the incursions of Islam and Christianity, neither of which was fully accepted into Chinese life. In modern times Confucianism suffered from the disrupting influences of Western culture.

Despite the many changes, Confucian tradition provided the thread linking Chinese thought. It became the basis for the most outstanding Chinese character traits and functioned as the state's political ideology over a longer period of time than any similar ideology. Its understanding of human nature and political astuteness, as well as its system of training bureaucrats (not so much with technical expertise as with moral and cultural sensitivity), has made it one of the most significant products of the human mind and spirit. On the other hand, it was also responsible for the traditionalism and conservatism of Chinese society, making it difficult to deal with new problems requiring decisive change. For this reason it has been resisted by many Chinese concerned with the task of technological modernization, even though the Confucian tradition embodied the best in the Chinese spirit.

THE CHINESE CLASSICS

The five classics of the Confucian tradition and the archeological material relating to the Shang people are primary sources of information for pre-Confucian religion. There are some obstacles to reaching a clear understanding of the ancient religion because the texts were edited to conform to the official philosophy in the Chou period and then destroyed in the Ch'in era, necessitating a reconstruction during the Han age. Disputes arose concerning the authenticity of the reconstructed texts.

The five major classics are the *Shu-ching* (*Book of Documents* or *History*), *Shih-ching* (*Book of Poems*), *I-ching* (*Book of Changes*), *Li-chi* (*Book of Ceremonies*), and *Ch'un-ch'iu* (*Spring and Autumn Annals*). A sixth text, the *Book of Music,* has been lost to history, but its existence is implied both in the importance Confucius ascribed to music and in the fact that Confucian studies were divided into six fields.

Probably composed around the ninth century B.C. when the Chou dynasty had reached its peak, the *Shu-ching* was the primary source for the legendary history of China. Through later additions to the text, the narrative reached 625 B.C. While much of the material is of late derivation, it contains the reflection of older religious ideas.

The *Shih-ching* is a collection of folk songs covering a period of more than a thousand years beginning with the Shang era. Though it is believed that more than three thousand poems once existed, tradition claims that Confucius selected three hundred and five of the best poems relating to piety, war, and love. Since many of the poems appear to have been ceremonial in origin and purpose they provide direct insight into the earliest religion of the Chinese. Confucius himself regarded poetry as a source of moral guidance and information. Consequently, Confucian tradition has overlaid the poems with orthodox interpretation.

Used for divination, the *I-ching* is perhaps one of the most important and fundamental of the classics. Through its system of interpretation of symbolic trigrams and hexagrams, it also provided a basis for philosophical and mystical speculation in later Chinese thought.

The system of hexagrams, composed of varying combinations of solid or *yang* lines and broken or *yin* lines, is traditionally thought to have been created by the ancient hero Fu Hsi in the initial trigram system of eight symbols. Later the symbols were doubled to form hexagrams giving sixty-four possible forms. Tradition attributes the expanded forms to either Fu Hsi or King Wen of Chou who is said to have composed the text of the *I-ching* while in prison in 1142 B.C. Confucius is reputed to have written a commentary to the text, and it became closely associated with his tradition.

The theory and practices based on the *I-ching* exhibit the Chinese organic view of Nature as a grand, dynamic, harmonious process of interacting yin-yang forces and interdependent elements. Since man and society are parts of the total natural order, their destinies are dependent on harmony with Nature. To achieve or maintain this harmony, it is necessary to discover the appropriate hexagrams governing the present situation. When the diagram is determined through selecting yarrow sticks or throwing coins, the practitioner may consult the manual and interpret their lines in relation to the client's contemplated choices and actions. A significant aspect of these diagrams and their use is the limitation on corruption by the diviner, since the patterns and the explanatory passages in the text are fixed.

Circular diagram of the sixty-four hexagrams of the I-ching. (*From Hellmut Wilhelm*, Change: Eight Lectures on the I Ching.)

The *Li-chi* (*Book of Ceremonies*) has considerable importance among the classics because Confucius considered ceremony and propriety essential to forming character and maintaining public peace. The work concerns ancestor worship, music, dancing, and the state sacrifices. The present version of the text derives from the second century B.C. and is clearly the work of later generations. In the twelfth century A.D. two chapters, *Ta-hsueh* (*Great Learning*) and *Chung-yung* (*Doctrine of the Mean*), were singled out for special regard in Neo-Confucianism. Other traditional texts of similar content are the *I-li* (*Ceremonies and Rituals*) and *Chou-li* (*Rituals of Chou*).

The final text, *Ch'un-ch'iu* (*Spring and Autumn Annals*), traditionally ascribed to Confucius, concentrates on the history of the kingdom of Lu, Confucius' home state. The narration begins with the rule of Duke Yin (722–712 B.C.) and continues through a series of twelve dukes to Duke Ai (481 B.C.). It is considered one of the first accurate historical texts of China. The text itself is only a statement of fact, but in its choice of terms depicting rulers, it implies criticism of leaders who assume titles they do not deserve. The book thus appears to conform to Confucius' teaching on the rectification of names, whereby the name of a thing must correspond with its reality.

The Confucians were more interested in the meanings and morals of the classics than in the more formal literary elements of presentation. Through their interpretations, they constructed durable and creative systems of thought, although frequently obscuring ancient religious beliefs.

HARMONY IN THE CLAN AND KINGDOM: THE RELIGION OF THE SHANG AND CHOU

Archeology and the poetry of the *Book of Poems* provide the basic information for the religious outlook of the Shang and Chou eras. Behind the later official interpretations of the poems, is the basic character of the communal religion which must have been the foundation of the royal religion represented mainly in the archeological finds.[1] The emphasis on the harmonization of man and Nature, which became the controlling motif of later Chinese thought, was expressed in tribal and royal rites.

The realization of the harmony of man and Nature appeared in the *Book of Poems* in the interrelation of marriage practices and seasonal fertility themes. Within natural settings such as mountains, woods, and junctures of rivers a variety of rituals were performed in spring and autumn, including purifications, bathings, contests, sexual rites, sacrifices, banqueting, rainmaking, and flower gathering. Though later expurgated as immoral, there are hints of orgies. Concerning the significance of these religious activities Marcel Granet writes:

Speaking generally, they are festivals of union, in which people become aware of the bonds which unite them, and, at the same

1. For a concise summary of the archeological discoveries relating to the religion of the Shang and Chou eras, see Jack Finegan, *The Archaeology of World Religions*, Princeton, N.J., Princeton University Press, 1965, vol. II, pp. 317–342.

time, of their oneness with their natural environment. To crown all, they also serve to guarantee, along with the prosperity of men and things, the regular working of Nature.[2]

The concern of the Shang and Chou to maintain the balance of forces in Nature indicates their awareness of interacting but unequal forces within Nature and life which could bring disaster on the community if proper means were not taken to achieve harmonization. From this awareness the yin-yang dualism which pervaded all Chinese religious and philosophical thought and the duality of *shen* (positive divine forces) and *kuei* (negative forces) have arisen.

The concept of yin-yang may have resulted from the confrontation of boys and girls in the ceremonial poetic competition preceding betrothal or from observation of meteorological phenomena, since the yin aspect is represented in Chinese by the character for rain-cloud and yang is represented by the symbol for the sun's rays. Consequently, yin stands for all characteristics which are dark, wet, cold, soft, and female. It is also square and even-numbered. Yang includes all qualities associated with brightness, dryness, warmth, hardness, masculinity, and is round and odd-numbered. Yang is naturally superior. It is to be noted that the duality is complementary and not conflicting. The traditional symbol implies the ultimate balance of the complementary interaction.

The contrast of positive and negative forces represented by the shen and kuei related to the development of the Chinese pantheon. The shen comprised all the good spirits which eventually came to be organized in a great hierarchy of gods headed by T'ien (Heaven) on the pattern of the feudal monarchy. Each deity had a particular function and rank within the whole.

Ancient thought regarded each person as a compound of the shen and kuei elements (also termed *hun* and *p'o*). The shen was man's superior aspect, the basis of intelligence and vital forces, while the kuei represented inferior features, the basis of physical nature. At death the shen proceeded to the palace of Shang-ti and became a beneficent deity as a result of pacification through the sacrifices of his descendants. The kuei resided in the tomb and along with the decay of the body sank to the underworld. If not appeased through sacrifices, the kuei could become a hostile spirit. The final residence of the keui was believed to be a place in the underworld called Yellow Springs.

The major deities associated with the ancient religion of the soil in China were the fertility deities Hou-t'u (Lord Soil) and Hou-chi (Lord Millet). Among the Chou the same cult was called She-chi (altar of earth and grain). The oldest and most universal cult in China, it has persisted to modern times due to the enduring importance of the soil in the life of the peasant.

In the early stages of Chinese religion the divine forces did not possess highly defined personalities. People did not attempt to relate to the deities in personal communion; they thought of them in

2. Marcel Granet, *Festivals and Songs of Ancient China*, New York, Dutton, 1932, p. 180.

P'an-ku holding in his hands the yang-yin, symbol of Heaven and Earth. (Courtesy of the British Museum.)

terms of function. All important natural objects were invested with divine power, undefined but effective. Eventually, however, the deities were historicized so that the earth deity She was identified with Yu, the reputed founder of the Hsia dynasty, and Chi, the grain deity, was identified with the founder of the Chou people. In addition to deities related to agriculture or ancestors, each home was guarded by a group of household deities who guaranteed the prosperity and security of the family. There were deities of the inner and outer doors, the well, the hearth, and the inner court. The ancient cult has continued into modern times.

The realization of harmony with Nature brought religion into close association with political power, as the king was the mediator between the total community and the forces of Nature and deities. The aim of the ritual activities of the king, like the peasants, was to secure the assistance of the ancestral deities in maintaining the continuity of the people and promoting food production. The Shang not only believed that the dead lived in the afterlife in a manner similar to this life, but that the ancestral spirits guarded the present world and guaranteed the authority of the reigning king. As imperial power grew, the supporting system of sacrifices became more elaborate.

The royal religion may be viewed as the religion of the central clan among the Shang which, as the power of the clan extended, grew to cover the entire body of associated clans. The deity Shang-ti, whose name means "Supreme Ruler" or "Supreme Ancestor," was the central deity of Shang times and may have originally been the ancestral deity of the leading clan. He was addressed as protector of the royal house and in connection with good harvests. With the transition to the Chou age, there was need for a deity who transcended tribal and clan connections. T'ien (Heaven) replaced Shang-ti. The ruler, as representative of T'ien on earth, was called T'ien-tzu (Son of Heaven), and the state defined as T'ien-hsia (Under Heaven). T'ien, in early Chinese thought, was a personal power who controlled the world.[3] There grew up about him a pantheon of deities who had various functions in maintaining the world.

The major religious practices of the Shang and Chou eras were sacrifice and divination. These practices, originally communal in nature, eventually became more individualized. Religious activities pervaded every area of life and were led by the head of the family or the ruler. The sacrifices were occasions to report to the ancestors on family matters or on the success of various ventures— military or diplomatic. Animals by the hundreds were slaughtered, as well as occasional prisoners of war. Methods included burning in open flame, drowning in rivers, or burial, depending on the occasion of the rite.

As the Chou state consolidated, sacrifice assumed central importance and the number of rites and feasts increased. The Shang were employed as ritualists, and the earlier forms of ritual were continued. The major state ceremonies, continuing until 1911, were the sacrifices made to Heaven in the spring and winter solstices. The Emperor performed them on the great altar of Heaven in the capital.

Under Chou rule the perspective on sacrifices shifted from an emphasis on clan relationships to rites centered on the personality of the founder of the dynasty, Wen-wang, to whom the divine mandate to rule had been given by the deity Shang-ti. His successors who were instrumental in the conquest of the Shang people also became

3. Yu-lan Fung, *History of Chinese Philosophy,* Princeton, N.J., Princeton University Press, 1952–1953, vol. I, p. 31, notes five meanings given to the term *T'ien* in Chinese thought. They should be clearly understood in order to avoid confusion in interpreting Chinese thought at various times. (1) There is the physical sky, as in the phrase "Heaven and Earth." (2) There is the anthropomorphic ruling Heaven, as "Imperial Heaven Supreme Emperor." (3) There is the fatalistic concept of Heaven applied to all events outside human control. It is equivalent to *ming,* decree, command. (4) There is Heaven used in the sense of Nature. (5) There is the ethical Heaven as the highest moral principle in the universe. In the Confucian *Analects* the anthropomorphic Heaven is most frequent.

The Altar of Heaven, Peking. (Photo by Fritz Henle, from Monkmeyer Press Photo Service.)

objects of reverence. Confucius particularly idealized the Duke of Chou for his many social and cultural achievements.

The interrelation of the religious and political was evident in the fact that only the Emperor was entitled to perform national sacrifices. For anyone else to attempt it was equivalent to a challenge to the throne. The term designating the overthrow of the state was "turning over the She-chi," which was to despoil the altars of the earth deity.

Although a more rationalistic attitude toward sacrifice developed in Chinese tradition, the basic beliefs and activities forged in the ancient period remained until recent times as the symbol of the political foundations of the state as well as the recognition of man's dependence upon the forces of Nature for his existence.

The second major practice of communal importance in ancient China was divination, since it was necessary to determine the will of the deity before engaging in activities affecting the whole society. In China the practice assumed special importance in view of the concern for the harmonization of Nature and society.

The major materials for divination among the Shang were ox bones and tortoise shells, or occasionally, sheep bones. The tortoise shells had particular significance, as they embodied in their shape the structure of the universe itself. The upper round part was like the vault of the sky, while the square lower section represented the earth. In the ancient thought tortoises were pictured as the foundation of certain islands and the world. Consequently, the ancient Chinese considered them important sources of information on worldly and heavenly affairs. The *I-ching* eventually became a major manual for acquiring counsel concerning one's future actions.

Numerous other methods of divination developed. Appeal was made to astrology; almanacs with observations on the seasons; arrangements of the five elements as earth, wood, fire, metal, and water; dreams; and the system of forms represented by phrenology. In later times coins were used in which the yang was the upper side, while the yin was the lower. Three coins were tossed at least six times and the combination was interpreted according to the *I-ching* series of sixty-four hexagrams. Also fortune-telling was performed through consideration of the correlation of the five basic elements, calendrical symbols, and one's birthdate (the year, month, and day). Divination not only pertained to matters of one's future destiny, but also to the use of the environment in placing a building. Geomancy, called *Feng-shui* (Wind and Water), was a conspicuous feature of the Chinese approach to the world.

As C. K. Yang [4] indicates, divination in earliest times was primarily a political activity dealing with war and peace. Divination gave a sacred character to political decisions and consequently contributed to their authority and popular acceptance. Yang notes that Confucian thought, though rationalistic at many points, did not alter this basic function. Only in later times was the activity extended to more private and individual concerns.

The religion of the classical period largely centered on the royal and noble clans. Through securing the support of their ancestral spirits all the land was peaceful and prosperous. Since it was the duty of the heads of the clans to perform the sacrifices, the formation of a specifically priestly caste was inhibited.

However, in connection with the sacrifices and divination performed by the king on behalf of the entire people, personnel of allied clans assisted in the prayers and sacrifices. Eventually they became specialized in function, and the performance of rites was transmitted through certain families. During the Chou period the organization of the ritual and personnel became formalized. Nevertheless, the officials of the state cult did not have mystic or magical authority.

Along with the development of official ritualists, there were functionaries termed *wu* (sorcerers or wizards). The status of these individuals in early times was quite high, sometimes second only to the king himself, who originally attained his position on the basis of magical charisma as a rainmaker. The functions of the sorcerers were divination, sacrifices, rainmaking, and ridding the community of evils. During the Chou period the status of the wu declined as a rationalistic view of government grew and the prestige of the literati advanced. Displaced through the growth of the Confucian school and its ritual functions, the wu also later faced competition from Taoist and Buddhist priests. The wu have persisted into modern times, performing fortune-telling, geomancy, prayers for the sick, exorcisms, and various forms of magic for individuals or groups out-

4. C. K. Yang, *Religion in Chinese Society*, Berkeley, Calif., University of California Press, 1961, pp. 107, 259–265.

Bronze ritual vessel from the Shang-Yin Dynasty, 1766–1122 B.C. (Courtesy of the British Museum.)

side the traditional religious structures. However, they are not regarded very highly.

In assessing the Chinese religion which emerged from the information available on the classical period, we may observe that it was rooted in an ancestral cult chiefly designed to maintain and unify the group by enlisting the powers of the departed members of the tribe and family. This cult with its seasonal festivals did not contain highly defined deities of concrete character, but rather an indefinite awareness of forces impressed on the imagination by natural phenomena. As the organization and function of society developed and as larger urban centers arose, the religion of the people evolved along a somewhat parallel course, resulting in the highly organized and multitudinous pantheon with each deity having its specific task in the divine bureaucracy.

During the Han period, the emergence of religious Taoism and the arrival of Buddhism spurred the proliferation of deities. The popular standing of religion as a means for attaining health, wealth, and security underlay this development and linked the modern Chinese religious perspective with its ancient precedents. There has been no significant alteration in the popular Chinese religious viewpoint, save in the scope and multiplicity of objects of worship and appeal.

The details of early Chinese religious beliefs and practices are not particularly unique when compared with other ancient religious cults revering ancestors or natural forces. Thus the specific features of the ancient cult do not explain the peculiar developments of Chinese religio-philosophic tradition. The outstanding feature of the religious history of China is the rationalization and moralization of the cult making man and the social order the central concern. This tendency was most conspicuous in the teachings of Confucius.

The basic presuppositions of Chinese religio-philosophic thought were clearly rooted in the earlier religious perspective. As we have previously noted, it was axiomatic that society was an integral part of Nature, and it was the duty of man through his ethical and moral behavior not to disturb the harmony basic to his life. Only those features of the ancient religious system which symbolized and strengthened this awareness in the people were retained and implemented in the official cult. All other elements were ignored or left to the common man for individual solution. Consequently, ancient Chinese skeptics ridiculed the rulers for their excessive attention to the spirits and superstition when the state was in danger.[5] Confucius also warned his followers not to be overly concerned about the spirits, while yet affirming the need for ceremony.

5. Fung, op. cit., vol. I, p. 31.

HARMONY IN SOCIETY: CONFUCIANISM

Confucius' life and his social ideals must be viewed against the background of the turmoil, social upheaval, and succession of intrigues and war that were destroying traditional morality, undermining old loyalties, and eroding the power of the royal house at the beginning of the Warring States period (481–221 B.C.). The magical and pragmatic traditional religion lacked sufficient moral and spiritual depth to contribute to social harmony.

In order to meet the problems of the age there appeared numerous private teachers and statesmen who offered their services to various lords. As politicians and administrators, they aided the ruler in cultivating and extending his power. These scholars were called *ju* (literati). The term itself meant weak or mild and may have first been applied sarcastically to those teachers who espoused a more pacifistic and moderate approach to human relations. Although there are numerous theories concerning their origin, they appear to have had skill in reading and writing, which enabled them to master traditional wisdom useful in administration. It is significant that Confucianism came to be known as *Ju-chiao* (the teaching of the literati) and that Confucius was perhaps most representative of that class. Undoubtedly his keen insight into human relations, the foundation of morality, and the function of leadership set the direction for later Chinese scholarship.

A major traditional source for information on the life of Confucius, apart from indications in the *Analects,* has been the *Historical Records (Shih-chi)* of Ssu-ma Ch'ien (d. 85 B.C.). According to his account, Confucius (K'ung Fu-tzu, 551–479 B.C.) was born in the state of Lu in the family of K'ung and given the personal name of Ch'iu and literary name Chung-ni. His parents died when he was very young. At an early age he showed great interest in sacrifice and ceremonies. Though his family was of poor and common background, the young Confucius was given responsibility in the house of Baron Chi. In the many positions which he came to hold, he had a reputation for fairness. When he was magistrate in Chung-tu, it became a model town. Under Duke Ting he became Grand Secretary of Justice, then Chief Minister. During this time, we are told, he reformed society so that mutton and pork butchers no longer sold spoiled meat; men and women used different roads; [1] things left on the street were not stolen; and foreigners were safe.

Despite his competence and moral character, Confucius ran into difficulty in the various principalities that he served, making it necessary for him to wander about seeking employment. He suffered from intrigue and slander. In the course of his travels he taught disciples the ways of a gentleman and government. Some of these pupils gained administrative positions in various states. In spite of his many problems, Confucius did not alter his ways, being convinced he had a mission which none could thwart because it was supported by Heaven. Besides carrying on his political and educational activities, Confucius also studied and edited the classics and composed the *Spring and Autumn Annals.*

His personal deportment and character are described in most eloquent terms as very much the example of what he constantly taught. Upon his death in Lu at the age of seventy-two, the Duke of Ai and his disciples deeply mourned his passing. Eventually his tomb became a shrine where his personal belongings were kept and ancestral sacrifices offered. The first Emperor of Han came to make sacrifice at the tomb in 206 B.C. At the end of his account, Ssu-ma Ch'ien poignantly contrasted the pervasiveness and lasting character of Confucius' influence with the perishability of worldly power:

> There have been many kings, emperors and great men in history, who enjoyed fame and honor while they lived and came to nothing at their death, while Confucius, who was but a common scholar clad in a cotton gown, became the acknowledged Master of scholars for over ten generations. All people in China who discuss the six arts, from the emperors, kings and princes down, regard the master as the final authority. [2]

Despite this legendary glorification, the life of Confucius does not suggest actions or characteristics which might lead to the formation of a religious movement or cult, and although Confucius himself was agnostic in religious matters, a cult of Confucius developed under the sponsorship of the state when Confucianism achieved supremacy as the orthodox ideology of the nation.

It should be noted, however, that this development was in line with the outlook of Chinese ancestor reverence and popular religion which, as an expression of gratitude and reward for their merit, exalted to the level of divinity individuals who benefited mankind.

---

1. In ancient Confucian thought the sexes were strictly segregated.
2. Lin Yu-tang, *The Wisdom of Confucius*, New York, Random House, 1938, p. 100.

Three sages—Shaka, Confucius, and Lao-tzu. (Courtesy of the Museum of Fine Arts, Boston, Bigelow Collection.)

Wang Chung, a critic of Chinese religion about A.D. 80, summarized the general Chinese attitude to such practices:

Two motives are underlying all sacrifices: gratitude for received benefits and ancestor worship. We show our gratitude for the efforts others have taken on our behalf, and worship our ancestors out of regard for their kindness. Special efforts, extraordinary goodness, merits and universal reforms are taken into consideration by wise emperors, and it is for this reason that they have instituted sacrifices. An oblation is offered to him who has improved the public administration, who for the public welfare has worked till his death, who has done his best to strengthen his country, who has warded off great disasters, or prevented great misfortunes.[3]

Although traditions claim that Duke Ai of Lu initiated the cult of Confucius, it did not really begin to take shape until the Han era when in A.D. 37 the Emperor Kuang Wu sponsored sacrifice at the grave of Confucius and conferred honors on his family. Even more important was the first regular cult paid to Confucius by Emperor Ming in A.D. 59, when he proclaimed that schools in the major cities should make sacrifice to Confucius. The cult became associated with education and the class of scholars in which Confucius functioned as a hero or patron saint.

Corresponding to the exaltation of the sage, there developed legends concerning his miraculous birth. While direct references to divinity were generally avoided, Confucius received honorific titles such as "Confucius, the perfectly holy teacher of antiquity." During the Ming period (A.D. 1363–1644) the cult was reformed. The image of Confucius was replaced by a tablet, and excessive titles were rejected. These changes led early Jesuit missionaries to regard the cult as reverence rather than worship.

The cult of Confucius was never a popular cult, but the reverence paid to him by the state naturally seeped down to the people so that on family and clan altars tablets, images, or pictures of Confucius were found along with Buddha, Kuan-ti, and ancestral tablets. As Hsu notes: "The popular gods in all family shrines were three: Kuan Kung (The warrior from Three Kingdoms), Confucius, and one or more Buddhas. A fourth popular figure is the Goddess of Mercy or Fertility."[4]

The Confucian cult was official instead of popular. The principle lying behind such official cults was that "the sages devised guidance by way of the gods and the (people in the) empire became obedient."[5]

In effect, the various cults receiving official authorization sanc-

3. John K. Shryock, *The Origin and Development of the State Cult of Confucius,* New York, Harper & Row, 1960, pp. 81–82, quoted from the *Lun Heng.*

4. Francis L. K. Hsu, *Under the Ancestor's Shadow,* New York, Doubleday, 1967, p. 184.

5. C. K. Yang, *Religion in Chinese Society,* Berkeley, Calif., University of California Press, 1961, p. 145.

tioned the ethical and political values of the society. The cult of Confucius had particular relation to the power of the state. According to C. K. Yang, it is a mistake to neglect the religious elements of this cult evident in the awe and reverence it induced among the people through its ceremonies and the dispersion of grand buildings through the country.[6]

After the death of Confucius his disciples, perhaps feeling need for his continued counsel and direction, culled from their memories his basic ideas and deposited them in a small manual now known as the *Analects* (*Lun-yu*), or "Words of Confucius."

CONFUCIUS' PHILOSOPHY OF HUMAN RELATIONS

Despite various textual problems concerning the present work, it is the most reliable source available for studying Confucius' thought. Its content is unsystematic, but there emerges a consistent system of values and insights on human behavior which have contributed to the formation of later Confucian philosophy and social theory. In order to grasp the distinctive features of his perspective, we must first consider the audience to whom the material is directed.

The audience assumed in the *Analects* was clearly the aspiring scholar-bureaucrats who sought positions in the courts of the various principalities. It was, consequently, a practical work with an aim to alert the individual to the problems of power in catering to powerful rulers and in controlling the common people. The practical advice given in the text, however, was susceptible to wider interpretation, since the problem of the man in power was only an intensified version of the problem facing all men—namely, how to develop and maintain successful human relationships.

Throughout the text there is an awareness of the limitations of sheer authoritarian compulsion and the use of force in gaining one's goals. There is also a recognition that society is structured with inevitable distinctions of superiority and inferiority. In every form of human relationship there is a leader and a follower. There is embodied in the basic philosophy the insight that individuals will accept any amount of authority provided they are permitted to retain their self respect and dignity. That government should benefit the people and that only the most morally competent should rule are two principles implied throughout the work. A basic element of governing or leading is knowing when to defer or yield. In view of these insights, the major issue confronting Confucius in the *Analects* is the formation of the appropriate moral character enabling the individual to wield power without force.

To realize the character for successful leadership Confucius advocates the cultivation of a number of principles and perspectives on human relations, all designed to contribute to harmony among men. These principles divide into interior and exterior aspects of moral life. Both dimensions are ultimately united in the ideal person. The central interior qualities of moral life essential to leadership are

6. Ibid., pp. 164–165.

jen, chung, shu, and *hsueh,*[7] while *li* and *hsiao* are the exterior elements of moral character.[8] All aspects are joined and harmonized in the ideal of the *chun-tzu* and *shih.* The power they manifest in human affairs is their *te.*

The achievement of ideal human existence requires the harmonization of the inner and outer aspects of man's life. The attainment of this harmony within himself would inevitably make the individual a leader among men through the attractiveness and magnetic quality of his character. In contrast to magical forms of charisma, Confucius asserts that the most real and effective charisma is rooted in the cultivation and expression of virtue. The durability of his thought rests on the fact that it is rational, being based on the realistic contemplation of the requirements for groups to maintain social life in the most meaningful way. It is not perfectionistic but only requires that those who subscribe to the ideal begin to move in that direction, starting where they find themselves at present. Heaven guarantees morality by responding to human actions with reward or punishment. Relying upon the classics, Confucius holds up the examples of the ancient sages and rulers such as Yao, Shun, Yu, Chou Kings Wen and Wu, and the Duke of Chou as the justification for his moral views and as models to be followed in the cultivation of virtue.

Jen stands as the supreme virtue and interior quality in Confucius' catalogue of values. As the symbol of Chinese humanism, the term embraces a wide range of meanings reflecting the importance of human relations. It may mean humaneness, humanity, human-heartedness, man-to-manness, love, benevolence, or goodness. In essence, jen is what one does when he is most truly human and implies that humanity is a task and an achievement.

As presented in the *Analects* the term jen has two dimensions. There is the level of expression in particular actions and attitudes, and a deeper dimension of perfection which can never be defined or exhausted in particular acts.

As Confucius believed that one must begin with lower things in order to arrive at the higher, we may begin to understand jen by indicating the types of action which may manifest that quality. When Jan Jung inquired about the nature of goodness, Confucius answered:

> *Behave when away from home as though you were in the presence of an important guest. Deal with the common people as though you were officiating at an important sacrifice. Do not do to others what you would not like yourself.*

> *(Analects XII.2)* [9]

7. Other correlative principles appearing in the *Analects* are *hsin* (faithfulness in keeping one's word) and *chi* (straightforwardness). Later, the quality *ch'eng,* usually translated as "sincerity," became a major virtue on the basis of the text of the *Chung-yung.*

8. The concept of *I* (righteousness) received greater stress in the teaching of Mencius as a correlate of *jen.*

9. Unless otherwise indicated, all quotations from the *Analects* are taken from the excellent translation by Arthur Waley, *The Analects of Confucius,* New York, Random House, 1938.

To Fan Chih he replied to the same question:

> In private life, courteous, in public life, diligent, in relationships, loyal. This is a maxim that no matter where you may be, even amid the barbarians of the east or north, may never be set aside.
>
> (*Analects* XIII.19)

In response to Tzu-chang, Confucius indicated that the good person would possess five virtues: courtesy, breadth, good faith, diligence, and clemency.

It is interesting to note in relation to the ultimacy and supremacy of jen that there are actually few passages delineating specifically the actions and qualities which constitute it. The *Analects* indicate that Confucius rarely spoke of jen, and never claimed to be good himself. As he pointed out, the man of jen is chary (jen) of speech because it is a quality difficult to attain. Confucius refused to judge the jen quality of specific persons or situations. However, it is possible to move in the direction of jen by turning one's merits to account and helping others to apply theirs, as well as using one's own feelings as a guide in helping others according to the principle of reciprocity. Everyone should compete in the pursuit of jen. One pursues it by making friends with those who manifest it.

Confucius recognized the problem of the inner reality and the external appearance. He maintained that jen came from within the man and could not be derived from someone else:

> For Goodness is something that must have its source in the ruler himself; it cannot be got from others.
>
> (*Analects* XII.1)

A true gentleman may lack jen, but all possessing jen would of necessity be true gentlemen. True jen avoids artifice as represented in clever talk and pretentious manners.

The pursuit of jen is not easy. If it is to be undertaken, it must be the primary goal of life, and, although it is a difficult task, it is the source of true happiness. While it enables one to bear up under adversity and eventually to achieve prosperity, it is an end in itself:

> The Good man rests content with Goodness; he that is merely wise pursues Goodness in the belief that it pays to do so.
>
> (*Analects* IV.2)

Finally, jen is the basis for the love of men, and it is the only means to make power durable after one's wisdom has brought him into power.

From the brief indications of jen provided in the *Analects* we can observe a studied attempt to avoid pinning the virtue down in such a way that one could assert that his superficial and limited efforts had fully expressed the quality. The nature of jen on its deepest level is a quality possessed by sages and heroes as a transcendental perfection. It is never fully present in living or historic persons.[10]

Although the political or social dimension of Confucius' thought appears to be its central interest, the ultimate indefinability of jen

10. Waley, ibid, p. 27.

and its crucial role in forming the basis for all successful rule and exercise of power make Confucius' thought more than mere politics or ethics. Rather, he seems to point toward a situation in which the moral order is embodied in men, enabling them to realize their full human potential.

According to Confucius, the "beads" of jen are strung on the threads of chung (conscientiousness, loyalty) and shu (reciprocity, altruism). The fulfillment of the human potential implied in jen requires a deep awareness of others and identification with them. When asked if there is a principle that would be applicable day or night, Confucius offers the quality shu expressed in the Golden Rule: Never do to others what you would not like them to do to you.

The character in Chinese for shu is a combination of the term for "like" and "similar" and the term for "mind." Behind this principle lies an idea of identification enabling persons to know the appropriate behavior for dealing with others through considering what they themselves need to live happily and securely. This principle is not to be applied mechanically. Rather, it can only be realized when there is a felt sense of oneness with others. It is in line with this principle that Confucius rejects action based on calculation of profit for oneself. The foundation for true ethical action in Confucius' view comes from contemplating what benefits all, and not merely oneself.

An ethic based on shu is more dynamic and inward than an imposed, external ethic. Shu does not exclude the existence and necessity of formal prescriptions of behavior, but it means that their application will be dictated in accord with the situation. Thus, morality is not fixed or static. Confucius is reputed to have said: "As for me, I am different from any of these. I have no 'thou shalt' or 'thou shalt not' " (*Analects* XVIII.8). Further, he was astute in noting that people with fixed principles are good when there is need for someone to take a position on an issue, but they cannot function in an emergency calling for flexibility and adaptation.

It is clear that Confucius was attempting to replace the traditional, tribal morality with an inwardly motivated morality based on one's awareness of his common humanity with others. In this view of morality he was far in advance of his time and mankind as a whole. E. R. Hughes succinctly summarizes the problem Confucius confronted:

> It was an age of marked individualism, individualism of the dangerous egotistical kind, and Confucius' achievement was to point out to all who would listen that a man is not more of a man because he has fiercer appetites and more power to gratify them, but when he can recognize his fellow man as having equal rights with himself.[11]

The quality chung, which generally accompanies shu, complements it. Chung represents the development of one's mind, while shu is the extension of that mind to others. According to Yu-lan

11. E. R. Hughes and K. Hughes, *Religion in China*, London, Hutchinson, 1950, p. 27.

Fung, though the concept chung is not defined in detail in the *Analects,* it carries the meaning of acting on behalf of others.[12] One is exhorted to be conscientious in dealing with all men, loyal to the prince one serves.

An indispensable quality or attitude in the cultivation of virtue was the desire for, and love of, hsueh (learning, study), or wisdom. While goodness (jen) is the goal of virtue, learning is its condition. It is significant that Confucius did not boast of his goodness or perfection, but rather of his love of learning. He regarded learning as an essential qualification for teaching, since only "he who by reanimating the Old can gain knowledge of the New is fit to be a teacher" (*Analects* VII.33). The learning advocated by Confucius was not restricted merely to the acquisition of information, but included the wisdom which recognized the limits of one's knowledge. Learning was to be pursued with utter seriousness and no possible source rejected, since it was only through such learning that the virtues could be kept in proper harmony without excess or distortion.

It is thus clear that for Confucius the purpose of learning was to build moral character and not merely to instruct in skill or impart information. Maintaining that "a gentleman is not an implement" (*Analects* II.12), he desired to develop leaders who were persons of broad moral quality rather than specialists in some activity. Consequently, he refused requests of disciples that he teach them farming and gardening.

Learning is for change. Confucius notes that the already wise and the stupid do not change. The wise probably do not need to, while the stupid do not want to change. The love of learning, though stated as a boast, is a confession of imperfection and openness to the future. Confucius complained that his moral power and learning remained imperfect.

Confucius' ideal of teaching was strikingly modern. He taught without discriminating according to class or economic ability. Only the desire to learn was necessary. He demanded, however, that the person who came to him for instruction must be committed and engaged in the effort to learn. He did not so much *give* education as he challenged the individual to gain his own.

> If I hold up one corner and a man cannot come back to me with the other three, I do not continue the lesson.
>
> (*Analects* VII.28)

He worked with students individually, adapting his approach to the student's need. He did not claim to have all wisdom, but remained open to thrashing out questions put to him even by the simplest peasant. Despite his willingness to work with all people, Confucius did not advocate indiscriminately using one's time and energy:

> The Master said, Not to talk to one who could be talked to, is to waste a man. To talk to those who cannot be talked to, is to

12. Yu-lan Fung, *History of Chinese Philosophy,* Princeton, N.J., Princeton University Press, vol. I, p. 71, n.1.

*waste one's words. "He who is truly wise never wastes a man,"
but on the other hand, he never wastes words.*

(Analects XV.7, VI.19, XV.15)

Since Confucius' philosophy of human relations was practical and not merely theoretical, the interior moral qualities had to find expression in supporting and complementary behavior. The concept li covered the whole range of human activities from the performance of religious rituals, such as practices of mourning, to dress, personal manners, and decorum within the family and among associates. In addition, Confucius stressed hsiao (filial piety) as an important aspect of moral behavior.

Although the Chinese character for li originally signified placing ritual vessels in proper order for sacrifice, the concept expanded to embrace all things properly done. In Confucian thought it came to represent the rationalized social order and conventions which aid in avoiding conflicts. As the practical means for achieving harmony, Confucius claimed that the people would respond to the goodness (jen) of the ruler if he would conform to li.

The necessity of li stems from the fact that the direct expression of virtue can at times be as destructive of human relations as creative. Li provides the fine polish and restraint needed to make virtue effective. Confucius states:

Courtesy not bounded by the prescriptions of ritual becomes tiresome. Caution not bounded by the prescriptions of ritual becomes timidity, daring becomes turbulence, inflexibility becomes harshness.

(Analects VIII.2)

Confucius is also aware that the li might become mere external show. He maintains that the inner and outer must be harmonized, since "only when ornament and substance are duly blended do you get the true gentleman" (*Analects* III.12).

Hsiao (filial piety) loomed important in Confucius' thought as a test of the actual moral character of the individual. His basic assumption was that without a deep sense of obligation toward one's parents who made his existence possible, an individual could not be trusted to have the necessary sense of obligation toward other members of society. Further, the discipline of family life was the foundation for the inculcation of the attitudes of loyalty, faithfulness, and submissiveness required for social harmony. Although Confucius regarded filial piety as essential to moral and social life, he did not consider it the supreme virtue which it later became in the *Hsiao-ching* (*Classic of Filial Piety,* written 350–250 B.C.).

Confucius held that sons should obey and defer to their parents. However, a son should also remonstrate with his parents when they fell into error. Should they fail to accept his admonitions, he must remain silent and unresentful out of respect for them.

All the virtues and qualities advanced by Confucius as the foundation and expression of moral character were combined in the ideal person termed chun-tzu. This word, originally referring to the son of a ruler or an aristocrat by birth, came to mean in the *Analects* the true gentleman or superior person as a result of his moral development. The term shih (knight, warrior) also came to signify a person of highest moral attainment rather than the virtues of warfare.

Fundamentally, the chun-tzu represents the fusion of all qualities in such a way that a person can respond to every situation benefiting mankind without sacrificing his principles. He is particularly distinguished by his faithfulness, diligence, and modesty. He neither overpowers with his knowledge, nor is afraid to admit error. He looks at all sides of any issue, is cautious and not concerned for personal recognition. Carrying himself with dignity, he appears imperturbable, resolute, and simple. He is exemplary in filial piety and generous with his kin. In his relations with others he looks for good points, though he is not uncritical. As a leader, he knows how to delegate responsibility and when to pardon or promote. He is sensitive to the feelings and expressions of others, knowing when to defer or desist. Always conciliatory, he does not merely accommodate.

In addition to the numerous qualities which depict the true gentleman, there are specific principles which govern his actions. Most important, he is committed to the good as an end in itself and to right before all else. He rejects seeking mere personal profit as well as doing wrong in order to advance or to serve an evil prince. He will not employ expediency. Honesty is essential to life. Ready to lay down his life for the good, he serves his master in faithfulness. He demands more of himself than of others. He holds to consistency (of principle), but not blind fidelity. He neither judges things by externals, nor by eloquence or status:

> A gentleman does not
> Accept men because of what they say,
> Nor reject sayings, because the speaker is what he is.
>
> (*Analects* XV.22)

In summary, the chun-tzu combines inner quality and spirit with outer form. He provides the harmony of substance and ornament. However, in such an ideal there is always the possibility of mere sham. Confucius notes that the gentleman may not always be good, meaning perhaps that the good could not be exhausted in any expression. Eloquence is not moral power, though they can be confused. A brave man is not necessarily good. One must be careful of those who put on solemn airs. Many passages scattered through the text criticizing the decadence of the age suggest that the true gentleman is a rarity, and Confucius almost despaired of creating or finding one.

The ideal of the chun-tzu in his nature and function created several issues which stimulated the development of later Confucian thought. These issues comprise a series of dichotomies, which, though interrelated, affect the cultivation and application of Confucian ideals. The first polarization is the conflict between devotion to self-cultivation and the ordering of society. The second dichotomy concerns the harmonization and mutual relation of inward moral capacity and the outer sphere of rules, rituals, and forms.

The third polarity was the relationship of knowledge and action. It was generally agreed that the basis of action was knowledge and learning. The problem was the nature of this knowledge and how it was developed. The earlier scholarly, historical, and factual approach of Confucius eventually developed into the more metaphysical approach of the Neo-Confucians, who sought intellectual enlightenment either by discovery of the essential harmony in the outer world or through intuiting it in the inner world of mind.[13]

As we have earlier pointed out, the fusion of moral qualities in the true gentleman endows him with profound effectiveness in creating and maintaining human relationships. The moral charisma which he generates is denoted by the term te, that peculiar efficaciousness resulting when a thing or person functions as it is designed to function. The essence of leadership is the ability to influence. Influence depends on character, in contrast to coercion which requires force. Te, as moral influence, is that power which causes people to do things on behalf of others through their own volition and desire. Confucius aptly sums up the meaning of te:

> Govern the people by regulations, keep order among them by chastisements, and they will flee from you, and lose all self respect. Govern them by moral force, keep order among them by ritual and they will keep their self respect and come to you of their own accord.
>
> (Analects II.3)

Although in theory te was practical, it appears that in Confucius' time men hesitated to enter fully into his way. He complained that only a few understood it and that he had not seen anyone in whom te was as strong as his sexual power. Some apparently were willing to apply te only in certain limited situations.

There were also dangers which obstruct te or destroy it. It is not to be confused with eloquence. Physical prowess is also no true indicator of te. Clever talk confounds te, while hearing the teaching and merely repeating without acting on it is to throw it away. The attempt to please everyone also undermines te.

As te is perhaps the inner force of attraction generated by the ideal ruler and official, its correlate, wen, is the exterior quality of culture, bearing, poise, and carriage expressed in the polite arts and ritual. Although the substance is prior to the decoration, the element of culture is indispensable. The attractive power of culture is expressed by Master Tseng:

> The gentleman by his culture collects friends about him, and through these friends promotes Goodness.
>
> (Analects XII.24)

Wen refers concretely to the arts of peace such as music and dancing, and literature in contrast to war. It is whatever beautifies

13. Benjamin Schwartz, "Some Polarities in Confucian Thought," in A. F. Wright, *Confucianism and Chinese Civilization*, New York, Atheneum, 1964, pp. 3–15.

human existence. Confucius believed that the true way to conquer a people was to spread culture. Although one may win the battle, in order to prevail completely one must have won. Illustration of the Confucian principle appears in the Greek cultural conquest of the Romans after they themselves had been conquered militarily. The principle has frequently been tested in Chinese history where invader after invader succumbed to the allure of Chinese culture.

Before concluding the study of Confucius' thought, we should note that he employed the concepts Tao (Way) and T'ien (Heaven) in the discussion of his philosophy. In contrast to later Taoist thought, the Tao of Confucius was represented by the chun-tzu as the highest ideal of human endeavor. For him the Tao was primarily social. Aware of rival views of Tao, Confucius claimed that when his Tao prevailed, society would be ordered and authority effective. The ultimate basis for his philosophy, according to Confucius, was T'ien. Heaven was the source of moral power which guaranteed virtue. Hence, the Tao set forth by Confucius was ultimately the will of Heaven. This view was based on his conviction that his system of morality conformed to the nature of man when he functioned as a true human being.

The concept of Heaven is important in strengthening the moral commitment of the true gentleman. It gives him confidence that a power greater than his own individual strength works through his efforts to attain its ends. The belief in the ordination of Heaven mitigates disappointment when things do not go as men might desire. For this reason the true gentleman must fear and understand Heaven, since it gives perspective to his efforts and keeps the necessary balance in his deportment and attitudes.

Heaven appears in some ways to be a personal force, but it is certainly unlike spirits and ghosts. Confucius does not speculate on its nature, but attributes all events outside the control of man to the will of Heaven. Sometimes he appeals to Heaven to avert the consequences of his errors.

Confucius' contribution to the history of moral and social thought lies in his articulation of a consistent system of inner values and qualities and correlation of external actions which must be the basis for effective government. His ideal of the true gentleman is a comprehensive and universal goal which, in its humane, compassionate, sensitive, and implicitly democratic character, is worthy of serious pursuit. Its relevance for this age of moral and social confusion will be apparent to thoughtful students. Nevertheless, Confucius does not speculate on the nature of reality or the nature of man to determine precisely what basis there is in reality or man for the achievement of these aspirations. The further exploration of his thought remained for his interpreters, especially Mencius (Meng-tzu, 372–288 B.C.) and Hsun-tzu (298–238 B.C.)

In the period after Confucius the political conflicts multiplied and intensified. At the same time more challenging solutions to the problems of human relations contended for acceptance, as indicated in the so-called Hundred Schools. Social thought swung between the

INTERPRETERS OF CONFUCIUS: MENCIUS AND HSUN-TZU

two poles of despair and rejection of social conventions of Yang-chu (440–369 B.C.?) and a more utopian idealism of universal love of Mo-ti (479–380 B.C.) The Confucianists followed a middle path between these extremes, applying the rational and practical outlook of the master.

Yang-chu became the symbol of social irresponsibility and indifference, espousing a hedonistic enjoyment of life. He was described by Mencius as advocating an "every man for himself" philosophy without any allegiance to a ruler and refusing to save the world even if it required only the plucking of a hair. His doctrine was pictured as a grand egoism because he put the enhancement and nurture of one's own individual existence before social obligations. The *Lu-shih Ch'un-ch'iu* quotes Yang-chu:

> *Now, my life is my own possession, and its benefit to me is also great. If we discuss what is noble and mean, even the honor of being Emperor could not compare with it. If we discuss what is unimportant and important, even the wealth of possessing the empire could not be exchanged for it. If we discuss peace and danger, were we to lose it for only one morning, we could never bring it back. These are three points on which those who have understanding are careful. There are those who care too much about life and so injure it. This is because they have not reached an understanding of the qualities of human life. Without such an understanding, of what avail is caution? . . . Among the rulers and nobles of the world, whether worthy or unworthy, there are none who do not desire to live long and see many days. Yet if they daily obstruct the course of their life, of what avail is such a desire? All long life consists in non-resistance to it. What causes such resistance are the desires. Therefore the Sage must first of all put his desires into harmony.*[14]

It is clear that Yang-chu did not promote licentiousness by his hedonism, but a principle of not being ensnared by things and affairs. Although from a later time, the sentiment of the Yang-chu chapter in the *Lieh-tzu* expressed succinctly the spirit of those ancient recluses who rejected conventional social striving as destructive to one's inner spirit and integrity:

> *Do we live for the sake of being cowed into submission by the fear of the law and penalties, now spurred to frenzied action by the promise of a reward or fame? We waste ourselves in a mad scramble, seeking to snatch the hollow praise of the hour, scheming to contrive that somehow some remnant of reputation shall outlast our lives. We move through the world in a narrow groove, pre-occupied with the petty things we see and hear, brooding over our prejudices, passing by the joys of life without even knowing that we have missed anything. Never for a moment do we taste the heady wine of freedom. We are as truly imprisoned as if we lay at the bottom of a dungeon.*[15]

14. Fung, op. cit., p. 137.
15. H. G. Creel, *Chinese Thought from Confucius to Mao Tse-tung*, New York, New American Library, 1953, pp. 82–83.

The tradition of iconoclasm and social criticism began very early in Chinese history. In the *Analects* (XVIII.5, 7) there appear several incidents when Confucius or his disciples encountered anarchistically inclined individualists who did not hesitate to criticize his activities. As we shall see, the Taoists, Lao-tzu and Chuang-tzu, were direct inheritors of these views, though providing them with a deeper mystical and philosophical basis.

At the opposite extreme from Yang-chu, Mo-ti advocated a utilitarian, utopian principle of universal or indiscriminate love (*ch'ien-ai*) as the ultimate solution to human problems. Although little is known of the teacher himself, he was, like Confucius, from the province of Lu and at first sought office as a Confucianist. Failing in his ambition, he turned to private teaching and developed a philosophy and way of life which criticized the Confucian emphasis on elaborate ceremonial music and uneconomic ostentation. In his own character he was an ascetic, combining intellectual acumen and moral intensity. Unlike the Confucianists, he formed a tight-knit organization by which he could direct the activities of his disciples more closely. Each student had to contribute to the master's upkeep. Through the control of his students, Mo-ti could refuse to serve rulers who did not accept his teachings.

The basic principle of his social thought by which he achieved fame was his exhortation of universal love. Although criticized by Confucianists, the concept is an extension of the Confucian principles of jen (love, humaneness) and shu (reciprocity) applied without discrimination to all people. In defense of his principle, Mo-ti appealed to the instinctive behavior of men to show that all people really accepted it, though in theory and word they might reject it. He pointed out that in a situation of crisis and disaster, people would appeal to rulers or individuals whom they knew to be inspired by generosity and social concern rather than to those they knew to be narrow and selfish. Such a reaction in his view testified to their tacit awareness of the necessity and truth of the principle of universal love. He stated:

> *It seems to me on such occasions as these there are no fools in the world. Even though he be a person who objects to universal love himself, he would choose the "universal" rulers. This is rejection of the principle in word but acceptance of it in actually making a choice—this is a contradiction between one's word and deed. It is incomprehensible, then, why the gentlemen of the world should object to universal love when they hear of it.*[16]

A corollary principle growing out of the assertion of universal love was the idea of utilitarian benefit as the basis of durable order. This concept of profit appears entirely contrary to Confucian rejection of profit, but the two perspectives may be reconciled when it is understood that Confucians denied personal profit while retaining concern for the total good. Generally Mo-ti espoused the greatest good for the greatest number as the objective of government. In re-

16. William Theodore De Bary, *Sources of Chinese Tradition*, New York, Columbia, 1964, vol. I, p. 43.

alizing this, rulers must promote productivity throughout the kingdom and stress frugality and simplicity in living.

Another corollary aspect of his philosophy was the rejection of aggressive warfare. Although opposed to violence, Mo-ti developed a reputation for defensive warfare and expertise in fortifications. He lent his services to besieged, weaker kingdoms.

Despite the apparent idealistic and sentimental character of the concept of universal love, Mo-ti supported strong central government to bring order to the world. He also urged the rejection of the Confucian concept of fate and the maintenance of belief in the gods and spirits in order to induce men to belief in universal love on pain of divine retribution. In addition, he preached obedience and submission to superiors, ignoring egalitarian implications of his doctrine.

The importance of Mo-ti's philosophy lies in his recognition that society must inculcate into people a broad concern for others beyond the limits of self and kin if it is to have stability. He should be credited with the astute insight that people always prefer others to be altruistic toward them, though they may act egotistically toward others. Further, in exalting material prosperity as the index of the achievement of a society he was very close to modern exponents who employ the standard of living as the basis for judging social progress.

Mencius, the St. Paul of Confucianism, lamented that the doctrines of Yang and Mo filled the world and had great appeal to the people of that time. He made it his mission to refute these philosophies and to revive the fortunes of Confucianism. Mencius' career paralleled in many ways that of Confucius. Born in the region of Tsou in Lu, he became a disciple of Confucius' grandson Tzu-ssu. In the course of his life he served numerous rulers. His thought has been preserved in the text called *Mencius*.

The *Mencius* differs conspicuously from the *Analects* in being more discursive in style. Whereas Confucius' ideas appear in epigrammatic form without elaboration, the arguments of Mencius are more fully articulated to meet the challenge of opponents. His arguments in defense of Confucianism are probably the basic reason for its eventual supremacy over other schools and its lasting influence. Though Mencius, like Confucius, is humble in attributing his views to the sages of the past, there can be no doubt concerning his creative intellectual insight.

The starting point of Mencius' thought was the Confucian assumption that to be a human being means to be a social being and that the principles of social behavior are rooted in human nature. Consequently, all theories are false which conflict with man's nature. A major consideration of Mencius and later Confucians was the definition of the nature of man.

It was from this standpoint that Mencius criticized Yang-chu for undermining allegiance to rulers, and Mo-ti for not recognizing the gradations of love in human psychology. Both, as panaceas for society, were extreme and one-sided, as well as unrealistic in understanding human nature.

With this theory of the goodness of human nature Mencius clarified the ambiguity of Confucius who simply declared without elaboration that men were "by nature, near together; by practice far apart." [17] Like Mo-ti, Mencius appeals to the spontaneous actions of people as evidence for his view. When people confront various human problems, they react with compassion, commiseration, shame, dislike, or modesty. These responses he terms "the beginnings" of the basic qualities that distinguish men from animals. When these innate potentialities of moral behavior are allowed to develop to their fullest, they express themselves in behavior embodying the qualities of jen (humaneness), I (righteousness), li (propriety), and chih (knowledge or wisdom). That men lack goodness is simply because they have not permitted their capacities to develop. Thus he argues:

The real kings of old were compassionate human beings, and so theirs was a government by compassionate men. And having thus brought order to the world, they turned it on the palm of their hands. It can be said that all men have a capacity for compassion because, even today, if one chances to see a toddler about to fall into a well, one becomes apprehensive and sympathetic. This is not because one knows the child's parents; it is not out of desire for the praise of neighbors and friends; and it is not out of dislike for the bad reputation that would ensue if one did not go to the rescue. In the light of all this we can conclude that without compassion one would not be a human being. And the same holds if there is no sense of shame, no ability to yield to others, no sense of what is correct and what is not correct. The sense of compassion marks the beginning of becoming man-at-his-best. The sense of shame marks the beginning of propriety. Submissiveness marks the beginning of a sense of ceremony. The sense of right and wrong is the beginning of wisdom. Every human being possesses these four beginnings just as he possesses four limbs. . . .
(*Mencius* II.A.6) [18]

A number of significant implications for the view of man and society flow from Mencius' theory of human goodness. He recognized the essential equality of all men in maintaining that every man could become a sage through proper cultivation of his nature. As a result of his high estimation of man, he interpreted the Mandate of Heaven as the basis for revolution against despotic kings, making government rest on the will of the people. He further insisted that the purpose of government was to benefit the people and enable them to fulfill their potentialities. To do this the ruler should provide universal education and sufficient work and income to make crime unnecessary to survive. He saw the necessity of a division of labor in society as represented in traditional class structure, but he maintained that it was functional and no real indication of the essential worth of

17. *Analects* XVII. 2. See also V. 12.
18. James Ware, trans., *The Sayings of Mencius,* New York, New American Library, 1960, pp. 68–69.

people. Mencius clearly understood that social institutions do not make people good, but enable them to express goodness.

In order to achieve this, it is necessary to have exemplary rulers who stimulate the people in their moral efforts. Accordingly, true kingship is realized when the ruler shares his benefits with the people and identifies with them. Through his compassion on their behalf he would be universally attractive to his own people and those beyond his borders. Ministers to kings must play the role of critic when occasion demands. A minister must never serve an evil king. Both the king and his ministers need self-scrutiny to evaluate their actions.

It is in this connection that Mencius proclaimed a type of moral mysticism which cultivated the discernment of and commitment to moral values even in difficult times. Though the precise method of meditation was not specified, it produced a state described as "being on top of oneself and the world" and embraced an intuitive conviction relating to the rightness of things. It was not a mysticism in which one lost his personality in an all-embracing reality. Rather, it related concretely to life in this world where, by moral exercise, the division of the egocentric world and the outer world was abolished through consistent goodness. Mencius related:

> It is difficult to describe. As power, it is exceedingly great and exceedingly strong. If nourished by uprightness and not injured, it will fill up all between heaven and earth. As power, it is accompanied by righteousness and the Way. Without them, it will be devoid of nourishment. It is produced by the accumulation of righteous deeds but it is not obtained by incidental acts of righteousness. When one's conduct is not satisfactory to his own mind, then one will be devoid of nourishment.
>
> (*Mencius* II.A.2) [19]

According to this passage, righteous action reinforced moral commitment, which in turn stimulated further action. Mencius forged the union of knowledge and action, later to be stressed in Neo-Confucianism, within a highly sensitive moral consciousness.

The deep moral concern of Mencius was reflected in his analysis of the profit principle which Confucianism has consistently rejected. He asserted that all ambitions motivated by desire for profit and advantage were open-ended and could never be fully satisfied until the ruler or individual had striven to attain complete possession and control. There would also be a competitive struggle for advantage once the challenge was issued. In true government, following correct procedure and propriety would naturally result in the satisfaction of all interests.

Mencius' thought in its turn received criticism from several quarters. He engaged in lengthy conversations concerning Kao-tzu, a non-Confucian who maintained the moral neutrality of human nature and asserted that one's goodness or badness depended on external

19. Wing-tsit Chan, *A Sourcebook in Chinese Philosophy*, Princeton, N.J., Princeton University Press, 1963, p. 63.

conditions. Within the Confucian tradition itself, the philosopher Hsun-tzu took issue directly with Mencius' thesis, declaring: "Mencius states that man is capable of learning because his nature is good, but I say that this is wrong. It indicates he has not really understood man's nature nor distinguished properly between the basic nature and conscious activity." [20]

In following out his argument, Hsun-tzu declared that man's basic nature was evil, while such goodness as he possessed was acquired. Nature, according to him, signified whatever man possessed that was neither learned nor worked for. He regarded ethical and moral conduct as determined by culture. Similar to previous thinkers, Hsun-tzu summoned the spontaneous behavior of individuals as evidence for his position. He observed that from the time of birth onward, man was egocentric and desirous of his own profit and advantage; that he possessed violent emotions of envy and hatred. Driven by desires, man naturally found himself in conflict with his fellow men. Certainly, the background of conflicts in the age of Warring States could furnish ample evidence of the thesis.

In order to deal with this fundamental selfishness in man, the sages had developed rituals and regulations in order to train (socialize) human behavior. The goodness of man was the result of restraining human nature just as "a warped piece of wood must wait until it has been laid against the straightening board, steamed and forced into shape before it can become straight. . . ." [21]

As a consequence of his view of man, Hsun-tzu, contrary to Mo-ti, regarded music, ritual, and ceremonies as indispensable in the cultivation and refinement of human emotion. He complained that Mo-ti did not understand human emotion. According to Hsun-tzu, "music is the great arbiter of the world, the key to central harmony, and a necessary requirement of human emotion. This is the manner in which the former kings created their music. And yet Mo Tzu criticises it. Why?" [22] "Therefore, I say that Mo Tzu's attempts to teach the Way may be compared to a blind man trying to distinguish black from white. . . ." [23]

As music exerted a beneficial influence on the spirit of man, bringing harmony and tranquillity, Hsun-tzu noted the function of ritual and ceremony in social control. According to him, the ancient kings established rituals in order to overcome disorder. However, the rites also had a deep root in human emotion, being a means of expressing human feeling in moments of depression, melancholy, or times of elation. He stated:

Hence the sacrificial rites originate in the emotions of remembrance and longing, express the highest degree of loyalty, love and reverence, and embody what is finest in ritual conduct and formal bearing. Only a sage can fully understand them. The sage

20. Burton Watson, *Basic Writings of Mo-tzu, Hsun-tzu, Han Fei-tzu*, New York, Columbia, 1967, p. 158.
21. Ibid., p. 157.
22. Ibid., pp. 113–114.
23. Ibid., p. 114.

understands them, the gentleman finds comfort in carrying them out, the officials are careful to maintain them, and the common people accept them as custom. To the gentleman they are part of the way of man; to the common people they are something pertaining to the spirits.[24]

Hsun-tzu's perspective on religious ritual was rationalistic, distinguishing between the true understanding of the sage and gentleman and the naive belief of the common man. Further, he regarded religion as a form of art or means of beautifying life. It ennobled existence with form, order, and meaning, impressing man with his relation to the spheres of Heaven, earth, and man.

His rationalistic, antisuperstitious tendency was also expressed in his concept of Heaven, which he regarded as an amoral, naturalistic process. His view contrasted sharply with the anthropomorphic, moralistic conception of Confucius and Mencius. According to Hsun-tzu, Heaven had its regularities which, without peering into the causes of phenomena, the sage could utilize beneficially. He rejected occult interest in heavenly phenomena, for man could only affect the actions of men, not of Heaven:

You pray for rain and it rains. Why? For no particular reason, I say. It is just as though you had not prayed for rain and it rained anyway. The sun and moon undergo an eclipse and you try to save them; a drought occurs and you pray for rain; you consult the arts of divination before making a decision on some important matter. But it is not as though you could hope to accomplish anything by such ceremonies. They are done merely for ornament. Hence the gentleman regards them as ornaments, but the common people regard them as supernatural. He who considers them ornaments is fortunate; he who considers them supernatural is unfortunate.[25]

Hsun-tzu manifested a deep scholarly interest and perspective and possessed a confidence in human intellect, believing that man could control his destiny through effort and reason. However, he appears gripped by pessimism concerning man's moral capacities. His social theory based on this pessimism contributed to the development of the authoritarianism of the Ch'in dynasty. Although Hsun-tzu carried forward the rationalistic and intellectual tendencies of Confucianism, his thought fell into the shadow before the more positive and inspiring view of man of Mencius.

CONFUCIANISM IN
THE TA-HSUEH AND
CHUNG-YUNG

In addition to the three major figures who laid the foundation for Confucian tradition, we must also call attention to two texts which became particularly influential in the Neo-Confucian philosophy of Chu-hsi (1130–1200). The *Ta-hsueh* (*Great Learning*) and *Chung-yung* (*Doctrine of the Mean*), as we earlier noted, were sections in the Chinese classic *Li-chi* (*Book of Ceremonies*). Although the dates

24. Ibid., p. 110.
25. Ibid., p. 85.

of composition of the works remain uncertain, they revealed at an early age the two basic tendencies of Confucianism, namely, rationalism and intuitionism or mysticism.

The *Ta-hsueh* is a short chapter, presenting in capsule form a summary of the Confucian basic approach to life. Though the work is attributed to Confucius himself, the authenticity is doubtful. It is an advance over Confucius' thought in the *Analects* because it is a more systematic presentation of his basic ideas.

The text opens with a statement of the three major concerns of Confucian teaching: manifesting clear character, loving the people, and abiding in the highest good. As an outline of Confucian teaching, they indicate that the basis of life rests in cultivating the inner self, applying oneself on behalf of the people, and striving to realize the highest good or jen. The text shows that the order of the world depends on the proper ordering of the self and all human relations based on the investigation and extension of knowledge. The world rests on character and character is founded on insight.

We may summarize its philosophy briefly, following the text's chain of reasoning. In order for the ruler to make clear his character, he must bring order to the state. Order is brought to the state through order in the family, and one may regulate his family by cultivating his personal life. In order to cultivate the personal life, one must rectify his mind. When the mind is rectified, the will will be sincere. Sincerity will result when one's knowledge is extended through the investigation of things. Working back through the chain, we can see that the life of man begins with knowledge as the basis for the cultivation of character and the proper functioning of every level of social existence. Implicitly the text affirms that society is no better than the people who make it up, whether ruler or common person.

The text not only emphasizes the fact that the health of society rests on the character of those who live in that society, but it stresses that it is of utmost necessity to have a proper ordering of values. We must know what is primary and what is secondary. The principle that the primary knowledge of the highest good yields inner tranquillity reveals a basic insight into the conduct of life. Knowing the goal and foundation of one's life makes possible the detachment and confidence required to reach necessary decisions.

The *Chung-yung* (*Doctrine of the Mean*) is a work of decidedly more mystical character, elucidating themes taught earlier by Mencius. Its mystical emphasis made it popular among Taoists and Buddhists as well as Confucianists. They were attracted by its philosophical character. As the title (the terms appear in *Analects* VI. 27) indicates, it is concerned with what is central (*chung*) and universal or harmonious (*yung*). It deals with human nature and its relation to reality. According to Yu-lan Fung, the terms have the meaning of equilibrium and normality which characterize the superior man in contrast to the small, petty man. In this view the superior man performs the proper actions fitting to the situation. The concept "mean" has the sense of hitting the mark or correctness, as in common speech we say that the person is right on target.

The consideration of human action and morality is set within the framework of the great harmony which exists between man and Nature. This harmony is realized through sincerity, which is not a passive attitude in man, but involves practical efforts to manifest in human affairs the ultimate harmony of man and Nature. Pursuing the harmony of Nature within human personality, Confucian ethical perspective receives a basis in Nature which differs from its earlier emphasis on the sages as models of human behavior.

Education is the process whereby man develops the capacity to express his fundamental unity with Nature. The natural sentiments of joy, anger, sorrow, and pleasure receive expression in proper measure through instruction. The true gentleman thus attains the equilibrium and poise required to manage affairs.

A major conception in the *Chung-yung* is *ch'eng* which may be variously translated as sincerity, reality, or truth. As reality, it is the way of Heaven and the foundation of harmony. It is the only basis of successful government and may be cultivated in man through the five steps of study, inquiry, thinking, sifting, and practice.

In contrast to the ordinary conception in the West of sincerity as an attitude of a person toward his actions, the concept of ch'eng signifies that a man is sincere when his actions and attitudes are in harmony with the highest reality and that reality radiates through his deportment. The background of the concept is the ancient Chinese view of the universe as a grand organic harmony of Heaven and earth. All phases of the cosmic process, including human existence, have a common essence revealed in the perfect equilibrium and harmony of the cosmic process. To manifest this harmony in human affairs in every situation is to be sincere.

LATER
DEVELOPMENTS
IN CONFUCIAN
TRADITION

As the basic perspective on life and the fundamental value system had been established in the classical period through the writings of the figures and texts studied above, there has been little decisive change in the character of Confucianism except in the direction of broadening the vistas of understanding reality and pursuing the realization of those values. After a setback in the persecution of scholars by the Ch'in despots, Confucianism, under the Han rulers, attained the position of the official ideology of the state. It never retreated from this position down to modern times. Despite the lack of great alteration in basic outlook through the centuries, there have appeared significant thinkers who amplified or refined its understanding. We may only mention them briefly here as a guideline to the further study of Confucian tradition.

Tung Chung-shu (179–104 B.C.) is noteworthy for the cosmological framework he gave to Confucianism, and his effort to relate the political order to the order of Nature. His thought was based on the *I-ching* and the theory of yin-yang. Accordingly, the universe was seen as a system of coordinated, interrelated parts in a continual process of transformation. Human life was a microcosm of the great system and the interaction between the human and natural orders was based on morality. In his concept of man Tung Chung-shu attempted to unite the theories of Mencius and Hsun-tzu.

Wang Chung (A.D. 27–100) was noted for his rationalistic approach to religion, and he was critical of the flourishing interest in divination and Taoism. He attacked the conception that Nature responds morally to man's actions by arguing that the yin-yang process was entirely impersonal, man being no more comparatively than a flea or a louse. He rejected belief in ghosts and afterlife. He appeared to be progressive in opposing reverence of the past for its own sake, and scientific in stressing factuality in assessment of the classics. In his understanding of man he attempted also to unite the theories of Mencius and Hsun-tzu.

The development of Confucian thought suffered in the decline of the Han empire and loss of confidence in the ability of Confucianism to solve pressing problems. As a consequence, Taoism revived and Buddhism began to attract intellectuals and assume spiritual leadership. After the Buddhist interlude which extended from the end of Han to the end of the T'ang dynasty, Confucianism again reasserted itself in the Neo-Confucian movement.

While we cannot go into the many reasons leading to the Confucian revival, such as the breakdown of empire, a weighty and positive cause lies in the continuing need for administrators to serve in the bureaucracy even during T'ang times. The Confucian examinations were reestablished after a long interval of neglect, and by the ninth century the intellectual class was thoroughly imbued with Confucian ideals. Consequently, the scholars expressed criticism of the religious practices of Taoism and Buddhism. Most outstanding was the famous memorial of Han Yu (768–824) who in 819 attacked the reverence given by the court to a bone of the Buddha.

The development of Neo-Confucianism, which began with such figures as Han Yu and Li Ao (c. 789), can be termed a "rediscovery" of Confucian ideals, though tailored to fit a new social situation. While its promoters intended to revive the original Confucian perspective, the movement became more metaphysical in orientation as it responded to questions posed by Buddhism. What emerged was a firmer foundation in philosophy and mystical experience for the traditional Confucian ethic. In effect, Neo-Confucianism synthesized all major thought streams which had developed in China to that time.

It is significant that the formulators of Neo-Confucianism had been either Buddhists or Taoists in their youth. Though drawing upon the experience of other traditions, Neo-Confucianism produced its own distinctive view. In particular it remained this-worldly in its concern for morality and ethic. Though influenced by Ch'an (Zen) Buddhism, it rejected Ch'an subjectivism by holding generally to the objective existence of the principle of universal order (li).

The Neo-Confucian movement can be divided into two stages or streams. These are the Reason school of the Sung era (960–1279), which culminated in the thought of Chu Hsi (1130–1200), and the Mind school of the Ming period (1368–1644), represented in the thought of Wang Yang-ming (1472–1529).

Building on numerous precedents in thought, Chu Hsi taught that everything has its li (principle or ideal prototype). The things of the world are formed through a combination of the li with the *ch'i,* a type of ether or vacuous gas providing the principle of individuation. The system of the whole exists within the Supreme Ultimate or absolute which cannot be defined and exists beyond time and space. The world is produced through a process in which the five basal elements, the yin-yang process, the li, and the ch'i interact. The embodied principle within a specific thing is its nature. It is within the Ultimate and the Ultimate is within it.

This interpretation was not developed simply for the sake of metaphysical speculation, but in order to understand man and his role in the world. The li of man consisted in the virtues of love, righteousness, propriety, and wisdom. Since he was conjoined with impure ether, man was unstable in his expression of virtue. If he purified himself, enlightenment would follow. The method to do this was to investigate things and extend knowledge according to the pattern established in the *Ta-hsueh.* Through the study of objective things and affairs one would eventually come to an understanding of the harmony of the whole which would animate his expression of virtue.

Wang Yang-ming was a scholar of broad attainments in religion, philosophy, poetry, and military and social affairs. Drawing on the thought of Lu Hsiang-shan, he emphasized three points in his Confucian philosophy. He maintained that there was a unity between li and the mind; that innate or intuitive knowledge may be cultivated without cognition or corrupting external influence; and that there was a unity of knowledge and action so that knowledge was expressed immediately in action. Whatever Buddhist influence can be discerned in his system was displaced through emphasis on selfless action in the world. In actuality, though his thought had mystical overtones, he was an activist attempting to remove the intellectualist blocks from one's commitment to action. In the background was the formalistic, rationalist Neo-Confucianism based on Chu Hsi. His thought became very popular for a time in China and was also introduced into Japan where exponents were active in the restoration of the Emperor in 1868.

In the period after the Sung and Ming philosophers there was little if any advance in the substance of Confucian thought. A major reason for the decline in the vitality of Confucian thought was the nature of the literary examinations which were the chief means to official position. Restriction of the content to Confucian dogma and authoritarianism made the system rigid. In the Ch'ing period (1644–1911) there was a reaction against Neo-Confucianism with attempted purges of the tradition of Taoist and Buddhist overtones. A major issue was the determination of the authentic texts of Confucianism giving rise to the Old Text-New Text controversy. While the movement had scientific and empiricist emphases, it did not issue in the formation of scientific theory or outlook. This limitation made the adaptation of Confucianism to modern challenges extremely difficult and contributed to the intellectual crisis in the confrontation with the West.

In the modern period, when China was challenged on all levels by Western thought, culture, and technology, there were various reactions among Chinese scholars. These reactions ranged from total rejection of the West, attempts to relate Chinese tradition to Western outlook, or total repudiation of the Chinese tradition in favor of Westernization. O. Briere has summarized succinctly the problem confronting Chinese thinkers at the end of the nineteenth century:

> All knew that it was necessary to change something in the governmental machinery, but remained faithful to the Empire; all knew that it was necessary to borrow from the Occident its scientific spirit, its spirit of organization, whatever made for strength and material greatness; but all wanted to conserve at all costs the Confucian morality which had in the past brought about the strength and greatness of China. They reckoned that Confucianism still had its word to say in modern times, and were convinced that the welfare of humanity depended upon putting this morality into practice throughout the world.[26]

The future of Confucian philosophy in view of the Communist takeover in 1949 remains in doubt. It is to be hoped that Marxian philosophers will better be able to assess the enduring insights of their tradition after they have recovered from the initial necessity to purge the tradition of elements inhibiting progress.

---

26. O. Briere, *Fifty Years of Chinese Philosophy 1898–1948*, New York, Praeger, 1965, p. 17.

HARMONY WITH NATURE: PHILOSOPHICAL AND RELIGIOUS TAOISM

PHILOSOPHICAL TAOISM

The "drop-out" philosophy expounded by earlier individualistic non-conformists such as Yang Chu received eloquent expression in the *Tao-te-ching,* traditionally attributed to Lao-tzu (sixth or fourth century B.C.), and the text of Chuang-tzu (between 399 and 295 B.C.). Our information concerning both sages depends on the accounts of Ssu-ma Ch'ien which are of doubtful historical value.

According to tradition, Lao-tzu, whose name means simply Old Sage, was identified by the historian with a historical individual Li Erh and the legendary archivist Lao Tan, indicating obscurity concerning the life of the teacher. Most famous in the story of Lao-tzu are the narratives of his conversations with Confucius which highlight the contrast between the Confucian and Taoist approaches to life.

In terms reflecting Taoist perspectives on morality, social responsibility, and inner freedom, Lao-tzu condemned Confucius for his attachment to the past and for excessive concern with external displaying of goodness. Then brusquely dismissing Confucius, Lao-tzu urged him:

> Get rid of that arrogance of yours, all those desires, that self-sufficient air, that overweening zeal; all that is of no use to your true person.[1]

On another occasion, Lao-tzu left Confucius with the observation that the exercise of intelligence and learning in making just criti-

---

1. Max Kaltenmark, *Lao Tzu and Taoism,* Stanford, Calif., Stanford University Press, 1969, p. 8.

cisms and exposing others' faults leads to an early death. He further declared that subordination to another, whether one's father or ruler, prevented a person from being his own man.

The mystery of Lao-tzu is heightened by the circumstances of his taking leave of history. After serving some time in court and witnessing its corruption, he set out in the direction of the state of Ch'in to the west. When he was about to pass through Han-ku Pass, the guard requested that he set down his teaching. He quickly composed the small volume of about 5250 characters now known as *Tao-te-ching*. His destination and place of death were unknown.

The *Tao-te-ching* itself appears to have been composed during the Warring States period and is regarded by scholars as a compilation of materials rather than the product of a single mind. Despite the implied historical priority of Taoism over Confucianism in the legendary conversations of Lao-tzu and Confucius, the *Tao-te-ching* can be understood better as criticism of the growing currency of Confucian thinking. A compact, poetical work of eighty-one sections, it has had wide influence in Chinese history, providing perspective and guidance for individuals in disturbed times. Through the centuries more than 950 commentaries have attempted to plumb its meaning, and there have been more than forty English translations, testifying to both its inherent attraction and the difficulty of rendering its sometimes obscure language. In Communist China also its thought is explored and interpreted along materialistic lines.[2]

Although the *Tao-te-ching* is commonly understood to contain a deeply personal mystical philosophy, it should be noted that it addressed itself to the problem of human relations and the functioning of society. Directed at rulers who wished to control their people, the text contains numerous passages commenting on government, the nature of the sage-ruler, criticism of society, war, and oppression. Later Legalist philosophers perceived the significance of the opportunistic political implications of the Taoist principle of acting according to Nature which discounted the past.

Although similar to the Confucian interest in morality and true leadership, there are significant differences in the Taoist approach to the problem. Where Confucianism proposes a specific system of values by which men could attain the durable society, the *Tao-te-ching* points to the requisite attitudes and personal traits which the individual must cultivate as the foundation of human relations. Confucian emphasis is on doing and acting, following specific rules of behavior. The teaching of the *Tao-te-ching* stresses one's mode of being in the world and the perspective which one must hold when dealing with the circumstances of life. The Confucians are more oriented toward the fulfillment of external obligations, while the Taoists attempt to develop their inner lives, enabling them to meet any contingency spontaneously. Although Confucius warns against

2. Wing-tsit Chan, trans., *The Way of Lao-tzu,* Indianapolis, Bobbs-Merrill, 1963, pp. 30–31; Holmes Welch, *Taoism, The Parting of the Way,* Boston, Beacon Press, 1966, pp. 4–5, presents a list of other major English translations.

externalism in the *Analects,* later Confucians tend to place greater stress on the exterior acts, opening the way for formalism, hypocrisy, and rigidity, which the Taoists acutely criticize.

As its name implies, the central concept of Taoism is the Tao, which means the Way or Path. Although all schools of Chinese thought had their respective Tao, for the Taoist school it refers to the process of Nature and the cosmos and to the underlying reality embracing all existence. It is the symbol of ultimate reality.

The opening passage of the *Tao-te-ching* initiates the reader immediately by means of a short, pithy statement into the metaphysical and mystical perspective of Taoism. As a warning concerning the limitation of speech to exhaust the meaning of reality, it declares unequivocally that the *"Tao* (Way) that can be told is not the eternal *Tao;* the name that can be named is not the eternal name." In a later passage, we are told that "He who knows does not speak. He who speaks does not know" (*Tao-te-ching* 56).[3]

The concept of Tao may have evolved from ancient observation of the fixed, unchanging process of Heaven or Nature. The religious beliefs concerning a female agricultural deity or the god Shang-ti may have contributed to its formation. However, in the *Tao-te-ching* the Tao has become the formless, nonactive-active reality and is essentially indefinable.

In keeping with the Taoist economy of speech in describing the nature of reality, cosmological concepts are kept to a minimum. The evolution of the world out of the Tao offers a model for the attitudes necessary in human relations and dealing with life. The concept has two aspects. It is at once the totality of the order of Heaven and Earth and at the same time the nameless, vital potentiality which is the basis of the order of Nature. As the ultimate ground of things, Tao can only be termed the nameless, or Nonbeing. It is beyond categorization, but is the necessary source of all. Among the world of things dualism is the fundamental mode of thinking. The term "Nonbeing," consequently, has two aspects. On one hand it is the basis of Being beyond thought. On the other it is the correlate of Being in the world of experience. As Nonbeing implies Being in the world of dualistic thought, so Being has mysteriously flashed forth from the midst of Nonbeing. Te is Tao manifest as the power of Being within the myriad things. It is that which makes (virtue) a thing to be what it is. Through te things fulfill their natures:

> *Tao produces them.*
> *Virtue fosters them.*
> *Matter gives them physical form.*
> *The circumstances and tendencies complete them.*
> *Therefore the ten thousand things esteem Tao and honor virtue.*
> *Tao is esteemed and virtue is honored without anyone's order.*
> *They always come spontaneously.*

3. Unless otherwise indicated, all quotations from the *Tao-te-ching* are from Chan, op. cit.

Therefore Tao produces them and virtue fosters them.
They rear and develop them.
They give them security and give them peace.
They nurture them and protect them.
(Tao) produces them but does not take possession of them.
It acts, but does not rely on its own ability.
It leads them but does not master them.
This is called profound and secret virtue.

(*Tao-te-ching* 51) [4]

In Western terms, Taoist cosmological thinking appears grasped by the mystery of existence expressed in the ancient question: Why is there something and not nothing? Taoists are deeply aware that individual objects are not self-explainable. Things point beyond themselves to their ultimate source. At the same time, that ultimate source is mirrored in things. Each element of the world embodies a significant aspect of Tao from which man may glean wisdom for living. Thus the only true existence is that which conforms to the wisdom of Nature.

Drawing inspiration from Nature, a wide variety of natural images depict the essential qualities of the Taoist way of life. In the figure of the valley there is the suggestion of characteristics such as breadth, openness, inclusiveness, humility, and lowliness. As female, the valley expresses qualities of passivity, receptiveness, tranquillity, and productivity. The flexibility and suppleness of grass and young trees are signs of vitality, while rigidity and hardness signify death. Strength in weakness is dramatized in the invulnerability of the infant. The eroding ability of water attests to the hidden power in softness and weakness in dealing with affairs:

There is nothing softer and weaker than water
And yet there is nothing better for attacking hard and strong
*   things.*
For this reason there is no substitute for it.
All the world knows that the weak overcomes the strong and the
*   soft overcomes the hard.*
But none can practice it.

(*Tao-te-ching* 78)

The uncarved block suggests qualities such as genuineness, simplicity, and naturalness. It is the condition before something is imposed on it. The one who cultivates eternal virtue is described:

He will be proficient in eternal virtue,
And returns to the state of simplicity (uncarved wood).
When the uncarved wood is broken up, it is turned into concrete
*   things.*

(*Tao-te-ching* 28)

4. Other passages employing the term "virtue" (te) are 10, 21, 23, 28, 38, 41, 54, 55, 56, 60, 65, 79.

Landscape with waterfall and two figures, from the Ming Dynasty, fifteenth or sixteenth century. (Courtesy of the Museum of Fine Arts, Boston.)

Objects of human invention could also provide insight into the nature of reality and life strategy. In this connection the *Tao-te-ching* develops the thesis of the utility of the empty:

> *Thirty spokes are united around the hub to make a wheel,*
> *But it is on its non-being that the utility of the carriage depends.*
> *Clay is molded to form a utensil,*
> *But it is on its non-being that the utility of the utensil depends.*
> *Doors and windows are cut out to make a room,*
> *But it is on its non-being that the utility of the room depends.*
> *Therefore turn being into advantage, and turn non-being into utility.*

(Tao-te-ching 11)

The most famous and significant quality advanced in the *Tao-te-ching* is the trait of *wu-wei* (nonaction). Many interpretations have been given to this concept which is repeatedly set forth as the ideal way of handling affairs and governing:

> *Tao invariably takes no action, and yet there is nothing left undone.*
> *If kings and barons can keep it, all things will transform spontaneously.*
> *If, after transformation, they should desire to be active,*
> *I would restrain them with simplicity, which has no name.*
> *Simplicity, which has no name is free of desires.*
> *Being free of desires, it is tranquil.*
> *And the world will be at peace of its own accord.*

(Tao-te-ching 37; also 48 and 57)

It is clear that wu-wei does not mean doing nothing. Rather, it is a special perspective on the nature of doing. Its basic meaning is to do nothing contrary to Nature or the Tao. It may also mean not to do anything with selfish motives and ends in view. However, since Nature is the model for all action, it refers to the fact that all events in Nature flow out from within Nature, and all appear to be spontaneously self-caused. They happen of themselves. The nonaction by which all is accomplished would imply that one is to cultivate his nature in order to act spontaneously from within without contriving or forcing himself or others externally in attaining a goal. If we consider that action refers to deliberate, contrived, externally imposed efforts toward some personally desired end, then nonaction is a *state of being from which* actions flow freely. Goals are not based on mere subjective desire. The difference in the two perspectives on the foundations of behavior may be illustrated in the contrast between two questions: What should I do? as against What kind of person should I be? In terms of Confucian-Taoist contrast, the Confucianist tended to specify actions which would bring a person into harmony with reality. The Taoist emphasized that harmony with reality is the basis of action.

While in relation to oneself nonaction means to act from inward and spontaneous impulse as one is harmonized with the Tao, dealing with others it also signifies that one can achieve his goals without deliberately imposing his will on others. Through the natural influence of his character, he can lead people toward desired ends in a manner corresponding to the concept te in Confucianism.

A correlative idea grows out of the understanding of nonaction. It is to let things alone. This aspect means not to intrude oneself and one's personal desires into the course of events in order to bend them to one's wishes. One should understand the course of events and allow things to work out by themselves in the light of the true way of influencing:

> Therefore the sage manages affairs without action
> And spreads doctrines without words.
> All things arise, and he does not turn away from them.
> He produces them but does not take possession of them.
> He acts but does not rely on his own ability.
> He accomplishes his task but does not claim credit for it.
> It is precisely because he does not claim credit that his accomplishment remains with him.
>
> (Tao-te-ching 2)

This passage urges the true leader to reject the ego which would attempt to dominate affairs. It is the quality of the sage that he does not intrude himself, while yet bringing to bear his influence. Letting alone may be illustrated in the image of cooking a small fish whereby, with too much poking, one may lose the fish (Tao-te-ching 60). Because action fails and grasping loses, the sage "supports all things in their natural state but does not take any action" (Tao-te-ching 64).

Two other traits are associated with letting alone. One is the noncompetitive approach to human relations, and the second is knowing when to stop. Contrary to the opinion that competition is the nature of life, hence inevitable, the sage indicates that it is willed by man, and to end it one must decide to stop it. Then there is no competition. Competition is the attempt to subjugate others to one's own ego. It is to win superiority over the other. When one has his own ego in proper perspective, however, there is no competition, as is evident in the pattern of Heaven's dealings with the world:

> The way of Heaven does not compete, and yet it skillfully achieves victory.
> It does not speak, and yet it skillfully responds to things.
> It comes to you without your invitation.
> It is not anxious about things and yet it plans well.
> Heaven's net is indeed vast,
> Though its meshes are wide, it misses nothing.
>
> (Tao-te-ching 73)

Knowing when to stop and discarding extremes suggest a necessary sense of moderation and balance:

To hold and fill a cup to overflowing
    Is not as good as to stop in time.
. . . .
Withdraw as soon as your work is done.
Such is Heaven's Way.

(*Tao-te-ching* 9)

The sage thus "discards the extremes, the extravagant, and the excessive" (*Tao-te-ching* 29).

In addition to appeals for cultivation of various general attitudes as the basis for fruitful human relations, the *Tao-te-ching* exhorts readers with more specific and concrete principles of behavior. It declares that "much talk will of course come to a dead end" (*Tao-te-ching* 5). It recommends closing the mouth and limiting the desires.

In dealing with affairs, it counsels care and foresight. Particularly when success is in sight the greatest care is necessary:

If one remains as careful at the end as he was at the beginning,
    there will be no failure.

(*Tao-te-ching* 64)

In one's dealings with others one does not justify himself, boast, or brag. One is to be honest and good with all. Whether dealing with the big or small, many or few, hatred is to be repaid with virtue. The sage observes:

To patch up great hatred is surely to leave some hatred behind.
How can this be regarded as good?
Therefore the sage keeps the left-hand portion (obligation) of a
    contract
And does not blame the other party.
Virtuous people attend to their left-hand portions,
While those without virtue attend to other people's mistakes.

(*Tao-te-ching* 79)

Again, keen insight into human relations is revealed in the admonition:

It is only when one does not have enough faith in others
    that others will have no faith in him.

(*Tao-te-ching* 23)

People's reactions to us are often reflections of our reaction to them.

The political philosophy of the *Tao-te-ching* rests on the principle that the best ruler is the one whose existence is hardly noted by the people. He rules by the principles of nonaction, letting alone, and moderation. Through the beneficent influence of his character, he brings peace and harmony to the kingdom. On this point the Taoists and the Confucianists both recommend example and moral influence over the imposition of laws as the ideal means of ordering society.

However, there are a number of passages in the *Tao-te-ching* which appear, at least on the surface, to express a despotic approach to government. They were employed later by Legalists to support their methods and outlook. While scholars agree that the passages in question have affinity with the Legalist philosophy, they also point out that the criticism of society and the Confucian system, as well as the general tendency of the Taoist perspective on human relations, would argue against their being Legalist in intent. Rather, they are paradoxical in their meaning when the value system of Taoism is kept in mind in interpreting them.

The passages in question are 3, 36, and 65. In verses 3 and 65 there is the suggestion that the ruler may despotically control the minds of his subjects by emptying their hearts, weakening ambitions, and limiting knowledge. Interpreted as advocating deceit, passage 36 has been widely condemned in Chinese tradition. While there is the suggestion of treachery, the text may also be intended to inform the king "that it is a common lot among men and kings to be built up for a fall." [5] By implication, the king should understand "that gentleness is stronger than harshness." [6]

Taoist criticism of society and war contains insights relevant in our own time. With respect to society, Taoists realized that appeals to virtue were an indication that society had already failed. Such appeals only arise when people have ceased spontaneously fulfilling virtues inspired by deep human relations.

As symptoms of a deeper problem, appeals provide no solution. Hence, calls for patriotism betray a condition in which people's patriotic fervor may be at low ebb. What is necessary is not exhortation to patriotism, but a rectification of the condition leading to a decline in the spontaneous commitment to the state. In a similar fashion laws are also seen as signs of society's failure and an attempt to gain by compulsion what should flow naturally from the human situation. The externalization of virtue and imposition of law lead only to competitive struggle, hypocrisy, and oppression in society. In essence it is a thwarting of human nature and hence society in its deepest sense. Thus the sage notes:

> *When the great Tao declined,*
> *The doctrine of humanity and righteousness arose.*
> *When knowledge and wisdom appeared,*
> *There emerged great hypocrisy.*
> *When the six family relationships are not in harmony,*
> *There will be the advocacy of filial piety and deep love to children.*
> *When a country is in disorder,*
> *There will be the praise of loyal ministers.*

(*Tao-te-ching* 18)

5. R. B. Blakney, *The Way of Life: Lao Tzu,* New York, New American Library, 1955, p. 89.
6. Ibid.

On the failure of law, the sage declares:

> *Govern the state with correctness*
> * Operate the army with surprise tactics.*
> *Administer the empire by engaging in no activity.*
> *How do I know that this should be so?*
> *Through this:*
> * The more taboos and prohibitions there are in the world,*
> *The poorer the people will be.*
> * The more sharp weapons the people have,*
> *The more troubled the state will be.*
> * The more cunning and skill man possesses,*
> *The more vicious things will appear.*
> * The more laws and orders are made prominent,*
> *The more thieves and robbers there will be.*
>
> *(Tao-te-ching 57)*

In view of the people's willingness to die in resisting oppression, the sage advises rulers not to be extravagant in extracting taxes or in spending and not to "reduce the living space of their dwellings. Do not oppress their lives" (*Tao-te-ching* 72).

War is also seen as a basic failure in society, though it is recognized that war is sometimes inevitable. It brings desolation and encourages disrespect for life. When undertaken, it is to be done with sad regret. Any rejoicing in war is a sign of lack of basic humanity and understanding of existence. The sage keenly notes the results of the use of force and war:

> *He who assists the ruler with Tao does not dominate the world*
> * with force.*
> *The use of force usually brings requital.*
> *Wherever armies are stationed, briers and thorns grow.*
> *Great wars are always followed by famines.*
>
> *(Tao-te-ching 30)*

The Taoist criticism of society made it the spokesman for the oppressed in society. Due to this feature it fostered secret societies responsible for popular uprisings aimed at political and economic reforms.[7]

The ideal state requires rejection of the superficial ways by which society measures people and demands the cultivation of awareness of the Tao rather than enforcement of externally imposed values and goals. The sage draws a picture of the ideal society which is essentially a primary group where values are spontaneously realized without legislation:

> *Let there be a small country with few people.*
> *Let there be ten times and a hundred times as many utensils*

7. C. K. Yang, *Religion in Chinese Society*, Berkeley, Calif., University of California Press, 1961, pp. 218–227.

But let them not be used.
Let the people value their lives highly and not migrate far.
Even if there are ships and carriages, none will ride in them.
Even if there are arrows and weapons, none will display them.
Let the people again knot cords and use them (in place of writ-
    ing).
Let them relish their food, beautify their clothing, be content with
    their homes, and delight in their customs.
Though neighboring communities overlook one another and the
    crowing of cocks and barking of dogs can be heard,
Yet the people there may grow old and die without ever visiting
    one another.

(Tao-te-ching 80)

While it may be argued whether this ideal can ever be realized in the modern context, the atmosphere and values it expresses are those which need to be cultivated wherever possible if the human spirit is not to be submerged within the structures it has created for its own protection and fulfillment. Passages like these serve to remind us that civilization extracts a price from the human spirit. With increasing civilization and organization comes the loss of spontaneity, naturalness, simplicity, and sheer delight in life itself.

The second major figure in the development of Taoist tradition is Chuang-tzu. According to the traditional biography provided by Ssu-ma Ch'ien:

Chuang-tzu was a native of Meng (in present Honan). His personal name was Chou. He held a small post at Ch'i-yuan, in Meng. He was a contemporary of King Hui or Liang (370–319) and Hsuan of Ch'i (319–301). His erudition was most varied, but his chief doctrines were based upon the sayings of Lao Tzu. His writings, which run to over 100,000 words, are for the most part allegorical. His literary and dialectic skill was such that the best scholars of the age were unable to refute his destructive criticism of the Confucian and Mohist schools. His teachings were like an overwhelming flood which spreads unchecked according to its own will, so that from rulers and ministers downward, none could apply them to any practical use.[8]

Despite the presumed factuality of this account the precise date of Chuang-tzu, his relation to Lao-tzu and his teaching, and his relation to his contemporary Mencius remain unclear and uncertain. It is also a problem whether the book *Chuang-tzu* was actually authored by that individual. Nevertheless, the text reflects the work of a penetrating mind (or minds) which gave new depth and scope to Taoist teaching.

The *Chuang-tzu* advocated a decidedly mystical approach to life in contrast to the activist views of other ancient schools of thought such as the Confucianists and Mohists whom it severely criticized. Although the *Chuang-tzu* was concerned with the problem of social

8. Fung, op. cit., p. 221.

harmony and the fulfillment of human existence in common with the other schools, it presented a radical solution by advocating emancipation from the world instead of reforming it. According to the *Chuang-tzu,* men created their own problems by the pursuit of virtue, fame, and wisdom.

Attempting to encourage men to transcend the world, the *Chuang-tzu* makes a determined effort to shake the mind loose from its addiction to words, values, conventions, and actions which have come to be regarded as natural to man and necessary to his existence. It strives to free the mind from the conviction that what it perceives, thinks, and understands is what really is. In order to bring about this loosening, the *Chuang-tzu* employs a number of strategies such as the non sequitur, paradox, "pseudological discussion," and humor.

To achieve emancipation the *Chuang-tzu* urges the practices of "free and easy wandering," "fasting of the mind," and "forgetting." Through mystical meditation resulting in the perception of the blinding effect of words and intellection, and awareness of the illusory nature of the world and life, one arrives at a true understanding of change and death.

Through "free and easy wandering" we journey in the vast spaces of reality where one "climbs up on clouds and mist, rides a flying dragon and wanders beyond the four seas." Traveling "beyond the dust and dirt, one wanders free and easy in the service of inaction." Following "any far-away, carefree, and as-you-like-it paths," we enter into the beyond where there is nothing and where there is no trail. Borne beyond the trivialities of mundane concern in company with the Creator and great Teacher we truly govern the world as the sage notes:

> Let your mind wander in simplicity, blend your spirit with the vastness, follow along with things the way they are, and make no room for personal views—then the world will be governed.[9]

Not all can make this journey, for bound by benevolence and righteousness, they are blind. For small minds and spirits the freedom of the sage is as incomprehensible as the flight of ninety thousand leagues by the great P'eng bird is to the cicada and the dove. To have evident skills and capacities means slavery:

> In comparison to the sage, a man like this is a drudging slave, a craftsman bound to his calling, wearing out his body, grieving his mind. They say it is the beautiful markings of the tiger and the leopard that call out the hunters, the nimbleness of the monkey and the ability of the dog to catch rats that make them end up chained.[10]

To wander in the world means neither to submerge oneself in mere conformity, nor to reject or withdraw from affairs. Rather, the

9. Burton Watson, *Chuang Tzu: Basic Writings,* New York, Columbia, 1964, pp. 90–94.
10. Ibid., p. 91.

true sage, flexible in confronting circumstance, is "able to wander in the world without taking sides, can follow along with men without losing himself." [11]

Embarking upon the path of free and easy wandering requires that "you strip away not your fine fur only, but every impediment of the body, scour your heart till it is free from all desire, and travel through the desolate wilds." [12] Through the "fasting of the mind" we transcend the intellect and enter the emptiness of the Tao. By means of true forgetting we attain union with the Tao as we "drive out perception and intellect, cast off form, do away with understanding." [13]

The spiritual ascent to enlightenment and the realization of the unity of all differences is a process of progressive emptying of the self:

> So I began explaining and kept at him for three days, and after that he was able to put the world outside himself. When he had put the world outside himself, I kept at him for seven days more, and after that he was able to put things outside himself. When he had put things outside himself, I kept at him for nine days more, and after that he was able to put life outside himself. After he had put life outside himself, he was able to achieve the brightness of dawn, and when he had achieved the brightness of dawn, he could see his aloneness. After he had managed to see his aloneness, he could do away with past and present, he was able to enter where there is no life and no death. That which kills life does not die; that which gives life to life does not live. This is the kind of thing it is: there's nothing it doesn't send off, nothing it doesn't welcome, nothing it doesn't destroy, nothing it doesn't complete. Its name is Peace-in-Strife. After the strife, it attains completion.[14]

This passage is noteworthy in that the stages outlined conform generally to the pattern of mystical experience throughout the world. Devotees pass through the stages of *purgation,* freeing them from bondage to the external world, *concentration,* leading to unification of the self, and *enlightenment* or union with reality.

Although the mystic path outlined in the *Chuang-tzu* implies disregard for the affairs of ordinary men, there is no call for rejecting any particular life context in order to become the perfect man. Rather, there is recognition that a man cannot always control the conditions of life about him:

> But though you may be one time a ruler, another time a subject, this is merely a matter of the times. Such distinctions change with

11. Ibid., pp. 137–138.

12. Arthur Waley, *Three Ways of Thought in Ancient China,* New York, Doubleday, 1956, p. 39.

13. Watson, op. cit., pp. 86–87.

14. Ibid., p. 79. The alternative translation in Fung, op. cit., pp. 238–239, suggests a vision of the One which enables the sage to transcend all distinctions, past-present, life-death, tranquillity-strife.

the age and you cannot call either one or the other lowly. There-
fore I say, the Perfect Man is never a stickler in his actions.[15]

It even suggests that mystic endeavor enables the ideal ruler to
manage affairs successfully. Rejecting the quest for fame or imposing schemes and projects as evidence of his wisdom, his mind will
be like a mirror: "going after nothing, welcoming nothing, responding but not storing. Therefore, he can win out over things and not hurt
himself." [16] He can call out troops and conquer nations without losing the hearts of the people, and he benefits countless ages, though
not having love for men.[17]

While the mystical pursuit appears useless from the conventional
standpoint, it actually provides man with his footing in the world:

A man has to understand the useless before you can talk to him
about the useful. The earth is certainly vast and broad, though a
man uses no more of it than the area he puts his feet on. If how-
ever, you were to dig away all the earth from around his feet until
you reached the Yellow Springs, then would the man still be able
to make use of it? [18]

The concept of the "usefulness of the useless" in the *Chuang-tzu*
corresponds to the idea of the utility of the empty in the *Tao-te-
ching.* As a practical approach to life, it suggests that the truly wise
person avoids grief and pain and fulfills his life by following a simple, quiet, obscure life which the world passes over as insignificant
just as the woodcutter and carpenter ignore the gnarled and bumpy
ailanthus or oak tree.

Free and easy wandering in the boundless beyond in meditative
endeavor produces keen awareness of the contrast of the heavenly
and the human. The heavenly is the natural, original, or fated endowment of any being just as horses and oxen naturally have four
feet. In contrast the human refers to man's intentional imposition
on, and manipulation of, Nature.

Heaven, like the nameless, formless Tao is beyond human categories and determinations. However, just as men cut a road through a
trackless field, they attempt to impose order on Heaven, making it
conform to their scheme of values:

What is acceptable we call acceptable; what is unacceptable we
call unacceptable. A road is made by people walking on it; things
are so because they are called so. What makes them so? Making
them so makes them so. What makes them not so? Making them
not so makes them not so. . . .[19]

Further, Heaven stands for what is essential and inward, while the
human is the external, artificial, and manipulative. Thus, while it is

15. Watson, op. cit., p. 137.
16. Ibid., pp. 94–95.
17. For eloquent description of the demeanor and bearing of the ideal
man, see ibid., pp. 75, 99–100.
18. Ibid., pp. 136–137.
19. Ibid., pp. 35–36.

according to Heaven that horses have four legs, it is the result of human intentions that horses wear halters and oxen have pierced noses. The timely word of the sage urges:

I say: do not let what is human wipe out what is Heavenly; do not let what is purposeful wipe out what is fated.[20]

Against the background of this distinction we must observe the attack which the *Chuang-tzu* launches against words and language. Fundamentally, words represent man's intellectual effort to order reality. When his words are believed to represent reality as it really is, they become a barrier to the full realization of his existence.

Perceiving that the preachments of moralists, i.e., Confucianists and Mohists, permit people to consider themselves superior to others or that the subtle word play of logicians deludes people into believing they truly understand reality, the *Chuang-tzu* emphasizes the relativity of words and views. Differences among people are only matters of degree and standpoint, not substance or reality:

If a man sleeps in a damp place, his back aches and he ends up half paralyzed, but is this true of a loach? If he lives in a tree, he is terrified and shakes with fright, but is this true of a monkey? . . . Men claim that Mao-ch'ing and Lady Li were beautiful, but if fish saw them they would fly away. . . . Of these four, which knows how to fix the standard of beauty for the world? The way I see it, the rules of benevolence and righteousness and the paths of right and wrong are all hopelessly snarled and jumbled. How could I know anything about such discriminations?[21]

The evaluations which men make of their experiences create endless dissatisfactions and struggles for more and more achievement. Man's life is bound and overwhelmed by fears and anxieties. Failing to see that human life is simply part of the ever-transforming process of Nature, change becomes threatening. Confusion and frustration in life result from not perceiving man's pettiness within the cosmic order.

To be able to accept and harmonize with change and to confront death with equanimity, one must press beyond the world of contrary distinctions and arbitrary evaluations. Attaining a vision of the unity of the Tao which unifies all the dualities of existence, one may keep his spirit whole, and his response to life will be like the hinge well-fitted to its socket or like a mirror which embraces and reflects all without stain. The person not touched by good or bad "just lets things be the way they are and doesn't try to help life along."[22]

It is important to notice that the man who perceives the Tao does not abolish the world of things. He understands its nature. Those who are close to attaining truth, according to the *Chuang-tzu*, are those who do not reject what pertains to Heaven nor neglect what pertains to man. He does not use "the mind to repel the Way" nor

20. Ibid., p. 104.
21. Ibid., p. 41.
22. Ibid., p. 72.

"man to help out Heaven." [23] "When man and Heaven do not defeat each other, then he may be said to have the True Man." [24]

Making a perfect adjustment to life, those who understand the Tao develop a skill in life and never exhaust their spiritual power just as the expert cook was able to use his knife for nineteen years without sharpening it because he merely passed his knife through the empty space between joints when butchering a cow.

It is clear that the major problem of existence is egoism and ego attachment. If one can attain a detachment from the self and world, one's spirit would not be disturbed by dramatic shifts in affairs. In order to drive home the relativity of existence and ego experience, the *Chuang-tzu* emphasizes that the line between dream and reality is difficult to maintain and the solidity of our ego may be merely the solidity of a dream from which we shall awake.

> *What's more, we go around telling each other, I do this, I do that —but how do we know that this "I" we talk about has any "I" to it? You dream you're a bird and soar up into the sky; you dream you're a fish and dive down in the pool. But now when you tell me about it, I don't know whether you are awake or whether you are dreaming. Running around accusing others is not as good as laughing, and enjoying a good laugh is not as good as going along with things. Be content to go along and forget about change and then you can enter the mysterious oneness of Heaven.*[25]

Concerning life and death, the *Chuang-tzu* emphasizes that the distinction is meaningless in the light of the dream nature of existence and the fact that the duality of life and death is wrongly evaluated by man. Both must be accepted as part of the nature of things. Death, particularly, is merely one of the many changes the individual undergoes through his process of living. They should not perturb his spirit.

When the spirit of Chuang-tzu's philosophy is apprehended, it enables the individual to approach life with a grand indifference. Although he is not entirely disinterested, the true man views with detachment all affairs as part of the same process whose secret he knows. He therefore refrains from trying to force it to conform to his desires.

We may compare Chuang-tzu's attitude toward fate and death with the stoic attitude of accepting everything as the working out of a universal reason. His philosophy does not guarantee success in every situation. Rather it teaches how to face every situation. When one loses, he has fortitude; when he wins, he is not prone to presumption or pride. Unless the person is certain of himself within, he cannot be sure facing the world. The nurture of the inner man, which is the foundation of all life's activities, forms the central concern of the *Chuang-tzu*.

23. Ibid., p. 74.
24. Ibid., p. 76.
25. Ibid., pp. 84–85.

NEO-TAOISM   At the end of the Han era the loss of prestige of Confucianism and the upheaval of society led to revived interest in Taoist philosophy. Two distinct trends appeared in the movement. On the one hand there was a group of philosophers with Confucian leanings and devoted to reconciling Taoism with the established teaching of Confucius. The other group appears more interested in the life-style engendered by Taoist principles. The Neo-Taoist movement was termed "Pure Talk" because of its concentration on philosophical issues and rejection of worldly advantage. It was also called "Dark Learning" because it focused on the relation of the abstruse and mysterious Tao to the world.

    Those concerned mainly with philosophical issues included such philosophers as Wang Pi (A.D. 225–249), who is considered the founder of the movement, Hsiang Hsiu (c. 221–c. 300), Kuo Hsiang (d. 312), and Chi K'ang (223–262). These philosophers wrote commentaries to the *I-ching,* the *Tao-te-ching,* and the *Chuang-tzu.* Through their commentaries they reinterpreted Taoism in the light of their own age and manifested considerable originality in the application of Taoist principles.

    A distinctive feature of these later Taoist philosophers was their attitude to Confucius, whom Taoists generally criticized and identified with sham and hypocrisy. The latter-day Taoists regarded Confucius as the greatest sage, even superior to Lao-tzu and Chuang-tzu. The reason for this was that according to Taoist principle, he who knows does not speak and he who speaks does not know. Since Confucius did not speak of Tao and its mysterious operations, he must know it, while the Taoist sages, who spoke about it, must not know it. The motivation behind this peculiar reconciliation was the fact that Confucianism was the official philosophy of the state, and one could hardly advance in any position without coming to terms with the sage. Taoist philosophers reinterpreted the Taoist sages in order to provide a basis for participation in society. Thus the reconciliation of the perspectives of both philosophies proceeded from two directions: the exaltation of Confucius and the interpretation of his thought in terms of Taoism, and the reinterpretation of Taoist principle to make it amenable to Confucian outlook.

    In general, Neo-Taoist philosophy focused attention on the problem of metaphysics, the relation of things to the source of their being and the relation of Being and Nonbeing which had been raised in the *Lao-tzu* and the *Chuang-tzu.* This type of inquiry was part of a wider interest at that time in analyzing terms and developing principles growing out of the School of Names tradition. By investigating the distinctions and meanings involved in names and terms, the principles governing reality could be discerned. Much discussion was devoted to these terms and principles, and little attention was paid to concrete actualities.[26]

    The second group, known as the Seven Sages of the Bamboo Grove, appear more significant for the attitude and style of life they embodied than for the contribution they made to Taoist thought.

26. For detailed discussion, see Fung, op. cit., vol. II, pp. 175–179.

Their philosophy was hedonistic in its exaltation of the enjoyment of life and pursuit of pleasure. Like Yang Chu earlier, they sought enjoyment and freedom from cares. They refused office, glorified drinking, and believed that following impulse was the expression of integrity. They were also sensitive to Nature. Their care-nothing attitude was represented by Liu Ling who, unabashed at criticisms of his nakedness at home, retorted:

I take the whole universe as my house and my own room as my clothing. Why, then, do you enter here into my trousers? [27]

The sense of equality of all things was demonstrated in the practice of the Juan family who enjoyed their drinking bouts by sharing the same large wine bottle, even to the extent of permitting the pigs to join in. Sympathy for animals was depicted in Chih-tun's freeing a captured crane. Sheer impulsiveness was represented in the tale of Wang Hui-chi. In the middle of the night he got the urge to visit his friend Tai K'uei, even though it was snowing. However, when he got to the door he did not knock. When asked why, he replied that the urge had passed and there was no need to knock.

RELIGIOUS TAOISM

While philosophical Taoism has provided the bureaucrat, scholar, or artist with a profound understanding of existence upon which to base his life and seek his satisfactions, it is religious Taoism which has functioned among the hosts of ordinary people to fulfill their desires for satisfaction in life and a bright destiny beyond this life.

Religious Taoism, as an institution, began about A.D. 143, established by one Chang Ling. However, the diverse beliefs and practices which make up the religion originated in more ancient times with the evolution of Chinese folk religion. Although Chinese folk religion employed elements from both Confucianism and Buddhism, religious Taoism has been the central element as the vehicle of folk beliefs. It has, however, never been supported officially by the state or advocated by scholars in the same fashion as Confucianism. At times individual rulers favored it as in the case of Emperor Kao Tsung of the T'ang who in 666 designated Lao-tzu the "Most High Emperor of Mystic Origin," a status above Confucius and Buddha.[28]

The origin or roots of religious Taoism may be traced to four sources which merged to form the complex of religious Taoism in the fourth century B.C. before any institutional establishment appeared. These sources include the philosophical Taoism of Lao-tzu, Chuang-tzu, and Lieh-tzu; a school of hygiene; the Five Element school of Tsou Yen, which later came to be regarded as a school of alchemy; and belief in the Isles of the Blest where the secret of immortality could be obtained.

The unifying element fusing these varied beliefs was the quest for

27. Ibid., p. 235.
28. Wing-tsit Chan, *Religious Trends in Modern China,* New York, Columbia, 1953, pp. 138–139.

immortality. It appears that magicians (*fang-shih*) were largely instrumental in promoting them. After unifying China, the first Ch'in Emperor sought his own immortality by turning cinnabar into gold in 133 B.C.

In the early centuries of the Christian era the quest for immortality developed in a hygienic direction. It became a quest for achieving longevity in this world through care of the body and deities within. According to the theory, everyone had thirty-six thousand deities dwelling within. Arranged in a hierarchy, these gods also ruled the universe. In order to maintain life, the deities must remain in the body. To assure this, certain rules of diet had to be undertaken, such as abstaining from wine, meat, and grain. Circulation was to be improved through gymnastics and breathing exercises termed "embryonic respiration," which meant to breathe like the baby in the womb. One held his breath as long as he could and directed the inhaled air to various parts of the body.

The hygienic practices, which required considerable expenditure of effort and time by the devotee, were also linked to performance of good works in order to achieve complete fulfillment. The devotee's actions contributed to his destiny from their resulting rewards or punishments.

The popular work entitled *T'ai-Shang Kan-ying P'ien* [29] illustrates the moralistic character of religious Taoism. Developed in the eleventh century, it became one of the most widely read religious books in China. Through a combination of Taoist, Confucian, and Buddhist ideas it reveals how morality and religious concepts were made available to the common people and enabled the Confucian elite to maintain their control over the people through fears of punishment inculcated by its text and drawings.

A conspicuous feature of Chinese popular religion and religious Taoism is its complex and multitudinous pantheon. For detailed study of this profusion of divinities, the reader may be referred to the study of Chinese peasant deities by Clarence Burton Day.[30] Among the most important Taoist deities, he notes the Jade Emperor, who is regarded as the father of the gods in Taoist lore. His palace is in the constellation above the North Pole where all the powers of Nature which influence earth are concentrated.

Below the more exalted deities are the popular Eight Immortals who work to bring blessings to mankind. Other widely revered deities are the Great God of Five Roads (also known as General of the Five Brigands) of evil omen and the positive God of the Five Bless-

29. Translated by Teitaro Suzuki and Paul Carus; discussions in Holmes Welch, *Taoism, the Parting of the Way,* Boston, Beacon Press, 1966, pp. 139–141. For a detailed study of this type of literature the reader may refer to Wolfram Eberhard, *Guilt and Sin in Traditional China,* Berkeley, Calif., University of California Press, 1967; also, C. J. Yang, *Religion in Chinese Society,* Berkeley, Calif., University of California Press, 1961, pp. 286–289.

30. Clarence Burton Day, *Chinese Peasant Cults,* Shanghai, Kelly and Walsh Limited, 1940. Also on the historical development of the pantheon, see Welch, op. cit., pp. 135–141.

ings. Very important is the god of the hearth, who keeps track of family doings and annually reports to the Jade Emperor.

As a survey of the many functions of the hosts of Chinese deities indicates, every aspect of the physical and social environment is overseen by a deity who assumes his office by appointment of the Jade Emperor (concretely through designation of the government, which regulated religious matters). The divine world is a replica of the bureaucratic world of the Chinese state.

Interaction with Buddhism imported from India contributed to the development of religious Taoism. Beliefs in Heaven and Hell, karma and transmigration, and Buddhist divinities expanded Chinese perspectives on human destiny.

The previously outlined beliefs took more concrete shape with the establishment of religious Taoism by Chang Ling in A.D. 143. Religion and politics were mixed in his work, resulting in the formation of a semi-independent state in the regions of Szechuan and Shensi. His group was called Five Bushels of Rice Taoism, since he charged that amount for membership. He also initiated a health cult to cure diseases by charms and spells, and emphasized abstention from alcohol, giving of charity, moral deeds, filial piety, meditation, repentance, and the reading of the *Tao-te-ching*. The movement continued to modern times, headed by descendants of Chang.

It is to be noted that during the period of the breakdown of the Han dynasty, the dissatisfactions of the people grew as the power of Confucianism waned. Land became concentrated in the hands of the few, and frequent floods, droughts, ruinous taxation, and banditry imperiled life.

Taoist religious organization provided a refuge for people seeking stability through a hierarchical system and offered the benefits of magic. In A.D. 184 Chang Chueh led the revolt of the Yellow Turbans, who promoted T'ai-p'ing Tao (Great Peace Taoism) in the region of Hopeh. According to this movement the age of Great Peace, the millennium, had come when all men would be equal. Yellow turbans, the color of the earth element, were their badge. Although it was put down with great effort by the Han government, the movement seriously disrupted the government itself.

In 189 Chang Ling's followers led a rebellion, gaining control over wide areas in Szechuan and Shensi. Taoist priests performed the functions of government administrators and collected taxes. In 215 they capitulated to the central government, but in return the government recognized the Taoist religion.

In the course of Chinese history numerous other rebellions have had a religious foundation in Taoism. Against the Chin and Mongols appeared the Chuan-chen-chiao (Complete Truth Religion). During the Ch'ing period there were rebellions of Taoist and Buddhist origins. The T'ai-p'ing rebellion of the nineteenth century, however, had Christian influence.

While Taoism as a religious and clerical organization has never shown an interest directly in politics, Taoist philosophy as expressed in the *Tao-te-ching* and the *Chuang-tzu* criticizes tyranny and oppressive government and society. Thus it appears to be on the side of the masses, upholding the principle of benefiting the people as the basis of successful rule. In times of stress and strain the people turned to Taoism for inspiration for their struggle. Also the magical notions of invulnerability and promises of immortality gave encouragement in face of danger.[31]

In modern times Taoist religion appears to be waning and heading for extinction, but at the same time it has inspired the formation of numerous religious societies. Largely secret in character, they require initiation into membership, vows, and the use of symbolic communications, chanting, and fasting.

Many societies began in the period preceding or just after World War I in the area of Shantung, a center of much civil and international conflict. Reflecting the general disillusion of the times, "they are all negative in outlook, utilitarian in purpose and superstitious in belief." Though they are rejected and attacked by intellectuals, Chan asserts they are not so easily dismissed, for they embody features which will influence the future of religious belief in China. He notes a number of tendencies latent in such organizations. It is a striking fact that Taoist schools and societies have generally begun as patriotic movements opposed to invaders. The Boxer Rebellion in 1900 was an outstanding modern example. They also opposed tyranny. They were this-worldly in attempting to obtain the fruits of salvation in this life. Though there are beliefs in Heaven and Hell, these were not the central religious concern. The quest of longevity was to increase life in this world. A strong ethical emphasis accompanied the attempt to achieve the good life on earth. Movements were laymen-oriented as each worked out his own salvation. Clergy performed ceremonies, but they did not control the people. The groups were syncretic, drawing from all major traditions of Confucianism, Buddhism, and Taoism.[32]

While Taoist religion continues to exist on Taiwan, its status on the mainland is in doubt. It faces severe problems in both regions from the rising influence of science and education and from its own emphasis on magical quests for self-benefit and lack of commanding leaders.

31. For discussion of the history and character of the Taoist church, see Welch, op. cit., pp. 113–123.

32. Chan, *Religious Trends in Modern China*, pp. 168–185.

HARMONY WITH REALITY: BUDDHISM

Buddhism represents the first major foreign religio-philosophical tradition to penetrate and seriously influence Chinese religious and cultural outlook. Buddhism, in its Theravada (Hinayana) or Mahayana forms, promoted an essentially Indian view of reality and life which at once contradicted the Chinese understanding and also amplified it.

Buddhism contradicted Chinese interpretations of existence by generally regarding the common world of human experience as a delusive product of passion-infected minds. Hence, truth lay beyond this world in a transcendent experience of enlightenment which would reveal things as unsubstantial and valueless. This effort was to be carried out by individuals within special communities devoted to the goal of emancipation apart from common social life. Monasticism and the rigorous discipline to control the mind and passions aimed at inducing an awareness of the voidness of things, leading to detachment, tranquillity, and egolessness. These qualities marked emancipation from bondage to finitude in this life and hereafter. The individualistic character of the Buddhist quest for enlightenment collided sharply with the Chinese sense of social or communal obligation and filial piety, as well as the positive acceptance and enjoyment of this world.

The interaction between the Indian and Chinese perspectives on the world took place on various levels of Chinese society. As a consequence, distinctive forms of Chinese Buddhism (such as Ch'an) emerged, advocating acceptance of this world and supporting participation in it.

Buddhism also broadened the scope of Chinese understanding of human destiny through the concepts of karma, transmigration, and mythical cosmology. The moralism of the karmic system fitted well with Confucian social concern. Confucian tradition showed little interest in the aspirations and hopes of ordinary individuals, and Taoist philosophy primarily enabled individuals to adjust to their life conditions. Taoist religion attempted to enhance the individual's prospects in this world, but it was mainly Buddhism which attempted to console ordinary people with hope for their future well-being beyond this life through Pure Land teaching.

Although Buddhism contained aspects alien to the Chinese outlook, it had a wide attraction for people on all levels of Chinese society. On the popular level Buddhism resembled religious Taoism which could confer benefits of long life, good luck, and help in misfortune by means of magical power. Buddha was early ranked with the Yellow Emperor (Huang-ti) and Lao-tzu as an important divine personage. Emperor Huan set up an altar to these three divinities in the capital at Loyang in the period A.D. 147–167.

While the popular masses looked upon Buddhism as a means to enhance their worldly fortunes, on higher levels of society it appealed to more cultured individuals who yearned for freedom and release from worldly burdens resulting from the collapse of the Han empire. Along with the resurgence of interest in Taoist philosophy, the life of retirement and withdrawal afforded by Buddhist monasticism invited the gentry of that time.

Buddhist teachers took advantage of the similarities between Buddhist and Taoist metaphysics through a practice of matching or paralleling terms rendering Buddhism more intelligible to the Chinese mind. Consequently, the Buddhist concepts of the Absolute (*Bhutatathata*) and the phenomenal world of change were paired with the Taoist terms *Wu* (Nonbeing) and *Yu* (Being). The distinction *Nirvana-Samsara* was interpreted in terms of *wu-wei* (nonaction) and *yu-wei* (activity). The Buddhist religious ideal of the Arhat was related to the Taoist immortal Chen-jen. The five precepts of Buddhism were matched with the five virtues of Confucianism. Buddhist texts were also translated in conformity with Confucian moral sentiments. The text *Mou-tzu on the Settling of Doubts,* the first apology for Buddhism by a Chinese composed sometime between the second and fifth centuries, employed traditional Chinese texts in order to demonstrate that there was no essential contradiction between Confucianism, Taoism, and Buddhism.

Despite initial efforts of early Chinese Buddhists to commend Buddhism to the Chinese people on the basis of the similarity of its thought and practices to traditional Chinese ways, the production of more accurate translations of Buddhist texts and more penetrating studies of Buddhist philosophy revealed its basic differences with Chinese thought. As a result, numerous Taoist and Confucian spokesmen throughout subsequent Chinese history criticized and challenged the religious and social implications of Buddhism in order to advance their own religious or social interests.

Taoists charged that Buddhism was inappropriate for Chinese society because of its foreign dress, ritual, and burial customs, as well as its strange rules for food and family. They objected to Buddhist celibacy, to the use of impure materials for medicine, and to the

Kneeling Bodhisattva, from the Northern Wei Dynasty, early sixth century. (Courtesy of the Museum of Fine Arts, Boston, Hoyt Collection.)

practice of begging. Taoists followed Confucianists in criticizing the unproductive labor and wealth of the monks. They also argued about the historical priority of Lao-tzu and Buddha or superiority of Taoist and Buddhist teachings. Forged texts and misrepresentation were widely used on both sides.

The Confucianists had two main objections to Buddhism which continually recurred in memorials to the throne. They claimed that Buddhism was contrary to the basic pattern of ruler-subject relationship and that the existence of a class of nonproductive priests meant less revenue for the state. Buddhism was charged with the decline of the government and society and had to be rooted out. Such indictments often became the pretext for persecution as illustrated in the attack on the order in 446 by Emperor Shih Tsu of the Wei dynasty.

In a memorial to Emperor Liang Wu-ti (502–549), Hsun-chi, a Confucian scholar, made seven charges against Buddhism of which sedition was the central issue:

(1) the Buddhists were imitating the imperial quarters with their monasteries and temples; (2) they were translating and circulating seditious works in disrespect of the imperial mandates; (3) they were soliciting contributions for exemption from punishment in hell, thus usurping the sovereign's power of imposing penalties and punishment; (4) the Buddhist designation of the three months for fasting each year, and six days each month, was an attempt to set up another calendar in opposition to that of the dynasty; (5) they implied the existence of hardship and suffering in the royal domain by portraying the peace and joy of the Buddha lands; (6) they regarded the great bell in the temple courtyard as a substitute for the clepsydra in the imperial palace; and (7) they hoisted banners and pennants that imitated the imperial insignias.[1]

Criticisms of monastic life and superstitions were made by Fu-yi (544–639) and Han Yu (768–824). Intellectual objections centered on the existence of the soul and transmigration which the Confucians denied, mainly on the ground that this opened the people to exploitation. Confucianists were interested in ideas which had social utility.

Buddhists countered the various criticisms of both Confucianists and Taoists by maintaining that Buddhism was not contradictory to Chinese social and moral concerns. Philosophically they asserted that Buddhism was universalistic while Taoism and Confucianism were inferior in being concerned only with this world and its petty affairs. The interdependence of all beings taught in Buddhism reduced selfishness and competition, according to Buddhists.

While the attacks on Buddhism were substantial and involved many forms of argument, Buddhism spread among the people by offering glorious salvation and many benefits. The attacks sometimes resulted in persecutions of the order and restriction of its activities and numbers of monks. Sometimes wealth was expropriated in land, money, or art treasures. However, the persecutions were never of long duration, because the restlessness of the common people who supported Buddhism caused the rulers to relent.

Further, Buddhism was able to answer objections in deed as well as word. The Buddhists engaged in social work and contributed to the economy of the country through its rolling mills, oil processing facilities, hostels, and the "inexhaustible" treasury used for welfare. Buddhism brought medicine to the poor, aided the sick and starving, built roads, wells, bridges, and planted trees. In the capital the only places for recreation were the open spaces provided by temples. Buddhism grew in the face of bureaucratic and official opposition, appealing to the common man with compassion and to the intellectual with a profound vision of wisdom and spiritual emancipation.

1. Kenneth Ch'en, *Buddhism in China,* Princeton, N.J., Princeton University Press, 1964, pp. 143–144.

From the early beginnings of the Buddhist movement in China some of the best Chinese minds devoted themselves to understanding, interpreting, and elaborating the content of Buddhist thought and experience. A brief role call will serve to remind us of the personal labors behind Buddhist growth. Tao-an (312–385) studied metaphysics and meditation. His interests extended to problems of translation, cataloguing sutras and rules of discipline. Hui-yuan (344–416) was noted for his discussions on karma and the indestructibility of the soul. He argued for the independence of the Buddhist Order, maintaining that monks should not bow before kings. He also promoted meditative practices based on faith in Amitabha Buddha. The monk Tao-sheng (360–434) advanced theories which eventually became hallmarks of Chinese Buddhism, such as the doctrines of instantaneous enlightenment and universal Buddha nature. Seng-chao (374–414) was an outstanding interpreter of the philosophy of Nagarjuna which he had learned as a disciple of the famous Indian missionary Kumarajiva (in Chang-an, 401–413). Hsuan-tsang (596–664) achieved eminence as a pilgrim to India, translator, and commentator. Chi-tsang (549–623) systematized the Madhyamika philosophy of Nagarjuna and earned the reputation of being one of the most virtuous monks.

THE SCHOOLS OF CHINESE BUDDHISM

As Buddhist teachings flowed into China from India, their many tendencies gave rise to a diversity of schools and interpretations. The history of the formation of Buddhist schools divides into two periods. The initial period was known as the age of the "Six Schools and Seven Branches." During the second stage, the encouragement and support of Buddhist scholarship by the Sui and T'ang emperors led to the formation of more distinct and well-defined systems of Buddhist teaching which had enduring significance as the zenith of Buddhist intellectual leadership and influence in Chinese culture. As these schools developed, they reflected the gradual assimilation of Buddhism to the Chinese mind.

The first scholarly movement in the "Six Schools and Seven Branches" exhibited the two basic interests of early Chinese Buddhism in meditation and *Prajna,* or Wisdom. Influenced by the contemporary ascendancy of Neo-Taoism, there was a concern for the nature of ultimate reality and its relation to things. The names of the individual schools reflected rudimentary traces of Indian Buddhist philosophical tendencies.

The later major schools of Chinese Buddhism developed during the T'ang age in an endeavor to interpret Buddhism on its own terms. Efforts were made to ensure orthodoxy by the construction of doctrinal lineages. Ten schools emerged of which five had distinct Indian character and were limited in their overall influence on the Chinese mentality. These schools represented the Hinayanistic Satyasiddhi, Abhidharma Kosa, and Vinaya teachings and the Mahayanistic Yogacara and Madhyamika philosophies. More consonant with Chinese spirit were the T'ien-t'ai, Hua-yen, Ch'an, and Ching-t'u schools, which have had wide influence in Japan as well as

Eleven-headed Kuan-yin from the T'ang Dynasty, early eighth century. (Courtesy of the Cleveland Museum of Art, gift of Mr. and Mrs. Severance A Millikin.)

China. The Mantra or Cheng-yen school, transmitting Tantric teachings, did not become fully systematized in China but was absorbed into the traditions of other schools.

The transformation of Indian Buddhism into Chinese Buddhism appeared as early as Seng-chao, the famous Madhyamika teacher, when he asserted: "Reality is wherever there is contact with things." [2] This statement contrasted with the Indian emphasis on the delusive character of the world motivating withdrawal. Chinese Buddhists were critical of the Indian tradition for attempting to abolish the spiritual domination of the world over man by doing away with the world. For the Chinese, wisdom was not divorced from the

2. Wing-tsit Chan, *A Sourcebook in Chinese Philosophy*, Princeton, N.J., Princeton University Press, 1963, p. 356.

things of the world but rather wisdom revealed their true nature. Seng-chao declared:

> *Hence the sage is like an empty hollow. He cherishes no knowledge. He dwells in the world of change and utility, yet he holds himself to the realm of non-activity (wu-wei). He rests within the walls of the nameable, yet lives in the open country of what transcends speech. He is silent and alone, void and open, where his state of being cannot be clothed in language. Nothing more can be said of him.*[3]

With reminiscences of Taoist terminology and thought, Buddhism took up the cause of world affirmation.

The Hua-yen School

The development of a more this-worldly interpretation of Buddhism received a strong philosophical support in the thought of Fa-tsang (643–712) who expounded a complex system based on the *Avatamsaka* (*Hua-yen*) *Sutra*. In his famous parable of the golden lion presented before Empress Wu (684–705) we have a striking illustration of the ability of Buddhist teachers to render abstruse doctrines intelligible through analogies from the everyday world. Commanded to demonstrate the truth of his school, Fa-tsang explained the ten basic principles of Hua-yen philosophy concerning the relationship of ultimate reality to things by referring to a golden lion standing in the hall.

According to Fa-tsang, the ultimate teaching of Buddhism was the principle of the mutual interpenetration of all things as a result of their being manifestations of the one, all-embracing Buddha-mind. Things in the world had a degree of reality as expressions of the absolute Buddha-mind within things. Corresponding to aspects of objective idealism in the West, the teaching combined logical and psychological insight, making it one of the most influential philosophies in Chinese and Japanese Buddhism. It not only synthesized major philosophical currents in Mahayana thought, but its universal vision and ideal of mutuality within the whole inspired mystical endeavor and contained sociopolitical implications.

The T'ien-t'ai School

The face of Chinese Buddhism began to show itself in the formation of the T'ien-t'ai school, whose name was taken from the mountain in South China where the founder Chi-i (531–597) resided. This fact suggests the Chinese concern and interest in this world.

The central texts for this sect were the *Lotus Sutra* (*Fa-hua-ching*). Its teaching combined in a unified system the central Mahayana doctrines of universal Buddha nature, mutual interpenetration of all things, and the theory of instantaneous enlightenment. Although there were several predecessors in the development of the school, Chi-i was the pivotal figure in completing the doctrinal system. His character, depth of learning, and intellectual power have been unparalleled in Chinese Buddhist history.

3. Yu-lan Fung, *History of Chinese Philosophy*, Princeton, N.J., Princeton University Press, 1953, vol. II, p. 268.

The T'ien-t'ai school attempted to confront the increasingly difficult problem of the diversity of teachings attributed to the Buddha flowing into China from India. Each doctrinal system claimed to be the direct teaching of the Buddha because all sutras opened with an affirmation that they had been originally recited by Ananda, Buddha's companion and original transmitter of his teachings.

It was Chi-i's contribution to develop a comprehensive historical-doctrinal organization of Buddhist texts and doctrine covering Buddha's lifetime which set the pattern for later thought in Chinese and Japanese Buddhism. He gave an account of the order of appearance of Buddhist teachings involving a theory of progression to the ultimate truth of the *Lotus* and *Nirvana Sutras*. His system came to be known as the theory of "Five Periods and Eight Doctrines."

Briefly stated, during the first period of twenty-one days the Buddha attempted to teach the profound doctrine of the *Hua-yen-ching.* However, his disciples did not have the capacity to understand. Consequently, he had to devote himself during the next twelve years to the propagation of Hinayana doctrine. In this time he hoped to induce individuals to higher aspirations by using a simple doctrine. In the third period, covering eight years, some individuals converted to elementary Mahayana teaching, while others were rebuked for rejecting this doctrine. The fourth stage of twenty-two years centered on the propagation of the *Prajna* (*Wisdom*) *Sutras.* The Mahayana concept of Voidness was stressed. In the fifth and final period of eight years the Buddha proclaimed the doctrine of the *Lotus* and *Nirvana Sutras* as the supreme way of Buddhism. Correlated with the different periods of Buddha's life and teachings Chi-i developed a set of criteria for distinguishing various forms of doctrine with the aim of showing the superiority of full Mahayana teaching over earlier Hinayana or elementary expressions of Mahayana philosophy.

The theory of five periods represented a quasi-historical attempt to place the Buddhist texts in their approximate historical order based on the perception of growth in the depth and breadth of Buddhist insight on the nature of salvation and the world in the development from Hinayana to Mahayana philosophy. The criteria for evaluating doctrines reflected pedagogical and mystical insight. Its major contribution to the development of Buddhist thought lay in its systematic and scholarly approach, drive for unity and coherence, and theory of religious development. Further, its universalistic philosophy, expressed in the theory of "three thousand in one moment (or instant) of thought," proclaimed, like the Hua-yen philosophy, that everything is the essence of every other thing from the standpoint of ultimate reality. Consequently, this philosophy also asserted the importance and reality of the things of this world as embodiments of the universal Buddha-nature.

The Ch'an (Zen) School

Ch'an (Zen) Buddhism appeared as the culmination of several trends within Chinese Buddhism. Combining with Taoist iconoclasm, it was, in a measure, a reaction to the scholasticism and lifeless formalism of T'ang Buddhism. It attempted, through the discipline of meditation, to bring to full practical and experiential realization the principles of universal Buddha-nature and instantaneous enlightenment. It also focused attention on life in this world, fusing with Taoist love of Nature. The emphasis on egolessness and nonduality (Buddhism) together with the resulting qualities of naturalness and spontaneity (Taoism) achieved the complete assimilation of Buddhism within the Chinese spirit.

The term Ch'an or Zen was derived from the word *dhyana*, meaning "meditation" in Sanskrit. In the sense that meditation is the heart of Buddhism, Ch'an claimed to be the most essential aspect of Buddhist life. Originally meditation was a discipline of regulated sitting, breathing exercises, and mental exercises designed to still the passions and bring discursive thought to a halt. Indian Yoga techniques provided the basic elements for this endeavor. In China, India's elaborate system of meditation underwent considerable modification in its adaptation to Chinese ways. Influenced by Taoist nature mysticism and Chinese interest in this life, meditation aimed at instantaneous enlightenment. Rather than merely bringing discursive thought to a halt, Chinese Buddhists directed their effort at realizing their fundamental identity with the absolute reality surrounding them in the world of Nature. This identity produced a new awareness of the world in which the singularity of things in the given world at the same time revealed the allness of the Buddha-nature.

As a specific tradition in Chinese Buddhism, Ch'an had a long history. Though shrouded in conflicting legends there appeared numerous schools claiming to transmit the true doctrine and practice of Ch'an. The main divisions were the Northern school, derived from the monk Shen-hsiu (605–706) who is described as maintaining a gradualist approach to enlightenment, while the Southern school, stemming from Hui-neng (638–713), emphasized instantaneous enlightenment. In the contest between these two factions the Southern school became the main stream of tradition for present schools. The basic text for this tradition was the *Platform Sutra* attributed to Hui-neng.

The story of Hui-neng and the teaching given in the *Platform Sutra* manifests certain religious characteristics of Ch'an noteworthy for their social implications. The account of Hui-neng's entrance into the monastic life and his eventual assumption of spiritual leadership depicts the democratic principle in Ch'an in which all beings equally possess the potentiality to manifest Buddha-nature. Lowly people are not to be despised. Thus Hui-neng, an illiterate woodcutter, attains enlightenment and displaces Shen-hsiu who, by virtue of training and background, is in line for leadership. The stress on illiteracy and lowly background of Hui-neng may be a comment on the scholasticism and formality in the great schools in much of Chinese Buddhism of that time. Hui-neng retorts to his master Hung-jen's assertion that he was a barbarian:

I replied: "Although people from the south and people from the north differ, there is no north and south in Buddha nature. Al-

though my barbarian's body and your body are not the same, what difference is there in our Buddha nature?" [4]

The spiritual revolution urged by Hui-neng discounted the external religious activities of building temples, giving alms or offerings, or mechanically reciting sutras. Merit in Ch'an Buddhism meant "inwardly [to] see the Buddha nature; outwardly, practice reverence." [5]

The rejection of externality and formality was carried further by the monk I-hsuan (d. 867) who declared the essence of Buddhism as the natural way of life:

The Master told the congregation: "Seekers of the Way. In Buddhism no effort is necessary. All one has to do is to do nothing, except to move his bowels, urinate, put on his clothing, eat his meals, and lie down if he is tired. The stupid will laugh at him, but the wise one will understand. An ancient person said, 'One who makes effort externally is surely a fool.'" [6]

The radicality of I-hsuan's rejection of the obstructive attachment to externalities and forms burst forth in his demand to his disciples to "Kill the Buddha if you happen to meet him. Kill a patriarch or an arhat if you happen to meet him. Kill your parents or relatives if you happen to meet them. Only then can you be free, not bound by material things, and absolutely free and at ease.[7]

As the Southern school of Ch'an developed after Hui-neng and his disciple Shen-hui (670–762), who led the attack on the Northern school, two other schools appeared which became most influential in the progress of Ch'an in China and in Japan to the present day. These two important streams were that of Lin-chi, established by the monk I-hsuan, and the Ts'ao-tung, formed by the monk Liang-chieh (807–869). The major difference between these two schools united in aim and philosophy was the method undertaken to attain enlightenment. The Lin-chi (Japanese *Rinzai*) employed a method whereby the disciple was catapulted into enlightenment through pondering a riddle (*kung-an, koan*) and subjection to physical shock by means of a shout or blow causing the individual to release his grip on reason. The Ts'ao-tung (*Sodo*) school was more tranquil and emphasized quiet meditation under the direction of a master which would lead to the realization of one's Buddha-nature.

As the Ch'an perspective took shape, five basic principles emerged to guide its basic way of life.[8] These principles were frequently dramatically presented in the many stories used in the training of the monk as the basis of his meditation.

The first principle, that "the highest truth or first principle is inexpressible," indicates that Ch'an strives for an experience of reality beyond words and is not satisfied with merely conceptual knowl-

4. Philip B. Yampolsky, *The Platform Sutra of the Sixth Patriarch*, New York, Columbia, 1967, pp. 127–128.

5. Ibid., p. 156.

6. Chan, op. cit., p. 445.

7. Ibid., pp. 447–448.

8. Based on the discussion provided by Fung, op. cit., pp. 388–406.

Hui-neng, sixth patriarch of the Ch'an sect, chopping bamboo at the moment of enlightenment, from the Southern Sung Dynasty, probably end of the twelfth century. (Courtesy of the Tokyo National Museum.)

edge. This experience is called Void because it cannot be defined, but it is also called Buddha-nature or Original-nature as a symbol of union with the root of our being.

Buddhist philosophy, unlike some contemporary philosophies, is one of experience, a self-evidential experience. Consequently Ch'annists generally refuse to engage in merely rational argument and appear pretentious in their retort: "Try it yourself."

The second principle, that "spiritual cultivation cannot be culti-vated," is a paradoxical assertion emphasizing the fact that reli-gious endeavors which may begin on the conscious level must eventually be made second nature and part of the instinctive, spontaneous reactions of our personalities. When this aim is at-tained, one does not practice Buddhism; one is in his deepest being Buddhist. The conquest of conscious goodness abolishes affected-ness and competition from religious life.

The third principle, that "in the last resort nothing is gained," re-fers to the fact that the world is not abolished, nor are we transferred to another realm by the fact of enlightenment. The true existence of this world is affirmed in all its depth. However, our un-derstanding is transformed: "When I began to study Zen, mountains were mountains; when I thought I understood Zen, mountains were not mountains; but when I came to full knowledge of Zen, moun-tains were again mountains." [9]

The fourth principle states: "There is not much in Buddhist teach-ing." This is not to be taken as an expression of doubt or unbelief. Rather, it is a declaration that concepts, doctrines, and words are inferior to the experience of enlightenment itself. From the highest perspective there is really neither Buddha, Buddhists, nor Bud-dhism. We noted above I-hsuan's instruction to his disciples that if they meet Buddha, they should kill him. If one perceives Buddha over against himself, he is still caught in the net of discriminating abstractions. The whole attempt of Buddhist discipline, generally, is to actualize in experience what is learned in concept.

Related to this principle also is the claim that Ch'an Buddhism is a transmission beyond scriptures. There are, of course, scriptures and important texts, but the experience to which Ch'an aspires is not gained from books but through persons. Famous stories of in-sight gained by disciples through striking encounters with the mas-ter under whom they were training emphasize the person-to-person contact which accounts for some of Ch'an's modern appeal.

The fifth principle declares that "in carrying water and chopping wood: therein lies the wonderful Tao." It is a vivid comment on the texture of religious existence. Ch'annists have developed their spe-cific forms of education and monastic life. Nevertheless, the senti-ment exists that enlightenment is not itself confined to definite prac-tices but may come instantly in the course of carrying out the most menial tasks. As the world is the world, and Buddha-nature is uni-versal, one may realize it anywhere. Such a viewpoint intensifies the

9. D. T. Suzuki, *Studies in Zen,* New York, Dell, 1955, p. 187.

significance of even the most elementary acts. Hence, Ch'an has
had extraordinary influence in art. In an age when the significance
of individuals and persons appears to be declining in mass society,
Ch'an stresses one's inner and ultimate identity in deep interper-
sonal relation with others. Artificialities are to be swept away. The
emphasis on the validity of daily life as the sphere of ultimate reality and meaning also supports the individual in his quest for self-
understanding.

The final major tradition of Chinese Buddhism which we must consider is the Pure Land tradition (Chinese *Ching t'u,* Japanese *Jodo*).
This teaching attracted the popular masses through its offer of a
simple way to salvation through reciting the name of *Amitabha* Buddha (Chinese *O-mi-to-fo,* Japanese *Amida*). The faith and practice of
recitation would permit the individual to be born in the Pure Land,
from which state he would eventually be assured the achievement
of Nirvana or realization of Buddhahood.

The Pure Land in Buddhist mythology was created by Amitabha
Buddha as the result of his vows to save all beings and the infinite
merit he acquired through aeons of practice. In the Chinese mind it
represented a glorious heaven beyond the travail of this world and
easily accessible through reciting the Buddha's name in faith. In
order to stimulate faith in the Pure Land, there were Buddhist texts
which depicted the alternative destiny of birth in one of many hells
for those who ignored or despised that faith. These teachings coincided with belief in heavens and the quest of immortality which had
developed in religious Taoist tradition.

Like other schools, the Pure Land teachers sought in Buddhist
tradition for texts and teachers in order to construct an orthodox lineage for the doctrine. They believed Buddha Sakyamuni taught the
doctrine in three central texts, the *Wu-liang-shou-ching* (*Great Sukhavati-vyuha Sutra*), the *O-mi-t'o'ching* (*Short Sukhavati-vyuha
Sutra*), and the *Kuan-wu-liang-shou-ching* (*Amitayur-dhyana Sutra*).
It was then reputedly passed on through the famous Indian Mahayana teachers Nagarjuna and Vasubandhu. Eventually it made its
way to China, where it was practiced by such outstanding monks as
Hui-yuan who formed the White Lotus Society for the purpose of
meditating on Amitabha Buddha.

T'an-luan (476–542) was responsible for the popular development
of the doctrine. He was followed by Tao-cho (c. 645) and Shan-tao
(613–681). In addition to this line of transmission, other teachers
promoted the doctrine either as a subsidiary aspect to one of the
more philosophical schools such as Ch'an or T'ien-t'ai or as the
central teaching.

The first major figure in the Chinese tradition was T'an-luan
from the area of Wu-t'ai-shan in North China. Living in an environment infiltrated with magical religion, T'an-luan engaged upon a
search for the elixir of immortality following a long illness. Having
obtained texts containing formulas from a Taoist master in the
south of China, he returned home. On the way, legend relates, he

The Pure
Land School

met the Indian monk Bodhiruci who convinced him that true ever-lasting life was attained through Pure Land teaching. Casting aside his Taoist texts, he became a teacher of Pure Land doctrine.

T'an-luan popularized Pure Land doctrine by joining it to the theory of the decline of Buddhism. According to this theory, which became basic to Pure Land doctrine in China and Japan, the purity of the Buddhist Order, doctrine, and discipline and the ability to achieve enlightenment decreased as the inspiration of Buddha receded into the historical past. Finally, the last age of the decline and disappearance of Buddhism arrived when no Buddha was present and extremes of egoism, passion, stupidity, anger, pride, and doubt dominated human life. During this age, men did not practice or attain Buddhist ideals, though the doctrine was taught.

On the background of the degeneracy of Buddhism, T'an-luan held that ordinary mortals could achieve salvation through the recitation of Amitabha's name. Rather than depending on one's own power (self-power), mortals had to rely on the saving power of Amitabha deposited in his name. This method of salvation was designated the "easy" way in contrast to the "difficult" ways of meditation and austerities of earlier Buddhism.

The teaching was later systematically organized by Shan-tao, who made the practice of recitation of Buddha's name the central Buddhist discipline. Analyzing the doctrine into the method of meditation, attitudes, and conditions of practice, he developed a comprehensive interpretation of religious life. Through his writings he defended Pure Land doctrine against proponents of the more traditional modes of Buddhist discipline and set the stage for its later flourishing in Japan.

The evolution of Pure Land teaching coincided with the Chinese tendency to affirm life in this world, despite its other-worldly emphasis, because it opened the doors of salvation to the lowliest common man. Through the simple vocal recitation, and without arduous or strict regimentation, individuals could achieve salvation, while fulfilling their family and social obligations.

BUDDHISM IN
CHINESE SOCIETY

As Buddhism spread through Chinese society it met sporadic opposition from either Confucian or Taoist exponents who regarded it as inimical to the health and progress of Chinese society and culture. As a consequence of their criticisms and the traditional control over religion maintained by the Chinese government, Buddhism was constantly under the surveillance of the state even when officials patronized the order for the sake of merit. The result of these conditions was to keep Buddhism institutionally weak but not to interfere with its permeation of the masses. Buddhism reached the peak of its influence in the Sui and T'ang periods, where it blossomed with great intellectual and spiritual creativity witnessed in the various schools.

The comparison of the state of Buddhism after the T'ang period with its prosperity during that age gives the impression that Buddhism entered into a state of continuing decline and lethargy with few signs of vitality. The persecution of Buddhism in 845, which was most severe and damaging, signaled the end of Buddhist influence on the higher levels of society. In addition, Confucian knowledge had begun to revive and spread during the T'ang age. Confucian scholars eventually displaced Buddhist intellectual leadership. Beginning with the memorial of the scholar Han Yu (786–824) against Buddhist superstition, the criticism of Buddhism mounted and reached its zenith in the Sung and Ming Neo-Confucian schools which attempted to deal with issues raised by Buddhism from a Confucian standpoint. In contrast to the other-worldly and mystical tendencies of Buddhism, the Confucianists stressed practical efforts in the world.

Further, Ch'an emphasis on practice and discipline and its anti-intellectualism limited efforts to educate monks and contributed to the waning intellectual influence of Buddhism. Buddhist scholarship did not progress beyond the lines established by the major schools of the T'ang era. In modern times reformist monks such as T'ai Hsu have advocated the education of monks and have endeavored to revive scholarly traditions, particularly the study of the Wei-shih (Consciousness-only) school of subjective idealism which T'ai Hsu thought was most compatible with the scientific era.

With the change of circumstance Buddhism lost prestige among the wealthy classes, which also meant a loss of income. The increased intellectual competition and resistance led to more government control. On the popular level the government permitted the spread of concepts and practices which aided in pacifying the people, but the aspects of asceticism and other-worldliness were made to conform to Chinese interest in this world. Nevertheless, Buddhist influence in Chinese society and culture has been extensive through its two thousand-year history, and it can be discerned in language, popular ideas, beliefs about afterlife, festivals, arts, literature, and philosophy.

Buddhism as a specific faith became relegated to a popular religion on the level of religious Taoism with which it generally fused. Among the common people the Buddhas and Bodhisattvas together with Taoist deities became the protectors of the common man in his struggle for existence. He implored divinities for aid in avoiding disaster and recovery from disease or misfortune. Buddhism became largely associated with the performance of funerals as a consequence of the promise of a glorious destiny promoted by the Pure Land cult. It also developed masses and memorials for the dead, such as the Avalambana festival designed to save ancestors as far back as seven generations from suffering. Such celebrations enabled Buddhists to fulfill filial piety demanded by Chinese morality. Although Buddhism entered into a comparative state of decline because of its changing fortunes in society, there were some positive features. During the Sung period the development of printing aided diffusion of Buddhist texts. The founder of the Ming dynasty (1368–1644), Chu Yuan-chang (1328–1398), had originally been a Buddhist. He placed Buddhism under strict regulation, knowing its hold on the masses, and also reorganized the order, testing the scholarship of priests, building and repairing temples, and contributing to publishing the canon of scriptures. Further, there were a number of Buddhist scholars during the Ming period such as Yun-ch'i Chu-hung (1535–1615) who advocated the unity of the three teachings of Buddhism, Confucianism, and Taoism as well as combining Ch'an and Pure Land teaching. He also defended Buddhism against Christianity.

During the three hundred year domination of the Manchus in the Ch'ing dynasty, Buddhism suffered from oppression and strict control under the influence of Confucian orthodoxy. Also the T'ai-ping rebellion (1864) resulted in a great destruction of Buddhist temples in southern China. Nevertheless, some emperors had personal interest in Buddhism and favored it.

With the confrontation of China and the West, like the Confucians the Buddhists have also had to struggle to discover ways to cope with the cultural crisis. In addition, Buddhists have had to deal with skeptical and reform-minded officials who wished to seize their institutions and transform them to schools or museums. While the founders of the republic in 1911 appreciated the high moral outlook of Buddhism, they did not believe it supported democracy, since it was apolitical and too passive. The crisis, however, served to awaken interest in Buddhism among laymen as well as clerics. This interest was also stimulated by a religious desire to acquire merit for their future destinies. Thus laymen sponsored Buddhist publications, lectures, and societies for the study of Buddhism. They were also moved by a desire to unite Chinese society based on Buddhist ideals as a means of meeting the modern challenge.

Although materials are now becoming more accessible for the assessment of the role of Buddhism in modern China, it has suffered from widespread misrepresentation by Christian missionaries, Chinese Confucianists, the Japanese, and Communists. The Christians regarded Buddhism as superstition and the priests lazy and ignorant, while the Confucianists looked on it as parasitic. The Japanese tended to despise it as inferior to their own forms of Buddhism, while the Communists saw it as exploitive and reactionary to social and political progress.

Due to the general negative views of Buddhism put forth by modern observers, there has been a tendency to interpret Buddhism since T'ang times as one of complete decline, degradation, and loss of vitality until a revival took place at the end of the nineteenth century and early twentieth century. This view has been challenged through detailed studies of Buddhist institutions and history in the modern period. In some measure the serious practice of Buddhism has always been carried on by a few dedicated monks in a number of monasteries widely respected for their purity and rigor. Buddhism has performed a positive role among the people in caring for their spiritual needs. The revival represented by the flurry of activity largely developed by laymen can be regarded as a shift away from the central core of Buddhism, since the major element of Buddhism was its system of meditation and discipline whose function was to provide an alternative for the human spirit to the tedium, anxiety, and struggles of conventional social life. The attempt to adjust Bud-

Kuan-yin seated in the "royal ease" pose, from the Sung Dynasty. (Courtesy of the Museum of Fine Arts, Boston, Hervey Edward Wetzel Fund.)

dhism to modern conditions in the effort to make it relevant may represent the secularization of Buddhism and signal a true loss of vitality and meaning for the religion.

In the present situation the future of Buddhism in China hangs in doubt. Though initially rejecting religion in 1949, the 1954 Constitution guarantees freedom of religion. Nevertheless, the Communist regime has seized property and forced monks in great numbers to become laymen and join the work force. In comparison to its treatment of Christianity, also a foreign and international religion, the Chinese Communists have recognized the cultural contributions of Buddhism and its utility as an instrument of foreign policy in dealing with the Buddhist countries of Asia. They have maintained the Chinese Buddhist Association which engages in studies of Buddhist tradition as well as serving as a spokesman for government policy to Buddhists outside of China. Whether the Buddhist spiritual outlook can survive its complete subordination and subjugation to the interests of a totally secular political order remains to be seen.

SECTION TWO

JAPAN: RELIGION OF A SACRED PEOPLE IN A SACRED LAND

INTRODUCTION: RELIGION IN JAPAN

The emergence of Japan as a major world power after centuries of isolation has focused world attention on her peculiar combination of old and new, conservative and progressive, particular and universal. A strong historical awareness has been coupled with a sense of the unchanging essence of her people.

Though these characteristics do not differ essentially from features previously noted in Chinese tradition, they have attained remarkable durability as a result of Japan's relative geographic isolation and racial homogeneity. Consequently, Japanese native traditions and spirit have survived waves of foreign cultural inundation from China and the West.

Japanese folk religion, as the piety of ordinary people, shares characteristics in common with other cultures in its this-worldly, communal, pragmatic, magical, and adaptive features. However, the Japanese folk religion also embodies a sense of the sacredness of the land and the people, nourished by the beauty, fertility, and relative security of the environment. As a result of this strong racial sentiment which asserts Japan's central role in the cosmic order, all freely accepted foreign cultural elements are transformed to bring them in harmony with Japanese sensitivities.

This process is clearly evident in the adoption by the Japanese of Confucian, Buddhist, and Taoist beliefs and practices. Christianity has had great difficulty in gaining broad acceptance, unlike Buddhism, despite popular fascination with and the overwhelming pressure of Western culture in all areas of social and cultural life.

The highly variegated elements of Japanese religious tradition drawn from early native religion, Buddhism, religious Taoism, and Confucianism have been fused into a complex whole. The superstructure of Japanese religious tradition rested on, and was nourished by, folk sentiment and religious piety expressed in the manifold festivals and other spontaneous religious activities. The qualities and attitudes of the Japanese outlook derived initially from the masses who lived close to the soil and reveled in its abundance and glory. While folk piety has sustained the superstructure, manifest social expressions of religion in Japan have played significant roles in the history of the people.

In the interaction of these traditions the Japanese, like the Chinese, did not sense any essential contradiction. In a somewhat simplistic way it has been true that Shinto and religious Taoism advanced human interests in this life, while Buddhism came to be concerned mainly with death and afterlife in addition to aiding endeavors of this life. Confucianism focused upon social and individual morality.

The integration of the various components of Japanese religious tradition can be more easily understood through a brief discussion of the Japanese perspective on religion. We can approach this perspective from three angles: this-worldly realism, communalism, and emphasis on purity.

THE JAPANESE PERSPECTIVE ON RELIGION

The dominant feature of this-worldly realism has manifested itself throughout Japanese history in frank acceptance and enjoyment of life and the world. Japanese landscape with its great diversity and beauty inspired ancient inhabitants with the belief that it was truly a land of gods. This faith was further borne out by the abundant fertility of the soil. The sense of sacredness of the land and its productivity banished any deep disillusionment with existence as implied in the mystical philosophy of Buddhism. The awareness of the goodness of the land stimulated all forms of art and efforts to transform even the most lowly object into a thing of beauty. There has been a conscious attempt to harmonize man-made structures with their natural surroundings, attesting to a sense of kinship and unity with Nature.

The sense of awe and wonder aroused by the creative forces of Nature has also provided the basis for accompanying traits of pragmatism, eclecticism, tolerance, and a more intuitive, sentimental and nonintellectual approach to religion among the Japanese.[1]

Ancient Japanese awareness that gods and spirits resided in natural objects which particularly arrested their attention led them to exalt the concrete phenomenon and made them especially open to novelty and influences from all areas of their world. Hence they not only welcomed Chinese culture with its religious beliefs and practices, but they continued the transformation of other-worldly Buddhism which had begun in China. Further, it is clear that eclecticism and tolerance resulted from the need to find alternative effective ways to cope with the erratic and unpredictable aspects of Nature.

---

1. H. Nakamura, *Ways of Thinking of Eastern Peoples,* Honolulu, East-West Center Press, 1964, pp. 350–406, 531–576.

The Japanese were receptive to claims that Buddhism possessed superior magic powers for dealing with divine forces.

The intuitive approach has expressed itself in the widespread Japanese sentiment that Buddhism and religion in general is mysterious and profound. Concern for the mood and beauty of a ritual outweighs in significance any intellectual consideration in its evaluation. Also group sentiment has played a great role in determining thought.

A good illustration of the predominance of intuition over intellectualization in Japanese thought is the contrast in the ways of understanding the nature of divinity in Japanese and Western tradition. In the West philosophers and theologians attempt to define what God is; then they seek the evidences of his existence in the world. The Japanese, however, regard the impressions of beauty, mystery, awe, goodness, or ugliness which arise in encounters with things in the world as signs of the presence of divinity within those things. Thus the idea of divinity begins with the recognition of the special character of the object which points beyond itself to a more fundamental reality behind and within. There is no need to define or prove divinity in this context as in the Western mode of thinking, because the recognition of the peculiar significance of the object constitutes its quality of divinity. Divinity is not limited to a specific class of objects nor to one set of attributes. Aesthetically, this perspective encourages art and the exaltation of the common and menial. Ethically, it may be criticized that religion becomes morally irrelevant when goodness and badness, beauty and ugliness, are equally divine. However, Japanese tradition emphasizes the aspects of productivity, growth, and creativity in Nature as the prime qualities in life. This stress has moral implications which counter the apparent indifference to values in the awareness of divinity.

Japanese communal feeling began with primary commitment to the clan and family in ancient times. Eventually this commitment extended to the central Imperial clan which gradually grew more powerful as the government transformed into a centralized bureaucratic state on the Chinese model. Supported by similar Confucian principles, the Japanese came to view their country as a great family headed by the Imperial parent.

As the family-nation concept indicates, religion throughout Japanese history has been inextricably interwoven with kinship, group, and national concerns and relationships. On the village level the Dozoku kinship unit (a group of related, nuclear families in hierarchical arrangement involving status and obligations) has been the major religious unit. The concrete activities of religious festivals generated a cohesive spirit as all the members, aware of their common destiny, strove to secure the life of the group through ceremonies designed to stimulate fertility or pacify the spirits of the dead. The centrality of the kinship group was expressed in ancestor reverence, which has been an essential feature in every tradition, native or foreign, in Japanese history.

A significant implication of the importance of the kinship group in social and religious matters has been the priority of the group over the individual in all vital social matters. As a consequence, religious commitment and belief have not been emphasized, though conscious voluntary adherence to a specific religious system is not entirely absent. In general, one's religion and religious activity depended on his group obligations. The social organization required in food production in ancient times imposed limitations on individual expression, since the good was not sought for oneself but for one's group.

In the sphere of politics and government the Emperor came to symbolize the unity of the people as the supreme mediator between the gods and the people. He was the concrete expression of the divinity of the nation being a direct descendant of the Sun Goddess. Because of the unique status of the Emperor, the Japanese differed from the Chinese in placing loyalty to the Emperor and nation ahead of one's family. The theory of Japanese society gradually crystallized in the concept of *Kokutai* (National Essence), which provided the ideology of modern Japanese nationalism.

Emperor reverence also relates to the tendency of Japanese to form strong bonds of devotion to concrete individuals, whether Emperor, Lord, or teacher. This characteristic contributed to factionalism and sectarianism in later developments of Japanese Buddhism.

Japanese emphasis on purity initially centered on the avoidance of actions giving rise to physical or ritual pollution or uncleanness which could threaten the well-being of the community and the individual. In common with other lesser developed peoples, the early Japanese focused their attention on the external, concrete act. Eventually consideration was given to motivation and inner character.

The Japanese concern for purification was early observed by the Chinese and a central ceremony was the *Oharae*, whose text is contained in the *Norito* (ritual prayers) of the *Engishiki*. From this passage we gain concrete indications of the idea of sin or pollution among the early Japanese. According to the prayer, sins were divided into heavenly and earthly. The heavenly sins were

> *Breaking down the ridges,*
> *Covering up the ditches,*
> *Releasing the irrigation sluices,*
> *Double planting,*
> *Setting up stakes,*
> *Skinning alive, skinning backwards,*
> *Defecation—*
> *Many sins (such as these) are distinguished and called the heavenly sins.*[2]

The earthly sins were:

> *Cutting living flesh, cutting dead flesh,*
> *White leprosy, skin excrescences,*

2. Donald L. Philippi, trans., *Norito*, Tokyo, The Institute for Japanese Culture and Classics, Kokugakuin University, 1959, p. 46.

The sin of violating one's own mother
The sin of violating one's own child,
The sin of violating a mother and her child,
The sin of violating a child and her mother,
The sin of transgression with animals,
Woes from creeping insects,
Woes from the birds of on high (sic),
Woes from the deities of on high (sic),
Killing animals, the sin of witchcraft—
Many sins (such as these) *shall appear.*[3]

The performance of the rite of purification caused the gods to take away all the sins recounted above. According to the ritual, the Goddess Se-ori-tu-hime who dwelled in the fast-flowing rivers carried the sins to the briny ocean where they were swallowed by the Goddess Haya-aki-tu-hime. When she swallowed them at a gulp, the deity Ibuki-do then blew them all to the underworld. With the sins gone, tranquillity reigned.[4]

As can be seen in this early listing, sins were primarily social in character. Good and evil were completely distinguished according to whether an act was beneficial for the community or dangerous. The term good (*yoshi*) covered a wide area such as beauty, excellence, good fortune, and nobility. Bad (*ashi*) signified something evil-omened, inferior, and unlucky. In the mythology the polarization of good and evil was expressed in the *Magatsubi-no-kami* (bending Kami) and the *Naobi-no-kami* (straightening Kami). The former were gods of pollution and disaster, while the latter were those who restored things to a normal condition.

Although early Shinto possessed awareness of purity and pollution and good and evil, it did not enunciate a formal value system. Rather than setting up a scale of values, it sought unity with the Kami in each action. To attain unity with the Kami meant to cultivate a bright, pure, correct, and straight mind. The characters *mei-jo-sei-choku* (brightness-purity-correctness-uprightness) provided an outline of the basic values eventually employed to express the Shinto ethic. It also contained the potentiality for a more spiritual ethic of inward purity.

Though the Japanese concern for purity became more inward, it was not guilt-oriented nor ascetic since it believed in the essential goodness of man and was optimistic. Many Imperial edicts stressed purity of heart or the honest and sincere heart. In the fulfillment of vows, an important element was the declaration that one's heart and intention was pure. This perspective in Japanese religion can be observed in the vow ascribed to the divinity Hachiman Bosatsu:

Though much I see as I tramp back and forth
Shall I ever forget the heart of a man
Who is innocent and pure! [5]

3. Ibid., pp. 46–47.
4. Ibid., p. 48. See also poem of Motoori Norinaga, in Tsunetsugu Muraoka, *Studies in Shinto Thought*, Tokyo, Japanese Ministry of Education, 1964, p. 152.
5. Muraoka, op. cit., p. 33.

Among the symbols of Imperial authority, the mirror represented the pure heart as interpreted by the Shinto thinker Kitabatake Chikafusa:

> The Mirror harbors nothing within itself. As it reflects all phenomena without a selfish heart, there is never an instance when the forms of right and wrong, or good and evil fail to show up. Its virtue consists in responding to these forms as they come. This is the basic source of correctness and uprightness.[6]

In addition to the ideals of purity of body and spirit which pervaded Japanese religious tradition, the principles of filial piety, loyalty, gratitude, and sincerity have been key elements in Japanese moral existence. A keen sense of duty and obligation has inspired individuals with serious purpose. These fundamental social values have received support and reinforcement from the religious traditions through the inculcation of ancestor reverence and the teachings of the various religious communities. Confucianism particularly strengthened Japanese moral sentiments and provided the theoretical structure for native morality.

As an outgrowth of the maintenance of purity and correctness, buttressed by the Confucian principle of li (propriety and decorum), the Japanese have developed a highly ceremonial and ritualistic culture. The necessities of recognizing status have shaped language, as well as social activities, extending from everyday ordinary affairs to major social and religious events.

The Japanese religious perspective harmonized well with religio-philosophical elements imported from China. Confucianism implemented moral and political tendencies through affirming hierarchy, authority, monarchy, filial piety, and duty. Religious Taoism amplified magical techniques and divination practices, while Buddhism expanded the scope of the Japanese understanding of human life and offered gorgeous imagery, ceremony, and pageantry appealing to Japanese aesthetic sentiment.

The study of the manifold characteristics and tenor of Japanese religious perspective may be further amplified through a brief survey of the basic trends arising from the mutual interaction of the various components of the tradition within the changing conditions of Japanese society.

RELIGION IN JAPANESE HISTORY

The indigenous Japanese religion emerging out of the obscurity of prehistoric times faced the subtle complexity and pageantry of Mahayana Buddhism which appealed to many facets of Japanese character. However, rather than fading from history before the pronounced sophistication and practicality of Buddhism, the two religions merged on the folk level, and the native tradition became more self-conscious through the compilation of its myths in the Kojiki (712) and the Nihonshoki (abbrev. Nihongi, 720) as a result of Imperial demand. Borrowing Chinese terminology, the native tradition came to be known as Shinto (the Way of the Gods).

6. Ibid., p. 39.

Despite the formalization of Shinto, Buddhist perspectives and activity dominated the Japanese religious world on institutional and intellectual levels, as witnessed by the great temples and Buddhist schools of the Nara (710–784) and Heian (794–1185) eras.

However, the national sentiment, grounded in Shinto faith in the divinity of the country and people, never permitted leaders to neglect their obligations to the gods of the people. While on the surface the foreign culture appeared stronger, the folk sentiment nourished the roots as an underground stream. Eventually, the foreign tradition transformed into the national image.

As a consequence of the combination of national sentiment and Buddhist tolerance, Shinto ritual and outlook on life persevered. In the Kamakura era (1185–1333) and in the later Tokugawa period (1600–1867) Shinto tradition became reawakened alongside the flourishing of numerous popular, lay-oriented Buddhists sects. Scholarly exponents of a pure Shinto without foreign accretions and associations appeared one after the other to lay the foundation for the restoration of the Emperor Meiji to political authority by appealing to the ancient Shinto awareness in the people. The modern political use of Shinto as the basis of Japanese nationalism depended on the latent sentiments in the minds of the people. Modern popular religious cults have drawn upon either Shinto or Buddhist traditions, taking advantage of the deep-rooted association of these traditions in the hearts of the people.

Despite tension and conflict in modern times, the two traditions complement each other, corresponding to the tension of universal and particular elements in the Japanese spirit. The universal, cosmic philosophy of Buddhism provides a vision of Japan as the kingdom of Buddha radiating Buddhist wisdom and compassion to the world. Shinto supports that sense of uniqueness and particularity in the Japanese which has prevented them from losing their identity in the midst of floods of foreign influence. It is perhaps not without significance that the Nichiren Buddhist tradition which incorporates both facets has burst forth, nationally and internationally, with some of the most active religious communities.

SHINTO: A DIVINE WORLD AND A DIVINE PEOPLE

The Shinto religious tradition has deep roots going back to the remotest times when the Japanese people established themselves on the islands, becoming enamored with their climate, beauty, and fertility. We have already noted that Japanese native beliefs mingled and fused with elements from China such as Confucianism, Buddhism, and religious Taoism, drawing from them moral, metaphysical, and magical features which supported their inner feeling of the essential sacredness of the land and its people. Traditional Shinto as it has come down in history has become a complex religion, making it difficult to separate native and foreign aspects. In this short summary we simply attempt to focus upon elements of Shinto belief, its thought and history, as background for understanding Shinto influence in modern times and its potentiality for the future.

The durability of Shinto religion can be highlighted by calling attention to features of that tradition which have maintained themselves from the earliest times. We gain our first glimpse of the religion in Chinese sources from the third century which describe Japanese religious and political conditions.

According to these texts, a major element in the ancient religion was concern for purification, achieved through water rites and maintaining taboos. The still-existing practice of clapping the hands when summoning or dismissing a deity was noted as well as the practice of divination. An outstanding feature of the religion of this time was the presence of a female shaman, Pimiko (Himeko, Sun Daughter), who acted to bring peace and order to the community after protracted strife. Her activity may have provided the model for

EARLY JAPANESE RELIGION

the myth of the central female Sun Goddess, Amaterasu-o-mikami.

As with other ancient societies, the early Japanese were concerned with securing food and maintaining the continuity of the group, or otherwise prospering their lives. As means to achieve these ends, the Japanese early came to revere mountains, worship spirits, and resort to shamans.

In relation to mountains, Japanese religious tradition reveals three types of beliefs concerning their sacredness. Conically shaped dormant volcanoes, supremely represented by Mount Fuji, have been objects of reverence. Mountains have also been associated with fertility as the sources of the vital water. They have also been conceived as either residences of the dead or the way the dead ascend to heaven.

The belief in mountains as the abode of the dead or the meeting place between this world and the other can be seen in the ancient practice of burying kings in natural or artificial mounds (yama). In the poems of the ancient classic Man'yo-shu some fifty-one view the dead as living on a mountain, while twenty-three place the dead in the sky or clouds.

Ancestor worship and concern for the spirits of the dead became especially prominent in Japanese religious life from the eighth to the twelfth century and appeared in the literature of the age. As Hori points out:

> All social and personal crises such as political changes, civil wars, epidemics, famines, droughts, earthquakes, thunderstorms and typhoons, as well as difficult childbirth, diseases, and deaths, were believed to be the result of revenge by the angry spirits of the dead. Sometimes they were believed to be caused by the angry or jealous souls of living men and women.[1]

Such beliefs have persisted to the present time and ceremonies must be held to pacify spirits of people who have suffered untimely death.

The origin of such beliefs and their gradual penetration to all levels of society perhaps lies in the interaction with early beliefs in shamans whom a deity had possessed, the deification of nobles after death, and the beliefs in spirits of the dead and the belief in the essential equality of all people transmitted through Buddhism and Taoism. The association of the spirits of the dead with Kami of ancient Shinto was a gradual development brought about through linking the activities of reverence for the dead and worship of Kami as a result of political interests. Initially the worship of the souls of the dead and ancestors was not really central to Shinto. When it appeared, it was promoted by political leaders rather than by popular religious feeling. In Buddhism the belief attained its strongest expression.[2]

1. Ichiro Hori, "Japanese Folk Beliefs," *American Anthropologist*, June, 1959, pp. 61–63, 419.

2. Delmer M. Brown, "Kami, Death, and Ancestral Kami," in *The Proceedings of the Second International Conference for Shinto Studies*, Tokyo, Institute of Japanese Culture and Classics, Kokugakuin University, n.d., pp. 169–182.

The reason for the eventual predominance of Buddhism in such matters can easily be understood in the light of its development in India and China. The myths of India concerning the hungry ghosts, *Preta,* became the basis by which Buddhism enforced and stimulated practices of filial piety on behalf of the dead as a way of accommodating Buddhism to Chinese and Japanese outlook. These practices with their pageantry and variety also appealed to the Japanese imagination.[3]

Like mountain worship and worship of spirits, the phenomenon of shamanism has deep roots in Japanese religion. The earliest evidence from outside sources concerning Japan indicate the presence of shamanesses as in the case of Queen Pimiko (see p. 343). Though it has never been institutionalized, it has persisted to the present, appearing even in contemporary religions. Lacking institutionalization, it has also penetrated and combined with alien traditions such as Buddhism and Taoism.

Shamanism in Japan has generally centered upon shamanesses, though shamans are also present. In addition, the Emperor possessed a shamanic charisma both through his descent from the Sun Goddess and as the head of the Imperial clan. Although the Emperor himself might receive divine words through dreams or ecstatic experience, he frequently received communications through other shamans and diviners.[4]

The Shugendo system of religious practices, carried out on mountains and generally associated with Buddhism, functions on the popular level as the virtual amalgamation of all the elements of early Japanese religion. The practitioners, who devote themselves to ascetic exercises on the mountains, combine Japanese reverence for mountains and beliefs in spirits, Buddhist esoterism, and Taoist wizardry and magic. Since the Heian period the movement has largely become associated with Buddhism because of the monasteries located on mountains.

The complex of Shinto tradition with many forms and nuances has emerged from the stream of Japanese religious and social history and can be studied from a variety of angles, none of which are sufficient to elicit a full understanding of its outlook and function in Japanese society. One may view it in terms of the various types of cults in the Japanese environment, such as an agricultural-fertility cult, local cults of mountains or other features of the natural environment, or aversive cults centered on attempts to appease the spirits of important personages whose death was considered unfortunate as illustrated in the cult of Sugawara Michizane. In addition, forms of Shinto can be classified as Shrine Shinto, Sect Shinto, Folk Shinto, Imperial House Shinto, or Domestic Shinto.

3. The comprehensive study of the use of Buddhist texts in ancient Japanese Buddhism by M. W. De Visser, *Ancient Buddhism in Japan,* 2 vols., Leiden, E. J. Brill, 1935, illumines the character of early Japanese Buddhism and provides ample illustration of such magical use of texts. Also, Shoko Watanabe, *Japanese Buddhism: A Critical Appraisal,* Tokyo, Kokusai Bunka Shinkokai, 1964, pp. 82–99, discusses the background and development of Buddhist ceremonies for the dead.

4. Joseph M. Kitagawa, *Religion in Japanese History,* New York, Columbia, 1966, pp. 17–19.

The term "Shrine Shinto" is a relatively modern one for that aspect of Shinto which was supported by the state in its efforts since the Meiji period to provide a basis for national integration and feeling. In earlier times it was simply called Shinto.

Over against the political use of Shinto to reinforce national sentiment, "Sect Shinto" refers to individually founded modern religious orders based on Shinto beliefs and practices. "Folk Shinto" is applied to the magico-religious beliefs which are the substratum of beliefs and sentiment in all other aspects of Shinto. These folk beliefs serve individual or communal purposes. Through Folk Shinto practices the individual attempts to satisfy his various needs for health, wealth, and security in life, while the communal cult is the focus for harmonization of the local society, politically and culturally. "Imperial House Shinto" refers specifically to those rites carried out by the Emperor and his family, while "Domestic Shinto" signifies the worship centered on the god-shelf in the ordinary home.

Further, as a consequence of the intimate relation to society and its needs, we find that Shinto, as the religion of natural groupings, has functions connected to blood-related groups such as the Dozoku and represented by the *Ujigami,* or Clan deity, land-related groups such as the village community and symbolized in the tutelary deity of the area, age-related groups in which young and old have various responsibilities in the cult, and occupation-related groups in which deities care for the interests of various trades and crafts. In addition, groups termed "Ko" have a more voluntaristic character in which people become associated for some spiritual purpose such as a pilgrimage to a famous shrine like Ise. The influence of location remains strong in the relationship of people to Shinto shrines. A distinction is made between the *Ujiko,* who are believers living in the general area, and the *Sukeisha,* who are believers from outside that region.

Beside the various structural forms and practices which can be discerned within Shinto, its mythology and beliefs reveal the nature of the folk beliefs and also provide the basis for the cult of the Imperial house and national self-understanding. A history of Shinto thought results from interaction with many influences in Japanese history. Because of the multiplicity of factors in this development, it is difficult to uncover the precise nature of early Shinto, since even its mythology, given in the *Kojiki* and *Nihonshoki* (abbrev. *Nihongi*), was organized and recorded under foreign influence. Though the popular religion is very conservative and is perhaps a good source for viewing what may have been the ancient Japanese outlook on the world, it is difficult to isolate foreign elements.

Although the various elements of ancient Japanese religion have become associated with Buddhism as well as Shinto on the folk level, it is Shinto which, through all changes, has continued to provide the foundation of the Japanese religious consciousness as a sacred people in a sacred land. As the basis of their awareness of being a particular people, Shinto has evolved into a complex system paralleling the transformation of the people from a motley group of clans to a modern industrial state. Just as the Japanese became more self-conscious through the impact of Chinese culture, so also Shinto became awakened and sought formulation of its tradition distinct from the foreign systems permeating the culture.

In view of the many aspects of the study of Shinto, rather than being exhaustive we shall simply attempt to survey several significant aspects of Shinto tradition which may enable the student to better appreciate this oft-misunderstood and inadequately known religion.

We shall first give an account of the conception of deity and the character of mythology which set the direction for the tradition. Second, we shall observe the way in which the foreign traditions of Buddhism and Confucianism came to terms and appropriated Shinto. Third, in the face of the prestige of foreign religio-philosophical traditions, we shall inquire into the struggle for a pure interpretation of Shinto. Finally, in modern times we witness the expression of Shinto as a patriotic cult and as the basis of religious communities. Through the study of Shinto in interaction with its environment we become aware of its profundity and its strength, refusing merely to be absorbed into more highly articulate traditions.

In approaching the discussion of Shinto we must rely mainly on the materials provided by the *Kojiki* and *Nihongi,* though we recognize that they were the product of a specific class of people pursuing special interests. In addition, we gain important insight from the ritual prayers called *Norito* in the *Engishiki* and such texts as the *Kujiki* and *Kogoshui.* In all probability the great deities depicted in the texts had little relation to the popular masses, but they do reflect something of awareness and understanding of deities among the people. It is also necessary to recognize that Shinto was not consciously cultivated in early times nor systematically organized. Such religious activity and thought as were present constituted the Japanese response to their surrounding environment. Wonder at the mystery of the universe inspired the Japanese from earliest times. It is this awe of the suprahuman powers in nature that penetrates all areas of religion and is the basis of their conception of deity.

The central core of Shinto lies in its peculiar awareness of divinity which, from the ethnological view, points in the direction of a mana-like conception common to the Polynesians, and from the religio-philosophical view, is the basis for the more pantheistic tendency observable in the development of Shinto theology as it is elaborated in interaction with Buddhism and Confucianism.

Unlike the conception of deity in Western tradition, the concept "Kami" in Shinto does not refer to an absolute being who stands distinct from the world and beings he has created. Rather, "Kami" refers more to a quality in things, persons, and forces, whether good or evil, which raises them above the ordinary level of evaluation through the sense of awe, wonder, fear, attraction, or repulsion which the object arouses in the person. The Shinto scholar Motoori Norinaga (1730–1801) summarizes most clearly the understanding of "Kami" in Japanese tradition:

KAMI: MYTH AND RITUAL IN TRADITIONAL SHINTO

I do not yet understand the meaning of the term, kami. *Speaking in general, however, it may be said that* kami *signifies, in the first place, the deities of heaven and earth that appear in the ancient records and also the spirits of the shrines where they are worshipped.*

It is hardly necessary to say that it includes human beings. It also includes such objects as birds, beasts, trees, plants, seas, mountains, and so forth. In ancient usage, anything whatsoever which was outside the ordinary, which possessed superior power or which was awe-inspiring was called kami. *It is needless to say that among human beings who are called* kami *the successive generations of sacred emperors are all included. . . .*[5]

Further included in this category by Norinaga are not only spirits of emperors or people of the past, but some people in villages in the present. Among nonhuman Kami are dragons, echoes, foxes, tigers, wolves, peaches, rocks, stumps, leaves, and thunder. These all may awaken awe and wonder in the human mind.

The permeation of the cosmos by deity even to the lowest form of life has made the division between divinity and profane existence difficult to draw in Japanese experience. Not only the spirits of the dead may be treated as divine, but living persons may also manifest divinity. An outstanding illustration is the Emperor himself who is termed *Arahito-gami* or "Manifest Kami."

The awareness of the divine activating Japanese religiosity has been crystallized in the mythological tradition in the conception of the *Yao-yorozu-no-kami,* the eight hundred myriads of deities (eight million deities). This conception embodied the sense of the Japanese of the abundance and pervasiveness of the divine power through the whole of the cosmos and life. According to Holtom, the number of deities, many nameless, reached untold numbers, while at the time of his research 214 deities were acknowledged in state shrines.[6]

Though Shinto is a clear polytheism, its belief may be positively evaluated in the light of its awareness of the creativity and abundance in life. As one scholar of Japanese religion states:

Life, by its very nature, tends to be infinite. Historians of religion, by penetrating more profoundly into the religious reality, have come to recognize that former generations have misjudged polytheism. What they understood to be "idolatry," was never practised in this manner by any religion. Religious people, by worshipping a variety of objects, always intended one thing, the SACRED, which they expressed in many forms.[7]

From among the superabundance of divinity acknowledged by the Japanese, the myths of the *Kojiki* and *Nihongi* focus on a modest

5. Quoted in D. C. Holtom, *National Faith of Japan,* New York, Paragon, 1947, p. 23.

6. Ibid.

7. Heinrich DuMoulin, "The Aspect of Creation in the Shinto Concept of Kami," in *The Proceedings of the Second International Conference for Shinto Studies,* Tokyo, Institute of Japanese Culture and Classics, Kokugakuin University, n.d., p. 26.

number of deities significant for Japanese religious tradition. In general, two groupings are important in the development of Shinto: (1) a triad of deities who are responsible for the creation of the cosmos and who initiate the cosmogonic process; and (2) deities directly related to the creation of Japan and the Imperial line.

The three deities—*Ame-no-mi-naka-nushi-no-Kami* (Kami Master of the Center of Heaven), *Taka-mi-musubi-no-Kami* (High Sacred Creating Kami), and *Kami-musubi* (Sacred Creating Kami)—began creation when there was still nothing but primordial chaos and no shapes had appeared. Unlike many other deities, they had no genealogy but appeared spontaneously and later disappeared. From the young earth which they had originated there eventually appeared a whole host of deities who make up the genealogical succession resulting in the creation of Japan and the Japanese people.

The very abstract and remote character of these deities made it possible in later times to employ them as more philosophical principles. Thus Hirata Atsutane in his interpretation of Shinto placed *Ame-no-mi-naka-nushi-no-Kami* as the central divinity, existing before Heaven and Earth. The elevation of this deity to absolute status, supported by the two assisting deities, had repercussions in the modern attempt to promote Shintoism politically.

The deities who initiated the process of creation or production of growth and life in the universe do not have highly concrete imagery reflecting the folk consciousness. However, the subsequent stories concerning the sexual activity, death, births, and conflicts of deities possess a vividness suggesting that originally those deities were once centers of cultic life. The myths were important in ancient Japanese attempts to secure food and the continuity of the group through ritual action. Analysis of various myths in the cycle in the light of myths of other cultures suggests that they reflect the conditions of the environment through their symbolism.

While these myths had their original locus in the cult concerned with food and sex, as they appear in the ancient texts of the *Kojiki* and *Nihongi,* they have a different function. In this context the original nature deities are transformed into ancestors and made the basis for the faith in the divinity of the Imperial house and the associated nobility. The narratives of the Age of the Gods lead to the history of the Age of Man which is carried almost to the point when the texts were composed.

As the society developed, the originally unorganized cult took firmer shape with more concrete conceptions of deity, formation of priestly functionaries, and establishment of shrines and rituals. In time various distinctions and nuances have grown up.

In the sphere of the divine a variety of classifications appeared. There were those Kami who represented the spirits of heroes or emperors of the past. These have had political and moral significance in the education of the people. There were deities which symbolized natural phenomena. Another category stressed functional deity. The creation deities could be viewed as the divinization of the power in growth. Certain objects came also to have the value of deity as the body of the deity (*shintai*). There were also divinities which resisted classification as illustrated in the head of the Idzumo pantheon, *Okuni-nushi-no-Kami*. Some deities were classified in terms of the region they oversaw, such as the *Ubusuna-Kami* or *Chinju-no-Kami*. Classifications also appeared in the types of spirits recognized in Shinto:

> *Traditionally, Shinto acknowledged four kinds of spirits—ara-mi-tama, those which rule with authority and power;* nigi-mi-tama, *those which bring about union, harmony, and recollection;* kushi-mi-tama, *those which cause mysterious transformation; and* saki-mi-tama, *those which impart blessings. There are suggestions that one and the same kami might have more than one* tama. *Spirits of enemies and those who might have met an unfortunate death, later known as* go-ryo, *were also believed to have potency. Moreover, the* mono *or* mononoke (*sometimes spirits of animals*) *were widely feared and venerated. All those kami and spirits could "possess" men and women, and those who were thus possessed were called* kami-gakari (*kami-possessed*) *and* mono-tsuki (*mono-possessed*), *respectively.*[8]

Originally priesthood was controlled by the head of the clan in group worship. Hence, initially there was no special priesthood. At a later time, now unclear, four classes of functionaries appeared. These were ritualists called the *nakatomi*, abstainers termed *imibe*, diviners or *urabe*, and musicians and dancers or *sarume*.[9] As early as the eighth century A.D. the control of the priesthood was located in the *jingi-kan* or office of Divine affairs.

The festivals of Shinto represented the people's active response to environmental changes in the quest for food and group survival. Many were thus seasonal. The major seasonal festivals of official Shinto were the Kinen-sai on February 4 with the object of praying for the year's crops, Niiname-sai on November 23–24 which was the harvest festival, and the Rei-sai or festival of the local shrine. Many of the national holidays celebrated in the system before the war were closely related to Shinto tradition.[10] According to Sokyo Ono the purpose of the festivals was:

> *to ward off or ameliorate any misfortune and secure or augment the cooperation of the kami in promoting the happiness and peace of the individual and community. They include prayer for divine protection, communion with the kami, praise of the kami's virtue, comfort for the kami's mind, reports to the kami on the affairs of daily life, and pledges offering the whole life to the kami.*[11]

The major elements of the shrine ceremony were purification, carried out by both priests and devotees. Offerings, prayer, and a symbolic feast composed the *matsuri* or service to the deity. In the

8. Kitagawa, op. cit., p. 14.
9. Holtom, op. cit., pp. 27–29.
10. Ibid., pp. 157–158.
11. Sokyo Ono, *Shinto the Kami Way*, Tokyo, Bridgeway Press, 1962, p. 50.

The creation of Japan. Izanagi and Izanami, Shinto gods, standing in the clouds creating islands out of sea water. Late nineteenth century. (Courtesy of the Museum of Fine Arts, Boston.)

deepest sense *matsuri* enveloped all life which was lived in awareness and communion with the gods. It also referred to specific occasions when the individual or community sought blessings from the gods or the prosperity of the people.

The more than eighty thousand shrines were formerly integrated into an overall system of classification. The status of a particular shrine depended on its national, regional, and local significance and received support accordingly. Presently, without government control or support, the shrines have become independent, though priests and shrines are generally related through the Association of Shinto Shrines.

Shinto mythological narratives and understanding of the nature of Japanese society have provided Shinto tradition with several theological themes which have been the subject of discussion in the development of Shinto thought. These were the distinction between the hidden and the manifest, the concept of *musubi* (growth, productivity), and the principle of *saisei-itchi* (union of religion and government).

The distinction of the hidden and manifest was important in the political and religious spheres of thought. On the political side, it suggested that the deities resided in the hidden world but gave the visible world over to men to govern. In religion it related to the contrast between the visible world of this life and the hidden world of the dead.

The concept musubi, generally rendered "creativity" or "productivity," has significant philosophical and ethical aspects as a basic value in the Shinto interpretation of life. Its fundamental importance is evident in the fact there are a number of deities whose name includes the term. The two assisting deities of *Ame-no-mi-naka-nushi-no-Kami* are *Taka-mi-musubi-no-Kami* and *Kami-musubi-no-Kami.* These three are considered the source of all creation according to the mythology. In addition, there are *Ho-musubi-no-Kami* (Fire-Creating Deity), *Waku-musubi-no-Kami* (Young-Creating Deity), *Iku-musubi-no-Kami* (Life-Creating Deity), *Taru-musubi-no-Kami* (Plentiful-Creating Deity). Further, the prolific generation of the gods depicted in the mythology directs our attention to Japanese awareness of growth, productivity, and vitality as the essential feature of the surrounding Nature.

The awareness of the productive goodness of Nature is the basis for the Japanese ethical recognition of *on,* the obligation one has to his benefactor and the gratitude which expresses it. To repay *on* is central to Japanese ethical outlook. Japanese concepts of purity and pollution are also related to the awareness of musubi in Nature. Emphasis on life and productivity leads to the identification of pollution with death as dramatically presented in the horrified flight of Izanagi from the decayed corpse of his wife Izanami in the land of Yomi. Life wins out over death and pollution. When Izanami declares she will strangle one thousand people every day, Izanagi promises that he will cause fifteen hundred children to be born every day.

Drawing upon these implicit themes within the tradition, contemporary exponents of Shinto have attempted to show that it can provide modern man with a viable view of life. Beginning with the affirmation of the life force, they hold that it becomes embodied in history through man's work and effort. There is frank recognition that religion cannot ignore the existential anxieties of modern life and it must seek voluntary commitment.

Another important theme which Shinto thinkers drew from the mythical tradition was the principle of saisei-itchi (union of government and religion). Forming the basis of the self-understanding of the nation, this concept teaches that the religious and political dimensions of life are essentially one, because the leader of the nation and its high priest before the gods is the Emperor. Commitment to the nation is an ultimate commitment and has manifested itself in modern times in the extremes of patriotic sentiment and sacrifice for which Japan has become famous in the reputation of the Kamikaze pilots of World War II. It has been manifested in traditional thought concerning religion and government in the word *matsuri-goto,* which refers both to actions performed toward the gods (*matsuri*) and civil affairs. The term *miya* also means shrine and Imperial court.

Although this principle was not strongly enforced during the periods when the Shogunate (military dictatorship) was operative, during the Meiji period the principle was stressed and attempts were made to establish Shinto as the state religion. The object of the effort was to develop national consciousness and cohesion in face of the transitions needed to industrialize and modernize the state. The principle was enunciated in the proclamation defining the relation of Shinto and the state as the basis for a broad effort of indoctrination:

> *We solemnly announce: The Heavenly Deities and the Great Ancestress (Amaterasu-Omikami) established the throne and made the succession sure. The line of Emperors in unbroken succession entered into possession thereof and handed it on. Religious ceremonies and government were one and the same (saisei-itchi) and the innumerable subjects were united. Government and education were clear to those above while below them the manners and customs of the people were beautiful. Beginning with the Middle Ages, however, there were sometimes seasons of decay alternating with seasons of progress. Sometimes the Way was plain, sometimes, darkened; and the period in which government and education failed to flourish was long.*

> *Now in the cycle of fate, all things have become new polity and education must be made clear to the nation and the Great Way of obedience to the gods must be promulgated. Therefore we newly appoint propagandists to proclaim this to the nation. Do you our subjects keep this commandment in mind.*[12]

This principle has had to be set aside as a result of the Shinto directive issued in 1945 declaring absolute separation of Church

12. D. C. Holtom, *Modern Japan and Shinto Nationalism,* New York, Paragon, 1947, p. 6. Quotation taken from Imperial Rescript of February 3, 1870.

and State in Japan. Despite the abuses of the concept in modern times, it does hold the ideal that human society is not only an organized secular arrangement, but a spiritual reality in which mundane and divine affairs are completely integrated and harmonious.

Shinto religion has displayed through the centuries a capacity for adaptation and a potentiality for philosophical and religious development, stimulated by interaction with Confucianism and Buddhism. It is this factor which has given hope to adherents that it will adapt to the necessities of the modern age.

BUDDHIST AND CONFUCIAN ACCOMMODATIONS

When Buddhism and Confucianism entered Japan from China, they gradually came to terms and fused with the Shinto awareness of Japan as a sacred people and sacred land headed by a divine Emperor. The Buddhist accommodation to Shinto was perhaps more outstanding because of the cosmic, metaphysical, and other-worldly character of Buddhist tradition. Confucian morality with its own hierarchial, social theory harmonized easily with Japanese sentiments. Some differences between the Confucian outlook and the Japanese appeared in their rejection of Mencius' implicit principle of the right of revolution in his concept of the Mandate of Heaven and the Japanese tendency to place the interest of the nation, ruler, or lord above the family, though it was generally viewed that these elements would never be in conflict. Also, Confucianism was not theological or speculative. However, it was chiefly among Buddhists that more detailed theories of the relation of Buddhas and gods had to be worked out.

Though Buddhism has easily adapted itself to native traditions in other lesser developed countries, in Japan it faced a problem of a more profound nature in attempting to harmonize itself with the deep-rooted sentiment of the sacredness of Japan. On the popular level of folk piety, Buddhism merged with the life of the people much as in other places. The latent awareness of the more fundamental issue of the true superiority of the Buddha over the gods was reflected in the development of more sophisticated and philosophical theories, grounded in Mahayana metaphysics, which attempted to demonstrate the essential equality of the Japanese deities with the Buddhist divinities.

In order to spell out the relationship of the two traditions, two theories gradually grew up within the major schools of Buddhism in the Heian period and attained full expression in the succeeding Kamakura era. The system of *Ryobu Shinto* (Double Aspect Shinto) was formulated on the basis of the Shingon esoteric doctrine promoted in Japan by Kobo Daishi (Kukai, 773–835). *Ichijitsu Shinto* (One Truth Shinto) or *Sanno Shinto* (Mountain King Shinto) embodied the theory of the Tendai school established on Mount Hiei by Dengyo Daishi (Saicho, 766–822).

The essential idea contained in both theories held that Shinto deities were fundamentally manifestations in the world of the universal Buddha-nature. Although the Buddha-nature was the source of fundamental reality (*honji*), and the deities were trace manifestations (*suijaku*), the relationship was virtually an identification, since the essence of the manifestation is the original source and the two could never be separated. On the practical and concrete level the theory maintained that specific deities such as the Sun Goddess (Amaterasu-o-mikami) and Toyo-uke-o-mikami of Ise shrine were identical with the great Sun Buddha Mahavairocana (Dainichi-nyorai). It was not without significance that the concept of the Sun Buddha was used as the symbol for the unity of the people in the construction of Todaiji in Nara as Japan grew into a centralized state.

Confucian Shinto refers to the interpretation given to Shinto by the exponents of Neo-Confucian philosophy during the Tokugawa period. In a similar fashion with Buddhist thinkers, Confucian teachers maintained the harmony of Shinto and Confucian thought. The most outstanding advocate was Hayashi Razan (1583–1657), a counselor to numerous Shoguns and an outstanding figure in promoting Chinese culture.

In maintaining the harmony of Shinto and Confucianism, Razan was continuing the work of his teacher Fujiwara Seika. According to Seika, Confucianism was but another name for Shinto, since in their respective countries both were teachings expressing mercy and compassion for all the people.

However, Hayashi Razan carried the ideas forward in a more positive way. He criticized both the Buddhist views based on honji-suijaku and teachings which attempted to set forth pure Shinto. His version of Shinto emphasized one's obligation to principle (li) or sense of duty. He interpreted Shinto as the Imperial Way along Confucian lines whose essence lay in conformity to the rule of the Emperor. He identified the virtues present in the three sacred regalia in accordance with the virtues of the Confucian classic of the *Chung-yung:* the mirror was wisdom; the jewel, humaneness; the sword, courage. His theory had great influence on all Confucianists despite their varying tendencies.

THE STRUGGLE FOR PURE SHINTO

Concurrent with the assimilation of Shinto in Buddhism and the unification of Confucian morality and political theory with Shinto beliefs in the divinity of the Imperial line and sacredness of the nation, there were exponents of pure Shinto who wished to keep the national traditions free from alien influence. In their interpretations they utilized ways of thought borrowed from foreign traditions but always in the name of Shinto itself. The effort to express a pure Shinto reached its culmination in the teachings of the National Learning (*kokugaku*) scholars, particularly Kamo Mabuchi, Motoori Norinaga, and Hirata Atsutane.

The reason for the emergence of a self-conscious Shinto polemic and apologetic may stem from what was believed to be remarkable interventions of the gods saving Japan from the Mongol invasions in 1274 and 1281 through great winds (*kamikaze*). As G. B. Sansom points out, Shinto religion flourished in times of danger when the rulers called upon the national deities to aid the nation.[13] The clan-centered character of the Kamakura regime also contributed to strengthening of Shinto clan cults. Additional influences came later from the development of historical studies by Confucian scholars and the increasing dissatisfaction with the Tokugawa leadership and its failure to solve pressing political and economic problems.

A variety of schools of thought attempted to give a pure Shinto interpretation to Japanese tradition through relying on Buddhist or Confucian philosophy for the exposition of Shinto theology. Buddhism contributed to the development of pantheism in Shinto thought, while Confucianism provided an ethical orientation and reinforcement for patriotic themes centering on reverence for the Imperial house.

In the background of the struggle for a pure Shinto, there were a number of contributory streams. *Ise* Shinto, developed by Watari Tsuneyoshi (d. 1339) and Watari Iyeyuki (d. 1355), aimed to purify Shinto of Buddhist influences, based on the *Shinto Gobusho* (*The Five Books of Shinto,* forged texts represented as ancient classics) which exalted the Sun Goddess as supreme. The famous Shinto scholar Kitabatake Chikafusa (1293–1354) continued this work in his important text: *Jinno Shotoki* (*The History of the True Succession of the Divine Emperors*). Though applying Confucian virtues to the interpretation of the three sacred Imperial regalia, he maintained the superiority of the Japanese way to the Indian and Chinese. The *Yuiitsu* (Unique, One and Only) Shinto was a reaction to the Double Aspect theory of Buddhism and reversed the relationship of gods and Buddhas. Buddhas became manifestations of the absolute Kami. *Suiga* Shinto, set forth by Yamazaki Ansai (1618–1682), employed Neo-Confucianism in order to exalt the nation and give a basis for patriotism. Ansai stressed strongly loyalty and reverence for the Emperor. The basic virtue advocated by Ansai was *tsutsu-shimi,* defined as "a circumspect attitude; an attitude carefully obeying precepts and rules; an attitude careful not to be guilty of disrespect or failure." [14] Other lesser trends directed attention to the practical application of morality, rituals, divination, or ceremonies for the dead.

The most important development for the evolution of Shinto thought was the emergence of the National Learning school which, as seen in the parallel term "Restoration Shinto," aimed at reawakening and purifying the national consciousness based in Shinto against Buddhist, Confucian, or Christian influences which had penetrated Japanese culture. Not only does the movement reveal the intellectual potentialities of Japanese thinkers and Shinto theology, but its patriotic fervor also sets the stage for the modern employment of Shinto as the ideological basis for nationalism and national cohesion.

13. G. B. Sansom, *A History of Japan,* Stanford, Calif., Stanford University Press, 1958–1963, vol. I, p. 445.

14. *Basic Terms of Shinto,* compiled by Shinto Committee for the 12th International Congress for the History of Religions, Jinja Honcho, Tokyo, Institute for Japanese Culture and Classics, Kokugakuin University, 1958, p. 75.

Portion of the Shinto Ise Shrine, dedicated to the Great Sun Goddess. (Courtesy of the Japan National Tourist Organization.)

In the development of this tradition of scholarship there were several important individuals whose accomplishments built one on the other, leading to greater refinement of thought. Keichu (1640–1701) developed philological studies in connection with the classic *Man'yoshu* and turned attention from Chinese ancient learning to Japanese ancient learning. Kada Azumamaro (1669–1736) developed the concept of National Learning (*kokugaku*). He was particularly concerned with the lack of interest in Shinto studies in his time. Kamo Mabuchi (1697–1769), as a poet, attempted to grasp the ancient spirit in the *Man'yoshu* and strove to clarify the Japanese outlook before Buddhism and Confucianism came to obscure it. He turned the anti-intellectual and intuitive perspective of Taoism to use in criticizing Chinese tradition. Motoori Norinaga (1730–1801) and Hirata Atsutane (1776–1843) were the key figures in the background of modern Shinto thought and scholarship.

Motoori Norinaga brought the National Learning school to its highest development in purging Japanese and Shinto thought from its Confucian and Buddhist influences. In his attempt to revive ancient Shinto, he employed the studies of philology and concentrated his attention on interpreting the ancient traditions in the *Kojiki, Nihongi,* and *Norito* in the light of linguistic study and on the basis of their internal thought. He also studied deeply the *Man'yoshu.* Though he was scholarly in his method, a pious faith inspired his devotion to study. This faith resulted from his contact with three intellectual movements penetrating his time, namely *Dazai* Learning,[15] *Suiga* Shinto, and Pure Land Buddhism.

Building on the foundations of earlier scholars of National Learning, Norinaga explored every sphere of that study and wrote prolifically in prose and poetry. His most important writing was his commentary on the Age of Kami period in the *Kojiki* (*Kojiki-den*).

15. A more independent trend of Confucian studies set forth by Dazai Shundai (1680–1747) in the tradition of Confucian Ancient Learning was developed by followers of the Wang Yang-ming wing of Neo-Confucianism.

Itsukushima Shrine, dedicated to Ichikishimahime Goddess, niece of the Great Sun Goddess. Located on "Shrine Island" in Hiroshima, this shrine is part of the Shinto nature worship. (Courtesy of the Japan National Tourist Organization.)

Norinaga particularly focused his attention upon the *Kojiki* for understanding the Japanese spirit, where earlier scholars drew from the *Man'yoshu.* Despite its limitations as a spiritual document, it provided Norinaga with a basis for cultivating spiritual sentiment in the adoration of the Sun Goddess and the elevation of the deities Taka-mi-musubi-no-Kami and Kami-musubi-no-Kami as symbols of the life force.

Norinaga gave expression in a telling fashion to the intuitive, emotional side of the Japanese spirit in his attempt to displace the dominant Confucian rationalism. Appealing to the myth of creation in the *Kojiki,* he emphasized the mystery which lay at the heart of creativity. On the same basis he asserted the superiority of Japan over other nations, pointing to the unbroken line of emperors as witness to the fact. He suggested a messianic destiny for Japan, because she possessed the ancient way of the Sun Goddess. His sentimentalism was expressed most clearly in his claim that the Buddhist monastic discipline was in contradiction to man's natural disposition and essentially insincere, though correct from a Buddhist standpoint. According to him, truth lay in the expression of human feeling and sentiment. Hence, Buddhist rejection of sexual relations was erroneous. The spontaneous outpouring of love and compassion in the Ancient Way contrasted with the formalized, external ways of the Chinese. The primary value for Norinaga was sincerity (*magokoro*):

*The heart that can be moved
Is a Sincere Heart.*

Those who boast
   That they cannot be moved—
Are they made of stone and wood?

To veil and hide
   The Sincere Heart,
To put on airs
   To pretend—
Such are the ways of China [16]

Hirata Atsutane represented the more intellectual side of the Japanese mind. He was unusual for his knowledge of Chinese thought and contact with Christianity and Western knowledge. His Shinto theology was influenced by ideas drawn from the writings of Matthew Ricci and Didacus de Pantoja, both Jesuit theologians. In general, his notions of creation and eschatology were derived from Christian sources.

Despite the Christian influences in his thought, Hirata was committed to the revival of Shinto and at the grave of Motoori he made a vow to be his disciple and to strive for the Ancient Way. He wrote numerous works including "treatises on maritime defense, Chinese philosophy, Buddhism, Shinto, medicine, and the art of poetry as well as elaborate commentaries on the Japanese classics and discussion of Japanese political institutions and history." [17] All his knowledge was permeated and woven together by his exaltation of Shinto as the highest knowledge. His major works were *Koshi Seibun* (*Composition of Ancient History*) and *Koshiden* (*A Commentary on "Composition of Ancient History"*).

Like Norinaga and other Shinto scholars before him, Hirata was an exponent of the superiority of the Japanese people in all areas, whether material, religious, moral, intellectual, or dynastic.[18] Particularly, the unbroken dynastic succession evidenced the superiority of the Japanese and their destiny to rule over all others.

Historically, Hirata's thought was of great significance as the basis for the establishment of Shinto in the Meiji era and a major influence in modern Japanese nationalism. This approach to Shinto did not differ greatly from his predecessors, except perhaps in the intensity of antiforeignism and nationalism. Though despising the West, he appreciated the value of Western science and the influence of Christian thought was evident in his concept of deity and afterlife.

According to Hirata the deities of Shinto were universal gods. Ame-no-mi-naka-nushi-no-Kami was the highest personified deity. The deity Taka-mi-musubi-no-Kami was the supreme creator of all. He used evidences from other religions concerning the existence of a supreme creator to support his contention of the truth of the Shinto teaching of creation. He wrote:

16. Tsunetsugu Muraoka, *Studies in Shinto Thought*, Tokyo, Japanese Ministry of Education, 1964, pp. 158–159.

17. Holtom, *National Faith of Japan*, p. 50.

18. Ibid.

> *Thus, in all countries, as if by common consent, there are tradi-*
> *tions of a divine being who dwells in Heaven and who created all*
> *things. These traditions have sometimes become distorted, but*
> *when we examine them they afford proof of the authenticity of the*
> *ancient traditions of the Imperial Land. There are many gods but*
> *this god stands at the center of them and is holiest of all.*[19]

He took great comfort in advocating his position from the Coper-
nican revolution which recognized that the earth revolved about the
sun. According to Hirata, Japanese tradition had always recognized
the centrality of the sun.

Hirata revealed his own independent thought in his conceptions
of the afterlife. Stimulated by Christian conceptions, he went beyond his teacher Norinaga to give a comparable Shinto view. For
him, the concealed and mysterious Kami world, which Norinaga had
identified merely with the amoral Yomi or the land of darkness, was
a world of souls where individuals who had become Kami on their
death resided. Kami possessed various capacities and powers to reveal the future. This world was a place of testing, and all accounts
would be squared in the world of souls. He also believed that souls
lived in the vicinity of their graves and the spirit of Motoori Norinaga lived at Mount Yamamuro.

His contribution to the establishment of Shinto as a patriotic and
national cult in the Meiji period lay in his interpretation of the ge-
nealogies given in the mythology and the association of the general
ancestor worship of the Japanese to the worship of the deities of
the Imperial House. He gave some attention to the problems of rites
and ceremonies.

In summary, the National Learning school of Shinto provided the
emotional, spiritual, and intellectual foundation of modern Japanese
national consciousness. It involved elements of sentimentalism, rational criticism, a logic of its own based on faith in the uniqueness
of Japan and her people, antiforeignism, and chauvinism. Though
penetrated by a religious faith, it was political in centering devotion
on reverence of the unbroken Imperial line, believed to be divine in
origin.

When the intention of the scholars of this tradition is seen in the
light of their nationalist faith, their scholarly capacity is more readily appreciated despite its distortions. They excelled in philology,
classics, and literature. They frequently combined a wide knowledge of Chinese and Japanese tradition, and in the case of Hirata,
knowledge of Western religion and science. The most pertinent criticism of their endeavor lay in the subordination of their scholarship
to the goal of exalting the supremacy of a particular national and
cultural tradition. This effort often resulted in the distortion of historical and religious understanding. Nevertheless, when viewed
within the context of the changing fortunes of the Tokugawa era,
they believed deeply that they were restoring the truth of their tradition which had been obscured through foreign influence resulting in

19. William Theodore De Bary, *Sources of Japanese Tradition,* New York,
Columbia, 1958, p. 546.

the social decline then becoming more and more evident. The later fortunes of Shinto in the Meiji period suggest, however, that nationalist and particularistic fervor were no real substitutes for a foundation in universal truth supported by sound scholarship in the solution of problems facing the nation.

In modern times the most significant outcome of the National Learning movement which stirred Japan during the Tokugawa period was the restoration of Imperial authority under Emperor Meiji and the establishment of Shinto as the official ideology and expression of patriotism. Japanese leaders responsible for preparing Japan to take its position in the modern world politically and industrially sought in Shinto the basis of national cohesion. They proclaimed that the restoration of the Emperor was the revival of the ancient Imperial way and the continuation of the creative work of Emperor Jimmu. Success in the effort depended on the citizen's revering the Emperor and worshiping the Kami and ancestors and on uniting religion and government.

SHINTO—
PATRIOTISM
OR RELIGION?

To realize the goals of the new regime, Shinto was proclaimed the state religion, and Buddhism was purged from any association with Shinto shrines and ceremonies. The motto was *shimbutsu-bunri* (the separation of Kami and Buddha). The antiforeign and anti-Buddhist feeling which the restoration engendered appeared at times in violent ways. Temples were burned and destroyed and the slogan *haibutsu-kishaku* (abolish Buddha, cut down Sakyamuni [icons]) was heard through the land.

Doctrinally, official Shinto did not go beyond that already presaged in the National Learning school, and it was based largely on the thought of Hirata Atsutane.

With the establishment of the Office of Shinto Affairs there was set up a Board of Shinto Missionaries to propagandize and indoctrinate the people concerning Shinto and patriotism. It aimed also to check the spread of Christianity, particularly in the area of Kyushu. Eventually Buddhists also came to participate in the effort of indoctrination centering on three major points: (1) Compliance with the spirit of reverence for Kami and love of country; (2) Clarification of "the principle of Heaven and the Way of man"; (3) Exalting the Emperor and obeying the Imperial Court.[20] Various teaching institutes for indoctrination on a variety of religious and political themes were set up throughout the country, with the central one being the Daikyoin in Tokyo.

This effort was a history of failure for numerous reasons, symbolized in the successive governmental bureaus charged with responsibility for Shinto affairs. The propaganda effort also went through repeated changes which indicate the problems encountered by the government, until finally the whole effort was abandoned in 1882.

Numerous factors led to the collapse of the endeavor. Among them was the growing dependence on Buddhist priests to carry out

20. Muraoka, op. cit., p. 206.

the teaching of essentially anti-Buddhist doctrine. Also, the existence of numerous Shinto bodies which sought more independence as separate churches revealed the fragmentation of the Shinto world. Other more fundamental reasons centered on the fact that this attempt to institutionalize an ancient religious tradition uncritically was not in harmony with the demands of modernization and the need for Japan to measure up to the West as indicated by Fukuzawa Yukichi (1834–1901). In addition, there was the theological weakness of Shinto itself.

Fundamentally, such Shinto theology as had developed could not be entirely free from dependence on foreign modes of thought in order to meet the challenge of those systems. Buddhist, Confucian, and even Christian influences had been turned to the defense of Shinto. However, in the period of the establishment of Shinto this factor ultimately worked against it, particularly in that Hirata theology was the basis of the political effort to ground patriotism in Shinto. Hirata's views of creation and afterlife became focal points of attack in demonstrating that Shinto was a religion which lacked an adequate theology. Further, Hirata's theology was not without criticism within Shinto itself.

Progressives and conservatives among Shintoists also disagreed. It was also realized that it was unwise to subject religion to political control. The attempt to establish Shinto religion politically led to a cry for religious freedom and the separation of Church and State. Buddhists were outstanding in this effort to establish religious freedom, since they were forced by their promotion of Shinto often to contradict their own basic Buddhist convictions. Representatives sent abroad to observe conditions in modern nations informed the Japanese government that establishment of a state religion contradicted the trend in modern nations to separate the political and religious aspects of life because of the conflict between those areas.

A leader in the effort to achieve freedom of religion was Mori Arinori (1847–1889) who had studied in the United States and put his thoughts on religious freedom into a text, *Religious Freedom of Japan,* which he presented to Prince Sanjo. His basic point was that religious freedom and freedom of conscience was a prerequisite to human progress and civilization. He predicted the failure of government policy in compelling religious belief and activity. Another was Shimaji Mokurai (1838–1911), a Buddhist of the Jodo Shinshu school, who noted that while the government might feel a threat to the National Polity (Kokutai) in modern thought, one could not actually compel belief.

Despite the fact that religion and government were officially separated in the Meiji period, Shinto, defined as a patriotic cult rather than a religion, continued to play a part in the government's efforts to inculcate national feeling. As a consequence of defeat in World War II, the new Constitution made it explicit that the government must henceforth refrain from any religious involvements. The Shinto Directive set forth by the allied powers demanded that the militaristic and ultranationalist doctrines, supposedly found in Shinto, be abolished.

The problems of Shinto within the modern development of Japan have raised the question whether it is a religion or merely a patriotic cult. In the postwar period since 1945 voices claiming a non-religious status for Shinto similar to that applied in the Meiji era have attempted to secure revision of the Constitution and financial support from the government for Ise and Yasukuni shrines, both shrines central to nationalistic concern.

Other Shinto thinkers have maintained that the future development of Shinto as a factor in the construction of a new and modern Japanese society lies in deepening the faith and theology of Shinto following the true intentions of Norinaga and Hirata. They have welcomed the loss of privileged status because it opens the door to free and voluntary commitment to the ideals of Shinto and is the only way to harmonize Shinto with the needs of contemporary Japan.

Although on the official levels of government and scholarship, Shinto was artificially established as the state cult in the Meiji era, during the Tokugawa period and into more recent times there have appeared numerous explicitly religious movements inspired by charismatic individuals and based on Shinto beliefs and outlook. The sociological and religious characteristics of these popular movements are important as part of the background of post-World War II movements commonly termed "New Religions."

The social background of these sects was the political and economic decline of the later Tokugawa period. Internal problems arose from economic and political conditions within the feudal system. Rising taxation and higher prices pressured the peasants and exacerbated the continuing economic decline of the samurai class. Increasing dissatisfaction with the Tokugawa regime was expressed in local uprisings. Confrontation with the West symbolized in the appearance of Commodore Perry's black ship off Japan in 1853 complicated the problems. Eventually a royalist movement succeeded in abolishing the Shogunate and restoring the Emperor to power in 1868. He set about reorganizing the government and meeting Japan's many problems.

The disturbed political and social conditions reflected themselves in religion in the emergence of sects emphasizing morality, nationalism, or ways of salvation. Some sects criticized contemporary conditions and issued proclamations of a coming age where all evils would be corrected.

The Japanese appear to respond religiously to times of crisis. This tendency can be observed at the time when the Shamaness Queen Pimiko was made the ruler in ancient Japan. It appears also during the Kamakura period in the revival of Buddhism, at the end of Tokugawa in the sects presently under discussion, and after World War II with the New Religions. Recent studies of mass movements represented by the Communist-Socialist movements and the Buddhist Soka Gakkai movement reveal clearly the religious orientation of Japanese in their approach to problems. Although the Leftist movement confronts problems in Japanese society, it is highly intellectual and divorced from the feelings and needs of the common man, where the many popular religious movements not only attempt to deal with current problems, but also provide for the emotional and spiritual needs of the people.

In the later Tokugawa period the most significant of the popular movements which have maintained their existence to the present, such as Tenri-kyo and Konko-kyo, originated with people of peasant origin. In the cases of Tenri, Konotabi, and Omoto-kyo the founders were sensitive women sharing characteristics derived from the shamanistic tradition of Japanese folk religion. While these movements were purely religious, they instilled in the pious devotee a sense that his faith would sustain him during upheaval, and they prepared people to accept the changes in society. Through advocating a broadly altruistic morality, emphasizing loyalty to the nation and Emperor and instilling confidence that one could better his life situation through the cultivation of one's spirit, these sects contributed to the orderly process of modernization which enabled Japan to confront the West with minimum disruption to her own way of life.

The most detailed analysis of these sects is provided by D. C. Holtom who classifies the thirteen officially recognized sects of Shinto into five categories. In addition to those thirteen, Anesaki adds the Konotabi sect founded by the peasant woman Kino (1756–1826), while Kitagawa mentions Omoto-kyo, Seicho-no-Ie, and Hito-no michi which developed later in the Meiji and Taisho periods.

For the sake of convenience, we shall follow the general categories given by Holtom in depicting the significant aspects of these movements. The group designated as Pure Shinto includes Shinto Honkyoku (Main Bureau of Shinto), Shinri-kyo (Divine Reason Teaching), and Taisha-kyo (Teaching of the Great Shrine). These sects were called Pure Shinto because they worshiped deities central to ancient Shinto Tradition and were devoted to the realization of the ideals of Shinto religion. Based on a pantheistic interpretation of divinity, they all promoted a universal ethic regarded generally as the fulfillment of the divine will in man and the expression of the true nature of man. In some cases it was claimed that the ills encountered in life, physical, social, and mental, were all due to the failure to cultivate the true spirit. They also included elements from folk religious practices and ceremony. Though the teachings were altruistic and universalist, all groups were committed to cultivating nationalism through adherence to the three principles set forth by the government's propaganda.

The sects described as Confucian also followed the basic tenets of Shinto, but they buttressed these teachings with moral and social concepts derived from Confucian tradition. Representative of this trend were the Shusei-ha and Taisei-kyo. Shusei was a term derived from the words *shuri*, meaning to repair, strengthen, or improve, and *kosei*, meaning to consolidate and make secure. These terms, taken from the myth of the creative actions of Izanagi and Izanami, set the perspective for moral cultivation in the interests of the development of Japanese society. *Taisei* meant Great Accomplishment and combined Confucian teaching, Shinto religion, and encouragement of science in the service of the nation.

The Mountain sects consisted of Jikko-kyo (Practice-Conduct teaching), Fuso-kyo, and Mitake-kyo. These sects were based on traditional Japanese reverence for mountains. The two former sects had Mount Fuji as their object of worship, while the latter had Mount Ontake. Their aim, like others, was the security and prosperity of the nation.

The Purification sects, which include Shinshu-kyo (Divine Learning) and Misogi-kyo (Purification), emphasized ritualism as the means to attain the goals of national, individual, and human existence. Particularly, they supported the practices of ancient Shinto.

The Faith-healing groups such as Kurozumi-kyo, founded by Kurozumi Munetada (b. 1780), and Konko-kyo (Metal Luster Teaching) were distinguished by their stress on material and bodily welfare through cultivating the spirit. They were significant also in that their founders believed they received their teaching through divine inspiration or were possessed by deity. The revelations put in writing have become the sacred texts of the sect.

In the case of Mrs. Miki Nakayama (1798–1826), who founded the Tenri-kyo sect, and Deguchi Nao (1836–1918), foundress of the Omoto-kyo, a prophetic quality was present. Through her revelations Miki foretold the coming of a new age when the world would return to the paradisiac conditions of the age of the Kami, while Nao proclaimed the coming transformation of the world and a new age of eternal peace.

The Sect Shinto religious organizations have maintained their existence down to the present time. Some of them have split into subgroups so that they now total about seventy-five groups. Those with the largest following are the Taisha-kyo, now known as the Izumo Oyashiro-kyo, and the Tenri-kyo, which is the most active of all. However, their development since the war has been affected by the formation of other "New Religions" which have many similar traits but are less conservative than the older groups.

In the postwar period after 1945 and the granting of complete religious freedom, there was another outburst of religious activity stimulated by the anxieties, upheavals, and turmoils of the war. In their overall character the new groups resembled those religious societies which originated in the earlier period. However, the freedom of the postwar age permitted the flowering of such groups in unprecedented numbers reaching several hundreds and including many fraudulent groups. An early listing indicates 735 sects. After some sifting of fraudulent organizations, the number was reduced to 377 as of 1956. Among this large grouping, those of Buddhist orientation mounted to 170, while Shinto-oriented sects reached 142. A miscellany of others had Christian (36) or other (29 unclassified) background.

It has been pointed out that though many groups are incorporated as independent sects, they are really subdivisions of the three traditional religions and only about twenty-nine can be accepted as

"New Religions." [21] According to one recent study, 171 groups are potentially religiously significant, and the author describes twenty-two of the most important organizations. [22]

Apart from the sects of primarily Buddhist derivation among the "New Religions" we may simply take note that the Tenri-kyo, which was earlier placed among the Shinto sects of the Meiji era, also continued to expand with vitality in the most recent period. The Omoto-kyo, also a Shintoistic organization developed in the early part of this century, continued to attract attention. Several sects developed out of Omoto-kyo and attained widespread notoriety. Among these were the Seicho-no-Ie, Sekai Kyusei-kyo, and P. L. Kyodan. A widely known group of mixed background was Ittoen.

The phenomenal growth of religious mass movements has attracted the attention of scholars in view of the slow, plodding growth of political mass movements such as Communism and Socialism which in actuality have not been very successful. The religious mass movements are a combination of ancient and modern themes. Five common factors which have led to the appearance of these organizations are (1) a social crisis, or upheaval in the cultural situation; (2) a charismatic leader or inspired personality; (3) performance of miracles and wonders; (4) forms of ecstatic behavior as trance; and (5) syncretic doctrines. The combination of these elements in the modern context has led Margaret Mead to describe the phenomena as "the ferment of the half abandoned old and the half understood new." [23]

In contrast to the highly intellectual, alien, and radical pronouncements of political mass movements which are out of touch with the feelings of the majority of people, the "New Religions" have been very successful in concentrating attention on the concrete needs of the people for health, wealth, and security in the highly competitive mass society. A major element in the appeal of most groups is the promise of benefits through magical practices and faith. In addition, they support popular aspirations for democracy and peace. They emphasize youth and attempt to win the minds of people through comprehensible indoctrination and publishing efforts. This element contrasts sharply with traditional endeavors in religious education and with the abstract and intellectualistic approach of the political ideologies. Further, they cater to the need of individuals for recognition and status through offering means of mobility within the organization for ordinary people of devotion and zeal. A quasi-intellectual cast is frequently given to the organization by titling leaders as lecturers, professors, and assistant professors. A democratic flavor is often present in the society through discussion groups where believers may raise questions and witness their faith. However, in many instances the charismatic leader is the final voice of authority. De-

21. *Japan's Religions: New Religions: Directory No. 4,* International Institute for the Study of Religions, February, 1958, pp. iii–iv.

22. Harry Thomsen, *The New Religions of Japan,* Rutland, Vt., Charles E. Tuttle Co., 1963, pp. 11–12.

23. H. Neill MacFarland, "Japan's New Religions," *Contemporary Religions in Japan,* December, 1960, 1–4, p. 60.

votion to the leader and loyalty to the group frequently supply the necessary ethical guidance for individuals whose family relations have weakened in the modern context. The modernity of such organizations is often symbolized through the construction of enormous centers for worship or administration.

Despite the use of all forms of modern media to reach people, the basic teachings of most groups are reconstitutions of traditional Japanese values drawn from Shinto and Buddhist background and reformulations of the general metaphysical outlook largely derived from Buddhism. The traditional characteristics of such societies often lead critics to regard them as reactionary, retrogressive, and fundamentally conservative. Nevertheless, it is clear that they have functioned to provide the individual with a stable and familiar basis on which he may stand to cope with the pressing problems of contemporary existence.

Our survey of Shinto tradition reveals that the ancient religion had a durability and vitality through the ages, and though permeated by various influences such as Buddhism and Confucianism has been able to provide spiritual orientation in the face of perplexing problems on the level of intellectual leadership as well as on the popular level. Its close association with the Imperial political institutions as the basis for their sanction created a situation in which the permanence of the Imperial line was supported by its religious foundation, and the religious ideology persisted through the prestige gained in the recognition of the unbroken line of emperors. Consequently, in recent times Shinto became the spiritual and ideological vehicle for the expression of nationalism. While this was consciously cultivated on the part of government, it was not unnatural in the consciousness of the Japanese. In the present postwar period Shinto has suffered from the shock of defeat, but as a whole it was more than a cult of nationalism and through its symbolism it could be reinterpreted to provide a philosophy of life adequate to attract modern intellectuals. The spiritual tradition also displayed great potentiality as a resource for the emergence of new religious communities, which could orient men and women in a difficult world and constantly renewed their sense of being a sacred people in a sacred land.

BUDDHISM IN THE LAND OF THE GODS

INTRODUCTION Though Buddhism initially entered Japan from the Asian continent by way of Korea and later through transmissions from China, it did not remain merely a foreign religion. Rather, it became absorbed into the Japanese way of life, adapting to the spiritual needs and social demands of the Japanese people, and became the second major religious tradition in Japanese culture.

The attitude of the Japanese toward Buddhism differed considerably from the Chinese who already possessed a highly developed and articulated cultural system. In China, Buddhism was always regarded as a foreign religion, at times subject to political persecution or criticism by Confucianists or Taoists, as well as favor by rulers. Buddhism, however, came to Japan as part of Chinese civilization, and its acceptance was thought to be a mark of a progressive nation. While Chinese Buddhism remained throughout its history institutionally weak, Japanese Buddhism developed firm organization and institutions which sometimes became formidable threats to the established order.

A key to the understanding of Japanese Buddhist history is the recognition that the Japanese awareness of being a sacred people in a sacred land eventually placed its stamp on the universal tradition of Buddhism itself. Our present study will attempt to trace Buddhist involvement in the political affairs of the nation, its fusion with the indigenous folk religious and magical perspectives, and the emergence of Buddhist schools or sects dominated by the Japanese spirit.

These various aspects of Buddhism have been interrelated and interdependent. The construction of temples, dissemination of Buddhist texts, and ceremonies of national Buddhism contributed to the spread of Buddhism among the people and supported the various technical schools whose leaders and teachers often functioned as the personnel of the national Buddhism. Popular Buddhism provided means of support and basis for the further development of the popular Buddhist schools, while the various schools and their associated temples provided the context for the development of Buddhist insight and experience and the maintenance of Buddhist tradition within Japanese society.

In contrast to the emphasis on ideological issues present in the development of Buddhism in China, our study of Japanese Buddhism will concentrate on social-cultural relations in order to provide a background for understanding the state of Buddhism in modern Japan. A survey of the various facets of Japanese Buddhism reveals the conditions which have contributed to the passivity and detachment of the Buddhist communities in the face of modern problems and the resultant criticisms by nonreligious intellectuals as well as by thoughtful devotees. The exploitation and political manipulation of Buddhism by the ruling classes in history as they attempted to unify and control the people, the magical and otherworldly outlook of traditional Buddhism, and the pronounced divisive sectarianism which dominates the tradition have created doubts in the minds of many modern people concerning its ability to contribute to the modernization of Japan or to turn back the growing secularization of the society.

NATIONAL BUDDHISM

According to the account recorded in the *Nihon Shoki,* Buddhism officially entered Japan during the reign of Emperor Kimmei in 552, though it may actually have been 538. On this occasion the king of Kudara (Paekche) in Korea presented the court with Buddhist images and texts. He declared that Buddhism would benefit the Japanese people and that it had been accepted by such leading countries as China. Though Buddhism had earlier infiltrated Japan carried by Chinese and Korean immigrants, its spread was greatly facilitated by the recognition of its political utility for promoting national interests.

Immediately upon its introduction it became involved in the political rivalry between the Soga and Mononobe clans, though neither side understood the true nature of the religion. The Soga, who supported Buddhism and adopted it as its own clan religion, represented the more internationalist and progressive leadership among the Japanese, while the Mononobe represented the particularistic interests of the clans.

The first major figure to appear in the formation of national Buddhism was Prince Shotoku (573–621). He implemented the Soga aim of establishing a strong central authority as the regent of the Soga-sponsored Empress Suiko (592–628). Admiration of China and a desire to restore Japanese fortunes in Korea also motivated him.

Because the Prince was deeply devoted to the teachings of Buddhism and recognized its spiritual role in the development of a unified nation, he was credited in history with the promulgation of a seventeen-point constitution which advocated reverence for the

Horyuji Temple, an early Japanese Buddhist temple. (*Courtesy of the Japan National Tourist Organization.*)

three treasures of Buddhism by all the people as the basis of social harmony. In addition, the Prince was thought to have composed commentaries on three major Mahayana sutras which reflected his critical and independent thought as he transformed Buddhism from an other-worldly religion to one promoting social harmony in this world. His emphasis on Buddhism as a religion of laymen greatly influenced later generations.

The Prince also encouraged Buddhism by inviting visiting priests to lecture, cultivating Buddhist scholarship, and commissioning the construction of numerous temples and works of art. Most prominent of the temples established by the Prince were the Shitennoji, which included social welfare facilities, Horyuji, and Chuguji.

Though Buddhism was supported by the court after Shotoku, it was subjected to greater control as a result of the Taika reform in 645 when the T'ang law codes were adopted in Japan. Private temples were prohibited, and monks had to be licensed. In addition, they could not work among the people.

A more positive approach to the Buddhist Order appeared, however, in the provincial temple system set up in 741 by Emperor Shomu who devoted himself to the prosperity of Buddhism. Symbolic of his efforts was the construction of the great Buddha of Todaiji (consecrated in 752). The Buddha selected for representation was Mahavairocana Buddha (Dainichi Nyorai), the great Sun Buddha. This Buddha symbolized the philosophy of the *Kegon Sutra* (Sanskrit *Avatamsaka,* Chinese *Hua-yen*), which taught that the essence of each thing contained the essence of every other thing. All reality was interdependent and mutually permeating. Hence, the world manifested the Buddha nature combined in a grand harmony.

The symbolism of the image and its many surrounding Buddhas carried a political message of the interdependence of the Japanese people and the Imperial house.

Emperor Shomu viewed Buddhism as a magical religion founded on the belief that the proper recitation of various nation-protecting sutras would bring prosperity and security to the nation. It was not the principles of Buddhist philosophy which brought harmony, but the use of Buddhist texts and institutions which granted security. According to these "nation-protecting" sutras the divine heavenly kings protected any country that materially supported Buddhism or copied and recited such texts. Eventually a whole system of provincial temples equipped with sutras, monks, and nuns was constructed with Todaiji as the head temple for the purpose of benefiting the nation through spiritual protection.

As a result of the efforts lavished on the construction of the system of national and provincial temples, corruption appeared when the official temples acquired great properties and wealth. The situation reached a climax when the monk Dokyo became the Prime Minister with apparent designs on the throne. However, at the death of Empress Shotoku (764–770) he was banished and the Buddhist Order was subjected again to strict regulation.

Another stage in the political relations of Buddhism opened when the monks Saicho (767–822) and Kukai (774–835) attempted to free themselves from the influence of the Nara temples after studying in China. The establishment of the Chinese Tendai and Shingon schools of Buddhism were in some measure attempts to reform and reestablish the true principles of Buddhism in Japan.

The reforming aspect was particularly strong in Saicho who asked the court for permission to set up his own Tendai ordination platform on Mount Hiei, which would then qualify his monks to serve in the provincial temples. Because the temples in Nara only followed the Buddha's instruction in words, Saicho maintained that Tendai Buddhism would provide monks who would be true national treasures and that the nation would be better protected spiritually. The court granted approval soon after his death in 822.

With the removal of the capital from Nara to Kyoto (794), Mount Hiei became continually involved with national politics. As its own economic and political power grew, organized warrior monks fought in the interests of the order. The problems of violence and corruption created by these militant monks became notorious in Japanese history. The *Heike Monogatari* depicted numerous instances of the terror which the monks of Hiei aroused in the people as they preyed upon the religious sensibilities of the people and court.

Kukai, who introduced the Shingon school to Japan (Sanskrit *Mantra,* Chinese *Chen-yen*), was at first allied with Saicho, but later they separated when Kukai taught that the esoterism of Shingon was really superior to the exoterism of Tendai. In addition, Kukai did not strongly oppose the temples of Nara and soon attained high rank in the official organization, becoming the abbot of the Toji temple in Kyoto. Here he performed the rite of *kanjo* (a form of ordination), as well as ceremonies for the pacification of the nation. Supported by the court, Kukai and his order attained wide influence. Even emperors received instruction in Buddhism under the tutelage of Shingon monks.

The relation of these schools to the Imperial house in the Heian age took a special form called Insei (Cloister) government, which involved the monasteries more deeply in politics. It became the custom for emperors to retire from active rule and to enter a monastery. This system was based on the principle that men of responsibility might retire to devote themselves to religious concerns, transferring their worldly burdens to others. In the political sphere it might also mean an escape from conspiracy. The purpose of the retirement was thus not always religiously motivated. In some instances the retired Emperor had more political power in this status than he had as actual Emperor. The involvement of Buddhism in political conflicts during this period tended to degrade it and to stimulate those forces of reform which later appeared in the Kamakura period.

The Buddhist schools of Nara and Heian held little concern for the ordinary person. Although individual monks engaged in social welfare and religious work among the people, the various official schools were more concerned with promoting their power and influence through the manipulation of spiritual forces and catering to the demands of the aristocracy.

Against the background of the corruption and spiritual decline of Mount Hiei and Mount Koya as well as the earlier Nara temples, a number of sects emerged during the Kamakura age which differed in their views of the relation of Buddhism and society and its function in providing spiritual protection for the state. On the one hand the Pure Land schools of Ryonin, Honen, Shinran, and Ippen were other-worldly and designed chiefly to bring birth in the Pure Land for individuals. On the other hand Eisai, who introduced the Rinzai (Lin-chi) Zen (Ch'an) tradition from China, maintained in his treatise *Kozengokokuron* (*Treatise on Spiritually Protecting the Nation through Prospering Zen*) that the nation could be spiritually protected only through promoting the true practice of Zen.

Dogen, Eisai's disciple and the founder of the Soto Zen sect, asserted that Buddhism was superior to the state. According to his view, human laws were merely based on precedents and ancient laws whose origins were uncertain. However, Buddhism had a clear transmission from the beginning. Thus the state was not absolute. Claiming extraterritoriality for the monk who did his duty by performing his discipline, Dogen refused to associate with the government and established his temple in a distant province.

Perhaps the most important expression of the relation between the nation and Buddhism in the Kamakura era was the teaching of the Buddhist prophet Nichiren. According to his basic work *Risshoankokuron* (*Treatise on the Attainment of Peace in the Country through the Establishment of the True Teaching*), the security of the nation depended on strict adherence to the true form of Buddhism. The true Buddhism was the Tendai school based on the *Lotus Sutra* as interpreted by Nichiren himself.

Insisting on the supremacy of the Lotus Sutra over all other teachings of Buddhism, he demanded that the government establish it as the national religion to the exclusion of all other forms of Buddhism. His intolerance was the result of his conviction that the many natural disasters and political upheavals which Japan had experienced had been prophesied by the Buddha as punishment for not adhering to the truth. Very soon, he taught, the final punishment would come with the invasion of the Mongols. He pointed to the prosperity of Pure Land teaching, Zen Buddhism, the use of Shingon practices, and the fame of Ritsu priests as evidence that the people had ignored and were blind to the truth originally declared by Saicho. Even traditional Tendai teachers had strayed from the truth by adopting Pure Land teaching and Shingon practices into their own system.

Although Nichiren employed traditional concepts of the relation of state and Buddhism, he held strongly to the primacy of Buddhism over the state in contrast to the traditional political subservience of Buddhism. His outspokenness and uncompromising attitude brought him persecution and banishment.

The period of civil wars and strife following the fall of the Kamakura Shogunate in 1334 until the establishment of the Tokugawa regime in 1615 frequently involved Buddhist orders as they carried on sectarian rivalry or attempted to protect their own interests. As Sansom points out: "Although most of the numerous sects of Buddhism in Japan were tolerant to the point of indifference in matters of doctrine, they were very jealous of their rights, and would fight hard on a point of privilege." [1]

The various dictators engaged in armed struggles to reduce the political and military threats of the great Buddhist institutions. While Ashikaga Takauji (Shogun, 1338–1358) had to retrench before the militant reaction of the forces of Mount Hiei, Oda Nobunaga (1534–1582) was eventually able to subdue the hosts of the Ikko (Single-minded sect of Pure Land devotees) and Mount Hiei. He even encouraged the propagation of Christianity to counter the influence of the Buddhists. Hideyoshi (1536–1598) pursued the monks of Kumano and Mount Koya. As the monks turned from warlike activities to works of piety, Hideyoshi began to restrain the Christians, ordering missionaries to leave the country in 1587. Oppression of Christians mounted under Hideyoshi and reached its peak with the martyrdom of twenty-six persons at Nagasaki in 1597. The persecutions and martyrdoms of Christians increased under the Tokugawas, reaching a climax in the Shimabara revolt which precipitated the policy of total isolation from foreign relations for the next 250 years.

The importance of the Christian persecutions lies in their relationship to the political control of the Buddhist Orders during the Tokugawa era. As a measure in the abolition of Christianity, Buddhist clergy began to function as police. In 1640 an investigating agency was formed in Edo and extended throughout the country. In

1. G. B. Sansom, *A History of Japan,* Stanford, Calif., Stanford University Press, 1958–1963, vol. II, p. 153.

order to seek out Christians, citizens were made to trample the cross, and local Buddhist temples were required to register all persons in their district on such matters as their personal history and activities.

The Buddhist religion declined because of the earlier attacks on its institutions and its reduction to a mere political tool in the Tokugawa effort to achieve total social stability and harmony. The dominant ideologies of the Tokugawa age were Confucianism and a renascent Shintoism, both of which were critical and negative to Buddhism. Buddhist institutions continued to function, and members of the government associated with it through their families as a matter of custom. However, it exerted little control or influence over the intellectual outlook or personal conduct of the national leaders.

Buddhist scholars regard the change brought about in Buddhism, resulting from the activities of Nobunaga, Hideyoshi, and the later Tokugawas, as a turning point in Buddhist history. During this period Buddhism completely capitulated to secular authority. The establishment of the parish system (*Danka Seido*) irrespective of doctrinal convictions, as well as the imposed clerical control, effectively cut Buddhism off spiritually from the people. Despite the fact that Buddhism had permeated daily life or that scholarship had developed within the monastic communities, the real vitality of Buddhism was lost when compared with its impact in the medieval periods of Heian and Kamakura. The position of Buddhism in the feudal period resembled only externally its role in the earlier period when the state was institutionalized. The important difference was that rulers in the earlier ages believed in Buddhist spiritual experience, and revering the three treasures (*Buddha, Dharma, Sangha*) prayed for the welfare of the nation. In the later period the Edo warriors, dominated by Confucianism, regarded Buddhism simply as a useful instrument of social control.

When the Tokugawa regime ended with the restoration of Imperial rule under Meiji in 1868, Buddhism was rudely awakened by the shout of "Expel Buddha, cut down Sakyamuni." The renascent Shinto sentiment held by leaders of government quickly overthrew the trappings of state support of Buddhism, and the new nationalism claimed it was merely a foreign religion. The attack failed because of the faith of the ordinary people in Buddhism which had given them some hope for their meager existences.

As we have seen in the study of Shinto, Buddhist leaders joined with Shintoists in promoting the new nationalism and thus linked themselves to the political absolutism of the new regime. Government officials welcomed the assistance of Buddhist clergy, since they had traditionally the closest relation to the people. While promoting religious freedom in order to gain its own autonomy, Buddhism was soon faced with the new threat of a spreading Christianity. In modern times in numerous ways, the various Buddhist Orders have attempted to commend themselves as supporters of the national destiny reinforcing the awareness of the sacredness of the land and people. However, institutional lethargy has inhibited serious grappling with the problems of modernization and social progress. Thus a major issue confronting the Buddhist sects has been their own relevance in a rapidly changing and more highly sophisticated, complex, industrial society.

Merely recounting the history of Buddhist institutions in Japanese society would be insufficient to convey the significance of Buddhism in the life of the people. The description of formal and external relations cannot replace an understanding of the impact on the people which has sustained the religion through periods of great social change. Buddhist influence, widespread in all areas of culture, is readily evident in the arts and literature. It is apparent in language where colloquial terms reflect Buddhist background. For example, "to drop dead" is *tachiojo-suru*. Literally it means to attain rebirth while standing. Rebirth refers to the Buddhist belief in transmigration. *Kara-nembutsu,* which means "vain talk," refers to an empty mouthing of the recitation of Buddha's name. The common phrase *jigo-jitoku,* which means "it's your own fault," summarizes the Buddhist karmic principle that what one sows one reaps.

POPULAR BUDDHISM

Buddhism infiltrated into Japan when immigrants from China or Korea carried their faith with them. However, official recognition of Buddhism also spurred the spread of Buddhism among the people as the more wealthy families built private temples in their domains. They tended to view the Buddhas as analogous to their ancestral and tutelary deities. From the death of Prince Shotoku in 622 when there were 46 temples in the country, the number grew to 545 in the time of Empress Jito (687–697).

As a rule, the growth of Buddhism was largely concentrated within the ruling class who displayed their social power through building temples, sponsoring images, and copying sutras. However, a few monks traveled about the country and preached Buddhism to the common people, despite government restrictions on such activity. In their alliance with the people such unauthorized and shamanistic priests naturally became critical of political exploitation and religious corruption,[2] having deep concern for the spiritual and material welfare of the common man.

Representative popular priests in the Nara period were Dosho (629–700) and Gyogi Bosatsu (670–749). Dosho was highly regarded as an ideal Buddhist monk and scholar of the Hosso school. Among his many contributions, he is credited with the introduction of cremation as the proper Buddhist way to dispose of the dead. During the later years of his life he gave himself to the welfare of mankind by constructing wells, bridges, almshouses and ferries, as well as monasteries.

Gyogi's efforts on behalf of mankind were so outstanding that he was given the title *Bosatsu* (*Bodhisattva*), which testified to the depth of his compassion for man. Although he was learned in Buddhist philosophy and meditation discipline, he engaged in works

2. Joseph M. Kitagawa, *Religion in Japanese History,* New York, Columbia, 1966, pp. 40–41.

of mercy by building bridges and river dykes, planting fruit trees, and constructing way houses for travelers, reservoirs, irrigation canals, ferries, and harbors. In addition, he was credited with opening thirty-four monasteries and fifteen nunneries. His popularity grew to such dimensions that the government prohibited his activity and banished him. However, because of his great influence the government sought his assistance in soliciting funds to construct the great Buddha of Nara, and in 745 he was elevated to the rank of *Daisojo* (Great High Priest).

In the succeeding Heian period several noted compassionate monks traveled through the country offering the hope of salvation to the common man through the recitation of the name of Amida Buddha. The simplicity of the Pure Land doctrine appealed to ordinary people and influenced all levels of society. The attraction of the other-worldly faith increased along with the social turmoil and upheavals at the end of the Heian era. During this period the popular preachers laid stress on the fact that it was the Last Age (Mappo) of corruption and strife, dramatizing the anxieties of the age.

Several priests drew particular attention in promoting the spread of Pure Land doctrine during this time. Kuya Shonin (903–972) was called "the Saint of the Market" as he went about proclaiming Pure Land faith and using a melodic form of recitation. The preaching of these priests was augmented by the work of Genshin (942–1017), a high-ranking monk and scholar on Mount Hiei, through his treatise on the essentials for rebirth in the Pure Land (*Ojoyoshu*). The text became a handbook for preachers by bringing together all scriptural passages relating to the Pure Land and Hell. The monk Ryonin (1071–1132) taught a doctrine of mutual salvation (*Yuzu-nembutsu*) which gave a social dimension to efforts for salvation. During the later Kamakura period, the priest Ippen (1238–1289) taught a distinctive interpretation of Pure Land doctrine which advocated reciting the *Nembutsu* at six specific times during the day and emphasizing that one should regard each moment of life as his last in reciting the sacred name.

Although the Pure Land teaching based on faith in Amida Buddha became the dominant Buddhist belief among the common people during the Heian era, other Buddhist divinities also were objects of devotion. Jizo (Sanskrit *Kshitigarbha*, Chinese *Ti-tsang*) assisted men in the afterlife and helped them to avoid going to hell. Merging with beliefs of folk religion, he was also regarded as a savior for those in trouble, particularly women in childbirth and children. Kannon (Sanskrit *Avalokitesvara*, Chinese *Kuan-yin*), the Goddess of Mercy, was widely revered. Tradition held that even Prince Shotoku was an ardent devotee. Emperors sponsored lectures and ceremonies on the *Kannon Sutra* and promoted the popularity of the cult. According to this text, Kannon symbolized the depth of Buddha's compassion. She promised to save men from all forms of calamity and to grant them health, wealth and security in life. Other popular deities were Kangiten (Sanskrit *Ganesa*), the elephant-headed deity dispensing wisdom, and Kishimojin (Sanskrit *Hariti*), a goddess of childbirth.

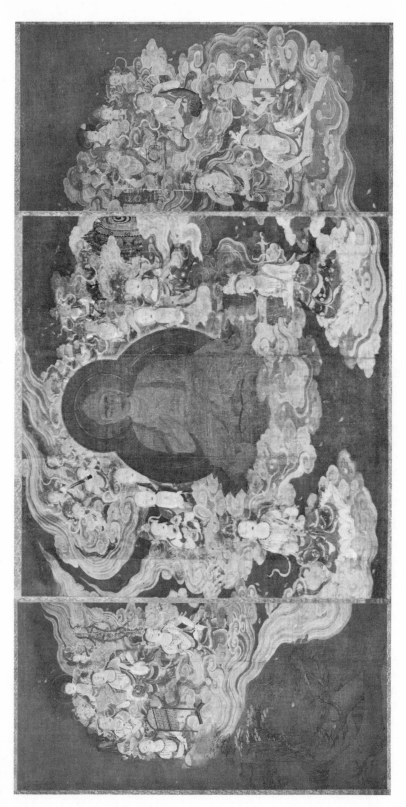

Amida Raigo triptych of the Pure Land school, from the Heian Period, late eleventh century. (Courtesy of the Koyasan Museum, Wakayama.)

Together with the beliefs in great Buddhist divinities there were numerous practices designed to gain desired benefits. Most popular and easiest was the recitation of magical phrases such as *Namu-Amida-Butsu* (*Hail Amida Buddha*) or *Namu-Myoho-Renge-Kyo* (*Hail Lotus of the Wonderful Law*). Shingon teaching became very influential because of the potent magical *Dharani* spells and incantations of Indian origin which it offered for every possible contingency. There were also mystic ceremonies such as the fire ritual, *goma,* which was thought to burn away impurity and to remove curses of demons. The ceremony was much used in the Heian period.

During the period when the manifold Chinese religious beliefs and practices spread into Japan with Buddhism, religious Taoism also came, though not in an institutional form. Whereas the teachings of Confucianism were first regarded as the required learning for rulers and politicians, religious Taoism had a wider influence and import, offering various methods for advancing one's life in this world and attaining longevity or good fortune. In addition to religious Taoism, yin-yang magic and divination, astrology, geomancy, and calendrical computations were combined with Buddhism. Taoist belief in sage-hermits contributed also to the formation of the Shugendo movement of Buddho-Shinto mountain ascetics. The practitioners of Shugendo functioned among the people as exorcists and shamans.

Ceremonies for the dead were also a prominent aspect of Japanese Buddhism. Not only was there the fear of dead spirits which emerged in the Heian period (see pp. 344–345), but there was also reverencing of the dead in filial piety. Masses for the dead helped to assure the good destiny of the departed. A calendar of memorials provided the dead with periodic assistance until they faded from living memory to become part of the general host of ancestors.

An important annual festival was the Urabon-e (Sanskrit *Avalambana, Ullambana*), based on the story of Buddha's disciple Mokuren (Sanskrit *Maudgalyayana*) who saw that his mother had become a hungry ghost. Thereupon began the rite of offering food for one's parents and ancestors. Related to the Urabon-e but of different origin was the Segaki ceremony of feeding the hungry ghosts. This ceremony is still regularly performed.[3] Other ceremonies connected with the dead occurred at the spring and autumn equinox and were called Higan-e.

Ancestors are venerated through masses and entertainments. Most important are visits to the grave which, despite the decline in religious activity among modern people, are still commonly carried out even by those of no specific religious commitment. Considerable criticism has been directed to Buddhism because of its predominant association with death. Watanabe states:

It is clear that funeral services were not the work of monks in Sakyamuni's Order. They were the task of hereditary Brahmins. In

3. S. Watanabe, *Japanese Buddhism: A Critical Appraisal,* Tokyo, Kokusai Bunka Shinkokai, 1964, pp. 88–91.

Jizo Bodhisattva, patron of the world of death, late twelfth century. (Courtesy of the Museum of Fine Arts, Boston.)

East Asia such was not the case. When Buddhism came to act as agent for the folk religion, it became responsible even for funeral rites. . . .

If one considers that Buddhism has a living road in the future, there is probably nothing else to do but to advance in the direction of rejecting the cloak of funeral rites which is satisfied with mere form, and both to have confidence itself concerning life and death and to indicate it to others.[4]

The elements of popular religion have penetrated all sects to secure support from the masses. The Shugendo movement was very instrumental in carrying these beliefs and ceremonies to the people, particularly in the Tokugawa period when the traditional sects had largely been deprived of their spiritual influence among the people.

In the modern era a gap frequently exists between critical intellectual priests and the ordinary persons in relation to the magical and pragmatic features of Buddhism. Despite the calls for reformation and modernization within Buddhism today, the great source of support and strength in the orders still derives from the magical and pragmatic faith which, for lack of a better alternative, supports individuals in dealing with the problems and anxieties of modern life.

DOCTRINAL BUDDHISM   Though Buddhism has functioned in the social and political sphere as a support for the state and ruling class, and on the popular level has fused with native folk religion with stress on magic and pragmatic, this-worldly interests, it also established its own thought tradition in which Japanese monks studied and researched Buddhist texts and principles and applied themselves to the practice of Buddhist disciplines in the effort to achieve their own enlightenment. Thus, while it is easy to criticize Buddhism for its political exploitation and superstitious elements, it is necessary to balance these judgments with the recognition of serious efforts to understand Buddhism and to realize its own distinctive ideals.

The development of Buddhist thought in Japan follows largely the major historical periods of Nara (710–784), Heian (794–1185), and Kamakura (1185–1333). In general we may describe each period as a step in the gradual assimilation or Japanization of Buddhism.

In the Nara period the highly scholastic and philosophic schools current at the time in T'ang China (618–907) commanded the center of interest. The schools in this introductory period had little relation to the common man and were little more than academic trends, representing the various alternative Buddhist perspectives which had developed in India and then China. Commonly referred to as the Six Schools of Nara Buddhism, they were Jojitsu (Sanskrit *Satyasiddhi*), Kusha (Sanskrit *Abhidharma Kosa*), Hosso (Sanskrit *Dharmalakshana, Yogacara*), Sanron (Three Treatise, Sanskrit *Madhyamika*), Kegon (Sanskrit *Avatamsaka*), and Ritsu (Sanskrit *Vinaya*). They were introduced at various times by Chinese or Japanese monks from about 625 to 754.

4. Ibid., pp. 98–99.

Of greater religious and historical significance was the introduction of the Tendai (Chinese *T'ien-t'ai*) school by Saicho and the Shingon (Sanskrit *Mantra,* Chinese *Chen-yen*) by Kukai. The doctrines and scholarship within these traditions laid the foundation for the flowering of Japanese Buddhism in the Kamakura period. Stressing the idea that there was really only one truth among the diversity of teachings in Buddhist tradition, they opened the way for greater sectarianism as later teachers asserted that they taught the "One Vehicle," or one truth necessary for salvation. In addition, they taught the universality of salvation based on the theory of mutual interpenetration of the Kegon school. The development of Pure Land teaching, particularly within the Tendai school, and the increasing emphasis on mystic rites and pageantry contributed to the broadening impact of Buddhism on all classes in the Heian era. These trends assured that Japan would be a Mahayana Buddhist country.

Against the background of dramatic social change and the deepening penetration of Buddhism into Japanese life, the flourishing of novel and creative movements in Buddhist tradition mark the Kamakura era in Japanese history as one of the most significant periods in the history of religion. While Buddhism reflected native aspirations and needs, closely identifying with the common man, it also offered universal paths of salvation unique in Buddhism.

With the rise to political dominance of the warrior clans, headed first by the Taira and then the Minamoto who established their center of power at Kamakura, a new virile and martial ethos displaced the formalistic and aesthetic outlook of the Heian nobility. The life of delicate beauty, peace, and ease of Heian changed to a way of life based on bravery and loyalty.

The repercussions of the transformation reverberated through all aspects of culture, whether art, literature, or religion. In religion the new era expressed itself in the emergence of several Buddhist leaders: Honen (1133–1212), Shinran (1173–1262), Dogen (1200–1253), and Nichiren (1222–1282). Their critical spirit and search for truth enable us to view them as reformers, much on the order of their European counterparts.

Each of these individuals attempted to achieve the ideals of Buddhism through the study of traditional doctrine and discipline either on Mount Hiei or in Nara. The general decline of studies and discipline and the activities of turbulent, warlike monks did not provide an atmosphere conducive to sincere religious pursuits. In each case, religious dissatisfaction stimulated the search for a new approach to Buddhist enlightenment. As a result of their various quests, these men were inevitably led to reject the traditional ecclesiastical system which had become formalized, sterile, ritualistic, doctrinally sterile, superstitious, and inwardly corrupt. Each found his solution in some aspect or tendency within Buddhist tradition which he elevated to a supreme position and proclaimed as the superior or true way to reach the goal of enlightenment.

In contrast to earlier Buddhism which was largely dominated by the interests and outlook of the nobility and Imperial house, the new movements appealed to the common man. Aristocratic support and outlook were rejected. In offering Buddhism to the common man, each of the major teachers strove for a simplified doctrine and religious discipline within the capabilities of the ordinary person. Drawing on the tradition of One Vehicle Buddhism which had developed within the Tendai tradition, out of which all these individuals had come, there was a strong tendency to sectarianism based on the conviction that each teacher had discovered the one fundamental truth of Buddhism.

As illustration of these various tendencies, there was Honen who wrote his "Testimony on One Sheet of Paper" just before his death, and Shinran who asserted that only faith was required for salvation. They represented the ultimate perhaps in the simplification of the abstruse and complicated systems of Buddhist philosophy and discipline. The rejection of the aristocratic life and political connections was portrayed in Dogen's rejection of favor with the Shogun and the construction of his monastery far from centers of power in distant Echizen province. He is said to have excommunicated the monk who brought him the message of the Shogun's gift of land. The sectarianism of the new Buddhism of Kamakura appeared most decisively in the four denunciations of Nichiren concerning the other contemporary schools. He declared emphatically that believers in the Pure Land teaching would go to hell; that the Zen sect had been created by devils; that Shingon was the ruination of the state; and that the Ritsu sect betrayed the country. Only the teaching proclaimed by Nichiren would save the nation from destruction.

It was the teacher Honen who, slightly before the onset of the Kamakura period, first gave himself to the attempt to discover in Buddhism a solid foundation for the spiritual life. According to his biography, his religious dissatisfaction was expressed in anxiety for his future destiny. Though having studied at the great Japanese centers of Buddhism, he had no spiritual peace until he happened on the Chinese teacher Shan Tao's Pure Land doctrine. Struck by this teaching, he abandoned religious life on Mount Hiei and eventually established his own school in 1175, later known as Jodo-shu.

The main characteristic of his school was the rejection of manifold practices of Buddhist tradition and the selection of the single practice of recitation of Amida Buddha's name as the only means of salvation. When he published his major work, *Senjakuhongannembutsushu* (*Treatise on the Nembutsu of the Select Original Vow*), for the regent Fujiwara Kanezane in 1198, the true nature of his doctrine became clear and eventually resulted in persecution and banishment.

Through analyzing traditional Buddhist doctrines in the light of the dawn of the Last Age in the decline of Buddhist teachings, Honen made it clear that the only certain way for ordinary persons in this age to achieve salvation was the recitation of the Buddha's name alone. Implicitly, the exaltation of this practice rendered all other Buddhist disciplines meaningless.

Apart from the theoretical foundations of his teaching, Honen was also motivated by a deep compassion for the common man, and he eloquently attacked the aristocratic Buddhism of his time which made salvation contingent on wealth or learning:

And so Amida seemed to have made his Original Vow the rejection of the hard and the choice of the easy way, in order to enable all sentient beings, without distinction, to attain birth into the Pure Land. If the Original Vow required the making of images and the building of pagodas, then the poor and destitute could have no hope of attaining it. But the fact is that the wealthy and noble are few in number, whereas the number of the poor and ignoble is extremely large. If the Original Vow required wisdom and great talents, there would be no hope of that birth for the foolish and ignorant at all, but the wise are few in number, while the foolish are very many.[5]

The essence of his faith and practice were given concisely in the famous "Testament on One Sheet of Paper":

The method of final salvation that I have propounded is neither a sort of meditation, such as has been practiced by many scholars in China and Japan, nor is it the repetition of the Buddha's name by those who have studied and understood the deep meaning of it. It is nothing but the mere repetition of the "Namu Amida Butsu," without a doubt of his mercy, whereby one may be born into the Land of Perfect Bliss. The mere repetition with firm faith includes all the practical details, such as the three-fold preparation of mind and the four practical rules. If I as an individual had any doctrine more profound than this, I should miss the mercy of the two Honorable Ones, Amida and Shaka, and be left out of the Vow of the Amida Buddha. Those who believe this, though they clearly understand all the teachings Shaka taught throughout his whole life, should behave themselves like simple-minded folk, who know not a single letter, or like ignorant nuns or monks whose faith is implicitly simple. Thus without pedantic airs, they should fervently practice the repetition of the name of Amida, and that alone.[6]

Shinran was a disciple of Honen and followed him in promoting Pure Land doctrine (Jodo-shinshu, true sect of the Pure Land). After a period of exile as a result of the persecution of Honen's band, Shinran taught in the eastern province of Kanto. In his latter years he returned to Kyoto and lived in retirement. During this period he produced various texts which are major sources for his thought. Among them are *Kyogyoshinsho* (*Treatise on the Doctrine, Practice, Faith and Realization*), various groups of hymns, some interpretative texts, and letters to his disciples. In addition, his disciple Yuiembo wrote the popular little text *Tannisho* (*Deploring the Heresies*), giving the essence of Shinran's thought.

5. Harper H. Coates and Ryugaku Ishizuka, *Honen the Buddhist Saint,* Kyoto, Society for the Publication of Sacred Books of the World, 1949, vol. II, p. 344.

6. Ibid., pp. 728–729.

While Shinran was in harmony with the spirit of Honen's teaching and motivation to aid spiritually the common man, his Pure Land doctrine went beyond Honen's in several important respects. Honen had concentrated attention on the adequacy of the practice of vocal recitation to bring salvation in comparison with traditional Buddhist disciplines, while Shinran directed attention to the foundation of the efficacy of this practice. He found its effectiveness rooted in the transfer of merit made by Amida Buddha as the result of his arduous effort to create a way of salvation for all beings. The transfer of merit gave potency to the name, and it also was the basic cause for the resultant faith in the Buddha's Vow and Work within the person. Shinran placed major emphasis on the experience of faith. He criticized all forms of Buddhism, including those advocating the repetition of Buddha's name, as expressions of man's egoism through attempting to achieve salvation by his own effort.

Since the experience of faith reveals that one's salvation has been assured by Amida Buddha, one may attain spiritual peace in contrast to the self-powered disciplines which always involve an anxiety of not knowing whether one has sufficiently purified himself in order to gain salvation. Consequently, the religious life undergoes a dramatic reinterpretation in which our lives and religious practice are to be viewed as expressions of gratitude for the salvation already assured rather than as desperate attempts to achieve spiritual security.

The life of gratitude had several social implications which eventually became clear in the history of the tradition. In contrast to traditional Buddhism Shinran rejected the magical principle of performing Buddhist practices in order to gain benefits in this world and salvation in the next. In the doctrines of Bodhisattvic return to this world after death (*Genso*), Shinran made the goal of religion the salvation of others. In rejecting self-powered, egocentric religious attitudes, all superstitious practices which had such a prominent role in popular Buddhism were cast aside. Further, with the assurance that one's status in the next world was already determined, one might give more attention to developing himself in this world. Abandoning the disciplines and precepts regulating the lives of monks in earlier Buddhist orders, Shinran's clerical followers were noted because they ate meat and married. Believers could also engage in occupations of their choice. With the decline of magic and a more ethically oriented interpretation of faith developed later by the patriarch Rennyo, Shinran's teachings assisted in the development of the merchant class in the Tokugawa period.[7]

Although Eisai is credited with introducing the Zen sect into Japan, it was the aristocratic and highly intellectual form of Rinzai (Lin-chi) Zen which employed the rigorous, demanding Koan or riddle method of revealing one's attainment of enlightenment. The characteristics of Kamakura Buddhism appear more within the Soto (Chinese *Tsao-tung*) tradition of Zen which Dogen introduced to Japan after his study in China.

7. Robert N. Bellah, *Tokugawa Religion,* New York, Free Press, 1967, pp. 117–122.

Like other Kamakura Buddhists, the priest Dogen had become dissatisfied with the religious discipline he encountered on Mount Hiei and at first went to study under Eisai. Because this did not meet his need either, he went to China where he studied under the master Ju Ching. There he discovered a form of Zen, which was based not only on monastic existence but also could be expanded to allow men of all walks of life—great ministers, woodsmen, hunters, and even women—to gain enlightenment. He rejected the Koan practice, enabling his form of Zen, based on the meditation practice itself, to spread more easily among the common people. While the popular spread of Zen could not compare with that of the Pure Land, it gained the name "Farmers' Zen" because of its greater adaptability to ordinary life.

Dogen inherited his master Ju Ching's insistence on the centrality of the practice of *Zazen* over all other Buddhist practices. According to his interpretation in such works as the *Shobogenzo* (*The Repository of Buddhist Teaching*), Zazen was the process wherein Buddha himself had attained the bliss of enlightenment. There was no temporal, cause-effect relation between meditation and enlightenment. To perform Zazen was thus in a mysterious manner to participate in the enlightenment of the Buddha. Practice and realization were identical.

The identity of the practice and attainment led Dogen to criticize other approaches to Zen which made the practice secondary and instrumental, merely a means to the effort to attain Buddhahood through perceiving one's true nature (as Buddha). He also rejected the Zen principle of a special transmission beyond scripture. He criticized the dichotomy this view implied between the Buddha's mind and his teaching as represented in the sutras. Thus Dogen was more scripturally oriented than the Zen of the Rinzai tradition. Further, because the doctrine of the Buddha's "one mind" did not allow dualities, everything was embraced within his enlightenment. The world, as it is, was Buddha's mind.

In addition to criticizing other Zen teachings, Dogen also denied the theory of the three periods in the decline of Buddhist teaching (Mappo) as emphasized in the Pure Land tradition. Buddha's enlightenment and the possibility of realizing it were not affected by time.

The attitude toward life and the world generated in Zen discipline of whatever school has made it significant in the development of Japanese society and culture. It has been the basis of such military arts as Kendo (swordsmanship) and Judo. The discipline and traits of character it cultivated made it attractive to the samurai (warrior) class. It influenced broadly such arts as architecture, gardens, literature, drama, painting, and calligraphy. Its experience was expressed profoundly in such activities as the tea ceremony and flower arranging.

Perhaps the most fiery and striking personality among the Kamakura Buddhist reformers was Nichiren. Unlike the other thinkers who appear to have had aristocratic or warrior background, Nichiren was the offspring of a fisherman's family in the eastern province of Awa. Impressed early by the impermanence of life, he decided to enter nearby Kiyozumi-dera monastery which belonged to the Tendai sect. While studying, he visited Kamakura, Kyoto, Hiei, and Nara. At first he became attracted to Pure Land teaching, but soon began to doubt its efficacy to assure salvation. Other doubts also began to assail his spirit and motivate his study. He was concerned about the problems of peace in the country, particularly in relation to the death of the boy-Emperor Antoku, whose divine personage should have assured him assistance from the gods. He knew also of other Emperors, such as Go-Toba, who had been exiled by the Hojo regents. He was also perturbed by the numerous Buddhist sects existing in the country. He believed that just as there may be only one rightful ruler in a country, there could be only one true teaching of Buddhism. After studying all the various schools, he concluded that only the *Lotus Sutra* (*Hokkekyo*) taught the supreme truth of Buddhism as Saicho had earlier proclaimed.

In a unique manner he connected the fortunes of the country with the nation's lack of clear support for the true form of Buddhism. Rather than the *Lotus Sutra* being the center of faith, the land was overrun by Pure Land teaching. In his work *Risshoankokuron* he pointed out that Japan had already suffered numerous penalties for failing to adhere to true Buddhism, but a final major one, namely invasion by a foreign country, would bring an end to the nation unless she adopted the true teaching. Implicitly Nichiren advocated the abolition of all other sects and the establishment of his own doctrine. He characterized himself as "the pillar of Japan." Although Nichiren claimed merely to be restoring the truth of Tendai, since the age of Mappo had arrived and the successors of Saicho had themselves perverted the tradition, he did not simply desire a return to an exact replication of traditional Tendai Buddhist teaching.

Nichiren, who believed he was the *Jogyo Bosatsu* promised by Buddha Sakyamuni in the Last Age in the *Lotus Sutra,* brought his missionary zeal to bear in challenging the government, people, and contemporary religious institutions, now including Zen, Shingon, and Ritsu, as well as Pure Land. As he began to win supporters, he soon experienced persecution. He was attacked by mobs, chased from temples, banished several times, and even once nearly met death. These events only strengthened his confidence that he had the truth. In addition to street preaching and other varied activities, Nichiren wrote voluminously.[8]

Nichiren's teaching embodied a response to a time of crisis in Japanese society. Though his predictive powers are not entirely clear, his admonitions concerning the invasion of the country as a final punishment by the Buddha and the gods appeared to be borne out when the Mongols attempted to invade Japan in 1274 and 1281. These events provided him with a greater following, though the nation did not turn as a whole to his teaching nor was it destroyed.

8. Five texts are basic for Nichiren's thought: *Risshoankokuron* (*Treatise on Attaining Peace in the Country Through Establishing True Buddhism*), *Kaimokusho* (*Treatise on Opening the Eyes*), *Hoonsho* (*Treatise on Requiting Gratitude*), *Senjisho* (*Treatise on Selection of the Time*), and *Kanjinhonzonsho* (*Treatise on the Meditation of the True Effect of Worship*).

Although along with other Buddhist schools Nichiren was concerned with providing a way of individual salvation, he was also moved by a strong national feeling. Buddhism was not purely an individual matter but of utmost importance to the life of the whole society. In relating Buddhism and the state, he differed from traditional thinkers in placing Buddhism above the state. He believed the destiny of the state depended on its adherence to the true form of Buddhism. In contrast to Pure Land other-worldly indifference to the state, and Dogen's rejection of the seductive influence of political connections, Nichiren sought to influence state policy through his religious views.

In view of the importance of maintaining true Buddhism, Nichiren's intolerance went beyond that of other schools in seeking the abolition of all other schools. The method of *Shakubuku,* forced conversion or a way of aggressively conquering evil, was widely employed by Nichiren, and by his later followers to the present day. His personal involvement in his teaching and his sense of divine mission gave greater intensity to his teaching so that the tradition stemming from him bears his own name.

Though he is doctrinally related to the Tendai tradition, he modified it by establishing his own Mandala (sacred symbolic diagram) based on the view of the eternal Buddha presented in chapter 16 of the *Lotus Sutra.* This is the ultimate Buddha who stands behind the historical Sakyamuni Buddha. The true Buddha is the timeless reality, not a person who at a specific time and place attained enlightenment. That mode of expression was only to accommodate men and guide them to deeper faith. In the Last Age in the decline of the Buddhist teaching the most profound teaching must be given just as a very ill person must be given the most effective and powerful medicine. On this point Nichiren differed with the Pure Land tradition in that the means of salvation must be correlated directly with the capacities of the people of that time. As it was a corrupt age, an easy way to salvation was necessary. Nevertheless, the religious practice of Nichiren was the recitation of the title of the *Lotus Sutra, Namu-Myoho-Renge-kyo.* This practice was probably influenced by the development of Pure Land, though the supporting philosophy differed.

Like Saicho, Nichiren wanted to establish the true ordination platform based on his teaching. Within the context of Japanese Buddhism this would signify state acceptance of his doctrine as a recognized religion and a participant in the effort to maintain the spiritual security of the state. In this case the ordination platform would represent official adherence only to Nichiren's interpretation of Buddhism, rather than the mere inclusion of his teaching with others.

With the acceptance of the Tendai philosophy of "Three thousand in one thought" by which all things in this world express the Buddha-mind itself, his interpretation of human existence is this-worldly rather than other-worldly in emphasis. One's mystic unity with the reality within things is achieved through the recitation of the *Daimoku* (title of the *Lotus Sutra*) rather than the elaborate meditations in Tendai. Nichiren is significant for the way in which he adapted the abstruse Tendai philosophy to the needs of ordinary men. As a result, his tradition has revitalized today with the outcropping of a multitude of sects drawing on his fervor and his thought in attempting to deal with modern problems.

The new impetus given to Buddhist thought by the Kamakura teachers determined the direction of Buddhist tradition down to the present day. Because of social circumstance, it became increasingly separated from the life of the people and largely functioned to attain health, wealth, and security, to dispense one's duties toward the dead, or become an instrument of the state in the pursuit of its ends. Nevertheless its fundamental insights were preserved in the scholarly, priestly traditions.

In the postwar period Buddhism shares significantly in the religious fermentation, with statistics indicating the establishment of some 170 Buddhist sects in contrast to the 56 prewar sects distributed within the thirteen traditional schools. The statistics are deceptive because the increase is largely due to secessions resulting from the freedom of religious competition granted by the new Constitution. Whether there is really a revitalization of Buddhism or religion in general may be questioned when one compares studies concerning the actual participation and interest in religion with the official statistics recorded by religious organizations. According to a recent study of religion in the urban context, hardly one third of the adult population expressed interest in religion, while the remainder affirmed the need for religion but would not presently join any group.[9]

Nevertheless, within the shifting urban situation of the postwar period, two Buddhist organizations have shown phenomenal growth corresponding to conditions of rising urban populations. The Rissho Koseikai and Soka Gakkai, both derivative from the Nichiren tradition, have attracted the attention of social scientists as well as religionists.

There are numerous reasons given for the striking progress of these sects. A major reason is that they have addressed themselves aggressively to meeting the needs of the new urban dwellers and their problems. In contrast to the traditional Buddhist organizations whose foundations are largely rural and familial, the new sects attempt to provide a personal ethic and sense of meaning for people released from traditional bonds of community and family. They provide a focus for positive dealing with the sense of frustration and dissatisfaction that attends the competitive life of the city. Where other sects wait for people to come when there is need, the newer groups reach out and contact the socially disorganized urbanite. The method of their spread emphasizes the personal aspect in that believers contact prospects and draw them into fellowship. Through educational programs and frequent meetings loyalty to the group

9. Fujio Ikado, "Trend and Problems of New Religions: Religion in Urban Society," in *The Sociology of Japanese Religion,* Kiyomi Morioka and William H. Newell, eds., Leiden, E. J. Brill, 1968, pp. 101–117.

and solidarity develop. These less tradition-bound groups have benefited from the experience of other organizations in propagandizing for they have borrowed tactics from such diverse sources as the Christian Church and the theories of Saul Alinsky.

Despite the roots which Rissho Koseikai and Soka Gakkai have in Nichiren tradition and in the *Lotus Sutra,* the styles of the groups contrast sharply. As a consequence they also appeal to different segments of the urban population. The former relies upon the rural middle class and the small businessman of the city for support, while the latter attracts laborers and the urban lower middle class.

The approach to the problems of contemporary life of these supporters helps to account for the differing attitudes represented by the sect. Rissho Koseikai is more tolerant, striving for a Buddhist ecumenicity as well as positive interfaith relations. Great emphasis is laid on filial piety as the prime ethical value. Soka Gakkai embodies the dogmatic and intolerant attitudes of the prophet Nichiren himself and holds itself aloof from any compromise with other forms of Buddhism. For individuals strongly dissatisfied with the prevailing social conditions, this form of religious outlook provides a rationalization that social ills are due to a failure to follow the true religion. Its zeal for bringing about change in society in conformity with its own ideals has led the Soka Gakkai movement to enter into politics by forming the Clean Government party (Komeito), whose name symbolizes its reformist attitudes. This party's meteoric rise to prominence and importance in the various local and national elections has led to apprehensions among other religious groups which fear its religious intolerance.

The Rissho Koseikai in its general orientation tends to be more individualistic in its emphasis on the development of one's personal life through faith in Buddhism and practice of filial piety. It is also interested in society at large and has developed numerous social welfare projects such as hospitals, schools, old age homes, and cemeteries. The Hoza group meeting is significant in bringing believers into active participation in a religious and social gathering of mutual fellowship and assistance.

The Soka Gakkai provides for the satisfaction of individual needs through the emphasis on the benefits which the devotee receives from the concentrated practice of reciting the *Daimoku; Namu-Myoho-Renge-Kyo.* It is most renowned for the practice of *Shakubuku,* which refers to the forceful exhortation and strong insistence on the truth of Soka Gakkai teaching. It is the obligation of each member to win his family and friends to this faith.

The effort is inspired by an eschatological perspective based on the doctrine of the Last Age in the Decline of Buddhist Teaching at which time the strong medicine of the *Lotus Sutra,* as taught by Nichiren and further elaborated through the recent teachers and leaders of Soka Gakkai, Tsunesaburo Makiguchi, Josei Toda, and Daisaku Ikeda, is required for the solution of modern social problems of peace, justice, and social welfare. The quasi-political concept of the true ordination platform (*Hommon Kaidan*) advocated by Saicho in Tendai Buddhism and Nichiren in his time symbolizes the perfect union of religion and the state for the promotion of universal human good. It is this theory imbedded in the doctrine of Soka Gakkai that arouses the fears of a religious totalitarianism and intolerance should it become the dominant political force in Japan. Each devotee is to work for realization of this ideal. This theory has not only motivated the political activity of the group, but recently has caused it to turn attention to the fields of labor and education to achieve its goals in society.

It should be noted also that its universalist goals extend beyond Japan. Soka Gakkai has experienced a rapid spread among Americans, first among servicemen with Japanese wives, but in more recent times on the basis of its own religious appeal. In the missionary context the political implications of the doctrine are muted.

While the development of Rissho Koseikai and Soka Gakkai has commanded the major attention of students of the Japanese religious world in recent years, the efforts of the traditional schools to adapt themselves to contemporary conditions should not be overlooked. In the many schools supported by these sects scholarly study of Buddhism in all aspects has rapidly progressed. The education of clergy has attained higher standards. Lectures, publications, and broadcasting bring the claims of Buddhism to a wide audience. Nationwide Buddhist organizations of lay persons and clergy attempt to unite the sects of Buddhism around common projects. There are also efforts to engage the interest of young people.

Despite the wealth of activities carried on in the various sects and chronicled in the many religious papers and periodicals, the traditional organizations are hindered in making an impact by the general stereotype that Buddhism is only for funerals and by the lack in the past of a concerted effort in religious education. Since intellectual commitment was never an essential part of the mode of religious belonging in the community or family, the average lay person understands little of the essential teachings of Buddhism. Statistics indicating that Shinto claims some seventy-nine million followers and Buddhism about seventy-eight million in a nation of ninety million people reveal that most Japanese appear not to sense any contradiction between the two traditions, and they show little consciousness of belonging to a particular religion.

In an age when customary and familial foundations for religion are weakening, the traditional Buddhist sects are at a disadvantage in maintaining social and economic support. With decreased income priests must often work as teachers or run kindergartens to maintain their livelihood. The result is that they lack adequate time for religious cultivation and evangelism.

Further, a hereditary clergy and a hierarchical organizational structure has tended to work against needed reforms urged by scholars and younger priests. As a consequence of these various factors, the older orders cannot match the vitality of the newer groups.

Although facing great difficulties, as the religious world stabilizes, the older organizations may benefit from their greater maturity and scholarship, as well as from the prestige that attends a lengthy history in Japan. A new age may be dawning when Buddhism will attain intellectual leadership as it comes to more adequate terms with the forces of secularism and modernization. In this connection, the understanding of Buddhism in the newer sects does not go beyond the traditional insight, though a greater attempt may be made to make those doctrines relevant to the contemporary situation. Thus from the intellectual standpoint the new and old sects are on much the same footing. The clash of claims, however, will encourage the refining and clarifying of views which will benefit the entire Buddhist tradition in Japan.

BIBLIOGRAPHY
Chinese Religio-
Philosophical
Tradition

General historical works:
    Creel, H. C., *Chinese Thought from Confucius to Mao Tse-tung*, New York, New American Library, 1953.
    Hughes, E. R., and K. Hughes, *Religion in China*, London, Hutchinson, 1950.
    Li, Dun J., *The Ageless Chinese: A History*, New York, Scribner, 1965.

Sourcebooks:
    Chan, Wing-tsit, *A Sourcebook in Chinese Philosophy*, Princeton, N.J., Princeton University Press, 1963.
    De Bary, William Theodore, et al., *Sources of Chinese Tradition*, 2 vols., New York, Columbia, paperback ed., 1964.
    Hughes, E. R., *Chinese Philosophy in Classical Times*, London, Hutchinson's University Library, 1950.

General works on Chinese perspectives in religion and philosophy:
    Eberhard, Wolfram, *Guilt and Sin in Traditional China*, Berkeley, Calif., University of California Press, 1967.
    Hsu, Francis L. K., *Under the Ancestor's Shadow*, New York, Doubleday, 1967.
    Nakamura, Hajime, *Ways of Thinking of Eastern Peoples*, Honolulu, East-West Center Press, 1964.
    Thompson, Laurence G., *Chinese Religion: An Introduction*, Belmont, Calif., Dickenson, 1969.
    Yang, C. K., *Religion in Chinese Society*, Berkeley, Calif., University of California Press, 1961.

Works on Chinese popular religion:
    Day, Clarence Burton, *Chinese Peasant Cults*, Shanghai, Kelly and Walsh Limited, 1940.
    Finegan, Jack, *The Archaeology of World Religions*, Vol. 2, Princeton, N.J., Princeton University Press, paperback ed., 1965.
    Granet, Marcel, *Festivals and Songs of Ancient China*, New York, Dutton, 1932.

General works on Chinese philosophy:
    Fung, Yu-lan, *A Short History of Chinese Philosophy*, ed. D. Bodde, New York, Macmillan, paperback ed., 1966.
    ————, *The Spirit of Chinese Philosophy*, trans. E. R. Hughes, Boston, Beacon Press, 1967.

Waley, Arthur, *Three Ways of Thought in Ancient China,* New York, Doubleday, paperback ed., 1956.

Works on Confucianism:

Creel, H. C., *Confucianism and the Chinese Way,* New York, Harper & Row, paperback ed., 1960.

Levenson, Joseph R., *Confucian China and its Modern Fate,* 3 vols., Berkeley, Calif., University of California Press, 1968.

Lin, Yu-tang, *The Wisdom of Confucius,* New York, Random House, 1938.

Shryock, John K., *The Origin and Development of the State Cult of Confucius,* New York, Appleton-Century-Crofts, 1932.

Verwilghen, Albert Felix, *Mencius: The Man and His Ideas,* New York, St. John's University Press, 1967.

Waley, Arthur, *The Analects of Confucius,* New York, Random House, 1938.

Ware, James, trans., *The Sayings of Mencius,* New York, New American Library, 1960.

Watson, Burton, *The Basic Writings of Mo-tzu, Hsun-tzu, Han Fei-tzu,* New York, Columbia, 1967.

Wright, Arthur F., *Confucianism and Chinese Civilization,* New York, Atheneum Publishers, 1964.

Works on Taoism:

Chan, Wing-tsit, trans., *The Way of Lao-tzu,* Indianapolis, Bobbs-Merrill, 1963.

Kaltenmark, Max, *Lao-tzu and Taoism,* Stanford, Calif., Stanford University Press, 1969.

Watson, Burton, *Chuang Tzu: Basic Writings,* New York, Columbia, 1964.

Welch, Holmes, *Taoism, the Parting of the Way,* Boston, Beacon Press, paperback ed., 1966.

Works on Buddhism:

Ch'en, Kenneth, *Buddhism in China: A Historical Survey,* Princeton, N.J., Princeton University Press, 1964.

Fung, Yu-lan, *History of Chinese Philosophy,* Vol. 2, Princeton, N.J., Princeton University Press, 1952–1953.

Suzuki, Daisetsu T., *Studies in Zen,* New York, Dell, paperback ed., 1955.

Welch, Holmes, *The Practice of Chinese Buddhism, 1900–1950,* Cambridge, Mass., Harvard, 1967.

Wright, Arthur F., *Buddhism in Chinese History,* Stanford, Calif., Stanford University Press, 1959.

Yampolsky, Philip B., *The Platform Sutra of the Sixth Patriarch,* New York, Columbia, 1967.

Works on modern China:

Briere, O., *Fifty Years of Chinese Philosophy (1898–1948),* New York, Praeger, paperback ed., 1965.

Chan, Wing-tsit, *Religious Trends in Modern China,* New York, Octagon, 1968.

Works on the historical backgrounds of Japanese culture:

De Bary, William Theodore, *Sources of Japanese Tradition,* New York, Columbia, 1958.

Sansom, G. B., *A History of Japan,* 3 vols., Stanford, Calif., Stanford University Press, 1958–1963.

————, *Japan: A Short Cultural History,* New York, Appleton-Century-Crofts, rev. ed., 1962.

Works on Japanese religious history:

Anesaki, Masaharu, *History of Japanese Religion,* Rutland, Vt., Charles E. Tuttle Co., 1963.

Kitagawa, Joseph M., *Religion in Japanese History,* New York, Columbia, 1966.

Kishimoto, Hideo, ed., *Japanese Religion in the Meiji Era,* Tokyo, Obunsha, 1956.

Works on Japanese religious perspectives and value orientations:

Anesaki, Masaharu, *Religious Life of the Japanese People,* Tokyo, Kokusai Bunka Shinkokai, 1961.

Bellah, Robert N., *Tokugawa Religion,* New York, Free Press, 1957.

Benedict, Ruth, *The Chrysanthemum and the Sword,* Rutland, Vt., Charles E. Tuttle Co., 1965.

Earhart, H. Byron, *Japanese Religion: Unity and Diversity,* Belmont, Calif., Dickenson, 1969.

Hori, Ichiro, *Folk Religion in Japan,* Chicago, University of Chicago Press, 1968.

Morioka, Kiyomi, and William H. Newell, eds., *The Sociology of Japanese Religion,* Leiden, E. J. Brill, 1968.

Moore, Charles A., ed., *The Japanese Mind,* Honolulu, East-West Center Press, 1967.

Nakamura, H., *Ways of Thinking of Eastern Peoples,* Honolulu, East-West Center Press, 1964.

Philippi, Donald L., trans., *Norito,* Tokyo, The Institute for Japanese Culture and Classics, Kokugakuin University, 1959.

Works on the Shinto tradition:

Aston, W. G., *Nihongi,* London, G. Allen, reprint, 1956.

Brown, Delmer, "Kami, Death, and Ancestral Kami," *The Proceedings of the Second International Conference for Shinto Studies,* Tokyo, Institute of Japanese Culture and Classics, Kokugakuin University, n.d.

Creemers, Wilhelmus H. M., *Shrine Shinto After World War II,* Leiden, E. J. Brill, 1968.

Holtom, D. C., *Modern Japan and Shinto Nationalism,* New York, Paragon, 2d ed., 1947.

————, *National Faith of Japan,* New York, Paragon, 1965.

Matsumoto, Shigeru, *Motoori Norinaga: 1730–1801,* Cambridge, Mass., Harvard, 1970.

Muraoka, Tsunetsugu, *Studies in Shinto Thought,* Tokyo, Japanese Ministry of Education, 1964.

Ono, Sokyo, *Shinto the Kami Way,* Tokyo, Bridgeway Press, 1962.

Philippi, Donald L., *Kojiki,* Princeton, N.J., Princeton University Press, 1969.

Ross, Floyd H., *Shinto: The Way of Japan,* Boston, Beacon Press, 1965.

Works on the Buddhist tradition:

Anesaki, Masaharu, *Nichiren the Buddhist Prophet,* Cambridge, Mass., Harvard, 1916.

Bloom, Alfred, *Shinran's Gospel of Pure Grace,* Tucson, Ariz., University of Arizona Press, 1965.

Coates, Harper H., and Ryugaku Ishizuka, *Honen the Buddhist Saint,* 5 vols., Kyoto, Society for the Publication of Sacred Books of the World, 1949.

DeVisser, M. W., *Ancient Buddhism in Japan,* 2 vols., Leiden, E. J. Brill, 1935.

Dumoulin, Heinrich, *A History of Zen Buddhism,* New York, Pantheon, 1963.

Matsunaga, Alicia, *The Buddhist Philosophy of Assimilation,* Rutland, Vt., Charles E. Tuttle Co., 1969.

Saunders, E. Dale, *Buddhism in Japan, with an Outline of Its Origins in India,* Philadelphia, University of Pennsylvania Press, 1964.

Watanabe, Shoko, *Japanese Buddhism: A Critical Appraisal,* Tokyo, Kokusai Bunka Shinkokai, 1964.

Works on new religions:

MacFarland, H. Neill, "Japan's New Religions," *Contemporary Religions in Japan, 1,* no. 4 (December, 1960), pp. 57–69.

MacFarland, H. Neill, *The Rush Hour of the Gods,* New York, Macmillan, 1967.

Murata, Kiyoaki, *Japan's New Buddhism,* New York, Walker-Weatherhill, 1969.

Offner, C. B., and H. Van Straelen, *Modern Japanese Religions,* Leiden, E. J. Brill, 1963.

A Short History of Tenrikyo, Tenri, Japan, 1958.

Thomsen, Harry, *The New Religions of Japan,* Rutland, Vt., Charles E. Tuttle Co., 1963.

PART FOUR

BIBLICAL RELIGIOUS TRADITIONS: JUDAISM AND CHRISTIANITY

JANET K. & THOMAS F. O'DEA

JUDAISM IN HISTORICAL PERSPECTIVE

Biblical religion is grounded upon the experience of God's presence, a presence which transcends and which transfigures the life of the individual and the group. The encounter of man with a reality beyond himself to which he is related and with which he communicates is the essence of biblical religiosity and the constituting foundation of Jewish peoplehood and the Christian church. For the Israelites of the biblical age and their descendants, the relationship with their God, Yahweh, determined the meaning, the order, and the goal of their existence. On this foundation all later Western religion rests.

The nature and course of Israel's relationship to Yahweh is disclosed in the Bible, which is itself a record and interpretation of historical events within the framework of religious faith. The Bible tells who Yahweh is, how he chose a group of tribes to receive his revelation, and how these tribes responded to him. Yahweh was the God who revealed himself to Moses in a burning bush as the God of the Hebrew patriarchs and as the future God of the entire Hebrew people. It was he, Yahweh, who would be present to lead the tribes out of their bondage in Egypt, who would guide them through the wilderness, and who would establish a permanent covenant with them. Yahweh disclosed his name to Moses, *eh'yeh asher eh'yeh,* "I am who I am," meaning he is the being who will be eternally present to his people, there whenever his people need and call upon him. Moses was commissioned by Yahweh to lead the suffering Israelites out of slavery and to carry the divine word to this people. With Moses as his representative, Yahweh promised to lead the Hebrews

GOD'S CALL AND
THE COVENANT
WITH ISRAEL

forth and to be with them eternally as a guide and protector in their course through history.

The Bible tells how Israel responded to Yahweh's call to recognize his sovereign lordship, to submit to his rule, and to receive his benevolent care. Moses proclaimed the word of Yahweh to the people:

> You have seen what I did unto the Egyptians, and how I bore you out on eagles' wings, and brought you to myself. Now therefore, if you will obey my voice, and keep my covenant, you shall be my own possession among all peoples; for all the earth is mine, and you shall be to me a kingdom of priests and a holy nation.
>
> (Exod. 19:4–7)

Yahweh has delivered Israel out of the hands of the oppressive Egyptians and has singled out this people to draw near unto him and to enter a special covenantal relationship with him. He has created the whole world and all is properly his. Yet he has selected one particular people to fulfill his demands, to benefit from his promises, and to be his instrument in history. Israel's response to Yahweh was immediate.

> And all the people answered together and said: All that the Lord has spoken we will do.
>
> (Exod. 19:8)

Having experienced Yahweh's presence, having witnessed his redeeming action in the Exodus, and having heard his words, the Hebrew tribes willingly accepted his demand. Israel and Yahweh bound themselves to a covenant, which would determine a total life relationship. The disparate tribes united to become a nation dedicated to the service of the Lord. They are to be a holy people in imitation of the holiness of their God and in obedience to his commands. The decision to enter into the covenantal relationship was the great decision of Israelite history, resulting in the emergence of a special religious consciousness. For the Jew, the Exodus from Egypt became the central event in religious history. In it God's saving power had been revealed to Israel and the people had responded with the promise of constant service to him.

> And Israel saw the great work which the Lord did against the Egyptians, and the people feared the Lord; and they believed in the Lord, and in his servant Moses. . . . The Lord is my strength and my song; and he has become my salvation; this is my God and I will praise him.
>
> (Exod. 14:31, 15:2)

Israel had perceived Yahweh's presence in history and had come to understand that his power was behind all events. According to the biblical vision, it was Yahweh who ruled, who alone was master of history, and unto whom the people submitted in trust.

The covenant is the central conception of the Bible. The content and implications of the covenant formed the framework in which Israel understood its social constitution and historical meaning. At Sinai the clear will of Yahweh had been revealed and the clear response of the people had been enunciated. They accepted the covenant as a gift of the Lord which would establish a permanent relationship between him and them. They also accepted the divine law of the covenant, committing themselves to follow God's commandments in all areas of national and private life. The Bible presented the nation as founded in a religious event, and its rule as always to be religious law. The loose tribes were transformed into a people united by shared loyalty to Yahweh, and ordered in the political and social realms by his religious code. The God of the Bible laid claim to the actions of man. Deeds, particular acts, whether ethical or ritualistic, were the form and expression of the relationship of God and man. It was in his deeds that man demonstrated his faithfulness to Yahweh or strayed from the Lord. Israel was commanded to actualize Yahweh's will in the world, to be his witnesses, and by imitating his holiness, to bear testimony to his presence. For this reason, Law became absolutely central in the religious life of Israel. The civil and moral ordinances believed to be revealed by Yahweh to Moses were the constitution of the people who had vowed to serve the Lord in the way prescribed. Yahweh was the author of a code which governed the entire range of human life. His majesty and holiness were embodied in the Law which he had issued. Israel, in fulfilling the Torah, this law which is the way of the Lord, actualized his word in history and fulfilled its covenant obligation. For in the covenant Israel had pledged to submit itself to the omnipotent will of Yahweh and to realize his rule in the concrete activities of national life. Obedience to the law was seen, therefore, as an expression of love for its author as well as an acknowledgment of his sovereignty, while ignorance of the law or disobedience was considered a sin. The Lord had spoken to Israel face-to-face at Sinai and had contracted a sacred covenant with the nation.

Not with our fathers did the Lord make this covenant, but with us, who are all of us here alive this day.

(Deut. 5:3)

Therefore it is incumbent upon every Israelite to hear the commandments, to learn them, and to perform them.

Hear O Israel: The Lord our God is one Lord; and you shall love the Lord your God with all your heart, and with all your soul, and with all your might. And these words which I command you this day shall be upon your heart; and you shall teach them diligently to your children . . .

(Deut. 6:4–7)

It is only because he loved them that Yahweh had chosen Israel to be his special treasure and to serve his special mission in the world. Israel must return his love in every generation by acting to fulfill the sacred obligations of the covenant. This is the clear imperative which issued from the covenant relationship.

> *For this commandment which I command you this day it is not too hard for you, neither is it far off.*
>
> (Deut. 30:11)

Every man of the nation is able to understand and participate in the covenant and thereby share in realizing the divine life.

> *See, I have set before you this day life and good, death and evil. If you obey the commandments of the Lord your God which I command you this day, by loving the Lord your God, by walking in his ways, and by keeping his commandments and his statutes and his ordinances, then you shall live and multiply, and the Lord your God will bless you in the land which you are entering to take possession of it.*
>
> (Deut. 30:15–16)

Israel thus understood its relationship to Yahweh and to the world within the covenant framework. Yahweh had revealed himself in history to his people and had determined their historical destiny. The Israelites interpreted events in their national history, such as the exodus from Egypt, the revelation at Sinai, the conquest of Canaan, as religious symbols and as part of a sacred history. They, as a people, were partners with Yahweh in carrying out his plan for mankind and the concrete events of their history were to be understood within the structure of the divinely ordered drama. Yahweh had intervened in history to guide the destiny of man.

The conception of a God who acted in history and who participated in an ongoing historical relationship with a community of men broke with prevailing notions of deity, of nature, and of man in the ancient Near East. Ancient Near Eastern man viewed the world of nature as being alive with divine forces, which were of the same substance and which experienced the same needs as he himself. The gods as well as man were born out of a primeval matter, were subject to natural processes, and were ultimately subordinate to the laws of nature or fate. It is because the gods and man were of the same substance and subject to the same laws that man could manipulate the gods through magic and could actually become a god or semigod.

In contrast to the mythological deity, Yahweh was conceived by Israel as the absolutely transcendent Lord of the universe whose being was beyond nature and completely other than man. He was the all-powerful God, who had not been created out of primeval matter but who had himself created the entire universe. He was totally independent of natural processes, could not be controlled by magic, and certainly did not need the gifts of man for his existence. Because his being was totally different from the world which was his creation, Yahweh could not be fully comprehended by man and could not be embodied in any concrete form. The existence of Yahweh was not in any way parallel to nor comparable with the existence of man.

And yet this all-powerful, totally other, infinite Lord had chosen to relate himself to man. Yahweh had entered into human history, had encountered his creature, and had made his will known to him. He had even invited man to enter into a covenant which made man a partner in realizing the divine design for the universe. To Israel it appeared that history was the sphere of its relationship to Yahweh and was filled with sacred moments of divine action. The past, present, and future all received meaning in relationship to the will and word of the Lord. If Israel fulfilled its side of the covenantal relationship, the progress of history towards its ultimate goal would be advanced. If Israel failed to uphold the covenant stipulations, the divine plan would be frustrated and God's instrument subject to chastisement and punishment. Biblical history is thus the record of successive fulfillments and defections, of faithfulness and waywardness, of social peace and social disorder.

The tribes of Israel, under the leadership of Joshua, settled in the promised land of Canaan, and there renewed the covenant pact. They pledged themselves once again to form a community dedicated to Yahweh, who alone was God and who alone would guide their national destiny.

KINGS AND PROPHETS: DISAPPOINTMENT AND HOPE

> *Then Joshua said unto the people: You are witnesses against yourselves that you have chosen the Lord, to serve Him. And they said, We are witnesses. He said, Then put away the foreign gods which are among you, and incline your heart to the Lord, the God of Israel. And the people said to Joshua, The Lord our God we will serve, and his voice we will obey.*
>
> (Josh. 24:22–24)

The Israelite tribes formed a confederacy whose unity was based upon the common covenant agreement. They came together for national worship and in times of danger, when Yahweh would raise up a leader to lead in the defense of the confederacy. These charismatic leaders, the judges of the Old Testament, were believed to be graced with the spirit of Yahweh and in a holy war carried the tribes to victory. In the consciousness of Israel it was the might of God and not the power of men which was decisive, and the charismatic judge served merely as a temporary instrument of God's will. The ideal form of Israelite communal life was most closely realized during this period of the judges. The tribes were linked by common faith and worship, and believed themselves to be protected by the spirit of Yahweh and his representatives.

However, the tensions between the ideal and the real were ever-present, and resistance to God's demands was constant. Throughout this period a rhythm of faithfulness and rejection, of fulfillment and defection, was evident. Israel forgot the commandments of Yahweh, turned to false gods and false pursuits, and was then punished by the Lord. However, because he was patient and anxious to restore his people, Yahweh delivered them from the punishment and accepted their penitent return unto him. This is the recurring pattern not only of the Book of Judges but it is indeed the recurring pattern of Israelite history. The inherent tension between divine demand

and human desires was experienced constantly as the nation developed. Would Israel submit to Yahweh's rule and adhere to the covenant or would it turn to the ways of man and the pursuits of nations? Who is ultimately the ruler of Israel and who determines the national destiny? The strain between the divine and human order became most intense when the question of monarchy arose, for with the institution of monarchy a permanent human ruler was placed over the people of God and secular interests were asserted over the moral and religious ideals of the Yahwist order.

In the story of the selection of Saul as the first Israelite king the conflict between the people's will and Yahweh's command is vividly portrayed. The people declared:

> But we will have a king over us, that we also may be like all the nations, and that our king may govern us and go out before us and fight our battles.
>
> (1 Sam. 8:19–20)

No longer were the Israelites willing to rely on Yahweh to raise up charismatic leaders to lead them, and no longer did Israel want to be distinguished from all other peoples. For these reasons the institution of monarchy threatened the foundations of covenant society.

> And the Lord said to Samuel, "Harken to the voice of the people in all that they say to you; for they have not rejected you, but they have rejected me from being king over them."
>
> (1 Sam. 8:7)

Although kingship was gradually integrated into the covenant religious order, the basic tension between divine and human rule was never overcome. The history of Israel under the kings was plagued by continual crisis both internally and externally. Political maneuvering in the international arena brought military defeat and finally downfall to Northern Israel in 722 and to Judah in 586. Conflicts arising from the economic exploitation of the common people by the ruling classes caused great social dissension in these kingdoms. The freedom and equality which the small farmers and sheep raisers had enjoyed during the period of the confederacy disappeared as peasants lost their land and had to work on state projects and became hopelessly indebted to the aristocracy. The social-ethical ideals of the covenant were abandoned as were the religious values. Israel turned to the false gods of the nations.

At the moment when Yahwistic religion and covenant existence were in the most extreme peril, the Bible describes the emergence of powerful religious leaders who opposed the secularizing idolatrous tendencies of kingship and called upon Israel to return to the covenant and to its God. These were the prophets, Yahweh's representatives, sent into the breach to war for the soul of the straying people. In the name of the religious and socioeconomic ideals of the covenant they battled against syncretism with foreign religions, economic oppression, social injustice, and international political involvement. The prophets called for an inner change, for a revival of the covenant, and a regeneration of religious life. From the ninth to the fourth centuries B.C., these unique individuals confronted the people and its leaders with the word of the Lord. Again Yahweh intervened in the history of Israel, revealing his will to his elect through the agency of his messengers, the prophets. With the spirit of Yahweh driving them on, often in the face of difficult internal conflict and external opposition, the prophets fulfilled this divine task assigned to them. They issued a sweeping critique of the social and religious aberrations of the present and interpreted Yahweh's actions for the future.

Elijah, the semilegendary prophet of the ninth century, in his figure and in his task was prototypical of the great classical prophets who followed him. This militant and eerie man of God completely dominates the First Book of Kings. Elijah waged a war to win back the allegiance of Israel to Yahweh and to demonstrate that the ethical imperatives of the covenant law were supreme over all men. Appearing suddenly from out of the desert, the prophet confronted Ahab, King of Israel, who had been led to worship the baalim, idols of Canaan, by his foreign-born wife Jezebel, and who had in turn misled the people of Israel. Elijah alone rose to challenge the baalists, in one of the most dramatic scenes in the Old Testament, and tested the religion of the idol worshipers.

> How long will you go limping with two different opinions? If the Lord is God, follow him; but if Baal, then follow him.
>
> (1 Kings 18:21)

It is only after the miracle Yahweh performed that the Israelites reply to the prophet's taunt.

> And when all the people saw it, they fell on their faces; and they said, "The Lord, he is God; the Lord, he is God."
>
> (1 Kings 18:39)

Responding to the religious fervor of the ecstatic prophet and the saving work of Yahweh, the nation finally reaffirmed that Yahweh is king over Israel and rededicated itself to the covenant.

The battle of Elijah was carried into the ethical sphere in the tale of Navoth and his vineyard. When Ahab, coveting the vineyard of Navoth, had requested to buy it, the Israelite farmer refused to sell the sacred ancient possession of his family. Jezebel, again the agent of corruption, had Navoth killed and turned the vineyard over to her husband. For this sin of arbitrary power, Elijah announced that destruction would befall the entire household of Ahab. The king could not raise himself above the commoner, for covenant law and justice were equal to all Israelites. The demands of Yahweh were defended by Elijah in both the religious and the ethical spheres. He stood as the prototype of the messenger, coming to recall an erring people and king to the traditional covenant order. Moses had revealed the order of Israel's society and Elijah defended it. The prophetic voice announced boldly that Yahweh would countenance neither apostasy nor immorality. He would punish the ordinary man and the king alike. The nation which long ago encountered Yahweh and accepted his covenant, stood responsible before him. In recalling the Law, issuing a warning, proclaiming judgment, and then offering a promise of salvation, Elijah the prophet outlined the tasks which those who followed him believed themselves commissioned to perform over and over again. For Israel persisted in its defection, the decline in religious life was unabated, despite the mighty effort of the prophets to return Israel to itself and thus save the nation from disaster.

The moral corruption of Israel deepened as the drive for economic, political, and social power increased. It was the prophet Amos who condemned this moral degeneration most thoroughly, finding Israel guilty in all manner of unethical behavior. The rich trampled the poor, crushed the needy, perverted justice, and were immersed in debauchery, sexual license, and drunkenness. Amos cried out against the oppression found everywhere in the land. He considered false religion to be chief among the sins of Israel, for the performance of cultic duties by immoral men was a base act reviled by Yahweh. Ethical behavior must precede ritual and the cult was secondary to the moral code. Those who trusted in the cult to satisfy Yahweh deceived themselves. Sacrifices and rituals were not the way to Yahweh,

> For I know how many are your transgressions, and how great are your sins—you who afflict the righteous, who take a bribe, and turn aside the needy in the gate.
>
> (Amos 5:12)

The demand of Yahweh was for adherence to ethical norms, and only then was the cult pleasing to him.

> I hate, I despise your feasts, and I take no delight in your solemn assemblies. Even though you offer me your burnt offerings and cereal offerings, I will not accept them, and the peace offerings of your fatted beasts I will not look upon. Take away from me the noise of your songs; to the melody of your harps I will not listen. But let justice roll down like waters, and righteousness like an ever-flowing stream.
>
> (Amos 5:21–24)

Through the prophet, Yahweh demanded righteousness and justice. It was only because the nation refused to meet this demand for ethical righteousness, because it continued to disappoint Yahweh and reject him, that he condemned them to grave punishment. Many times the warning had been given and ignored. Therefore the prophet announced, "prepare to meet your God, O Israel" (Amos 4:12). The compassion and mercy of Yahweh were not unending, and punishment was due the nation obdurate in its faithlessness and sin.

Amos proclaimed that according to the religion of Yahweh ethics was more significant than cult and that moral behavior would determine the national fate of Israel. This same proclamation was issued by later prophets.

> How the faithful city become a harlot, she that was full of justice! Righteousness lodged in her, but now murderers. Your silver is

*become dross, your wine mixed with water. Your princes are reb-
els and companions of thieves. Every one loves a bribe and runs
after gifts. They do not defend the fatherless, and the widow's
cause does not come to them.*

(Isa. 1:21—23)

And when the holy city resembled Sodom and Gomorrah in its iniquity, the performance of the cult would only be an abomination to
the Lord.

*What to me is the multitude of your sacrifices? says the Lord.
. . . Bring no more vain offerings; incense is an abomination to
me. New moon and Sabbath and the calling of assemblies—I
cannot endure iniquity and solemn assembly. . . . When you
spread forth your hands, I will hide my eyes from you; even
though you make many prayers, I will not listen; your hands are
full of blood. Wash yourselves, make yourselves clean; remove
the evil of your doings from before my eyes; cease to do evil,
learn to do good; seek justice, correct oppression; defend the fatherless, plead for the widow.*

(Isa. 1:11—17)

To Isaiah, the worst of Israel's sins was pride, the self-assertion
and self-confidence of man which inevitably led to rebellion against
God. This basic pride caused Israel's leaders to pursue expansionist
military policies. The monarchy was filled with arrogance and illegitimate ambition. Rather than seeking to establish a just state and
trusting in God's power for protection and guidance, the ruling class
trusted in its own might and political prowess. According to the
prophet, reliance upon the work of man's hands and the accomplishments of man's power was leading Israel into disaster. He proclaimed that history was controlled by Yahweh and that human
force did not determine its order. Trust in self was idolatry, a sin
which Israel committed constantly. And punishment for this sin
would come,

*for the Lord of hosts has a day against all that is proud and lofty
. . . the haughtiness of men shall be humbled; the Lord alone will
be exalted in that day.*

(Isa. 2:12—17)

The idolatry of self-assertion was only one aspect of the general
sin manifested in Israel: forgetting of Yahweh and his covenant.
Men worshiped idols because they had forgotten the true Lord.
They were unjust, impious, and unrighteous because they had lost
sight of the covenant ideals. According to the prophets, knowledge
of God and knowledge of the covenant were absolutely essential if
Israel were to realize its true national destiny, and yet it was just
this knowledge which had been lost.

*Hear, O heavens, and give ear, O earth; for the Lord has spoken:
"Sons have I reared and brought up, but they have rebelled
against me. The ox knows its owner, and the ass its master's crib;
but Israel does not know, my people does not understand."*

(Isa. 1:2—5)

The great Northern prophet Hosea bemoaned the consequences which followed from Israel's sin of forgetting Yahweh.

Hear the word of the Lord, O people of Israel; for the Lord has a controversy with the inhabitants of the land. There is no faithfulness or kindness, and no knowledge of God in the land; there is swearing, lying, killing, stealing, and committing adultery; they break all bounds and murder follows murder.

(Hos. 4:1–2)

Life without God had led to life without righteousness, life without truth, and life without mercy. These basic moral attributes are what Yahweh has demanded of Israel. Lack of them must result in punishment and national calamity, as every prophet warned. Yahweh had revealed himself to Israel, had let himself be known intimately to the people, and had actually betrothed himself to them. Yet his intimacy had been rejected and the betrothal bonds broken. Israel had gone awhoring after false gods, after idols, military might, economic gain. Man had erected false ultimates, rather than remaining faithful to the only true ultimate, Yahweh. This was the great wickedness of Israel, that they put man in place of God. They relied upon the kings, who knew not the Lord, upon fortifications, and upon warriors. They believed that alliances with idolatrous Egypt and Assyria would bring great success. And, further, in forgetting God they had lost their own selves, sinking into drunkenness and license. To Hosea, loss of self implied loss of the relationship with Yahweh and it was this sin of which Israel was guilty.

Return, O Israel, to the Lord your God, for you have stumbled because of your iniquity. Take with you words and return to the Lord.

(Hos. 14:1–3)

Hosea knew how deep was the corruption of Israel. He also knew how deep was the longing of Yahweh that his people would repent of this corruption and return to him. The special relationship of Yahweh and Israel had to be reestablished, and the love between them renewed. Israel did not repent, did not hearken to the warning, and did not seek to avoid the punishment.

My people are destroyed for lack of knowledge; because you have rejected knowledge, I reject you from being a priest to me.

(Hos. 4:6)

The Northern Kingdom of Hebrew tribes was finally defeated and crushed in 722 B.C. by Assyria. Towns were destroyed, the land ruined, and large sections of the population exiled. Throughout that century and the next, Judah too was threatened with subjugation. Her kings, in continuing to maneuver and maintain independence from the international powers of Assyria and Babylonia, brought her closer to disaster at the hands of these powers. In the eyes of the prophets the wrath of Yahweh had indeed been visited upon his people. Only return to him in genuine repentance could avoid for Judah what had already overcome her sister, Israel. Trust in military power would not insure national security. The safety and prosperity of Israel depended upon the protection of Yahweh alone, and this was granted only when the moral conditions of the covenant had been fulfilled. Isaiah and Jeremiah, prophets speaking at the height of the national danger, called Judah to repent, to cleanse herself, and thus to avoid catastrophe. It was not Yahweh who failed to protect his people, but his people who failed to respond to his call, to actualize his rule in their lives, and who thus brought doom upon themselves. As defection continued and the moral crisis deepened, the prophets looked away from the present toward the future. Israel persisted in disappointing Yahweh, yet this did not mean that Yahweh's plan for history was permanently overthrown nor that his promises were void. There was complete disorder in Israelite society, darkness covered all, but the prophets perceived meaning in this condition and projected new hopes for a renewed covenant people.

From 617 to 586 Jeremiah stood as a solitary defender of the covenant tradition and relationship which the people had abandoned. He represented the order of Yahweh against its enemies from within, announcing the will of God, warning the king and the people of the doom to come, and then finally promising hope for the righteous few who would survive the holocaust. Jeremiah, believed to be chosen from the womb to perform this critical task, was the personal servant of Yahweh, suffering deeply in empathy with the suffering of both the nation which he loved and the chastising father with whom he identified. Of all the prophets, the fate of Jeremiah was the most tragic. He prayed for the people, interceded on their behalf, and tried to turn them from the road of destruction. However, his warnings were ignored by the nation and his prayers rejected by God. The terrible strain of the prophetic task is reflected in the moving autobiographical outcries of Jeremiah, in which the prophet sought rest, consolation, and hope.

> *Woe is me, my mother, that you bore me, a man of strife and contention to the whole land!*
>
> (Jer. 15:10)

> *For I am called by thy name, O Lord, God of hosts. I did not sit in the company of merrymakers, nor did I rejoice; I sat alone because thy hand was upon me, for thou hadst filled me with indignation. Why is my pain unceasing, my wound incurable . . . ?*
>
> (Jer. 15:16—18)

To such depths of despair did the prophet sink that in the midst of great spiritual agony he cursed the day of his birth. The darkness which overwhelmed Jeremiah was the darkness overwhelming the nation, and in his own suffering he foreshadowed the suffering of the people. In his own personal experience Jeremiah depicted the terrible problems of prophetic existence, of the one who alone faced both man and God with knowledge that though his message would not be heard, he must persist in his efforts in obedience to the word of the Lord.

Jeremiah predicted that defeat would come upon the erring nation, but not complete doom. There would be suffering but there would also be salvation. This hope for salvation was tied to the entire prophetic theodicy, which attempted to make sense of the religious crisis and give meaning to the severe difficulties which the covenant people was to undergo. Jeremiah knew that punishment was inevitable, for there was no other way to atone for the massive sins of the generations.

Because your guilt is great, because your sins are flagrant, I have done these things to you.

(Jer. 30:15)

THE EXILE: ISRAEL'S ABIDING FAITH

And that punishment, the doom which Jeremiah and the prophets before him had foreseen, came upon Judah in 587–586 B.C. Continuing to trust in her military capabilities, Judah participated in a rebellion of minor powers against Babylonia, which was crushed in 598. Jehoiachin, the newly crowned king, along with government officials, a number of important citizens, and priests, was exiled to Babylonia. Zedekiah became king of Judah. Having learned little from the recent defeat, rather than remaining an obedient vassal he began plotting another rebellion. Warnings from Jeremiah could not deter the fierce patriotic drive for political independence. In 589 the rebellion broke out. Babylonian forces arrived and laid siege to Jerusalem in 588. They took the major fortified cities throughout Judah and in July, 587 broke through the walls of Jerusalem. Zedekiah was captured, tortured, and died in exile, the last king of Judah. Another major portion of the Judean population was sent to Babylonia, and Jerusalem, the eternal holy city, was razed to the ground by fire in August, 587. Thus the Judean kingdom fell in ruin, and the defeated nation was cast into despair.

The survival of Jewry and Judaism can only be explained in terms of the religious faith which the prophets had instilled in the people and which they continued to teach them in the moment of crisis. Jeremiah had spoken. He had foretold destruction and exile, but he had also promised forgiveness and reconciliation that would come after the terrible judgment.

Behold the days are coming, says the Lord, when I will make a new covenant with the house of Israel and the house of Judah, . . . for I will forgive their iniquity, and I will remember their sin no more.

(Jer. 31:31–34)

This is the vision of the new covenant which would herald salvation for Israel, which became the comfort and hope of the disillusioned people. Man who had not been able to fulfill the old covenant would be changed in his nature. God would plant in him a new heart, a heart of obedience. Man would come to affirm God spontaneously, there being now but one heart and one way for both God and man. Man had been unable to change himself, so that God had had to transform him inwardly.

The promise of a new age was reaffirmed by the exilic prophet Ezekiel, who sought to comfort and give understanding to the community of Jews exiled in Babylonia. With tremendous zeal, imagination, and power he called out to the captives to repent. He was a watchman over Israel, rebuking and comforting, teaching and curing. First, he taught that God's actions were just, for the sins of Israel had merited the wrath he visited upon them. Every man suffered for his own deeds and Jerusalem had been destroyed because of the sins committed by its citizens. But to the plaintful cry, "Our bones are dried up, and our hope is lost we are clean cut off" (Ezek. 37:11), the prophet answered that while God is just he is also merciful. The real yearning and searching of the people would be heard by the Lord, who would raise up his elect, redeeming Israel and his own name from disgrace and suffering.

> I will make with them a covenant of peace and banish wild beasts from the land, so that they may dwell securely in the wilderness and sleep in the woods. . . . And they shall know that I, the Lord their God, am with them, and that they, the house of Israel, are my people, says the Lord God.
>
> (Ezek. 34:25–30)

The dead bones of the exiled people would be revived and live in a new manner of existence. Like Jeremiah, Ezekiel promised that the people would return to Jerusalem and there fulfill the covenant perfectly. Ezekiel offered sustenance to a disillusioned people with his explanation of history and his trust in a forgiving God.

> Let us test and examine our ways, and return to the Lord!
>
> (Lam. 3:40)

In this verse the court poet expressed the understanding of destruction which the people adopted. God was just and therefore the sins of Israel had caused the national catastrophe. In severe pain and suffering the people acknowledged their guilt.

> The Lord is in the right, for I have rebelled against his word; but hear, all you peoples, and behold my suffering.
>
> (Lam. 1:18)

And the people would now turn to Yahweh for forgiveness.

> The steadfast love of the Lord never ceases, his mercies never come to an end.
>
> (Lam. 3:22)

This basic understanding of sin causing punishment, the need for repentance, and the mercy of God which would bring salvation assuaged the soul of a broken people. This theodicy, that is, the justification of God's ways, enabled the exiles to recover the inner strength required for the reconstruction of a community dedicated to Yahweh's service on foreign soil.

The most elevated expression of Israel's renewed faithfulness to Yahweh, in the face of political and social conditions which might lead to total apostasy, is to be found in the writings of the anonymous exilic prophet whose message is contained in the latter part of the Book of Isaiah. Defeat of the government, ruin of the land, destruction of the Temple, and exile to Babylonia—these were sufficient to cause a people to question the power and justice of its God. In the midst of the attractions of pagan culture, as a defeated community, the exiles could have easily accepted the gods of the conquerors and the verdict of might. Yet the Jewish captives would not abandon Yahweh and denied that he had failed. The Bible tells how they yearned to return to their ancient God and to reestablish their ancient relationship with him. To this people the second Isaiah came with a message of consolation from the Lord. His words are found in the latter part of the Book of Isaiah and are close in style and in spirit to the original Isaiah, whose prophecies fill the first thirty-nine chapters of that book.

Comfort, comfort my people, says your God.

(Isa. 40:1 ff.)

In magnificent passages, rich in splendid visions and language, he captured the hearts of the people and brought hope to the sufferers. Deutero-Isaiah spoke of the great power of the Lord of the universe, who had created the cosmos and who was above all creatures. It was this cosmic creator God who had promised salvation to Israel and surely his word endureth forever. Soon

the glory of the Lord shall be revealed, and all flesh shall see it together.

(Isa. 40:5)

He who created Israel would soon redeem Israel.

The closeness of Yahweh to Israel was revealed in the joyous warm promises he made to the people.

I bring near my deliverance, it is not far off, and my salvation will not tarry; I will put salvation in Zion, for Israel my glory.

(Isa. 46:13)

It is true that Israel has suffered, but it is a temporary condition.

For a brief moment I forsook you, but with great compassion I will gather you. In overflowing wrath for a moment I hid my face from you, but with everlasting love I will have compassion on you, says the Lord your Redeemer.

(Isa. 54:7–10)

Yahweh had a plan for universal redemption, and it involved the special participation of his chosen people. Israel must spread the message of redemption and must demonstrate God's saving power to the nations. The task would be difficult, entailing suffering and humiliation.

Behold my servant, whom I uphold, my chosen, in whom my soul delights; I have put my spirit upon him, he will bring forth justice

to the nations . . . I am the Lord, I have called you in righteous-
ness, I have taken you by the hand and kept you; I have given
you as a covenant to the people, a light to the nations.

(Isa. 42:1–6)

Yahweh addressed his servant, an idealized figure, commissioned to
perform the weighty labor. At present the servant is himself despised and considered abominable. No one would take notice of
him and no one would hearken to his message. But in the future all
would listen to him, kings and princes would recognize the truth.
The servant must suffer, but his suffering has redemptive value. For
the suffering of the servant would atone for the sins of mankind
and would bring liberation to others.

But he was wounded for our transgressions, he was bruised for
our iniquities; upon him the chastisement that made us whole,
and with his stripes we were healed.

(Isa. 53:5–6)

Deutero-Isaiah's image of the servant became the model for Israel, which interpreted its suffering of the present as having redemptive value. The pain of exile was necessary not only for self-
purification and atonement, but the pain was also necessary for the
sake of the salvation of mankind. Israel must become the servant,
bearing witness to Yahweh. The servant, like the prophet, performed
a mission which demanded suffering for the sake of all men.
Through his example of righteousness, others would become righteous and would be led back to their creator. First, Israel itself
would return and be redeemed. Then all flesh would know God, acknowledge his saving work, and seek to become part of his covenant.

This elevated universal message of salvation is reminiscent of the
earlier universal messages of the first Isaiah. This man had prophesied that when the idols had fallen, when human pride and self-
confidence had been unmasked as false trust, all men would turn
to Yahweh and follow his ways.

It shall come to pass in the latter days that the mountain of the
house of the Lord shall be established as the highest of the
mountains, and shall be raised above the hills; and all the nations
shall flow to it, and many peoples shall come and say: "Come let
us go up to the mountain of the Lord, to the house of the God of
Jacob; that he may teach us his ways and that we may walk in
his paths."

(Isa. 2:2–3)

This was the great messianic hope of Israel. At the end of time,
when all nations acknowledged Yahweh as sovereign king and true
God, then universal peace would reign. At that time the cosmos itself would be transformed. Righteousness and peace would prevail
among all creatures. The prophet conceived Yahweh's plan to be
the progressive revelation of himself to the nations through the special mission of Israel toward the end goal of universal knowledge
and universal peace.

Give thanks to the Lord, call upon his name, make known his deeds among the nations, proclaim that his name is exalted. Sing praises to the Lord, for he has done gloriously; let this be known in all the earth. Shout and sing for joy, O inhabitant of Zion, for great in your midst is the Holy One of Israel.

(Isa. 12:4–6)

Israel, defeated and exiled, believed in its sacred historic task and understood the meaning of its punishment. As a nation, Israel possessed and bore the saving religious truth which would eventually be the possession of mankind. Until that great day, Israel was obligated to fulfill the commandment of Yahweh in its communal life, whether in the Holy Land or in exile. The paradoxical fact that in reality this weak and defeated nation could not well represent the power of Yahweh to the world did not seem to disturb the Jews' self-conception, for they denied that political destiny and external reality testified to truth. The Jewish community determined to live by the reality of internal spiritual truth, in which Yahweh's relationship to his people and his plan for history had been revealed. They understood their role in history according to this internal reality and dedicated themselves to fulfilling their task in the face of whatever exigencies external reality might present.

The destroyed national institutions of Jewish life were replaced in Babylonia by two key religious institutions, around which community life was ordered. These were the synagogue and the Torah. With the Temple in ruins, a substitute for the official cult had to be found. To the challenge of how the Lord could be worshiped on profane foreign soil, the response was given that he could indeed be worshiped with a new cult, a cult not located in the Temple and not dependent upon sacrifices. Prayer in sanctuaries consecrated by the people, fasts, and the Sabbath celebration formed the core of the new worship. Israel might be estranged but it was not totally cut off from Yahweh, and the institution of prayer, the expression of the heart of the community and the individual, preserved the living relationship of the faithful to the Lord.

There were individuals who did assimilate to the culture of Babylonia. However, the Jews, as a community, resolved not to accept the gods of Babylonia and not to assimilate to its culture. Rather, they determined to exist as a distinct community, loyal to its national past, guarding its religious tradition, and anticipating a national-religious restoration. The religious and national unity of Israel had been gravely challenged by the destruction and exile, and the challenge was met by the resolution to remain loyal to Yahweh and the religious values of the covenant tradition. The cornerstone of the exilic community was the Word of God, recollected in the sacred literary traditions of the past. Yahweh had disclosed himself to Israel, had spoken through his messengers and through his own acts, and this self-disclosure would now serve as the source of his continuous presence to his people. The traditions telling of Yahweh's acts and his relationship to Israel were gradually gathered to-

A fourteenth-century manuscript depicting Haggadah, service for the Eve of Passover, illustrating the bondage of the Children of Israel in Egypt. (Courtesy of the British Museum.)

gether in Babylonia by the priests. These men, on the basis of these traditions, compiled a history of the world from Creation, preserved in ordered form the words of the prophets, and formulated a priestly code of ritual laws grounded upon earlier cultic prescriptions. These literary traditions became the foundation of exilic life, being the record of Yahweh's words and acts and thus the source of his holiness. They served as a guide to the community in its daily life. Study of the traditions revealed what was demanded in the present. Acquiring knowledge of the past and fulfilling God's commandments became the most sacred activities in the religious life of the Jew. Having accepted the prophetic theodicy and having rededicated itself to Yahweh's service, Israel found in its history and law the means whereby it might remain a holy people, although uprooted from its natural environment.

The duty to remain a holy people dedicated to Yahweh was interpreted by Israel as a duty to remain separate and distinctive. The kingdom of priests and holy nation, in imitation of the holiness of the Lord, would have to be vigilant in avoiding profane contacts with the profane idolatrous environment. A later rabbinical statement found in a commentary to the Book of Leviticus says, "If ye are separated from the nations, ye belong to me; if not, ye belong to Nebuchadnezzar, the king of Babylonia and his companions" (Sifra, Lev. 20:26, 93d). The measure of exclusiveness, which was necessary in order to constitute and maintain the holy community under the conditions imposed by exile, could be attained through legal prohibitions. The prohibitions against mixed marriage and the elaborate dietary laws prevented intimate contact with non-Jews. In addition, the calendar of special religious observances separated Jews from non-Jews and symbolized the determined separate existence of Israel.

The inner will of the exiles succeeded in enabling them to establish an integrated community life within the framework of the religious self-understanding and rule set out in the compilation of ancient traditions and interpreted by the priests. While remaining loyal to this framework and united within this community, the exiles acculturated to a certain extent to the Babylonian environment, achieved success in material pursuits, and reached high positions in the political and economic system. However, this success did not extinguish the sense of exile nor snuff out the hope for eventual restoration to the homeland. The prophet of exile had predicted a speedy redemption, in which all Jews would return to Israel and all nations would come to recognize Yahweh. The rise of Cyrus and his victory over Babylonia seemed to many Jews to signal the world-historical change, which Isaiah had prophesied and which Yahweh had promised. Indeed, in the first year of his conquest of Babylonia, Cyrus issued a decree permitting Jews to return to their land and to reestablish the cult there. This was part of the general policy of moderation through which Persian rulers encouraged local cultural and political autonomy. Thus in 538, permission had been granted and a restoration to the homeland could take place.

RESTORATION   Historical knowledge of the period of the restoration is quite scanty. However, it is certain that the initial response of the Babylonian exiles to the opportunity to return was weak. Under Sheshbazzar and Zerubbabel some did make the trip and did resettle in the homeland. However, most Jews, comfortably established in Babylonia, preferred to support the few returnees morally and financially, but themselves remain in exile. The newly established Palestinian community struggled for its very survival economically, politically, and religiously. The ideal of a glorious material and spiritual renewal was far from realized, and the great disappointment of religious leaders reflected the real situation. True, the Temple was rebuilt in 515 B.C., but only after a twenty-year struggle to obtain funds and labor. It was only with the administrative and religious reform work of Nehemiah and Ezra that order was restored. Nehemiah, appointed by the Persian court, arrived in Palestine between 444 and 440 and proceeded to set up a strong and honest government. He fortified the walls around Jerusalem, thereby providing residents with security from external threat, and he attempted to introduce religious reforms in neglected cultic and ethical law. A thoroughgoing reform in these areas was not instituted until the arrival from Babylonia of another imperial appointee, Ezra the Scribe. Of a priestly family, Ezra brought with him to Palestine the code of the law of Moses, consisting either of the entire Pentateuch or large parts of it compiled by the priests in Babylonia, and this code he proclaimed as the law of the land in the name of the King of Persia. The Law of Moses would be enforced as if it were the law of the Persian monarch, and all those claiming membership in the Jewish people and loyal to Jerusalem would be obligated to observe it. Ezra introduced the Law dramatically by gathering the residents of Jerusalem around him and, while standing upon a platform elevated above the crowd, read aloud from the book of the Hebrew Law. The assembled Jews were apparently quite struck by the reading, and recognizing their sins of violations, repented, knelt down, and worshiped the Lord. The reading was explained to the listeners in Aramaic, the language of daily speech, by the Levites so that all could understand. Study of this law continued in the following days while the Feast of Tabernacles was celebrated. At a later time the people confessed their sins to Yahweh and made a solemn pledge "to observe and act in accordance with all the commands of Yahweh, Our Lord, with his judgments and statutes" (Neh. 9:1–37; 10:29).

During this period the Five Books of the Law were finally canonized. This "Torah" was disseminated among the people; it was taught by the priests throughout the land and became the possession of every Jew. The ideal of piety as devotion to the Torah was accepted and the righteous Jew was one whose "delight is in the Law of the Lord; and on his law he meditates day and night" (Ps. 1:2). Thus, through the combined efforts of Ezra and Nehemiah the small and poor Palestinian community was reconstituted around the Law and recommitted to the fulfillment of Yahwist demands. Zion was once again the dwelling place of God and Jerusalem the cultic center of Judaism. The community based upon the Law was not

An elaborate eighteenth-century Persian silver case used to preserve the Torah in the synagogue. (Courtesy of the Jewish Museum, New York.)

simply a national or ethnic unit, but essentially a religious one. The Jew, no matter where he lived, was to be defined as one loyal to the Law of Yahweh, one devoted to the ancient beliefs and traditions recorded in the Torah.

The following four centuries, from the conquest of Alexander through the first century A.D., were tumultuous and crucial years in the history of the Jews and the evolution of Judaism. It was the time of national hopes and national frustration for the community in the homeland. It was the time of great growth of communities outside Palestine. And it was during this time that the institutions and ideas which would be the foundation of Jewish life until modern times emerged in clear form. By the end of the first century A.D., Judaism had proven that it would survive the spiritual and physical conflicts of the age, and by the third century A.D. the framework had developed, giving meaning and order to the lives of the Jews for the following fifteen hundred years.

The Persian Empire fell to the advance of Alexander's armies in 333. Following the division of Alexander's conquests, Palestine was first ruled over by the Ptolemies, and then by the Seleucids, who defeated the Ptolemies at Banyas in 198. The Seleucid king, Antiochus III, guaranteed autonomy to the Jews and supported the leadership and cult of Jerusalem, in the hands of the High Priest and wealthy aristocracy. The incorporation of Palestine within these successive empires brought Greeks with their economic and political institutions and culture into the land, thus introducing a strain between traditional Judaism and the advanced foreign ideas and values. This strain became increasingly severe. The same tension existed in all diaspora communities where Jews lived within their own religious framework and maintained allegiance to their national homeland but were attracted to and absorbed in part by the hellenistic culture of the environment. This clash between a self-enclosed and self-perpetuating Judaism and the influence of foreign culture, seen in the hellenistic situation, was in fact repeated throughout Jewish history. Later, under Islam, Jews were open to the penetration of Greek culture in Arabic forms and responded by creating a rich Judeo-Arabic culture. The interest in poetry and philosophy, both secular and religious, aroused by the mixing of cultures produced beautiful and highly significant works within the Jewish world. On the other hand, Jewry in Poland and Russia from the sixteenth to the eighteenth centuries responded negatively to foreign influences and gradually shut itself off from creative interaction with them. The tension between the native and the foreign was constant and was experienced as particularly difficult by the exilic communities within the Christian world, which struggled for their very existence.

During the hellenistic period acculturation to Greek ways was quite widespread. Jews became "hellenes" through *paidea* (education), but did so without abandoning their own religious and national culture. The translation of the Torah into Greek, somewhere around 250 B.C., and the translation of other Jewish works attest to this acculturation. The Jews of Alexandria, where the Scriptures were translated, who numbered up to two-fifths of the city's population by the first century B.C., were especially influenced by hellenistic ways and responded to them by adopting much of Greek culture into their own patterns. Philo, the great Jewish thinker of Alexandria, produced a Jewish theology in response to the thought of Plato and earlier Greek philosophers.

While they absorbed much of the new and the foreign, Jews propagated their own religious culture with apparent success. Adherence to Judaism by non-Jews was certainly not a new phenomenon. Deutero-Isaiah described "those who joined themselves to Yahweh"

"And thou shalt smite on the rocke, and water shall come out of it, that the people may drink," a color lithograph by Marc Chagall from The Story of the Exodus, *published by Leon Amiel, Paris, 1966. (Courtesy of the Museum of Modern Art, New York. Gift of Lester Avnet.)*

(Isa. 56:3–7), and there were occasional converts from the Babylonian period on. However, large-scale religious conversion dates from the hellenistic period, especially during the second and first centuries B.C. Many residents of the Roman Empire were searching for significant religious experience and meaning because philosophical sophistication and urbanization had undermined traditional paganism but had not provided any replacement for the religious relationship. The faith of Yahweh and the community of the faithful Jews were quite attractive, and many accepted Judaism fully or in part. Jewish missionaries carried the message of Yahweh throughout the hellenized world, emphasizing its universal and ethical aspects. It has been estimated that by the first century A.D. the Jewish population of the empire reached eight million and that one out of ten members of the empire was Jewish, and in the Eastern Mediterranean area one out of five was a Jew. Yet as Jews converted gentiles, they were themselves hellenized to one extent or another.

The hellenization of the Jews was not limited to the diaspora. The penetration of the universal hellenistic civilization, the civilization of the conquerors, into Palestine was quite extensive. A coterie of hellenized Jerusalemites, centered around the Greek gymnasium built within the holy city, attempted to spread their newly adopted cultural patterns to the majority of the Jewish population. The hellenizers, drawn mainly from the upper class, abrogated Jewish law in order to come closer to the life-style and ways of the non-Jewish powers. Under the leadership of Jason and then Menelaus, appointed High Priests by Antiochus IV Epiphanes, a policy of national hellenization was instituted. A fortified Greek polis called the *acra* was erected opposite the Temple mount, constituting a pagan city within the holy city. Engaging in Greek sports, imitating Greek styles in dress and appearance, and worshiping Greek gods were open activities within the precincts of the polis. Further, Yahweh was transformed by the hellenizers into a Greek high god, being identified with Zeus Olympus and becoming part of the hellenic pantheon. The cult of the emperor was also accepted.

To the traditional Jews of Jerusalem and the countryside, the ways of the hellenizers were a scandal and an abomination. The loyal and pious, the *hasidim,* were uncompromising in their refusal to adopt the innovations. Such intransigence frustrated the efforts of the aristocracy and angered Antiochus IV, who was intent upon establishing cultural and political unity within the lands under his control. Opposition to hellenization on the part of the faithful resulted in the proclamation of the oppressive decrees of 168 B.C. by the king. These decrees, which were fully supported by the Jewish hellenizers, prohibited regular sacrifices in the Temple; forbade the observance of the Sabbath and Jewish festivals; did away with circumcision; ordered the introduction of the cult of Zeus Olympus into the Temple, the construction of pagan altars in the land, and the sacrifice of swine upon them (forbidden in Jewish law); and finally commanded the destruction of Torah scrolls. The intent was to extirpate Judaism completely, and the response of the loyal Jews could only be one of total resistance. As the measures were enforced, many who refused to comply with them were slaughtered. Finally, full rebellion broke out, led by the priest Mattathias and his five sons. When Mattathias died in 166, his son Judah, called the Maccabee (which probably means hammer), took command. Jews, mainly from the peasantry, who would not be coerced into pagan ways, joined the rebel band and engaged in guerilla warfare. They were highly successful in raiding and harassing the more organized and technically advanced but less mobile Seleucid army. In a major engagement in 165, Judah defeated a large Syrian force under Lysias, and Antiochus, fighting a war against the Parthians in the east, was obliged to sue for peace. The hellenizing decrees of 168 were rescinded, the religious persecution ended, and the attempt to suppress Judaism defeated. Judah marched triumphantly into Jerusalem, removed the statue of Zeus—"the abomination of desolation" (Dan. 9:27, 11:31)—from the Temple, and reestablished the Law of Moses in the holy city. In 164, after thorough purification, the Temple was reconsecrated in a feast of dedication, Hanukah, which was then proclaimed as a national-religious festival for all Jews.

The victory of the Maccabees and the independent government which their descendants, the Hasmoneans, maintained for about one hundred years represents a brief chapter in the total history of Judaism. But it represents the victory of both national and traditional religious forces, the resistance of the old Yahwist order to forced hellenization. The yoke of the heathen was indeed removed from Israel. Although the conflict with hellenism, with foreign physical and spiritual forces, went on, the victory of the Maccabees lies in their reversal of the policy of total submission and total assimilation pursued by the hellenizing elite. During the following centuries Jews did accommodate to and adopt foreign values and ideas, but they were able to do so without abandoning their national and religious traditions. Judaism could develop creatively, remaining true to its essential self and yet open to the influences of outside culture.

The political independence established under the Hasmoneans was short-lived. In 63 B.C. the armies of Pompey conquered Palestine and the Jews became subjects of the Roman Empire, the greatest and most powerful empire of the ancient world. This loss of political autonomy had serious consequences for Jewish consciousness. First, the Hasmoneans had disappointed the hopes of the people by failing to inaugurate anything resembling the just and prosperous state projected in the religious ideals of the nation. And now once again a foreign power had subjugated Israel, bringing pagan ways and pagan authority into the Holy Land. Israel had been a worldly people whose deep religious hopes rested in the establishment of a kingdom of God on this earth. However, successive disappointments led to the development of more radical eschatological ideas. In this period of conflict and turmoil the notion that only a supernatural catastrophe could change the world and that only a totally new world order could save corrupt mankind became part of the Jewish consciousness. The world was too evil and men too sinful for the traditional religious conceptions of repentance, atonement, and renewal to be any longer sufficient. Nothing less than a total transformation, begun on the initiative of God and carried out by his transcendent agent, would effect an end to the sufferings of this-worldly existence.

Between the third century B.C. and the first century A.D. a rich literature describing the future catastrophic events which would bring about the longed-for total transformation developed in Palestine and in the diaspora. This literature is called "apocalyptic"— meaning the revelation of secret things, referring to the secret

THE EMERGENCE
OF THE
APOCALYPTIC
SPIRIT

events of the end of days—and is characterized by rich fantastic visions and descriptions. The apocalyptic writer allowed his imagination to sketch freely a historical sequence in which the powers of evil are to be crushed by the powers of good; death, sickness, and suffering are to end; and the just, so long persecuted, are to be redeemed. This next world-age will be a transcendental one, totally different from the hopelessly corrupt world of the present. History, as it is known in this world, will come to an end, and an unknown and unearthly time will be inaugurated. Apocalypticism posits an inherent dualism between good and evil, between this aeon and the future aeon, a dualism founded in continuous frustration and disappointment. The visions of the prophets seemed to recede, as the course of history progressed steadily away from the paths of Yahweh toward the paths of evil.

Already in the time of Antiochus Epiphanes the limit of suffering in this world was being reached and apocalyptic hopes began to emerge. How long would the captivity endure? How long would the chosen people bear persecution? The author of the Book of Daniel asked these questions and presented a developed apocalyptic answer to them. In the seventh chapter he depicted the four horrible beasts representing the four successive oppressive international powers, which come before the throne of the Ancient of Days, Yahweh, to be judged for their evil deeds. Daniel described the execution of the divine sentence upon the evil powers and the establishment of the longed-for kingdom of the saints. He also described the apocalyptic figure of the "son of man," God's representative, who comes surrounded by clouds to bring in the kingdom. He is the apocalyptic Messiah, a semidivine and semihuman figure, called forth to accomplish the miraculous events of the eschaton.

> *I saw in the night visions and behold, with the clouds of heaven, there came one like a son of man, and he came to the Ancient of Days and was presented before him. And to him was given dominion and glory and kingdom, that all peoples, nations, and languages should serve him; his dominion is an everlasting dominion which shall not pass away, and his kingdom one that shall not be destroyed.*
>
> (Daniel 7:13–14)

Daniel forsaw an end to national and religious adversity. God's victory over evil would soon come and man's victory over suffering and death would be accomplished. To Israel the apocalyptic message brought consolation and hope.

> *And at that time shall arise Michael, the great prince who has charge of your people. And there shall be a time of trouble, such as never has been since there was a nation till that time; but at that time your people shall be delivered . . .*
>
> (Daniel 12:1–3)

The people of Israel, still trusting in the covenant, still atoning for their sins and enduring suffering, were promised redemption in the near future. Yahweh's kingdom would be established and the world utterly changed.

Of course, Daniel's vision was not actualized, but his hopes were adopted and intensified as political conditions worsened. Books like Enoch, 4 Ezra, the Sibylline Oracles, Jubilees, and the Testaments of the Twelve Patriarchs, known as pseudoepigraphical works because of their erroneous ascriptions to authors, developed legendary portrayals of the great end of days, which was always seen as near at hand. Jews yearned for that age to come, and found consolation in the apocalyptics' depictions of it. One group of Jews, the Essenes, separated themselves from the people in order to prepare for the end of days. Living an ascetic communal life on the shores of the Dead Sea, they formed an army of the purified elect, who would aid in the great process of transformation. The Essenes cultivated apocalyptic literature, fully believing in the immediate reality of its promises. Other Jews, not as radically inclined, were still highly influenced by the apocalyptic movement. Within Pharisaic circles (the more moderate but progressive stream of Judaism) certain apocalyptic notions, such as the radical breakthrough of a new order and the resurrection of the dead, were accepted and indeed cherished.

During this same period another trend within Judaism developed, based upon the desire for total change found in apocalypticism. This new religious development was *merkavah* mysticism, whose literary productions date from the first century B.C. and continue until several centuries after the common era, and whose doctrines became highly significant for all later Jewish and Christian mystical movements. The first-century mystical tradition is related to both apocalypticism and gnosticism. Indeed, it is rooted in the apocalyptic and gnostic rejection of history and in their desire to find meaning and solace in some ahistorical visionary reality. The mystic turned away from this world to speculate on a prehistoric age, the age of Creation, or the future posthistoric age. The story of Genesis (*maaseh bereshit*) and the chariot vision of Ezekiel (*maaseh merkavah*) served as his texts and formed the constant basis of Jewish mystical speculation.

The earliest mysticism was confined to small groups of men, drawn from apocalyptics and from important rabbinic circles, who elaborated an esoteric tradition around the interpretation of Ezekiel's famous first chapter, the chariot (*merkavah*) vision. Desiring desperately to find an escape from the cruel fate history had visited upon their people, these men yearned to step outside of time. They believed that the soul was imprisoned in an earthly cage, and they sought a route for its escape and return to its true spiritual home. The *merkavah* mystics described the ascent of the soul through seven heavenly spheres toward the throne of God, an ascent marked by obstacles presented by demonic powers and constant danger. The mystic trained himself for this ascent through ascetic exercises and intense spiritual reflection. He armed himself with magical devices which offered protection against the evil demons.

And he patiently labored to rise up, to overcome all barriers, and to reach his ultimate goal—a vision of the true King upon his throne. The Jewish mystical quest ended in vision rather than union. The distinction between man and God, the gulf between the finite and the infinite, was not to be overcome. Therefore, the mystic did not seek to lose his self in a final union with the deity, but attained a vision of the divine majesty which would enable him to live on, to survive in the reality of earthly existence. In a great mystical tract of the first century, the *Greater Hekhalot,* the true goal of the mystic quest is stated explicitly: "When will he see heavenly majesty? When will he hear of the final time of redemption? When will he perceive what no eye has yet perceived?" The Jewish mystic hungered for release from the evils of this world and the knowledge which would bring release for all men. He believed that what he in his individual ascent might learn would eventually become the property of mankind, in the end of time when all men would be redeemed and would all witness God's glory.

Although the masses of Jews did not join in mystical speculation, they shared the longings and hopes of the mystics. Rooted in more traditional religious concepts, they saw themselves as members of a community which politically and spiritually opposed those who ruled over that community. They desired freedom from the oppressor and freedom from the sufferings of this-worldly existence. The Jewish community of the first century B.C. and first century A.D. waited for redemption, mixing prophetic eschatological hopes with newer apocalyptic visions, but always trusting in God's speedy intervention. It was in the midst of this atmosphere of expectancy and hope that Christianity arose.

CHRISTIANITY IN HISTORICAL PERSPECTIVE

Christianity came into existence within Judaism and within the Judaic world of the first century of our era. It was the product of Jewish messianic hopes and expectations and was considered by its adherents to be their fulfillment. It was at first one more tendency or point of view within Judaism, but it soon gained gentile converts and before long became a separate and predominantly gentile religion. Christianity arose within a Judaism which had been restored to Jerusalem and the surrounding country when the Persian intervention put an end to the Babylonian exile (537 B.C.). It was a Judaism resulting from the renewal of Jewish religious life and national existence under Ezra and Nehemiah and which had seen the partially successful attempt of Judas Maccabeus to restore national independence and rid Judaism of alien intrusions into its religious life (165–161). It was a time when apocalyptic expectations had come to play an important part in Jewish psychology and when hopes abounded for God's intervention into the history of the people to bring about its fulfillment. Many related such intervention to political rebellion against the Roman rule as in the revolt led by Judas the Galilean about the beginning of the Christian era as we now reckon it.

Judaism after the exile developed several tendencies of religious opinion, and the religious and national situation into which the central figure of the new religion, Jesus of Nazareth, was born was a complex one. Aside from smaller sects, at least four groups may be distinguished, each of which had some influence upon the career of Jesus and the development of the early church.

First and most important are the Pharisees, probably derived from the "pious ones" (*hasidim*), who supported and were involved in the Maccabean revolt against Greek paganism. Josephus, the Jewish writer of the first century and historian of the Jewish War against the Romans in A.D. 66–70, considered them to be the leading Jewish religious group and the most accurate interpreters of the law. The Pharisees placed great emphasis upon obedience to the law, but they also looked forward to a fulfillment of Israel's sacred destiny and believed in the resurrection of the dead. Before the defeat of the uprising of 66–70, which was a terrible disaster, they probably shared the widespread apocalyptic hopes and messianic expectations. They were not simply concerned with Israel as a group; their expectation of the resurrection indicates the importance they gave to individual as well as group religiosity, to individual as well as group hope for delivery and salvation.

The next important group was the priestly aristocracy, the Sadducees, who controlled the ritual sacrifice and worship of the Temple. This aspect of Jewish life had declined in importance at a time when a majority of Jews lived outside Palestine and when the synagogue in Palestine and abroad had come to be a new center for the study of the law and for nonsacrificial worship. Yet Jerusalem with its Temple was the center of Judaism and the symbolic heart of its national and religious existence. All Jewish groups shared in its forms of worship, and the earliest Christian literature depicts not only Jesus but the early Church members in Jerusalem participating in its life. The Sadducees held their position as priests by hereditary right and were often wealthy. They practiced a kind of cooperation and compromise with the Roman power. They accepted only the word of scripture, tried to minimize the application of the law to the details of daily life in opposition to the Pharisees, and did not believe in the resurrection of the dead.

The third group important in the Jewish world in which Christianity arose were the Essenes, who unlike the first two, are not mentioned in the New Testament. Josephus speaks of them as cultivating "peculiar sanctity," shunning pleasures, and regarding self-control as "a special virtue." The discovery of the Dead Sea Scrolls less than two decades ago and the study of their texts has shed considerable new light upon this group. The Qumran group who left the scrolls behind were in all probability Essenes. They withdrew from the common life of the Jewish people and set up monastic communities taking the radical view of rejecting the evil and darkness of ordinary existence. They looked forward to a coming triumph of good over evil which would be both a culmination of history and a fulfillment of Israel. They saw themselves fulfilling the call of Isaiah to prepare a highway in the desert for God's coming. They lived in the tension of eschatological or apocalyptic hope and expectation and saw themselves as helping to hasten the blessed day.

A fourth group, of which the New Testament indicates that at least one of Jesus' disciples had been a member, is that of the Zealots. They probably originated around the time of the revolt of Judas the Galilean against the census taken under the Roman procurator Quirinius. They were absolutely opposed to foreign domination and the payment of taxes to the foreign rulers. They were a dis-

The rock fortress of Masada, overlooking the Dead Sea, the site of major drama in the first century A.D. when Jewish rebels committed mass suicide rather than submit to the Romans. (Courtesy of the Israel Government Tourist Office.)

tinct minority and appear to have been regarded with disapproval by the majority of Jews. They practiced political violence and the Romans referred to them as *sicarii*, or "stabbers," because of their prowess with the dagger. They became important in 66 as the leading advocates of war against Rome and remained important enough to take part in another rebellion three generations later.

The relation of Christianity to these groups is a difficult and a complex one, and we have little historical evidence allowing us to see it in detail. The New Testament speaks critically of the Pharisees and accuses them of hypocricy, yet Jesus and his followers shared their belief in the resurrection of the dead and their emphasis upon the individual as well as the collective aspects of religious life. Jesus also appears to have generally followed the Pharisaic religious discipline. Paul, who was most influential in setting aside the details of the Jewish Law for the new Church, was himself a former Pharisee.

The similarities of the teachings of Jesus to those of the Teacher of Righteousness mentioned in the Dead Sea texts has engaged the attention of scholars. The followers of Jesus soon came to set themselves apart, somewhat like the Essenes, though they did not form monastic communities, and, like them, they saw the present age as corrupt and evil. The new Christian Church did not insist upon the detailed Hebraic law as did the Qumran group, although they shared with them the high significance attached to moral standards.

The influence of the Sadducees upon the early Church appears in any immediate sense to be that of opposition to Jesus and his followers. However, they may be said to have had a remote and indirect influence upon the development of Christian ideas of worship. This becomes visible later on, when the Church began to interpret its own worship as a transformed version of temple sacrifice.

The relation of Jesus and his followers to the Zealots has fascinated some. It has been suggested that Jesus could have been a Zealot and that he expected to bring about a rebellion against the Roman power which would initiate God's intervention and the beginning of the messianic age. To hold this point of view one must interpret the peaceful messianic message of the New Testament as a later reaction coming after the defeat of Jesus and his alleged revolutionary plans. The evidence for such a connection of Jesus with the Zealots is fragmentary and like so much such evidence is open to contrary interpretations. It can at best be evaluated only by scholars thoroughly familiar with the data and it has certainly not been given credence by the vast majority of them.

Despite the divisions which we have indicated in Jewish life, Jewish religion at the time possessed a deeper unity. A complex of apocalyptic and eschatological ideas was central to it in quite strategic respects. The idea of God as Lord of history about to intervene to bring about its redemption and apotheosis, the centrality of the Jews as a covenant people in this historical and cosmic drama, the emphasis upon a sharp division between good and evil, and the tendency to see the Jewish role as an increasingly universal one bringing the light of Yahweh to the nations—all constitute a significant core of Jewish religiosity at the time. Jewish history had been a history of frustration and defeat punctuated by brief periods of triumph or respite. The Jewish religious writers who interpreted the meaning of that history for the nation, providing what became the widely accepted interpretation, saw all this as the favor and disfavor of Yahweh. Israel's misfortunes, so many and so harsh, were God's judgments upon his chosen people for their transgressions. Yet faith was not lost. Indeed, misfortune seemed to strengthen the abiding hope that God would intervene, would send his anointed one, would redeem Israel and begin a new age of the world for all men.

Those converted to Christianity felt that it was the fulfillment of these hopes. It took over the major Jewish ideas and wove them into the fabric of its own teachings. It saw itself as the renewal and fulfillment of the covenant and its extension to all who would believe. It embraced as central to the religious life the Jewish emphasis upon morality—upon righteousness as a personal disposition and sin as an offense against God himself. It saw God as the Lord of history and itself as the new community based upon the renewed covenant resulting from his intervention through Jesus in the "fullness of times." It saw Jesus as the Messiah of Israel, the expected one anointed of Yahweh, and it looked forward to his return to earth to be followed by the end of the present world, the resurrection of the dead, and the final judgment of all men.

Though Jesus was an innovator because he spoke and embodied God's revelation in a new time and became the bearer of its message to later gentile generations, the Jewish character of his central moral teaching is clear. The oldest Gospel records that when he was challenged by an opponent, " 'Which commandment is the first of all?' he answered, 'Hear, O Israel: The Lord our God, the Lord is one; and you shall love the Lord your God with all your heart, and with all your soul, and with all your mind, and with all your strength!' The second is this, 'You shall love your neighbor as yourself. There is no other commandment greater than these' " (Mark 12:28–31). It is significant that here Jesus quotes from the sixth chapter of Deuteronomy and from the nineteenth chapter of Leviticus. Jesus quoted what is known as the *Shema*, recognized from time immemorial as the central Jewish confession of faith and standard of morals. It is this which the devout Jew recites three times daily as the fulfillment of divine command. In faith and morals Christianity took its stand on the basis of the Judaic revelation. Moreover, all three Synoptic Gospels (Matthew, Mark, and Luke) show Jesus leaving Galilee after a time of preaching and teaching in his native region and going to Jerusalem. They all three show him at this time telling his disciples that he was the Messiah, thus identifying himself with the deepest yearnings and aspirations of the Jewish people.

And Jesus went on with his disciples to the villages of Caesarea Philippi; and on the way he asked his disciples, "Who do men say that I am?" And they told him, "John the Baptist; and others say Elijah; and others one of the prophets." And he asked them, "But who do you say that I am?" Peter answered him, "You are the Christ [that is, the anointed one, the Messiah]." And he charged them to tell no one about him. And he began to teach them that the Son of man must suffer many things, and be rejected by the elders and the chief priests and the scribes, and be killed and after three days rise again. And he said this plainly.
        (Mark 8:27–32; see also Matt. 16:13 ff. and Luke 9:18 ff.)

Thus was Christianity founded by a prophetic Jewish figure who took his stand within the Jewish religious tradition and in the consciousness of his messianic mission announced its imminent fulfillment.

JESUS OF NAZARETH We shall not attempt here to essay the impossible task of presenting the preaching, teaching, healing, and suffering of Jesus of
Nazareth apart from the memory of them, the commentary upon
them, and the development of their meaning to be found in the New
Testament. Nor shall we try to reconstruct the image of the figure of
Jesus himself as the historical personage which lies behind his impact on the Gospel narratives. The New Testament itself is the
product of the early Christian community, which before the end of
the first century began to write down its earlier oral traditions and
to collect letters and other written matter which had circulated
among its various churches. By the end of the second century these
writings had been subjected to the critical appraisal of the Church,
some accepted and some rejected, and what is called the canon
(Greek *kanon,* "rule" or "norm") established. Twenty of twenty-
seven books making up the present New Testament were accepted
as canonical in the Church by the year 200, and the differences that
did exist were decidedly of a minor character. Thus what the New
Testament presents to us are those characteristics of Jesus and
those aspects of his career which were the foundation of the faith
of the Church seen in the light of the development of that faith that
had taken place within the community in the first three or four generations.

According to the Gospel narratives Jesus preached, taught,
healed, died, and rose from the dead. He preached the imminence
of the Kingdom of God and called for repentance. "The time is fulfilled, and the kingdom of God is at hand; repent, and believe in the
gospel" (Mark 1:15; see also Mark 4:17). The kingdom which Jesus
proclaimed was an inner condition and relationship to God and an
outer expression of moral behavior and compassion with respect to
one's fellow man and also a personal and ethical reality which
moved toward an imminent eschatological fulfillment as may be
seen from his parables as set forth in the synoptic gospels.

In these Gospels one also sees the high esteem in which his followers and the early Church held Jesus. In the nativity stories (Matt.
2; Luke 1–2) Jesus' birth, which probably took place between 4 and
2 B.C., is told as accompanied by the apparition of angels, the visitation of gentile religious leaders bearing gifts, the alarm and violence of Herod threatened by the event, and by prophetic witness
from pious Jews, which proclaimed the child "a light for revelation
to the Gentiles and for the glory to thy people Israel" (Luke 2:32).
Indeed he is born of a virgin and of the Davidic line, signifying his
relationship to God and his special mission. Mark's account of his
baptism by John the Baptist states that "when he came up out of
the water, immediately he saw the heavens opened and the Spirit
descending upon him like a dove; and a voice came from heaven,
'Thou art my beloved Son; with thee I am well pleased'" (Mark
1:10–11), an event which later gospels present somewhat more as
an external happening. In the story of the transfiguration the three
apostles Peter, James, and John see Jesus transformed in appearance and standing with Moses and Elijah, the two great archetypal
Jewish figures symbolizing the Law and the prophets. Jesus' central

Rembrandt, Christ Preaching. (*Courtesy of The Metropolitan Museum of Art. Bequest of Mrs. H. O. Havemeyer, 1929. The H. O. Havemeyer Collection.*)

position symbolizes the Christian belief that he is the final fulfillment of both the Law and the prophets, which he declared he had "come not to abolish but to fulfill" (Matt. 5:17). In the temptation narrative we see Jesus challenged by the powers of evil and offered this-worldly success and glory which he spurns, quoting Deuteronomy, "Man shall not live by bread alone but by every word that proceeds from the mouth of God" and "You shall worship the Lord your God and him only shall you serve" (Matt. 4:4 and 4:10; see also Luke 4:1–13).

Central to Jesus' teaching was love of God and one's fellow man. Jesus accepted and took his stand upon the Hebraic conviction of the immediacy of God and the centrality of ethics, and in typical Jewish fashion he saw them as inseparable parts of a single reality. Central to his preaching was a call for repentance, a demand for justice and righteousness from men, and an assurance of mercy from God. Jesus stressed the importance of love—of man's love for God and God's love for man—thus giving renewed emphasis to ideas found in Hosea, Jeremiah, and Isaiah. The biblical idea of love is not, however, a phenomenon of structureless sentimentality to which everything is indifferently permitted. While it is a deep emotional reality characterized by man's yearning and God's mercy and consolation, it involves the ethical demands of Old and New Testaments as central to its essential character, and while it envisages God as the forgiving father and the good shepherd, it also sees him as the stern judge of the unrighteous and unrepentant. Indeed the Gospel of Matthew presents Jesus himself acting as judge on the day of final judgment separating the righteous from the evil ones "as a shepherd separates the sheep from the goats" and calling the righteous to God saying, "Come, O blessed of my Father, inherit the kingdom prepared for you from the foundation of the world; for I was hungry and you gave me food, I was thirsty and you gave me drink, I was naked and you clothed me, I was sick and you visited me, I was imprisoned and you came to me . . . [for] as you did it to one of the least of these my brethren, you did it to me." But to the evil and the unrepentant he says, " 'Depart from me, you cursed, into the eternal fire prepared for the devil and his angels' . . . and they will go away into eternal punishment, but the righteous into eternal life" (Matt. 25:31–46).

Like the pious Jew that he was, Jesus emphasized the importance of prayer although he was critical of some current practices. He counseled his followers against long prayers in public and admonished them to pray briefly and in private. Before his death we find Jesus subduing his own interior turmoil through prayer. Jesus teaches men to pray with assurance that prayer is answered. The only formal prayer attributed to Jesus himself by the New Testament is found in the Gospels of Matthew and Luke, where Jesus says: "Pray then like this:

Our Father who art in heaven,
Hallowed be thy name.
Thy kingdom come,
Thy will be done,
On earth as it is in heaven.
Give us this day our daily bread;
And forgive us our debts,
As we forgive our debtors;
And lead us not into temptation,
But deliver us from evil."

(Matt. 6:9–13)

The Gospel narratives depict Jesus performing miracles or what the Greek text sees as expressions of power (*dynamis*), feeding the hungry, healing the sick, and curing the tormented whom the New Testament sees as possessed by demons. Matthew reports that it was said of him with astonishment, "He has done all things well; he even makes the deaf hear and the dumb speak" (Matt. 7:37). Peter in The Acts of the Apostles is reported as saying that "God anointed Jesus of Nazareth with the Holy Spirit and with power; . . . he went about doing good and healing all that were oppressed by the devil, for God was with him" (Acts 10:38). These miracles so bothersome to modern thought were seen by the early Church as the breakthrough of divine power into the life of men, as mighty works of God heralding the kingdom, the signs (*semeoin*) and portents (*teras*) of its imminence. They were also understood in the early Church as the evidence of Jesus' victory over the demons which the popular thought of that period conceived as ubiquitous powers of present evil.

Of central significance to the meaning of Christianity and to the teaching of the churches for centuries is the passion and death of Jesus. All three Synoptic Gospels show Jesus deliberately going to

Jerusalem for the celebration of the Passover feast, an event he appears to have anticipated as closely bound up with the manifestation of his own messianic mission. At Jerusalem he entered the city riding upon an ass and receiving the acclamation of the multitudes according to the synoptic accounts, an expression of messiahship reminiscent of the ass-riding princes of the early Israelite confederation as portrayed in the Song of Deborah and recalling the words of Zechariah,

> *Rejoice greatly, O daughter of Zion!*
>   *Shout aloud, O daughter of Jerusalem!*
> *Lo, your king comes to you;*
> *triumphant and victorious is he,*
> *humble and riding on an ass,*
> *on a colt the foal of an ass.*
>
> (Zech. 9:9)

These Gospels show him driving out "those who sold and those who bought in the temple" (Mark 11:15), another act displaying messianic claims. On Thursday evening of that week he ate a supper with his disciples which has become the archetype of the basic Christian act of worship ever since. The bread and wine of the traditional seder were interpreted by Jesus as his body and blood.

> *And as they were eating, he took bread, and blessed, and broke it, and gave it to them, and said, "Take; this is my body." And he took a cup, and when he had given thanks he gave it to them, and they all drank of it. And he said to them, "This is my blood of the covenant, which is poured out for many."*
>
> (Mark 14:22–24)

After appearing before the Jewish Council (Sanhedrin), where he affirmed his messianic mission and made reference to the messianic Book of Daniel, and before the Roman procurator, he was put to death. On the cross on which he died the Roman procurator nailed a sign stating that this man was king of the Jews. Thus in the eyes of this world and by its standards the life of Jesus ended in bitter defeat and utter failure. He died forsaken. One of his own chosen twelve had betrayed him to his enemies and their senior member had denied him. After his death the others apparently returned to Galilee, their native region, disillusioned and discouraged in the death of him who they had hoped "was the one to redeem Israel" (Luke 24:21).

A short time after these seemingly disastrous events the followers of Jesus, except for him who betrayed him, who, according to Matthew's Gospel, hung himself in remorse, are found back together in Jerusalem and are actively propagating the messiahship of Jesus. It was the conviction of these men and the belief of the early Church which resulted from their efforts that Jesus had risen from the dead and that his death and resurrection taken together represented the beginning of that messianic kingdom which Jesus had proclaimed in

Marcello Muccini, Crucifixion, *1947; a plate from the portfolio* 6 Acqueforti di Muccini, Urbinati Vespignai. (*Courtesy of the Museum of Modern Art, New York. Purchase.*)

his own earthly ministry. The resurrection became the keystone of the Christian faith, the guarantee that Jesus was of God and the sign of the general resurrection to come. In one of the earliest Christian writings (A.D. 51 or 52) we find the Apostle Paul saying:

Now if Christ is preached as raised from the dead, how can some of you say that there is no resurrection of the dead? But if there is no resurrection of the dead, then Christ has not been raised; if Christ has not been raised, then our preaching is in vain and your faith is in vain. We are even found to be misrepresenting God, because we testified of God that he raised Christ, whom he did not raise if it is true that the dead are not raised. If Christ has not been raised, your faith is futile and you are still in your sins. Then those who have fallen asleep in Christ have perished. If for this life only we have hoped in Christ, we are of all men most to be pitied. But in fact Christ has been raised from the dead, the first fruits of those who have fallen asleep.

(1 Cor. 15:12–20)

There are several New Testament sources in which we find versions of the tradition of Jesus' resurrection as it existed in the early Christian community. Chief among them are 1 Corinthians 15:3–8, Mark 16:1–8, Matthew 28:1–20, Luke 24:1–53, and John 20:1–21:25. They differ among themselves in considerable detail. In the Pauline account Jesus after his death appears first to Peter, although in the Synoptic Gospels there is no mention of an appearance to Peter. In the Gospels of Matthew and Mark only the women visit the tomb, but in Luke's, Peter follows by himself. Such differences could be listed at length. But the testimony of all traditions is that Jesus, whom the early followers had known in his earthly existence, had been put to death, was interred in a tomb, had been raised from the dead, and had appeared to numerous eyewitnesses. This Easter event was the foundation of the Christian faith. It was not only a beginning of the new age, not only a victory over death, but a victory over sin. "For we know that Christ being raised from the dead will never die again; death no longer has dominion over him. The death he died he died to sin, once for all, but the life he lives he lives to God. So you also must consider yourselves dead to sin and alive to God in Jesus Christ" (Rom. 6:9–11). In this death and resurrection the followers of Jesus have been "set free from sin," and as a result share in "sanctification and its end, eternal life" (Rom. 6:22). The new messianic age had commenced. Jesus had returned to the Father but he would come again. The earliest gospel has Jesus saying at his last supper, "Truly, I say to you, I shall not drink again of the fruit of the vine until that day when I drink it new in the kingdom of God" (Mark 14:25). The new communities which came together in response to the preaching (*Kerygma*) of Jesus' disciples repeated the communion of bread and wine in which they felt the hidden presence of their risen Lord and in which they proclaimed "the Lord's death until he comes" (1 Cor. 11:26). They lived in the expectation of the return of Jesus in glory, an event which they apparently felt would come in their own lifetimes.

Following the four Gospels in the New Testament is found the Book called The Acts of the Apostles. It was written by Luke, the author of the third synoptic gospel, sometime during the last two decades of the first century. It has often been called the first Church history

THE EARLY CHURCH

because it gives us a picture of the young Christian community in the Apostolic age. Though it is not a history in our modern sense of the word, since it is written as a kind of apologia and from a particular theological point of view, it does reflect the early Church and provides valuable insights into its life. It begins by raising the question asked of the risen Christ of when the new messianic age would achieve its full realization.

> *So when they had come together they asked him, "Lord, will you at this time restore the kingdom to Israel?" He said to them, "It is not for you to know times or seasons which the Father has fixed by his own authority. But you shall receive power when the Holy Spirit has come upon you; and you shall be my witnesses in Jerusalem and all Judea and Samaria and to the end of the earth."*
>
> (Acts 1:6–8)

Then is recounted what Christians call the ascension of Jesus: "he was lifted up, and a cloud took him out of sight" (Acts 1:9). The second chapter begins with an account of the Pentecost event in which Christians believe the close followers of Jesus "gathered together in one place" were "filled with the Holy Spirit" which sent them forth preaching the message of the new church (Acts 2:1–13).

Thus does a document of the early Church present the fundamental conditions characteristic of the infant Christian community—the absence of Jesus now believed to be risen and returned to the Father, the expectation of his return and the lack of knowledge of the times and seasons fixed by God for its occurrence, and the orientation to proselytism. We next read the preaching of Peter, giving us an example of the early *Kerygma*. Following this the book is divided into two parts, the first showing us the progress of the Church within Palestine, the second the development of missionary work abroad and its triumphant expansion in the gentile world. In the preaching of Acts we see the presentation of Jesus' career and its meaning and the liberal use of Old Testament quotations to support the argument and show Jesus as the promised one, as may be seen in the sermon of Peter in the second chapter and that of Paul in the thirteenth. The book reflects the conviction of the author that the promises to Israel were being fulfilled in the new Church, which was the new Israel and heir to the old. Here we see the new Church defining itself as the authentic covenant community and oriented to the conversion of gentiles, although it appears still predominantly Jewish in its composition.

We see in Acts the confrontation by the early Christian group of the first basic decisive issue of Christian history—the one whose outcome would decide whether or not there would be any Christian history. Will the new group, believing in the messiahship of Jesus and awaiting his second coming, remain a sect within the confines of Judaism or will it become an independent religious community with its own essential character and destiny? Of course the question, like all significant historical questions, was neither grasped nor met in this abstract form, but rather in terms of concrete incidents in the historical experience of the group. In Acts we see the author's conviction that the Jewish nation will not as a whole accept the new proclamation of Jesus' disciples, although Luke obviously considered it to be the legitimate continuation and fulfillment of the entire Jewish past. Thus, in speaking to Cornelius and his friends, Luke has Peter at the beginning of the gentile mission declare that "God shows no partiality, but in every nation anyone who fears him and does what is right is acceptable to him" (Acts 10:34–35). And the Book of Acts ends with Paul preaching to the Jews of the diaspora living in Rome and "trying to convince them about Jesus both from the law of Moses and from the prophets. And some were convinced by what he said while others disbelieved" (Acts 28:23–24). To those who disbelieved Paul quoted Isaiah and declared that "this salvation of God has been sent to the Gentiles; they will listen." In the speech and death of Stephen we find another incident and one in which Paul was involved in quite another way. The charges against Stephen indicate that he and other members of the new community were questioning the temple worship and the law, and the speech which Luke attributes to him sets forth a developed theological position, accuses the Jewish authorities of Jesus' death, and questions the efficacy of temple worship. Here we see not only difficulties between the new group and the religious authorities of Judaism but also the internal conflict within the new Church with respect to its own Judaic character. Chapter 6 of Acts speaks of two groups of Christians, Hellenists and Hebrews, and speaks of the murmuring of the former against the latter. Stephen apparently represents an extreme hellenist position which the dominant leadership of the new group and the Christians in Jerusalem are not ready to accept. A third expression of this fundamental historic choice facing the new Church is to be seen. We learn that there is a disagreement concerning whether or not the male gentile converts must be circumcised. Jews in the diaspora would not accord such gentiles a full membership, but admitted them to a kind of half membership in the synagogue without circumcision, a painful and possibly dangerous experience for adults under the conditions of the times. What should be their status in the new Church? Conversion of gentiles raised a question concerning the Jewish dietary prescriptions, which though less elaborate than later must have seemed difficult to understand and onerous in practice to gentiles. Acts attempts to solve the second question by recounting a vision of Peter setting them aside. Chapter 11 of Acts gives us the impression that Jewish Christians challenged the conversion of gentiles to the Christian fellowship but came to accept it as right and proper seeing that they "received the Holy Spirit just as we have" (Acts 10:47). It raises the dietary problem and suggests a permissive answer. Chapter 15 raises the question of circumcision of the converts and shows us a council of the early Christian group discussing and apparently deciding the issue. "For it seemed good to the Holy Spirit and to us to lay upon you no greater burden than these necessary things: that you abstain from what has been sacrificed to idols and from blood and from what is strangled and from unchastity" (Acts 15:28–29). This question is discussed by Paul both in Galatians and Romans where he declares that Abraham himself was justified by his faith rather than by circumcision. The church which issued from the experience of Jewish followers with Jesus of Nazareth was coming to seek its own fulfillment in the gentile world.

The Book of Acts, as we have noted, is not a reliable history in the modern sense. The author is trying to present an idealized picture of the early Church. Actually the early Christian community at this time was divided among a number of trends both within Palestine and among the Christian gentile groups. Despite its statement that "the company of those who believed were of one heart and soul" (Acts 4:32), the book does reveal the existence of the severe inner conflict that divided the Church over the status of the law and the temple in nascent Christian life. In addition to what we have already discussed, Acts shows us the followers of Stephen driven out of Jerusalem, Peter after his escape from arrest departing and going "to another place" (Acts 12:17) leaving James totally in authority, and the conflict of Paul and Hebrew Christians and his arrest in Jerusalem. In his own writings Paul reveals the depth of feeling aroused in the conflict. He tells the Roman Christians that he is going to Jerusalem with the collection money raised from the gentile converts for the poor in the church there. This collection was a symbol of unity between the conflicting groups and between the Christians of Jewish and of gentile origin; a symbol of the debt owed to the Jewish Christians by the gentiles, "for if the Gentiles have come to share in their spiritual blessings, they ought also to be of service to them in material blessings" (Acts 15:27). It symbolized Christian unity, as Jewish unity was symbolized by the temple tax paid each year by the Jews of the diaspora. In this situation Paul asks the Roman Christians to pray to God that he may be "delivered from the unbelievers in Judea" and that the collection which he presents and his work of proselytism for which its stands "may be acceptable to the saints" in Jerusalem (Acts 15:31). When Paul arrives at the holy city, James and the other leaders tell him that Hebrew Christians "all zealous for the law" believe that he is telling the Jewish Christians of the diaspora to "forsake Moses" and to give up circumcision (Acts 21:21), and are aroused against him. There follows Paul's arrest which eventuates in his martyrdom which, however, the book does not relate.

THE GENTILE WORLD   Since the Babylonian exile Jews had started to settle in places outside Palestine—in Egypt and elsewhere—and, as we have seen, there arose groups of Jews living abroad known as the dispersion communities or the diaspora. Diaspora Jews were removed from Palestine and the close relationship of religion, temple, nationality, and land characteristic of the Holy Land was loosening in their minds. They were under these circumstances beginning to feel more like members of a religious group rather than a nation, although they did maintain an ethnic identity and a kind of social separateness. New forms of worship developed in the synagogue more like the later "church services" than like the temple. In short, a kind of growing universalism was becoming characteristic of diaspora Judaism and the kinds of questions about circumcision and proselytism plaguing the early Church were being raised there too.

At the time the early Church began its gentile mission in Antioch, where "the disciples were for the first time called Christians" (Acts 11:26), and Paul went "over to Macedonia" (Acts 16:9), most of the Jews of the diaspora spoke Greek. Alexander the Great (356–323 B.C.) in his conquests, which united southeastern Europe with much of western Asia, sought to spread Greek culture and the Greek language. This former student of Aristotle looked forward to a mixing of Greek and non-Greek cultural elements and the intermingling of biological stocks as well. He advocated the development of a unified culture based upon Greek throughout his empire. The world of the eastern Mediterranean and beyond, embraced in the Macedonian Empire, was a world which followed upon centuries of cultural development among Greeks, Persians, Egyptians, and others. It was a sophisticated world and to a considerable extent a highly urbanized one—in fact more urbanized than Europe would be again until after the Industrial Revolution. Moreover, Alexander made the cities of the region Greek cities and throughout the area hellenistic culture—the blend of Greek and indigenous elements Alexander had sought to bring about—flourished in the urban centers. Early in this hellenistic period of eastern Mediterranean culture, the Jewish Bible had been translated into Greek. This version, the so called Septuagint, was translated in Alexandria, in Egypt, sometime around 250 B.C. for the use of the sizable Jewish community resident there. Moreover, a form of common Greek speech and writing somewhat simpler than the Attic Greek spoken by Plato and Aristotle and known as the *koine* developed at this time. It became the *lingua franca* of the literate population. Although Alexander died prematurely and his empire did not hold together as one unit, his cultural efforts remained and the successor states maintained their hellenistic character. Thus a common language, somewhat of a common culture, and an available translation of the Hebrew Scriptures were part of the gentile world to which the early Church turned. The Church wrote its own scriptures in the common Greek of this world and soon became there a predominantly gentile religious phenomenon.

The gentile world into which the new religious movement came had been united into one political whole by Rome, and the Palestine in which Christianity originated had been incorporated into a Roman province with the dissolution of the Seleucid kingdom which had been one of the successor states of Alexander's empire. The Roman Empire, at the height of its expansion in the period when the New Testament was written, occupied the Mediterranean world from Syria and Palestine in the east to the Iberian Peninsula and the island we know as Great Britain in the west. It did not extend as far east as the empire of Alexander, which penetrated what is now India, but this was more than compensated for by its bringing together the regions of Britain, Gaul, and Spain with Italy and North Africa into one political unit with the Greek- and Semitic-speaking lands of the East. The Roman genius for order and administration and the power of Roman arms gave the world of the empire political stability and peace, which, though at times interrupted, exhibited a marked continuity and dependability. This was the period of the *pax romana*, the peace organized and enforced by Rome which lasted for two and a half centuries at the beginning of the Christian Era. Rome not only provided a condition of order and developed an advanced legal system, it also developed the most advanced system of roads on land and of sea transportation on the Mediterranean that had been seen up to that time, making possible orderly and secure transportation throughout the large extent of the empire. Thus Christianity came into an urban society, a society sharing a common language and culture to a marked extent, a society where travel though difficult by modern standards was easier than ever before, and a society enjoying peace and order.

The ancient world had known at an earlier period profound and bitter social and political conflicts, but these were greatly diminished and generally may be said to have ended since the time of Alexander. With the return of order came a return of prosperity and a marked bettering of economic conditions. Moreover, Greece and Rome had earlier aspired to a kind of fulfillment of man's hopes in the life of the city-state, but with the empire of the Caesars such political life ended and with it such political aspirations. The *pax romana* meant a reduction of the slave markets and political order as the basis for economic recovery. Consequently there was a gradual improvement in the conditions of urban life. The world of the Roman Empire and the *pax romana* was one in which an orderly world was ruled more and more by a skilled bureaucracy under the centralized authority of the monarchy, although there was at the same time the persistence of older republican forms now devoid of their former substance. It was a world of moderate economic prosperity in which urban lower middle classes achieved in some measure the minimum material means of life. In this situation human aspirations and human mobility tended to turn inward and the latter part of the ancient period sees a marked development of religious sensitivity and of creative religious experience. Into this world Christianity brought its religious message. It made converts first probably among diaspora Jews and proselytes who had been admitted into half membership in the diaspora synagogue. It soon, as we have seen, admitted gentiles and before long these constituted the vast majority of its members and converts. It made converts in all social classes as time went on but for the first many decades its members in the majority belonged to the lower middle classes of the cities. After the reign of Marcus Aurelius (161–180), upper-class people more and more became active in the life of the Church. The Christian message issued a call which the historical and social developments of the empire had prepared many to hear and disposed many to respond favorably to.

The period when Christianity entered the world of pagan antiquity was one in which the older popular religion was in decline. The educated no longer believed literally in the gods of the Greco-Roman pantheon and allegorical explanations and philosophical meanings were suggested by those philosophically inclined. Yet naive popular piety did remain and the traditional public religion of the empire, which Augustus (the emperor when Jesus was born) attempted to preserve and promote. Moreover, from this time the emperor himself began to be regarded as divine and libations were offered to him. Since such offering was seen as a kind of test of political loyalty and since the Christians refused to offer libations on religious grounds, it became a cause of difficulty and finally of persecution for them. Yet the loss of national independence for those peoples who had been incorporated into the empire and the mixing of peoples which the urban life and improved travel conditions of the empire made possible helped undermine the old traditional religions while the advance of learning made them unsuitable to the educated.

This world which saw the decline of the traditional religions remained, however, a religious world. Indeed it witnessed a deepening of religious concern and a decided turn toward religious interests and the interior life. Mystery cults rose, appealing to the individual and promising him some kind of renewal or regeneration. Most of them appear to have derived from older fertility rites, but to have become highly individualistic. They emphasized the individual and his needs and survival of the individual soul after death. They all had certain structural elements in common. They all secretly engaged in esoteric rituals which the adherents were sworn not to reveal. As a consequence, we do not have extant explicit descriptions of what went on and what we do know is reconstructed from fragmentary evidence—such as the paintings of the initiation rites of the mysteries of Dionysius found on the walls of Pompeii. The rites all appear to involve as their central element the ritual reenactment of archetypal events of the particular myth which was the cult's basic statement of meaning. The Eleusinian mysteries, for example, which originated in Greece, near Athens, were made part of the general state religion in the classical period. They were based on the myth of the rape and carrying off of Proserpine, daughter of Demeter, the goddess of earth and crops, by Pluto, god of the underworld, and of her mother's recovery of her annually for half the year. The myth and the rites reenacted represent the cycle of vegetation and the yearly death and rebirth of life. Through the rite the individual is integrated into this cycle and derives special strength from his relation to it. The mystery of Adonis which originated at Byblos in Phoenicia presented in a similar manner the dying and rising of the god of vegetation. This was a typical pattern—the death and rising of a fertility god. Frequently, the regeneration and renewal of life also involved survival after death; the older fertility and regeneration elements being given an interpretation in relation to the life and death of man. The Orphic mysteries, whose origins are lost in the obscurity of antiquity, possessed a developed cosmogony and theogony and explained the origin of man and his ultimate

THE RELIGIOUS
TEMPER OF
LATER ANTIQUITY

destiny, including a doctrine of the transmigration of souls. Orphism was one of the more profound of these groups and its ideas influenced Plato, the Pythagoreans, and others. The Isis and Osiris mysteries brought the Egyptian concerns with immortality to large numbers in the cities of the empire. The mystery of Mithra which originated in Persia was based upon a solar myth. It was extremely popular among the Roman soldiers and Mithraic archeological remains have been found as far west as Great Britain. It was probably the chief rival to Christianity among the mysteries in the late second and third centuries. The rites were the reenactment of these myths, a reenactment which was understood as a re-presentation, for the mythic events are understood as eternally present, making possible a participation of the individual adherent in them and his gaining of strength and immortality through them. They all seem to have involved an initiation rite, a ritual progress through various graduated stages of purification and a final achievement of perfection, such perfection involving the final insights arrived at in the ritual enactment. Human sexuality was often seen as closely related to this final insight and sexual elements were often important in the rites.

Not only have these cults embraced and dramatized the cycles of nature but they have extended them to cosmic rhythms which lead man beyond this earth to a future life. The similarities among these cults do not seem to be based upon borrowing but rather upon certain perennial religious needs which though originally concerned with man's relation to the earth and its mysterious powers of life and death came to be seen as centered upon individual life and individual psychological needs. In fact, the mystery cults would seem to express certain archetypal characteristics of religious thought and behavior—the need for some kind of strength from ultimate sources outside oneself and the longing for some kind of regeneration and transformation. They represent specifically religious groups organized around a complex of ritual and myth. They are typical of urban settings where people have been uprooted from the traditional relationship to the soil and the older kinship structures of human relations so closely connected with it. As such, it is not difficult to see why they flourished in the cities of the hellenistic and Roman periods. They were not state religions but private associations and they were not just widely believed as the older paganism but required voluntary adherence and admission by initiation. Yet they were not exclusivist in their demands. A person could be a member of the mysteries and also take part in the traditional or state religion. He could worship Mithra and Jupiter and together with the worship of both of them offer libation to the divine emperor. The early Christians considered most of these groups to be immoral and under the influence of demons and to be engaged in immoral rites. While this impression is probably exaggerated, the fact is that only Mithraism, which was based upon the ethical and ontological dualism of Zoroastrianism, saw existence as a struggle between right and wrong and took a serious ethical position. As the traditional religion declined, these groups increased in popularity and by the beginning of the third century Christians concentrated their polemics against them as chief rivals rather than the older paganism.

It was at one time a scholarly hypothesis that as Christianity developed its own ritual of worship and its own theology it was influenced by the mysteries against which it had long contended. Indeed Christianity has made use of and integrated into its thought and liturgy certain rites and concepts which antedate it. However, the hypothesis of significant Christian dependence upon the mysteries has generally been given up and the archetypal elements of Christian rites appear to be structural archetypes of religious thought and ritual behavior rather than the product of obscure cultural diffusion. Indeed many of them appear to be taken over from Judaic prototypes.

While these new groups were voluntary, specifically religious organizations, they did not represent new communities and new religions demanding the exclusive commitment of the individual. These cults involved parts of a man; they required his partial involvement, not all his heart, all his soul, all his mind, and all his strength as did the commands of Deuteronomy and Leviticus quoted by Jesus. Perhaps Orphism is an exception here, for there was talk of an Orphic way of life which involved an ascetic discipline. Orphism seemed addressed to suffering souls and to involve some real idea of conversion and salvation. Such profundity was not general. Even Mithraism with its moral elements was not something that demanded the whole man. This stands in sharp contrast to both Judaism and Christianity which demanded a genuine conversion—a profound interior turning around of the whole person—of those who joined their ranks. Moreover, in the mysteries one does not find the belief that their sacramental rituals in any way help men to lead a moral life here and now. Such profound conversion demands as those made by Judaism and Christianity appear elsewhere in the ancient world only in philosophy.

Greek philosophy exhibited two interests: one speculative or scientific and concerned with understanding the world in which men find themselves, the other concentrating upon the significance of human existence and seeking a basis for right conduct. The former interest began in the sixth century B.C. in Ionia, where human thought gradually emancipated itself from the mythic imagination and took its stand in the abstract conceptual formulation of man's experience. The latter interest may be said to have begun in Athens in the fifth century, when Socrates turned his attention to the examination of human life. Socrates set ancient men on the quest for understanding what man ought to do to live well and properly. His idea of knowledge was not simply intellectual; it involved an interior motion of the inner man to embrace truth when he found it, a motion that changed him in a profound manner. Pythagoras had given rise to a movement that was philosophical and highly concerned with mathematics but which was also of a marked religious cast. It was a philosophy, a way of life, and a community of believers as well. Plato, Socrates' outstanding disciple, developed the insights of his master and created the first rational theology making the transcendent good the measure of all things and urging the reformation of human life in its light. Early in his career Plato hoped to bring about general political change; he was without success and consequently turned his attention to the inner world and the perfection of inner man.

Following the end of the city-state and the rise of the Hellenistic Empire, further philosophical developments are to be seen in answer to the spiritual and psychological problems of men in the new kind of society which developed. Men were more alone, more individuated, less a part of stable groups with temporal continuity. They lived in a larger and more complex world. Already at the end of the classical period we see souls in need of cure and men becoming identified with philosophical movements. This need now greatly increased, and there arose to meet it two significant philosophical schools—Stoicism and Epicureanism. The latter was a materialist doctrine which saw the world outside of man as offering no guide and sanction to human life. The Epicureans did not deny the existence of gods but saw them as having no relation to men. Death is the dissolution of the human being and is final. Man must therefore find within himself a guide to a satisfactory life. The modern use of the term "Epicurean" is a caricature of its original meaning, for it was not a life of pleasure. Men were to seek freedom from pain, and in so doing they were to avoid involvement in pleasure or any other activity which might upset the steady unruffled way of life which was advocated, a life characterized by *ataraxy*.

The Stoics gave a quite different response to ancient man's new situation. They saw an ordered universe which was the expression of reason. Indeed, reason was seen as the soul of the universe, the god which is also referred to as nature. Man was made up of a spark of this reason as well as of lesser material elements. His true happiness was to be found in cultivating the former and leading a life in harmony with nature. The usual ways of the world were seen as errors and man must avoid them and find the true way beneath them. Thus will man recognize folly and find wisdom. He will lead a life of justice and restraint; he will not give himself to vanities. Like Epicureanism, the Stoic philosophy offered man freedom, but it offered it through identification with and cultivation of the divine element within himself and within nature as a whole. Stoicism too, like Plato, had intended to revolutionize political life and in fact did have some effect upon it, especially under the first emperor Augustus, who attempted far-reaching reforms of the political and social structure. The spirit of Stoicism had an effect upon the conception and spread of Roman citizenship in the empire and upon the development of Roman law. Its ideas influenced the later revival of Platonism and the development of Christian thought. St. Augustine tells how at the age of eighteen he was deeply affected and prepared for his later conversion to Christianity by reading Cicero's *Hortensius*. The Cynics (this word also is not being given its modern meaning but signifies a disregard for established customs and manners), too, developed a notion of a basic reality behind particular cultures and customs in relation to which men found or sought to find detachment and freedom.

The rise of philosophy was accompanied by the development of what we might characterize as a prototype of higher education. In the imperial period educated people learned grammar, then rhetoric, and then some went on to philosophy. Moreover, among the Romans the study of law was important. There were famous centers where men went to study philosophy such as the Platonic Academy in Athens, but most men learned philosophy from private teachers who were located throughout the empire. This study of philosophy with private teachers was at its height in the first century when Christianity came into the gentile world. Not only could one study philosophy in one's youth, but public lectures made it possible for older people to become involved as well. Philosophical literature received a wide circulation and exercised considerable influence. Moreover, a large number of elementary philosophic introductions and summaries were found. When Christianity came to face the challenge of ancient philosophy, its concepts were widely diffused among the literate classes.

These philosophical schools in the first century were less concerned with pure philosophical speculation and more involved in preaching the need for and way to a good life. They demanded something closely akin to religious conversion. They offered meaning and direction to men who could no longer find it in the older religious culture of paganism and whose needs had been deepened and made conscious by the intellectual and social developments of the preceding centuries. They made the universe intelligible and offered a way of life, an intellectually planned and justified mode of living. They offered an ascetic discipline for the taming of human passions based upon the understanding of man's nature and place in the universe. Stoicism later emphasized doing good and performing the duty of one's station in life. Its doctrine of moral progress gave the individual a path to self-development and improvement. In short these philosophical schools and movements offered intelligible explanations of the world and man's place within it and at the same time a life based upon an intelligent design or plan, a disciplined and intelligible mode of existence. They also offered a kind of brotherhood, and even held up heroic and ideal human examples before their followers, examples which would affect later Christian hagiography. For the deeper student, philosophy offered the joy and satisfaction of mystic and scientific contemplation, both of which involved an intellectual relationship with the deeper ground of existence. Ancient philosophy saw the life of contemplation as a higher expression of the human potential than the active life, a fact that reflected the inward turning characteristic of the ancient world after the classical period.

Such philosophy was a kind of religion. It was more profoundly religious in the sense in which that word can be applied to Judaism and Christianity than the older popular religion or even than the mysteries, since it demanded genuine inner change. Its literature urged repentance, conversion, deliverance, etc. In Seneca's words, it involved not only improvement but transformation. And it related men to what it saw as the basic ground of their existence and all existence.

Some time after the appearance of the mystery cults, the philosophical and religious phenomenon known as Gnosticism appears in the Greco-Roman world. It expresses severe disillusion with life in this world, as may be seen in various conflicting dualisms—spirit versus flesh, soul versus body, light versus darkness, life versus death, good versus evil, and God versus the world. In it we witness the effort to break out of the here and now to find salvation carried to exaggerated lengths. Where Gnosticism originated is not clear. It has been called Greek, Near Eastern, and Egyptian and its syncretic character shows elements of all these kinds. There was a Jewish Gnosticism which was considered heretical just as later there was a Christian Gnosticism which was considered heretical and combated vigorously as a dangerous heresy.

Gnosticism held the world in which man found himself, the world of matter and our daily existence, to be radically evil and man, or at least the spiritual element in him, to be imprisoned in it and in the body composed from its substance. Man is an alien here and is lost and out of touch with his original home, which was in the presence of a radically other-worldly God outside and beyond the world. He can find delivery from this predicament through a kind of secret knowledge (*gnosis*). This involves a knowledge of God and the divine realm, the nature of the transcendent world and the pathway leading to it. The reception of this saving knowledge is by means of learning esoteric doctrine and is often accompanied by a transforming experience of inner illumination. Thus is the spiritual element in man related to the hidden God and emancipated from its material and worldly prison. Moreover, the more intellectual forms of Gnosticism developed these doctrines in theoretical form, setting forth ideas concerning the nature of God, the universe, man's condition, and the way to salvation. Man's condition is one of radical and thorough alienation of his spirit from the world. His salvation is rescuing that spirit, promoting its escape, and allowing its return to the radically other-worldly God. Some Gnostic doctrines involved the notion of a divine agent sent to help man, an idea probably developed in imitation of Christianity. Christian Gnosticism saw Jesus in this role. The Christian Church was highly involved with and thoroughly challenged by the intrusion of Gnostic ideas and the Gnostic heresy came to comprise a dire threat to Christianity in the second century. Such Gnostic doctrines see the God of the Old Testament as an evil God related to or creator of this world, in opposition to the good God who is beyond this world. Saturninus of Antioch, for example, declared that Christ came to destroy the God of the Jews. Evidence of the conflict with Gnosticism can be found in such Christian writings as the New Testament books attributed to John, Colossians, and the Pastoral Epistles. There is also a large Christian literature of polemics against Gnostic ideas and practices, the most notable of which is *Against Heresies* by Irenaeus, a Church

Father of the late second century. We have also some Gnostic interpretations of Christianity, such as the Gospel of Thomas and the
Gospel of Truth. This radical Gnostic dualism found two quite opposing interpretations of human behavior. Some Gnostics withdrew
from the world and lived a disciplined life not indulging themselves
in its pleasures or vices. For some, Gnosticism demanded asceticism. Others felt that since the flesh and the world were negative
values, one could indulge oneself as much as one wished and it
would not affect the spiritual reality of man's make-up. They felt
sexual pleasure could be pursued without limit. Both groups, however, did not see the possibility of meaningful participation in the
world's activities.

The Christian Church that went out into this complex gentile world   THE UNDERSTANDING
was one whose faith and hope were centered upon the figure of   OF CHRIST:
Jesus. A number of understandings and interpretations of Christ as   PAUL AND JOHN
the founding figure existed and eventually they were expressed in
Christian writings—in the canonical New Testament and others.
Paul presents us with what is probably the earliest extant statement
of belief characteristic of that Church:

> *For I delivered to you as of first importance what I also received,
> that Christ died for our sins in accordance with the scriptures,
> that he was buried, that he was raised on the third day in accord-
> ance with the scriptures, and that he appeared to Cephas, then to
> the twelve. Then he appeared to more than five hundred brethren
> at one time, most of whom are still alive, though some have fallen
> asleep. Then he appeared to James, then to all the apostles.*
>
> (1 Cor. 15:3–7)

Jesus was seen as the suffering servant of God who was "wounded
for our transgressions" and "bruised for our iniquities" (Isa. 53:5).
He had returned to the Father and was now "exalted at the right
hand of God." He was the stone which the builders rejected that became the cornerstone (Acts 4:11; Ps. 118:22). Christian thinking
would continue to ponder this figure, his meaning, and the implications of his career. He would be seen as

> *the image of the invisible God, the first-born of all creation; for
> in him all things were created, in heaven and on earth, visible
> and invisible, whether thrones or dominions, principalities or
> authorities—all things were created through him and for him. He
> is before all things, and in him all things hold together. He is the
> head of the body, the church; he is the beginning, the first-born
> from the dead, that in everything he might be preeminent. For in
> him all the fullness of God was pleased to dwell, and through him
> to reconcile to himself all things, whether on earth or in heaven,
> making peace by the blood of his cross.*
>
> (Col. 1:15–20)

We have seen that Christianity originated in Jewish apocalypticism
and we know that the young Church expected an early return of

Jesus. But Jesus was seen to be more than was implied in the usual ideas of the Messiah. In him God had revealed himself in a special way to all men. The intellectual clarification of what the Church meant by Jesus as Christ and the character of his mission would be a cause of considerable conflict as time went on. The earliest contributions to this clarification (which is known as Christology) and the most basic are those found in the writings of Paul and the writings attributed to him and in the writings attributed to the apostle John.

Paul was a Jew who saw Jesus as the Messiah, but as more than the Messiah in the traditional sense. Paul was learned in Jewish thought and aware of the Judaic idea of the divine wisdom as present with God "at the first, before the beginning of the earth," as an entity which beside him "was there" when God "established the heavens" (Prov. 8:23, 27). He was also aware of Stoic ideas and the notion of God as divine reason. Paul, who is second to Jesus himself in his influence upon Christianity and its development, saw Jesus as a preexistent figure, "the power of God and the wisdom of God" (1 Cor. 2:24). Jesus was indeed the Davidic Messiah "according to the flesh," but he was "designated Son of God in power according to the Spirit of holiness by his resurrection from the dead" (Rom. 1:3 and 4). God is the creator of the universe; he is "our Father." Jesus, Paul calls "Lord" (*Kyrios*), the term Greek-speaking Jews had used for the Hebrew *Adonai* which was substituted for Yahweh in the reading of the Scriptures by Jews because pronunciation of the proper name of God had become taboo because of its sacred character. Jesus is a preexistent divine being who existed before the creation of the world, who had taken on human form and died for the sins of men, and who will return at the end of the world. Paul sees Jesus' death as a voluntary expiation of man's sins which reconciles God and man. The basis of man's relation to God and the condition of his reconciliation is faith. Paul also placed great emphasis upon man's justification—that man was "justified by God's grace as a gift, through the redemption which is in Christ Jesus, whom God put forward as an expiation by his blood to be received by faith" (Rom. 3:24–25). But he was no less insistent upon righteous conduct though salvation was not by works of the law. Paul concerns himself with the meaning of Jesus—his life, death, and resurrection—and approaches this meaning within the ideas of Judaism and its understanding of the relationship between man and God. For Paul the basic question is how man who is sinful and fallen can be reconciled with God and be counted as righteous in his eyes. In this context Paul deals with problems which will be central to Christian theology for centuries to come, problems of justification through good works versus justification by grace through Christ's death. In Christ, God gratuitously reconciled man to himself, not because man deserved it, but out of God's generosity. Man's way of acceptance was through faith. Man must believe in Jesus as the Christ—the Messiah and reconciler—and in the work of reconciliation which God has wrought through him. In this faith the believer begins to share in the new life which will be fulfilled after the Parousia, when Christ will come again. This enables him to walk in righteousness and to withstand suffering patiently. Yet in this context Paul makes much use of the imperative mode calling the Christians to live up to this new state.

Another important discussion of the meaning of Jesus for the Church is to be found in the Fourth Gospel. This book was written toward the end of the first or near the beginning of the second century. Here, as in the writing of Paul, Jesus is seen as a preexistent being closely associated with God's creativity. The Christian tradition long attributed this Gospel to the apostle John, the son of Zebedee and brother of James, who together with his brother and Peter are seen in the synoptics as specially close to Jesus. The Gospel contains references to "the disciple whom Jesus loved" (John 21:20) and identifies him as the author of the work. This was early thought to be the apostle John. Modern scholarship, however, considers such an authorship to be highly unlikely if not impossible.

In this work the words of Jesus are presented in discussions which are not like those of the Synoptic Gospels. The latter are collections of Jesus' sayings, the most famous being the Sermon on the Mount in Matthew's Gospel. In the Fourth Gospel a discourse develops each theme. Each discourse arises from some episode which symbolizes the theme presented in the discourse itself. The discourse has a kind of mystical character appealing to the religious intuition. Jesus moves through the Johannine Gospel as a sublime divine figure somewhat mysterious. We see this mode of presentation, for example, in the fourth chapter where Jesus asks the Samaritan woman for a drink of water. In the discussion that follows, Jesus makes statements that reveal his real identity and significance to the reader. "If you knew the gift of God, and who it is that is saying to you, 'Give me a drink,' you would have asked him and he would have given you living water" (John 4:10). In this Gospel Jesus' statements about himself are much different from those in the first three Gospels.

I have come in my Father's name.

(John 5:43)

My teaching is not mine but his who sent me; if any man's will is to do his will, he shall know whether the teaching is from God or whether I am speaking on my own authority.

(John 7:16–17)

I and the Father are one.

(John 10:30)

If any one serves me, he must follow me; and where I am, there shall my servant be also; if any one serves me, the Father will honor him.

(John 12:26)

I am the true vine, and my Father is the vinedresser. Every branch of mine that bears no fruit, he takes away, and every branch that does bear fruit he prunes, that it may bear more fruit.

(John 15:1 and 2)

He who abides in me, and I in him, he it is that bears much fruit, for apart from me you can do nothing.

(John 15:5)

As the Father has loved me, so have I loved you; abide in my love. If you keep my commandments, you will abide in my love, just as I have kept my Father's commandments and abide in his love.

(John 15:10)

The Father himself loves you, because you have loved me and have believed that I came from the Father.

(John 16:27)

I glorified thee on earth, having accomplished the work which thou gavest me to do; and now, Father, glorify thou me in thine own presence with the glory which I had with thee before the world was made.

(John 17:4–5)

Such are the sayings of Jesus in this Gospel. Jesus speaks of his union with God and of the mystical life man can have in union with him. He calls to a life which is not of "this world." "I chose you out of the world" (John 15:19). Moreover, in this Gospel Jesus is often spoken of as glorified or as manifesting his glory, a tendency found in far less striking manner in the synoptics. In fact here he is described as "making himself equal with God" (John 5:18).

The Fourth Gospel is a product of a later time in the history of the new Church. There had been somewhat of a waning of eschatological expectations and a consequent need to emphasize and develop a present relation to God in Christ. The Church at this time was also developing as an institution with its own needs, among which is an understanding of the meaning of Jesus under these new conditions. Moreover, the portrayal of the relationship between Jesus and the Jews reflects the later time the Gospel was written, a time in which, following the destruction of the Temple by the Romans, the Jewish Council at Jamnia, and continued separate Christian existence, increased hostility between Christians and Jews is evident.

Perhaps nowhere is the theology of the Fourth Gospel so succinctly stated and stated as a whole as in the opening or so-called prologue to the work. In it Jesus is called the "Word" (Greek, *Logos,* "Wisdom" or "Reason"). The term was a long-standing one in Greek philosophy going back to Heracleitus. Philo of Alexandria (20 B.C.–A.D. 50), a devout Jew learned in Greek thought, and Plato in particular, had used the term to designate the divine intermediary between God and the world, the divine reason which was the instrument of God's creativity. It is also found in Gnostic sources. But in the Johannine work the Divine Word or *Logos* takes on human nature and lives among men. Reminiscent of the opening of Genesis, the Fourth Gospel starts from the "beginning."

In the beginning was the Word, and the Word was with God, and the Word was God. He was in the beginning with God.

(John 1:1–2)

Thus is Jesus presented as the preexistent divine reason. He then is seen as the source of God's creative action:

All things were made through him, and without him was not anything made that was made.

(John 1:3)

The text now introduces those words so laden with religious meaning for the mystical tradition—life and light—both of which Jesus as *Logos* brings to men:

In him was life, and the life was the light of men. The light shines in the darkness, and the darkness has not overcome it . . . The true light that enlightens every man was coming into the world.

(John 1:5 and 9)

The Fourth Gospel sees the role of Jesus as enlightening men with the divine life which he communicates to men. It then summarizes his earthly career:

He was in the world, and the world was made through him, yet the world knew him not. He came to his own home and his own people received him not.

(John 1:10–11)

Both the other-worldliness of Jesus' followers and their separation from the Jews is now emphasized. But this is background for the enlightening and almost divinizing mission with which the prologue is concerned.

But to all who received him, who believed in his name, he gave power to become children of God; who were born, not of blood nor of the will of the flesh nor of the will of man, but of God.

(John 1:12–13)

Unlike Gnostic other-worldliness, however, the Fourth Gospel does not reject the flesh but rather sees Jesus' human condition as the medium through which is manifested his divine origin and character, and his gifts given to men.

And the Word became flesh and dwelt among us, full of grace and truth; and we beheld his glory, glory as of the only Son from the Father . . . And from his fulness have we all received grace upon grace. For the law was given through Moses; grace and truth came through Jesus Christ.

(John 1:14, 16–17)

The Fourth Gospel is concerned with Christology and in his discourses in this Gospel Jesus talks about Christology. We are given an explanation of the character and role of Jesus as Christ which Christians at the time could feel appropriate to their own feelings of his significance, glory, and power—and the relationship to him in which they were sustained by the spiritual food and drink he gave and by his light in which they walked. When in the fourth and fifth centuries the Church would be concerned with credal formulas, it would find important sources here.

THE MAKING OF THE INSTITUTIONAL CHURCH

By the end of the first century the Christian Church had communities (or churches) in many places throughout the Mediterranean world. These groups did not enjoy full legality and Christianity was not granted the status of a licit religion under Roman law. Indeed this first century saw the churches persecuted. There was the violent turning against Christians in Rome under Nero in A.D. 64 which cost the lives of Peter and Paul, making that city the memorial city of the two great apostles. The persecution under Domitian followed in 95. The new religion, however, saw a rapid and wide expansion in the second century, following the trade routes of the empire. From Mesopotamia to the southern coast of Britain, on the Rhone and the Rhine, along the eastern shores of the Adriatic, and in North Africa into Egypt, Christian groups were to be found. At the same time the Church continued to grow in its older locations of Greece, Syria, Italy, and Asia Minor. This growth was basically an urban phenomenon, as the country districts remained traditionally pagan. In this century sporadic persecutions continued under the otherwise greatly admired Antonine emperors, Antoninus Pius and Marcus Aurelius, but it was not until Decius' reign in the third century (250–259) that systematic and thorough persecution got under way.

The second century was a most significant one in Christian history. It was the time when the Church put order into its beliefs and into its internal organization. Was Christianity to remain a Jewish sect or was it to become a universal religion addressing its message to the gentiles? We have seen that not without considerable conflict, the Church decided for the latter course. The second century presented four major issues of decision to the new religious movement which would eventually provide the basic direction of the Church in the entire later period of its history. Each of these fundamental challenges is a complex story in itself and many of the important details have been lost. We shall present here merely summary statements of the issues and their outcomes. It must also be remembered that human movements, religious or otherwise, do not face such questions in the abstract form in which we discuss them. Such movements are involved and embedded in specific historical circumstances and meet the problems as they arise concretely in different concrete settings, a process that is often gradual, confused, and even marked by contradictions.

The first of these major issues with which we shall deal is the failure of the Parousia, or second coming of the Risen Lord. We noted that Christianity began as a messianic and apocalyptic movement and that the first Christians expected the return of Jesus and the beginning of the new age of the world in their own lifetimes. In the writings of Paul and those attributed to him we note a movement from imminent expectation to an acceptance of postponement. At times the Synoptic Gospels give the impression that the Parousia is imminent, but like the Pauline writings they affirm that no man knows the time of the Lord's coming. The Fourth Gospel, which is the latest gospel, is hardly to be characterized as eschatological. In that work Jesus's glorification is already a fact and the believer is to share in it. The terms used, such as judgment, life, and and resurrection, do not carry the vivid apocalyptic connotations to be found in the Synoptics. In the Fourth Gospel we find the kind of present, here-and-now relationship to the Risen Christ which will more and more replace eschatological expectations as the core of the Christian religious relationship to God and the basic orientation of Christian devotion.

The post-Apostolic church contained a number of different ways of expressing the faith and hope of the Christians. Alongside the expectations of the Parousia there were also elements of an important present religious relationship. This is seen particularly in the Eucharistic worship in which a here-and-now relationship with the Risen Christ as well as an expression of the hope in his second coming was constitutive of the rite from the beginning. This meant for the earliest Church a close and intimate participation in the life of the Lord. In this rite Christ united himself with his followers. Also alongside the hope of an imminent second coming there were Christian hopes formulated in terms of the Greek ideas of the immortality of the soul, ideas which also quite possibly affected the Jews of the diaspora. Thus Christian fulfillment seemed to be expressible in two idioms—the Jewish one of Parousia and resurrection of the body, and the Greek one of immortality and life with Christ in another world after death. In fact we see both of these conceptions in the Pauline literature. Moreover, important as the expectations of the Parousia were in the early Church, they did not rule out vigorous missionary work in the present.

Thus in the Church of the first and early second century there appear to be temporal dynamic apocalyptic conceptions along with static ontological ideas of a present relationship to God through Christ. There appear to be ideas of a passing of the old world-age and the inauguration of the new one with Christ's appearance, and also ideas pointing to the significant division between life in this world and the life in the next, between the earthly and the heavenly life as most important. In the earlier period the Church as a whole seemed to give the dominant and presiding position to the dynamic eschatological ideas and orientations and to have fitted the others into their general context. In the later period the ontological ideas with their conception of a present relationship to the Risen Christ and a heavenly reward after death were given dominance and eschatology remained but was generally subsidiary to them. The change was one of enormous significance and the details of transformation are to be obtained only through the fragile and hypothetical reconstructions of scholarship.

When Christianity came into the gentile world in which the learned strata partook to one extent or another in Greek culture, it necessitated that the adherents of the new religion take this culture into account. The historic problem facing the new Church may be stated in this way: What of the wisdom of the gentiles? We have noted earlier that Philo, the Jewish philosopher, had sought to reconcile Plato and Moses. What would the Christian Church do?

The Church not only offered a sense of salvation to its converts, it also offered a definition of man and his world, and this definition of the meaning of man found itself in competition with the philosophy of the Greeks. Moreover, this competition existed in an atmosphere of official and unofficial hostility. In response to this situation there arose in the second century a group of Christian writers known as the Apologists. The term is used in its classical sense, to designate those who present and defend a doctrine or point of view. There were Apologies written by Aristides, Justin, Tatian, Athenagoras, Clement of Alexandria, Tertullian, and others. These men attempted to defend the faith and to show its superiority to Greek philosophy. In so doing they made use of Greek ideas and helped to introduce a Greek philosophical idiom into Christian theology. For example Justin Martyr, who was put to death in Rome in 165, speaks of the "Word" (*Logos*) as do other Apologists, and of "God who begat him" and sees the Word as "Teacher . . . the Son and Apostle of God the Father and Master of all, that is Jesus Christ, from whom we have received the name of Christians" (*Apology* I.12). He sees this *Logos* always at work in the world teaching Greeks such as Socrates and Heracleitus and Jews such as Abraham and Elijah and so he finds all those that "lived by Reason" to be in some way Christians (*Apology* I.46). The life of the historic Jesus is little stressed by Justin except as the great instance of the incarnation of the *Logos* and the occasion for the revelation of true philosophy. Writing to influence Greeks toward tolerance for the Church, Justin and the Apologists stressed similarities between Christianity and Greek thought and presented the former as a fuller version of what was present in less perfect form in the latter. Yet religion is not reduced to philosophy and Justin does speak of the passion and crucifixion of Christ which he suffered "cleansing by his blood those who believe on him" and also saying that "men of every nation will look forward to his coming again" (*Apology* I.32).

The problem of how the new Church should react to Greek thought was however a matter of conflict. In Justin we see a positive approach to the question. "Whatever has been uttered aright by any men in any place belongs to us Christians; for, next to God, we worship and love the Word which is from the unbegotten and ineffable God; since on our account he has been made man, that, being made partaker of our sufferings, he may also bring us healing" (*Apology* 11.13). We find a similar attitude at the end of the century in the writings of Clement of Alexandria, who saw philosophy as "necessary to the Greeks for righteousness, until the coming of the Lord," and after that as assisting "toward true religion as a kind of preparatory training for those who arrive at faith by way of demonstration" (*Stromateis* 1.5.28). Yet this point of view met significant opposition as we see in the writings of no less a figure than Tertullian, who found his pagan analogies in Roman law rather than Greek philosophy. "What is there in common between Athens and Jerusalem? What between the Academy and the Church? What between heretics and Christians? . . . Away with all projects for a 'Stoic,' a 'Platonic' or a 'dialectic' Christianity" (*De praescriptione haereticorum* 7). The mode of relationship started by the Apologists persisted and the Church proceeded later to construct its theology on the basis of the Greek philosophical heritage and using the Greek philosophical language.

The historical process of bringing into contact philosophical ideas and the primitive Christian tradition was a chronic condition characteristic of the position of Christianity in the second century and reached an acute stage in the relations between Christianity and Gnosticism. Gnosticism appealed to many of the best minds in the early Church and at the height of its influence in the middle decades of the century threatened to infuse and change the beliefs of Christianity in a thoroughly substantial manner. At this time the Church was weakly organized; its beliefs were still largely undefined though they made up a common but differentiated tradition. We have already seen some of the resemblances between Christian and Gnostic ideas. These similarities made it easy for Gnostic meanings to penetrate the faith. Then Christ was seen as the emissary of the good but hidden God sent to rescue men of spiritual character by revealing secret knowledge. While Paul was certainly not a Gnostic, the Gnostics were able to use much in his teaching, as for example his idea of "a secret and hidden wisdom of God" (1 Cor. 2:7). The God who is the creator of the world was seen as an evil deity or at best an inferior demiurge. It was held in accordance with Gnostic dualism that Christ did not really become man, did not really assume human nature, but only maintained the appearance of so doing—a heresy designated as Docetism. Perhaps the most important figure here was Marcion, a man from Asia Minor converted to Christianity in Rome. Under the influence of a Roman Gnostic, Cerdo, Marcion began to develop a Gnostic Christianity. He was excommunicated from the Roman Church in 144. He then set up a separate church of his own, compiled a canon of Christian literature in which he accepted only the Gospel of Luke and ten Pauline epistles which he edited to meet his own Gnostic standards.

Much of ordinary Christian life in this century had become legalistic as people sought to work out practical everyday ways of living by their faith. From the Apologists and other Christian writings such as the *Didache* or *Teaching of the Twelve Apostles,* a church manual, the writings of Hermas, and the writings of early bishops known as the Apostolic Fathers, we get some idea of ordinary life in the Church. It was both ascetic and marked by a certain legalism. Wednesdays and Fridays were days of fasting. Prayer and almsgiving were held in high regard. Satisfaction as well as repentance was necessary for the forgiveness of sins. Marcion established his new church in part as a protest against the growing legalism in the Church.

Despite superficial similarities to Christianity, Gnosticism was

Christianity's most dangerous enemy and threatened to distort and transform the meaning of its faith from within. The result was a general Christian counterresponse in which the Christian intellectual leadership took up the fight to defend the faith from what was seen as a demonic subversion. The Church indeed responded in two spheres, in that of doctrine and that of organization. In response to Marcion the canon of the New Testament was established as we have already seen. Moreover, a formal credal statement was developed which became known as "The Apostles' Creed," an attempt to state in formal language the content and import of the Christian faith. The earliest confessions of faith which were used when converts were baptized were simple and consisted chiefly in declaring Jesus to be Lord. But now more detailed statements were developed, though not as detailed as they would become later. At the end of the second and the beginning of the third century the baptismal candidate in Rome was asked three questions.

Do you believe in God the Father Almighty?

Do you believe in Jesus Christ the Son of God, who was born of the Holy Spirit and the Virgin Mary, who was crucified under Pontius Pilate and died, and rose the third day living from the dead, and ascended into heaven, and sat down at the right hand of the Father, and will come to judge the living and the dead?

Do you believe in the Holy Spirit, and the Holy Church, and the resurrection of the flesh?

(Hippolytus, *Apostolic Tradition,* 21.12 ff.)

In the sphere of organization the response to Gnosticism was a development of the ecclesiastical institution. The Christian truth was seen to reside in the Church and the core of Church organization was the office of the bishop. Earlier the local churches were presided over by a council or group and this collegial leadership constituted what was later known as the clergy. This form of leadership began early to give way to a single ruling figure, the bishop, probably because collegial leadership is always unstable and tends to give rise to a one-man form. But this process was hastened considerably by the crisis in the inner life of the Church which Gnosticism had brought about. Christian faith came to be seen as entrusted to "those who, together with the succession of the episcopate, have received the certain gift of truth" (Irenaeus, *Against Heresies,* 4.26.2). The true faith was that of the apostles which is "preached to men, which has come down to us through the successions of bishops." Moreover, the Roman Church, indicative of much that was to come, was being accorded a certain strategic position in this transmission of the apostolic faith. It is that faith which is to be seen in "the tradition and creed of the greatest, the most ancient church, the church known to all men, which was founded and set up in Rome by the two most glorious apostles, Peter and Paul" (Irenaeus, *Against Heresies,* 3.1).

The second century and the struggle against Gnosticism saw the development in the Church of what we might call "Catholic consciousness" and "Catholic organization." What had emerged was an ecclesiastical structure and an institutional point of view. This was in part no doubt necessary and would have come about under any circumstance, for if Christianity did not define its basic ideas and achieve some kind of uniformity with respect to them it probably would not have survived, at least not as the significant cultural force that it became. In fact we see the beginnings of these developments before the Gnostic crisis. What was emerging was the "Catholic" Church. The word was first used in a letter from Ignatius to the church at Smyrna, written around the year 112, in which he also points to the significant position of the bishop (Ignatius, *Epistle to the Smyrnaeans,* 100.8). It is found again in another letter written around 156 by the church at Smyrna concerning the martyrdom of their bishop, Polycarp, which refers to "the whole Catholic Church throughout the world" (*Martyrium Polycarpi* 8). Between 160 and 190 the Church developed marked Catholic characteristics. The older situation of local churches was replaced by a greater degree of union, the older collegial leadership gave way to the monarchical episcopate, the older charismatic freedom was giving way to defined doctrine, the clergy were emerging as a leading and indeed an intellectual stratum in the Church, and the laity were entering a kind of status of religious tutelage. The Church based itself on what it called an apostolic succession of office and teaching. The Church repelled the Gnostic danger, but it changed itself considerably in the process. Yet it must be recognized that the necessity for objective intellectual and organizational points of reference for Christian life and thought—a requisite for Christian survival—would have demanded changes in the general direction in which they actually occurred. We may well suspect, however, that the depth and seriousness of the crisis gave these developments an exaggerated form. In this struggle we see the rise of a church characterized by explicitly defined doctrine, integrated organization, and law. The end of the second century saw one Catholic Church throughout the expanse of the empire and around it a number of sects calling themselves Christian as well but considered heretical and enemies of the faith by the Catholic Church itself. The beginning of the third century saw the emergence of the Church in the basic form which it maintained until the Reformation and which the Eastern Orthodox and Roman Catholic churches maintain to this day. Later developments were important but they were built upon the foundation already present by the year A.D. 200. In the following century these features were strengthened. The authority of the bishops was enhanced and the spontaneous character of church life—the "gifts of the spirit" characteristic of the first century—tended to become memory and a tradition, and such charismatic gifts became possessions endowed by clerical status. By the year 250 Cyprian of Carthage (who was martyred in 258) could say that the Church was based upon the unity of the bishops (Cyprian, *Letters,* 66–68.8). By now the word "clergy" (*kleros*), first found in a document of the year 95 (1 Clem. 93–97), designated a separate and superior order of men, while the word "laity" (*laikos*), used once in the New Testament in an un-

Third-century synagogue on the shore of the Sea of Galilee at Capernaum. It marks the site of an older synagogue in which Jesus preached. (Courtesy of the Israel Government Tourist Office.)

technical sense (1 Pet. 5:3) to designate those ministered unto, became the designation for the mass of the people. Many of these latter were by that time ignorant converts from paganism or "cradle Christians" born into the Church and lacking the enthusiasm of earlier generations, making for the coexistence within the Church of a kind of naiveté and a kind of worldliness. The bishops, who lead the services of worship and were increasingly seen as a priesthood, were the guardians of orthodoxy, and defined what was heresy. They were disciplinary officers as well. The lower clergy were their assistants. Hence in the last part of the third century the clergy had emerged into the status of teachers, rulers, and celebrants of worship possessing graces and gifts not available to the mass of believers. Admission to the clerical estate was, by ordination, a rite which went back to the earliest days of the Church as a mode of setting men aside for special duties, showing the early roots of these later developments. The election of bishops was still ratified by the total congregation, however, a practice that in time would disappear.

This tendency toward a loss of former spontaneity and the growing importance of structure led to protest within the Church. In fact the concept of protest is one of major significance in understanding the development of a religious movement. As such a movement becomes a stable institution, which it must do if it is to survive, there develops in response currents of antagonism and revolt against the loss of formerly prized characteristics of the group. And when the institutionalization process is advanced, completed, and even carried to excess and tends to stifle a living spontaneity, we see such protest asserting itself again. The great historical example of protest and of the protest of the latter type is to be seen in the Protestant Reformation of the sixteenth century. We have already noted that protest of the former kind increased the appeal of Gnosticism and strengthened that religious tendency. The second century saw another example of such protest rise up to challenge the Catholic Church and its ecclesiastical development. All such revolts come into existence in concrete historical circumstances and are affected by the ideas available in the tradition. They see the spirit tending to be smothered by form and they try to reassert what they see as its former vigor. Moreover, both in the second and the sixteenth centuries, revolt was at the same time a reaction to an increasing worldliness in the church.

We have seen that the early Church considered Christ divine and as such worshiped him with the Father. By the beginning of the second century, Christian thought had differentiated the Holy Spirit from Christ and had seen it as preexistent with Father and Son. This is seen in the Trinitarian baptismal formula to be found in Matthew's Gospel. There developed in the second century the idea that the Holy Spirit would come and bring a more abundant spiritual fulfillment. Thus the failure of the Parousia to come about and the fading of the earlier spontaneity in the Church which had been seen as the gift of the Holy Spirit gave rise to a hope in a new outpouring of the spirit. This would be the end of the old world-age and the beginning of a new one. This hope was expressed in Montanism. Around the year 156 Montanus announced himself to be the passive instrument through which the Holy Spirit was revealing himself. Thus the promise of Christ ("But when the Counselor comes, whom I shall send to you from the Father, even the Spirit of truth, who proceeds from the Father, he will bear witness to me" [John 15:26]) was being fulfilled, and the new age, the age of the Holy Spirit, was here. The end of the world was seen as imminent and the Montanists advocated that all should go to Phrygia, whence Montanus had come and where ecstatic religion was popular, for there the new age would soon commence in all its fullness. An arduous ascetic discipline was advocated including celibacy, fasting, and abstinence from meat. The movement achieved genuine popularity and the bishops of Asia Minor called the first synods of bishops in church history to combat it in the seventh decade of the second century. The Montanist doctrines were found in Rome around the year 170 and remained for some time a source of inner conflict in the Roman Church. Around the year 200 the great African apologist and Latin father, Tertullian, became a Montanist. Although the Church overcame this threat, Montanism was but the first example in the new Catholic Church of protest against formalism and worldliness assuming a radical apocalyptic stance combined with an ecstatic religious attitude and a highly puritanical moral orientation. In it we see a precursor of the more radical groups of the Reformation. Indeed, did not Tertullian anticipate at that time Luther's reassertion of the priesthood of believers—"Are not even we laics priests?"

If protest is a universal category of religious history, monasticism is one of its classic expressions. Monasticism involves the founding of separate and special ascetic communities, a phenomenon found not only in Christianity but in Judaism and in nonbiblical religions in

THE RISE OF
MONASTICISM

many parts of the world as well. Monasticism is indeed a protest movement expressing withdrawal from or rejection of the world and of the Church which compromises with the world, with its sinfulness and halfheartedness. But monasticism is also more than protest. It represents the attempt to live in harmony with the highest and strictest ideals of a religious tradition, to assert those ideals, and to form an ideal community of believers. Already in the early Church before the beginning of monasticism there was considerable emphasis upon asceticism and avoidance of the temptations and dangers to the life of the spirit to be encountered in the world. In contrast to the developing worldliness and the consequent compromise of worldly Church members—conditions which were no doubt favored by the fading of apocalyptic hopes, the rejection of Montanism, and the increasing importance of form and structure—there were large numbers who sought to live according to a stricter interpretation of what they considered the counsels of the Gospels. "If you will be perfect, go, sell what you possess and give to the poor, and you will have treasure in heaven; and come, follow me" (Matt. 19:21). The same Gospel represents Jesus as saying, "there are eunuchs who have made themselves eunuchs for the sake of the kingdom of heaven" (Matt. 19:12). Moreover, superior pagan spirits also looked upon the world as morally questionable, advocated a restrained and austere life, and saw human fulfillment in contemplation rather than in action. This last idea was taken over by the Christians. The second century looked upon a life of voluntary poverty, celibacy, and contemplation as the Christian ideal and there were many who practiced it within the Church, without, however, separating themselves from the general community.

This situation gave rise to a kind of double standard. There were those who attempted to do the maximum in terms of the Christian ideal and there were others of whom this ideal could not be expected. A compromise with the world was inherent in the new existence of the Church as an established religious institution. As part of such a compromise, the Church evolved a higher and a lower morality. This expression of the more rigorous ideal led men into the desert as hermits where they led lives of extreme self-denial and even self-torture. The most important of these was Anthony (251?–356), an Egyptian who first took up the ascetic life in his native village but soon went into the wilderness. Many imitated him and the deserts were soon the scene of men alone or in small groups seeking extreme and zealous expression of their religious ideal. Much attention has been given to the demon-haunted life of Anthony and the inhuman austerities to which he subjected himself, but they were the gross expressions of an ideal of renunciation and of developing the power of the human will to follow an ideal. This hermit life was changed into a community, or cenobitic, form by Pachomius (292–346), who established the first Christian monastery at Tabenna on the Nile between 315 and 320 and a convent for women somewhat later. At one time he is said to have had seven thousand men and women living under his rule in a number of congregations. The rule he established called for a community of men or women involved in worship and work on a regular schedule, wearing similar dress, living in cells close together under the presiding governance of a paternal or maternal superior, an abbot or an abbess. Indeed a traveler to Egypt around the end of the fourth century felt there must be as many people in the desert as in the cities. Pachomius' monastic idea gained considerable following and it was reformed by Basil (330–379), who worked for its propagation from about the year 360 on. Basil's monastic rule is the basic constitution of monasticism in the Eastern Orthodox Churches to this day.

Monasticism was brought to the West by Athanasius, archbishop of Alexandria, and a friend of Anthony's. It was first looked upon with considerable suspicion although it met the approval of such great Latin Fathers as Ambrose, Augustine, and Jerome (a monk and the translator of the Bible into Latin). Western monasticism was disorganized until around 529 when Benedict of Nursia established the monastic rule since known as Benedictine and established his community at Monte Cassino, about halfway between Rome and Naples. Benedict built his way of life around worship and work. Worship took up four hours of each twenty-four-hour day. Work was both mental and manual, for it was concerned with intellectual as well as agricultural endeavors. Thus the Benedictines became important transmitters of culture. Moreover, their emphasis upon worship made their monasteries centers for the development of liturgy and for the development of the Christian culture of the early Middle Ages in which liturgy was a central element. Their concern for work made them pioneers in agricultural development and they made tremendous contributions to the progress of European agriculture in the early Middle Ages. But most significant was their missionary work, for Monte Cassino was a veritable schoolmaster of Europe and from it and its sister monasteries missionaries went to the North to bring Christianity to Teutonic and Celtic peoples. When the fall of the civilization of antiquity (from the late fifth century onward) brought retrogressive political and social conditions to the Empire, the disorder and misery of the age magnified the attractiveness of the monastic life and further exaggerated the contrast between the ordinary and higher morality which we have seen beginning in the second century. From the beginning, monasticism attracted the best people in the Church, and after the foundation of the famous Benedictine monastery at Cluny in eastern France in 910, and particularly in the eleventh and twelfth centuries, this was even more the case. Out of Cluny came a great reform movement to purify the Church which was bogged down and almost overcome by all the evils of that gross and violent age between the fall of the Empire and the rise of the civilization of the High Middle Ages. This movement known as the "cluniac reformation" fought simony, advocated clerical celibacy, and held before the world the monastic interpretation of the gospel ideal. It culminated in the election of the cluniac monk Hildebrand to the chair of the bishop of Rome, now long since the central, presiding, and ruling bishopric of the entire Church, but particularly of the West, since the East long contested Rome's claims. As Gregory VII (1073–1086), this reforming Pope became the outstanding figure of the time, journeying throughout much of Western Christendom, purifying the Church, and struggling against the political domination of the Church by the Christian emperor.

In contrast to Benedictine monasticism and its moderate ascetic ideal there arose in Ireland a recrudescence of the stricter Egyptian monasticism which flourished from the fifth to the seventh centuries in the Celtic British Isles. It combined ascetic rigor of an extreme sort with the most arduous missionary work in the British Isles themselves and on the continent. The Celtic Church was in fact organized around monasteries rather than the bishops, and their episcopal sees and Celtic monasticism adapted itself to the Celtic clan system so that monasteries were also clan organizations and abbots were hereditary offices. Irish monks played a strategic part in the conversion of Northern Europe, but in the later consolidation of the Church there the moderate and well-organized Benedictines proved superior. The practice of private confession had developed among the monks of both the East and West and the Irish missionaries of the sixth and seventh century introduced the practice to the laity as a whole, and with it a penitential literature which had flourished in Ireland. This practice replaced an earlier public confession of the community and became throughout the Middle Ages a long training school in introspection and self-examination for the individual Christian, a training school without which Martin Luther and his profound interior religious problems in the sixteenth century would hardly have been possible.

Monasticism gave an outlet to Christian ideals in the new ages into which the Church's existence was prolonged and offered a life of heroic piety and liturgical participation. It made possible some kind of realization of the ideal Christian community presented in the Book of Acts. As the gifts of the spirit were now attached to the charisma of office in the clerical order, so life according to the gospel ideal was now to be found in the institutionalized monastic form. The distinction between clergy and laity, a distinction of function, became a difference of religious worth and dignity. With monasticism there arose a new distinction—between people formally seen as "religious" and people living in the world. At first monasticism was a lay movement and indeed one with antiecclesiastical potentialities. But the rules of Basil and Benedict domesticated monasticism, so to speak, and brought it not only within the Church, but in the West especially put its huge religious energies at the Church's service. With the concentration on worship in Benedict's rule and the central position given to liturgy, monks soon became clerics or at least something closely akin to clerics. A third division had arisen in the church—between religious and nonreligious. When, in 1140 at Bologna where Roman law was again being studied, Gratianus, the great canonist and monk, collected his concordance of Church law and attempted to put order into it, he recorded a canon (which he says was authored by Jerome) which states that there are two genera of Christians—the first comprised of those dedicated to worship, the clergy, and those seeking the improvement of their lives

Late twelfth-century enameled cross with five scenes from the Old Testament, attributed to Godefroid de Claire. (Courtesy of the British Museum.)

according to Christian counsels, the monks; the second made up of lay people who live in the world and are compromised by it. And when Pope Honorius II in that same century confirmed the establishment of a new monastic order, the Premonstratentions, he declared, "From her beginning the Church has offered two kinds of life to her children: one to help the insufficiency of the weak, another to perfect the goodness of the strong." Hugh of St. Victor (d. 1141), a monk, a Christian Platonist, and by his own admission a man who loved all forms of learning sacred and profane, represented the

Church as two peoples—one following the pope made up of clerics and monks, the other following the emperor made up of princes, nobles, knights, and ordinary men and women, a representation that became more frequent in the fifteenth and sixteenth centuries.

THE CHRISTIAN
TRADITION

By the fourth and fifth centuries the traditions of Christianity had assumed the major forms which would characterize them for many centuries to come. First there were the scriptures of the Old and New Testaments, the basic sources of Christian thought and piety for all time. With the growing acceptance of revelation as finished and closed, the importance of these was enhanced. There was also (visible in the New Testament and in the formulation of creeds) the development of Trinitarian ideas which became the distinctive core of Christian theology. There were the efforts to relate Christian thinking and Christian life to the ideas and ideals of the higher secular culture, and to meet the intellectual challenge of sophisticated secular learning. Visible and central also were the ecclesiastical and institutional traditions, already expressed in the writings of the Apostolic Fathers and embodied in the Church seen as the safeguard and transmitter of the deposit of faith and the traditions of the fathers, a church speaking with the authority of the Holy Spirit, judging orthodoxy and proper morality, and disciplining its followers, at times to the point of excommunication. The Church of Rome, early the largest and most esteemed of the churches, rose to a position of leading influence, then to a primacy of honor, and finally to the Pope as a bishop of bishops and a ruler of the Western Church —a trend which despite opposition and reversals continued in Catholicism in the nineteenth century when the First Vatican Council defined the Pope as infallible when he speaks on matters of "faith or morals." Along with this development are the traditions of opposition to papal dominance, first in North Africa and later in the East, opposition which eventuates in a final rejection of papal claims by the Eastern Church and in rebellion against them by large numbers in the West at the time of the Reformation.

By the fourth and fifth centuries the Christian tradition of worship and prayer and the here-and-now relationship to God through Christ which flowers in later liturgical and mystical developments were well established. The cultivation of Christian feeling in connection with the Mass and the Divine Office, and the development of Christian mysticism, represents a profound deepening of the spirituality of Western man and his relation to God. Well established also was the tradition of asceticism—of self-denial, of an other-worldly orientation and a high estimation of virginity for men and women, of fasting and abstinence. Such asceticism is seen as part of the development of the Christian person, both as penance and reparation for past sins and as training in self-control in accordance with higher demands necessary for the achievement of "perfection." This emphasis often enough resulted in an extreme other-worldliness to the neglect of legitimate worldly demands and values, and a dark suspicion of sexuality which exaggerated and exacerbated the problems

Mont-Saint-Michel, a town and abbey built on a huge rock off the coast of France. Crowned in prehistoric times by a Celtic temple, the island was fortified during the Hundred Years' War. Portions of the monastery date from the ninth century. (Photo by Engelhard, from Monkmeyer Press Photo Service.)

of spirit and flesh throughout Christian history. Such extremes appear to have been conditioned by the lamentable moral and even physical conditions of sexuality in late antiquity and by the extremes of the reactions of the Gnostic groups as seen in their dualistic ideas and in both their asceticism and licentiousness. It was soon to be seen (with the early hermits and the first monks) to what extremes self-denial and asceticism could be carried. In the reaction of the institutionalized Church we see the beginnings of the tradition of official moderation and suspicion of extremes long characteristic of the Church in these matters.

Visible as well were the traditions of protest asserting freedom in the face of constraint and spontaneity in the face of form, as will be seen still alive in the medieval sects such as the Cathari and the Waldensians and later in the new churches of the Reformation. This tradition of protest was visible in two forms of expression—one in the groups which leave the great Church and pursue independently their own understanding of the Christian calling, and those who remain within as religious orders and are reconciled to the life of the great Church but find for themselves a special, separate, and often reforming status within. Noticeable also was the marked split between men of religion and men of the world which will long remain characteristic of the Western world and which even the best efforts of the Reformation will not overcome.

Finally we see the apocalyptic tradition out of which the Church came still rising to the surface. Men continued to expect a second advent or an age of the Holy Spirit and to find in the catastrophes of each age the propadeutic and initiating conditions of the coming of the New Jerusalem, a tradition ever driven underground and ever rising again. Chiliastic phenomena remained characteristic of Christian history from Montanist expectations in Phrygia in the second century to Millerite hopes in New York State in the nineteenth. So did the attempts to construct an ideal Christian community from Benedict's rule in 529 in Southern Italy to Joseph Smith's efforts in Kirtland, Ohio, in the 1830s. The expectation of an age of the Spirit was a real force in the Joachimite movement in the Middle Ages which saw it as an "age of monks" which was imminently expected. It remained important for the more radical groups in the Reformation. These traditions would be expanded, developed, and cast in novel forms of expression, but by fourth and fifth Christian centuries they were already present and already recognizable. From the religious life—the efforts, the sufferings, the hopes, and the disappointments—of these first centuries there had come into existence that religious and cultural phenomenon which we call Christianity.

SECOND EXILE: ISRAEL RECONSTITUTES ITSELF

The bitter and harsh defeat of the Jewish rebellion in A.D. 70 left the population of Judea despoiled and depressed. Once again the nation had failed to achieve independence, the Temple lay in ashes, and the people of Yahweh were subjugated to the rule of a pagan power. Reminiscent of the destruction of 586 B.C., a crisis of order and meaning arose. And again reminiscent of the first destruction, this crisis, the situation of disillusionment and chaos, was overcome through a communal reaffirmation of religious faith and a reconstruction of the religious foundations of the community.

Jewish legend attributes the rescue of the community from total crisis to Rabbi Yohanan ben Zakkai. According to the legend, Yohanan, recognizing that defeat was inevitable, had himself smuggled out of Jerusalem in a coffin during the final stages of the battle. Carried to Vespasian, he pleaded and received permission from the Roman commander to found an academy at Jamnia. Whatever the historical accuracy of the legend, this academy of rabbis maintained stability and self-government after the defeat and exercised decisive leadership in reconstituting the Jewish people. The disastrous results of military efforts seemed to vindicate the more moderate nonactivist position of the Pharisaic party. That party now came to rule. Its leading rabbis, gathered at Jamnia, declared what was binding upon the community in all areas of activity. The Jewish people, with the experience of the first reconstruction behind them, accepted both the rule of the rabbis and the traditional explanation of this latest disaster which had come upon them. This is revealed in the following Apocryphal quotes:

> *Righteousness belongs to the Lord our God, but confusion of face to us and our fathers, as at this day. All these calamities with which the Lord threatened us have come upon us . . . for the Lord is righteous in all his works which he has commanded us to do.*
>
> (Bar. 2:6, 8)

> *Why is it Israel that you are in the lands of your enemies? . . . You have forsaken the fountain of wisdom. If you had walked in the way of God you would be dwelling in peace forever.*
>
> (Bar. 3:10, 13)

The ideas and institutions which emerged from the crisis of A.D. 70 reenforced the religious structure and religious self-understanding which already existed, and became the permanent foundation of Jewish religious and communal life until modern times.

It was most important, in the emergency situation following the fall of Jerusalem, that a legitimate authority emerge which would organize communal life. The rabbis who gathered at Jamnia derived their authority from their knowledge of Scripture (the Written Law) and their ability to interpret it. Their interpretations of the Law formed the Oral Law. These men were considered to be legitimate successors of the priests and scribes, empowered to interpret the word of the Lord. In the *Mishnah* of *Avot* it is written: "Moses received the Torah on Sinai, and handed it to Joshua; and Joshua to the elders, the elders to the prophets; and the prophets handed it down to the men of the Great Synagogue . . ." (*Avot* 1:1). The rabbis of the Pharisaic party claimed and were recognized as the next step in this continuous chain of tradition. Descendants of the great sage Hillel became heads of the Academy at Jamnia and held power from A.D. 85, under Gamaliel II, to 425, when permission to appoint a successor was denied by the Byzantine emperor. While the Patriarch of the house of Hillel held ultimate authority, decisions were generally made on the basis of a majority vote among the rabbis who constituted the academy. They debated issues brought to their attention and then passed a ruling. Local courts and schools ruled on local cases and referred problems to the central academy when difficult disputes arose. The Jamnia body produced the laws, judges, and teachers necessary for the governance of a community whose life was framed within the religious structure of the Torah. The rabbi, from this time forward, was the head of the Jewish community, rendering decisions in religious matters and wielding the authority which gave order to the life of that community.

Jews living in the diaspora were organized in the same way as those living in Palestine. They were governed by rabbis, who from their schools issued decisions in social and religious matters. In Babylonia, the largest diaspora community, civil administration was in the hands of the Jewish exilarch, who deferred to the rabbis of the leading academy in religious concerns. The schools of Babylonia grew rapidly and renowned rabbis emerged there who would eventually become the chief authority of Jewry when the Palestinian

The Wailing Wall in Jerusalem, part of the western wall of the Temple, believed to be part of Solomon's Temple. Since the Middle Ages, Jews have come to this wall to lament the destruction of the Temple and to pray for the restoration of the Jewish people. Frequently prayers and requests are written on slips of paper and inserted in the crevices between the ancient stones. (Courtesy of the Israel Government Tourist Office.)

schools had declined. In the first centuries A.D. all diaspora communities turned to Palestine for final guidance, used the Palestinian traditions as the basis of their own rulings, and regarded the Palestinian academy as the spiritual center of Jewry. This recognition of Palestinian leadership was crucial in evolving generally uniform patterns in religious order and communal organization.

The emergence of the rabbis as the effective authority in self-governing Jewish communities must be understood as a consequence of the function which the Torah fulfilled within Jewish life. This in turn must be understood within the Jewish concept of covenant and religious law. Within Judaism the religious experience of revelation, the disclosure of God to Israel, had been given specific definition and content within the structure of biblical law. The Law was considered to be a gift of Yahweh, which established a permanent relationship between him and his chosen, and which provided a constant source of his presence to his people. From its earliest stages, Judaism concentrated upon the sphere of action, emphasizing fulfillment of God's commandments as the essential activity of the religious life. One was a member of the covenant community upon obligating oneself to observing covenant law. Commitment to God's law was an expression of commitment to God himself, an acknowledgement of his revelation and a positive response to it. This is the context of meaning within which the elaboration and observance of specific commandments must be understood. Underlying the detailed structure of law is the concept that the love of God, a vital binding relationship to him, must be actualized in concrete deeds. Every aspect of behavior was seen as an opportunity in which the Jew asserted his commitment to the Lord by fulfilling the divine will.

It is this basic concentration on commandment, on the deed which fulfills the Word, which was responsible for the development within Judaism of the Oral Law and the neglect of intellectual definition in the form of theology. This is not to say that the Jew did not embrace specific beliefs, but rather that these basic beliefs were assumed, implicitly accepted, and generally not transmitted in objectified formulated creeds. The distinctive religious creation of Judaism is the *halakah,* the law. It is this law which has sustained the order and given the form to Jewish life, a life constantly threatened by the many disruptive and disintegrative forces inherent in the situation of exile. *Halakah* in its broadest sense is more than *nomos,* that is, law as statute. *Halakah* refers to a universal cosmic principle, which is contained in the Torah and its commentaries. It is really the way of the universe established by God for the governance of man. In rabbinic literature one reads that the Torah preexisted the world and that God fashioned his creation on the basis of the Torah. God himself is said to study this law, such activity being the highest value. Indeed, it is claimed that the whole universe is maintained for the sake of the Torah.

Study of the law and the interpretation of its meaning, both for the sake of practical behavior and for the attainment of answers to the questions of meaning, became the most valued activity in Jewish society. At Jamnia, the immediate need was for a codified body of law which would establish norms and give a degree of uniformity to Jewish life both in Palestine and in the diaspora. The rabbis set themselves to this task, and during the first and second centuries A.D., they gathered opinions on all issues, evaluated them, and ruled between conflicting views. Finally in A.D. 200, Rabbi Judah the Prince issued the *Mishnah,* a practical code of law which set definite standards in civil and religious matters. This work, the first and most important code, was accepted throughout the diaspora. As the rulings in the Mishnah are interpretations of biblical law in application to concrete life situations, so the decisions of the Mishnah were further interpreted within constantly changing circumstances. The process of interpretation has been continuous throughout Jewish history, and centers of learning have been established from Babylonia to Egypt, North Africa, France, Germany, Poland, and Russia. Following the decline of the Palestinian schools, the main decision-making institutions were the academies of Babylonia at Sura and Pumpedita. Learned rabbis from all over the diaspora consulted the Babylonian authorities. The compilation of the Babylonian interpretation, the Babylonian Talmud, became the authoritative code of Jewish law and the primary text of study for all later periods.

Commentaries upon commentaries have been elaborated to guide the community of the pious along what was considered to be the proper path of life, the path pleasing to God. While this heavy corpus grew, there remained the underlying notion that the total body of law could be reduced to the essential precept to love man and to love God. Hillel had said, "Be of the disciples of Aaron, loving peace, pursuing peace, loving men, and bringing them near to the Torah" (*Avot* 1:12). In bringing them near to the Torah one led them to God's precious gift, the source of his love and the source of righteousness. Rabbi Akiba, one of the greatest rabbis of Jewish tradition who lived in the first century A.D., stated, "Thou shalt love thy neighbor as thyself, that is the greatest principle of the Law" (*Sifra* 89b). All of the commandments and all of the commentaries could be leveled down to this essential moral precept, without which the entire elaborate structure was meaningless. Micah had stated the demand of God, "to do justice, and to love kindness, and to walk humbly with your God" (Mic. 6:8), and this ethical demand remained primary.

The rabbis did not consider mere external observance of the law, even in its most minute detail, to be proper or sufficient. Conformity to the law was to be based upon an inner intention. Certainly, the fixed objective structure was to be followed, but the interior subjective attitude was of decisive importance. The heart was to be directed toward heaven. Hillel is said to have said, "Let all thy deeds be for the sake of heaven." The law was indeed compared to a yoke which brought freedom and purification to man. This was its true goal—spiritual perfection.

This sense that the law brought freedom and that it was a source of benefit to man underlay submission to the "yoke." The traditional pious Jew assumed the regimen of the religious life because he trusted that the word of the Lord, as interpreted to him by his rabbis, was binding upon the chosen people and that he personally, as an elect member of that people, was responsible for realizing the word. Through his actions, carried out in conformity to the objective structure and with the proper intention of true service, he felt that he contributed to the perfection of himself and to the perfection of the world. It is not possible to understand the continuous devotion of the Jewish community and the determined will to survive in exile unless one understands this basic religious trust and positive faith. The law was a total way of life which segregated the Jew from the environment of the non-Jew. This rigorous segregation and the full structure of Jewish practice which maintained it could not have survived without the conviction that such a way of life was a sanctification which brought man near to God. "It is not an easy thing, but it is your life" (Deut. 32:47). Such was the lot of Israel, singled out to be God's special agent in history. The law was God's own gift to his people and a symbol of his love for his chosen son.

> With everlasting love hast Thou loved the house of Israel. Thou hast revealed to us a Law and commandments, statutes and judgments. Therefore, O Lord our God, when we lie down and when we rise up we shall attend to thy statutes. Yea, we shall rejoice in the words of Thy Law and in Thy commandments forever and ever. They are our life and the measure of our days and we will meditate upon them day and night. Mayest thou never take away Thy love from Israel. Praised be Thou, O Lord, who lovest thy people Israel.
>
> (Prayer from the Evening Service)

The development of the *halakah,* the legal literature, served to give structure and organization to Jewish life. At the same time there arose the *aggadah,* the literature concerned not with practical behavior but with the ideas and values which are the ground of that behavior. The rabbis speculated upon things divine and things human. They asked questions of why and wherefore, and sought to understand the basic questions of meaning inherent in human life. In traditional Jewish manner, they went to the Bible for clues to the answers to such questions and developed their own notions as exegesis upon the biblical text. Their folkloristic opinions of metaphysical and theological problems are contained in the various volumes of the *midrash,* written at the same time as the legal matter contained in the Mishnah. In addition to these separate works, one-third of the Babylonian Talmud, and one-half of the Palestinian Talmud, consists of aggadic material. The importance of such material in expressing the religious insights and deep sentiments of the Jewish soul has been enormous. Indeed, without the *aggadah,* Judaism would be a petrified legal system. The rabbis recognized this when they commented upon the blessing which Isaac gave Jacob, "God give thee the dew of heaven, the fat of the earth, and plenty of corn and wine. Dew of heaven is Scripture, the fat of the earth is mishnah, corn is halakah, wine is aggadah" (Genesis Rabbah 27:28).

Aggadah is thinking about man, his relation to God and his relation to his fellowman. It is insight into the mystery of the universe, and speculation upon God's presence in the universe, in history, and his relationship to man. The entire legal structure of Judaism rests upon these insights. *Halakah* and *aggadah* are mutually dependent. Judaism teaches that there must be both objective obedience and subjective understanding; there must be discipline but also freedom. The dialectic of the external act and the internal intention is constant. Both *halakah* and *aggadah* developed continuously wherever Jews engaged in the study of tradition.

Judaism accepted the notion that the Torah, revealed to Moses on Sinai, was eternally true and binding. This Torah was made relevant to everyday life by the constant process of interpretation on the level of both *halakah* and *aggadah*. In the area of *halakah,* general prescriptions and proscriptions, such as not cooking a calf in its mother's milk or not working on the Sabbath, had to be applied to concrete situations and elaborated fully. From such elemental negative commands, a complicated body of dietary laws and a full regimen for Sabbath observance emerged. In the area of *aggadah,* explanations for the acts of God and of man in concrete situations had to be sought. In order to apply Scripture, years of study were required. Indeed, study of the tradition was considered the highest religious duty, and education became an ideal value to all Jews. Had it not been commanded that "thou shalt meditate upon them day and night, that thou mayest observe to do all that is written therein" (Josh. 1:8)? Study, like prayer, was a religious act which must be directed heavenward. It was to be the occupation of a lifetime, beginning with the learning of Scripture at the age of five and continuing into advanced exegetical interpretive work of mature scholars. Rabbi ben Bag Bag had said, "Turn it over and over again, for everything is in it, and contemplate it, and wax gray over it, and stir not from it" (*Avot* 5:25). His suggestion became the ideal of the people of the book. The structure of belief and law evolved by the rabbis saved Judaism from destruction following the fall of the Jewish state in A.D. 70. From that time until the period of Emancipation in the eighteenth century, Jewish life became a spiritual reality, with the laws of God serving as its ordering constitution, its principle of national coherence, and its source of ultimate meaning.

FAITH AND THE THEOLOGICAL TRADITION

WHO IS CHRIST? Christianity confronted the intellectual culture of antiquity and related itself to it in a positive way. It is true that such a positive reaction was opposed in the spirit of Tertullian who declared that "after Christ Jesus we desire no subtle theories" (Tertullian, *De praescriptione haereticorum,* 8) and that the positive reaction itself was selective. Christian thinkers and writers were indeed inclined to take over and use those elements of the philosophy and ethics of late antiquity which exhibited an affinity for Christianity and expressed the inward-turning and growing other-worldly orientation of the period. It found its chief material in this respect in Platonism and in the Stoic ideas of a rational ethical natural law which it related to Hebraic ideas of morality. The history and the criticism of the secular culture were neglected, and in harmony with the general spirit of declining antiquity its empirical scientific elements were not taken up. Yet this adaptation of the intellectual heritage of the Greeks to serve Christian ends was a most significant one for the future. The struggle against Gnosticism had already given an intellectual cast to the clerical mentality. The acceptance of the Platonic and Stoic heritage would impart to the Christian tradition two characteristics which would remain constitutive of it throughout its history. First, faith was conceived as not standing in contradiction to understanding, religion as not opposed to secular knowledge. Second, yet despite this deep and deeply significant orientation to the harmony of faith and reason, a conflict between the claims and implications of the two became characteristic of the development of Christian thought forever after.

The first fruits of this coming together of Christian faith and the philosophical culture of the Greek world can be seen in the theological controversies of the fourth and fifth centuries. Here indeed "subtle theories" would appear to be both causing and expressing bitter division. The religious experience of the Christian Church had encountered God in three fundamental modes. It had met the transcendent God who revealed himself in history in the Old Testament and in the earthly career of Jesus of Nazareth. It had experienced God's Word become flesh and mediate the relationship between men and the Father. Finally, it had experienced what it saw as the Holy Spirit in the life of the Church itself. A transcendent, a mediational, and an immanent mode of God's self-revelation and of his relation to the world that he created were characteristic of the Christian experience. This found its formulation in the early Trinitarian formulae which we have already seen. But the intellectual mode of speculative philosophy which the Church had now adopted found such statements inadequate and demanding further explication. How was this fundamental Christian experience to be given adequate intellectual form as the Greek philosophical mind insisted it must? The distinctions between the three had been established by the end of the first century, but how could they be given precise and consistent definition and how were the relationships of the three to be stated in philosophical terms? By the third century there had evolved in the West a near unanimity on the answer to these questions but the East was divided. The East, moreover, was culturally more thoroughly Greek and more inclined to speculative theology than the West and much of the outstanding intellectual ability in the Church was found there.

The next century and a half saw the working through and fighting out of these issues. It was a process which exhibited three characteristics that remained with the Church throughout its history in one form or another. First, as we have already seen, is that mixture of faith and philosophical speculation which leads to the objectivized, formulated, intellectual statement of the content of faith, giving high salience to the element of intellectual assent. In the sixteenth century Martin Luther, himself a figure of intellectual eminence, challenged such intellectualization and presented faith as a more holistic acceptance of and dependence on Christ as Savior. This intellectual bent gave rise to the important status granted to the "correct" formulation and turned the understanding of faith into a sophisticated philosophy of religion accessible in this form only to a trained specialist. While the Church always admitted the equal personal worth of the faith (often implicit) of the simple believer, the intellectual statement became the accepted standard for official teaching and the measure of orthodoxy. A second characteristic long to be found in the Christian tradition also comes into existence at this time. When these theological conflicts reached their full force, the Church was no longer a community of the withdrawn, in the world but not of it, establishing and maintaining its own way of life alongside the life of the Roman Empire. Decius who became Emperor in 249 initiated the first really general persecution of the Church and sought to bring about its extermination. There followed both apostasy and heroic martyrdom. Such persecutions continued under the emperors Gallus and Valerian and reached the greatest proportions under Diocletian. But persecution came to an end with the Edict of Toleration in 311 "allowing Christians the right to exist again and to set up their places of worship" (Lactantius, *De Mortibus Persecutorum,* 24) and the identification of the new Emperor Constantine with Christianity in 312. Constantine saw in the Christian faith a means for constructing a foundation for unity and stability in the empire, a basis for developing that "consensus" which Cicero had seen as requisite to political order. Thus Christianity now became involved in the political life of Europe, subject to political pressures, and manipulated for political purposes, a fact of life for Christian existence which lasted until the nineteenth century and may still be seen in many parts of the world. A third element visible in these controversies is the amalgamation of religious points of view with the cultural interests of national and ethnic groups so that religious antagonisms often admit of analysis upon two levels—one concerned with the manifest content of religious thought, the other with the cultural, psychological, and political needs of various nationalities. In the post-Reformation period this aspect of religious phenomena became very prominent, and nowhere more palpable than in the history of the assimilation of European immigrants into American society in the nineteenth century.

The issue of how Christ was to be understood had already produced formulations considered heretical. There were those who identified Christ and the Father, saying "that the Father himself descended into the virgin, was himself born of her, himself suffered; in fact that he himself was Jesus Christ," a point of view Tertullian attributed to the devil (Tertullian, *Against Praxeas,* 1), or those following Sabellius, who held "that Father, Son and Holy Spirit are one and the same being in the sense that three names are attached to one substance" (Epiphanius of Salamis, *Against Heresies,* 42.1). There were also those who believed that Christ's humanity was not genuine but only an appearance (the Docetists) and those who saw Jesus only as a man chosen and adopted by God at the time of his baptism by John (the Adoptionists). The conflict came to a head in the formulation of Arius, a learned and pious priest of Alexandria, which stated that "the Son has a beginning, but God is without beginning," that before the Son "was begotten or created or appointed or established, he did not exist" ("Letter to Arius to Eusibius of Nicomedia," Theodoret of Cyprus, *Church History,* 1.5). He was opposed by Alexander, Bishop of Alexandria, and by the year 320 the conflict was widespread and bitter. Constantine desiring the unity of the Church as a basis for the stability of the empire called a council, which was held at Nicea in 325, the first in Church history, and presided over it although he was himself only in catechumen status—not yet baptised. There were some 308 bishops present with only about a half dozen of them from the West, where opposition to Arius was strongest. There were among the Council Fathers two small minorities, one supporting the Arian position and one holding with Alexander that the Son was eternal, of like essence with the Father, and uncreated. The majority were not deeply cognizant of the issues of the controversy. A creed was adopted using the terms "begotten not made" and "of one substance with the Father" (*homoousion*), representing the view of Alexander and of the West in general. The influence of the emperor was a decisive factor in the decision of Nicea and the Nicene formulation was almost immediately the subject of bitter controversy. Indeed, the real conflict only began with the Council's end.

There then arose Athanasius who became the champion of the Nicene formula, and bishop of Alexandria. He was a robust figure, strong in his convictions, and unlikely to be moved by political pressures or court considerations, and he led the Nicene party to ultimate success. Athanasius saw the problem as most intimately related to the understanding of salvation which he understood in harmony with the Johannine as well as the Pauline tradition: "He was made man that we might be made divine," "his task was to restore the corruptible to uncorruption" (Athanasius, *De incarnatione*, 53.3, 7). The conflict continued to rage for years, each side making use of and being used by political manipulation. Many of its leaders would see several terms of exile, including Athanasius who was exiled four times. At first it looked like a victory for the anti-Nicene party—a group made up of the Arians and a large conservative middle group which was not really of Arian convictions but disagreed with the Nicene use of the term *honoousion,* which sounded to them like Sabellius. This victory, like the earlier one of the Nicene group, was made possible by imperial influence. Moreover, the debate was broadened to include a discussion of the relationship of the Holy Spirit to the Godhead. Athanasius and his party saw that relationship as similar to that of the Son and the Father. With the death of Athanasius the leadership passed to the three great figures of the Eastern Church, Basil and the two Gregorys. These men were greatly responsible for the victory of the Athanasian point of view. In 380 an imperial edict was issued declaring that all should hold the faith as taught by Damasus, Bishop of Rome, and Peter, Bishop of Alexandria. Thus there was set up one religion in the empire and that was based upon the Nicene formulations. In 381 a synod, recognized as an Ecumenical Council, was held at Constantinople, which adopted the Nicene statements. A creed which became the standard belief of the Church came into general use and was finally approved by the Council of Chalcedon in 451. We reproduce it here as found in the writings of Epiphanius, in the lectures of Saint Cyril of Jerusalem, and as presumably read and approved at Chalcedon as the creed of "the 318 Fathers who met at Nicea and that of the 150 who met at a later time," that is, at Constantinople, and known since as the Nicene Creed or the Niceano-Constantinopolitan Creed,

We believe in one God the Father All-sovereign, maker of heaven and earth, and of all things visible and invisible;
And in one Lord Jesus Christ, the only-begotten Son of God,
Begotten of the Father before all the ages, Light of Light, true God of true God, begotten not made, of one substance with the Father, through whom all things were made; who for us men and

for our salvation came down from the heavens, and was made flesh of the Holy Spirit and the Virgin Mary, and became man, and was crucified for us under Pontius Pilate, and suffered and was buried, and rose again on the third day according to the Scriptures, and ascended into the heavens, and sitteth at the right hand of the Father, and cometh again with glory to judge living and dead, of whose kingdom there shall be no end;

And in the Holy Spirit, the Lord and Giver of Life, that proceedeth from the Father, who with Father and Son is worshipped together and glorified together, who spake through the prophets;

In one Holy Catholic and Apostolic Church;

We acknowledge one baptism unto remission of sins. We look for a resurrection of the dead, and the life of the age to come.

In this creed we see the belief of the West in one God in three divine persons and the belief of Athanasius and his followers in the East in one essence (*ousia*) and three "subsistencies" (*hypostasis*) established as the faith of the Church. However, this decision did not set well in the East, where revolt threatened immediately. The creed of Chalcedon, in addition to enacting the Niceano-Constantinopolitan doctrine, further explicated it by speaking of "two natures," one of the same substance as the Godhead, the other of the same substance as our manhood (Council of Chalcedon, *Actio V, Mansi,* 8). Many in the East saw this as destroying the unity of Christ, and before long Palestine and Egypt were in revolt and there arose the Monophysite heresy and divisive religious and political conflict in the eastern empire. For more than two centuries the imperial government strove to adjust the ensuing controversies. These conflicts exhibited that combination of religious and national elements to which we have referred; non-Greek nationalities in the East struggled against the imposition and restraint of Greek ideas and against rule from Byzantium, the new Greek capital of the eastern half of the empire, as well as against the content of the religious ideas themselves. The exhaustion which resulted from these fierce struggles prepared the way for the conversion of most of the area to Islam, in which the non-Greek inhabitants of the region found a new religious form and one possibly much more in harmony with their indigenous culture than post-Chalcedon Christianity. Yet the definition of the triune God at Chalcedon became the faith of the overwhelming majority of Christians, the Eastern Orthodox, the Western Catholics, and most Protestant groups to this day. The West would, however, make one addition not accepted in the East. It would in the sixth century add the word *filioque* to the Latin creed, thereby declaring the Holy Spirit to proceed from the Father "and the Son." Monophysite (anti-Chalcedon) churches are still found, however, in Egypt, Ethiopia, and the Middle East.

In the Creed adopted at Chalcedon we see a combination of the sophisticated Greek philosophical ideas and the historical elements of the career of Jesus of Nazareth, a combination characteristic of Christian thinking in the centuries to follow. Moreover, we see an acknowledgment of the expected second coming and of the resurrection of the dead and the beginning of a new world-age. Together with this we see a growing reverence for the Church itself as the guardian of orthodoxy and the community of succor. This found expression by the end of the second century in describing the Church as a "mother." In the middle of that century we already see the Church appearing under various symbols, as for example in the *Shepherd of Hermas,* the brother of Pius, bishop of Rome (140–154), where among other forms that of an exhorting mother is to be found. By the end of the century we find Clement of Alexandria calling the Church "a mother" who feeds her children the spiritual food of the *Logos* (*Paedagogus* 1.6.42.1). The tradition of affection and respect for "Mother Church" had begun.

The Christological controversies had raised the question as to the genuineness of Christ's humanity, which involved some understanding of the role of his virgin mother, for the Church had very early accepted the idea of the virgin birth (Matt. 1:20 and 23; Luke 1:34 ff.). At the Councils of Ephesus (431) and Chalcedon (451) the title *theotokos* (Godbearer) for Mary, which had come into use by theologians by the fourth century if not earlier, was approved. This confirmed a growing attention to Mary's role and importance by Christian thinkers and a popular devotion to her and belief in the efficacy of her intercession which was already well established. This term was translated into Latin as *Dei Genetrix* (Mother of God). Thus was confirmed the devotion to Mary which would increase with the years and become a basic and central devotion in the Medieval Church and after the Reformation in Catholicism. Indeed, in the nineteenth century Pope Pius IX promulgated the dogma of her Immaculate Conception, the belief that she was born without the stain of original sin which Christians believe all men have inherited from Adam, although of natural parentage, and in the mid-twentieth century Pius XII promulgated the dogma of her Assumption—that is, the belief that after her death her body was miraculously transported to heaven. Indeed, some Catholic theologians have even conceived of Mary as a kind of mediator with Christ between God and man, a view never given dogmatic status. Protestantism rejected this emphasis upon Mary and the devotion to her as a nonscriptural accretion and as a kind of semiidolatrous activity.

Head of the Virgin, *a drawing by Leonardo da Vinci.* (*Courtesy of the Metropolitan Museum of Art. Harris Brisbane Dick Fund, 1951.*)

There also began early in the Church a devotion to martyrs and to other esteemed Christians, seeing them after their deaths as intercessors before God, that is, as those who offer prayers to God for the living and to whom the living pray to ask their intercession. This devotion spread rapidly from the fourth century on. It was approved by the later Fathers, the theologians of late antiquity, and in the Middle Ages was a prominent feature of popular and official worship and devotion. It found its way into the liturgy of the Mass, where Saint Augustine speaks of its presence in the fifth century (*City of God* 22.10) and the Divine Office of the monastic daily worship in which lives of the Saints were read. It has remained characteristic of Catholic practice but was repudiated thoroughly by the Reformation. Even the Church of England, although in some ways undecided on other Reformation issues, speaks of it as a "fond thing vainly invented" (*Thirty-Nine Articles,* art. 22).

HOW ARE WE SAVED? The Christian East was concerned with problems of speculative theology and had centered its attention upon the Godhead and particularly on the character of Christ, as the pagan East had earlier been concerned with speculative philosophy. The Christian West was more humanistic in its emphasis as the pagan West had earlier been in its study and development of administration and law. The chief theological controversy in the West concerned the relations between God and man and the relation of each to the problem of the existence of evil and the nature of salvation. Moreover, in line with its humanistic emphasis the West was concerned with problems involved in the functioning of the Church, and the relationship between the Church and the secular world and particularly the state. The great figure who brought together and developed these themes was Augustine, Bishop of Hippo in North Africa. Augustine had been a Manichaean, a member of a religious group which held to a sharp dualism of good and evil, seeing an evil agency as an eternal part of the cosmos engaged in continual conflict with the good God. He later became a skeptic, taking up the ideas of the New Platonic Academy which denied the possibility of genuinely knowing truth. He then became a Neo-Platonist, which opened up to him a transcendent world of being and goodness above and beyond the material world he had previously conceived as total and ultimate. Neo-Platonism was most significant in preparing for his conversion to Christianity and in providing him with the philosophical concepts in terms of which he would develop his Christian theology after his conversion. He was converted in 387 after a personal religious experience of a semimystical character.

> *But when a profound reflection had, from the secret depths of my soul, drawn together and heaped up all my misery before the sight of my heart, there arose a mighty storm, accompanied by as mighty a shower of tears . . . I flung myself down, how, I know not, under a certain fig tree, giving free course to my tears . . . and weeping in the most bitter contrition of my heart, when, lo, I heard the voice as of a boy or girl, I know not which, coming from a neighboring house, chanting and oft repeating, "Take up and read; take up and read."*

He then picked up the copy of the scriptures which he had left nearby and opening it "in silence read that paragraph on which my eyes first fell" (*Confessions* 8). The paragraph which Augustine read was from Paul's Epistle to the Romans, "not in revelling and drunkenness, not in debauchery and licentiousness, not in quarreling and jealousy. But put on the Lord Jesus Christ, and make no provision for the flesh to gratify its desires" (Rom. 13:13–14). This experience was the culmination of a long period of interior suffering and it completely changed Augustine who had unsuccessfully up to then attempted to restrain his lusts and his ambitions. While Augustine was learned in scripture and ecclesiastical tradition, while he knew the philosophy of the age and was possessed of a towering intellect, his development of Christian theology was tremendously affected by the impact of that conversion experience. Augustine's thought evolved in the years before his conversion—from Manichaeism to skepticism, from skepticism to Neo-Platonism—but afterward he saw the whole of reality from one point of view, that of the supremacy of and centrality of God in human experience. Like Paul before him, Augustine reshaped theology in terms of his own profound experience of its meaning. Augustine's experience was whole and deep, involving both the profoundest emotion and the most sophisticated intellect and his theology reflected that experience. Moreover, Augustine considered his conversion and the transformation which he immediately experienced and which was to be seen and felt in his daily life, as a gift of God for which he himself deserved no credit.

In his life Augustine confronted three viewpoints either heretical or antagonistic to Christianity. He countered the first, Manichaeism, by asserting and explicating the infinite goodness of God, the creator, and the essential goodness of his creation. He saw evil not as a positive force, as did the Manichaeans, but as a privation of good, a lack in an essentially good creation. The source of moral evil he found in the human will. Classical philosophy had neglected the concept of the human will, which Augustine now subjected to brilliant intellectual analysis.

While he was Bishop of Hippo, Augustine came into conflict with the Donatist heresy. The advocates of Donatism, protesting immorality in the Church, held that sacraments administered by unworthy clergy were invalid. Augustine defended the objectivity of the Church's sacraments against this point of view, holding that they are not the work of men but of God and that therefore they do not depend on the spiritual condition of the minister. This conflict made Augustine examine the conception of the Church and the sacraments and to develop them beyond what had taken place up to his time. Augustine saw Baptism, the Holy Eucharist, and Holy Orders as the three chief sacraments, but recognized other ecclesiastical rites as sacraments as well. The Catholic Church would eventually define seven sacraments which it saw as outward signs instituted by Christ and endowing the communicant with God's grace—his gratuitous aid to the human spirit—operating *ex opere operato:* Baptism, Confirmation, Holy Eurcharist, Penance, Anointing of the Sick, Holy Orders (the ordination of the clergy), and Matrimony. The Reformation contested all of these except Baptism and Holy Eucharist, and the attitudes of various Protestant groups toward them differ. Moreover, Augustine emphasized the significance of the institutional church. He stands as the great prototypic example of that union of profound subjective religiosity and an objective ecclesiastical and sacramental system characteristic of the Middle Ages and the Catholic piety of the post-Reformation period. He felt that the "Holy Spirit may be said not to be received except in the Catholic Church" (*Baptism* 3.16), although he recognized that there were men outside the Church who were really within it in spirit (*Baptism* 5.28). However, "the church even now is the kingdom of Christ, and the kingdom of heaven" (*City of God* 10.9), though she contains both good and bad individuals who will not be separated out until the day of judgment. He also gave his attention to the relationship of the Church to the state. He accepted the state as part of God's providence but saw it as good only insofar as it was founded on the concept of justice. Yet he saw actual states as ambiguous, as the embodiments of human ambition and pride as well as God's instrument in punishing evil and maintaining peace and order. He felt that the state should support the worship of God and should help in counteracting heresy, although he rejected the idea of the death penalty for heretics. In his concepts of the Church and the sacraments and in his ideas of the function of the state and the relations of Church and State, Augustine was the great source of ideas for Christianity in the Middle Ages and indeed in modern times. His Platonic philosophy as he applied it in the explanation of Christian doctrines became the guide of Christian thinking up to the thirteenth century when St. Thomas Aquinas shifted the philosophical basis of theology from Platonism to Aristotelianism. Yet in Thomas himself the influence of Augustine and Augustinian Platonism is serious enough to be characterized as constitutive.

Important as these ideas of Augustine are, he is perhaps most significant in his ideas on grace and free will. Men were redeemed by Christ, but the question arose as to what role the individual performed in his own salvation and what part was to be attributed to divine initiative and support. Christ's death was the basis of salvation, but how? There are variations in Augustine's answer to this question—Christ had offered himself as our sacrifice to God; he had ransomed us by his death from the power of Satan; he had died in our stead and paid the human debt to God's justice. But of one thing Augustine was sure, basing himself upon the Scriptures and tradition viewed in the light of his own personal experience. The initiative was God's and the transformation was made by God. Salvation is the work of grace and it is neither deserved nor earned by man; it is God's free gift. All men fell in Adam's sin and all are in a sinful state until they receive God's grace. These ideas were formed in Augustine's mind early in his Christian life but they reached their full development and their most vigorous expression in the controversy with Pelagius and his supporters.

Pelagius was a Celtic, possibly Irish, monk who came to Rome during the time when Anastasius was pope (399–401). He and his followers, especially Celestius and Julian of Eclanum, taught that a man was himself responsible for both initiating and achieving his own salvation. The Pelagians insisted that the human race was not fundamentally damaged by the sin of Adam. Pelagius, who was a man of great ethical seriousness and shocked by the state of morality he found in Rome, believed that to say that a man was not responsible for his own deeds was to give him permission for self-indulgence and sin. Like the Stoics he saw most of the human race as bad in practice, but like them also he saw as paradigmatic the slogan, "If I ought I can."

What the Greek Fathers, the great religious thinkers of the Eastern Church, had taught about the relation of Adam's sin to the condition and guilt of the human race is far from clear. They seemed to hold that it had some effect making man corruptible, but their language is vague and there is no precise kind of statement on which they agree. In the West, however, Fathers such as Tertullian, Cyprian, and Ambrose were of the opinion that all men were somehow involved and implicated in Original Sin, an involvement transmitted to oncoming generations by heredity through the sexual act. Pelagius is said to have started his teaching in response to a sentence in Augustine's *Confessions,* "give what Thou commandest, and command what Thou wilt" (*Confessions* 10.29). Augustine soon replied and there followed a bitter controversy on the issue. In the course of this, Augustine set forth definite ideas on Original Sin and predestination.

It was Augustine's own personal experience that the transformation which came with and developed after conversion was not his own doing. He believed from all the depths of his fervent soul and with all the power of his vigorous mind that his own delivery had come from God. God had chosen and changed him, it was not his own initiative nor effort that was responsible. This was in harmony with the teaching of Ambrose, who had been influential in his conversion. It was in this light that Augustine read the Scriptures:

Sin came into the world through one man.

(Rom. 5:12)

For those whom he foreknew he also predestined to be conformed to the image of his Son . . . and those whom he predestined he also called; and those whom he called he also justified; and those whom he justified he also glorified.

(Rom. 8:29–30).

He destined us in love to be his sons through Jesus Christ according to the purpose of his will, to the praise of his glorious grace which he freely bestowed on us in the Beloved.

(Eph. 1:5–6)

The issue became a central one for the Church and the conflict saw the fortunes of both parties change from time to time. But the anti-Pelagian party eventually won the inner struggle and in 418 Pelagianism was condemned by an imperial rescript which ordered the exile of its adherents; a large council at Carthage was held that approved a moderate position, and Pelagius and Celestius were condemned by Pope Zosimus, who earlier had shown some sympathy for the Pelagians. Augustine's reassertion of the Pauline position established the doctrine of Original Sin as Church teaching, although it continued forever afterward to be a matter of controversy from time to time, and especially in the Reformation.

With respect to predestination, the doctrine that some persons are foreordained by divine decree to eternal salvation, Augustine developed the Pauline ideas. He felt that God had indeed foreordained to salvation and glorification and had given the gift of perseverance to those chosen. This depended not upon human attitudes of acceptance but on God's decree. Why God does as he does, Augustine saw as a mystery, beyond our human comprehension. God does not cause evil but he permits it for a greater good which we cannot understand here on earth. God is loving, generous, and just and the doctrine does not in any way impugn these divine qualities but may only seem to do so to our darkened intelligences. Moreover, man's will, though not responsible for his salvation but rather for his sin, is seen by Augustine as free and the doctrine of predestination as he teaches it does not violate the existence of free will. It is a subtle and difficult doctrine that Augustine develops and one which will cause great conflict in the future. Augustine and Pelagius seem to have been looking at different aspects of the general problem and from quite different points of view. Augustine was a man who has had a great religious experience which changed and transformed him, the impact of which ever remained fresh and clear to him. He also had a great theoretical mind, indeed he may be justly said to be the father of all Western theology, as Plato is the father of all Western philosophy. He saw the problem from a combination of a deeply personal and subjective and a lofty intellectual perspective. Pelagius, on the other hand, was a practical moralist concerned with developing ethical habits in individuals. To Augustine, Pelagius appeared to dwarf and parody the mystery and majesty of the conversion experience and the biblical doctrine of God as Lord of history electing and foreordaining crucial events affecting human destiny. To Pelagius, Augustine appeared to make sin man's normal condition and any goodness in him to be God's work, not his. This would make the achievement of virtue an extrahuman gift. The implication for Pelagius was that man is heartily discouraged from trying to be moral; in fact, he is encouraged to be what he is and to enjoy sinning since he cannot do otherwise of his own accord. Both points of view appear to be speaking of different levels of the problem which are brought together under a single conception. The issues they raised long continued to be a bone of contention in the Church.

The fifth century saw more moderate or "semi-Pelagian" positions (a word coined in the sixteenth century when the issues were again being debated) put forward. John Cassianus in 429 stated that "the will always remains free in man, and it can either neglect or delight in the grace of God" (Cassianus, *Collationes,* 12). In 434 Vincent of Lerins wrote a work which gave his oft-quoted and difficult definition of what the Christian tradition was—*Quod ubique, quod semper, quod ab omnibus,* "the faith that has been believed everywhere, always and by all" (*Commonitorium* 2.4)—and in which he characterized Augustine's distinctive ideas on grace and predestination as not meeting this criterion. Faustus of Rhegium declared in 473: "Man's effort and endeavor is to be united with God's grace;

man's freedom of will is not extinct but attenuated and weakened; he that is saved is in danger, and he that has perished could have been saved" (Faustus, *Epistle ad Lucidim,* P.L. 53.683). The Synod of Orange in 529 took the position "that through the sin of the first man, free choice was so warped and weakened that thereafter no one is able to love God as he ought, to believe in God, or do anything for God that is good, except the grace of God's mercy first come to start it in him (*Praeveniret*)."

In Pope Gregory the Great (590–604), the first monk to hold the papal office, an energetic, wise, and temperate man, who was the real ruler of Rome in secular as well as ecclesiastical affairs, we see a prefiguration of much of the Middle Ages. Although Gregory expected the world to come to an end before too long a time and felt he was living in the final age, he built the Church and the Papacy in a manner that would stand them in good stead in the difficult years ahead. His great practical wisdom may be seen in his advice on the conversion of the English—to disturb the indigenous culture as little as consonant with the new faith—and in his book *Pastoral Rule.* His theology is that of Augustine but with changed emphasis, and it reflects the growing loss of intellectual vigor of the declining Roman West. He accepts predestination but he often seems to see it merely as divine foreknowledge. He saw man truncated by Original Sin but rescued from this state by the death of Christ to which he becomes heir in baptism, an idea long accepted. For sins which a man commits after baptism, he must render satisfaction. This he can do by works of merit, which are done with the assistance of God's grace. The Church offers aids in this effort, especially the Eucharist, which he saw as a repetition of Christ's sacrifice. The prayers of the saints are also available and of help. Gregory put forward as a matter essential to faith an idea that began much earlier in the Church, the idea of purgatory. In some form this idea of a state after death in which those do penance who have not made adequate satisfaction and are still guilty of smaller sins was taught by various fathers. We find hints of it in Hermas, a clearer notion in Clement of Alexandria, and a more systematic treatment of it in the West, as in Ambrose. Indeed, the idea of purifying pains in the next life is also found in Augustine himself. Gregory declared, "It is to be believed that there is a purgatorial fire before the judgment for certain light sins" (Gregory, *Dialogues,* 4.30). Although the Eastern Church did not follow the West in such a precise and defined answer to the problem, it held a similar doctrine and continues to hold it, that some kind of intermediate state exists after death in which souls exist and can be helped, as they can also in the Western conception, by the prayer and sacrifice of the living. The doctrine became a basic one for the Middle Ages. Around it all sorts of abuses arose, including the sale of indulgences which set souls free from suffering in purgatory. It was completely repudiated by the Reformers of the sixteenth century, but was reaffirmed by the Catholic Church at the Council of Trent (1545–1563).

The Middle Ages accepted the doctrine of Original Sin as basic to Christian belief, and medieval theology was concerned with its implications and with its mode of transmission. They also were much influenced by Augustine's ideas on predestination but at the same time they held with the Greek Fathers that God desired and willed the salvation of all men. Moreover, they accepted, like Gregory, the idea that "the good that we do is both of God and ourselves" (*Moralia* 33.22). St. Augustine had seen man's fallen state as one in which the appetites of the flesh are no longer subordinated to reason. This was accepted in the Middle Ages but there was some question on how it was to be understood. St. Bernard (1090–1153), who was probably the most influential churchman of all Christian history, wrote in his treatise "On Grace and Free Will," "Remove free will, and there is nothing to Save; remove grace and there is left no means of Saving. The work of Salvation cannot be accomplished without the cooperation of the two." A more sophisticated and optimistic position was developed by St. Thomas Aquinas, who gives the matter considerable attention. Thomas, who made the great intellectual revolution of shifting Christian theology from a Platonic to an Aristotelian basis, recognized an autonomous nature which he separated from the sphere of the supernatural. Thus Adam before the Fall was not perfect in human nature only because that nature was brought to a perfection beyond itself by supernatural grace. In this state of grace there was in man a harmony between his supernatural end and his natural end and hence a harmony within his own composite make-up. The Fall deprived man of supernatural grace and hence of the internal order with which it had endowed him, thus wounding but not vitiating his capacities.

> Hence in the state of the integrity of nature, man needs a gratuitous strength added to natural strength for one reason, viz., in order to do and will supernatural good; but in the state of corrupted nature he needs it for two reasons, viz., in order to be healed, and, furthermore, in order to carry out works of supernatural virtue which are meritorious.
>
> (*Summa Theologica,* Part II, Ques. 109, art. 2)

Original Sin is thus a condition of the human race after Adam had lost the added gift of grace which put order and direction into man's make-up and behavior by relating him beyond the powers of his own nature to God and God's help.

The problems involved here rise again in full view at the time of the Reformation. Martin Luther, another great religious personality like Paul and Augustine, who combined knowledge of Scripture and tradition with profound personal religious experience, reformulated Christian tradition in keeping with his reading of the Scriptures in the light of his own profound inner struggles and religious experience. His deeply pessimistic view of man is to be seen in his denial of freedom of the will and in his affirmation of the total depravity of fallen human nature. Luther, who was himself an intellectual of impressive dimensions, suspected reason, considering it a harlot willing to serve any cause. Man is hopelessly sinful and is saved because God deigns to regard him as righteous because of the saving merits of Christ's death. As he said in his famous hymn, *Es ist doch unser Tun umsonst, auch in dem besten Leben,* "All we do is in vain, even in the best life." Justification of man is God's work and salvation is based upon faith alone—on man's total reliance upon God's mercy. This position had come to Luther as the solution of his own personal internal anguish which, like Augustine before him, he took as paradigmatic for the human problem as a whole. It was God attributing Christ's merits to man without human cooperation that brought salvation. Luther stood in the long medieval Augustinian tradition and he exaggerated its theological pessimism. However, he refused to teach the complete sinfulness of all human acts.

Augustinianism found its most radical and most intellectualized expression in John Calvin's *Institutes of the Christian Religion* (1536–1539). Calvin taught that before the Fall man could live in relation to God by his own natural powers. The Fall, however, which was willed by God for reasons that lie hidden in his transcendent inscrutability, so corrupted and vitiated man's nature that all he can do since is sin. He is no longer possessed of free will but follows of necessity either the attractions of his own fallen nature—his worldly desires and appetites of the flesh—or the call of divine grace. All human acts are sinful and all human glory is filth.

"Therefore original sin is seen to be an hereditary depravity and corruption of our nature, diffused into all parts of the soul." Moreover, this corruption is not just a weakening, for this sin we inherit possesses "positive energy." "For our nature is not merely bereft of good, but is so productive of every kind of evil that it cannot be inactive." Indeed, "whatever is in man, from intellect to will, from the soul to the flesh, is all defiled" (*Institutes of the Christian Religion,* Book 2, chap. 1).

This spirit of a hyper-Augustinian pessimism is found coming to the surface in the seventeenth century within the Catholic Church in a rigorous moralistic movement known as Jansenism and causing no little theological controversy. Its basic point of view is stated by Cornelius Jansen (1585–1638) in his book on grace and human nature entitled *Augustinus,* which was published after his death in 1640, and which is based upon the anti-Pelagian writings of Augustine. Five propositions extracted from this work were condemned by Pope Innocent X in 1653. Jansen and his followers held that obedience of God's commandments is impossible without a special grace from God, and that grace was irresistible by man. The problem of grace, how to understand its workings and its relationship to man's natural powers and psychological dispositions, gave rise to a large controversial literature in the seventeenth century. It was the subject of conflict between Protestants and Catholics and within the two groups themselves.

Paul had accepted predestination and free will but did not attempt to work out a rational theological context in which both positions were put together. Augustine also followed him in this, although Augustine presented considerable theological commentary upon the problems involved. The Middle Ages inherited these problems and attempted to put together the mystery of divine predestination with the belief in the universal saving will of God. In the ninth century we find a controversy over the meaning of the doctrine of which the leading figures were the monk Gottschalk (805–868) defending a hyper-Augustinian position and his chief opponents Archbishop Hincmar of Reims (806–882) and Johan Scotus Erigena (810–877). Here again Thomas, commenting on Romans 8:30, attempts a synthesis by viewing predestination as part of God's providence in which he directs men beyond the sphere of their own proper nature to eternal life. Behind predestination Thomas sees God's love, "all the predestinate are objects of election and love" (*Summa Theologica*, Part I, Ques. 23, art. 4). Most important is the fact that for Thomas God's predestination, his calling and electing of some, does not destroy free will.

> *Predestination achieves its effects most certainly and infallibly, and yet it does not impose any necessity, such that its effects should take place from necessity. For it was said above that predestination is a part of providence. But not all things subject to providence are necessary; for some things happen from contingency, according to the disposition of the proximate causes which divine providence has ordained for such effects. Yet the order of providence is infallible, as was shown above. So also is the order of predestination certain; and yet free choice, from which the effect of predestination has its contingency is not destroyed. Moreover all that has been said about the divine knowledge and will must also be taken into consideration; since they do not destroy contingency in things, although they themselves are most certain and infallible.*
>
> (*Summa Theologica*, Part I, Ques. 23, art. 6)

Luther had made salvation by faith alone (*sola fide*) the cornerstone of his theology and emphasized the all-pervading divine mercy which clothed the sinner with righteousness. Calvin, a man of stern temperament and logical rigor, insisted on pushing the notion of predestination to its logical implications without the saving qualifications which had long hedged its meaning. He indeed accuses his predecessors, not excluding Augustine himself, of a "superstitious fear" deriving "from motives of piety" which makes them "often shrink from the straightforward acknowledgment of the truth in this matter" and suggesting that biblical references to " 'hardening' and 'blinding' refer not to the operation of God, but to his foreknowledge" (*Institutes of the Christian Religion*, Book 2, chap. 5). Calvin says:

> *No one who wishes to be thought religious dares outright to deny predestination, by which God chooses some for the hope of life, and condemns others to eternal death. But men entangle it with captious quibbles . . . . By predestination we mean the eternal decree of God, by which he has decided in his own mind what he wishes to happen in the case of each individual. For all men are not created on an equal footing, but for some eternal life is preordained, for others eternal damnation.*
>
> (*Institutes*, Book 3, chap. 21)

Thus Calvin denied the universal saving will of God and taught that Christ's atoning death affected only the elect.

The Westminster Confession of Faith in 1643 established this Calvinist doctrine as the credo of Presbyterianism. "By the decree of God, for the manifestation of his glory, some men and angels are predestined unto everlasting life, and others foreordained to everlasting death." Yet "neither is God the author of sin or is violence offered to the will of his creatures." Moreover, "neither are any redeemed in Christ . . . but the elect." The First Baptist Confession of Faith, drawn up by seven congregations in London in 1646 declared, "God hath, before the foundation of the world, foreordained some men to eternal life through Jesus Christ, to the praise and glory of his grace: leaving the rest in their sin, to their just condemnation, to the praise of his justice." The Quakers, however, took a different view of the matter. Robert Barclay presented their view in 1678 in *Apology for the Quakers.* While finding all men "fallen, degenerated and dead" as a consequence of Adam's sin, the Quakers emphasized God's "infinite love" and declared, "Therefore Christ hath tasted death for every man . . . even unto those who are necessarily excluded from the benefits of this knowledge by some inevitable accident."

A strong reaction against the Calvinist theory of predestination was initiated by Jacobus Arminius, a professor of divinity at Leyden, in 1603, when he put forth views similar to those adopted by the Catholics at the Council of Trent. He explained election by God's foreknowledge of man's merit. In 1618 these views were condemned at a synod of the Reformed Church at Dort and the Arminians expelled, but Arminianism increased in popularity in time and became a strong current in Protestant theology, greatly affecting the Methodists in the eighteenth century.

In the year 410 Alaric, a Visigothic noble and an Arian by religion, who had been commander of the barbarian troops of the imperial army, proved successful in his third seige of Rome and led his troops into the city. It was a shocking event to the men of that time and the cause of widespread consternation. In response to it Augustine wrote his *City of God.* The work was a reply to pagans who charged the reason for the fall of the city was the decay of the traditional religion. In it Augustine examined the relationship of Christianity to the world and set forth for the first time a Christian philosophy of history. Augustine presents human history as consisting of the careers of two cities, an earthly city and a city of God. In these two cities we find the key to an understanding of human destiny. "Accordingly, two cities have been formed by two loves: the earthly by the love of self, even to the contempt of God; the heavenly by the love of God, even to the contempt of self. The former, in a word, glories in itself, the latter in the Lord" (*City of God,* Book 14, chap. 28). The city of this world, the earthly city is self-oriented, the heavenly city, the City of God, is oriented to God. No institution can be wholly identified with one or the other, but the Church is seen as embodying in human terms the heavenly city. The real heavenly city is made up of those who have received God's grace and the Church contains others who have not. Yet the Church "even now is the king-

kingdom of Christ" (*City of God,* Book 20, chap. 2). Human history is the working out of the destiny of these two cities. Basing himself upon the Hebraic and Christian tradition, Augustine sees history as proceeding in a straight line and not a cyclical and repetitive process as had been held by Greek thought. In this work which consists of twenty-two books, Augustine presents not only a view of history but a discussion and explanation of Christian doctrine, and a consideration of other philosophical opinions. This involves Augustine's presentation of world history, a history in which the City of God is gathered together and triumphs in its ultimate peace and in its final glory. But before that time it is a society of pilgrims. Yet "in its pilgrim state the heavenly city possesses this peace by faith" (*City of God,* Book 19, chap. 17).

THE JEWISH RELIGIOUS TRADITION

The God who loved Israel was also the God who had punished it. The conviction remained that it was only because of Israel's heavy sin that the suffering of exile had been imposed. "Because of our transgressions we were exiled from the holy land and banished from its borders." Exile and redemption—the one, reality, and the other, expectation—were crucial concepts in the consciousness of the Jew and quite essential notions in the development of Judaism. To account for its historical destiny, Israel looked inward. Its deeds and the will of God, not external political forces, had determined its fate. The exile was viewed as a time of terrible suffering and penance which the Jews had to endure in order to atone for the sin of forgetting God's law and will. At the same time, just as living in exile accomplished atonement for Israel's sin, it was also thought to be part of the process of atoning for the sins of the world. Jews saw their own suffering as redemptive for mankind, in the image of the servant of God according to Isaiah. The task of the Jewish people was to suffer in humility and with patience. Their despised and rejected condition, the condition of degradation and suffering, testified to the fulfillment of their mission and the consequent hastening of the redemption.

Thus the pain of exile could be considered a positive blessing, since it was the opportunity God offered to realize the historic role for which Israel had long ago been chosen. According to the Jewish conception, world history depended upon Israel's fulfilling that role, and hence responsibility for the course of world history devolved upon the shoulders of the individual Jew. Knowledge and acceptance of this responsibility constituted the spiritual power of the politically powerless people. Of course, the Jews knew that they could not force the redemption, as had been shown by the crushing of their rebellions and the failure of their pseudo-messiahs. But Israel could pray, could study, and could perform righteous acts—behavior prescribed by the Lord and pleasing unto him—and thereby move history closer to its end station.

The actual reality of exile was often bitter and difficult to bear. In times of persecution the question as to God's intention had to arise. "God, do tell me why I suffer, for I am no doubt unworthy to know why, but help me to believe that I suffer for your sake." Rabbi Akiba believed that sufferings were a gift of God. They served to bring man to a recognition of his own sins, to cause him to repent, and then to bring him to an unquestioning love of God. Akiba refused to challenge divine justice, believing that whatever God did must be for the good. "One ought not criticize Him who said 'let the world be.' Everything He does in justice and truth . . . the judgment is just" (*Avot* 3:20). Although there were many who did not accept Akiba's position and did question the ways of God, the notion that suffering ennobled and was hence a positive value penetrated the Jewish consciousness and brought consolation to the nation. "According to Rabbi Azariah: David said before God: show me the way of life! God said to him, if it is life you seek, seek suffering" (*Pesikta Derekh Kahanna,* p. 152, l. 7). It is this view of suffering which led Jews to accept martyrdom willingly. During the Crusades, which at times led to Christian attacks against Jews, martyrdom became the ideal act of devotion to God. This period witnessed numerous cases of self-slaughter, in which the victims, identifying themselves with Isaac, sacrificed themselves ritually to God, in the belief that this was his wish and part of his divine plan. The Jews of Mayence, attacked by the soldiers of the first Crusade,

> declared with their whole heart and willing soul, After all one must not have any doubts concerning the ways of the Holy One blessed be He who had given us His Torah and the commandment to suffer death in behalf of the unity of His holy name. Happy are we if we fulfill His wish and happy is he who is slain and slaughtered for the unity of His name. Such an one will be prepared to enter the world-to-come. . . . More, he will have exchanged the world of darkness for a world of light, a world of suffering for a world of joy, the transitory world for a world enduring forever.

(Chronicle, Solomon)

The Jews lived, in a certain sense, ahistorically and apolitically. They had no share in actual political power, and hence were not very much interested in it. Throughout the Middle Ages, in Christian lands, the Jews lived in the status of "Serfs of the Kingdom." This meant that they were considered serfs of the ruling power and that their residence and privileges were entirely dependent upon the will of that power. As long as they were useful, in an economic sense, they could remain. However, if their economic value declined, or if, for some reason, ecclesiastical authorities objected to their presence, the residency right was withdrawn and the Jews exiled. Completely dependent upon the will of the sovereign, the will of the

Church, and often the threats of the townsmen or peasants, the Jews lived in a state of constant insecurity. They were unable to determine their own fate, and hence did not really participate actively in the making of contemporary history. Their historical world was that of the past, of the Bible and the Tradition, which was a spiritual world out of time but in the midst of time. The condition of exile led the Jew to live with his eye toward the future, when existence in this world would end and all would be changed. Understanding of the present and hope for the future is summarized in the following statement of Rabbi Judah ha-Levi:

> If his mood is disturbed by the length of the exile and the diaspora and the degradation of his people, he finds comfort in acknowledging the justice of the divine decree . . . then in being cleansed from his sins; then in the reward and recompense awaiting him in the world to come, and the attachment to the Divine Influence in this world.
>
> (Kuzari II.33, 36)

The belief which sustained Israel and was of primary significance in Judaism was messianism, that is, the certain conviction that in God's appointed hour a messiah would come to deliver Israel and the world from travail. "For the vision is yet for the appointed time. And it declareth of the end and doth not lie; though it tarry, wait for it, because it will surely come and not delay" (Sanhedrin 97b). Every day the Jew prayed for the speedy fulfillment of the messianic promise. "Manifest to us the dawn of the Messianic deliverance and cause it to flourish by the grace of thy salvation. Thy redemption we want every day. Praised be Thou, O Lord, who causest deliverance to arise." Restoration of self-rule, of the ancient city of David, Jerusalem, return of the exiles, and the return of God himself to Zion—these were the ardent desires of the expectant nation. Jews also prayed for universal deliverance, for the day

> When we shall behold the triumph of thy might, when idolatry will be uprooted and falsehood utterly destroyed. We hope for the day when the world will be perfected under the dominion of the Almighty and all mankind will learn to revere thy Name; when all the wicked of the earth will be drawn in penitence to Thee. O may all the inhabitants of the earth recognize that unto Thee every knee must bend every tongue vow loyalty.

The messianic age would be filled with glories. First, Israel would be gathered together and restored as a national entity to its homeland to enjoy there the bounties of political freedom and material wealth. Following this age of material and national prosperity, the world-to-come would dawn. Conditions would be totally changed and a new order instituted. According to Jewish belief, at this time a universal judgment would take place and the righteous of all nations would be rewarded with eternal bliss. Descriptions of all stages of the future world and golden age abound in Jewish literature, providing hope and comfort to a people discredited in the eyes of the world and suffering the grave anxieties of exile.

The apex in the development of Jewish messianic thought is to be found in the doctrines of the Lurianic school of mysticism, which flourished in the mid-sixteenth century in the small Palestinian town of Safed. The devotees of this school, followers of Rabbi Isaac Luria, reinterpreted the traditional concepts of exile and redemption in light of their intense mystical experience and gave a radically deepened meaning to these keystones of Jewish belief. In 1492 the Jews had been exiled from Spain. This event had profound consequences upon the religious consciousness, manifested in the bursting forth of mystical speculation and activity concerning redemption, and the wide response to it. Around the time of the catastrophic exile and immediately following, messianic expectations ran high. Jews felt that the cruel events of reality could only be the signal and birth pangs of the long-promised ultimate deliverance. It is told that a group of Spanish Jews, confident of immediate redemption, marched headlong into the ocean, expecting it to part and let them pass. As late as 1560 a rabbi wrote that "No Jew has lived in Spain for seventy years, and we are sure that no Jew will ever pitch his tent there, for God will soon gather together the scattered remnants of his people of Israel" (*Baer* 69). However, when it became clear that the exile of 1492 was but another link in the chain of tribulations and not the beginning of the redemption, when the depth of the tragedy penetrated the Jewish consciousness, an explanation was sought. Why had the new darkness descended upon man? What had brought the evil fate? The Lurianic school of mystics, engaged in this inner process of soul searching, developed a doctrine of redemption which both offered an explanation of the external reality of intensified suffering in exile and presented a new path for internal spiritual salvation.

Lurianic mystical thought rested upon the notion that God, in order to create the world, had to impose limits upon himself. He had to retreat into himself in order to make space for the creation of the universe, so that in the very first act of creation a negative element was present. When God created the world he sent out his divine light, which was contained within form-giving vessels or spheres. However, the light was too much for the vessels to hold, and they burst, allowing the divine light to be scattered. Some of the sparks managed to return to God himself, but some descended to earth, to be diffused in the evil of the world and imprisoned below. Thus, in the process of creation, God himself went into exile. First, he exiled himself when he imposed limits on his being, and second, he was exiled when the spiritual and pure light was mixed in the impure world of man.

Through this mythological sketch of creation, the mystics revolutionized the Jewish concept of exile by giving it cosmic proportions. With God in exile, with exile built into the very nature of the universe, the exile of Israel became merely one sign of a total cosmic condition. The world had been broken from its very inception. Being itself had been distorted, had been ruptured, and the divine source of all suffered constantly from loss of wholeness. Exile, in this conception, was seen as a phenomenon characterizing all being, a matter of the inner nature of the universe. And redemption consequently was to be deliverance of the entire universe from its broken state of being. In the hands of Lurianic mystics, the traditional Jewish concepts of exile and redemption were deepened, interiorized, and universalized.

According to this school of mysticism, the task of the Jew was still to participate in the process of redemption, but in a new way. Within the framework of the traditional paths, of fulfilling the commandments, engaging in study, and devotion to prayer, the Jew had to now work for the inner salvation of the entire cosmos. He acted with a new intention, knowing that he participated in a universal process and that his deeds had cosmic power. The Jew had to help to redeem the fallen sparks and thus restore God to himself. It is this labor which he had to intend when he performed a religious commandment. With this concept, Lurianic mysticism radicalized the value of religious practice and the role of the individual Jew. The regimen of prescribed Jewish law would now be performed with the inner knowledge that such performance effected a cosmic change because with the fulfillment of commandments the diffused sparks were uplifted and returned to God. Man was thus a necessary agent in the process of reuniting God with himself and in healing the rift in creation. Through his actions he either hastened or delayed redemption.

The Lurianic mystic, when he observed the commandments and when he engaged in mystical prayer, believed that he helped to free his own soul from the bonds of earthly existence, and at the same time, that he helped to free the world itself. The great power of this doctrine lay in its awarding each man a vital role in the process of cosmic redemption and thereby the highest worth as a man. For the Jew who lived in the darkness of disappointment, in the brokenness and impotence of exile, Lurianic mysticism gave nobility and power. It enabled him to reach a new spiritual dimension of meaning and validation. To be sure, he and his people were defeated and unsuccessful when judged according to the standards of the external world. But he and his people alone possessed the internal spiritual power to redeem that exile. Thus, when judged according to the truth of inner reality, the Jewish condition was an elevated one. In the suffering of exile, reflecting the broken state of the cosmos, lay the opportunity to redeem the sparks and restore the world.

The concepts of Lurianic mysticism caught on and had great influence among large segments of the Jewish people. The rise and widespread acceptance of Sabbetai Zevi, the false messiah of the mid-seventeenth century, was made possible by the messianic expectations which Lurianic doctrines had encouraged. And in Hasidism, the great modern mystical movement, certain Lurianic notions live on, still providing great spiritual strength to those who participate in the hidden inner reality of the redemptive process. In Hasidism the emphasis is on the individual and his subjective religious experience. But his relationship with God is one which involves the act of redeeming the sparks and contributing to the restoration of the world. To the *hasid*, as to every traditional Jew, the basic fact of existence was exile, and redemption the basic need. In hasidic prayer ecstasy, the individual came close to God, achieved a degree of inner redemption, and returned to lead others to the same reality.

Judaism is a religion of revelation, in which ultimate authority resides in the word of God as found in Scripture and interpreted by legitimated scholars. The meaning of Jewish life and the order of its society was determined by an understanding of the revealed word. Religious ideas, values, and ways of behaving provided the framework for the total existence of the Jewish community throughout exilic history. However, the Jewish community was not a completely self-contained closed-off world, but was part of a larger environment and was subject to influences from it. In the hellenistic period, Greek ideas and values penetrated the Jewish consciousness and had a marked influence upon several levels of Jewish society. It was when the Jews came under Muslim rule, however, during the Arab conquests of the eighth and ninth centuries, that they were most deeply affected by outside influences. Through Arab writers and thinkers, the classical tradition of Greece and the traditions of the Hindus and Persians were presented to Jewish readers. In natural science, medicine, astronomy, history, literature, and philosophy Jews learned and responded to new ideas and new forms. The centuries under Islam proved to be among the most creative in Jewish cultural and religious history, producing a vast literature of a religious and secular nature.

The rise of Islam and the claims of the new religion challenged Judaism to respond in defense of its own claims to possess the original and true revelation of God and hence to be the one true religion. Rivalry with Christianity at other times evoked similar controversy and polemical activity. Jews were spurred to justify the beliefs and practices of their tradition in the rational philosophic language which would be understood by exponents of challenging beliefs. Influenced by the writings of Muslim philosophers and theologians, Jews were often themselves perplexed, and sought to examine the biblical tradition in the light of reason. From the ninth century to the eleventh, Jewish philosophic activity flourished in the Arabic lands.

The issues with which Jewish philosophers dealt were those which concerned all philosophical proponents of biblically derived religion, who attempted to integrate the doctrines of revelation with the ideas of Plato and Aristotle. There was the primary question of the role of reason within the structure of revealed religion and the relationship of philosophy and religious knowledge. Then questions as to the existence and nature of God, his relationship to man, and the role of man in the world were most significant. For the Jew in particular, proof of the eternal and absolute truth of the Torah, and validation of the election of Israel, were of great concern. An understanding of the commandments, both ritual and ethical, was also demanded as part of the attempt to rationalize the entire traditional way of life.

The first great Jewish philosopher of the Islamic period was Rabbi Saadia Gaon, who became head of the Academy at Sura in

The Dome of the Rock of the Temple Mount in Jerusalem, a sacred Moslem and Jewish site. The Dome marks the site of Solomon's Temple and is believed to be the place where Abraham prepared Isaac for sacrifice. (Courtesy of the Israel Government Tourist Office.)

Babylonia in 928, and who wrote his major work, *The Book of Beliefs and Opinions,* in 933. Saadia was impelled to write this work not only because of the challenge of Greek and Islamic ideas but also because of the internal threat posed by the Karaites, a Jewish sect which denied the authority of rabbinic interpretation, and hence the validity of the definitions, concerning law and ideas, handed down in the Talmud. Saadia was most influenced by the Aristotelian, the Mutazilite school, within Islam, and his defense of Jewish beliefs, such as the existence of God, was Aristotelian in nature. Saadia claimed that the truths of reason and revelation were completely harmonious. What God had revealed to the Jews, the content of the Torah, could not be contradicted by the knowledge which man would attain through reason. The specific value of revelation in contrast to reason was that revelation offered the truth to all men, many of whom could not otherwise attain it, and revelation, because of its final absolute nature, offered this truth in a form free of the inconclusiveness and uncertainty inherent in the process of reasoning. For these reasons, God's gift of revelation was necessary for man. Saadia believed that the exercise of reason in pursuit of the same basic truths was also a necessary, and indeed, a religious act. The philosopher is charged to engage in philosophical inquiry, with the assumption that he has already accepted the truths of revelation and hence knows the end to which his reasoning will lead. Saadia was as certain of the identity of natural knowledge and revelatory knowledge, as he was of the truth of Israel's special revelation. The indisputable historical fact that the Mosaic Torah, unlike any other revelation, was disclosed in a public event to an entire people guarantees its validity.

The writings of Saadia enjoyed widespread circulation among Jews in the Islamic lands and encouraged the development of Aristotelian philosophic thinking. Among the many figures to participate in this philosophic movement, the greatest by far was Moses ben Maimon, or Moses Maimonides (1135–1204). Maimonides was born in Cordova, Spain, fled with his family from anti-Jewish attacks to Fez, and finally settled in Fustat, outside Cairo, where he practiced medicine and served as the head of the Egyptian Jewish community. In his life and in his writings, Maimonides harmonized the Greek and Jewish traditions. He was pious in his religious practice, engaged in the rabbinic tasks of teaching and study and legislating, advised the Jewish community on public affairs, and at the same time was interested in general cultural ideas, devoting himself to bringing together Greek philosophy and biblical revelation. The first literary task which Maimonides undertook was a commentary on the Mishnah, followed by a systematic compilation of Jewish law. These works reflect his basic concern with traditional pursuits, and his desire, derived from acquaintance with Greek forms, to impress a logical order upon the traditional legal material. In the *Commentary,* Maimonides explained the concepts necessary for understanding the contents of each of the six volumes of the Mishnah, and prefaced the entire work with a chapter on the nature of Jewish tradition as it developed from the original Mosaic revelation into the halakic and aggadic writings of the rabbis. In the *Mishneh Torah,* Maimonides summarized the voluminous legal material of the Oral Law and codified the law in fourteen parts, corresponding to the fourteen types of legal commandments. He intended his work to be a lucid authoritative compilation of the law. Its merits were soon recognized and the *Mishneh Torah* became a basic guide to practice and a subject of study for all later generations.

It was in the *Guide to the Perplexed* (1190) that Maimonides expounded his philosophical ideas, which were decisive in the development of Jewish thought and which greatly influenced Christian Aristotelians, such as St. Albert the Great and St. Thomas Aquinas. As its title indicates, Maimonides composed the *Guide* for the perplexed of his time, for those troubled by the challenges which philosophy presented to biblical faith and concepts. He addressed the book to his student, Joseph, and intended it to be read only by those trained in traditional Jewish disciplines, mathematics, logic, the sciences, and who were thus fully prepared for the perils which philosophical speculation presented. Free rational inquiry was not

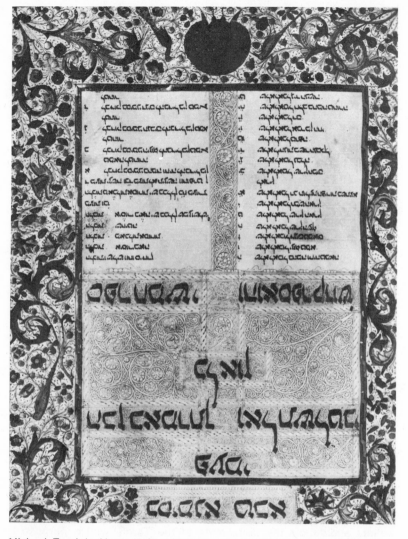

Mishneh Torah *by Moses Maimonides, showing the title and contents.* (*Courtesy of the British Museum.*)

to be pursued by all Jews, but only by an elite, whose minds and spirits could bear the doubts which such inquiry inevitably aroused.

The first concern of Maimonides was the relation of faith and reason. Like Saadia, he argued that natural knowledge and revelation were identical, and hence that there existed a harmonious relation between religion and philosophy. He did not propose that all philosophic knowledge was contained in Revelation, but that philosophic knowledge was the highest and truest way to reach an understanding of the content of Revelation. To Maimonides, philosophy was a religious task, and the pious man one whose faith has been understood and thereby deepened. He considered the greatest good of man to be the attainment of knowledge, for through metaphysical knowledge of the divine reality and divine truths, man entered into a relationship of love with God and achieved communion with him.

Therefore, contemplation, reflection, and the pursuit of understanding were the highest values of the religious life.

This view of Maimonides as to the value of contemplation and philosophical speculation represents a distinct shift in emphasis from the traditional Jewish evaluation of religious virtue. While contemplation was never disregarded, the traditional Jewish emphasis has been upon positive action, based upon loyal acceptance of the law. Maimonides' evaluation of intellectual activity and the internalization of divine knowledge, as the main activity of the religious life, does not imply a rejection of practice nor a denigration of tradition. On the contrary, Maimonides prescribed complete faithfulness to the ceremonial and ethical law of the Torah and assumed that philosophical study would be based upon mastery of the religious tradition. Further, he was himself involved in practical rabbinic tasks and wrote two major works on rabbinic tradition. His God was always the moral Lord of the Bible, who was concerned that men follow in the divine paths. Yet, despite this obvious loyalty to tradition, there is no doubt that Maimonides did shift emphasis when he postulated that knowledge would lead men to imitate God, and that this knowledge ought to underlie external conformity to religious imperatives.

Recognizing that most men were incapable of a life devoted to philosophic speculation, Maimonides postulated certain basic beliefs, which he felt were religious truths available to everyone and necessary for the salvation of every man. These thirteen creedal articles, listed in the *Commentary to the Mishnah,* include the existence of God, the unity of God, his incorporeal nature, his eternity, the obligation to worship God, the existence of prophecy, the recognition of Moses as the greatest of all prophets, the acceptance of the Torah revealed to Moses as divine in origin, the acceptance of the eternal validity of the Torah, the notion that God is omniscient, that he will reward and punish men on the basis of their actions, that he will deliver men through his messiah, and finally, that he will resurrect the dead. The ordinary Jew was required to affirm these beliefs and follow the commands of the Torah, whose purpose it was to lead men to an ordered moral and social life.

In the *Guide* Maimonides presented concise discussions and definitions of the classical religious questions. His doctrine of the attributes of God, based upon the notion that only negative attribution is possible in predication about God, was brilliantly presented, and became highly influential in later philosophical discussion of this problem. Altogether, his rational explanation of Jewish beliefs and practices is the most thorough and complete in Jewish literature. Its greatness was immediately recognized by his contemporaries and the *Guide* met with much success among those who felt the challenge of rationalism to their faith and experienced the need to work out a harmonization between reason and revelation. However, the intellectualization of Judaism accomplished by Moses Maimonides, his elevation of philosophical knowledge to the rank of the greatest perfection over the virtues of traditional study and practice, offended certain sectors of the Jewish population and eventually stirred protest against the entire philosophical enterprise. The basic motive of the protest was the desire to delimit reason and the autonomous activity of man. It was felt by the antiphilosophical party that human rationality could not go beyond a certain point. Maimonides and his followers were said to have exceeded the boundary, thereby distorting the simple precepts of Judaism and introducing alien forms and ideas into Jewish consciousness. Tradition could not be subordinated to the intellect and piety relegated to a position secondary to intellectual endeavor. During the thirteenth and fourteenth centuries the controversy between the advocates of philosophy and their opponents raged. It was the latter who eventually won out, and Jewish philosophical development was largely stemmed. However, the work of Maimonides was not lost and the attempt to rationalize faith was continued by many individual thinkers. The great work of Rabbi Nahman Krochmal (1785–1840), *The Guide for the Perplexed of Our Time,* indicates in its very title the influence of Maimonides and represents a significant attempt to do in the nineteenth century what medieval Jewish philosophers had attempted from the tenth through the fifteenth centuries.

Another development in Jewish religious thought, related to Neoplatonism rather than Aristotelianism and much closer to distinctly Jewish ideas and sentiments, is presented in the writings of Judah Halevi (1085–1141/42), the greatest poet and one of the greatest thinkers of the medieval period. In his major philosophical work, the *Kuzari,* Halevi endeavored to prove the uniqueness and truth of Judaism in opposition to Christianity, Islam, and philosophy. He did not base his claim on metaphysical proof, but rather denied that rational method could achieve absolute certainty in this area at all, calling attention to the innumerable differences between philosophers on all critical issues. The single proof for the truth of Judaism is a historical one, according to Halevi, namely, the historical facts of God's mighty deeds, his public revelation to the Jewish people, and his providential care for them. It is thus that Halevi stated his position:

> I believe in the God of Abraham, Isaac, and Israel, who led the Israelites out of Egypt with signs and miracles; who fed them in the desert and gave them the Holy Land, after having made them traverse the sea and the Jordan in a miraculous way; who sent Moses with His Law, and subsequently thousands of prophets, who confirmed His Law by promises to those who observed, and threats to the disobedient. We believe in what is contained in the Torah—a very large domain. . . . I made mention to thee of what is convincing for me and for the whole of Israel, who knew these things, first through personal experience, and afterward through an uninterrupted tradition, which is equal to experience.
>
> (*Kuzari* I.11, 25)

Halevi denied that the rational intellectual efforts of man could ever reach knowledge of God. Such knowledge is available only when God discloses himself because of his own desire to communicate with man. God has chosen and revealed himself to Israel, the object of his greatest affection. He has given Israel a special religious sense, a faculty to perceive the divine, which is of course superior to any other faculty with which man has been endowed. However, this special faculty is not fully actualized even in Israel, but must be nurtured by obedience to the divine law. And even with the religious faculty, not all Jews can come really to understand God, to see him fully, but only the prophets among them. To these men God reveals himself directly and sensually. The knowledge of the prophet cannot be reached by the philosopher, and the latter can never enter into the relationship of love and communion which the prophet has with God.

According to Halevi, Israel is essentially different from all other human groups in its religious endowment, and has a crucial role to play in history because of this endowment. The ultimate redemption of the world is dependent upon the relationship of Israel to God. The pious Jew who cultivates his religious faculty, who sanctifies his life by fulfilling the word of God, not only ascends toward communion with the Lord but hastens the salvation of all men. In the messianic age, what Israel alone possesses will become the property of all, and all men will enter into communion with God.

Halevi's views on the peculiarity of religious as distinct from philosophic truth and the peculiarity of Israel as bearer of this truth, essentially distinguished from all other religions, provided answers to the dilemmas which rational speculation and the rival claims of seemingly more successful faiths presented to the Jews of his time. Further, the historical stress of Halevi and his emphasis upon the uniqueness of the religious sense appealed to the traditional Jew greatly. Yet, despite the differences between them, Halevi and Maimonides both represented the philosophical strain in Jewish spiritual life. Of much more significance for the common man, and consequently of greater popularity, was the developing pietistic literature. In the Middle Ages, the greatest work in this area was Bahya Ibn Pakuda's *Duties of the Heart,* which became a standard guide to the meditational, devotional, and ethical life. In the spirit of his time, Bahya expounded proofs for the existence of God and presented a discussion of the divine attributes. However, his main concern was not with such rational doctrines nor with external ethical behavior, "duties of the limbs," but with the development of the inner soul, which was the relation of man's heart to God. In his central chapters on worship, trust in God, submission to God, humility, repentance, self-examination before God, withdrawal from the world, and finally, on love of God, he attempted to direct man toward the most intimate relationship with God which the soul could attain. Although man must labor in the world and live a life of righteousness, Bahya taught inner withdrawal and concentration upon the true task, which was ascent to God in order to communicate with him and serve him more perfectly. It was the appeal to the soul of the pious man which drew Bahya's writings to the soul of the Jewish people. His stress on the life of devotion and meditation, his emphasis upon the sentiments of trust and love rather than knowledge and wisdom, responded to the needs and exercised lasting influence upon the Jewish religious spirit.

Concentration upon the inner life, the life of the soul in relation to God, was most highly developed in medieval Jewish mysticism, known as the Kabbalah. Literally, the term *kabbalah* means "tradition," and refers to the mystic's claim that his knowledge of divine mysteries has been received through revelation. The tradition of mystical speculation and mystical practice was a continuous one from the days of *merkavah* mysticism. However, it was only during the thirteenth and fourteenth centuries that kabbalistic ideas spread to large segments of the Jewish population and became for many as significant a force in religious life as was traditional learning and practice. The classical kabbalistic work, the *Zohar,* assumed a position alongside the Bible and Talmud as a basic religious text of the people and maintained this position for three hundred years. The desire to understand the mysteries of God's being, the mysteries of his creation, and the secret relation of man's soul to God was a powerful one shared by all levels of the Jewish population. The *merkavah* mystics, the German *hasidim,* the Spanish kabbalists, the school of Isaac Luria, the Eastern European *hasidim,* and other groups form a continuous chain. A vast literature on theory and practice emerged from this mystical tradition, which aroused the soul of the Jewish people and drew many into participation in the inner religious life of mystical learning and into the intense social life of a mystical community.

The great development of the Kabbalah, which carried mysticism outside small esoteric circles to large numbers of the people, began in 1200 in southern France and Spain. Leaders of the movement were more often laymen than rabbis and were not committed to a life devoted to talmudic learning. They could approach the Jewish tradition from a new perspective and find in it new depths of spiritual insight and meaning. Largely uninfluenced by non-Jewish cultural forms or ideas, the kabbalists developed their tradition in the typical exegetical manner, but probed to hidden levels and interpreted scriptural passages in a novel, and often mythical, and highly imaginative way.

The *Zohar,* the *Book of Splendor,* is the most significant work in the kabbalistic corpus. The book was issued anonymously, and its authorship has been clouded in mystery. However, modern research has attributed it to Moses de Leon, a Castilian Jew, who is said to have composed the main body of the work c. 1280. The form of the *Zohar* is quite complex. It consists of many sections, not systematically ordered and not unified, which include homiletical interpretations of biblical passages, dramatic descriptions of persons and places, and epigrammatic revelations of divine mysteries. The use of Aramaic, and the ascription of large parts of the work to the first-century sage and saint Rabbi Simon bar Yohai, add further to the *Zohar*'s mystery and difficult nature.

The *merkavah* mystics had attempted to ascend to the throne of the Lord and to contemplate the majesty of the divine presence in the palace, throne, and garments of the seventh heaven. The kabbalists sought to go beyond this level of appearance in order to see the Lord himself. They perceived levels closer and closer to the real being of God, and penetrated deeper and deeper into his very essence. The kabbalists called the levels of divine being which they perceived the *sephirot,* the spheres. They were the manifestations of the hidden God, the *En Sof,* embodying specific attributes of his nature. According to the kabbalists, men could grasp God in the *sephirot* and could thereby enter the hidden and true reality of the divine being.

The kabbalists believed that the Torah contained a hidden meaning, which could be discerned if the text were interpreted in the mystical mode. Delving into the mysteries of revelation in order to penetrate to the mysteries of the universe, the kabbalists constructed, through their homilies, a world of mythical symbols to describe the divine mysteries and the mysteries of the spheres. They disclosed these secret meanings to the initiated, a group which grew steadily as men sought new paths to understand the ways of God. The mystical search for the beginning and the end, the search of the soul to reach God himself, has been embarked upon by generations of pious Jews, in the hope that this quest would lead to ultimate understanding and ultimate redemption.

During the long history of Judaism, many streams of religious thought and religious life developed. Rabbinic learning, rabbinic values, and rabbinic definitions of practice always constituted the mainstream and were the base from which innovative ideas and forms emerged. At the foundation of Jewish life was the original revelation to Moses and its interpretation by the successive schools of rabbis. Every Jew knew the Scripture and was acquainted with the most lucid and brilliant commentary upon it, that of the great French scholar Rabbi Solomon bar Isaac (1040–1105), known as Rashi. Rashi's commentary transmitted to the student, by way of exegesis upon the biblical text, an understanding of the literal meaning of that text and an understanding of its religious insights. With a knowledge of the Bible and Rashi, the Jew was anchored in the sacred traditions of his people, and had absorbed the religious ideas which gave meaning to the life of the community in which he participated.

Study of the Law and cultivation of the spirit were handmaidens in the history of Judaism. The ideal man was a saint and a scholar, who neglected neither mind, soul, nor body in the attainment of religious perfection. "Simon the Just was one of the last of the Great synagogue. He was wont to say: Upon three things the world stands —upon the Torah, upon worship, and upon the doing of righteous deeds" (*Avot* 1:2). The embodiment of this precept is to be found in innumerable heroes of Jewish tradition, one of whom, Rabbi Joseph Karo (1488–1575), may be taken as exemplary. Karo was recognized as the leading legist of his day and his legal writings have become classics in the rabbinic heritage. He composed the *Bet Joseph,* four large volumes tracing the sources and development of the Law, and the *Shulhan Aruch,* a concise summary and codification of the Law. The latter became the most widely used legal guide throughout the Jewish communities of the exile. However, legal activity was only one side of Karo's complex personality. On the other, he was constantly engaged in mystical experiences, which are recorded in a diary of his spiritual life, the *Maggid Mesharim.*

Karo had studied the Law intensely and had wrapped himself in his work in a most profound way. He had been devoted particularly to the Mishnah and had somehow become part of that code himself, so that the angel which appeared to him is identified as the Mishnah. This Mishnah-angel came to Karo during the night to advise, admonish, encourage, and teach him the mysteries of the tradition. Karo was commanded by the angel to devote himself more to the Kabbalah and to the devotional study of Bahya's *Duties of the Heart.* The greatest rabbinic scholar and authority of his day lived a double existence, always in contact with the inner world of the angels and the heavens. He believed that in his own work on earth he reflected in microcosm a heavenly reality, which the angel-mentor expressed in his greeting, "Peace from the College of Heaven." Karo labored on his legal tomes in the shadow of the heavens and in anticipation of the world to come, where he would sit with the righteous in the presence of God.

Karo's rabbinic school was established in Safed. At the same time and in the same town, the greatest school of Jewish mysticism arose and thrived, the school of Rabbi Isaac Luria. Karo had taught Moses Cordovero, leader of the Safed mystics before Luria, and Karo and Luria were in contact during the latter's years in Safed. This association of the mystics and scholars was certainly not unique, for it was common in Jewish history that the same man was both a rabbinic sage and mystic, while mystical movements arose and lived alongside rabbinic centers. Thus, in the eighteenth and nineteenth centuries the main center of talmudic learning was in Vilna, in Lithuania, where the great scholar Elijah Gaon lived and studied. Refusing any official position of authority, the Vilna Gaon was still recognized as the leading figure in rabbinic interpretation and was regarded by his contemporaries as a great saint, whose guidance was to be sought on all matters. In his personal life the Gaon was totally absorbed in his studies and dedicated his entire life to them. His example and his method inspired many disciples, and the great yeshivah at Voloshin owes its foundation to the work of Elijah of Vilna. This school stands as a symbol of the heights to which rabbinic learning in Eastern Europe rose. Here hundreds of boys and men submitted themselves to the discipline of talmudic study, laboring from early morning till late in the evening throughout the week, in the belief that such labor lifted the mind, deepened the spirit, and was a service to God.

At the same time that the Vilna Gaon wrote his commentaries and rabbinic studies flourished in schools throughout Eastern Europe, the mystical movement of Hasidism developed and captured the hearts of thousands among the simple pious folk and among the educated. In the figure of the Baal Shem Tov, the founder of Hasidism, one sees a complete contrast to the Vilna Gaon, for the Baal Shem (1760–1810) was an unlearned enthusiast, a wonder-worker, as his name indicates. He was a simple man, whose miraculous powers and marvelous character attracted followers and soon led to his being elevated to the position of a popular saint and legendary figure. The Baal Shem and his followers created a dynamic revivalist movement which encompassed large parts of Polish and Russian Jewry, arousing deep devotion and piety. Hasidic mystical activities regenerated a religious life which had become alien and ossified for many.

Although in its initial stages Hasidism's emotional subjective religiosity was in part a protest against the objectivity and intellectualism of rabbinic Judaism, and did represent the virtues of the simple and pious in opposition to the learned and aristocratic, the movement did not become antinomian, and did not long maintain an opposition stance. Hasidic leaders were also rabbis and the rabbinic tradition was integrated with hasidic ideas and practices in the formation of new vital religious communities. The *Habad* movement within Hasidism represents the coming together of subjective enthusiasm in worship, deep devotion to traditional subjects and methods of study, and dedication to mystical doctrines and practices, the enthusiastic revival of immediate religious experience, and the reaffirmation of popular mysticism. The Hasidic movement occurred within the structure of rabbinic Judaism, demonstrating the continuing ability of the traditional ideas and forms to develop and accommodate the multiple needs of the religious spirit.

MAN'S RELATION TO GOD

We have been considering here the chief elements of the Christian tradition as they developed from the messianic career of Jesus of Nazareth and the primitive Church. In considering tradition, we naturally concern ourselves with what is believed, for it is beliefs that make up traditions, and the content of beliefs that tradition transmits from past to future. But we must remember that important though belief indeed is, it derives from something more basic and more central to the religious life. Most basic to religion is the religious experience, the believer's experience of God. Man responds to what he experiences above and beyond the mundane happenings of his workaday life—to an aspect of the environment which he neither comprehends nor manipulates, but which calls to him and is related to him in an intimate way. That response is the central religious act—the act of worship.

Worship is a universal human response found in all cultures and traditions. It embodies and expresses man's basic relationship to what really is—to what is apprehended as real, fundamental, and in some way constitutive of all reality. Worship is a response in depth which points beyond experience to a realm of being and mystery. It points toward and expresses a relationship to transcendence. In worship men feel related to the source and origin of their own being, and of all being, and to the deepest end and goal of their own existence. Worship places man in a subject-object relationship to the Beyond, but it is an unequal and asymmetrical relation. Before the mystery which he confronts in the religious relationship, man feels a vast reverence, a kind of fear, mingled with an experience of being called to a closer intimacy. This complex attitude finds its expression in the acts of adoration which become the religious practices of the various religious traditions.

In the Judeo-Christian tradition this Beyond is revealed as the creator of the world and the Lord of history, the author and sustainer of nature, and the God who reveals himself in historical time. It is he to whom all honor and worship are due. "I am the Lord your God, who brought you out of the land of Egypt, out of the house of bondage. You shall have no other gods before me" (Deut. 5:6–7). Christianity finds the progressive revelation of this God in the history of the Jewish nation brought to its fulfillment in Jesus. "In many and various ways God spoke of old to our fathers by the prophets; but in these last days he has spoken to us by a Son, whom he appointed the heir of all things, through whom also he created the world" (Heb. 1:1–2). Jewish and Christian worship is centered on God and in it man is believed paradoxically to find his highest self-expression and fulfillment in relating himself to God and making God the center of his life. This worship has taken two general forms. It has found communal expression in a corporate form, a public prayer of the community, as seen in the early Temple sacrifices and the later worship services of the Jewish synagogue and the Christian church. It has also found an individual expression as seen in the importance attached to individual prayer. This individual expression reaches its highest development in mysticism.

The central act of worship for Christianity is the celebration of the Eucharist, called the Mass in the Latin church. In this service we have the ritual repetition of the last supper which Jesus ate with his disciples on the night before he was put to death, a ritual in which it is believed that his presence is experienced again. The New Testament contains four accounts of the institution of the Eucharist by Jesus and tells of its celebration in the early Christian community. From the beginning two things appear to have been held generally concerning it: It involved a real present relationship with the risen Christ and it was instituted by Jesus himself. From the first centuries it was generally accorded that it brought to the receiver the body and blood of Christ as stated in the words of Jesus quoted in the celebration. The Eucharistic celebration is a public external act of worship which is held to reenact and represent the Last Supper of Jesus and his sacrificial death upon the cross of Calvary the next day. The Mass is held to be not only the reenactment of and sharing in the sacred Passover meal of Jesus with his disciples but also an unbloody re-presentation and participation in the mystery of Christ's redemptive death—his offering of himself as the sacred victim to his Father for the redemption of men, his blood shed for the "remission of sins." Jesus was the Suffering Servant of Deutero-Isaiah and this death was his great redemptive act. It is in this that all share in the Mass. It is this public corporate act which provides to the worshiper the occasion for his own deepest subjective interior relation to God. The Eucharistic service of which the consecration and reception of the sacrament are central and basic involves also preparatory prayers and readings of Scripture obviously influenced by the synagogue as well as final prayers of thanksgiving. Indeed, the word "Eucharist" means thanksgiving and the celebration is also considered a thanksgiving service. At once individual and collective, both ritualized and eliciting spontaneous participation, objective and shared and subjective and individual at the same time, the Eucharistic celebration remains the central dramatic expression and fulfillment of the religious response in Western Catholic and Eastern Orthodox Christianity. Protestantism simplified much in the years following the Reformation, yet the meaning of the Eucharistic service remained in some sense central for most of the Reformation churches.

It is remarkable that although theological precision has been so prominent a Christian concern and the resulting controversy so prominent a feature of Christian history, the first several centuries of the Church witnessed hardly any real attempt at precise Eucharistic definition or any real controversy concerning Eucharistic faith. We find Cyprian stating that Christ "first offered himself as a sacrifice to the Father, and commanded this to be done in remembrance of himself" (Cyprian, *Epistle,* 63.14), Ignatius saying that "the Eucharist is the flesh of our Saviour Jesus Christ" (*Epistle to the Smyrnans* 6), and Irenaeus proclaiming that "the bread of the earth, receiving the invocation of God, is no longer common bread but Eucharist, consisting of two things, an earthly and a heavenly" (*Against Heresies* 4.18.6). From the fourth century on we find a general use of terms indicating that the elements of bread and wine are transformed into Christ's body and blood (anticipating the later Catholic definition), while some writers speak of a continued presence of the natural elements as well as of the body and blood of the Lord in the consecrated sacrament (anticipating Luther's later definition). It was not until the eleventh century that a significant conflict is to be found on these matters which will become so controversial in the Reformation period. At that time Berengarius denied the generally taught and accepted doctrine of the Real Presence but twice retracted his denial under pressure before his death in 1088. Some of his followers held a doctrine of a kind of hidden and obscure presence of Christ's body and blood covered and concealed by the presence of the bread and wine. Peter Lombard, who was the theologian who most influenced education in the Middle Ages, held that Christ was substantially present in the Eucharist but conceded the difficulties involved in any precise definition. In 1215 the Fourth Lateran Council declared in a dogmatic definition that "the body and blood are truly contained in the sacrament of the altar under the species of bread and wine; the bread being transubstantiated into the body and the wine into the blood by the power of God." Later in the same century this doctrine was given detailed definition in the works of Thomas Aquinas, who held in Aristotelian terminology that the elements were changed into the substance of Christ while the accidents of bread and wine remain and are present to our sense perception.

The Reformation saw great controversy on the meaning of the Eucharist. Luther found that transubstantiation "must be considered as an invention of human reason, since it is based neither on Scripture nor sound reasoning." He proposed a doctrine of consubstantiation which held that in the sacrament both the bread and wine and the body and blood of Christ coexist—"the bread and wine are really bread and wine and the true flesh and blood of Christ is in them." Ulrich Zwingli (1484–1531), the great Swiss Reformer, took the most radical view of the Eucharist of any major Reformation figure. Zwingli denied any doctrine which affirmed a real flesh-and-blood presence of Christ in the sacrament, and the differences between him and Luther on this question prevented any unity of the Reform efforts in Germany and Switzerland. Unlike Luther, Calvin had no sympathy with the worship practices of the old Church. He was overwhelmed by the transcendence of God, a God "wholly other," who "hath no image." Calvin reacted negatively and radically against all ceremonial and gestural symbolism and saw himself called to purify the Church. To him the Roman Mass was composed of "a criminal godlessness." For him there was not really a present and spontaneous here-and-now relation to God enacted by the worshiper aided by God's grace. Nor was a sacrament an established medium for this kind of present relationship. It was rather an "external symbol by which the Lord attests in our consciences his promises of goodwill towards us to sustain the inferiority of our faith, and we on our part testify to our piety towards him as well." Of the Eucharist Calvin says that as "the visible sign is offered to us to attest the granting of the invisible reality, then, on receiving the symbol of the body, we may be confident that the body itself is no less given to us." Calvin really did away with the old act of consecration, yet he saw the Eucharist as a "holy mystery" and was convinced that it involved a real relation to the Divine Presence, though this presence was not "enclosed in the bread and wine." He held that the recipient of Holy Communion received the power or virtue of the body and blood of Christ.

The Roman Catholic Church at the Council of Trent reaffirmed the Real Presence, the doctrine of transubstantiation, and the idea of the Mass as a sacrifice. The last doctrine also went back to the earliest times of the Church but like the Eucharist itself it was not given any precise definition for many centuries. From the fourteenth century on, however, a tremendous literature developed concerning the matter. In 1551 Trent declared that it has always "been held in the Church of God, and this holy Synod now declares anew, that through consecration of the bread and wine there comes about a conversion of the whole substance of the bread into the substance of the body of Christ our Lord, and of the whole substance of the wine into the substance of his blood." The tridentine declaration used the term "transubstantiation," but it did not give the Thomist definition of the term as part of its own statement. Most Reformation theologians tended to deny the element of sacrifice or to explain it away. The Westminster Confession drawn up in 1643, which became the basic document of Presbyterianism, rejected the idea of the "Popish sacrifice of the mass" and stated that "In this sacrament Christ is not offered up to his Father, nor any real sacrifice made at all . . . but only a commemoration." Reformation churches and the Church of England, which often hesitated before decisions on Reformation issues, also generally rejected the idea of sacrifice. Although Cranmer had used the word "Mass" in his first Book of Common Prayer, the term came for most Protestants to signify those aspects of Eucharistic worship which they had rejected as unwarranted, unscriptural "accretions."

In the Roman Catholic Church attendance at Mass on Sundays and on certain feast days is obligatory. The tendency for the observance of the first day of the week, or the "Lord's Day," in place of the Jewish Sabbath began in New Testament times and was based upon the commemoration of the Resurrection. From the fourth century we find both ecclesiastical and civil regulation of this observance, as in the decree of Constantine in 321 which commanded observance and forbade all nonagricultural work. Increasingly strict legislation continued in the Middle Ages. The Reformation churches also emphasized the importance of Sunday rest and worship, and in England and Scotland gave rise to that form of rigorous enforcement known as "sabbatarianism." Under the Puritan Commonwealth in England the observance was imposed by legislation which prohibited all kinds of recreation, including taking a walk. This strict tendency took its start with the book of Nicholas Bound, published in 1595, *True Doctrine of the Sabbath,* which proposed and defended a strict observance of Sunday comparable to the Jewish observance of the Sabbath. It became a political issue in 1618 when James I issued his *Book of Sports* which enjoined abstention from work but permitted and advocated recreational activities. The Puritans were particular rigorists in this respect and in 1643 the Puritan parliament, having beheaded James's son, proceeded to burn his book.

As Christians followed Jews in observing one day a week as holy, they also followed the Jewish practice of marking the passage of the year by special days of prayer. In the Western Church a liturgical year developed characterized by two chief seasons, that of Easter and that of Christmas. The former, centered on Easter Sunday itself, involves also forty days of penitential preparation following the example of Jesus' forty days' fast in the desert, and known as Lent; the feast of Pentecost, commemorating the descent of the Spirit as described in Acts, and Ascension Day, fifty and forty days after Easter, respectively. The latter, the season of Christmas, begins with the first Sunday of Advent, which comprises four weeks of penitential preparation commemorating the four thousand years which by traditional reckoning the world waited for Christ's coming and includes the feast of the Nativity or Christmas itself, the feast of Jesus' circumcision, January 1, and the feast of the Epiphany, January 6, which commemorates the showing of the child to the Magi. Easter is a movable feast, originally connected with the Passover, and hence is still observed on the lunar calendar, showing its link with the Jewish year. Christmas was fixed on December 25 in the fourth century to coincide with the pagan celebration of the solstice and thus follows the solar calendar and is linked with the ancient Roman year. Moreover, during the year thus commemorating the life of Christ there is a continual celebration of the feasts of saints, the most solemn being those dedicated to the Virgin Mary. These days and seasons all have their own special prayers which are incorporated into the Mass. A similar liturgical calendar is followed in the Eastern Church, divided into three parts: *triodion,* the fourth Sunday before Lent to the Saturday before Easter; *Pentacostarion,* Easter to the Sunday after Pentecost inclusive; and *Octoechos,* the remainder of the year.

Besides the Eucharistic celebration the Western and Eastern churches recognize another public prayer, the Divine Office, which is required of priests and many others in formal religious life. It is recited or sung at various times of the day and night in monasteries and religious houses, but more individually and informally by others. Those prayers which have variations according to the season and day are found in the Breviary and are composed of psalms, hymns, and readings. The psalms which make up the present psalter in the Jewish Scriptures are basically liturgical prayers, and the Book of Psalms has often been called the "Hymnal of the Second Temple." It is not surprising that Christians put it to similar use from the earliest times. Outside of its use in such public prayer where it is completely recited once a week (or once a month in the office of the Church of England), the Book of Psalms has been a favorite for private devotion not only in the Western Catholic and Eastern Orthodox communions but among the Protestant churches as well. Among Roman Catholics another popular prayer since the late Middle Ages has been the Rosary. A tradition which goes back at least to the fifteenth century holds that this prayer was introduced by Dominic, the founder of the Dominican Order, in the thirteenth century, but actually it seems to have developed gradually under the influence of both Dominican preachers and Cistercian monks. It consists of saying three sets of five "mysteries" composed of the recitation of ten Ave Marias, preceded by the Lord's Prayer and followed by a doxology praising the Trinity. The mysteries themselves commemorate important events in the salvation history of man from the Annunciation of the Angel to Mary that she would bear a son, through the Passion, death, and resurrection of Jesus, to Mary's own Assumption and coronation as "Queen of Heaven." This form of devotion was rejected by the Reformation as at best a pious accretion, but it has remained extremely popular among Catholics. It is said privately and in a semipublic setting as in homes and other informal gatherings as well as in devotions held in churches.

Like Jewish prayer the prayer of Christians receives its specific characteristic form from the belief in a God at once transcendent and personal, a God who although "wholly other," at the same time calls men to a profound personal relationship. In the prayer of Christians this relationship is centered upon the redemptive and mediating figure of Christ, who comes to us as God and who as fellow man leads us to the Father. We have seen that in the prayer life of Catholic and Orthodox Christians, devotion to saints to implore their intercession and to honor them is a significant form of religious expression, and most especially devotion to the Blessed Virgin Mary. Yet the official prayer of the Church in the Mass and in the Divine Office is christocentric and offered through Christ to the

The Journey of the Magi *by the Quattrocento painter Sassatta. (Courtesy of the Metropolitan Museum of Art. Bequest of Maitland F. Griggs, 1943.)*

Father, in the majority of cases, although prayer directly to the Father as taught by Jesus, to Christ himself, and to the Holy Spirit is also considered proper. Prayer to the saints possesses a different character than prayer addressed to the Godhead. It represents rather a communion between the members of the church in heaven (the church triumphant) and the church on earth (the church militant), in which the former intercede for the latter before the Divine Presence. Jesus taught prayer to his disciples by both precept and example. The one prayer he taught as recorded in the gospel remains a most significant model of prayer and is found prominently in the public and private prayers of Christians.

The Lord's Prayer contains the basic elements of prayer— adoration and praise together with petition for earthly and spiritual needs, including the penitential request for forgiveness. All prayer is an expression and often a combination of these elements. Another important element in prayer is thanksgiving. Moreover, Christian prayer is meant to be an activity of the entire person—of mind, will, and affection. But prayer is not simply a spontaneous expression, it is a duty, and it is moreover an art. This is recognized in the Christian exclamatory petition: "Lord, teach us to pray!" Moreover, in more profound prayer, adoration of God as the supreme and ultimate good and thanksgiving to him as the author of being and life are intimately related. In the words of the great prayer giving glory to God in the Mass:

Glory to God in the highest,
And on earth peace to men of good will.
We praise thee, we bless thee.
We adore thee, we glorify thee.
We give thee thanks for thy great glory.

Perhaps the most significant distinction made concerning prayer is that between vocal and mental prayer. St. John of Damascus, the great theologian of the Eastern Church, gives one of the earliest and clearest formulations. "Prayer is either the ascent of the mind to God, or the decently beseeching him" (*Concerning the Orthodox Faith* 3.24). By mental prayer is meant practices of meditation and contemplation which though rejected by many Protestant groups are of tremendous significance in Catholic and Orthodox religious life. Mental prayer is often classified as ordinary and extraordinary. The former refers to discursive meditation, forms of affective prayer, and finally contemplation—a more advanced, nondiscursive mode of lifting up the whole person to God. The latter refers to such prayers when they are marked by authentic mystical elements culminating in true mysticism.

Mysticism is the name given to a profound personal relationship between man and God in which man achieves a real experience of the relation—a vision or union with God in this life. In the Christian tradition this union does not lead to the annihilation of the individuality of the human person; the ontological gulf between creator and creature remains. Yet God's grace and love is felt by the great mystics as bridging that great chasm, and individuation is in some sense transcended. What is involved is a relationship in which God gives himself to man and man aided by God gives himself to God. It is a relationship of love. Whether in the Judeo-Christian tradition or in the other religious traditions of the world, mysticism must not be thought of as some kind of vaporous and unreal state characteristic of some adepts at psychological self-manipulation or self-hypnosis. It is a relationship which is achieved fully only by a few, and if achieved at all, only after long and rigorous preparation involving difficult mental prayer and ascetic exercises. In all true mysticism a difficult state of purification precedes the achievement of understanding and enlightenment, and the final relationship of vision or union achieved by the great religious geniuses of the mystical tradition is a final crowning of a long process. Moreover, in Christian mysticism the genuineness of the mystical experience is seen by the mystics themselves as attested to by its effects in the attitudes and actions of those involved—in an increase of such virtues as humility, patience, and charity. Accompanying phenomena such as visions and the hearing of voices have long been recognized as accessory and secondary. What is basic is the relation to God—the experience, in the words of Jacopone da Todi, of God's Presence, "ineffable love, imageless goodness, measureless light." What exhibits the marks of authenticity are its fruits. "What fruit dost thou bring back from thy vision?" asked Jacopone.

Institutional religion has often suspected mysticism as a kind of religious individualism outside its sphere of effectiveness, and indeed in periods when the institutional church has faltered for one reason or another in its ability to provide for men's religious needs, mysticism has increased in popularity. But mysticism needs and is a part of the institutional church, for without an authentic religious tradition and the religious environment provided by the institution there would be a severely truncated basis for its own development. Yet the suspicions are not without some basis nor are they all based upon institutional self-interest by any means. Mysticism offers the most profound fulfillment of the religious experience but it is a difficult path and its demands and the attendant strains can give rise to various illusions and to dangerous temptations. There is the temptation to extreme emotionalism, to antinomianism and immorality, and of fascination with secondary psychological phenomena. There is an old talmudic story of four rabbis who set out to study mysticism. One lost his mind, a second lost his faith, and a third died. The fourth one, Rabbi Akiba, came out a better Jew.

Protestant thinkers and writers have taken various positions on mysticism and in the Reformation period both the Catholic and Protestant institutions derived considerable inner strength from the mystics within their ranks. In our day men such as Emil Brunner and Reinhold Niebuhr have considered mysticism to be Neoplatonic rather than Christian and have characterized it as actually unchristian and antichristian; whereas a member of the Church of England such as Dean Inge and an Orthodox thinker like Nicholas Berdyaev consider it to be the essence of Christian religiosity. In the Western Catholic and Eastern Orthodox churches mysticism has remained an important element of religious life into our own times.

That Christian mysticism owes much to Neoplatonism is undeniable, but it has used what it has received to seek a relation to God on a profound level which would be consonant with the New Testament tradition. The Fourth Gospel and the Pauline Epistles, not to mention the Book of Revelation, all show mystic elements. The great theological rethinking of the Western tradition by St. Augustine was deeply affected by the mystic element in his experience. Such elements are found in many early Fathers. It is true that Christianity is a historical religion based upon a historical revelation now considered to be closed. It is true that morality—personal righteousness and social justice—are of the very essence of biblical religion. But it is also true that man's relation to God is central to all religion and that religion must in all ages base itself in experience. The mystical tradition has provided that experience and that relationship at its highest point of God's gift and man's achievement. The great mystics are to the religious life what the great artists are to the life of the senses and the great philosophers to the life of the mind.

The choice is not between a morally committed Christianity and a withdrawn mystical one. We have innumerable examples from Paul to our own time to illustrate the superficiality of such a distinction. The biblical tradition is one of both morality and a personal relation to God as part of one undivided religious attitude. "You shall love the Lord your God with all your heart, and with all your soul, and with all your mind." This is the great and first commandment. And a second is like it, "You shall love your neighbor as yourself" (Matt. 22:37–39). The mystical tradition has deepened the first side of this unity for us to the immense enrichment of the second.

The Jewish communities, in exile, without political power and dependent upon internal religious order for their continuity, relied upon the cultivation of the spirit and the mind, upon the constant dedication to conserving and upbuilding of religious sources, for their survival. Therefore, the school, the *yeshivah,* was a vital institution for the maintenance of Jewish life, and the rabbi, as teacher and exemplar of the tradition, society's most honored man.

Alongside the school, the synagogue as house of prayer and assembly was a crucial institution in the continuity of communal life and in the enrichment of that life. Soon after the destruction of the Temple in A.D. 70, the task of establishing a fixed order of prayers and rituals, which would be surrogate for the Temple worship, was completed. The time of the daily services—morning, afternoon, and evening—substituted for the Temple sacrifices which were offered at those hours. A supplementary service on the Sabbath and festivals filled in for the special sacrifices which would have been made on those occasions. In addition to set prayers, scriptural readings were incorporated into the service on Mondays, Thursdays, the Sabbath, and festivals. The full development of the prayer service enabled Israel to find a new outlet for its deeply felt emotions in relation to the divine. Joy, adoration, praise, and also sorrow, question, and anger could be expressed within an institutional framework. Israel was certain that this was in conformity with the will of God, who desired to relate to his people, and who was listening to their cries.

Prayer is an obligation upon every Jew. At the same time as it is a required matter, a duty to be performed at fixed times and according to a fixed ritual, it is also a matter of subjective intention: ". . . to love the Lord your God, to serve Him with all your heart . . ." (Deut. 11:13). "What is the service of the heart? It is prayer" (*Taanit* 2a). The quality of one's prayer, its intentionality (*kavannah*), is considered of supreme importance. "Better is a little with kavannah than much without it" (*Tur Orah Hayim,* p. 61). "Let him who prays cast his eyes downward but his heart upward" (*Yebamoth* 105b). In prayer the worshiper addresses himself to God and attempts to participate in the reality of the divine. He praises, he offers thanksgiving, and he petitions the Creator and Ruler of the world. Prayer is not to be used as a magical technique whereby man automatically receives what he requests. Rather, it is an act through which man can establish contact with God. In prayer man opens his heart, trusting that God does come near, that he hearkens, and that he understands the words of his creature. It is even suggested that God longs for the prayers of man, considering them more beautiful than sacrifices and even than good works. Hoping that God is present and listening, man turns toward him, seeking to go beyond his self to participation in the beyond. He seeks to establish a living vital relationship with the divine, and this is the essence of Jewish prayer. The Jew, throughout the ages, sensed that God guarded his people, took an interest in the concerns of each individual, and could be moved by prayers which expressed the joys, hopes, and agonies of these men. "O Lord our God, hear our cries!

Late thirteenth-century miniature in North French style showing Aaron the High Priest filling the Menorah from a Bible and prayerbook. (Courtesy of the British Museum.)

Have compassion upon us and pity us. Accept our prayer with loving favor. You, O God, listen to entreaty and prayer. O King, do not turn us away unanswered, for you mercifully heed your people's supplication. Praised are you, O Lord, who is attentive to prayer." The outpouring of the heart found in the Jewish liturgy attests to the profound conviction that God was present, that he cared, and that he would answer the address his people directed toward him.

The scriptural Book of Psalms and the *siddur,* the prayerbook of later Judaism, have served to bridge the gulf between man and God, enabling the Jew to expose his most profound feelings to the deity and to sense that God responds. Prayer has been the fundamental religious act of piety, both preceding and going beyond rational reflection and speculation. The Jew who stands before God blesses, sanctifies, and magnifies a reality which he knows instinctively is present. Knowledge of God's infinite transcendence exists, while "God is near in all kinds of nearness" (*Jerusalem Talmud, Berakoth* 13a). One kind of nearness is the nearness of prayer. ". . . when a man enters a synagogue and prays, God listens to him, for the petitioner is like a man who talks into the ear of a friend" (Ibid.). Throughout the centuries prayers were added to the liturgy, and reflected the ever-evolving piety and religious consciousness of the people. The *siddur* expresses in poetic form the soul of the Jewish people as it stood before God, and hence contains the highest thoughts and deepest sentiments of the religious spirit.

The life of the religious man is devoted to sanctification, to the act of making ordinary events and ordinary things holy. He is engaged in transforming the profane into the sacred by allowing a reality beyond the level of ordinary appearance to enter and to transform that appearance into something beyond itself, into something holy. The entire ritual order of Judaism serves to accomplish this act of sanctification in as many areas of man's life as possible. Reciting a blessing over food and drink transforms the mere intaking of food into a sacred act. Reciting a blessing over crops, over a house, over children, are acts which transform the ordinary into the extraordinary, the secular into the sacred. Whether it be the most mundane and trivial areas of life or the most significant and elevated, this process of transformation lifts the existence of the religious man into the dimension of the holy and the divine.

The religious year is a sanctification of time, in which precious moments are consecrated through ritual celebration and reenactment. Judaism, a religion founded upon the experience of God's appearance in time, possesses a full sacred calendar, in which the moments of divine revelation and the moments of sacred acts are recalled and relived. The year is marked by religious holidays, during which the eternal, the transcendent, is felt to enter time and thereby to transform it. The secular or profane cycle is raised to the dimension of the sacred. The pious Jew lives in the world, in secular time and space, but constantly anticipates the moments when, through participation in religious holidays, he will enter into another world, the world of the eternal and of the holy. He looks forward to the holy days, prepares for them, and longs to taste of their reality, which to him seems to be alone truly real and truly ultimate.

The Jewish ritual year is founded upon the Sabbath, the weekly sanctification of Creation. The entire spiritual year is marked off by the sequence of the Sabbaths. They provide a constant source of renewal and sanctity to the pious man, who in some way is re-created himself as he celebrates the creation of the world. "Wherefore the children of Israel keep the Sabbath, to observe the Sabbath throughout their generations, for a perpetual covenant. It is a sign between Me and the children of Israel forever, for in six days the Lord made heaven and earth, and on the seventh day He ceased from work and rested" (Exod. 31:12–17).

The Sabbath is thus a memorial to the work of God's creation. It is also a day of rest, in which the toil of the workweek is to be laid aside for prayer, celebration, and reflection. The rules of Sabbath observance have been prescribed in order to preserve its character as a day of rest. They allow man to separate himself from the cares of daily ordinary existence and thereby free himself to participate in the sanctification of time. According to Jewish tradition, participating in the Sabbath, celebrating God's own deeds of creation and rest, is of supreme importance. "Rabbi Levi said: If the Jewish people would observe the Sabbath properly even once, the son of David [the Messiah] would come. Why? Because it is equal to all the other commandments in importance" (*Exod. Rabbah* 25:12).

There are three festivals in the Jewish year, which are agricultural in origin, but which have been transformed into historical holidays marking sacred events in the religious history of Israel. The first is the feast of Deliverance, the Passover, or *Pesach,* which recalls the miraculous redemption from Egypt. Yahweh had revealed himself to the people in this mighty act of Exodus, personally leading them out of the house of bondage into freedom. Therefore:

> *In every generation a person is obligated to see himself as though he personally came out of Egypt, as it is written, "You shall tell your son on that day saying: This is because of what the Lord did for me when I left Egypt." It was not our ancestors alone that the Holy One, praised be He, redeemed, but he redeemed us as well, along with them. . . . Therefore we are obliged to thank, praise, laud, glorify and exalt, to honor, bless, extol, and adore Him who performed all these wonders for our fathers and for us.*
>
> (Passover *Haggadah*)

This great event, which was so engraved upon the consciousness of the Jew, is celebrated in the *seder,* a ritual meal in the home preceded by a recitation of the Exodus narrative. By participating in the recitation and the meal, the Jew returns and participates in the historical events. He feels himself one of the redeemed, and praises the Lord for the gift of freedom.

The festival of Weeks, *Shavuot,* occurs in late spring, forty-nine days after Passover, and celebrates the revelation of God at Sinai, when the Ten Commandments were presented to the newly formed nation. The third festival, called *Sukkot* (Booths), is an autumn harvest holiday, and marks the historical incident of the forty years' wandering in the wilderness when the children of Israel dwelled in booths. The final day of this festival is the day of Rejoicing in the Law, because on this occasion the yearly cycle of Torah readings is concluded with the last chapter of Deuteronomy and is begun again with the first chapter of Genesis. All three festivals are joyous holidays in which man recalls God's interventions in history. In so doing he participates in these symbolic events which are the core of Israel's religious history.

Two other holidays are of major significance in the ritual year and they are the High Holy Days of *Rosh Hashanah*, the New Year, and *Yom Kippur*, the Day of Atonement. *Rosh Hashanah* occurs on the first and second days of the month of Tishri, corresponding to September in the Gregorian calendar, and on the tenth day of Tishri is *Yom Kippur*. These are the Days of Awe, the most solemn period in the Jewish year, for it is thought that at this time each Jew is judged by God and his destiny for the coming year determined. In legend, God is pictured as sitting over a book and inscribing in it the fate of every individual, according to that man's actions of the past year. Judgment is thus not reserved for a final day at the end of life, but is meted out every year during these critical days, which are set aside for self-examination, repentance, and reconciliation, both between man and man and between man and God. At this time the individual stands alone, as he seeks forgiveness for his sins, purifies himself, and prays that he be judged favorably.

Rabbi Kruspedai said, quoting Rabbi Johanan: On Rosh Hashanah, three books are opened in the heavenly court; one for the wicked, one for the righteous, and one for those in between. The fate of the righteous is inscribed and sealed then and there: Life. The fate of the wicked is inscribed and sealed then and there: Death. The fate of those in between lies in doubt from Rosh Hashanah until Yom Kippur. If, during those days, they show their worth through their deeds, they are inscribed and sealed for Life; and if not, they are inscribed and sealed for death.

(*Rosh Hashanah*, 16b)

On *Rosh Hashanah*, the day which celebrates the creation of the world, the process of judgment begins:

The great shofar is sounded, and a still small voice is heard. Angels are seized with fear and trembling as they proclaim: This is the Day of Judgment! The hosts of heaven are to be arraigned in judgment, for in your eyes even they are not free of guilt. All who enter this world pass before You as a flock of sheep. As the shepherd musters his flock, causing each one to pass beneath his staff, so You pass and number, record and visit every living soul, setting the measure of every creature's life and decreeing its destiny.

On the most solemn day of the year, the Day of Atonement, which is

The shofar, or ram's horn. Played in synagogues at Rosh Hashanah and Yom Kippur, the shofar was blown by the ancient Hebrews in battle and at high religious observances. (*Courtesy of the Israel Government Tourist Office.*)

given over completely to prayer and fasting, the judgment is concluded.

> *On New Year's Day the decree is inscribed and on the Day of Atonement it is sealed: How many shall pass away and how many shall be born, who shall live and who shall die, who shall attain the measure of his days and who shall not, who shall perish by fire and who by water, who by the sword and who by the beast, who by hunger and who by thirst, who by earthquake and who by plague, who by strangling and who by stoning, who shall have rest and who shall wander, who shall be at ease and who shall be disturbed, who shall become poor and who shall become rich, who shall be brought low and who shall be exalted. But Repentance, Prayer, and Righteousness avert the severe decree.*

From *Rosh Hashanah* through *Yom Kippur*, the Jew has repented and sought mercy. He has confessed his sins innumerable times, and has layed himself open before the righteous Judge.

> *What shall we say before You, who dwell on high, and what shall we recount before You, who abide in the heavens? You know all things, hidden and revealed. You know the mysteries of the universe, and the hidden secrets of all living. You search out the innermost reasons and probe the heart and mind. Nothing is concealed from You or hidden from Your sight. May it therefore be Your will, O Lord our God and God of our fathers, to forgive us for all our sins, to pardon us for all our iniquities, and to grant us atonement for all our transgressions.*

After a full day of prayer, the worshiper, humbly trusting in God's mercy and goodness, finally bursts out in joyous affirmation: "The Lord is God, this God of Love, He alone is God!"

Thus ends the most sacred day of the religious year. Man reenters the cycle of life, purified and hopeful, but with the knowledge that he will sin again, that he is again embedded in the evils inherent in profane existence, and that his only salvation lies in reliving once again in the coming year the entire cycle of holy days, experiencing through them renewal and redemption. The meaning of the ritual year in the life of the Jew is summarized in the following statement taken from the closing prayers of the Sabbath:

> *Praised are You, O Lord our God, King of the universe, who has endowed all creation with distinctive qualities and differentiated between light and darkness, between sacred and profane, between Israel and the nations, and between the seventh day and other days of the week. Praised are You, O Lord, who differentiates between the sacred and the profane.*

Throughout its religious history, Israel has been certain of two things: that the transcendent God was present in history and that he had singled out the Jews to participate with him in bringing redemption to the world. God was understood as the Creator and Universal King, but also as the Father who had selected Israel to be his son. This choice was one of love, and is Israel's greatest blessing. "Beloved are the Israelites because they are called sons of God; still greater love that it was made known to them that they are called sons of God." (*Avot* 3:14). The traditional Jew felt God's presence in nature and in history. The great Hebrew poet and thinker of medieval Spain, Judah Halevi, wrote, "Lord where shall I find thee? High and hidden is thy place and where shall I not find thee? The world is full of thy glory. I have sought thy nearness; with all my heart have I called thee. And going out to meet thee, I found thee coming towards me." It is true that the Jews had been exiled from their holy land and had been chastised by God for their sins. However, even in exile, God was near. His *shekhinah,* his "presence," had followed Israel into exile and abided there, sharing in its suffering and homelessness.

Israel sensed that although God was not man, he shared the feelings of his creatures. "In the hour that the Temple was destroyed, and Israel exiled, and the Sanhedrin uprooted, God wept bitter tears" (*Pesikta Rabbati* 28). Judaism accepted the paradox of the infinite omnipresent Lord who is still found in specific places, the God who is totally other than man but who chooses to come close to man and to be involved in his fate. Jewish tradition stated that God actually needs man, and this is implied in the concept of Israel's election. "And you are my witnesses," said God, "and I am God" (Isa. 43:12). "When you are my witnesses, I am God, and when you are not my witnesses, I am not God, as it were" (*Pesikta Derrabh Kahannah, Bahodesh,* 102.6). It was said that God derived pleasure from hearing the prayers of man and from seeing his righteous deeds. This sense of God's abiding presence and his involvement in the particular fate of Israel was summarized in the statement, "My Torah is in your hands and the end is in my hands, so that the two of us need each other. As you need me to bring on the end, so I need you to keep my Torah and to hasten the rebuilding of my house in Jerusalem" (*Pesikta Rabbati* 31.144b). It was such faith in their election and in the critical role assigned to them in realizing God's plan, which inspired Israel and gave purpose to their struggle in exile.

ECCLESIA SEMPER EST REFORMANDA

PROTEST, REFORM, REVOLT

Christianity brought to Western man a new insight into and the possibility of a new relationship to transcendence, gathered to itself the parallel and sympathetic philosophical thrusts of antiquity, especially Neoplatonism and Stoicism, reworking them in relation to the Bible, and thus became the religion of Europe. It was a religion that could move simple folk and at the same time inspire great minds and sublime spirits. This biblical religion showed itself capable of great interior development and of receiving the insights and meeting the needs of the Teutonic and Celtic peoples of the North, who by and large had remained outside the civilization of Mediterranean antiquity. It was this religion that remained when the civilization of antiquity went down, brought low by the onslaught of the barbarian and its own inner decay and fatigue. It was this religion which nurtured the rise of the new Europe which, beginning in the tenth century, has had such an enormous influence upon the entire globe. It is this religion that provided Western man with the basic dimensions of his world view and the fundamental elements of his personal consciousness. The fact that Western men were the first to reach out and explore first the globe and now to begin the exploration of space, the fact that they first developed science with its transcendent and manipulative mental leverage over the elements of the human situation, the fact that they first developed a marked secularization of thought and a demythologization of their understanding of man and the world, the fact that they first built an enormous secularized social structure based upon commercial rationality and scientific technology and thereby changed irretrievably the character of life on this earth, have all been seen by many scholars as closely related to the religion of the Bible and as representing to a considerable extent a further working of insights already embryonic within it in Patristic times. That these complex developments were also often achieved in conflict with religious institutions and religious faith does not seriously detract from the fundamental character of the religious background which for so many centuries was the training school of the Western mind and spirit. Biblical religion rested upon the foundation of breakthrough and transcendence. It taught man to see himself seriously engaged in history but at the same time not enclosed within it. It brought him to a sense of universality. It showed him an ethical ideal which could not be attributed to his own creations and which raised his critical acumen above all mere localisms and provincialisms. It gave him a sense of individual worth and dignity. It taught him the rationalism of the Greeks which it had incorporated into itself. Though Western men honored these insights as much in the breach as in the observance, they had their effect upon the formation of minds and characters and became the basic core-meaning structure of Western culture.

When we use the word "religion," we may use it in three distinct but interrelated senses. First, it may designate that inner relation to the Beyond, however characterized and understood, which lifts man above himself and the effort of men to sustain and live by the implications of that relationship. Second, it may also be used to refer to the beliefs and practices which give objective intellectual and ritual expression to the meaning and significance of that relationship, making it available to men in general and transmissible from one generation to the next; or it may refer to the religious tradition as developed and passed on within a religious group. Third, it may denote the organizational and institutional framework which evolves as the communal structure providing a community for the individual believer and a social basis for the tradition. While the first usage points to the most basic and profound religious phenomenon, to that which gives rise to and nurtures the others, it is not accessible to direct observation and to scholarly study. It is the real essence of religion and we can know it directly only in our own inner lives and indirectly insofar as we are capable of appreciating the reports of others who have known it directly themselves. What we can know and study is the objectified and available second and third aspects. In this presentation so far we have drawn heavily upon the second in the attempt to suggest to the reader the quality and character of the religious experience with which biblical religion is concerned. We must now examine briefly the institutional framework.

We have already noted the importance of this side of religious life in the significance which is to be seen in the precise form of organization and life in the world characteristic of the people of Israel in the biblical period. We also noted the significance for the continuation and development of the Christian tradition of the rise of defined and stable ecclesiastical organization in the second century. It is the Church which acts as the institutional expression and instrument bringing the message of Christianity to men. Problems of the Church therefore become significant problems of the Christian tradition.

The Church came to see itself as the institutional continuation of the life and mission of Jesus, performing through its liturgy and sacraments his mediating role between heaven and earth. Its original emphasis upon transcendence and on man's destiny beyond the mundane here and now was transformed by the experience and spiritual affinities of late antiquity into a pronounced other-worldly point of view. The Church mediated between heaven and earth, and man was here below on probation in preparation for a better life in the world beyond. These tendencies of the declining ancient world were strengthened in the centuries which followed its fall—centuries of near barbarism in which the Church alone attempted to hold up spiritual ideals and maintain a degree of civilized order, efforts which bore fruit in the rise of the medieval civilization.

The Church came to the world to bring to it its message of salvation, and in entering that world to convert it, it was itself in the process unable to remain "unstained from the world." As in all social institutions, men brought to the Church a great variety of motives and sought from it a variety of satisfactions. Ambition, desire for esteem, will to power—such motives came in to qualify and corrupt the orientation to the meaning and propagation of the gospel. Like all social organizations the Church represented both the concrete expression and application of the values it preached and their compromise and indeed corruption at the same time. Already in the second century we saw lukewarmness and a superficial formalism alongside fervor and authenticity. From the first we find immorality alongside asceticism and moral rigor. The separation of clergy and laity into two distinct estates turned the latter into passive participants in important respects, while it gave the former opportunities for psychological and often material aggrandizement not conducive to a high level of religious performance. The picture within the Church was in fact a spotty one and we see an enormous variety from heroic sanctity to harsh political manipulation. The Christian community was never without moving witness; it was also never without an ever-present need for reform. It is a permanent continuing condition of the Church—to be in need of reform. *Ecclesia semper est reformanda.*

We have already noted that protest is a significant category of religious behavior. Such protest is directed against conditions in the Church. Monasticism was in part a protest against increasing worldliness. The Patristic age saw many movements of protest—in Montanism, in some Gnostic movements, etc. The Middle Ages saw the rise of protest movements and the secession and driving out from the Church of groups embodying such protest. The role of protest, however, is an ambiguous one. It is a necessary element in the forward movement of the Church in time, which places obstacles in the way of the Church's deserting or neglecting its basic mission, and calls it back from the varied temptations of the world. But it may also reveal itself as standing in the way of developments and innovations which have become necessary under new conditions. It is always the significant question whether protest is against what actually is corruption and vitiating compromise or whether it is directed against justifiable development and necessary adaptation.

Plaster casts of two Apostles from the chancel arch of Kilpeck Church, England, c. 1125. (Courtesy of the Victoria and Albert Museum. Crown Copyright.)

The distinction between the two in many historical cases may be anything but clear-cut, and conflict and contention on such issues play a prominent part in Christian history. We may ask this question in another way. We may say that the real issue is always this: Is protest the expression of authentic reform? To reform the Church means to alter its internal condition so that under the circumstances of its existence it is able to bring the basic message of Christianity to men. Consequently, efforts for reform always involve definite convictions concerning what is basic and central to that message. The history of the Church is at the same time the history of efforts to reform it, and contention concerning which aspects of its religious message are most basic.

Elements of protest and reform were often found in the Church to be related to apocalyptic ideas and their millenarian expectations. They also were at times embedded in situations of social and economic frustration so that the impulse for protest and the desire for reform were often both religious and social and political at the same time, but the reality of their religious aims and motivation is not to be doubted. The Middle Ages saw the founding of a whole series of new monastic orders, such as the Carthusians founded by St. Bruno in 1084, the Cistercians by St. Robert in 1098, and the Premonstratensions by St. Norbert in 1120. Perhaps most significant were the Mendicant Orders, the Franciscan Order founded by St. Francis of Assisi in 1209 and the Dominican Order founded by St. Dominic in 1220. These two orders, based in towns and not in the countryside as were the older monastic groups, became the dominant religious influence of the late Middle Ages. The Franciscans emphasized poverty and the issue became the cause of a bitter internal struggle ending in the excommunication of the "Spirituals," the party which advocated maintaining the early ideal of corporate as well as individual poverty as the rule of life. The chief interest of the Dominican Order was educational and it produced Thomas Aquinas, the greatest Christian thinker of the entire medieval period. Such monastic and mendicant groups brought a new spiritual vigor to the Church and affected the religious life of many among the laity. Such groups by precept and example advocated a reform of religious life. The most impressive example of the reform role of religious orders is to be seen in the history of the famous Benedictine monastery at Cluny in Burgundy. Cluny was established in 910, and by the power of its high example of the religious life, and its reform of financial and economic management, it grew to be the center of some 314 affiliated establishments and came to exercise a decisive influence in the Church in the eleventh and twelfth centuries. The reforming efforts of this group reached their culmination in the election of the cluniac monk Hildebrand to the papal office as Gregory VII, a pope who repressed simony, enforced clerical celibacy, and removed numbers of offending churchmen from office. Religious orders appealed chiefly to upper-class youth who gave up the world of the nobility (and later the bourgeoisie) to dedicate themselves to the call of the gospel. The protest and reform carried out by such groups did not usually challenge the established ecclesiastical and social order, although this was definitely not the case in the Franciscan struggle in which the demand for poverty had significant social and political implications.

The Middle Ages also saw protest and the demand for reform of a sort that was not contained within the Church and which sooner or later resulted in an antiecclesiastical stance. The Cathari of the eleventh century, encouraged by Pope Gregory VII and his agitation for reform, rose in revolt against the political-ecclesiastical establishment in the cities of Lombardy. The thirteenth century saw the rise of the Waldensians or Poor Men of Lyons, whose advocacy of poverty and simplicity of life also contained serious social implications. The fourteenth century saw the rise of the Lollards—precursors of the more radical groups of the Reformation—and Hussites, in which nationalist expression and religious interests would be found together. The two figures perhaps most significant in connection with protest and reform efforts thoroughly challenging the form in which Church polity and doctrine had evolved were Huss and Wycliffe. John Wycliffe (1329–1384) wrote on the concept of "dominion" or legitimacy of rule and found that only those in a state of grace could legitimately exercise ecclesiastical and even civil office. Considering the condition of the Church a sinful one, he suggested that the Church should be disendowed and deprived of all temporal properties. He advocated the centrality of the Bible for faith and its translation into English, and accepted predestination. He also attacked the Papacy, monasticism, and transubstantiation, as well as abuses in the Church. His teachings were popularized by the Lollards in England and became popular in Central Europe. John Huss (1369–1415) was attracted to Wycliffe's doctrines, especially their political implications of the abolition of property and the hierarchical structure of society. The teachings of these men were condemned and Huss was burned at the stake as a heretic. The teachings of Wycliffe appealed to the poor and oppressed in English medieval society, and although he had nothing to do with the 1381 Peasant Revolt his doctrines may indeed have had their effect in it. In these figures we see protest and reform passing over into revolt.

Another significant figure in medieval Christian thought with respect to the relation of Christian teaching to Church and society was Joachim of Fiore (1132–1202). Joachim's ideas had a tremendous impact upon many in the centuries following his death, who often, like the Franciscan Spirituals, tended to act on their revolutionary implications, although he himself was quite submissive to duly authorized ecclesiastical authority. Joachim wrote three chief works in which he put forth the idea that the history of the world was divided into three periods. The first was the age of the Father, which was a social and political order of the laity and lasted from the Creation to the end of the Old Testament period. The second was the age of the Son, which was an order of clerics and a period of grace which began with the New Testament period and in which he and his contemporaries still lived. This age of clerics he predicted would last for forty-two generations of about thirty years each. It would be followed by an age of the Holy Spirit, which was to be an order of monks and a time of freedom and blossoming of the spirit of man in relation to the Holy Spirit. He expected this age to begin in 1260. In this third age, new religious orders would arise and convert the whole world and would thus inaugurate the time of the spiritual Church. In these movements of protest, reform, and revolt we see the way in which Christian ideals and influences entered into the evolution of Western man's aspirations and his responses to the problems of various ages.

The people of Israel had considered themselves a "holy people" set apart and chosen by God, and the Church had inherited this idea, which it accepted and applied to itself. Israel was at first, and for long aspired to be, a national and political as well as a religious entity, but by the beginning of the Christian era the Jews of the diaspora tended to be a confessional group with ethnic identification rather than a nation, the tendency which the defeat of A.D. 66–70 would implement and increase. The Christian Church, seeing itself as the new Israel, was in the first centuries a community within the general community. It did not even in the times of the bitterest persecution question the legitimacy of the Roman state. Its response to the world it rejected was a peaceful one as was that of the rabbinical Jews after 70. Hence, when it became the general and established religion of the empire, it did not challenge the political authority structure but merely posited its own ecclesiastical authority alongside it. Even when Rome fell and the Church became the ruler in fact in much of Europe, it never sought to supplant the idea of civil rule with one of a total monocratic theocracy. What resulted was a community in which there were two authority structures, each granted to be legitimate, but one of them, the Church, claiming more ontological value and religious dignity. Both historical experience and religious beliefs seemed at first to confirm this superior position of the Church, but it became increasingly questioned. Hence, in the Middle Ages there took place within Christendom a conflict between these two structures, a struggle to define their spheres of competence, to separate their powers, and grant the primal position to one or the other of them. It took European man a long time to work out these problems in any generally satisfactory way.

The European community had two authority structures; that is to say that it was really two communities, but that the membership of the two communities was the same. One was organized around religion—around the hierarchically organized and functioning mediational role between God and man carried out by the Church in public worship, teaching, and the administration of the sacraments. The other was organized around the secular state, maintaining political order as the requisite social context for civil life with its thisworldly pursuits. The New Testament insistence on the supremacy of religious values had come to mean in this situation the supremacy of the religious institution and its sacerdotal authority structure.

CHURCH
VERSUS
STATE

The conflict between Church and State—pope and emperor, bishop and king—was also a conflict to define the proper ends of man's communal life, although the Christian theological language used by both sides most often kept this element potential and implicit. From the spokesmen for secularization of authority, ideas of reform were also forthcoming. The most celebrated work in this respect was the *Defensor Pacis* of Marsiglio of Padua which appeared in 1324 in the middle of a war between pope and emperor. It presents a proposal for a radical disestablishment of the Church and placing of it under the civil rule of the state. It was of course a radical statement in line with the interests of one party to the conflict, but at the same time it shows how severe the problem had become. The Church, now a hierarchically organized community of prayer and mediation, was ruled by a clerical structure far removed from the lives and interests of the laity in many respects. What was seen by churchmen as a conflict between the Church and the world—between the spiritual understanding of man and his end and the ambitions and pleasures of the world—was seen by others as a conflict with a vast institutional structure inhibiting the normal development of the European political community. Indeed, such issues were subtly and inextricably intertwined. Marsilgio cut through them with his radical proposals.

The *Defensor Pacis* states that the civil government is the proper unifying authority in society. It derives its authority from the people, an authority institutionalized in the emperor, who may be criticized and even deposed by popular action. The Church should be subject to the civil power. It has no rights of its own but only those given it by the state and which the state may withdraw. It has no right to own property, but only to use that which is lent to it by the state. The book also denies the divine origin of the ecclesiastical hierarchy and that the primacy of the Church was given to Peter. Marsiglio suggested that the rule of the Church belonged properly to a general council which should be composed of both clergy and laity. This work contradicted the basic presuppositions of the Middle Ages with respect to civil authority and its relation to the Church, but it anticipated much that was to come.

The fourteenth and fifteenth centuries however saw an attempt to make use of the general council to reform the Church. The Church was an old organization deeply involved in the world in terms of its interests, though having developed few new ideas to aid it in adapting Christianity to the needs of the new complex commercial and political society which was developing in Europe. This Church stood in need of reform on several levels—in thought, in organization, and in religious practice. Moreover, internal fighting in the Church—the existence of two rival popes, for example—made the situation all the more difficult and discouraging. At several councils, efforts at reform were made, often combined with efforts to place a general council above the papal office. At the Council of Constance (1414–1418) there were considerable efforts in this respect. Here a schism over the papal office was finally healed, but three commissions appointed to propose reforms accomplished little. The Council did however adopt some reform measures against simony and other abuses. It also condemned Huss as a heretic and handed him over to the secular power for execution. It has been said by many historians that the failure of the conciliar movement and of the Council of Constance to affect real reform in the Church was one of the main causes of the Reformation.

Despite a degree of secularization, despite the reality of political conflicts, Europe was still at the beginning of the sixteenth century an entity not inaccurately described as Christendom, a *Republica Christiana,* but it was a Christendom in severe crisis. All the problems of the medieval civilization—problems of religious faith, its meaning and significance, problems of the value and worth of the lay life, problems of the functioning of an overstructured and often corrupt ecclesiastical organization, problems of the relation of the Church to the new national consciousness developing in places like Germany and England, and problems of the relation between Church and State as two separate but necessarily interrelated authority structures—remained unsolved and exacerbated by time, and the resulting internal ferment brought tremendous pressure against the institutional structures of the old Church. The last half of the fourteenth century and the entire fifteenth century was a time in which religious life in Europe was in shambles, if by religious life we mean the functioning of the Church organization and its relationship to the civil power. In these years the moral prestige of the Papacy waned, and this together with its claims to authority and the widespread and often contradictory feelings of discontent throughout the lands of Christendom made it a central target for attack. At the beginning of the sixteenth century all literate Europe agreed that the Church was sadly in need of reform; all knowledgeable Christians saw the need for some kind of change in the structure and functions of the ecclesiastical institution. But as we have seen, how the Church should be reformed was a question that could be answered only in relation to another more basic and fundamental question: What aspects of the Christian faith are central and should be given emphasis? Hence, while all agreed on the need for reform, while all cried out against abuses, in many cases one honest Christian's abuse was seen by another equally honest as a necessary and defensible practice. When churchmen spoke of the need for reform, they did not usually mean change of belief as that belief was represented and taught by the Church and even by the pope. It was the Church's legal system, its bureaucracy with its inefficiency, its corruption and graft, and the worldliness and immorality of important and unimportant clerics alike to which they referred. Some who were interested in humanistic culture and were effective in the development of that intellectual phenomenon known as the Renaissance—the revival of ancient humanistic letters, the flowering of art, and the continued development of science—desired intellectual changes as well. What was desired was an organizational, a moral, and an intellectual reform and renewal. To bring that about

THE RELIGIOUS AND
ECCLESIASTICAL
CRISIS OF THE
SIXTEENTH CENTURY

within the structure of the old Church, so deeply embedded in the secular civilization to which it had given rise, proved impossible. Yet down to the very beginning of the great Reformation movement in the sixteenth century radical anticlericalism and deep divergence from Catholic doctrine were unusual in any open or pronounced sense.

In the course of its development as a separate and even primary authority structure, the Papacy had become a political power in the complex Italian political situation and in Western Europe. Its needs for revenue increased tremendously in the new commercial society and it made use of its bureaucratic system to collect money and bring it to Rome. These efforts often involved highly questionable practices, such as the sale of indulgences which originally aroused the protest of Luther. Moreover, Rome had been greatly affected by the new Renaissance flowering of art and architecture and had become its most lavish patron. As a part of this, the papal court had become the most magnificent of any ruler in Europe, a fact seemingly not inappropriate to many for Christ's vicar and the visible ruler of Christ's Church. The abuses of papal finance and the demands upon Northern Christians to support the political and artistic requirements of the Papacy proved to be important elements leading to a new protest movement and strategic to the outbreak of revolt and schism.

Yet the Church had become elaborated in such a way that it would be difficult to sustain any movement for reform that penetrated to the grass roots of the Christian population without a considerable amount of dismantling on all levels—doctrinal, organizational, and cultic. As we noted before, men brought a variety of motives to the Church and sought the fulfillment of a variety of needs within it. Now two decades into the sixteenth century, men would divide in terms of these complex internal alignments of their values and interests and give rise to equally complex external arrangements among friends and foes. When Luther in 1517 protested against Tetzel's sale of indulgences to raise money for the support of the pope's renovation of the basilica of St. Peter's in Rome, his expression of such grievances was not in itself an unusual phenomenon. But when he developed his protest to involve far-reaching theological changes issuing in his basing Christian faith upon the outcome of his own deep interior spiritual experience of salvation by faith alone, he opened the way for impulses to reformulation which had lain deep beneath the surface of European religious life.

Many of the basic ideas of the Reformation had already been expressed by the sectarian protests of the Middle Ages. Indeed, in the revolt of the laity in the eleventh century, a revolt supported and aided by Gregory VII, we see in anticipation many of the chief phenomena of the Reformation and post-Reformation periods, including lay preaching, rejection of the sacraments from corrupt clergy, an emphasis upon poverty of worldly goods, abrogation of taxes and tithes, indifference toward the state, advocacy of independent study of the Bible, and the raising of the example of the primitive Church as the standard for ecclesiastical life. The idea that the sacraments possessed no objective validity was as old as Montanism. Moreover, the medieval sects often advocated the doctrine of predestination in radical form, and when this was combined with some moralistic doctrine of signs of election in those who lead "good lives" the whole sacramental structure of the old Church became unnecessary at best, a spurious and evil development at worst. The revival of immediate eschatological expectations gave rise to an atmosphere of crisis and urgency which made the institutional church seem irrelevant, and if unreformed in its abuses, about to be condemned. Medieval sectaries also rejected the Mass and the sacraments and thereby questioned the central mediational function which the Church understood as constitutive of its earthly mission. Together with this they often attacked Church authority.

Moreover, developments in intellectual life in the fourteenth and fifteenth centuries contributed to a further weakening of the ground and sense of sufficient reason concerning the Church's doctrines. Nominalism had become the philosophical viewpoint of the late Middle Ages, and denying the existence of universal concepts with significance in reality, it severed the relation between faith and reason which the earlier medieval thinkers, and Thomas preeminently, had labored to build. For Ockham, the originator of this point of view, human knowledge consisted merely in conventions which though of practical use possess no objective value. The consequence was a radical skepticism. Nominalism became the accepted view of the leading theologians of the pre-Reformation period, and thus theology was cut off from any rational justification and from any positive rational criteria of judgment as well. Religious truth could only be held by faith, a faith no longer seen as harmonious with, though going beyond, reason. Hence authority was in certain respects enhanced, being freed from the critical oversight of rational thought, a kind of freedom likely to prove most detrimental to its functioning. Moreover, the critical and skeptical spirit of Nominalism undermined authority even as based upon faith. Since universals did not exist but were only conceptions, the Church as such did not exist but was only a collection of individuals so far as being a repository of truth is concerned. Truth was not in the Church but in individuals. But which individuals? Ockham stated that the pope was not infallible and composed a compendium of errors which he attributed to Pope John XXII with whom the Franciscan Order, of which Ockham was a member, was involved in profound conflict. He held that since Christ promised that the gates of hell would never prevail against the Church, someone in the Church would always be right but we cannot know unerringly who it is. We can only rely on the Bible. However, in the decades before Luther the Bible for the first time was being subjected to critical study, as may be seen in the work of Erasmus, who however rejected Luther and remained in the old Church. Moreover, there developed at this time a revolt against the sterile hyperintellectualism of the late medieval university and its academic theology. This movement, known as the *devotio moderno,* called for a simple piety and an end to theological subtleties. Its most famous expression was found in Thomas à Kempis' *Imita-*

tion of Christ (long a devotional work among Catholics and Protestants alike) and the Brothers of the Common Life to whom Thomas belonged. It elicited the sympathy of such humanist intellectuals as Erasmus.

Luther's protest was one more protest and Luther's break with Rome was one more schism, yet for subtle and complex reasons on which historians are by no means in agreement they turned out to be much more. Although Luther's general cast of mind was conservative and medieval and although even the most radical reformers saw themselves as bringing back the pristine purity of the primitive Church rather than making innovations, the Reformation turned out to be a quite new phenomenon in European religious history. In its complex development, conditioned by the specific historical circumstances which it encountered, the Church had responded on both the doctrinal and organizational level to the problems which time and place presented. In meeting these problems it gave shape and form to itself and to its beliefs. The faith of the early Church gradusually assumed the form of a sophisticated and elaborate philosophy of religion whose development we have already followed, especially with respect to the doctrines of Christology and grace. The Church was gradually transformed into a vast hierarchical structure administering a highly objectified system of worship and sacramental mediation. This structure was functioning badly as the sixteenth century began. Change in it was necessary, but change in it could not but involve a more and more radical questioning of the whole system and the specific form it had assumed in the course of its long history.

CHRISTIANITY
AND JUDAISM
The traditions of biblical religion had assumed a fixed form which would be thoroughly challenged in the modern age, which began in the sixteenth century. Those traditions which we sketched here split early into two strands, a minority strand which became the majority in Christianity and a majority strand which became the minority in Judaism. These two communities, grounded in a common past and common basic religious premises, differed over the significance to be attributed to the life and mission of Jesus. Judaism rejected the claims of Christianity with regard to the messiashship and meaning of Jesus, the doctrine of election, and the abrogation of the law. To the Jews it appeared that redemption had not come. None of the changes which were expected to accompany the coming of the Messiah had taken place. The Jews themselves remained defeated, paganism continued, and the world was still evil. They rejected the Christian belief that Jesus' suffering and death had brought redemption and saw in the Trinitarian ideas and Christological conceptions of the Church something like idolatry. The claim of the Church to be the true Sarah now chosen over the synagogue which it saw in the role of Hagar was sheer usurpation in Jewish eyes. Israel, they felt, could not be superseded, since the promises to it were eternal. Because the world had not been redeemed, the Law was still absolutely binding. The kingdom had not come and there-

fore men must live under the Law's yoke, fulfilling Gods commands in the attempt to purify themselves and to remain obedient. The Jews did not claim to be justified by their obedience, but only to be approximating the realization of God's will. "The congregation of Israel spoke before the Holy One, blessed be His name: Lord of the universe, though I am poor in meritorious acts yet nonetheless I belong to thee and it is within thy power to help me" (*Pesahim* 118b). They held that the Torah, in its entirety, was an everlasting guide to the way of life which God expected from his chosen people and that through faithfulness to its commands they were brought close to him. The growth of Christianity was not seen by them as an evidence of the truth of Christian faith but rather as the continuing dominance of a power outside the covenant over the defeated and scattered people of Israel reduced to a tolerated and too often abused minority within the confines of Christendom.

Two communities, a vast majority and a small minority, professing faith in God and an ethic in which love was central, lived together in a strange combination of hostility and symbiosis. Underneath their differences there remained the fundamental elements of agreement and similarity. Yet to members of the two groups it was the differences which were salient to their consciousness. Differences, especially since it was a matter of differences within a common tradition, meant rivalry and competition, and all the antagonism to which they give rise. Differences, especially since it was a matter of differences concerning profound religious beliefs, made that antagonism abiding and often bitter. To many Christians, Judaism was not merely a rival but a blasphemous one, since it rejected Christ; to many Jews, Christians came close to idolatry in placing a human figure next to God and were themselves guilty of blasphemy. As the majority group with political power in its hands, the Christians could make the rules. As a large majority, it contained groups who would make an unpopular minority a scapegoat. In popular thinking the existence of Judaism was often seen as an affront to the religious sensibilities of Christians, and Jews a people punished for Christ's death. To the Jews such conditions were a continuation of their exile and they looked for God's deliverance.

In periods of social and political unrest from the late eleventh century on, the Jews found themselves the victims of pogroms from time to time. Such matters of religious identification and antagonism as always became inextricably intertwined with other more mundane interests and the outbreak of anti-Jewish violence reflected this. Yet the history is not one of complete antagonism, for despite controversy and opposition Jews in practice had friendly contact with Christians in certain areas of life and in theory did develop a more tolerant attitude toward Christianity. Thus in the Paris debate of 1240 Jews stated that the talmudic restrictions on the relations of Jews to idol worshipers did not apply to Christians and that the negative evaluation of the seven foreign nations found in the Bible and the Talmud did not refer to contemporary Christians. At the end of the thirteenth century the great French Jewish scholar Ha-Meiri enunciated the principle that Christianity is not idolatry and that

Christians share with Jews basic ethical and religious truths evident to all men of reason. In the developed Jewish view the seven Noahide commandments are universally binding and all men who fulfill them will be recognized by God and share in the redemption to come.

In the early Christian Fathers we find harsh language used in expressing hostility to the synagogue and those who worship there. Yet the Fathers, despite the hostility of rivalry, saw the Jews as somehow continuing their testimony to God's revelation—indeed, to what the Fathers saw as the Christian fulfillment of that revelation. Augustine, who could see the Jew in the image of Judas Iscariot, could also recognize the importance of his continued existence.

> *Today, if the Jews are dispersed through all nations and lands, that is due to God's design; so that if idols, altars, sacred groves and temples are destroyed all over the earth and the sacrifices forbidden, it could still be seen from the Jewish books that all this was prophesied long ago; and although the prophecies, fulfilled in the Christian religion, may be read also in our own holy books, no one can accuse us of having composed them ourselves after the event.*

> (*City of God* IV.34)

Moreover, more profound Christian thought beginning with Paul was aware of a continuing special religious meaning and destiny for Israel. For Paul things happened as they happened by God's providence. The Jews now stand aside that the gentiles may be gathered. "Through their trespass salvation has come to the Gentiles"; but Paul asks, "have they stumbled so as to fall?" He answers, "By no means!" (Rom. 11:11). For Paul, "a hardening has come upon part of Israel, until the full number of the Gentiles come in," but when that is accomplished "all Israel will be saved" (Rom. 11:25–26). He says to gentile Christians, "As regards the gospel they are enemies of God, for your sake; but as regards election they are beloved for the sake of their forefathers. For the gifts and call of God are irrevocable" (Rom. 11:28–29).

Following Paul, the Christian view saw the Jews as both acting out God's will and subjectively unfaithful, and granted them a kind of secondary legitimacy. They should be permitted to exist, since that is God's will, and since they bear testimony to the truth of Christianity. But they should exist in a subject condition since they rejected the fulfillment of the truth and this subjection was the sign testifying to their infidelity. Proselytism of Christians by Jews continued well into the Middle Ages but it was forbidden by law; Christian attempts to convert Jews were of course perfectly legal. Jews were forbidden to hold public office in the Christian society of the Middle Ages and the public character of their worship was limited, as was the number of synagogues they could build. In the eleventh century the ghetto or special Jewish quarter arose as a pattern of residence and in the fifteenth century Jewish residence there was made compulsory, especially in Spain and the papal domain in Italy.

And the modes of contact between Jews and Christians were regulated by Church law. They were also regulated by Jewish law, and a strange symbiosis grew up in which the regulations of both communities worked to maintain Jewish identity and separateness. The condition of the Jews worsened greatly during the Crusades, when they were often victimized and massacred by adventurers and mobs.

St. Thomas held that although the Jews were in the status of bondsmen to the civil powers of Christendom, they did not by that fact lose their natural rights nor their special religious rights to practice their own religion. He held also that Jewish children could not be baptized without the consent of their parents (*Summa Theologica* Part II, ques. 10, art. 12, and Part III, ques. 68, art. 10). The policy of the Church followed Thomas in this, but there were those who disagreed with it and it was violated in practice at various times. The Church and the civil power did act at times to protect the Jews, but the policy of restricting their influence in a Christian society was generally accepted by all. As Malcolm Hay said: "The Popes of the Middle Ages often intervened, not always effectively, to defend the Jews against personal violence, but seldom wrote a line to condemn the ill-will which made such violence inevitable." Religious rivalry and the sense of threat which each group offered to the other left little room for their seeing each other as neighbors whom they were commanded to love by the commandment they both accepted.

Geography and history rather than the content of faith led to a further split in the majority tradition, and finally in 1054 Eastern and Western Churches split into two distinct groups, each considering the other to be schismatic. Several attempts were made to heal this rift but they failed. Finally in the Reformation, Western Christianity itself split again, unable to compose its differences, and the Protestant camp split up still further into numerous denominations as time went on. Medieval Europe had gradually and toilsomely built the foundations of a secular society within the confines of a sacral civilization with its institutions justified by their own functions and rationale. That this was the case would become apparent by the mid-seventeenth century, but the great changes would begin their long process of development at the commencement of the sixteenth.

THE REFORMATION

The Europe that saw the beginning of the Reformation was still religious and the Reformation was a religious movement. But once the issues had been joined on basic questions of Church reform, including questions of belief itself, it was unavoidable that all other aspects of European life would be drawn into the struggle. The Reformation could not help become at the same time a political phenomenon. It was in part a conflict of princes against the pope. It was in part a revolt of the Teutonic North against the Latin South; it was in part a revolt of new middle classes against the older aristocratic society and culture. And although it sought to deepen the religiosity of European man, it eventuated in a marked secularization of culture and a frank admission on the part of strategic classes in

Europe of the practical primacy of this-worldly aims and aspirations in politics and in business. Over a century of religious wars following the Reformation began with wars in which religious interests were dominant although intertwined with worldly interests, and ended in palpably secular struggles for power and wealth. There are times in the development of societies and cultures when the social structures and the modes of comprehension of man and his destiny which have evolved are no longer appropriate. The new situation which has slowly developed and the old forms which have been carried over into it from the past no longer fit. Men in such situations are for long unaware of the true dimensions of their problems, but as they seek to act on them they act as though forced to more and more extreme positions by the logic of the situation itself. Perhaps we live in such a situation in our own day. Certainly the men of the sixteenth century did, and what they started as a return to an imagined and idealized past eventuated in a greatly changed society and culture, although it would take some two or three centuries before all its implications would make themselves apparent.

The Reformation may be said to have begun in 1517 with the protest of Luther against the sale of indulgences and to have expanded in the next three years as he took a position against the validity of "good works" as aids to salvation, denied the primacy of the pope and the infallibility of general councils, attacked clerical celibacy, transubstantiation, and the indelibility of priestly ordination, and demanded far-reaching reforms of religious orders. By 1520 Luther had broken with the old Church, and after a period of pronounced religious conflict in Germany, Rome excommunicated him on January 3, 1521. Although at first placed under ban by the Holy Roman Emperor, he attracted sympathy from a number of rulers of German states, and his support of authoritarian secular government during the Peasant War ensured that he would be backed by powerful princes. In 1524–1526 the German peasants rose in rebellion, demanding the abolition of serfdom and certain taxes, as well as certain religious privileges, such as the right to elect their own pastors. It was another of those movements of mixed socioeconomic and religious motivation and it soon led to extremes of violence in the burning of castles and monasteries. Luther at first tried to mediate, but this proving unsuccessful he turned against the violence of the lower orders and wrote his own intemperate denunciation of them, advocating that they be stabbed and killed to extermination, a stand that effectively reduced his popularity if it brought him powerful support. Yet Luther's ideas spread throughout Germany, and popular religious enthusiasm as well as official protection and support brought many victories. The old order crumbled in many places as priests married and religious deserted the cloister. Many Catholic religious practices were given up. In 1524 Luther put aside his monastic habit and married a former Cistercian nun.

What had developed was a new form of Christianity designated as Lutheranism. Its basic doctrines proclaimed salvation through faith alone and the priesthood of believers. It tended to follow Luther in seeing all men totally depraved and human reason as useless in the search for religious truth. It emphasized the centrality of the Bible and had Luther's magnificent translation into German as its own vernacular scripture. Lutheranism became the faith of about two-thirds of Germany and all of Scandinavia.

In 1523 under the leadership of Ulrich Zwingli, who claimed that he took no ideas from Luther, but who brought forth many similar notions and some far more radical as in Eucharistic and social doctrines, reform gained control of the city of Zurich. There, with the backing of the civil authorities, Zwingli broke with Rome and abolished the ecclesiastical hierarchy and monasticism. The Zwinglian Reformation made rapid advances in many Swiss cantons and in South Germany as well.

The most dynamic of the Reformation tendencies came forward in Geneva under John Calvin, who replaced Zwingli as the reform leader in Switzerland when the latter was killed fighting against the Catholic cantons. Calvin was an austere and intelligent man; he was a logical expositor of doctrine and often extreme in his views, some of which we have already considered. Here for the first time the new religious agitation produced a massive, rigorously argued, and intellectually constructed theological system based upon predestination by a transcendent God far beyond the reach of man's understanding and saturated with a hyper-Augustinian pessimism. Calvin held that the Bible contained all we need to know about God and the moral life. He denied freedom, held that all human acts were sinful, but that in those who were of the elect they were covered over by the merits of Christ's death. He emphasized God's inscrutable and transcendent omnipotence and unlike Luther paid little heed to his mercy or his justice. In 1541 Calvin took over control of Geneva, which had become the center of the Swiss Reformation. Here he established a rigid theocracy and used the most coercive supervisory and repressive measures to keep people in line. He enforced an austerely ascetic life, and all forms of mere pleasure such as dancing and game playing were outlawed.

Calvin was the father of ascetic Protestantism which advocated a strict ascetic mode of life characterized by a high degree of self-control. Calvinism imparted a dynamic quality to the Reformation, which Lutheranism never really achieved. Whereas the latter rested content to concern itself with the inner life and left government and the worldly pursuits to the state, thereby effecting a kind of passivity which long remained one of its distinguishing characteristics, Calvinism set out to create Christian communities after the Calvinist model and under the supervision of Calvinist leadership. This austere ascetic religion appealed to the rising middle classes of a Europe experiencing commercial expansion and its consequent social change. It also combined with the national interests and sentiments of such groups as the Dutch and the Scots. Even more than Lutheranism it became involved in the political struggles of the time, as may be seen in France, in the Netherlands, in West Germany, in Scotland, and in England. It has been said that Calvinism provided the new rising bourgeoisie in many places with a form of Christianity which fitted the psychological and religious needs of rising individualists cut off from meaningful participation in the old Church, whose modes of worship and ways of belief they found as barriers to any religious experience and against which they turned in fury, and from real involvement in traditional national life as well. It is one of the unexplained ironies of the Reformation period that the religious point of view which most appealed to the highly activist and energetic capitalist classes was one that held man to be unfree and incapable of good by his own efforts. Yet the notion of election must have given a profound basis of inner security, providing it could be maintained. To maintain it was in fact difficult, and various compromises with it soon developed. Indeed, wherever the bourgeois classes got the upper hand they tended radically to reform the notion of predestination or to reject it entirely, although it remained the official doctrine of the United Presbyterian Church in the United States until 1965.

In England the Reformation got its opportunity when a small group of clerical intellectuals took advantage of the marriage problems and dynastic worries of a conservative Catholic king to bring about a break with Rome and to introduce change in doctrine and church structure. There evolved the Church of England, governed by bishops, but with its headship vested in the monarch. That church, in the settlement under Elizabeth I which gave it its definitive form, held to a kind of middle way on most of the controversial issues of theology. Yet Calvinism made important inroads in the Church of England in which, however, a Catholicizing tendency also remained important. Outside the established Church in England, Calvinism became an important force. In the Puritan Revolution (1640–1660) it abolished the monarchy and established a Commonwealth controlled by the more extreme religious groups. This movement split into numerous competing sects and led eventually to the restoration of the king and the established Anglican Church. It was never able to convince the English as a whole to accept its more extreme positions, not to mention its rejection of the monarchy.

The idea of the Church as it emerged in the Reformation took varied forms, and the working out of a definition of what the Church was became an important task of Protestant theologians. Whatever it was seen to be, it is obvious that it was conceived quite differently from the way it had been viewed in the preceeding centuries. The vast overarching superstructure of the medieval Church with its objective means of grace and its elaborate theology had to be replaced by other conceptions. All Protestant variations had one thing in common; they all rejected to one degree or another the Catholic emphasis on a centralized teaching office and an objective sacramental system. A new emphasis upon the Bible was characteristic and preaching came to take up a large portion of the time given to Sunday worship. Despite the variations to be found in reformed conceptions of the Church, perhaps three general tendencies may be distinguished. There was first a more traditionalist tendency which held that Christ intended a visible universal Church, but because that Church had been corrupted by ignorance and sin, national schisms in the interests of reform were justified. This conception gave some significant place to an objective, at times hierarchical, ecclesiastical institution. A second tendency held that the Church was really an invisible body comprised of the elect or those saved by a personal act of faith, and its true membership was known to God alone. Yet it also held that the Church needed a visible social organization as a means of existence in this world. This outward Church should enforce high standards so that its membership would correspond so far as possible with the inward Church, though there would never be a one-to-one correspondence of the two. It held that this visible organization would ideally be universal, but in fact, since that was now impossible, national churches and churches coterminal with political entities and established by law in them should be sought. Hence the Lutheran and Calvinist churches took hold in Germany and Sweden and in Holland and Scotland.

A third tendency may be seen in those who substantially agree with the second tendency respecting the ideas of the visible and invisible Church but who held that no form of unity between congregations was necessary, and some who even held such unity to be evil. This view may be best described as a sect ideal, which held up as the true model of the Church of God a small austere brotherhood withdrawn from the world or militantly hostile to it. In the Puritan Revolution the original aim of the Commonwealth was to establish a Calvinist Church, and in 1643 an Assembly of Divines convened for that purpose drew up The Westminster Confession as its basis. But the composition of the supporters of the Commonwealth, especially in the army, was decidedly of independent and sectarian stamp, and sectarian freedom had to be given legal approval.

The more extreme Reformation movements have often been lumped together under the label of "Left-Protestantism." They present a varied array but they all approach to one extent or another to the sect ideal. They are often radical in both theology and social ideas and apocalyptic at the same time combining communitarian social ideas, emotional enthusiasm, and millenarian expectations. Though often condemned by the great reformers and the official Reformation churches at least in their more extreme forms, these groups, at times made up of the poor and oppressed, represent a genuine and significant religious phenomenon. Just as sectarian and semimystical groups emerged in the pre-Reformation period, becoming either religious orders or excommunicated sects, and affected the life of the Church as a whole, so they emerged in the Reformation and post-Reformation periods as well. From the start such groups were present and the tendencies they embodied were widespread. Official Protestantism, however, was conservative in important respects and moreover needed time to work out its conception of the Church, and under those circumstances such groups found little place. From the middle of the seventeenth century, however, these groups began to have an increased effect on the more conservative Protestant churches. Among the important and quite varied groups of which we speak are Levellers, Mennonites, Diggers, Millenarians, the so-called Anabaptists, and the less extreme Congregationalists, Independents, Baptists, and Quakers.

THE CATHOLIC
COUNTER-REFORMATION
AND ATTEMPTS
AT UNITY

Luther's original demand for reform may indeed be viewed as part of the religious revival which was developing in the Church, a revival which was to be seen in the founding of such lay groups as the Brothers of the Common Life and in a marked renewal of religious fervor in the religious orders. New religious orders were founded in the 1520s, the Capuchins, the Theatines, and the Barnabites, and in 1540 the Jesuits, established by the austere militant Basque Ignatius Loyola who soon became the vanguard of the movement to defend, reform, and extend Catholicism in Europe, in the Americas, and in the Far East. A small but highly influential group founded in Rome in 1517 was the Oratory of Divine Love, made up of men who were of contemplative mind and who put together many humanistic ideas of the Renaissance with their Catholicism to produce an authentic Christian humanism. They led lives of prayer and devotion, as well as of responsible thought and action. Two of their prominent members, Cardinals Contarini and Pole, attempted to mediate between the Catholics and Protestants and to negotiate a compromise which would reestablish the unity of the Church. This idea of compromise and union appealed to important figures on the Protestant side as well, for after all had not Christian unity always been the ecclesiastical ideal, and wasn't it supported by men as significant as Bucer and Melanchthon? These leaders sought such a compromise at the Colloquy of Regensburg (or Ratisbon) in 1541. Pole and Contarini had agreed that the formal statement of Lutheran faith, the Confession of Augsburg, need not be an obstacle. Two groups of three each—for the Catholics Eck, Pflug, and Gropper; for the Protestants Bucer, Melanchthon, and Pistorius—drew up a statement on justification by faith which was agreed upon. It mentioned neither freedom of the will nor subjective certainty of salvation. Evidently other doctrinal matters proved negotiable in a similar manner but not the Mass, invocation of the saints, and papal supremacy. Bucer brought about a second Regensburg meeting in 1546, but it got nowhere. Luther was unfriendly to the whole affair, and Calvin who was present at one of the meetings was less willing to compose differences than the other reformers. The compromise party of Pole and Contarini was suspect by other Catholics, and Protestant princes were against any reunion being effected. Catholic and Protestant opinion had diverged widely in the two decades of separation and conflict, and vested interests had become invested in continuing disunity.

This effort after unity was but one expression of the reform tendency which had been gathering strength and energy in the old Church since the beginning of the sixteenth century. The other sought to combine an effort to combat the spread of Protestantism with the renewal of religious life and the promotion of austerity, discipline, and devotion within the Church. This tendency found its spokesman in Gian Pietro Caraffa who also had been a member of the Oratory and later became Pope Paul IV. Pope Paul III, whose personal life was far from presenting a model to churchmen, but who was however an effective promoter of reform in the Church, sympathized with both tendencies but sided with the more militant approach of Caraffa, partly perhaps in response to the aggressive expansion of Calvinism. Orthodoxy was enforced by a renewed Inquisition (1542) and the so-called Catholic Counter-Reformation began. In 1540 the Jesuit Order was formally established. It attracted much Catholic idealism eager to strive and suffer in defense of the Church. This new order gave the Catholic side a dynamism and a militancy to match that of the Calvinists. Largely through Jesuit efforts South Germany and Poland were won back to Catholicism and Catholic foreign mission work vastly stimulated. The battle between Protestants and Catholics was joined and Europe would now pass through an awful period of the religious wars. As well as efforts to mend the split in the Church at large, there were also efforts to bring about Protestant unity. A number of conferences were held, many of them initiated by Bucer, but they were unsuccessful. The ideal of Church unity was held by many, but it was not possible any longer. For nearly all it involved imposition of belief. One man, Sabastian Castellio, whom Calvin had expelled from Geneva, suggested toleration of differences in belief, but this found little favor among reformers trying to reestablish some kind of religious order and to domesticate the religious individualism which had been released by reform and rebellion. Consequently the seventeenth century saw a greater division among Protestants and the formation of the so-called Left-Protestant groups.

The Council of Trent also represented an attempt at unity in that Protestants were invited, but after appearing they soon left, refusing to take part in a meeting led by the pope. What Trent actually did was to provide a tighter formulation of Catholic doctrine and to increase the significance of strict and proper belief as the criterion of orthodoxy. Also, Trent carried out significant internal reform. After Trent there continued a magnificent flowering of the religious life within the Catholic fold. Yet it is another great irony of the religious history of the West that this most authentic and most long-lived renewal of spiritual life took place within the confines of a Church which was defensive in posture, closed to rethinking of its doctrinal positions, and now with its renewed purity of intention even more rigid in its structure. Trent indeed stamped upon Roman Catholicism the imprint of an intolerant age; Trent imparted to the Catholic mentality a sense of being under siege and of facing Protestant Christians as adversaries to be fought to the end. This feeling was of course reciprocated from the Protestant side but there disunity kept uniformity and rigidity of structure from dominating the entire religious scene.

SECULARIZATION AND SCIENCE

Europe had seen from the twelfth century a rise of secular states, which though Christian asserted their own competence and autonomy, and a vast development of commerce which carved out of rural and traditional medieval society an autonomous market becoming ever larger and more ramified. By the outbreak of the Reformation, Antwerp was the Wall Street of Europe and many modern business practices were to be found there. The break in Christian unity, which yielded to no attempts at reunion, gave the secularizing tendencies favorable conditions for their further development, and the consequent secularization of culture made religious unity seem less urgent and less important. It could loom large in the mind of Leibnitz in the seventeenth century, as can be seen in his correspondence with the French Catholic Bishop Bossuet, but it never again took on such significance with such an illustrious intellectual figure. The most significant element in these developments came in the seventeenth century in what is called the rise of modern science. The stage had been set for a far-reaching secularization of culture, and the revival of humanism in the late Middle Ages and early Renaissance led to an eventual break between humanistic and religious thought and feeling. There was no longer a grand overarching Church with its largely undisputed doctrines whose leaders could realistically hope to be the key influential elite keeping the conscience of a whole civilization. Now with science would come an element radically solvent of traditional thought and feeling. What commerce was doing to disenchant the world of human relations by introducing quantitative calculation as a dominant mode of relationship, scientific thought would do to the intellectual cosmos. The scientific development of the seventeenth century was a complex process and represented the continuation of a long development going back to the university life of the High Middle Ages and the numerous useful inventions which were made in Europe in the medieval period. When Luther began his protest, Western Europe was in fact the most technologically advanced society the world had seen up to that time. But in the seventeenth century there came a breakthrough in the scientific development—from Galileo to Newton—which justifies being described as a scientific revolution. It was much more than a continuation of the use of experiment and mathematics which had taken place since the thirteenth century. Nor was it merely the consequence of new data gradually accumulated and slowly changing men's outlooks. It was an abrupt and radical shift in ways of thinking which led men to look at their world in a new kind of abstract way. Moreover, in this development the earth itself had been thrown out of center and a new heliocentric astronomy became accepted. This development threatened religion directly, for the older geocentric view was held, at least superficially, to harmonize with religious ideas and to reinforce them with common pragmatic prejudices. The scientific endeavors of centuries came to sudden fruition and men found themselves with a new mathematized mode of thought which gave them distance from their world and a means of manipulating it symbolically in their heads. To the already proceeding secularization of culture was added an incomparably more powerful solvent of tradition which in less than two centuries would transform both man's world and his way of thinking about it. Thus there began a new and tragic division of the Western mind—a conflict between science and religion, a conflict in which religion was often reactionary and obscurantist despite the fact that the great pioneers of science, its greatest founding figures, were sincere Christians. It took a long time—even until our own day—for

The chapel at Ronchamp. Designed by Le Corbusier, it replaces a war-damaged church built in the thirteenth century. The structure is so fashioned that mountain winds playing between the columns under the roof and through archways make musical sounds heard for miles. (Religious News Service Photo.)

the idea to become evident that science and religion see experience from different standpoints, respond to their worlds in different modes of response, and require different languages to express their meanings. There is here a vast field yet to be explored and understood. The fact is, however, that by the year 1800 Christianity existed in a world which was increasingly secularized for dominant classes and in which science provided more and more the model of thinking for the literate. Religion was definitely on the defensive, though numerically most Western men were still believers; it was in fact definitely in retreat. Yet traditional religion would remain in a secularized world the repository of the riches of the religious heritage and the source of the profoundest Western values and aspirations.

This breakdown of a unified Catholic Europe and the emergence of a secularized bourgeoisie meant also the creation of a neutral public sphere free from the domination of religious values. This led to a gradual but drastic change in the status of churches in society, as can be seen in such countries as England and Sweden which officially still have established churches but are in fact about the most secularized in the world. But perhaps the greatest changes to result were found in the traditional Jewish communities of Europe. New ideas penetrated the ghetto and influenced the minds of many. The entire structure of exilic existence, which rested on the foundation ideas of election, exilic suffering, and ultimate redemption, was threatened by a rationalistic reconsideration of accepted truths. What Christianity was undergoing in the larger world was now coming with more sudden impact to be a fact within the Jewish communities themselves. The new secular spirit penetrated the ghettos

THE JEWISH
RESPONSE TO
SECULARIZATION

and captivated sections of the Jewish population, challenging the religious framework of the community. In the eighteenth century, the so-called age of reason, the values of this world, especially material values, were elevated above the values of the next. Bourgeois man tended to dedicate his efforts to the pursuit of gain and the betterment of his mundane condition, using his autonomous reason to do so. The bourgeois Christian had little need of the God of the Bible, and the Church's inability to speak to him in any depth left the matter to take on its own shape and form. What developed was the notion, seemingly confirmed by the facts of bourgeois existence, that realistic, practical rational activity would lead to continuous progress in the betterment of human life. Such ideas now penetrated the Jewish community and as a consequence some Jews adopted this rational spirit and found that for them too the God of the Bible was obsolete. They rejected the Torah culture and the religious values of traditional Judaism. No longer could they be satisfied to live in expectation of a future redemption while fulfilling the religious duties of the present; no longer would they look upon worldly success and the practical activities that led to it as secondary to religious activity with its future expected reward. Jews affected by this new modern spirit and its attendant ideas dedicated themselves to ending Jewish exile by achieving prosperity and success in this world. The emerging Jewish bourgeoisie, embodying this spirit, soon abandoned the religious practices which hindered its progress. Abrogation of the Law was common, and such abrogation rent the fabric of the traditional community. The emerging Jewish intellectual stratum, espousing secular ideas, abandoned religious beliefs and practices which could not be justified according to the canons of reason, and thus attacked the very foundations of Jewish life. Desiring to become part of the developing secular society of Western Europe, to become one socially and culturally with the general secular European world, now replacing what had once been Christendom, these Jews rejected self-segregation and the all-encompassing cultural world of the Torah tradition. They sought to share in the open society of European rationalism and humanitarianism.

The history of Judaism in modern times is a history of response to the challenges which the scientific and philosophical ideas of the past three centuries and the social, economic, and political changes in European society presented to the biblically derived religion and those which opportunity for assimilation into the new kind of general society presented to the isolated self-enclosed exilic community. The Jewish religious reforms proposed by German Jewish reformers offered one solution to these challenges by developing a system of religious beliefs and practices which conformed to the spirit and ideology of their time. This system legitimated the separation of the secular and the sacred and the truncation of Judaism and its relegation to one fragment of the individual's life. It also sanctioned a definition of Judaism which denied the necessary link between faith and the Jewish people as an ethnic unit, and thus justified the assimilation of the Jews and the end of their existence as a separate national community. In opposition to the radical reform movement, a more conservative trend developed, which did not reject whatever could not be rationalized according to contemporary standards, but which sought to accommodate tradition to the present without completely destroying what had been sanctified by the past and had long been considered essential to the sacred nature of Judaism. The more conservative reformers did not oppose ceremonial practices as irrational, nor did they reject the ethnic base of Judaism, yet they did make adjustments in belief and practice to render Judaism more viable under modern conditions. The efforts at reform along both radical and conservative lines have continued so that within Judaism today, Conservative, Reform, and Reconstructionist movements exist alongside many Orthodox groups to offer alternative definitions of belief and practice.

Another response of Jews to secularization has been the total abandonment of traditional religion and the substitution of nationalism for religion as the basis of Jewish unity. As Christendom broke up, the importance of the national group for men's basic identity and its significance as their basic community was greatly enhanced. Although such national developments offered rivalry to traditional Christianity, they did not usually seek to replace it. The Jewish proposal was more radical, reflecting perhaps how thoroughly challenged was Judaism by the conditions of modernity. Moreover, the rise of Jewish nationalism took place mainly in Eastern Europe, where ethnic group life was the dominant pattern and where assimilation into the general society was never a realistic possibility. Within Russia and Poland, Jews found themselves necessarily identified as Jews by external forces, but often at the same time lacking the religious convictions that had grounded that identity in the past. No longer accepting the traditional religion, these men sought a new ground for Jewish unity and identity and suggested national loyalty to a common past and present community now seen in secularized terms. They maintained that national sentiment, rather than religious belief, had always really been the primary factor in Jewish exilic survival and that now this same sentiment would continue to give purpose to Jewish existence and preserve Jewish unity. Nationalism as a political and cultural movement has provided a secular substitute for religion to many Jews, grounding their identity in a secular ideal and an ongoing community. As secularization continued in Western Europe, nation-states provided similar contexts for community and common values to lands and peoples where traditional Christianity was waning. In these conditions, biblical religion, both Judaism and Christianity, both Catholicism and Protestantism, remain as the embodiments of the great religious tradition of the West. Each and all they face vast problems of reinterpretation to bring their spiritual riches to a greatly transformed world so much in need of them. A first step of such reinterpretation is certainly understanding. Jewish attempts at restructuration offer many lessons whose meaning requires comprehension and which once understood may point out important general lessons.

THE CHRISTIAN
RESPONSE TO
SECULARIZATION

Catholic efforts to retain the integrity of the tradition, though distorted by the defensive post-Tridentine mentality, revealed an important lesson for all Christian institutionalism—the necessity of preserving the many-sidedness and the universality of the Christian tradition and its connection with the past as well as its expression in liturgical worship of great aesthetic value and capable of tremendous impact upon the interior psychological make-up of men. The internal renewal of the Roman Catholic Church in the period following the Reformation, although closed in upon itself and avoiding the real issues which history was presenting to Western man—in a word reactionary, despite its indubitable spiritual worth and beauty—remains a model for certain aspects of Christian life. In St. Francis de Sales, St. Teresa of Avila, St. Charles Borromeo, St. John of the Cross, and many others we see an austere yet human Christian piety which provides authentic examples of religious experience. The Protestant efforts to rework the tradition and to shed accretions which stood in the way of its contemporary relevance and to develop a Christianity cognizant of the changing world of the sixteenth and seventeenth centuries and its demands revealed another lesson no less significant. It demonstrated with the irrefutable confirmation of history itself that a great religious tradition could not become identified with any single intellectual expression or any one institutional form and remain a living flexible spiritual reality providing guidance and meaning to an evolving human society. It showed that all human realizations are relative to time and place, that even when they represent the realization of ultimate values and the expression of an ultimate religious relationship, they are realizations of ultimacy conditioned by specific historical and cultural circumstances, and cannot not be regarded as absolute. It is one of the tragedies of the period that if Catholicism rejected this Protestant principle, Protestantism itself failed to understand it.

THE CONTEMPORARY
SITUATION OF
BIBLICAL RELIGION

Indeed the Reformation conflict may be seen in retrospect as the manifest and surface expression of a great problem which man did not recognize as a whole and in the round, let alone solve. That problem is still to be formed, still to be stated, and the effort to solve it still to be begun. The tradition of biblical religion is one which tells us that God is central to man's fulfillment and that only through a relation to God can authentic human existence be cultivated. Man is called to live in that relationship, to grow in it, to prosper in it, to have life more abundantly in it. For the Hebrews and for the earliest Christians that was understood as awaiting, in the tension of hope and in the practice of the commandments, God's intervention into human history to redeem it and to lead human life to its apotheosis. When that hope receded under the specific conditions of declining antiquity, another interpretation developed. Jews in isolated communities, often persecuted for their loyalty to their religious convictions, awaited the end of God's strange exile and his sending of his Messiah. They combined this with other doctrinal adaptations to make life possible in the prolonged interim of this-worldly existence. Christians spread their good news throughout the European world and gave central place to a here-and-now relation to God through Christ and through the Church which continued his mediational mission. In this situation men also lived in the world. The world was a sinful place and Christians and Jews were sinners. But the world was more than this. It was also a place of human achievement and accomplishment, a place where men rose to nobility and towering human stature in spite of their offenses. European man built a civilization which incorporated many of these values, although being human it was also permeated by avarice and ambition. Yet while European man built that civilization, drawing his values from his religious tradition to provide its foundation, the religious tradition itself did not recognize the genuine worth of men's this-worldly accomplishments. By 1500, as we have seen, Christianity had become overelaborated in its doctrines, overrigid in its liturgies, and corrupted in its social organization. It was moreover formed and conditioned by earlier ages and presented its religious truths encapsulated in the ideas and expressive forms of the past. It was this situation which demanded reform; it was this condition that called for renewal. Nominalism attempted to dismantle the old elaborated intellectual forms and Marsiglio to give the this-worldly community a proper value. Protestantism tried to find a new way to state the implications of Christianity and render it contemporary. But a new and satisfactory solution was not found. Yet it was more than this that lay at the root of the trouble. The conditioned form which biblical religion had assumed was incapable of proclaiming its own values and at the same time recognizing the true worth of building a human community, a human culture, and a human civilization in this world. It was incapable of providing men in the world with a view at once religious and worldly, at once showing man his way in history and raising him above it in relation to transcendence. This problem neither the Catholics nor the Protestants nor the Jews were able to formulate explicitly in a form that would enable them to work for its solution. In the aftermath of the conflict Catholicism became even more set in its original form of other-worldliness, while Protestantism in disunion and disagreement with itself gradually experienced a vast secularization of thought and life which led to a recognition of the world but also a loss of religious consciousness, and the impact of modernity on self-enclosed traditional Jewish communities commenced a ferment whose end is not yet evident. As a consequence in the modern period of European history, civilization and culture have continued to rest unconsciously and implicitly upon the secularized versions of the values of biblical religion, while men have spent their efforts in mastering their environments and in emancipating themselves from all tradition so far as possible. Yet the tradition of biblical religion remains with its immense spiritual worth to confront that secularized world now in profound crisis and torn asunder by its own unbridled ambitions. Biblical religion remains to confront that world with that still unformulated question: What should man be doing on this earth being called to a living relation with God? Biblical religion remains confronting the modern secularized world to which it must explain the profound implications for a life of authentic value of the greatest commandments: You shall love the Lord your God with all your heart, and with all your soul, and with all your mind. You shall love your neighbor as yourself.

BIBLIOGRAPHY

Judaism in Historical Perspective

God's Call and the Covenant with Israel:

Bright, John, *History of Israel,* Philadelphia, The Westminster Press, 1959.

DeVaux, Roland, *Ancient Israel: Its Life and Institutions,* New York, McGraw-Hill, 1961; also available in paperback.

Eichrodt, Walther, *Theology of the Old Testament,* trans. J. Baker, 2 vols., Philadelphia, The Westminster Press, 1961 and 1967.

Kaufmann, Yehezkel, *Religion of Israel,* ed. M. Greenberg, Chicago, The University of Chicago Press, 1960.

Noth, Martin, *The History of Israel,* 2nd ed., New York, Harper & Row, 1960.

Orlinski, Harry M., *Ancient Israel,* 2nd ed., Ithaca, N.Y., Cornell, 1960; also available in paperback.

Ringgren, Helmer, *Israelite Religion,* Philadelphia, Fortress Press, 1966.

Speiser, Ephraim, ed., *Genesis,* Anchor Bible Series, Garden City, N.Y., Doubleday, 1964.

Von Rad, Gerhard, *Old Testament Theology,* 2 vols., New York, Harper & Row, 1965.

Kings and Prophets: Disappointment and Hope:

Buber, Martin, *The Prophetic Faith,* New York, Macmillan, 1949; paperback ed., New York, Harper & Row, 1960.

Frankfort, Henri, *Kingship and the Gods,* Chicago, The University of Chicago Press, 1948.

Heschel, Abraham J., *The Prophets,* New York, Harper & Row, hardcover and paperback eds., 1962.

Scott, R. B. Y., ed., *Jeremiah,* Anchor Bible Series, Garden City, N.Y., Doubleday, 1965.

The Exile: Israel's Abiding Faith:

McKenzie, John L., ed., *The Second Isaiah,* Anchor Bible Series, Garden City, N.Y., Doubleday, 1968.

Restoration:

Bickerman, Elias, *From Ezra to the Last of the Maccabees,* New York, Schocken, paperback ed., 1962.

Meyers, Jacob M., ed., *Ezra and Nehemiah,* Anchor Bible Series, Garden City, N.Y., Doubleday, 1965.

Tcherikover, Victor, *Hellenistic Civilization and the Jews,* Philadelphia, Jewish Publication Society of America, 1961.

The Emergence of the Apocalyptic Spirit:

Charles, R. H., ed., *The Apocrypha and Pseudoepigraph of the Old Testament,* 2 vols., New York, Oxford, 1913.

Klausner, Joseph, *The Messianic Idea in Israel,* New York, Macmillan, 1955.

Rowley, Harold H., *The Relevance of Apocalyptic,* London, Oxford, 1944, rev. ed., New York, Associated Press, 1964.

Simon, Marcel, *Jewish Sects at the Time of Jesus,* trans. J. H. Farley, Philadelphia, Fortress Press, paperback ed., 1967.

The Beginnings of Christianity:

Barrett, C. K., ed., *The New Testament Background: Selected Documents,* New York, Harper & Row, paperback ed., 1961.

Bultmann, Rudolf, *Primitive Christianity in Its Contemporary Setting,* trans. R. H. Fuller, New York, World Publishing, paperback ed., 1956.

Grant, F. C., *Roman Hellenism and the New Testament,* New York, Scribner, 1962.

Grant, Robert M., *Gnosticism: A Sourcebook of Heretical Writings from the Early Christian Period,* New York, Columbia, 1959, 1966; paperback ed., *Gnosticisim and Early Christianity,* New York, Harper & Row, 1966.

Jonas, Hans, *The Gnostic Religion,* Boston, Beacon Press, paperback ed., 1963.

Nock, Arthur Darby, *Early Gentile Christianity and Its Hellenistic Background,* New York, Harper & Row, paperback ed., 1964.

Jesus of Nazareth:

Cross, Frank Moore, Jr., *The Ancient Library of Qumran,* Garden City, N.Y., Doubleday, paperback ed., 1961.

Daniel-Rops, Henri, *Daily Life in the Time of Jesus,* trans. Patrick O'Brian, New York, Hawthorn, 1962; paperback ed., New York, New York, New American Library, 1964.

Davies, W. D., *Sermon on the Mount,* New York, Cambridge, paperback ed., 1966.

Enslin, Morton Scott, *Christian Beginnings,* New York, Harper & Row, paperback ed., 1956.

————, *Literature of the Christian Movement,* New York, Harper & Row, paperback ed., 1956.

Flusser, David, *Jesus,* New York, Herder & Herder, 1969.

New Testament.

Smith, D. M., Jr., and R. A. Spivey, *Anatomy of the New Testament,* New York, Macmillan, 1969.

The Early Church:

Bettenson, Henry, ed., *Documents of the Christian Church,* New York, Oxford, 1947.

Cadbury, H., *The Book of Acts in History,* New York, Harper & Row, 1955.

Lebreton, Jules, and Jacques Zeiller, *The Emergence of the Church in the Roman World,* New York, Macmillan, paperback ed., 1962.

————, *Heresy and Orthodoxy,* New York, Macmillan, paperback ed., 1962.

Walker, Williston, *A History of the Christian Church,* rev. ed., New York, Scribner, 1958.

Christianity
in Historical
Perspective

The Gentile World:
  Bultmann, op. cit.
  Jonas, op. cit.
  Nock, Arthur Darby, *Conversion,* New York, Oxford, paperback
    ed., 1961.
  Tcherikover, op. cit.
The Religious Temper of Later Antiquity:
  Bultmann, op. cit.
  Jonas, op. cit.
  Nock, *Conversion.*
  Nock, *Early Gentile Christianity and Its Hellenistic Background.*
The Understanding of Christ: Paul and John:
  Beare, F. W., *St. Paul and His Letters,* Nashville, Tenn., Abingdon,
    1962.
  Brown, Raymond E., ed., *The Gospel According to John, One to
    Twelve,* Anchor Bible Series, Garden City, N.Y., Doubleday,
    1966.
  Dodd, C. H., *Historical Tradition in the Fourth Gospel,* New York,
    Cambridge, 1963.
  ————, *The Interpretation of the Fourth Gospel,* New York,
    Cambridge, hardover ed., 1959; paperback ed., 1968.
  Nock, Arthur Darby, *St. Paul,* New York, Oxford, 1938; paper-
    back ed., New York, Harper & Row, 1963.
The Making of the Institutional Church:
  Bettenson, op. cit.
  Dawson, Christopher, *The Making of Europe,* New York, World
    Publishing, paperback ed., 1956.
  Heer, Friedrich, *The Medieval World: Europe 1100–1350,* trans.
    Janet Sondheimer, New York, New American Library, paperback
    ed., 1964.
  Southern, R. W., *The Making of the Middle Ages,* New Haven,
    Yale, hardcover and paperback eds., 1961.
  Walker, op. cit.
The Rise of Monasticism:
  Daniel-Rops, Henri, *The Church in the Dark Ages,* trans. Audrey
    Butler, Garden City, N.Y., Doubleday, 1962.
  Duckett, Eleanor Shipley, *Monasticism,* vol. 3 of *The Gateway to
    the Middle Ages,* Ann Arbor, Mich., University of Michigan
    Press, hardcover and paperback eds., 1961.
  Verheyen, Boniface, ed., *The Holy Rule of Our Most Holy Father
    Benedict,* Atchison, Kans., The Abbey Student Press, 1949.
  Waddell, Helen, *The Desert Fathers,* New York, Barnes & Noble,
    1936; paperback ed., Ann Arbor, Mich., University of Michigan
    Press, 1957.

Second Exile: Baeck, Leo, *The Essence of Judaism,* New York, Schocken, hard-
  Israel   cover and paperback eds., 1961.
  Reconstitutes   Baron, Salo W., and Joseph L. Blau, *Judaism: Postbiblical and
  Itself   Talmudic Period,* New York, Liberal Arts, 1954; also available in
                     paperback.

Cohen, D. Gerson, "The Talmudic Age," in Leo Schwarz, *Great Ages and Ideas of the Jewish People,* New York, Random House, 1956, pp. 143–212.

Ginzberg, Louis, *Legends of the Jews,* 8 vols., Philadelphia, Jewish Publication Society of America, 1919–1925; rev. ed., hardcover and paperback, New York, Simon and Schuster, 1961.

Goldin, Judah, "The Period of the Talmud," in Louis Finkelstein, *The Jews,* Philadelphia, Jewish Publication Society of America, 1956, vol. 1, pp. 115–215.

Guttmann, Julius, *The Philosophies of Judaism,* trans. David Silverman, New York, Holt, Rinehart and Winston, 1954; paperback ed., Garden City, N.Y., Doubleday, 1964.

Katz, Jacob, *Tradition and Crisis,* New York, Free Press, 1961.

Maimonides, Moses, *The Guide to the Perplexed,* trans. S. Pines, Chicago, The University of Chicago Press, 1963; paperback ed., M. Friedlander, trans., New York, Dover.

Scholem, Gershom, *Major Trends in Jewish Mysticism,* New York, Schocken, paperback ed., 1954.

Scholem, Gershom, ed., *Zohar the Book of Splendor,* New York, Schocken, paperback ed., 1963.

Zangwill, Israel, ed., *Selected Religious Poems of Solomon Ibn Gabirol,* Philadelphia, Jewish Publication Society of America, 1923.

Worship and Prayer in Christianity:
Cullman, Oscar, *Early Christian Worship,* London, SCM Press, 1953.

O'Brien, Elmer, *Varieties of Mystic Experience,* New York, New American Library, paperback ed., 1965.

Otto, Rudolf, *Mysticism East and West,* trans. Bertha L. Bracey and Richenda C. Payne, New York, Collier, paperback ed., 1962.

Underhill, Evelyn, *The Essentials of Mysticism,* New York, Dutton, paperback ed., 1960.

———, *Mysticism,* New York, World Publishing, paperback ed., 1955.

———, *Worship,* New York, Harper & Row, 1936; paperback ed., 1957.

Worship and Prayer in Judaism:
Agnon, Samuel Joseph, *Days of Awe,* New York, Schocken, paperback ed., 1948.

Daily Prayerbook, ed. Ben Zion Bokser, New York, Hebrew Publishing Company, 1957.

Gaster, Theodore H., *Festivals of the Jewish Year,* New York, William Sloane Associates, 1953; paperback ed., New York, Apollo Editions, Inc.

Idelsohn, A. Z., *Jewish Liturgy and Its Development,* New York, Holt, Rinehart and Winston, 1932; paperback ed., New York, Schocken.

Schauss, Hayim, *The Jewish Festivals,* Cincinnati, Ohio, Union of American Hebrew Congregations, 1938.

Man's Relation to God

Ecclesia
Semper Est
Reformanda

Bainton, Roland H., *The Age of Reformation*, New York, Van Nostrand, paperback ed., 1956.

Baron, Salo W., "The Modern Age," in Leo Schwarz, *Great Ages and Ideas of the Jewish People*, New York, Random House, 1956, pp. 315–484.

Berger, Peter L., *The Sacred Canopy*, Garden City, N.Y., Doubleday, 1967; paperback ed., 1969.

Blau, Joseph L., *Modern Varieties of Judaism*, New York, Columbia, 1966.

Burrell, Sidney A., ed., *The Role of Religion in Modern European History*, New York, Macmillan, paperback ed., 1964.

Butterfield, Herbert, *The Origins of Modern Science*, New York, Macmillan, 1951; rev., paperback ed., New York, Free Press.

Chadwick, Owen, *The Reformation*, Baltimore, Penguin, paperback ed., 1964.

Daniel-Rops, Henri, *The Catholic Reformation*, 2 vols., Garden City, N.Y., Doubleday, paperback ed., 1964.

Davidowicz, Lucy S., ed., *The Golden Tradition*, New York, Holt, Rinehart and Winston, 1967; paperback ed., Boston, Beacon Press.

Davis, Moshe, *The Emergence of Conservative Judaism*, Philadelphia, Jewish Publication Society of America, 1963.

Gay, Peter, *The Enlightenment*, 2 vols., New York, Knopf, 1966.

Glazer, Nathan, *American Judaism*, Chicago, The University of Chicago Press, hardcover and paperback eds., 1957.

Groethuysen, Bernard, *The Bourgeois: Catholicism Versus Capitalism in Eighteenth-Century France*, trans. Mary Ilford, New York, Holt, Rinehart, Winston, 1968.

O'Dea, Thomas F., *Alienation, Atheism and the Religious Crisis*, New York, Sheed, 1969.

Pauck, Wilhelm, *The Heritage of the Reformation*, rev. ed., New York, Free Press, 1961; paperback ed., New York, Oxford, 1969.

Philipson, David, *The Reform Movement in Judaism*, rev. ed., New York, Macmillan, 1931.

Tawney, R. H., *Religion and the Rise of Capitalism*, New York, New American Library, paperback ed., 1947.

Vidler, Alec R., *The Church in an Age of Revolution*, Baltimore, Penguin, paperback ed., 1961.

Ware, Timothy, *The Orthodox Church*, Baltimore, Penguin, paperback ed., 1967.

Weber, Max, *The Protestant Ethic and the Spirit of Capitalism*, trans. Talcott Parsons, New York, Scribner, hardcover and paperback eds., 1948.

Willey, Basil, *The Seventeenth Century Background*, New York, Columbia, 1942; paperback ed., Garden City, N.Y., Doubleday, 1953.

PART FIVE

THE ISLAMIC RELIGIOUS TRADITION

CHARLES J. ADAMS

THE BACKGROUND
AND THE LIFE
OF THE PROPHET

About the year A.D. 610 (the precise date is unknown) a hitherto obscure citizen of Makkah (Mecca) named Muhammad launched himself upon a public career as preacher and religious leader. As a
member of one of the poorer clans constituting the tribe of Quraysh,
who occupied the valley of Makkah, Muhammad had small claim to
distinction among his fellows. For some time, however, he had cultivated a habit of seclusion and meditation in the barren hills surrounding the city. These solitary vigils came to a climax in a series
of intense religious experiences in which Muhammad felt himself
overborne by divine power and compelled to take up the burden of
preaching a message to the people of his time. The message
emerging from these experiences, which continued to be repeated
until the end of Muhammad's life, proved at the same time to offer a
new world view of great profundity and to contain the resolution of
vexing social problems which then disturbed Arabian life. From it
came the basis for the formation of a new community about Muhammad which in subsequent centuries evolved into the bearer of the
most brilliant culture of the era. In our own day between one-sev-
enth and one-sixth of the human race still acknowledge that message as divine truth and as the normative insight for human life in
the world. In the beginning Muhammad was much disturbed by his
experiences, even to the extent of doubting his own sanity and of
suspecting that he had been possessed by an evil spirit. He endured
a crisis of personality that was traumatic in the extreme, driving him
almost to suicide. Finally, however, Muhammad won through to a
clear conception of the meaning of what had happened to him and
to acceptance of the role of prophet. He began thereupon to declare himself a prophet of the one God and to warn his fellow Arabs
of the catastrophic consequences of their misguided way of life.

That to which Muhammad summoned his fellow citizens he called Islam. The summons was twofold, to recognize a sovereign divine power which fashions and controls human destiny, and to commit oneself in ever renewed obedience to following the pattern ordained by the divine will for men. Islam is, of course, an Arabic word, most often translated as submission, surrender, acceptance, or obedience. Each of these terms partially renders its sense if only it be remembered that the reference is to an inner attitude which should be continuous and always renewed, an attitude of willingness to place all of one's will and action under the divine control. Islam is the resignation of oneself into the hands of God, throughout life and in all respects. A man who holds this attitude is known as a Muslim, meaning literally that he commits himself to make the divine will the norm of his life.

Very little certain knowledge exists about Muhammad's early life before he rose to prominence as the Arabian prophet. Even the date of his birth, which must have occurred within a few years of 570, is unsure, though it is known that he was orphaned at a very early age by the death of his mother, his father having died before he was born. Muhammad was brought up in straitened circumstances in the household of a kindly uncle, Abu Talib, who, although he protected Muhammad against the hostile Makkans, never became a Muslim. We know also of his marriage to the wealthy widow, Khadijah, a union that seems to have been happy and which was blessed with several offspring. Khadijah played an important role in helping Muhammad to grasp and understand his prophetic calling, both by her personal support and by bringing him into contact with other men who were preoccupied with religious quests. For as long as his first wife lived, Muhammad took no other, his only serious disappointment in the marriage stemming from the failure of the male children to survive childhood. In later life, however, he contracted a number of marriages. Muhammad's life does not emerge into the full light of history until the point was reached that he had collected a number of followers who began to take a sharp interest in his activities. Thus, our information about the last ten years of his career in Madinah (Medina) is vastly fuller than for the period in Makkah, and the end of the Makkan period is better known than its beginning.

The immediate relevance of Muhammad's message of one sovereign God who demands men's obedience may be better appreciated against the background from which Muhammad himself emerged. As we have said, he was a citizen of Makkah, then a thriving city located on the coastal plain of the Red Sea at a point which commanded two important trade routes, one connecting the ports of Hadramawt and Yemen to Egypt, Palestine, and Syria, and the other joining the same ports with Mesopotamia across the Arabian deserts. Profiting from this favorable geographical situation and from the disruption of trade created by the hostility between Byzantine Rome and Sassanian Persia, the two great powers of the Middle Eastern region, the Makkans had become both wealthy and powerful. They were the middlemen in a rich commerce of luxury goods, producing nothing themselves but dealing in the products of others and supplying the transportation, the financial and diplomatic assistance, and other arrangements necessary for this commerce. At Muhammad's birth his tribesmen, the Quraysh, were the most prestigious and influential group in the whole of Arabia. The connection of Quraysh with Makkah, however, had been of only short duration. Less than one hundred years earlier this group of nomads, under the leadership of a soldier of fortune named Qusayy, had captured the valley from a rival tribe and settled there. The transition from a wandering nomadic existence based upon the keeping of flocks and herds, to a settled life involving highly sophisticated arrangements for commerce over great distances, wrought profound changes in the outlook of Quraysh. Although they attempted to preserve the social organization appropriate to life in the desert and clung to its values, these prior attitudes proved inadequate to the new conditions of life in Makkah. Change in the economic basis of society brought in its train sweeping erosion of old ways of thinking and acting and produced new ones. Makkah was a society in a state of transition and, therefore, of social stress and disruption. Dissatisfaction was evident in many areas but especially centered around the breakdown of traditional tribal values which had protected the weak under the bond of kinship, around the emergence of a new merchant oligarchy whose power was based upon its wealth, and around the concentration of wealth in private hands. For any sensitive intelligence these conditions must have been a stimulus for reflection; in Muhammad's case an instinctive grasp of the realities of life about him was reflected in the revelation which pointed to a still different kind of social order based upon a comprehensive world view.

The older outlook which the Quraysh had preserved from their days of wandering in the desert was common to all of the Bedouin Arabs. At the time of Muhammad's appearance the majority of the Arabs, those who lived in the central highland known as the Najd, were nomads eking out a meager existence from flocks of camels, goats, and sheep. Their custom was to venture into the sand deserts separating the Najd from the surrounding regions during the months of spring when the annual rainfall brought a brief bloom of vegetation. When the feed and water for their animals were exhausted, they returned again to the central plateau, each tribe to a territory it claimed for its own. The competition among tribes for the sparse resources was fierce and constant, and the barren countryside was implacable in its demands of those who would survive. Stronger tribal groups would often overrun and drive out weaker ones, and in years when the rains failed or were inadequate, there was much hardship and even death. From time to time tribal groups were forced to migrate, always to the north since there was nowhere south for them to go. Life was harsh and normally quite short, affording but a few fleeting pleasures such as the wine cup, the glory of military conquest, or a couplet of poetry well-turned.

It is, perhaps, the experience of life's meanness which explains the character of extremeness that has often been noted in the life and actions of the pre-Islamic Arabs. They were a reckless, passionate, and vibrant people. Drinking and gambling, both of which they loved, they indulged in to excess. In their military exploits they showed utter disregard for personal danger and courted death for the glory which it might briefly bring to one who had met it as a hero. Even their prized virtues such as generosity and steadfastness, not to speak of courage, they evidenced in exaggerated and extreme form. Given but a short time to live and that in one of the cruelest environments known to man, they sought to wring life dry of its few rewards and pleasures. Theirs was literally a philosophy of "eat, drink, and be merry, for tomorrow we die."

The quality of pre-Islamic Arab life is also explained by the Arabs' lack of any religious conviction or mythology which gave life a meaning beyond the here and now. To be sure the pre-Islamic Arabs recognized certain deities, usually connected with the heavenly bodies, and also recognized and propitiated a host of demons and spirits who inhabited springs, groves, and other places. These, however, did not form a connected pantheon or coalesce into a religious outlook which gave the Bedouin assurance of their place in the order of things. On the contrary, these numerous supernatural powers which threatened men on every hand if they were ignored or trespassed upon constituted an additional element in the general insecurity and fearfulness of life. Some of the deities had shrines dedicated to them, and pilgrimages were made to these shrines for paying homage. Such was the case with the three goddesses al-Manat, al-Lat, and al-'Uzza, revered by Quraysh and called the "daughters of Allah." These three figured in an important incident early in Muhammad's career when for a time he seemed to waver in his devotion to the one God and to relapse into paganism. There was also an important shrine known as the Ka'bah (the word means "cube") in the center of a sacred area in Makkah. Pilgrimages were made to this shrine, whose principal god seems to have been Hubal, every year during the sacred month when fighting was forbidden. When Muhammad at last captured the city of Makkah, he destroyed the gods of the Ka'bah but incorporated the shrine itself and the pilgrimage connected with it into Islam. There is evidence of religious dissatisfaction and questing in Arabia in the existence of a vague group of men called Hanifs, of which Muhammad claimed to be one. The Hanifs appear to have come very near a belief in monotheism even before the advent of Muhammad's prophecy.

The closest approximation to a conception of an ultimate power controlling human destiny among the pre-Islamic Arabs was their notion of *dahr,* or time. In their poetry, the best source of information about them, *dahr* is spoken of as the destroyer against whom no man can stand, an inexorable force which eventually swallows up all things. As the one thing which no one could resist, it was the most powerful of the forces affecting man. Such a view is pessimistic in the extreme and must have reinforced the tendency to make the most of life while we have it. Also, however, it deprived life of all meaning or purpose beyond the effort to gain a reputation through deeds which would ensure one's being remembered for a time. The pre-Islamic view accepted the world for what it appears to be, a transient stage for a brief and difficult existence, totally under

The Ka'bah, the holiest structure in all Islam. It contains the sacred Black Stone believed to have been sent down from Heaven by God in ancient times. Pilgrims circle the Ka'bah, in the great courtyard of the Sacred Mosque, seven times. (Courtesy of Aramco.)

the control of capricious forces. It neither provided deep principles for ethics nor did it reveal any cosmic or eternal dimension to man's life.

The Arabs of that time, like those still living in Arabia today, were divided into tribal and clan groupings. The tie of kinship was the primary source of the individual's identity, and the Arabs took great pride in their descent. Enormous attention was paid to genealogy, each group claiming and believing its nobility to be superior to that of others. The bond of kinship also provided protection to the individual in the hazardous circumstances of desert life. A clan group considered itself a unit, and an offense against any of its members constituted a crime against the whole. If a clan member were killed or injured by an outsider, it was looked upon as a primary obligation to avenge the wrong suffered. Individuals who had lost relatives took the burden of revenge with awesome seriousness, swearing terrible oaths and refraining from the pleasures of life until their duty should have been fulfilled. The obligation of blood revenge was, perhaps, as close to a genuine religious and moral imperative as the Arabs recognized. Clan solidarity (*'asabiyah*) to some degree mitigated and policed the warlike tendencies of the Arabs for whom raiding was a sport—as well as a way of gaining prestige— and military prowess the greatest of virtues. In their raids designed to steal cattle, take captives for ransom, or simply to humiliate rival groups, the Arabs were careful to avoid the spilling of blood in order not to create a blood feud. When such feuds did erupt, they were often lengthy and devastating; in some instances entire tribes were wiped out.

In times of plenty all clansmen shared alike, as in times of want, and each rose to the protection of the other. Without the support of kinsmen no man could hope to survive, for he might become the victim of any whom he met. It was the withdrawal of his clan's protection after the death of Abu Talib that finally forced Muhammad to quit Makkah, just as it had been that very protection which had enabled him to endure against the fierce hatred of the Makkans during the previous years.

The mutual rivalry and hostility of clan entities was another factor of precariousness in desert life. Although solidarity formed some kind of shield against the more aggressive, weaker groups were at any time subject to depredations from their neighbors. Violence was, thus, an element in the unease which pervaded tribal society on the eve of Islam. The effect of Muhammad's message was to set aside loyalty to the tribe for loyalty to the newly formed religious community cutting across tribal lines, while at the same time preserving the values of solidarity, mutual protection, and mutual interest within the Islamic *ummah.* So far as the relations among its members were concerned, the Islamic community was a new and all-inclusive tribe in which all Muslims owed the duty of brothers to all others regardless of blood kinship. The coming of Islam also blunted the mutual hostility and aggressiveness of the Arab tribes by channeling their warlike energies into the service of a nobler cause. In this, as in many other areas, Islam preserved and built upon the pre-Islamic tradition while also subtly reorienting the pagan values by basing them upon a comprehensive world view whose fundamental element was a sovereign creative deity.

We do not know how long before he began his preaching it was that the first of the revelations collected in the Islamic Scripture, the *Qur'an,* came to Muhammad. Muhammad was far from an immediate success, being able in the beginning to attract only certain members of his family and a few other individuals to follow his call. In fact, during the entire ten or more years of his preaching in Makkah he never gathered more than a handful of the prominent men of the city into his following. Most of the believers were slaves or members of the lower classes. Even this small group was beset with problems. As time passed, opposition to Muhammad formed and intensified. Although his own clan could protect him from physical harm, nothing could stop the verbal abuse which the Quraysh poured upon him, and those followers who could not claim the protection of a prominent clan were often dealt with very harshly. At some point one group of his followers emigrated to Abyssinia. The reasons for the emigration are not altogether clear though Muslim tradition sees the move as an attempt to escape persecution. Recent scholarship, however, has tended to suggest that the move may reflect other motives, possibly a controversy and division within the young Muslim community.

The opposition to Muhammad in Makkah had several bases. At first there was a general refusal to take him seriously or a tendency to dismiss him as another of the soothsayers familiar to the pre-Islamic Arabs. This criticism had force, since the revelations were couched in the mode of speech used by these diviners. More important was the Makkans' response to Muhammad's attacks upon their forefathers for whom he predicted punishment in hell as a consequence of their misguided and contumacious lives. Among people to whom descent was the chief ground of nobility, suggestions that the way of the fathers was misguided and evil was not only an insult of a direct kind but, by questioning the authority of tradition, was a threat of destruction to the whole social fabric. Most frightening of all to the Makkans was Muhammad's very claim to be a prophet. If it were accepted that Muhammad truly spoke in the name of a divine power, there would have been no choice but to accept him as the chief man in the community. That the Makkans apprehended the implications of prophecy correctly is borne out by Muhammad's role as ruler when he had established himself in Madinah and later when he captured Makkah itself. The rich merchants were not likely willingly to see their place of primacy taken over by another. Muhammad also attacked the pagan gods of the Makkans, but these attacks as seen in the *Qur'an* were not frequent nor particularly virulent. At no point did he attack the cult of the Ka'bah. From all appearances the Makkans were not a strongly religious people, and they would have resented criticisms of customary beliefs and practices as much for the fact of their being departures from the hallowed tradition of the forefathers as for their religious implications. The Makkans tried a number of techniques short of outright violence to muzzle Muhammad, at one time enforcing a boycott against his entire clan, who despite the pressure refused to withdraw their protection. The breaking point was reached for the Makkans when Muhammad began to enter into relations with persons in other places, seeking alliances against his own people. In the end he was forced to flee for his life, having first sent away most of his followers to the oasis of Yathrib, some 200 miles to the north of Makkah, which in later times has been known as Madinat al-Nabi, the City of the Prophet. The departure from Makkah is the famous *hijrah* which not only marks a decisive turning in Muhammad's career but is also the date from which the Islamic calendar is reckoned to begin. The year was A.D. 622.

In Madinah Muhammad's situation was utterly different from that in Makkah. For one thing, Madinah was an agricultural community. Some time prior to the *hijrah* Muhammad had entered into negotiations with certain Madinese who came to Makkah for pilgrimage to the Ka'bah. These people became his followers and arranged that he should act as arbitrator in a bitter dispute about the ownership of land which had pitched the settled tribes of the oasis against one another in a destructive blood feud. Muhammad went to Madinah, therefore, with a recognized status, already having followers there, and bringing yet others with him, the *ansar* (helpers) and the *muhajirin* (emigrants) as they are known. In the oasis itself were several different tribal groups, some of them Jewish in religion though Arabic speaking. Muhammad's task was to consolidate his position into one of real strength and to weld these diverse elements into a unified community under his leadership. One of his first acts was to

A sixteenth-century Turkish painting depicting Muhammad the Prophet preaching. Muhammad is rarely depicted in Islamic art; when he is shown, as here and in the miniature on p. 596, his face is almost always obscured. (Courtesy of the Metropolitan Museum of Art, Rogers Fund, 1955.)

draw up a document, afterward called the Constitution of Madinah, declaring all the Madinese—Muslims, Jews, and pagans alike—to be one community under his leadership. As time passed the Prophet's conception of the community both narrowed and clarified until in the end it came to include only Muslims, those joined together by their common submission to the divine will.

The struggle to establish himself firmly in Madinah was difficult and long. Although all had agreed to the terms of the Constitution of Madinah, there were many who opposed Muhammad and feared his growing power. The *Qur'an* condemns these "hypocrites" for their deviousness. With the Jews Muhammad soon came to an open break, some of them being driven out and others killed or sold into slavery. In this case the cause of conflict was the steadfast Jewish refusal to accept Muhammad on his own terms as a genuine prophet; this religious intransigence produced a stream of ridicule against Muhammad for being uninformed or misinformed about the history of Jewish prophecy. Such attitudes must have stung the Prophet with great sharpness because of his expectation that the Jews (and Christians) would recognize and acknowledge him as a prophet like the others whom they revered.

Once he felt sufficiently secure in Madinah, Muhammad turned his attention to the countryside round about. A combination of shows of force and skillful diplomacy soon created a network of alliances with Bedouin tribes that rapidly expanded Muhammad's influence to the point where he was able to challenge even the power of the haughty Makkans. His objective was to disrupt the Makkan trade on which the life of the city depended. In 624 when he attempted to intercept a rich Makkan caravan, the Makkans sent a force against him and engaged the Muslims in battle at a place called Badr. This engagement, where a greatly outnumbered Muslim detachment won a resounding victory over superior forces, played a great role in confirming the community's sense of divine mission though, militarily, it was of little consequence. On two later occasions the Makkans attempted to deal with Muhammad by military force but without significant success. They actually won a victory over the Muslims at the Battle of Uhud, near Madinah, but were unable to follow it up. In the Battle of the Ditch, which saw the greatest army yet assembled in Arabia ranged against Muhammad, the Makkans proved utterly inept and allowed their effort to founder on bad leadership and tribal divisions. Military power was neither effective against Muhammad nor was it the method which he himself used to build his power. The secret of his success was a masterly diplomacy based upon an instinctive understanding of tribal relationships on the one hand and of the nature of Makkan power on the other. When Makkah fell to Muhammad in 630 and the Ka'bah was cleansed of its pagan symbols, this victory was achieved without a single sword stroke. The greatest military threat which Muhammad was compelled to face came in the Battle of Hunayn against the Bani Hawazin, after he had already won Makkah. The capitulation of Makkah broke whatever remaining resistance to Muhammad the tribesmen may have felt; they came flocking in thousands to accept Islam and to pledge their allegiance to the Prophet.

Muhammad died unexpectedly in 632 after a brief illness. In the short ten years between his arrival in Madinah and his death, he rose from the status of a hunted fugitive to become the most powerful man in Arabia. His life accomplishment was the double one of having propagated a new world view and of having founded a community. These two were to become the twin bearers of a brilliant civilization that may claim both past greatness and continuing contemporary relevance.

THE RIGHTLY GUIDED KHALIFAHS AND THE EXPANSION OF ISLAM

The Muslims were not adequately prepared for Muhammad's death; and when it came, it was a shock that almost destroyed the infant community. There is some evidence that certain prominent men did not expect Muhammad to die at all and even refused to believe the reports of his death. Immediately upon hearing the news, the community plunged into a crisis. Personal and tribal rivalries posed such obstacles to the choice of a successor that there was genuine threat of civil war. Only a desperate act of acclaiming one of their number *khalifah* or successor to the Prophet on the part of his closest companions averted a disaster. The man chosen was Abu Bakr, an intimate associate of Muhammad and one of the early prominent converts in Makkah. He was already an old man however, and after a reign of two years, died, passing on his authority to the able and fiery 'Umar ibn al-Khattab, the most brilliant of the Rightly Guided Khalifahs, as the first four successors to Muhammad are known. 'Umar fell victim to the dagger of an assassin in 644 and was succeeded by 'Uthman ibn 'Affan with whom the decline of the pious caliphate had already begun. 'Uthman was murdered by a group of dissidents who accused him of corrupt rule, and his successor, the last of the four Rightly Guided Khalifahs, 'Ali ibn Abi Talib, the cousin and son-in-law of Muhammad, was never firmly established in power. From the beginning his claims to rule were contested by a powerful party who suspected him of complicity in the murder of 'Uthman, and after a protracted struggle he lost out to Mu'awiyah of the powerful Ummawi clan. Mu'awiyah's power derived from the support of Syrian tribesmen, and for this reason he established his capital in Damascus rather than Madinah, thus founding the Arab Kingdom which survived for a century until overthrown by the 'Abbasis in 750. In spite of the violence and unrest that characterized the period, Muslims have always looked back to the pious caliphate as the time of Islam's greatest purity and glory. The *khalifahs* themselves are among the most revered figures of Islamic history.

The accomplishments of the pious *khalifahs* were considerable. First of all they succeeded in maintaining the unity of the community in spite of break-away attempts by some Bedouin groups who considered their loyalty to have been to Muhammad and to have been dissolved with his death. Second, they laid the foundations of a polity which kept the Arab armies intact in their camp cities and which provided means of governing the new territories. Third, and perhaps most important of all, were the great conquests themselves. The outreach to other lands beyond the peninsula began under Abu Bakr but came to full flowering in the reign of 'Umar. In rapid succession the rich provinces of Syria, Iraq, Palestine, and Egypt came under Muslim control. As a result of the Battle of Nihavand (641) the entire Sassanian Empire was brought crashing down to disappear from the pages of history, and the whole of the Iranian plateau was added to the Muslim territories. By the end of the century North Africa had been overrun on the west, followed soon afterward by the establishment of an Ummawi state in Spain, and on the east the Muslims were penetrating the vast regions of Central Asia beyond the Oxus River. These initial conquests are notable not only for their rapidity but for their permanence. All of the land which the Muslims overran in their first great expansion, with the exception of Spain and portions of Central Asia, has remained under Islamic control until this day.

Today the greatest number and concentration of Muslims in the world live outside the regions taken in the earliest conquests. One of the later waves of Islamic expansion brought the faith to the Indian subcontinent in a decisive way, and although Muslims have never been the majority there, from the establishment of the Sultanate of Delhi by Muhammad Ghori in 1192 until 1857 they were rulers of a vast Indian Empire. At present something more than 160 million Muslims are found in India and Pakistan. A still later wave of growth introduced Islamic faith into the islands of the Indonesian archipelago, this time through the agency of traders and wandering mystics. The emergence of important Muslim influence there cannot be precisely dated, but it was a factor in the life of the islands by the twelfth century. In the fifteenth century the first important Muslim sultanate took form, and today the majority of Indonesians, more than 100 million in a rapidly growing population, are counted as Muslims. When the Bedouin Arab warriors under the Rightly Guided Khalifahs burst out of the Arabian peninsula, their arms quickly carried them to the borders of Anatolia but not beyond. It was left to the Turks, who began to enter Islamic territories and the service of rulers in large numbers in the tenth century, to subdue the vast region of Anatolia and Asia Minor for Islam. The Saljuq Turks were the first to establish themselves but eventually gave way to the Ottomans who at last overthrew Christian power in Constantinople (1453) and drove their armies far into Eastern Europe. At the height of their strength the Ottomans dominated the Balkan countries, sending a great army to the gates of Vienna as late as 1683. Thus was another important region added to the domain of Islam, and the permanent influence of Islam on European soil established.

THE QUR'AN

The message which Muhammad preached to the Arabs came to him
as a series of revelations, given in piecemeal fashion throughout his
prophetic career until the very end of his life. After his death the
various revelations were collected into a book called the *Qur'an,*
which, as Scripture, is the fundamental authority for Muslims in all
matters of religious belief or practice. The name comes from the
pages of the book itself where some of the individual revelations
are referred to as Qur'ans. This name is somewhat puzzling, but it
is probably to be understood as meaning discourse or recitation. In
reference to the Prophet's work it indicates Muhammad's function
of reciting or discoursing a message that he had been chosen to
deliver by a divine agency.

Both Muhammad himself and later Muslims have believed the
Qur'an to derive from a heavenly original, a book that is with God, a
"Well-Preserved Tablet that only the pure may touch." Also called
the "Mother of the Book," this heavenly depository of truth, which
may be taken as a symbolic embodiment of the Divine Will, has
been partially revealed to men from time to time through a series of
prophets. Throughout history the normal mode of divine communication with men has been the sending of books drawn from the heavenly prototype. Adam, the very first man created, was chosen a
prophet and given a book so that he and his descendants might
have guidance in the proper way to live and so be rescued from the
aimless groping to which their creaturehood would otherwise have
condemned them. When succeeding generations failed to appreciate the importance and sanctity of this guidance and began first
to ignore it, then to distort it, the original act of divine mercy was
repeated in the sending of another prophet who reestablished the
race on the "right path." As seen in the light of the Islamic doctrine
of prophecy, history is a process of mankind's having repeatedly
fallen away from the path marked out by divine guidance and likewise having been continually restored to it again by renewed acts of
mercy through the institution of prophecy.

The prophets who have appeared in the past are numerous, perhaps as many as one hundred thousand, one to each people, speak-

ing in its own language. Among those whom the *Qur'an* mentions specifically are well-known figures from the Bible such as Moses whose book was the Torah, David who brought the *Zabur* or Psalms, and Jesus through whom was revealed the *Injil* or Gospel. Because these books were recognized as Scripture by Jews and Christians, the *Qur'an* grants these communities special recognition as Peoples of the Book or of Scripture. It was against this background that Muhammad's expectation of being favorably received by Jews and Christians grew up. Still other prophets, unknown to the biblical tradition, are spoken of also, for example, Salih and Hud. All prophets have spoken a message identical in content (if not form), and those who brought books as part of their missions were all delivering a revelation stemming from the Mother of the Book. Muhammad's prophecy and the book which he spoke or recited under the stimulus of inspiration were continuations of an already established divine method of communication with men as old as the world itself. The significance of Scripture was further underlined by theologians in the third Islamic century in the doctrine that the *Qur'an* is uncreated and coeternal with God; not, to be sure, the marks made with ink on paper and bound in covers, but the divine message itself.

The Muslim understanding of the *Qur'an* is shown clearly in the most common story of Muhammad's call to prophecy. According to tradition one night when Muhammad was keeping a lonely vigil of meditation and prayer in a cave on Mount Hira' near Makkah, an angelic being appeared to him and commanded, *Iqra'* ("Recite"). Muhammad's reply was a refusal, born perhaps of fear and confusion, or perhaps of misunderstanding. Thereupon the angel seized him by the throat and choked him while reiterating the command. Still a third time was the command repeated with such vigor that Muhammad's very life was threatened. Having been thus forced to give his consent, Muhammad received the first of the revelations, that which the majority of authorities identify with Surah 96:1–5:

> *In the Name of God, the Merciful, the Compassionate*
> *Recite: In the Name of thy Lord who created,*
> *   created Man of a blood-clot.*
> *Recite: And thy Lord is the Most Generous,*
> *   who taught by the Pen,*
> *   taught Man that he knew not.*

This story makes indubitably clear that there was no initiative on Muhammad's part in seeking prophecy. Rather the revelation came to him against his will and in spite of his resistance through the compulsion of a force from outside himself. Nor was the message itself of Muhammad's own invention. The words which he spoke were given him by the angel, and his sole task was to repeat what was communicated to him. Muhammad claimed no special qualities for himself and assigned no significance to his person as such. Many verses in the *Qur'an* begin with the imperative, Say! (addressed to Muhammad), indicating in this unmistakable fashion the heavenly source of the words that follow. The intermediary who brought these revelations from heaven to speak them into Muhammad's ear was a "spirit" or a "holy spirit" which later Islamic tradition identified with the angel Gabriel. In the revelation experiences the thing of consummate importance is that God himself has spoken; both the content of the message and its form were "sent down" upon Muhammad. There was no element of conscious manipulation on his part and no factor of historical conditioning. Muhammad had been "chosen" as the instrument of a greater power who utilized him for transmitting a message of warning and guidance, a message which was eternal and which Muhammad neither originated nor formulated. The *Qur'an* is *Kalam Allah,* the word or speech of God.

The divine origin and character of the *Qur'an* are emphasized also by the common Muslim belief that Muhammad was illiterate and thus incapable of having composed a book of his own or of having copied, as some of his Makkan enemies charged, from the Scriptures of the Jews and Christians. Indeed, the *Qur'an* is miraculous in its quality, its revelation being the only miracle which the Prophet claimed in proof of his mission. Later Muslims interpreted this Qur'anic teaching of miraculousness in literary terms, claiming that the beauty and perfection of the *Qur'an,* incapable of duplication by mere men, are self-evident proofs of its heavenly origin.

The Muslim conviction that the *Qur'an* is the very words of God himself, preserved exactly to the last syllable as they were revealed, explains many things about religious attitudes and practice in Islam. First of all, it allows us to understand clearly why the *Qur'an* should rank as the foremost authority in all matters of religion or law. It is inconceivable to the pious mind that any other source of information or teaching should be placed above the expression of the divine will in its definitive and eternal formulation. From this fact also we gain insight into the basis for the characteristic Muslim method in solving religious problems or expounding normative belief and practice. Essentially, the method is deductive, one of unfolding or extracting from the revelation its implications for a host of particular situations. Religious thinking among Muslims is bound most closely to the text of the *Qur'an,* to which it constantly returns as the fountainhead of all guidance.

The devoted and tender reverence paid to the *Qur'an* on every occasion is also a reflection of the sacred character of the book. The *Qur'an* is never placed on the floor, allowed to come into contact with unclean substances, or otherwise dishonored. Perhaps the most eloquent expression of this regard is the widespread practice of memorizing the *Qur'an* text in its entirety. One who does so is a *Hafiz,* and his accomplishment is considered an act of great piety. Even in those parts of the Islamic world where Arabic is not spoken and understood, devoted men in the thousands labor to commit the divine words to memory. In almost every Muslim area there exist special schools for teaching young children to memorize and recite the text.

In size the *Qur'an* approximates the New Testament. It is divided into one hundred and fourteen chapters, each of which is known as

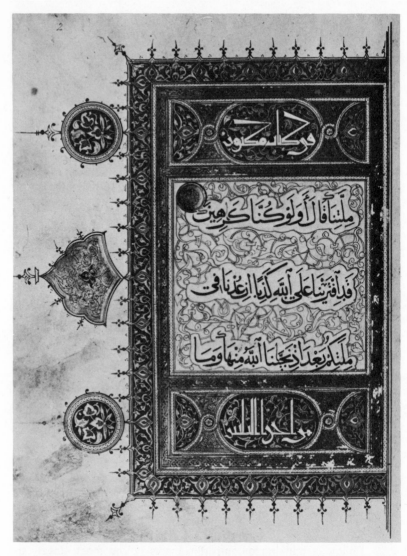

An Arabic manuscript of the Qur'an from fourteenth-century Egypt. (*Courtesy of the British Museum.*)

a Surah, and these are arranged roughly in the order of their length, with the longest coming first. Each chapter of the *Qur'an* has a name derived from something mentioned in it, though in recent times it has increasingly become the custom to cite Qur'anic passages by the number of the chapter. The Surah of the Believers (Surah 23), for example, gets its designation from the occurrence of the word "believers" in the very first verse, and the case is similar with other chapters. The division between chapters is marked by the formula *Bismillah al-Rahman, al-Rahim,* "In the Name of God, the Compassionate, the Merciful." With only one exception (Surah 9), every chapter of the *Qur'an* is introduced by this formula which also is repeated at many other points in the Muslim's life as a kind of in-

vocation or blessing. The division into Surahs is very old and probably goes back to the time of Muhammad himself, but the further division of the Surahs into verses or *ayahs* is later and was done for
the sake of convenience in locating passages easily. The word *ayah*
means a "sign" or "indication," and the term is used numerous
times in the *Qur'an* where the Prophet pointed to the wonders of
nature about him as signs of the existence and sovereignty of the
unique God. Its application to portions of the *Qur'an* is a reinforcement of the Muslim doctrine of revelation, for the "sending down"
of this heavenly book is the most important and most convincing of
all the evidences of God.

Unfortunately we do not know the exact state in which the materials composing the *Qur'an* were left at the death of Muhammad.
There are indications in early Muslim histories that some of the text
had been written down under the Prophet's personal supervision,
but it is certain that he had decreed no definitive order for it. The
Qur'an which we have today was collected and ordered under the
initiative of the third Khalifah, 'Uthman, who feared conflict in the
community over disagreements about the sacred book. He therefore
appointed a certain Zayd ibn Thabit, who had been a kind of secretary to Muhammad, to prepare an official text based on a document
in the possession of the daughter of the second Khalifah, 'Umar. At
the time there were already other versions of the *Qur'an* in circulation among the Muslims, at least four of which are known from extensive references to them. Eventually, with pressure from the state
authorities, the Uthmanic *Qur'an* came to displace these others, and
today it is the sole text recognized and used by Muslims. The work
of collecting, preserving, and writing down the revelations "sent
down" upon the Prophet was begun in his lifetime and finished
soon after his death. Furthermore, available information about the
earliest versions of the *Qur'an* shows a great similarity of content
between them and the official version. Thus, critical scholarship and
Muslim faith both agree that the *Qur'an* is an authentic record of
the message which Muhammad declared to the Arabs.

For the uninitiated person a first encounter with the *Qur'an* is
likely to create some puzzlement. Those responsible for its collection appear to have paid scant attention either to the chronological
sequence of the revelations or to the logical interconnection of subject matter. Further, the content ranges from vivid warnings of the
punishment soon to befall the "ungrateful," to stories of former
prophets, the exposition of detailed rules for different aspects of Islamic life, and passages of a sublime mystical content. The impression of the whole is likely to be that of disorganization. One should,
however, remember the nature of the *Qur'an*. It was not composed
as an ordinary book to be read; indeed, Muslim faith insists that it
was not composed at all. Rather, it is a collection of inspired utterances delivered over a long period of time, each one couched in a
rhetoric appropriate to the occasion when it was pronounced. The
revelations were intended to be heard, not read, and only when one
who understands Arabic hears the *Qur'an* recited can he begin

fully to comprehend its unique force and attractive power. So compelling is the sonorous language of the sacred book that its skillful recitation will often reduce strong men to tears.

The *Qur'an* is perhaps the most widely read and studied book in all of human history. It is contemplated, recited, and commented upon daily in every land where Muslims dwell and in all of the numerous languages which they speak. In one sense the whole body of Islamic literature in theology, law, and mysticism may be considered as nothing more than an extended exposition of the sacred text. The most precious possession of Muslims is a body of truth, a definitive guidance for life and the hereafter, which God himself has vouchsafed in his own words.

ISLAMIC THEOLOGY

Although the *Qur'an* lays down religious fundamentals for Muslims, including doctrines of the unity of God and the prophethood of Muhammad, it is not in any sense a book of theology. Nowhere in its pages will one discover religious doctrine presented in a systematic, comprehensive, or consistent manner. Everything about the *Qur'an* bespeaks its origin in the intensity of prophetic inspiration rather than in essentially intellectual motives. At many points the *Qur'an* is unclear in its teachings or incomplete, and in certain vital areas it even appears as inconsistent. With the passing of time Muslims found it imperative to be more precise in the intellectual statement of their religious faith. When after one hundred years or more they became acquainted with the modes of thought of Greek philosophy, a true Islamic theology was born. At the same time there was a parallel development of religious beliefs at the popular level. These popular beliefs were often in conflict with the opinions of the learned and sometimes depended heavily on doctrines of other religious groups, but they conveyed great meaning for the thousands who held them.

The stimulus to the development of a precise statement of religious doctrines was twofold: It arose on the one hand from tensions within the Islamic community and on the other from the confrontation with outsiders whom the Muslims encountered in the conquered territories after the great expansion. Internal problems, particularly those of political leadership, led to debate and the marking out of firm positions on such matters as predestination and free will, the nature of faith, and big and little sins. Predestination and free will, a problem that is especially confusing in its Qur'anic presentation, became of prime importance in the political controversies surrounding the Ummawi rulers after the establishment of the Arab kingdom in Damascus. There were many who accused the Ummawis of deserting the true faith and of gross worldliness as a result of their attempts to develop ways of ruling the vast territory which they controlled. For such pious people it became a religious duty to defy the Ummawi rulers and oppose them. To counter this pious criticism the rulers began to mount a religious propaganda, in which they employed a number of learned and respected men, arguing that all things happen in the world according to God's will by the principle of predestination. It followed, therefore, that Ummawi rule was legitimate and that to oppose it was to resist God's manifest will. Their pious opponents adopted the polar opposite stand, arguing that man has freedom to choose his actions and the duty to fight against tyranny and wrongdoing wherever they occur. Neither side faced difficulty in finding *Qur'an* verses to support its views. Although the issues were political and of life and death importance to the individuals concerned, the mode of argument was religious. From these early controversies arose several sectarian groups who have lent their names to the various positions on the problem of predestination and free will. The Qadariyah were those who accepted human freedom of choice and action, i.e., the anti-Ummawi faction; the Jabariyah were those who on the contrary believed in absolute divine compulsion in all things, i.e., the supporters of the rulers.

Early Muslim discussions about the nature of faith (*iman*) and about big and little sins also had to do with the political conflicts raging around the Ummawis. One party in the early days held that true faith is indistinguishable from pious works and the fulfillment of all a Muslim's religious duties. The commission of sin was nothing but apostasy from Islam, and according to the *Qur'an,* punishable by death. These fierce and puritanical fanatics, known as the Khawarij (the Seceders, because they withdrew from the majority of the community), bitterly opposed the Ummawis and made unrelenting war against them. For the whole of the first two centuries of Islamic history, before the sect was finally put down, the threat of Khawarij uprisings or assassins was a continuing nightmare to Muslim rulers.

Others, however, took a more moderate position. They drew a distinction between great sins (*kaba'ir*) and lesser ones (*sagha'ir*), holding that great sins, such as associating partners with God (*shirk,* or polytheism) or characterizing the revelations as lies (*takhdhib*), were unforgivable and plainly rendered a man outside the fold of Islam. Smaller offenses, however, were capable of finding pardon from a merciful and forgiving God and did not exclude one from membership in the community and all its rights. So long as the rulers were not guilty of great sins, it followed that the believers still had the duty to obey them.

Still others emphasized the difference between faith (*iman*) and works (*islam*) rather than their equivalence. According to their analysis, faith is an interior and personal matter, occurring within the heart of a man, and not visible to those about him, while one's actions do not necessarily indicate the state of the heart. From external evidence it is impossible to know whether or not faith abides in the heart. Such a stand did not escape the problem of why a man of faith would still commit sins, whether big or small, and some Muslim thinkers began to query whether faith might diminish or increase to account for lapses from piety in an individual's life. This issue like those above has been of continuing interest to Muslim religious thinkers through the centuries. The fourteenth-century theologian al-Taftazani, in a statement which represents the consensus of the greater part of Islamic opinion, defines faith as:

1) confession with the tongue; and,
2) assent in the heart.

Along with many others, al-Taftazani also holds that faith may increase and decrease. One sectarian group, the Murji'ah, took as their principle the suspension of judgment on the question whether a man is a Muslim in the true sense or not. In their view "who is a Muslim?" can be answered only by God, since he alone can see into the hearts of men. Their stand, in practical terms, was equivalent to supporting the Ummawis since they refused to judge the rulers, or anyone else who claimed to be Muslim, as falling outside the community.

The external stimulus to the growth of an Islamic theology arose when the Muslims became aware of the religious traditions of the peoples whom they overran in the great conquests. Both the Sassanian Persians and the hellenized peoples of the Mediterranean basin were inheritors of highly complex and sophisticated cultural traditions. These included well-articulated religious systems of much subtlety. In their first encounters with Zoroastrian, Buddhist, Christian, etc., thinkers, the Muslims, in spite of their ardor, were hard put to uphold the validity of their faith. Elements from these rival religious systems proved attractive to many Muslims, and pious men felt the need to defend the superiority of Islamic views against those of others. Formal debates between learned men of different persuasions were also a feature of the time, often sponsored by rulers at court for their own amusement or enlightenment. We know for example of the debates between St. John of Damascus and Muslim divines in the presence of the Ummawi prince. The challenge of rival religious systems produced a Muslim effort at self-expression and self-justification. The theology born under this impulse was largely apologetic, and Muslim theology retained that coloring throughout its subsequent development. Indeed, many Muslim thinkers, including the great al-Ghazali (d. 1111), have criticized the community's theological development as having been essentially negative, a reaction against unacceptable opinions rather than a positive outreach.

A sectarian group called the Mu'tazilah may be given the credit for having been the first among Muslims to develop a true theology. This group which appeared toward the end of the first Islamic century had gained fairly extensive acquaintance with Greek philosophy. Their leaders such as Wasil ibn 'Ata and al-Nazzam began to levy criticisms against the views of their more traditional contemporaries, using conceptual tools drawn from the Greeks. Their objections to traditional views were largely demands for more of rationality and consistency in the formulation of Islamic belief. For this reason they have sometimes been characterized as rationalists, but it should be clearly understood that they in no way sought to renounce or undercut their commitment to Islam. On the contrary, they saw their effort to build an intellectually more adequate system of belief as a move to rescue true Islam from those who were misrepresenting it in vulgar fashion. The Mu'tazilah were firm believers in revelation and prophecy and even in the authority of prophetic tradition.

The principal teachings of the Mu'tazilah are conveyed in their being called the "people of unity (*tawhid*) and justice ('*adl*)." Unity refers to the fundamental Islamic doctrine of the oneness of God. In the *Qur'an,* where God's uniqueness is much emphasized, the point is (1) to underline the exclusive sovereignty of God over the many powers recognized by the pagan Arabs, and (2) to call the Arabs' attention to the divine power which controlled their destinies. The Mu'tazilah, however, brought forward a more philosophical view of *tawhid* by interpreting God's unity in reference to the divine nature. They taught that God is one in the sense of being simple and uncompounded, not made up of parts, and incapable of any division in his constitution. Hence they would grant no independent and separate status to the divine attributes in spite of the *Qur'an*'s frequent mention of God's knowledge, will, power, etc. All of these qualities or attributes they held to be identical with the divine essence whose uncompromised unity was eternal. In similar fashion they denied all anthropomorphism in connection with God. The motivation in these doctrinal stands was primarily religious. Through their acquaintance with the Greeks the Mu'tazilah had gained a vision of a transcendental rational order, and they insisted that to speak of God in any other terms was untrue to his divine nature. Thus, they invoked rational criteria for assessing the validity of religious doctrines.

The same considerations apply in respect to their teachings about divine justice. The Mu'tazilah could not accept the predestinarian views of the majority of their traditionalist contemporaries. If God predestines men to do evil and then punishes them for it, he is guilty of injustice, which is inconceivable for the divine being. It follows that men must have free will and that reward or punishment must be in accord with the freely chosen actions of men. God by his nature always does what is best. Although this stand poses problems about the origin of evil in the world (does God create it, or is there another sovereign power alongside God responsible for evil?) the teaching of God's justice was one of the marks of the Mu'tazilah.

After some limited success that included the patronage of the 'Abbasi rulers, the Mu'tazilah were decisively rejected by the Muslims and the group passed out of existence. However, they made a permanent contribution to Islamic life by bringing the apparatus and approach of Greek philosophy into the service of Islam. They were the first to create a *kalam* (discussion) of Islamic doctrines, that is, the first to employ rational argumentation to express the community's faith. The subtlety and power of their methods obliged their opponents to adopt the same tools for self-defense. Thus was born the science of *kalam* (theology), i.e., the science of the rational defense of religious doctrine.

The individual who more than any other is responsible for the acceptance of *kalam* among traditionalist Muslims was Abu-al-Hasan al-Ash'ari (d. 873). In his early days al-Ash'ari had been a Mu'tazilah, but after a crisis of some sort he broke with his teacher, the famous al-Jubba'i, and renounced Mu'tazilah teachings in favor of more traditional views. To uphold his own stand, however, al-Ash'ari used the methods and vocabulary he had learned from his teacher. Whereas the Mu'tazilah had employed rational criteria in some degree as the judge and criterion of religious doctrine, al-Ash'ari made only an instrumental use of the reason. The doctrines which he espoused were derived from the authority of the revelation and the Prophet; the role of reasoned argument was only to defend and bolster what had been received as the truth. His purposes were, thus, primarily defensive, to ward off the attacks of those who questioned certain aspects of traditional Islam.

Al-Ash'ari was a literalist in his attitude toward the declarations of the *Qur'an,* insisting that they must be taken for what they say. Thus, he affirmed the reality of God's attributes (*sifat*) and upheld the Vision of God on the Last Day as a reality, both of which the Mu'tazilah denied as contrary to reason. His approach, however, was not naively anthropomorphic, and he was in the beginning subjected to bitter attacks from traditionalists who felt that any use of dialectical argument was heretical. Characteristic of al-Ash'ari was a kind of middle position on these controversial matters. While on the one hand affirming the reality of the divine attributes, on the other he refused to state precisely the nature of their relationship to the divine essence. He taught that God has attributes in reality, but "without saying how and without making comparisons." This convenient formula which was devised by al-Ash'ari's conservative predecessor, Ahmad ibn Hanbal (d. 780), was given even greater refinement by al-Taftazani who said of the divine *sifat* that "they are not He nor are they other than He." Al-Ash'ari believed with the *Qur'an* that God has hands and that he sits upon his throne, but the hands and the sitting are not like those of human beings.

Al-Ash'ari also took a strong stand in favor of predestination. He taught what is, perhaps, as strict an interpretation of the doctrine as can be found anywhere. Everything which happens is the result of divine initiative. When a man performs an action, it is God who creates in him the will, the power to act, the intention to do so, and the final impulse which precipitates the act itself. None of what happens is the cause of any of the rest; rather all comes about by the direct intervention of God. Al-Ash'ari's doctrine of predestination grew out of his vivid perception of the sovereignty of God which he would in no way compromise. He could not admit the existence of any power alongside God in the universe. In later years among al-Ash'ari's followers the implications of this doctrine were worked out in a metaphysical system of absolute consistency. Al-Baqillani, its chief author, taught that reality consists of a series of monads or atoms without connection among one another. The world may and does exist only as God re-creates it at each moment in time. Thus there is nothing which functions independently from God's direct stimulation, and what appear to men as "natural laws" or as "causes" are but God's habitual modes of behavior. Once more, however, in his doctrine of predestination al-Ash'ari exhibits the tendency to take a middle position. Although all things, including human action, are predestined, man is responsible for what he does. It is God who in reality acts, but man acquires (*kasb*) the action and accountability for it. This doctrine is of great subtlety and has been a puzzlement for Muslim thinkers through the ages.

In the course of Islamic development the theological position enunciated by al-Ash'ari has gained the assent of the great majority of Sunni Muslims, so much so that it is sometimes referred to as Islamic orthodoxy. His teachings were carried on and developed in a school of thinkers that includes some of the greatest names in Islamic history, al-Baqillani (above), ibn Furak, al-Juwayni, and the incomparable al-Ghazali who may be considered the climax of the development. With but small differences his views are accepted as normative by conservative Muslims to our own time.

THE ISLAMIC LAW

Islam has often been called a religion of law, and this ascription of a central place to the law is more than justified. Perhaps the most fundamental of all words in the Muslim religious vocabulary is guidance (*hudan*), for it is guidance in all the manifold situations of life that the Muslim expects from his religion. Considered in one sense the law of Islam is nothing more than the effort to make divine guidance as explicit and detailed as possible so that at no point will the Muslim faithful be left in bewilderment about the course to be followed. In its broadest sense of general principles the law is spoken of as the *shari'ah,* a word meaning pathway or roadway, the course along which God intends that men should walk. What came to Muhammad in the revelations was the *shari'ah,* a guidance, a road map to successful life in the world and to communion with God in the hereafter. The *shari'ah* is thus a transcendental expression of the eternal divine will for men. The Islam or commitment which God demands is commitment to following the *shari'ah,* for in no other way can men be pleasing to God and escape his wrath.

The first and most important thing about the *shari'ah* is the fact that it is a divine law. In the history of mankind many different sanctions for legality have emerged, some having derived the authority of law from the traditions of old, others from the decree of rulers, others from the consent of the governed, etc. Islamic law accepts none of these but claims its origin, and authority, from the very words of God himself. According to the Islamic understanding, man, a mere creature, with his unaided faculties is incapable of distinguishing between right and wrong or of determining how he should live. God has decreed a way of life for men, and this decree is the sole and determinative norm. All obligations as well as all rights arise because God in his wisdom has decreed them; their character

Left, enameled glass mosque lamp, early fourteenth-century Syrian. (Courtesy of the Metropolitan Museum of Art, Bequest of Edward C. Moore, 1891); right, brass bowl inlaid with gold and silver, mid to late fourteenth-century Persian. (Courtesy of the Metropolitan Museum of Art, Rogers Fund, 1941.)

is juridical. There is no question of human rights or of other "natural" bases of moral judgment. What is right is right because God has decreed it and not the other way around. If he had so chosen, there would have been nothing to prevent God in his freedom from making what he decreed as right to be wrong, for there is no moral order apart from his eternal decree. A law which thus represents the eternal will of the universe's Creator is infallible, and man's attitude toward it should be one of humble submission.

Furthermore, the divine *shari'ah* is comprehensive in that it offers all of the guidance necessary to humankind and, indeed, touches every sphere of life. Islamic law along with the usual areas of legal concern also regulates a great number of things which in the modern understanding fall outside the scope of law altogether. Not only contracts, criminal matters, marriage and divorce, etc., but also dress, foodstuffs, ritual, and even the forms of greeting and courtesy are decreed by the law. The subject matter of the law is traditionally divided into (1) obligations owing to God (*'ibadat*), such things as the profession of faith, performance of prayer and other religious duties, and (2) obligations owing to other men (*mu-'amalat*) or all those things which affect individual and social morality, the conduct of state, etc. Among the obligations to God proper belief is one of the foremost. Technically speaking, therefore, theology is an aspect of law though the science of *kalam* has tended to assume an independent status in the course of Islamic history. In later Islamic times the jurists have emphasized the comprehensiveness of the *shari'ah* by classifying all human activity without exception under one of five headings, thus showing that the *shari'ah* is indifferent to nothing. Actions are either *fard* (obligatory, like confessing the unity of God and the prophethood of Muhammad), *mandub* (recommended), *mubah* (permitted), *makruh* (disapproved but not outright forbidden, like divorce), or *haram* (absolutely forbidden, like eating pork). In another simpler scheme things are characterized as being *halal* (permitted) or *haram* (forbidden). All of the obligations under the *shari'ah* arise from an identical source and have ultimately an identical sanction. None can be more or less important than the others, for all represent the will of God which it is man's duty to fulfill.

Another characteristic of the *shari'ah* is the fact that most obligations arising under it fall upon individuals. Each man stands in an immediate relationship of accountability with God, and none can substitute for another. Although there are some aspects of the *shari'ah* that may be called public law, for the most part it does not imply enforcement by the state through police power or a system of courts, nor does it recognize many obligations that fall upon a collectivity as such. Even criminal offenses are considered as injuries to individuals, and it is the individual's responsibility, not the state's, to seek redress from the judge of the religious court (the *qadi*). In certain respects therefore the *shari'ah* is not really law at all as we understand it and should perhaps be designated by another term.

Every functioning legal system must have, in addition to ultimate sanctions, some trustworthy method of applying its broad principles to specific situations in life in the form of rules of law. This is no less true of Islamic law than of others. The process of finding definite rules from the broad principles is what we know as jurisprudence, in the Islamic case as *fiqh*. The word *fiqh* means understanding, and in connection with the law it refers to two things. On the one hand it is the name accorded the process of deriving explicit rules of law from the transcendental *shari'ah,* and on the other it is used for the result of that process, that is, for the books of rules compiled through the jurists' efforts. One customarily speaks, not of the books of *shari'ah,* but of the books of *fiqh.* A person who is skilled in the science of jurisprudence is called a *faqih* (pl. *fuqaha'*).

The impulse toward developing a science of jurisprudence came from the brevity and frequent unclarity of the revelations in the *Qur'an.* The book is, after all, relatively small in size, and as the Muslims spread out from the Arabian peninsula over the vast territories which they conquered, they began to confront a multitude of problems and situations for which the *Qur'an* had no specific provisions. It was necessary both to find additional sources of authority and to achieve a more precise statement of the Muslim's religious duties. For more than two centuries there was uncertainty and some controversy among the learned men of the community about the way in which Muslims might arrive at normative decisions on matters not specifically treated in the *Qur'an.*

The discussion about the sources of legal authority came to a climax in the work of a brilliant lawyer and polemicist of the late second and third centuries, al-Shafi'i (b. 767). Through an extensive series of writings in which he analyzed and discussed the rival opinions of jurists he worked out a concise and clear theory of the sources or roots of Islamic law. Although it was some time before his view was generally accepted, in due course it won universal assent among Sunni Muslims.

Al-Shafi'i held that there are four roots (*usul*) of the law, which stand in a definite order of precedence. The first and most authoritative is the *Qur'an,* the words of God, which no other authority may supersede. If on a given subject there are clear Qur'anic command-ments, these are unqualifiedly to prevail above everything else. The scope of such clear Qur'anic dictums, however, is very small, and it was precisely this fact that gave rise to the science of jurisprudence and the search for other authorities.

The second source of norms in order of importance was the cus-tomary usage or *sunnah* of the Prophet. Where it could be estab-lished on the basis of reliable reports that the Prophet had acted or judged matters in a particular way, such a precedent was not only trustworthy but constituted an obligation upon the Muslims to follow it. It cannot be too strongly emphasized that the Muslim tendency to look to the past as a storehouse of valid and normative guidance is of the very essence of the Islamic mentality. The pre-Islamic Arabs were a strongly tradition-bound people, taking it as their duty to re-vere the generations gone by, as in the case of their pride in ge-nealogy, and to preserve the time-honored ways of their fathers. The early Islamic community preserved this familiar Arab attitude but changed its focus to concentrate upon the Prophet and his companions. Instead of emulating the heroes of the glorious "Days of the Arabs," the Muslims found their tradition in the exploits, say-ings, and actions of Muhammad and those around him. These they endlessly repeated, sometimes embroidered, and always respected. The content of the Islamic understanding of the world was different from that of pagan Arabia, but the attitude toward the importance of the past was identical.

Al-Shafi'i's contribution to the elaboration of the prophetic *sunnah* as a norm was particularly significant. Although almost all Muslims had resort to tradition as one basis of legal judgment, there was widespread disagreement about precisely what constituted tradition. Some held that anything coming from the companions of Muham-mad was authoritative, while others preferred the practice of the people of Madinah where Muhammad had passed the latter and most successful part of his career. Still others based their legal thinking on customary usage in the particular region where they happened to reside or upon the teachings of a learned man whom they respected. Al-Shafi'i cut through this confusion by maintaining against many opponents that the normative *sunnah* was that of the Prophet and the Prophet alone. What must be sought is Muham-mad's example, and those of all others are irrelevant.

The content of the Prophet's *sunnah* is known to Muslims through a series of oral reports about him which record his sayings, doings, and implicit approbations. Such an oral report is called a *hadith,* and it consists of two parts, the *matn* or text and the *isnad* (lit. "foundation") or chain of authorities through which it has come down. Virtually all the information we have about early Islamic his-tory, the life of Muhammad, etc., has reached us in the form of such oral reports, gathered, written down, and preserved by men of later times.

In view of their consuming desire to remain true to the traditions of those before them, when they confronted a difficulty or a novel situation, the Muslims would, almost instinctively, search for a report which would supply guidance by way of precedent. The normal form of religious and/or political disputation among Muslims has been the citation of *Qur'an* verses and of oral reports of the earliest and most respected generation, but especially those relating to the Prophet. In the early centuries when no such report was found readily to hand, Muslims often supplied one of their own devising that served to make the desired point, that is, they deliberately put into circulation reports about the Prophet which had no basis in fact. Sometimes the motives for such fabricated *hadith* were cynical, but more often they were an expression of pious belief resting upon the conviction that the Prophet would have adopted the position taken in the fabricated report were he still alive. Such people thought that they understood the mind of the Prophet, and instead of stating what he might have said, chose simply to put words into his mouth.

By the end of the second Islamic century there was in common circulation a vast body of traditional material purporting to come from the earliest generations, but a major portion of which was fabricated to answer the changing needs of a growing society. Inevitably this situation provoked a reaction from more pious and conservative people who apprehended that the genuine prophetic example would be lost among the multitude of reports. In consequence there emerged a science for the criticism and authentication of *hadith* which has remained until today one of the central preoccupations of Islamic learning. The noteworthy feature of this science is that it concerns itself only with the *isnads* of the *hadith* and not with their subject matter. The purpose is to investigate the process of transmission to determine whether or not it is sound and uninterrupted. The students of *hadith* (*muhaddithun*) paid great attention to the personal histories and characters of the individuals constituting the chains of transmission, and under the stimulus of this inquiry, called "impugning and justifying," there grew up a large biographical literature dealing with the companions of Muhammad and the learned men of the early generations. This information allowed one to discover whether the relater of a *hadith* had actually known the man from whom he claimed to have heard it, whether he was generally trustworthy and honest, etc. There also emerged an elaborate system for the classification of *hadith* according to the number of channels through which they were transmitted and according to the characteristics of their *isnads*. In the most general terms the investigation of a *hadith* by applying the principles of this science permits one to judge it as *sahih* (sound), *hasan* (good), or *da'if* (weak).

In the late second Islamic century the criticism of *hadith* and the effort to separate the true from the false came to fruition in certain carefully sifted collections that have an authority for all Sunni Muslims second only to the *Qur'an*. These collections are the so-called Six Sound Books of tradition of which the most respected and best known are those by al-Bukhari (b. 810) and Muslim ibn al-Hajjaj (b. 821). Al-Bukhari is said to have sifted more than 600,000 separate *hadith* in order to arrive at his collection of 2,762 which he considered authentically to have come from the Prophet. The organization of al-Bukhari's famous book under headings drawn from legal discussions of the time shows clearly that the endeavor to achieve authoritative collections of *hadith* was stimulated by considerations of jurisprudence.

In spite of the special recognition given to the Six Sound Books, Muslims do not hesitate to make use of a great number of other works on *hadith*. The literature in the field is extensive, and the *faqih* or learned man ranges freely through it to find the *hadith* that help him to solve whatever problem may be under consideration.

In modern times there has been an attack on the authenticity of *hadith* from both without and within the Islamic camp. Some Western scholars, having noted that the Six Sound Books contain *hadith* that are contradictory, tendentious, and anachronistic, look upon even these authoritative collections as being composed largely of fabricated materials. In their view the *hadith* collections, though they tell us little that is trustworthy about Muhammad and his sayings, are very important as an index of the religious and legal doctrines most widely held in the Islamic community at the time of their collection. Taking their point of departure from this critical approach, some Muslim reformers in the twentieth century have declared their freedom from the authority of *hadith* altogether. Rejection of the *hadith* has liberated these thinkers from the rigid confines of the medieval Islamic schools of law that based their systems for the most part on tradition.

We may return now to take up the thread of al-Shafi'i's theory of the roots of law. After the *Qur'an* and the *sunnah* of the Prophet, the third source of legal guidance which he recognized was the consensus or *ijma'* of the community. If in looking at the past one discovers that the community at large or its most learned men have generally agreed upon a doctrine or a practice, he may take this consensus as sanction, provided always that the consensus does not go against *Qur'an* or *sunnah*. It is to be emphasized that the consensus is always that of past generations; in al-Shafi'i's terms it is, thus, not a power of legislation given to the contemporary community though some modernist Muslims take it to be precisely that. The appeal to *ijma'* underlines the Islamic attitude toward the past, for in the final analysis it is nothing more than another name for tradition, in this case the well-known and firmly established way of doing things in the community as a whole. The principle involved is nowhere more clearly expressed than in the saying attributed to Muhammad: "My community will never agree in an error." If one reflects deeply on the implications of this saying, he will perhaps be able to understand the agonized crisis of soul of many present-day Muslims as they contemplate the military, political, and economic subordination of Muslim peoples to outside powers.

The last of al-Shafi'i's four *usul al-fiqh* (roots or sources of the law), to be resorted to only when the preceding ones have not produced the required guidance, is *qiyas* or analogical reasoning. This technique, however, may be used only under the strictest control. In certain circumstances it is legitimate to extend the implications of an explicit rule of law arrived at on the basis of one of the three preceding *usul* to cover a different but analogous situation that is

The seventeenth-century Sultan Ahmad Mosque in Istanbul, known as the Blue Mosque. In the foreground is the obelisk constructed by Emperor Constantine Porphyrogenius, grandson of Emperor Basil, the Macedonian. (Courtesy of the Turkish Tourism and Information Office.)

not specifically provided for. For instance, the Qur'anic prohibition of wine on the basis of its being an intoxicant allows the *faqih* to judge that other intoxicants are also to be forbidden. Analogical thinking must always proceed from a previously established rule and can never in any way be innovative or serve to overturn or supersede judgments based on one of the other *usul*. The principle of *qiyas* is, therefore, by no means a license for speculation or the exercise of personal opinion in legal matters. In fact, it is clear from al-Shafi'i's entire stance that the thing which he most abhorred was the intrusion of arbitrary, unsubstantiated personal preference or whim into the formation of legal judgments. His criticism on this point was most severe, especially against the 'Iraqi jurist, Abu Hanifah (d. 767), whose use of *qiyas* was much less restrained.

Al-Shafi'i was but one of several prominent and creative jurists who did their work in the first and second Islamic centuries. The first important figure was Malik ibn Anas (d. 795) who passed most of his life in Madinah where he sought to uphold the usage and custom of that place as a norm for Muslim conduct. To him goes the credit for having compiled the oldest surviving book on Islamic law, his famous *Kitab al-Muwatta'* (*The Book of the Paved Path*). By the third Islamic century several distinct schools of law had emerged under the influence of prominent men who had passed down their teachings through a series of disciples. Many of these schools passed away or were displaced by others in the course of time, such as those founded by the Syrian al-Awza'i (d. 722) and the famous historian al-Tabari (b. 839), but four of them have survived to the present. A school of jurisprudence or legal interpretation is called a *madhhab* (a path). The four great *madhahib* (Arabic plural of *madhhab*) of Islamic history are the Maliki, after Malik ibn Anas; the Hanbali, after Ahmad ibn Hanbal; the Hanafi, after Abu Hanifah; and the Shafi'i after al-Shafi'i.

Among Sunni Muslims it is the custom to adhere to one of these schools which each man is free to choose for himself. In the content of their teachings there is very little difference among them, differences being confined for the most part to certain items of detail. All the four are considered to represent true Islam and to offer acceptable teachings. Important centers of Islamic learning such as the al-Azhar University in Cairo give instruction in the doctrines of all four schools, and in many Muslim countries it was formerly the custom to maintain religious courts with judges drawn from different schools so that each man's cause might be heard according to the legal doctrine which he accepted.

Each school is also associated with a certain region of the Islamic world where its acceptance has become customary for the majority of people. The teachings of Malik ibn Anas, for example, are the norm in North Africa and in much of the rest of Africa where Islam has penetrated, excepting Egypt. Probably the most widespread school is that of Abu Hanifah which prevailed in the Ottoman Turkish Empire and in Central Asia from where it was taken to India by the Turkish Muslim conquerors of the subcontinent. The strictest school in doctrine and that having the smallest number of followers today is the Hanbali *madhhab*. In the past this school was widespread throughout Iraq and Greater Syria, but at present its adherents are concentrated in the Arabian peninsula where the puritanical Wahhabi sect has opted for its strict view of Islamic teaching. The legal opinions of al-Shafi'i prevail in the largest of the Islamic nations, Indonesia, and in Egypt, Syria, and East Africa. Although in certain areas two or more of these schools exist side by side in the same society, there is an attitude of mutual acceptance so that relations among them are peaceful.

As in much else in their history the Muslims have shown a decidedly traditionalistic attitude toward the science of jurisprudence. The early great jurists and their followers for several generations after were engaged in a systematic unfolding of the *shari'ah* in all its implications for human activity. By applying themselves to understanding the source materials of the law, they built up elaborate systems of rules of conduct in every sphere of life. The process of striving to understand the sources of the law and to derive the rules of law from them is called by the technical term *ijtihad*, meaning to make a personal intellectual effort. Through their personal effort the founders of the *madhahib* had worked out the broad principles of *fiqh* while their followers in subsequent generations strove to elucidate the details. A time came, however, when the generality of Muslims began to consider that the fundamental work of expounding the law in both its principles and details had been completed. From that time the "Door of Ijtihad," to use the classical expression, was closed, and the duty of men was no longer to return to the sources of the law to make their own judgments but rather to accept as authoritative the opinions of the doctors of the *madhhab* to which they adhered. From that point the study of the law became exclusively the perusal of the works of the founders of the schools and their most important disciples rather than of the sources themselves. One who thus binds himself to the teachings of a particular legal school, as virtually all Muslims in medieval and early modern times have done, is said to be *muqallad* (tied) to that school. Although men learned in the law (*faqihs*) have always had freedom to offer legal opinions (*fatwas*) on questions put to them, their task has not been to seek new directions or principles in the law but only to discover from the writings of the authoritative teachers of their respective schools what resources may be brought to bear on the question at hand. The result of the attitude of *taqlid* (i.e., the attitude of a *muqallad faqih*) has been to make all later writing on Islamic law take the form of commentaries on earlier works and so effectively to cut Muslims off from fresh insights into the basic sources of Islamic piety.

Throughout Islamic history there have been isolated individuals who rejected *taqlid* and who claimed the right of studying and expounding the fundamental Islamic sources for themselves. In recent times an insistence that the "Door of Ijtihad" is still open has become one of the pillars of Islamic modernism. Many modernists see *taqlid* as perhaps the chief cause for the failure of their community to keep pace with the rival civilization that has come to dominate it. So long as Muslim religious leaders remain *muqallad,* just so long will they be caught up in a static understanding of law and society and so be unable to adapt to the changed conditions of modernity. For modernists Islam is dynamic and progressive, incorporating in such principles as *ijtihad* the means for its own perpetual self-regeneration and self-adaption to new circumstances. For these men *taqlid* is a grave misunderstanding of Islam which denies its very spirit.

The strenuous efforts of many countries in the Islamic world to modernize their societies has also affected Islamic law in recent times. While in the Arabian peninsula things have remained much as they were, in other places the trend has been to restrict the functioning of the traditional *fiqh* in an ever-increasing variety of ways. A majority of contemporary Muslim states has adopted constitutions patterned after Western models, and many of the same states have enacted legal codes that are virtually identical with the French or Swiss civil law. Criminal law also is now for the most part built upon bases that have little to do with the *shari'ah*. The religious courts of a few years back have also generally been abolished. Where the Islamic *fiqh* continues to have certain influence in the modern world is in the sphere of family and personal law. To the extent possible, many Muslim states attempt to regulate inheritance, marriage, divorce, patrimony, etc., in the ways traditional to the Islamic community. Even here, however, there have been profound changes. In Tunisia and Pakistan, for example, recent legislation has regulated both marriage and divorce in ways unknown to the Islamic *fuqaha'* of the past. The dual tendency to displace Islamic law by other systems and to change its provisions in ways more pleasing to modern minds has brought about a crisis of conscience for many pious people. If, as we have said, Islam is primarily a religion of law, it could not be otherwise. There is no question more fraught with significance or more hotly debated than that concerning the role which the *shari'ah* should play in the emergent national states of the Islamic world.

ISLAMIC WORSHIP AND RELIGIOUS PRACTICES

The most basic religious duties of Muslims, those usually described in the sections on 'ibadat (obligations owing to God) in books of fiqh, are known as the Five Pillars of Islam. These five essential obligations are witnessing (shahadah), ritual prayer (salat), fasting in the month of Ramadan (sawm), almsgiving (zakat), and the pilgrimage to Makkah (hajj). They are accompanied by a great series of other religious celebrations, occasions, and practices of varying degrees of merit in Muslim eyes.

It is obligatory upon every Muslim to give public testimony of his faith in the unity of God and the prophethood of Muhammad by verbal declaration. The customary formula reads, "I testify that there is no God but the one God, and Muhammad is his prophet." The willingness solemnly to affirm this statement in the presence of witnesses is the mark of a man's being a Muslim for purposes of membership in the community and sharing in its rights and duties. Other articles of belief deemed essential but not included in the witnessing formula are belief in angels, in the books of God, in all the apostles, and in the coming Judgment Day.

Perhaps the most visible mark of Islamic piety is the ritual prayer which adult Muslims of sound mind and body everywhere are expected to perform as an absolute obligation five times each day. Any who have visited the Islamic world will have seen this simple but impressive ceremony performed in streets and public places as well as mosques. The prayer consists of a set ritual that differs slightly for the different times of day. The worshiper begins in a standing position facing toward Makkah with his hands crossed before him, and as the prayer proceeds, he assumes positions of kneeling and then of bowing in prostration with the forehead touching the ground. These acts are accompanied by the recitation,

Pilgrims rest and worship at the Sacred Mosque at Mecca (Makkah). (Courtesy of Aramco.)

mostly silently, of portions from the *Qur'an,* of the witnessing formula, of praises to God, and of prayers. *Salat* may be validly performed only when the worshiper is in a state of ritual purity; therefore, it is always preceded by a washing, or a full bath, depending
upon the degree of impurity that has been incurred. Because of this
requirement it is customary that mosques include the facilities for
purification when they are constructed. In general it is considered
preferable that *salat* be performed in the company of others, but it
is perfectly permissible to observe the ritual alone. On Fridays, however, there is a special value given to the performance of *salat*
along with a congregation. On these occasions the prayers are led
by one called simply the leader (*imam*) who stands in front of the
ranks of worshipers, facing as they do toward the niche in the wall
of the mosque (*mihrab*) that marks the direction of Makkah (the *qiblah*). This congregational prayer is normally followed by a sermon

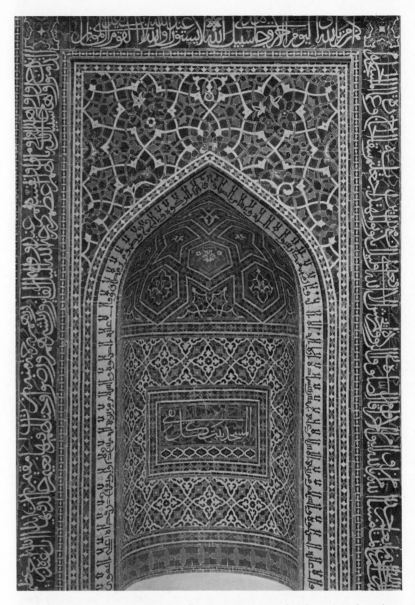

A mosaic mihrab, or prayer niche. Fourteenth-century Iranian; glazed earthenware set in plaster. (Courtesy of the Metropolitan Museum of Art, Harris Brisbane Dick Fund, 1939.)

(*khutbah*) preached from the pulpit which in many mosques is the only furniture to be found. The times of prayer (before sunrise, dawn, noon, afternoon, after sunset) are today, as throughout the whole of Islamic history, announced to the faithful from the minaret of the mosque by a *mu'adhdhin* (one who calls to prayer). The common observance of this time-honored ritual throughout the Muslim lands constitutes a great bond of unity for Islamic peoples everywhere.

In addition to the obligatory *salat,* Muslims know and observe many other kinds of prayer. Special prayers are often added at the end of the *salat* itself by pious worshipers, while others are reserved for special vigils and meditations. There is, in fact, an entire catalogue of prayers to accompany each act and undertaking of life. This aspect of Islamic religious life is often overlooked by observers, with the consequence that its devotional richness is missed.

Fasting during the entire month of Ramadan, the sacred month "when the *Qur'an* came down," is another of the duties incumbent upon every adult Muslim in possession of his faculties. The fast continues for the entire day, beginning from the first light when it becomes possible to distinguish a white thread from a black one and ending only when the sun has set. During these hours it is forbidden to take anything into the body, food, drink, tobacco smoke, etc., even to a prohibition of swallowing one's own saliva where it is avoidable. Since Muslims follow a lunar calendar for religious purposes, the month of Ramadan moves successively through all the seasons of the year. In the more arid and hot regions of the earth the fast can become a great burden when it falls during the months of summer; nonetheless, faithful Muslims subject themselves to its discipline scrupulously. Throughout the month much of each night is passed in the mosques where the *Qur'an* is recited in divisions that allow it to be completed within the span of thirty nights. The end of the month of fasting is marked by the greatest festival of the Islamic year, the 'Id al-Fitr or festival of the breaking of the fast. The occasion is one of great joy. After congregational prayers, which are the most universally attended of the entire year, there is feasting, for on this day fasting is categorically forbidden. In many countries it is the custom to wear new clothing, to visit friends, and to exchange gifts. As with most of the other pillars of Islam there are some exceptions to the requirement for fasting in special instances. The ill and infirm, travelers who have begun their journey before sunrise, those who must perform strenuous physical labor, and some others may be excused, though the *shari'ah* provides in many instances that the days of fast shall be made up at a later time.

North Persian (probably Tabriz) nineteenth-century wool prayer rug. (Courtesy of the Metropolitan Museum of Art, Mr. and Mrs. Isaac D. Fletcher Collection, Bequest of Isaac D. Fletcher, 1917.)

Fasting at times other than the month of Ramadan is also widely practiced by Muslims as an act of self-discipline and dedication to God. Such fasting is voluntary though religious authorities have advocated it especially in connection with days of religious importance, with certain days of the month or the week, or with religious festivals. The famous al-Ghazali, for example, recommended in particular that the first, middle, and last days of each month be marked by fasting and especially during the months of the year that are considered sacred. Islam, however, generally counsels moderation in fasting as in other things, and most authorities forbid fasting more than four days continuously outside Ramadan. Fasting also serves as a form of penance for Muslims when they have neglected or broken certain aspects of *shari'ah*.

In the early days of Islam the payment of alms, along with the performance of *salat*, was particularly emphasized as the sign of submission to the authority of the Prophet. The basis for this religious tax is the Islamic emphasis on the virtue of charity which runs through the *Qur'an* as a continuing and important theme. Muslims are obligated to pay fixed amounts on various types of property, and the revenue so collected may be employed only for specified purposes of which the most important are help to the poor and needy and to the wayfarer, and support for the cause of God, i.e., to finance the holy war against infidelity. Through much of Islamic history rulers and states have provided arrangements for the collection of *zakat,* but the individual has also been free to pay his *zakat* directly to those who may legitimately receive it. There has been great irregularity, however, in the state-organized systems of collecting the tax, both in the manner of its collection and in the uses to which the revenue has been put. With the growth of other taxes and the assumption of a considerable financial burden by peasants, it becomes increasingly difficult to realize *zakat* revenue. In modern times the adoption of legal codes based on Western models and the use of a great variety of secular taxes has created new problems for the state administration of *zakat*. Nevertheless, the payment of this annual sum remains a firm obligation of religion for every adult Muslim possessed of property beyond the minimum designated in *shari'ah,* and the devout are scrupulous in fulfilling it.

The last of the Five Pillars is the duty to perform the pilgrimage to Makkah at least once during a lifetime. Every healthy adult Muslim of either sex who can command the means should make this journey of piety. Each year during the month of pilgrimage thousands upon thousands of devoted Muslims pour into the sacred city by every conceivable mode of transport to participate in the complex rites. The great majority, when they have finished the obligatory ceremonies in Makkah and its vicinity, complete their journey of faith by also visiting Madinah to pray at the tomb of the Prophet and perform other ceremonies. For countless Muslims the pilgrimage to Makkah is the dream and goal of a lifetime, and many labor and struggle for years to save the sums necessary to accomplish it. Most of the ceremony of the *hajj,* which requires several days for its fulfillment, dates back to pre-Islamic times, and the rite is an outstanding example of the manner in which Muhammad adapted certain of the practices of his ancestors to the new world view of Islam, both maintaining continuity with the past and promoting a new perspective on life at one and the same time. The principal parts of the ceremony are the assumption of pilgrim dress upon entering the sacred area, circumambulation of the Ka'bah, climaxed by kissing the black stone set in one of its corners, running back and forth between the hills of Safa and Marwah, standing (*wuquf*) at the hill of 'Arafat, and casting stones at Mina. The latter is a ceremony whose meaning is far from clear; it consists in throwing seven stones onto one of three piles of stone. Muslim commentators have explained it as "stoning the devil." With the completion of these rites the pilgrimage proper is finished, but it is customary to observe yet other ceremonies, the most important of which is the sacrifice of an animal. This occasion at the end of the *hajj* provides the Islamic world with its second great festival of the year, the 'Id al-Adha, or festival of sacrifice. Not only the pilgrims but all Mus-

Pilgrims in the courtyard of the Khaif Mosque at Mina, near Mecca. (Courtesy of Aramco.)

lims who can afford it make sacrifice on that day. Much of the meat from sacrificial animals goes to the poor, and in recent times it is customary for religious associations to collect the animal hides from whose proceeds they support a variety of charitable and religious activities.

It must never be thought that the range of Islamic ceremony and religious celebration is limited to the Five Pillars, although they are the fundamentals of Muslim worship. Many other times in the year also take on special significance and are marked by rites and celebrations. For example, it is customary throughout the Islamic world to celebrate the birthday of the Prophet though this festival has no *shari'ah* status. Among all the Shi'ah the most important day of the year is the tenth of the month of Muharram, on which the martyrdom of Imam Husayn is remembered and lamented. For the millions of Muslims drawn to Sufi forms of piety, each Thursday night is a time of particular importance, when the Sufi circles meet to "remember" the name of God, for on that night God is believed to draw close to the earth to hear the petitions of the faithful.

MYSTICISM

During the same period when the *kalam* and the *fiqh* were being formed and given their classical expressions another element made its appearance in Islamic religious life. From small beginnings in the ascetic practices of a few isolated but influential individuals there emerged a mystical movement that rapidly swelled until it dominated the religious horizon. The rise of the movement had many causes, but important among them was the increasing distance between ordinary Muslims and their religious leaders. As *kalam* and *fiqh* became established sciences, they also grew more specialized and made greater demands upon their practitioners. For the majority of people it was impossible to follow the involved arguments and reasoning of the learned who became always more technical; in consequence, there was little of personal inspiration or religious guidance to be gained from them. With mystical leaders, however, the situation was entirely different. These men offered not only personal association and guidance at the level of the common man's spiritual needs, but as well, their piety was highly charged with emotional content that provided warmth of religious experience otherwise lacking for many. By the sixth Islamic century mysticism had such a hold in the life of the community that it touched virtually everyone; even the learned custodians of the legal tradition were caught up by it. For more than five hundred years, and continuing well into our own century, some form of mystical piety has been the effective religion of most people in the Islamic world. The hold of mysticism has somewhat lessened in recent times under the impact of criticisms from Muslim reformers and modernists, but in such areas as Sindh, the Frontier Province of Pakistan, Afghanistan, and Iran, especially among rural people, it is still the reality of Islam for the majority.

In Islamic dress mysticism is known as Sufism or more properly as *tasawwuf,* and one who practices it as a Sufi or *mutasawwif.* Many etymologies have been suggested for the word by Sufi writers themselves, but it is most commonly agreed to derive from *Suf,* Arabic for "wool." It was the practice of ascetics in the early days to wear a rough garment of white wool which then became the trademark of their peculiar religious practice. Definitions of Sufism are almost as numerous as Sufi writers, but the following may be taken as characteristic. Abu al-Hasan al-Nuri is reported to have said: "The Sufis are they whose spirits have been freed from the pollution of humanity, purified from carnal taint, and released from concupiscence, so that they have found rest with God in the first rank and the highest degree, and have fled from all save Him." [1] Another Sufi saint put it in this way: "He that is purified by love is pure (*saf*), and he that is absorbed in the Beloved and has abandoned all else is a Sufi." [2]

There are many elements in the *Qur'an* and the life of Muhammad which have given spiritual nourishment to persons of mystical temperament. Such verses as "Whether ye turn to the East or the West, there is the Face of God," and "God is nearer to thee than thy jugular vein," bear a mystical import that is evident at first reading. Perhaps the most significant *Qur'an* passage for the mystics is the famous "Light Verse" of Surah 24:35 ff.:

> God is the Light of the heavens and the earth;
> the likeness of His Light is as a niche
> > wherein is a lamp
> > (the lamp in a glass,
> > the glass as it were a glittering star)
> > kindled from a Blessed Tree,
> > an olive that is neither of the East nor of the West
> whose oil well nigh would shine, even if no fire touched it;
> > Light upon Light.[3]

These words have been contemplated and commented upon by thousands of Sufis who see them as an unambiguous teaching of God's ubiquitous presence in all things, places, and times. Even the mode of the *Qur'an*'s coming to the Prophet has a mystical significance, for it was accompanied by visions of a spiritual being, and consisted of direct communication with an order of reality above and beyond the mundane. The Sufis, however, have not contented themselves with contemplating only straightforwardly mystical verses but have seen the entire *Qur'an* as a great allegory of the soul's quest for union with God. Beyond the outward and evident sense of the words lies a hidden and more profound meaning which is uncovered in the tradition of esoteric knowledge which God has bestowed upon his saints.

The Prophet's life is equally rich in material for Sufi contemplation. Whether or not Muhammad could be called a mystic in the technical sense is debatable, but he had cultivated the habit of meditation, fasting, and prayer in his lonely night vigils; and his mode of life, even during the time of his greatest success, had been

1. Al-Hujwīrī, *Kashf al-Maḥjūb*, trans. Reynold Nicholson, London, Luzac and Company, 1936, p. 37.

2. Ibid., p. 34.

3. A. J. Arberry, *The Koran Interpreted*, New York, Macmillan, 1955, vol. 2, pp. 50–51.

modest and self-denying in the extreme, almost to the point of asceticism. Thus, the Prophet could be seen as a model of Sufi discipline to be followed and emulated. Most important, however, was the legend of Muhammad's miraculous Night Journey from Makkah to Jerusalem, thence ascending through the Seven Heavens to meet face to face with God before the Throne. Based on a verse in the *Qur'an* (Surah 17:1), this legend has given rise to many interpretations. For some it has portrayed the soul's rise from earthly involvement to divine truth, and for others it has generated a cult of imitation of the Prophet whose access to the Divine Presence is seen as the unique key opening the way for other men to attain that high prize. Thus, there was no lack of elements of a mystical nature in the early period of Islam. Although at a later point the mystical thought and practice of others, especially Christians and Neoplatonists, and perhaps even Buddhists, to some extent influenced the Muslims, there is no reason to seek further than the fundamental Islamic experience itself to explain the rise of Sufism. Sufism is a thoroughly Islamic phenomenon that sprang from the prime sources of the community's faith.

The first stage in the growth of a specifically mystical movement was the appearance of ascetics (*zuhada'*) among the Muslims as early as the first Islamic century. The most famous of them was a certain al-Hasan al-Basri (d. 728) whose name is also associated with the beginnings of the Mu'tazilah sect. Al-Hasan was noted for his piety and his courage in outspoken criticism of the Ummawi rulers. His ascetic ways appear, as also for others showing the same tendencies, to have been an expression of protest against the increasing worldliness of the state. To keep themselves and their faith pure the ascetics found it necessary to withdraw from the world. In the beginning they were interested only in physical self-denial and purity, but in time they also developed an elaborate practice of inner or spiritual asceticism as well. Just as the first was intended to break the seductive hold of the world upon the ascetic, the latter sought to destroy even the hold of his thoughts, emotions, and desires and to discipline the inner life so that he might be free entirely to seek God.

Asceticism, however, is not necessarily in itself mystical. The self-denying disciplinary practices of the *zuhada'* soon took on a different coloring as they began to see the culmination of their flight from the world in the contemplation and love of God. Rabi'ah al-'Adawiyah (d. 801), a renowned woman who is looked upon as a kind of ideal mystic, gave eloquent expression to this all-consuming love in her prayers: "O God, if I worship Thee for fear of Hell, burn me in Hell, and if I worship Thee in hope of Paradise, exclude me from Paradise; but if I worship Thee for Thy own sake, grudge me not Thy everlasting beauty." Or again: "O God, whatsoever Thou hast apportioned to me of worldly things, do Thou give that to Thy enemies; and whatsoever Thou hast apportioned to me in the world to come, give that to Thy friends; for Thou sufficest me." [4]

4. A. J. Arberry, *Muslim Saints and Mystics*, London, Routledge, 1966, p. 51.

Sixteenth-century Iranian miniature from the Safawi period depicting Muhammad's ascent to Heaven. (Courtesy of the Seattle Art Museum.)

From these beginnings emerged a complex Sufi system of thought. It is perhaps paradoxical to call attention to mystical philosophies as an important aspect of mystical life in Islam, for to the Sufis it is not intellectual teaching but the actual experience of immediate intimacy with God that is the goal desired. The mystical reality is ineffable, utterly beyond the possibility to be expressed in words. Nevertheless, as part of their instruction to followers and disciples, Sufi masters found it necessary to give verbal expression to their goals and the means leading to them. The details differ with individual Sufis and schools, but in general all agree upon a spiritual pilgrimage that leads the devotee through ascending spiritual stages (*maqamat*) that are attainable by sheer human effort until the limit of man's self-perfectibility is reached. Thereafter the pilgrimage traverses a variety of states (*ahwal*) which are the gift of God's grace to those who seek him. The spiritual journey reaches its culmination and climax in *tawhid* or unification with God, an experience in which the mystic in some sense merges with the Divine Reality in the most intimate way. As one of the Sufis' favorite expressions states, the goal of the mystic quest is a "taste" of God's being. *Tawhid,* however, has a double aspect. On the one hand it is a passing away or disappearance of the devotee's personality and identity into that of God so that nothing remains of distinction between the two. For the mystic there is only God. Such snuffing out of the personality bears the name *fana',* a word used for extinguishing a fire, and it represents the absolute loss of the mystic's own identity, even to the renunciation of the desire for union with God itself. The goal, however, is not simply to attain *tawhid* but to sustain that state of ineffable blessedness; thus, on the other hand the peak experience of *fana'* is followed by *baqa',* remaining or subsisting in God as a permanent condition even though one may continue to be physically present in the world and attending to its mundane affairs. It is given to but few to make this arduous journey in full, but they, who are saints, live in unutterable bliss.

Sufi thought has exhibited differences of view at many points. For example, there are variant interpretations of the exact nature of unification, thinkers being divided in their opinion of how it takes place and whether and to what extent there remains any possibility of distinction between the mystic and God. Sufis also disagree on the metaphysical systems which they teach. Followers of Muhiy al-Din ibn al-'Arabi, a highly influential Andalusian mystic of the twelfth century, teach outright pantheism, that there is only one reality, God, who is the sum of all things. This view is echoed in the most famous of the Persian mystic poets, Jalal al-Din al-Rumi (d. 1273). Such a view was highly offensive to numerous Muslims otherwise sympathetic to Sufism, and there have been many to condemn it. Another polar question in discussions among Sufi theorists has been the mystic's attitude toward the observance of the *shari'ah.* While the great majority have held unswervingly to the need for observing all its injunctions as the first step on the mystic path, others have taught that the Sufi adept, having attained unification with God, is beyond good and evil and the need to bestow attention on the law. One prominent group has gone so far as deliberately to flaunt the *shari'ah* in order to incur the blame and censure of men as part of their renunciation of the world.

The earliest Sufis encountered considerable opposition from traditionalist Muslims, and the reasons are not far to seek. Not only were Sufi teachings innovations, departures from tradition, and equivalent, therefore, to heresy; but in their public utterances the Sufis were often guilty of radical statements that outraged traditionalist sensibilities. The best-known instances are those of Abu Yazid al-Bistami who reportedly said, "Glory be to me! How great is my glory!" and of al-Hallaj whose passionate utterance, "I am the Truth," brought about his crucifixion in 922. The reconciliation of Sufism with traditionalist Islam is commonly said to be the work of the great al-Ghazali. This man, who was a brilliant jurist, theologian, and philosopher, became a teacher in one of the religious schools established by the Saljuq rulers of Baghdad in the late eleventh century to combat the Isma'ili and other heresies. Although he found much success in his profession, al-Ghazali underwent a profound spiritual crisis that debilitated him both spiritually and physically. After several years of wandering and searching, the reintegration of his personality was achieved with his conversion to Sufism. His monumental work, *Ihya' 'Ulum al-Din* (*The Revivification of the Religious Sciences*), which embraces the full scope of the Islamic sciences, is thoroughly mystical in its basic orientation.

In the twelfth century still another dimension was added to Sufism with the introduction of organized Sufi brotherhoods. The first of those still surviving is reputed to have been found by 'Abd al-Qadir al-Jilani (d. 1166), and the so-called Qadariyah order continues to have many thousands of followers in different parts of the Islamic world even today. Other major orders also bear the names of the great mystics responsible for their foundation. A brotherhood is known as a *tariqah* (another word meaning road, path, way, or method, in this case to true knowledge of God) and is characterized by several distinguishing features, such as the belief in saints, possession of a peculiar ritual all its own, and a communal life.

The doctrine of the saints or friends of God (*walis*) is essential to later Sufism. Each *tariqah* takes its authority from a *silsilah* or chain of saints, every one of whom has received from his predecessor a store of esoteric knowledge which alone illuminates the means of attaining unity with God. Great importance is given to the chain of authority, and the orders are virtually unanimous in tracing their beginnings back to 'Ali ibn Abi Talib, though, of course, they diverge from this beginning. Because of his intimacy with the Prophet, 'Ali received instruction in the most profound mysteries not made known to others. The fundamental conception is that of a store of secret insight, a spiritual truth lying behind the externals of religion, spread through the world by a network of divinely chosen pious men. The bliss of union with the Divine Reality and the means toward it could never have been known but for God's grace in revealing them to his specially chosen "friends." For all others guidance in the exercises and spiritual discipline that lead to union with God must be had by association with the *wali* and subjecting oneself in obedience to his direction. A *wali* is a person who is himself of the highest spiritual attainment, and this penetration to the very Divine Being has conferred on him miraculous powers (*karamat*), by which he may be recognized. Even after death many of the *walis* are believed to retain their miracle-working ability. One of the most common expressions of popular Sufi piety is visitation at the tombs of great saints to bring gifts and to benefit from their blessedness (*barakah*) or to ask their miraculous help in solving some of the problems and difficulties of life. Tombs of Sufi saints are scattered throughout the Islamic lands, and some of them, like that of Mu'in al-Din Chishti at Ajmer in India, annually attract hundreds of thousands of pilgrims at celebrations in the saint's honor.

The doctrine of the saints has also taken the form of cosmological and metaphysical schemes among Sufi theorists. It is thought that there exists in the world at any given time a comprehensive hierarchy of saints whose many degrees and stages culminate in the highest spiritual authority who is called the *Qutb,* the pole or pivot. Whenever some member of the hierarchy passes away, he is replaced by another, so that the invisible spiritual structure of the universe remains always intact. These saints represent the means of the mediation of Divine Truth (*haqq*) in the world; they are literally the essential being and reality of things, the principle of wisdom and order without which there could be no existence at all. In this manner the cult of the saints is closely tied with the teachings of philosophy.

Just as the teaching of each Sufi brotherhood is in some degree different from that of others, so each also has its unique form of worship. The mystics refer to their worship as *dhikr*, remembering the Name of God, in obedience to a verse of the *Qur'an* that commands: "Remember God always." Typically the members of a brotherhood in a particular locality meet once each week for the celebration of the *dhikr,* which is the richest ceremonial known to the Islamic tradition. The ritual is based upon the continued repetition of a verbal formula that is different for each brotherhood. In some cases only the name of God, *"Allah,"* is spoken while others may chant, *"Allahu akbar"* ("God is most great!"), *"Subhan Allah"* ("Praise be to God!"), etc. Often the *dhikr* is accompanied by swaying movements of the Sufis who stand with arms linked, and its tempo tends to increase with the length of the repetition. The object of this form of devotion is to fix the mystic's mind on the unique reality of God so that all else is driven from the consciousness. Its climax is an ecstacy which to a greater or lesser degree for individuals approximates the desired union with the Divine Nature. Probably the best known *dhikr* in the Western world is that of the Mawlawiyah or so-called Whirling Dervishes of Turkey, the order founded by Jalal al-Din al-Rumi in the thirteenth century. Wearing a peculiar costume, the Mawlawi brothers perform a spectacular whirling dance, often around a pillar of the building where the *dhikr* is held. Another unusual aspect of this order's devotion is that the dance is accompanied by music, something that is normally considered against the tenets of religion by Muslims. The authentic Mawlawi *dhikr* can no longer be seen, however, for the order, like all others in Turkey, was abolished by law at the time of the Turkish Revolution in the 1920s.

Although Muslims have generally resisted anything resembling monasticism, the Sufi brotherhoods are marked by a strong communal life. Sufi adepts gather about themselves disciples and inquirers and establish a center from which the work of instruction and propagation and other activities of the order may be conducted. The resultant institution (Arabic *zawiyah;* Turkish *tekke;* Persian *khanqah*) somewhat resembles a monastery, though the Sufis may not always be resident there but rather engaged in the life of wandering mendicants. A Sufi leader of this kind is called a *pir, shaykh, murshid,* or *rahbar* while those who have been fully initiated into the lore of the order are known as *darwishes.* At the lowest level stand those who are only beginning the Sufi quest as inquirers, the *murids,* or seekers after knowledge. Life together affords the Sufis opportunity for association with the *shaykh* who is their source of guidance and allows him in turn to supervise their meditation and spiritual development. Each head of an order customarily chooses from among the most advanced *darwishes* one who shall be his *khalifah* to maintain the spiritual tradition of the brotherhood after the *shaykh*'s death. The Sufi *khanqahs* have historically also served important social functions. They have been places of resort for men in difficulty and in need of help. Not only advice and spiritual comfort but also food, shelter, medical attention, and sometimes even money were available to the needy under Sufi auspices. These centers were supported in part by contributions from lay people but more often by pious endowments which guaranteed a fixed income from agricultural land or some other such capital asset. In several notable instances the *shaykh* of an order has acted as a virtual ruler of the surrounding territory, being responsible for the maintenance of law and order and the well-being of the inhabitants. Such is the case with the well-known Sanusiyah order of North Africa which led the struggle for independence from Italian colonialism in the first part of this century. The Safawi dynasty, probably the most brilliant of the Islamic rulers in Iran, had its origin in a Sufi order of Ardabil in northwestern Iran, where the brothers organized themselves into a military fraternity about their *shaykh.* A close relationship is also to be discerned between the communal aspects of Sufism and the craft guilds and chivalrous organizations (*futuwah*) which were such vital institutions in the life of the medieval world.

At the present Sufism is passing through a period of decline, though it is still very much alive. The modernization of Islamic society has weakened virtually every one of its traditional institutions in a more or less radical way, and the Sufi brotherhoods are no exception. To many of those who are leaders of the struggle toward development and modernization Sufism has appeared as a villain in the recent history of the community. They see the Sufi cult of the saints, the visitation to tombs, and the belief in miracles as departures from true Islam and as reasons for the loss of spiritual vitality.

Furthermore, they consider Sufi cosmological and philosophical teachings to be obscurantist and to act as an impediment to the acceptance of progressive and scientific ways of understanding. Thus, there is virtual unanimity among the leadership, both intellectual and religious, in turning away from Sufi practice and condemning it.

THE SHI'AH AND THE SUNNIS

In a tradition popularly ascribed to the Prophet, Muhammad is alleged to have said, "My community will divide into seventy-three sects of which only one is correct." In fact, Islamic history has produced vastly more sectarian groupings than the traditional number of seventy-three. Muslims have been no less fruitful than other religious communities in multiplying their internal divisions. We have spoken above of some of the early sects, such as the Khawarij and the Murji'ah, but a catalogue of the whole is impossible because it would occupy us far beyond the space available.

One schism, however, is of such importance that particular attention must be paid to it. The Islamic community falls into two great divisions, the Sunnis (sometimes, and in our opinion erroneously, called "orthodox") and the Shi'ah. Sunni Muslims speak of themselves as *ahl al-sunnah wa al-jama'at,* the people of established custom and of the (genuine) community. Plainly this terminology carries a connotation of positive judgment; it amounts to a claim to be the living representatives and bearers of true Islam, of the practices, beliefs, and expressions that have consistently characterized the majority of the community throughout its history. Another way of explaining the Sunnis is to say that they see themselves as the traditionalists of the community, for their claim is to maintain the ways established by pious men of old. This notion of a living community which embodies and unfolds the divine guidance in its practice in continuingly relevant form is basic to the Islamic understanding of religious authority. In addition to continuity with the past, such a concept of the community provides a means for expanding the guidance to meet changed needs and conditions without compromising the fundamental belief in revelation.

The other great division of Muslims, the Shi'ah, date their origins from, at latest, the death of Muhammad and perhaps even earlier. The word *shi'ah* means party, and the group got its name from its partisanship for 'Ali, the cousin and son-in-law of Muhammad, in the early struggles for leadership in the community. Those who favored 'Ali believed that succession to Muhammad's role as ruler should remain within his family, the *ahl al-bayt* (people of the house) of whom the most qualified was clearly 'Ali. They justified their stand by citing traditions from Muhammad and even *Qur'an* verses where the Prophet is said to have designated 'Ali as his successor. Thus, they opposed the election of the first three *khalifahs,* whom to this day the Shi'ah consider as usurpers; and after the short and unsettled reign of 'Ali, which was brought to an end by a Khawarij assassin in 661, they took up the cause of his sons, Hasan and Husayn, as legitimate claimants to the leadership. In Arabic the word for leadership is *imamah,* and the exclusive claim to the *imamah* for Muhammad's family has been a cardinal Shi'i doctrine through history. Although at various times there have been Shi'i states in the Islamic world, the descendants of 'Ali were never successful in establishing their rule for any length of time.

From the very beginning, however, the political interests and claims of the Shi'ah were tinged by religious elements. Even during Muhammad's lifetime there were individuals who paid a degree of respect to 'Ali that was nothing short of pious. With time the religious concern of the Shi'ah strengthened and diversified, producing many sects and exhibiting great richness, particularly in theology and philosophy, but also in religious practice and piety. Gradually these more religious elements took the foremost place as the political ambitions of the Shi'ah were frustrated.

Among the religious elements peculiar to the Shi'ah the most important are the passion motif and the doctrine of the *imamah,* which are closely interrelated. The passion motif came into prominence around the history of 'Ali's younger son, Husayn. After 'Ali's murder, the Shi'ah looked to the elder son, Hasan, to take up his father's cause, but Hasan had no spirit for the struggle and resigned his claims to the caliphate. Thereupon, Husayn, the younger brother, launched into a campaign against the Ummawis in which he was pitted against hopelessly superior forces. Ultimately he and his family were trapped by Ummawi troops and killed in pitiable circumstances on the battlefield of Karbala' in southern 'Iraq. This tragic event occurred on the tenth day of the month of Muharram in A.H. 61 (A.D. 680), and the annual celebration of this tragedy is the most important festival of the year for Shi'ah Muslims. Husayn's martyrdom and the great role it has played in Shi'ah thought have introduced the elements of sorrow, suffering, of the just man unjustly killed, and of pious sacrifice into the Shi'i strain of Muslim religiosity. There is, thus, a warmth and emotional fervour in Shi'i religious life that is one of its most noteworthy characteristics. During the Muharram celebrations each year the story of Husayn is repeated by preachers and storytellers and dramatized in passion plays called *ta'ziyahs.* The Shi'ah march in processions where they exhibit symbols of the slain martyr while beating their breasts and wailing or engaging in self-inflicted flagellation. The occasion is one of great grief that purges the souls of the worshipers while at the same time it is cause for rejoicing in the salvation and guidance which Husayn's noble self-sacrifice has bestowed on the faithful. The passion motif is not tied exclusively to the events surrounding Husayn, however; rather the Shi'ah believe that all of their *imams* (see below) and other members of the holy family, including the Prophet himself, have suffered martyrdom at the hands of unjust men. In the passion plays, which often last for days, the history of these martyrdoms is traced in a recurring pattern while the worshipers mourn and weep. According to the Shi'ah most of the *imams* have died by poison, usually administered at the instigation of the *khalifahs* who usurped the *imam*'s rightful place of rule.

The word *imam* means simply a leader, and it is used for several purposes. The one who stands before the congregation to lead the prayer is called an *imam;* an especially learned man may also gain the title, as in the case of the founders of the four Sunni schools of law, or certain other distinguished individuals. Among the Shi'ah the word is invested with a meaning that goes far beyond the usual one, however. Upon Muhammad's death the Shi'ah believe that not only his function as ruler but also his role as religious guide devolved upon his descendants beginning with 'Ali. The divine guidance did not stop with the decease of the Prophet but continued to be shed in the world through his family, each of whom under divine direction, designated his successor in the *imamah* just as Muhammad had designated 'Ali. The series of visible *imams,* living openly in the world, however, came to an end with the mysterious disappearance of the last *imam.* For a time the *imam* retained contact with his followers through representatives who had direct access to him, but soon even this was broken off. The *imam* remains in the world but is hidden until he will come again at the end of time as the *Imam Mahdi* to establish the kingdom of God. Meanwhile the learned men of the Shi'i community act as interpreters of the divine will through their exercise of *ijtihad.* This doctrine gives a distinctive character to Shi'i religiosity, for the *imam* constitutes a living source of guidance in the world at all times. The importance of the doctrine is shown in the saying: "He who dies without knowing the *imam* of the age dies in unbelief."

The precise nature of the *imam* is understood differently by the numerous Shi'i sects, but the belief in the *imamah* is common to them all and is, indeed, their distinguishing characteristic. For the more extreme Shi'ah (the *ghulat*) the *imam* is considered as virtually an incarnation of God. There is a veritable indwelling of the divine spirit in the *imam* so that in knowing him one experiences the full reality of divine presence in the world. The *imam* is the localization of the supreme mystery and creative force that has brought the universe into being and that continues to sustain it. Should the *imam* ever be withdrawn, the entire order of reality would literally collapse because of the absence of its essential principle. Such a view of the *imam* is almost precisely parallel to the Sufi understanding of the *Qutb,* or great saint around whom the whole order of reality turns. At the other extreme of Shi'ah opinion, as for example among the Zaydi sect of the Yemen, the *imam* is considered only to be inspired or divinely led, much as the Prophet himself was. Between the two extremes stand the great majority of Shi'ah who hold a kind of doctrine of metempsychosis with respect to the *imams.* According to their understanding a spark of the eternal divine wisdom was implanted in Muhammad and upon his death was transplanted into 'Ali and from thence into the series of his descendants whom God has chosen. Although there is, thus, an element of the divine in each of the *imams,* there is not the complete indwelling in which the *ghulat* believe. In every case the importance accorded the *imam* in Shi'i thinking has radical implications for the understanding of religious authority, for so long as the *imam* is accessible either personally or through his representatives in the form of learned men, there is a living source of guidance always at hand.

There have been some differences among the Shi'ah also about the number of *imams* and their identity. The major distinction is between those who accept a series of seven and those who accept a series of twelve. They are called respectively the Seveners and the Twelvers or the Isma'ilis (after the last *imam* they recognize) and the Ithna 'Ashariyah (Arabic for "Twelvers"). Generally speaking, the Isma'ilis have been more radical in their views than the Twelvers. For a great part of Islamic history the Isma'ilis existed as secret societies which, in the effort to spread their creed among Muslims, engaged in revolutionary activities against established rulers and states, often, as in the case of the famous Assassins, using terrorism as one of their methods. Isma'ili propaganda gained impetus and support with the rise of the Fatimi dynasty of Egypt (969–1174) whose rulers reckoned themselves in the line of descent from Muhammad ibn Isma'il, the last *imam* of the Isma'ilis. The Fatimi state was, thus, self-consciously Isma'ili in its constitution, and the period of its ascendancy must be reckoned as among the most brilliant eras of Islamic history. The founding of modern Cairo, the establishment of the famous al-Azhar University in that city, and many other feats testify to the greatness of the Fatimis. Numerous subgroups of Isma'ilis continue to flourish at the present time, among which are included the Druze and Nusayris of Syria, and perhaps best known of all, the followers of the Agha Khan, the majority of whom are found in India and the areas around the Indian Ocean where Indians have immigrated. Isma'ilis are also sometimes known as Batiniyah (from *batin,* hidden) because they profess an esoteric teaching accessible only to those who have gained initiation to this secret knowledge. This esoteric teaching is an elaborate philosophy, strongly influenced by Neoplatonic and gnostic ideas, whose basis is a doctrine that everything in the external and visible world represents or prefigures on a small scale the realities (*haqa'iq*) of a spiritual and invisible world. Penetration beyond the external to knowledge of the spiritual realities is the aim of the teaching.

The Twelver Shi'ah are much more numerous than the Isma'ilis. At present they may be found spread over a great area with the majority concentrated in Iraq, where they are more than half the popu-

Koutoubya Minaret in Marrakesh, Morocco, as it looks today. The 220-foot minaret, built by the Andalusians, was completed in 1195. (Courtesy of Mr. and Mrs. S. C. Isler.)

lation, in Iran, and in the Indian subcontinent. Twelver Shi'ism received a great boost to its fortunes in the sixteenth century when the founders of the Safawi dynasty in Iran chose to make it the official religion of the state. It has continued to enjoy that favored status, and Iran is now the stronghold of the group. Although the principal Shi'i shrines are located at Najaf and Karbala in Iraq (the burial places of 'Ali and Husayn), Iran also has holy places and centers of pilgrimage in Mashhad and Qum where great theological schools maintain the tradition of Shi'i learning and teaching.

Apart from the doctrine of the *imamah*, the Shi'ah are also distinguished from the Sunnis in several other ways. There is a separate and distinct Shi'i *fiqh* which recognizes completely different authorities from those of the four "orthodox" Sunni schools. In actual content the rules of law differentiating Shi'ah and Sunni are small, being limited for the most part to minor details. The greatest variation arises in jurisprudential theory because of the preponderating role of the *imam* in Shi'i thinking and the continued Shi'i espousal of *ijtihad*. The Shi'ah also have their own distinctive collections of traditions such as the book entitled *Al-Kafi* (The Sufficient One) by al-Kulayni (d. 939) and others. One must not be misled by the word "Sunni" into thinking that the Shi'ah have any less reliance on the authority of tradition than their fellow Muslims; if anything, the contrary is the case, for the Shi'ah pay full respect to the sayings and reports of the men of old, though, to be sure, the authorities they recognize are not the same as for Sunnis. Another important area of difference between the two major groups lies in the area of theology. On the whole the Shi'ah have inclined in a far more rationalistic direction than has Sunni Islam. Much of the doctrine of the Mu-'tazilah has survived among the Shi'ah, and in their theological method they show a preference for rational argument above traditionalist views. No doubt, the inclination to rationalism accounts in large part for the great richness in philosophy, theology and speculative science generally among the Shi'ah.

At various times in Islamic history there has been sharp conflict between Shi'ah and Sunni over both political and religious issues. Even today in Lebanon, India, and Pakistan, for example, civil tranquillity is sometimes marred by altercations between the groups, especially at the time of the Muharram celebrations when Shi'i fervor is at its highest. These unfortunate conflicts should be seen, however, against the background of the strong Islamic sense of community and the feeling of kinship among all who belong to it, no matter what their differences. As great as the disagreements may be between Sunnis and Shi'ah, they have not shattered the *ummah*'s sense of its own distinctiveness and unity. In modern times in particular, because of the pressures of outside forces and ideologies, there has been a determined effort to play down the divisive effect of religious differences and to recapture the community's sense of oneness.

ISLAM IN MODERN TIMES

The modern period of Islamic history has been marked by a reawakening of the Muslim peoples that has touched their lives in virtually
every sphere of activity, including the religious. Underlying this new
dynamic are a pervasive and profoundly disturbing sense that something has gone wrong with the community's life and a determination
to rectify it. Preceding the reawakening was a long period of relative decline which saw the Muslim nations outstripped and then
dominated by the rising civilization of Western Europe, and it is this
fact, together with some elements internal to the community, that
has created the sense of crisis and malaise. A once proud and brilliant people whose religious faith assured them of worldly success
in addition to future reward had become the pawns of others. How
was this disaster to be explained, and what was to be done about
it? Contemplating these questions has produced a ferment among
Muslims that has led to searching examination of traditional modes
of life, to reforms, and to political revitalization.

In the seventeenth century there were three great Islamic empires
in existence, each exercising an important influence in the world. In
comparison with the small states of divided Europe, still in the early
stages of their modern evolution, Islamic power represented a massive force that seemed secure in the control of its own destiny and
which for a time threatened even to engulf Eastern Europe. As late
as 1683 a great Ottoman army stood before the gates of beseiged
Vienna, and it required the combined powers of a number of East
European princes to turn it away. These three empires, the Ottoman
in Turkey and the Mediterranean Basin, the Safawi in Persia, and
the Mughal in India, were each culturally creative as well as militarily strong.

By the nineteenth century, however, the situation had changed
radically for the worse in the Muslim lands. The great Safawi dynasty, whose era saw the flowering of some of the finest elements in
Persian culture, art, and thought, had succumbed to fissiparous ten-

dencies and to the attacks of wild Afghan tribesmen. The Ottoman Turks who only shortly before had been the masters of the Eastern Mediterranean were now recognized as the "Sick Man of Europe," overpowered by the diplomacy or the outright military might of the rising Western powers. Throughout the nineteenth century and climaxing in the revolution of the 1920s, Turkey struggled desperately with a series of reforms and political experiments designed to restore her power and to insure her growth as a modern nation. With the death in 1707 of its last great ruler, Awrangzeb, the Mughal Empire began the long slide toward its eventual destruction. Bitter wars of succession shattered its unity and fostered the growing influence of the empire's Maratha and Sikh rivals. By 1800 the British were the strongest power in the subcontinent, and they put an end to even the fiction of Mughal sovereignty in 1858 after the great Indian Mutiny by incorporating India directly into the British Empire and declaring Queen Victoria to be her sovereign.

This decline in imperial strength coincided with the emergence of European colonialism that resulted in outright European rule over vast regions of the Islamic world. In the 1860s and 70s the armies of the Tsars overran Islamic Central Asia and brought the region permanently within the Russian sphere. The peoples of the area were able briefly again to reassert their independence after the Russian Revolution of 1917, but the Bolsheviks soon broke the Khanates and brought them within the Soviet system. The Dutch who had gained a commercial foothold in Indonesia from an early time ruled the islands of the archipelago with a firm hand. The British were established in Egypt, in addition to India, after 1882, and they exercised control as well in Adan at the southern entrance to the Red Sea, in the Persian Gulf, along the southern coasts of Arabia, and in Malaya. In an elaborate diplomacy aimed at keeping the borders of their Indian Empire safe from Russian encroachment, the British also wielded considerable influence, involving coercion at times, upon the rulers of Persia and of Afghanistan. French military activity in North Africa had given them control of Morocco after 1830, and their intense rivalry with the British for the upper hand in Egypt led them eventually to extend their sphere in the Maghrib until it included also Algeria and Tunisia. As a result of Turkey's decisive defeat in World War I, the eastern Arab regions also fell under European hegemony. The system established by the Sykes-Picot Agreement (1916) divided Greater Syria between the French and the British and allowed to Britain a kind of tutelage over Iraq. In short, there was no important region of the Islamic world that was untouched by European power or safe from European colonialism. To even the most uninstructed observer, Muslim political, military, and economic weakness was abundantly evident. The decline in worldly power was accompanied also by disruption of traditional institutions and social forms as a result of reform measures, by a dependence upon authority in the religious sphere, and by a degree of cultural stagnation. As Muslims became increasingly aware of the state to which they had fallen, partially through the efforts of a series of brilliant leaders who emerged in the last quarter of the nineteenth century, there was a gradual reawakening that first centered in efforts at religious reform but in its later phases turned increasingly to political and secularist alternatives.

The earliest efforts at religious reforms in the modern period were not, however, a response to the impact of the West as an external force but seem rather to have been the result of Islamic awareness of internal decay. The outstanding instances are the Wahhabi movement of Arabia and the activities of Shah Waliyullah of Delhi and his disciples. The Wahhabis are so called after Muhammad ibn 'Abd al-Wahhab (1703–1792), who launched the movement. This man traveled widely in the Near East and devoted himself to religious studies at several leading Islamic centers of learning, including those in Iraq and Iran where Shi'i views were propagated. Eventually he came to hold a very strict view of Islam that most closely resembled the position of the classical traditionist, Ahmad ibn Hanbal. 'Abd al-Wahhab was outraged by what seemed to him the great corruption of pure Islamic teaching that had come about in the course of time, and he set out to purify the body politic of these foreign and debilitating elements. His particular wrath fell upon practices associated with Sufi worship, especially the cult of the saints. He condemned the building of mausoleums, the visitations to saints' tombs, the bringing of gifts, the invocation of saints' names in prayer, the belief that saints might intercede for their devotees or otherwise assist them, and the doctrine that the saints possess special means of communication with the divine. Coupled with this attempt to return to a more pristine Islam was a strong puritanism that would use the power of the authorities to enforce performance of the prayer and to forbid such un-Islamic practices as drinking and smoking tobacco. To 'Abd al-Wahhab it seemed that the Muslims had forsaken the path of true religion; his was, thus, not a reform movement but an effort to restore or revive the genuine Islam of the earliest generation, the faith that had brought success, strength, and spiritual blessing to the early community.

The movement, whose strict teachings in themselves attracted many who were concerned about the state of the community's life, took on added significance when a cooperative relationship was contracted between the founder and the Su'ud family of Arabia. Under the leadership of the Su'udis the sect came into armed conflict with other tribesmen in Arabia, and the military strength of the Wahhabis grew steadily until by the turn of the nineteenth century they were in actual control of large areas of Arabia proper, of Syria, and Iraq. The revivalist zeal was given a military and political expression. Apprehending a danger to their suzerainty, the Ottomans took vigorous steps to suppress the sect; an expedition was despatched under Muhammad 'Ali Pasha, the ruler of Egypt, to recapture the holy cities of Islam and subdue the Wahhabis. There were important victories in 1812 and 1813 for the Egyptians, and in 1818 a second Egyptian expedition under Ibrahim Pasha put an end to the first phase of the Wahhabi empire by capturing their headquarters at Dar'iyah. The sect did not disappear, however, but by slow degrees reestablished its rule over the regions around the Persian

Gulf and some of the interior parts of Arabia. It gained a new lease on life in 1901 when 'Abd al-'Aziz ibn Su'ud captured the city of Riyadh and reestablished the Su'udi dynasty, which rules Arabia to this day. The dynasty has officially espoused Wahhabism and the strict teachings of the school of Ahmad ibn Hanbal, but in the years since World War II it has evidenced considerable flexibility in encouraging the modernization of the country and its intercourse with foreign states. The major factor in this change is the economic upswing following the discovery and exploitation of enormous petroleum resources in the eastern portion of the country. Nevertheless Wahhabism is the foremost attempt at Islamic revival that the modern world has witnessed, and it has had repercussions in every Islamic land.

The life of Shah Waliyullah (1703–1762) of Delhi coincided with the beginning of the Mughal decline. As a child he witnessed the fratricidal wars of succession among the sons and heirs of Awrangzeb and saw the power of the emperor eroded until the ruler scarcely exercised authority over the capital city, Delhi, itself. Shah Waliyullah has been called the "thinker of crisis," for it was in his day that the Muslims of India had for the first time to face the fact that they could no longer live in the subcontinent as its rulers. With the rise of indigenous Indian powers on one hand and Western colonialism on the other, the former custodians of Islamic greatness in India were doomed to play a lesser role. Waliyullah responded to the challenge of the time by launching a campaign of Islamic revival. In its negative aspects, like Wahhabism, it was concerned with purifying Islamic practice of historical accretions that had robbed the Muslims of their vitality and obscured the genuine faith. For an Indian Muslim the principal target of concern was a great variety of Hindu customs that Muslims had inevitably adopted through their centuries long association with their Hindu fellow countrymen. Waliyullah was also opposed to the excesses of Sufi thought and practice, but his attitude was less rigorous than that of the Wahhabis, and he himself was a Sufi adept who used certain Sufi institutions to forward his cause. The principal means of realizing his program of revitalizing Indian Islam was teaching. He gathered about himself in a *madrasah,* or theological school, founded by his father in Delhi a variety of disciples and imparted his views on Islam to them. A list of impressive works came from his pen, wherein he set out an interpretation of Islamic doctrine that was dynamic and which sought to resolve many of the religious issues that had spawned disunity among the Indian Muslims. Through a series of letters he also strove to awaken in the decadent Mughal nobility some sense of responsibility toward salvation of the Islamic cause in the subcontinent. In his view the matter of primary concern was to restore Muslim hegemony in a deteriorating situation, and to this end he initiated correspondence with Muslim rulers in Afghanistan and Iran, whom he besought to intervene in India on behalf of the Islamic cause. Both politically and religiously the vision of society he labored to realize was that of a restored and strengthened medieval Islam.

The result of his effort was a greatly increased consciousness among Muslims of their Islamicness and of its implications. A continuing stream of disciples propagated and worked out his ideas in the years that followed his death. His four sons in particular were instrumental in passing on his influence, and one of them, Shah 'Abd al-'Aziz, provided the religious and intellectual stimulus to a major movement in the Frontier area in the first decades of the nineteenth century. The movement, sometimes called Indian Wahhabism because of its similarity to the program of revival of 'Abd al-Wahhab but more properly known as the Mujahidin, recruited Muslims and collected funds all over India for the conduct of an armed struggle in the Frontier and Panjab to reestablish Muslim power against the Sikhs. Eventually the Mujahidin came into conflict with the British, and their principal leaders were killed at the Battle of Balakot in 1831. Remnants of the movement persisted and continued to have influence, however, throughout the century. The many Islamic movements of the Indian subcontinent in the nineteenth and twentieth centuries all owe some debt to Shah Waliyullah, who first called forth a new burst of interest in what it means to be a Muslim. The thrust of his efforts was toward the purification and reestablishment of the ancient ideal that had guided the community in the past, but at the same time his teachings offered a dynamic and provided principles that others have used to build a more modern interpretation of Islam.

Of greater relevance to recent times are those religious reformers whose thought appears to be a direct response to the threatening impact of Western Europe upon Islamic society. They are called Muslim modernists, in contrast to Muslim revivalists or fundamentalists such as 'Abd al-Wahhab and Shah Waliyullah, because their principal purpose has been to demonstrate the viability and relevance of Islam in the modern world. Islamic modernism has been a powerful force that has affected governing and intellectual classes in every Islamic country and that continues today as one of the important alternatives for Muslims who face the problems of modernity.

We may gain some understanding of Islamic modernism by looking at one of its most important and influential representatives, the Egyptian savant Muhammad 'Abduh (1849–1905). 'Abduh came from humble beginnings in a lower Egyptian village and showed an early bent toward mysticism. His life, however, was oriented in a radically new direction from the year 1872, when he came into contact with the fiery Jamal al-Din al-Afghani (1839–1897), whom he quickly espoused as his master. Al-Afghani is one of the towering individuals of modern Islamic history, an indefatigable worker for the liberation of Muslims from European dominance, who traveled extensively throughout the Islamic world and Europe preaching the need for Islamic unity and the requirement of a revived Islam as the key to renewed Muslim strength. Al-Afghani's powerful personality left a legacy of ferment throughout the Islamic regions, but he did not possess the qualities of a systematic thinker and wrote but little outside the journalistic field. It was 'Abduh who gave intellectual expression to the bases of a modern Islamic religious reform in a series of lectures, articles, and books. In his later life 'Abduh held a number of important posts in Egypt, as Chief Mufti (consultant on Islamic law), as member of the Superior Council of the leading institution of religious learning, the Azhar University, and as member of the Legislative Council which was Egypt's first step toward representative political institutions. These places of influence allowed him the opportunity to put many of his ideas and theories into practice. Even after his death his ideas continued to be vigorously propagated—with some new interpretation, to be sure—by his disciple Rashid Rida in the journal *Al-Manar.*

Like al-Afghani, 'Abduh was interested primarily in the liberation of the Muslims and the regaining of their vitality and strength. The desired end, he felt, could be achieved through Islam's own resources by restoring it to its original purity. Thus the solution to the modern dilemna of Muslims was to be found in a return to religion and its purification. Since in his opinion no civilization could flourish whose moral foundations were not firm, the central place in the rehabilitation of Muslim fortunes had to be given to religion. Unlike some conservative Muslims who opposed him bitterly, 'Abduh welcomed the changes which European influence had wrought in Egyptian society, as, for example, in the revolutionary reforms of Muhammad 'Ali Pasha at the beginning of the nineteenth century. He considered such developments to be an inevitable part of modernity, and the problem for one concerned in preserving the Islamic spiritual heritage was to bring such changes within an Islamic framework. This 'Abduh did by demonstrating that the essential element of Islam is its rationality and its faithfulness to the reality of things. Thus, he held that science, which, in common with all the modernists, he identified as the secret of European success, was a genuinely Islamic activity, the extension into practical affairs of the very spirit that lay at the heart of Islamic commitment. The generation of modernists who had preceded him had argued negatively, that science is not incompatible with Islamic faith; 'Abduh passed from this defensive stance vis-à-vis European thought to take the offensive by proclaiming that Islam is the very origin and inspiration of science, even of the science of Westerners, who had made their first steps in its direction under the influence and tutelage of Arab thinkers from classical Islamic times. In similar fashion he proclaimed the progressiveness of Islam and its inherent flexibility which permitted accommodation even of its law to the changing circumstances of human life. 'Abduh conducted an uncompromising polemic against the doctrine of *taqlid,* or of the obligation to follow blindly the teachings of one of the four accepted schools of law, calling instead for the reopening of the gates of *ijtihad,* for the right of exercise of personal judgment, and for a new *ijma'* in the community that would approximate the function of legislation in modern society. In the latter teaching 'Abduh exhibits a general characteristic of Islamic modernism to equate traditional Islamic concepts with institutions or values of modern times. 'Abduh also joined battle with Christianity in a sharp polemic aimed at upholding the superiority of Islam and putting down, once and for all, any suggestion that Europe's dominance might be attributable to Christianity or the weakness of Muslims due to faults in their fundamental conception of the world. His views on such traditional theological doctrines as free-will and the concept of prophecy reflect his bias toward a rationalistic interpretation of Islam. In many respects his foremost theological treatise, *Risalat al-Tawhid* may be seen as an attempt to rehabilitate the status of the long despised Mu'tazilah of a previous time. Conscious always of the European threat to Islam looming somewhere over the horizon, 'Abduh wrote, spoke, and worked for the betterment of Muslim fortunes through a revival of the true and genuine Islam. What is notable about his stance, and that of virtually every other modernist, is the steadfast refusal, however, to grant any shortcoming or deficiency in original and genuine Islam, whose truth he held to be enduringly valid. Although he admitted change in the social sphere and, indeed, welcomed it from an Islamic perspective, neither he nor his disciples saw any need for reconstruction or reformulation in the fundamentals of Islamic faith.

Many of 'Abduh's ideas were echoed in other parts of the Islamic world by men acting either independently or under his or similar influence. Very like notions may be read, for example, in the writings of Sir Sayyid Ahmad Khan (1817–1898), the founder of the 'Aligarh Muslim University in India, or in stronger and more exaggerated expression in the famous book of Sayyid Amir 'Ali (1849–1928), *The Spirit of Islam,* which has been called the Bible of Islamic modernism. In greater or lesser degree modernist Islam, in all its many contexts, has a unity in showing the following characteristics: (1) a strong sense of dynamism, i.e., that the meaning of Islam in modern times is a call to action; (2) a need to counter explicit or implicit criticism of Islam arising out of the Western impact; (3) a preference for rational methods in the interpretation of religious doctrine with a tendency to deny supernatural, legendary, or miraculous elements in the tradition; (4) a romantic interpretation of Islamic history, particularly of the earliest generations, that is part of the general defense of Islam; (5) an insistence upon the agreement between Islamic teachings and those of science; (6) a preoccupation with the personality of the Prophet and a tendency to exalt his moral and intellectual qualities; (7) the identification of Islamic teaching with liberal and humanitarian values compatible to the present age; (8) an anti-Sufi attitude which looks upon later Islamic mysticism as obscurantist and the partial cause of Muslim weakness; and (9) a rejection of the authority of the medieval legal schools and a refusal to adhere to their methods. In this body of teachings the modernists offer massive reassurance to the contemporary Muslim who in this light finds his spiritual heritage to be more than capable of meeting his needs as a modern man.

Far from dissolving in the acids of modernity, Islam has gained a new grasp on life; indeed, the resurgence of the Muslim peoples in every sphere, not the religious alone, is one of the principal facts of the twentieth century. In the period since the close of World War II one Islamic country after the other has thrown off foreign domination and gained its independence. The only major region still controlled by non-Muslim power is Soviet Central Asia where Islam is rapidly disappearing among the younger generation under the relentless pressure brought to bear upon it. In other countries, however, such as Pakistan, which emerged as a separate state for Muslims after the British departure from India and the partition of the subcontinent in 1947, there have been sustained attempts to work out the implications of Islamic commitment for social and political life. Islam is entering upon a new stage in its history, one in which its expression is taking new forms and where it faces novel problems, but as the spiritual cradle of a major portion of mankind it continues to provide a satisfying answer to men's deepest needs.

The most important reference work for students of Islam is the *Encyclopædia of Islam* in its various editions. The original edition, consisting of four volumes and a supplement, was edited by M. T. Houtsma (Leyden, E. J. Brill, 1913–1938). The encyclopedia is in process of republication in a completely revised and expanded form under the title *Encyclopædia of Islam, New Edition,* edited by H. A. R. Gibb and J. H. Kramers (Leyden, E. J. Brill, 1960–   ). Two volumes and most of the fascicles for the third have appeared by the time of this writing. There also exists a *Shorter Encyclopædia of Islam* (Leyden, E. J. Brill, 1953), edited by H. A. R. Gibb and J. H. Kramers. This volume contains articles on religion taken from the new edition of the larger encyclopedia.

BIBLIOGRAPHY
General
Works

The best guides to periodical literature on Islam are:

Pearson, J. D., and Julia F. Ashton, eds., *Index Islamicus, 1906–1955,* Cambridge, Heffer, 1958.

Pearson, J. D., ed., *Index Islamicus Supplement, 1956–1960,* Cambridge, Heffer, 1962.

The best currently available general work on Islam is H. A. R. Gibb's *Mohammedanism* (New York, Oxford, 1949, reprinted 1950; now also available in paperback). For general reading the following are also recommended:

Lammens, Henri, *Islam Beliefs and Institutions,* trans. E. D. Ross, London, Methuen, 1929.

Levy, Reuben, *The Social Structure of Islam,* New York, Cambridge, 2nd rev. ed., 1957; also available in paperback.

Von Grunebaum, G. E., *Mediæval Islam,* Chicago, The University of Chicago Press, 1953; also available in paperback.

The following anthologies of Islamic writers are useful:

Jeffrey, Arthur, ed., *Islam: Muhammad and His Religion,* New York, Liberal Arts, paperback ed., 1958.

———, ed., *A Reader on Islam,* New York, Humanities Press, 1962.

Schroeder, Eric, ed., *Muhammad's People,* Freeport, Me., Bond Wheelwright, 1955.

Williams, John A., *Islam,* New York, George Braziller, Inc., 1961; paperback ed., New York, Washington Square Press, 1961.

Pre-Islamic
Arabia

Much of the writing in this field is highly specialized, but the student of Islam can gain information on things important for his purposes from the following:

Izutsu, Toshihiko, *The Structure of the Ethical Terms in the Koran,* Tokyo, Keio Institute of Philological Studies, 1959.

Lewis, Bernard, *The Arabs in History,* London, Hutchinson, 1950; paperback ed., New York, Harper & Row, 1966. A short but splendid volume.

Nicholson, Reynold A., *A Literary History of the Arabs,* New York, Cambridge, 1953; also available in paperback.

Muhammad
the Prophet

The most important sourcebook in English is *The Life of Muhammad* translated by Alfred Guillaume (London, Oxford, 1955; also available in paperback). This volume is a translation of the most important Arabic biography of the Prophet; the original is the work on which all biographical studies of Muhammad depend.

The best modern biography and study of Muhammad is to be had in the works of W. Montgomery Watt, *Muhammad at Mecca* and *Muhammad at Medina,* both published by the Clarendon Press at Oxford, in 1953 and 1956 respectively.

The Qur'an

The translation of the *Qur'an* that best renders the traditional Muslim understanding of the text is Marmaduke Pickthall's *The Meaning of the Glorious Koran* (Hyderabad, Dakkan, 1938; paperback ed., New York, New American Library, 1953). Those interested in a translation of high literary quality and in the interpretations of modern scholarship should consult A. J. Arberry's two-volume work *The Koran Interpreted* (London, G. Allen, 1955; paperback ed., New York, Macmillan).

The foremost critical study of the *Qur'an* in English is R. E. Bell's *Introduction to the Qur'ān* (Edinburgh, Edinburgh University Press, 1953.)

For an exacting study of the *Qur'an*'s teaching two books by Toshihiko Izutsu are recommended: *Ethico-Religious Terms in the Qur'ān* (Montreal, Institute of Islamic Studies, 1967) and *God and Man in the Koran* (Tokyo, Keio Institute of Cultural and Linguistic Studies, 1964).

The Prophetic
Tradition

The only complete translation of one of the *sahih* books is in French:

Houdas, O., and W. Marçais, *Les traditions islamiques,* 3 vols., Paris, Imprimerie Nationale, 1903–1914.

Selections from the *hadith* can be found in the second edition of Muhammad Ali's *A Manual of Hadith* (Lahore, Ahmadiyyah Anjuman Isha'at Islam, n.d.).

The best critical work in English on the *hadith* is Alfred Guillaume's *The Traditions of Islam* (Oxford, Clarendon Press, 1924).

Kalam,
or Theology

The writing in this field is not as far advanced as one might like, but the following can be recommended as introductions to a vast and complex subject:

MacDonald, Duncan Black, *Development of Muslim Theology, Jurisprudence, and Constitutional Theory,* New York, Scribner, 1903.

Watt, W. Montgomery, *Islamic Philosophy and Theology,* Islamic Surveys Vol. 1, Edinburgh, Edinburgh University Press, 1962.

Wensinck, A. J., *The Muslim Creed,* New York, Cambridge, 1932.

Those who are interested in studying an original piece of Islamic theological writing in detail should peruse Walter Klein's translation of Al-Ash'ari's *Al-Ibānah 'an Usūl al-Diyānah* (New Haven, American Oriental Society, 1940).

The following are the best introductory works for this highly technical subject: The Law

Coulson, Noel J., *A History of Islamic Law,* Islamic Surveys Vol. 2, Edinburgh, Edinburgh University Press, 1964.

Schacht, Joseph, *An Introduction to Islamic Law,* Oxford, Clarendon Press, 1964.

Books by missionaries constitute the best introductory sources for   The Shi'ah
information on the Shi'ah. The two books by the following are especially good:

Donaldson, Dwight M., *The Shi'ite Religion,* London, Luzac and Co., 1933.

Hollister, John N., *The Shi'a of India,* London, Luzac and Co., 1953.

The best general work in English on this subject is *Sufism* by A. J.   Sufism
Arberry (London, G. Allen, 1950). There is a fine anthology of Sufi ideas and writing in Margaret Smith's *The Sūfī Path of Love* (London, Luzac and Co., 1954). Those who wish first-hand acquaintance with a basic Sufi work should consult Reynold A. Nicholson's translation of *Kashf al-Maḥjūb* by Al-Hujwiri (London, Luzac and Co., 1911).

The literature on this subject is vast and grows with each passing   The Modern
day. A good introduction to the nature of modern Islamic develop-   Period
ment may be had from the following:

Berkes, Niyazi, *The Development of Secularism in Turkey,* Montreal, McGill University Press, 1964.

Gibb, H. A. R., *Modern Trends in Islam,* Chicago, The University of Chicago Press, 1947.

Hourani, Albert, *Arabic Thought in the Liberal Age, 1798–1939,* New York, Oxford, 1962.

Smith, Wilfred Cantwell, *Islam in Modern History,* Princeton, N.J., Princeton University Press, 1957.

See the chapter "Islam" in Charles J. Adams, ed., *A Reader's Guide*   Additional
to the Great Religions, New York, Free Press, 1965.   Bibliography

PART SIX

THE PRESENT AND FUTURE OF RELIGION
W. RICHARD COMSTOCK

Religions are not static entities, existing in a state of immoble perfection outside time and history. Religions are cultural phenomena that exist *in* time; and to exist in time is to change, to be in process, to grow, develop, and be transformed. Religion, as part of the human process, exhibits such capacity for change and transformation.

The phenomena that we call religion do not present us with settled answers. On the contrary, whether the reader is a member of one of the existing communities that comprise the historic religions of man or is a neutral observer viewing them from the "outside," he will find that these religions present him with certain pressing problems that remain to be solved. Two questions are particularly pressing. The first is the problem of the relation of historic religions to one another; the second is the relation of historic religions to the rise of scientific and technological cultures in both Eastern and Western countries.

THE PRESENT AND FUTURE OF RELIGION

So long as a given society is in relative isolation from its neighbors, it remains concerned primarily with its indigenous symbols and rites. The problem of relationship among religions only becomes a dominant issue when there is communication and interaction among a number of cultures.

We have already noted that during the expansion of Rome into a world power, interest in the problem of religion increased and the comparison of religions of various cultures became a vital intellectual issue. At a later period, contact between the medieval Christian civilization of Europe and the civilization of Islam generated some interest in the problem of how those two great religions—Christianity and Islam—were related. Finally, the development of efficient transportation, extensive trade, and rapid systems of communication in the post-medieval world has created a sharper awareness of the existence of a number of impressive religious systems as parts of the interacting cultures of the contemporary world.

This problem of the relationships of the world religions to each other is, of course, of greatest concern to those who are a part of one of the historic religious traditions [1] and who must thus face the question of the significance of the presence of other religious traditions in the history of mankind. A number of options are open.

First is the stance that we may call *exclusivism*. According to this

---

1. See Part One, The Historical Forms of Religion, for the meaning of the term "historic religions."

view only one religion is true or valid and the others are false or misguided. Some representatives of this view can be found in every religion.

A second possibility is the argument that one religion is the fulfillment of what is best and true in the others. We might call this view a *teleological* one. Thus, some Christian theologians have argued that other religions have contained aspects of truth that are most clearly revealed in Christianity. Or again, since, of the major religions, Islam has most recently appeared in history, many Muslims argue that Judaism and Christianity are not false religions, but rather were preparations for the final revelation of Muhammad.

A third option might be called *pluralism.* According to this view, the various religions are diverse paths leading to a single goal, just as many different roads can ascend a mountain from different sides and finally meet at the top. The historian Arnold Toynbee adopts this view when he declares: "I believe that all the higher religions, and indeed, religions of all kinds, have in common an inkling of an identical truth about Reality and of an identical goal of salvation for human beings." [2] This pluralism can take several forms. It might assert, as we have noted, that all religions have an identical goal. Another possibility is the belief that each religion is valid according to its own terms and concerns, even though it has a different purpose from the others. Those who take this approach recognize that the generic term "religion" misleads one into looking for a common essence of religion, when in fact each religious system may be doing something different from the others.

In the eighteenth century the philosopher G. E. Lessing illustrated the dilemma of pluralism with an interesting parable in his play *Nathan the Wise.* According to the story, a sultan had three sons. As the sultan approached death, each son desired the father's opal ring, which possessed magic power and was a symbol of the sultan's authority. The sultan loved all his sons and did not know how to decide which of the three should have his ring. He finally decided on the following plan. He had two counterfeit rings made that duplicated the appearance of the original in every way. Each son was given one of the three rings, and after the father's death each claimed that he had received the authentic ring. After much tension, the sons went to a wise man who gave the following advice:

> . . . My counsel is:
> Accept the matter wholly as it stands.
> If each one from his father has his ring,
> Then let each one believe his ring to be
> The true one.—Possibly the father wished
> To tolerate no longer in his house
> The tyranny of just one ring!—And know:
> That you, all three, he loved; and loved alike;
> Since two of you he'd not humiliate
> To favor one.—Well then! Let each aspire
> To emulate his father's unbeguiled,

2. Arnold Toynbee, *Reconsiderations,* New York, Oxford, 1961, p. 100.

Left, a religious artifact of man's archaic past, the Megalithic stone pillars of Stonehenge in Wiltshire, England. (Photo by Bis, from Monkmeyer Press Photo Service.) Right, one conception of a religious artifact of man's technological future, the monolith from Stanley Kubrick's film 2001: A Space Odyssey. (©1968. Metro-Goldwyn-Mayer, Inc.)

Unprejudiced affection! Let each strive
To match the rest in bringing to the fore
The magic of the opal in his ring!
Assist that power with all humility,
With benefaction, hearty peacefulness,
And with profound submission to God's will!
And when the magic powers of the stones
Reveal themselves in children's children's children:
I bid you, in a thousand thousand years,
To stand again before this seat. For then
A wiser man than I will sit as judge
Upon this bench, and speak.[3]

Lessing's play and the parable therein took as their subject the medieval world, which was very much concerned with the relation among three basic religions: Judaism, Christianity, and Islam. Clearly, many more "rings" are to be considered today, now that Western man and Eastern man have become increasingly aware of each other's religious traditions.

A fourth option advocated by many religious thinkers and scholars might be characterized as *dialogic interaction.* Those who take this view consider it premature to decide whether all religions are "one," essentially diverse, or whether one is superior to the others. What is desirable, rather, is that members of each religion learn how to communicate with members of other religions. The point of dialogue is neither to attack another nor to repudiate the distinctive claims of one's own orientation, but to learn the art of listening. Perhaps through the act of dialogue and creative openness to each other, say the advocates of this view, religions will grow in unexpected ways and their future relationship may be different from that anticipated now.

3. G. E. Lessing, *Nathan the Wise,* New York, Ungar, 1955, pp. 79–80.

An even more pressing problem than the relationship among religions is that generated by the encounter of the historic religions with modern secular and technological civilization. The term secularism is as elusive and many-faceted as the term religion. The word secular is derived from a Latin root that means "this age" or "this world." It is usually used to refer to the worldly order, as contrasted with a sacred order. In early Christian and medieval thought, we find references to the secular activities of this world contrasted with sacred activities directly oriented toward God and the divine order of existence. The artisan and the farmer perform "secular" tasks, while the priest, who has been consecrated, is considered to pursue a "sacred" vocation.

With the breakdown of medieval society in the West, a new set of meanings became attached to the word secular. If we agree to use the word "modern" to refer to the new form of cultural and political life that emerged in Western Europe from the fifteenth century to the nineteenth century, we can say that during the early part of this modern period the word secular took on the meaning of freedom from the influence, authority, and direction of the Christian Church and other religious groups oriented toward the sacred order of existence. As Peter L. Berger puts it, "by secularization we mean the process by which sections of society and culture are removed from the domination of religious institutions and symbols." [4]

In the early modern period this "liberation" took primarily three forms. The first was the liberation of politics from Church authority and control. This movement was closely allied with the rise of nationalism. Many of the new nations of Europe and America became secular in the sense that they insisted that the political order be in no way subject to the authority of the Church. In the United States the principle of "separation of church and state" is a clear example of secular liberation.

The second form of liberation was economic. The Middle Ages were dominated by a feudal economy over which the Church had sizable influence. Many theologians promulgated laws on usury, interest, and trade that had an important effect upon the society as a whole. In the early modern period, the advocates of new forms of economic activity, particularly capitalism, insisted on their freedom from Church authority and control and to that extent affirmed a secular stance.

The third aspect of secular liberation was the emergence of modern science in the fifteenth and sixteenth centuries. Copernicus (1473–1543), Galileo (1564–1642), Kepler (1571–1630), and Newton (1642–1727) were among the pioneers who established the model of scientific investigation that has dominated the modern world. The work of these men and others produced a major scientific advance that was due partly to developments in mathematics, partly to the invention of new instruments of observation, and partly to increased sophistication in methodology, whereby scien-

4. Peter L. Berger, *The Sacred Canopy*, Garden City, N.Y. Doubleday, 1969, p. 107.

tists adhered to very exact and rigorous principles of observation and verification.

To the extent that technology is a by-product of science, secularism is closely related to the emergence of an industrial and technological society in the early modern period. All cultures, even the most primitive, have such technical devices as the ax, the plow, and the wheel. Since the sixteenth century, however, the modern period has seen the increase of technological inventions at such a rate that the term "revolution" is an understatement. People still living who remember the change from the horse and buggy to the automobile have also witnessed on television the landing of men on the moon. The radical difference between such a mode of existence and that of pre-modern civilization, in which technological change occurred at a much slower pace, cannot be overemphasized. More important than any particular invention is the *rate* of technological change and the *value* placed on change, as against stability and repetition: These mark the modern era as something new in world history.

The term industrial revolution refers to the increasing rationalization of the forces of production that took place in the eighteenth and nineteenth centuries. Inventions like the steam engine (1784) were an important part of the process. Even more significant are the factory system and the development of capital investment in industry that led to methods of industrial organization and production, creating modern societies capable of rapid, and seemingly limitless, multiplication of goods and services.

There is no doubt that the religious of the world face an important problem. All of the major world religions, Hinduism, Buddhism, Confucianism, Taoism, Judaism, Christianity, and Islam, emerged in prescientific and pretechnological societies. These traditional societies in both the East and the West have become modern technological societies. The pressing question remains whether the historic religions have within them the capacity for transformation and creative involvement with this new environment.

A crisis is a time of dramatic change, either for the better or for the worse. Most sensitive observers of society, from both religious and nonreligious camps, agree that the emergence of modern technological societies occasions dramatic changes in the religious forms of those societies. There is, however, much less agreement as to what these changes entail. For purposes of discussion we might distinguish three main possibilities.

The first, a conservative interpretation of the phenomenon of change, affirms that religion in its essence has a focus and orientation completely independent of society. Therefore, it is argued, the dramatic changes in society need have no fundamental effect on any religion. According to this view the task of any religion existing in the contemporary world, whether in the East or in the West, is to maintain its integrity and to achieve an understanding of the modern world only for the purpose of defending the true meaning of the *religion* from a false identification with the *culture*. At the other end of the spectrum is the radical interpretation that the new secular form of modern society requires, or must inevitably produce, the dissolution and demise of all forms of traditional religion. Finally, there is a third possibility, a more moderate solution, that suggests that in any religion there is both continuity and change. Thus it would be argued that modern society requires that religions change, but not to such an extent that they lose all sense of continuity and relationship with their past.

The first interpretation is taken by many people, but it is a difficult opinion to maintain without qualification. Throughout this book we have seen evidence of the close relationship between religious phenomena and the social, political, and cultural forms of the society in which they operate. If this relationship indeed exists, it follows that dramatic changes in the cultural and political forms of a society must surely be accompanied by a corresponding change in the religions that exert a vital influence on that particular society.

What is the nature of these changes? According to our second option, the total excision of religion from both societal and personal life is to be expected in the imminent future. Thus references are made to the "death of God," the "end of religion," and the dénouement of the religious age of mankind. It cannot be said, however, that it is a matter of hard sociological fact that religion is in a state of inevitable decline. The evidence at the moment is mixed. Some forms of religion are declining; others are flourishing to a remarkable degree. In this connection we must be careful to distinguish between the continued vitality of personal religion—an *individual's* religious orientation—and the decline of importance of the *institutional* forms of religion. It is true that at the present time some institutional forms of religion have experienced a period of decline, but even this fact must be qualified: Some Eastern religions have acquired new vitality with the emergence of modern nationalistic attitudes. Furthermore, all institutions have their periods of growth and decline, which often take a cyclic pattern. A decline at the moment may well be countered by a resurgence in the future.

Even if it is true, however, that religion is declining in its institutional form, we must recognize that the future of religious activity in the life of man and the future of religious institutions are two distinct things. It is possible that in a future world in which religious institutions have little influence on the political, economic, and scientific activities of man, large numbers of men might still pursue forms of religious practice and symbolism that are less structured and socially coerced than has been the case in the past.

We must also realize that the demise of a *particular* religion in history is not identical with the demise of *all* religions. We have already noted the rise and fall in the history of mankind of many distinctive religious forms. The once flourishing religions of ancient Egypt and of Mesopotamia died with the civilizations in which they were bred. We have also seen new religions emerge within the matrix of an old one. The relationship of Buddhism to Hinduism and the complex relationship of Christianity and Islam to the ancient religion of Israel are cases in point. Sometimes the new, burgeoning religion seems about to overwhelm and completely destroy the old; in many such instances, however, the old, after a period of retreat, again makes a remarkable advance. This is true of Hinduism in relation to its "stepchild" Buddhism and of Judaism in relation to Christianity and Islam. What is taken to be the demise of a religion may simply be a conscious or unconscious recognition of some dramatic change in that religion or a transition from one religion to another. There is a famous story of a pagan writer who meditates upon the emergence of a strange new religion called Christianity. As he thinks about this new faith he seems to hear from a nearby river a loud cry, "Great Pan is dead." The death of Pan was not the demise of all religion, however. Similarly, the death of a present-day god, even if verified, may simply be a preparation for the birth of a new form of faith tomorrow.

Nevertheless, some scholars feel that there are characteristics in modern secular society that are inimical to religious attitudes and behavior in any form. According to this view, as technology and science dominate the life of modern man, he will lose all interest in both institutional and personal religion. He will become pragmatic, manipulative, technical in his response to human problems, and will lose all sense of wonder, mystery, adoration, and contemplation.

There is certainly some evidence that society is moving in this direction. It is too early to decide whether it is an irreversible trend and one that will encompass all mankind. While some "technological" men seem to be devoid of traditional religious interests, others evidence a continued capacity for wonder and awe. For example, the recent film *2001* presented vistas of technological marvels in the future of man; it also surprised many viewers by its touches of mysticism, mystery, and numinous feeling.

In the light of these considerations, some religious thinkers suggest that, instead of the demise of all religion, forms of "secular theology" or "secular religion" will be developed. These phrases can be interpreted in different ways. If secularism is defined as "liberation from the control of religious institutions," then secular theology might urge the religious believer to accept his situation and not resist such changes in the political and economic world. On the other hand, if secular is defined as "this-worldly," a secular theology might be one in which the religious man seeks to put his religion at the service of the secular world. A third possibility is that a secular theology would change traditional emphases and beliefs by diminishing concern for a transcendent life or "other world" and cultivating an ultimate concern for the issues of this world. Traditional religions emphasize stability and order; secular religions might emphasize change and dynamic growth. Traditional religions are oriented toward nature and agriculture; secular religions might cultivate more positive feelings toward the city, machinery, and technological devices.

It is in the midst of these questions and possibilities that we leave the student. Religious man, whether in decline or resurgence, is still in process, is still on the way. His present and future are undecided, and scholars differ both about his nature and about his destiny on the plane of history.

Perhaps the present ambivalent approaches toward religion can be summarized by comparing two documents written at about the same time, around the end of the first quarter of this century. Each was written by an outstanding representative of the contemporary intellectual world. The first is by Alfred North Whitehead, who collaborated with Bertrand Russell in the *Principia Mathematica*, a major influence on twentieth-century logicians and mathematicians. In 1925 Whitehead offered the following ideas about religion:

> *Religion is the vision of something which stands beyond, behind, and within the passing flux of immediate things; something which is real, and yet waiting to be realised; something which is a remote possibility, and yet the greatest of present facts; something that gives meaning to all that passes, and yet eludes apprehension; something whose possession is the final good, and yet is beyond all reach; something which is the ultimate ideal, and the hopeless quest. . . . The vision claims nothing but worship; and worship is a surrender to the claim for assimilation, urged with the motive force of mutual love. The vision never overrules. It is always there, and it has the power of love presenting the one purpose whose fulfilment is eternal harmony. . . . That religion is strong which in its ritual and its modes of thought evokes an apprehension of the commanding vision. The worship of God is not a rule of safety—it is an adventure of the spirit, a flight after the unattainable. The death of religion comes with the repression of the high hope of adventure.[5]*

Sigmund Freud is best known as a pioneer in the field of human psychology. In 1927 he made the following judgments about religion, which are clearly much more negative than those of Whitehead:

> *When the growing individual finds that he is destined to remain a child for ever, that he can never do without protection against strange superior powers, he lends those powers the features belonging to the figure of his father; he creates for himself the gods whom he dreads, whom he seeks to propitiate, and whom he nevertheless entrusts with his own protection. Thus his longing for a father is a motive identical with his need for protection against the consequences of his human weakness. The defense against childish helplessness is what lends its characteristic features to the adult's reaction to the helplessness which he has to acknowledge—a reaction which is precisely the formation of religion. . . . But surely infantilism is destined to be surmounted. Men cannot remain children forever; they must in the end go out into "hostile life." We may call this "education to reality." . . . And, as for the great necessities of Fate, against which there is*

5. Alfred North Whitehead, *Science and the Modern World*, New York, Cambridge, 1929, pp. 238–239.

no help, they will learn to endure them with resignation. Of what use to them is the mirage of wide acres in the moon, whose harvest no one has ever yet seen? As honest smallholders on this earth they will know how to cultivate their plot in such a way that it supports them. By withdrawing their expectations from the other world and concentrating all their liberated energies into their life on earth, they will probably succeed in achieving a state of things in which life will become tolerable for everyone and civilization no longer oppressive to anyone. Then, with one of our fellow-unbelievers, they will be able to say without regret:

> Den Himmel überlassen wir
> Den Engeln und den Spatzen.

("We leave Heaven to the angels and the sparrows." From Heine's poem Deutschland *[Caput I]).*[6]

Here are two statements of opposing points of view. There are others perhaps more viable than either. Hopefully, you have now acquired tools and perspectives with which to make your own estimation of the place of religion in the modern world.

BIBLIOGRAPHY

For the relation of the religions of the world see:

Smart, Ninian, *A Dialogue of Religions,* London, SCM Press, 1960.

Tillich, Paul, *Christianity and the Encounter of the World Religions,* New York, Columbia, 1963.

Toynbee, Arnold, "The Relativity of a Human Observer's Approach to Religion," *Reconsiderations,* New York, Oxford, 1961, pp. 68–102.

For the relation of religion to secularism see:

Bellah, Robert, *Religion and Progress in Modern Asia,* New York, Free Press, 1965.

Berger, Peter L., *The Sacred Canopy,* Garden City, N.Y., Doubleday, 1969.

Martin, David, *The Religious and the Secular,* London, Routledge, 1969.

Szczesny, George, *The Future of Unbelief,* trans. E. Garside, New York, George Braziller, 1961.

6. Sigmund Freud, *The Future of an Illusion,* Garden City, N.Y., Doubleday, 1964, pp. 35, 81–82.

GLOSSARY

PART 2

Pronunciation of Sanskrit

Accent the first syllable of two syllable words. In longer words accent the penult when it is long vowel, otherwise the antepenult. A long syllable is one which contains a long vowel or diphthong. The vowels e and o are diphthongs, as are ai and au. For introductory purposes, one can ignore the dots that are sometimes found beneath certain consonants (ṭ, ḍ, etc.). The following can be taken as a general guide to pronunciation:

ā	as the a in father
a	(short) as the u in but
e	(long) as the a in say
ī	as i in machine
i	(short) i as in pin
o	as in go
ū	as in rule
u	(short) as in full
ṛ	(a vowel) usually as ri in river
c	as ch in church
g	as in get
ṣ or ś	as sh in shun
bh	as in abhor
th	as in anthill (not as in that)

Abhidhamma Piṭaka (*Abhidhamma Pitaka*). The third basket of the Pali Canon, containing doctrinal refinements.

Acharyas (*Āchāryas*). Teachers; those who, like Ramanuja, provided a philosophical base for theism.

Adhvaryu. Those priests of the Vedic sacrifices who are responsible for the manual operations of the sacrifices.

Adi Granth. The sacred book of the Sikh Community.

Advaita. Lit. "non-dual"; a philosophical system associated with Shankara.

Agni. The Vedic god of the fire, the priestly archetype.

Agnishtoma (*Agniṣṭoma*). Soma sacrifice, performed annually in the Spring.

Ahimsa (*Ahiṁsā*). Non-violence; non-injury to any living being.

Ahura Mazda. The one supreme being of Zoroaster.

Ajiva (*Ajīva*). The unconscious, matter; one of the two Jaina categories which compose the universe.

Alaya-vijnana (*Ālaya-vijñāna*). Yogacara doctrine of store-consciousness, accounting for deeds which do not reach immediate fruition.

Alvars (*Āḻvārs*). Lit. "those who are immersed in God"; the twelve successive poet-saints of South India who were devoted to Krishna.

Amesha Spentas. Six divine abstractions which, for Zoroaster, were aspects of Ahura Mazda. They later became deities in their own right.

Amitabha. Lit. "Infinite Light"; Buddha of the Western Paradise.

Anatta (Pali; Skt. **Anātman**). Denial of Atman, the concept of a permanent self.

Anicca (Pali; Skt. **Anitya**). Impermanence.

Apramanani (*Apramāṇāni*). The four immeasurables of Theravada morality: loving kindness (*mettā*); compassion (*karuṇā*); sympathetic joy (*muditā*); and equanimity (*upekha*).

Apsaras. Water nymphs, wives of *gandharvas*.

Aranyakas (*Araṇyakas*). Lit. "forest texts"; the third part of the Vedas, secret and private sayings which later led into the Upanishads.

Arhat. One who is worthy to be honored, one who is enlightened; the ideal of the Pali Canon.

Asha. The Parsi concept of truth or justice; counterpart of the Rigvedic *Rita*.

Ashram (*Aśram*). A monastery.

Ashramas (*Aśramas*). The four stages in life: student (*brahmacarin*), householder (*grhastha*), forest dweller (*vanaprasthya*), and wanderer (*sannyasin*).

Ashvamedha (*Aśvamedha*). The Vedic rite of horse sacrifice, made by a king to signify that he was a universal monarch.

Ashvins (*Aśvins*). The heavenly twins, Vedic deities; possessors of horses.

Asuras. Vedic demons, enemies of the *devas;* good deities to the Parsis.

Atharvaveda (or **Atharvasaṁhitā**). The fourth collection of the Vedas, consisting mostly of magical formulae.

Atman (*Atman*). The essence within man which is identical with the essence of the universe (*Brahman*).

Atyashramin (*Atyaśramin*). Lit. "he who is beyond the ashrams"; the fourth stage of life, later called sannyasin.

Avataras (*Avatāras*). Incarnations or descents, particularly the descents of Vishnu.

Avesta. The sacred text of the Parsis.

Avidya (*Avidyā*). Ignorance.

Ayatanas (*Āyatanas*). The classification of sense organs and sense data, analyzed in the *Abhidhamma Pitaka*.

Bhagavad Gita (*Bhagavad Gītā*). Part of the great epic the *Mahabharata*. The *Bhagavad Gita* is a book of devotion to Krishna as the Supreme deity.

Bhagavan (*Bhagavān*). Lit. "the Adorable One"; an epithet of personal devotion used of various deities, particularly of Krishna and the Buddha.

Bhajans. Hymns.

Bhakta. An adept who practices *bhakti*.

Bhakti. Lit. "Devotion"; a religious orientation including faith, love, surrender and devotional attachment, most often expressed to a personal deity.

Bhikkhu (Pali; Skt. **Bhikṣu**). Almsmen; the title for the followers of the Buddha who entered the *Sangha* and lived by the rules of the *Vinaya*.

Bhikkunis (Pali; Skt. **Bhiksunis**). Members of the monastic order for female devotees of the Buddha.

Bodhisattva. A Buddha-to-be.

Brahma (*Brahmā*). The creator god; sometimes placed in a triad with Siva (destroyer) and Vishnu (preserver).

Brahmacarin (*Brahmacārin*). The first stage of life, that of student.

Brahman. Devotion; food for the food offering; chant of the Sama singer; magical formula or text; great; the essence which pervades the universe; pure consciousness devoid of all attributes and categories of the intellect. Also, the highest class.

Brahmanas (*Brāhmaṇas*). Prose commentaries on the Samhitas or basic collections of the Vedas.

Buddha. Lit. "Enlightened One"; the title of Siddhattha Gotama.

Cakra. Wheel, circle; *cakra-puja* is left-handed tantric worship in which worshipers sit in a circle.

Dakmas. Towers of silence for the disposal of Parsi dead.

Dasyas. Dark-skinned worshipers of the phallus; foes of the Vedic Aryans.

Devadasis. Lit. "servants of God"; girls who were dedicated to temple deities and engaged in dancing and temple prostitution.

Devas. Lit. "gods"; a class of Vedic deities; "demons" to the Parsis.

Dhamma (Pali; Skt. **Dharma**). Law; the principle of order in society and in the universe; the teaching of the Buddha.

Dhatus (*Dhātus*). The irreducible elements of the universe: earth, fire, water, air, space (*akasha*), and consciousness.

Digambaras. Lit., "clothed in space"; a Jaina sect which gave up all attachments including clothes.

Din Ilahi. "The Divine Faith," promulgated by Akbar, which was intended to be a synthesis of "the best" of several Indian faiths.

Drishti (*Dṛṣti*). Dogmatism, viewpoints.

Druj. The Parsi personification of the Lie.

Dukkha. Suffering or "ill."

Dvaita. Dualism, the philosophical position of Madhva.

Gandharvas. Cloud spirits, husbands of the *apsaras*.

Gayatri (*Gāyatrī*). A verse to Savitri, recited daily by Brahmans.

Gopis. Cowherd lasses who are the lovers of Krishna in the *Bhagavata Purana*.

Grihapati (*Gṛhapati*). Lit. "lord of the house"; used as both an epithet of Agni and a term for a domestic priest.

Grihastha (*Gṛhastha*). The second stage of life, that of householder.

Gurdwaras. Lit. "gates of the Guru"; Sikh temples.

Guru. A spiritual teacher; a cult of the guru involves devotion to him as a divine manifestation.

Hanuman (*Hanumān*). The monkey god of the *Ramayana*.

Harihara. The deity who is a combination of Vishnu and Shiva.

Harijans. Children of Hari; people of god; Gandhi's term for the "untouchables."

Hinayana (*Hinayāna*). The "Little Vehicle"; a pejorative name given to the Theravada ("Way of the Elders") by the Mahayana, or followers of the "Great Vehicle."

Hotri (*Hotṛ*). Lit. "pourer of oblation"; a reciter of the verses of the *Rigveda*.

Indra. One of the principal deities of the *Rigveda*, a storm god attendant to the Buddha.

Ishvara (*Iśvara*). A supreme personal deity, Ultimate Reality for Ramanuja; in *advaita*, Brahman as qualified Lord or Saguna Brahman.

Jainas. Followers of the *jinas* who attained release and enlightenment; religion stemming from Mahavira.

Japji. Morning devotional prayer of the Sikhs.

Jinas. "Conquerors" or "victors."

Jiva (*Jīva*). The conscious or living principle, one of two Jain categories which compose the universe; the phenomenal personality in Shankara.

Jivan-mukti (*Jīvan-mukti*). Liberated while living; the state of perfection in this life after realization of unity with Brahman in the thought of Shankara.

Jnanamarga (*Jñānamārga* or *Jñānayoga*). Lit. "the way through knowledge", i.e., through meditation and discriminative thought.

Karma (Pali **Kamma**). "Deed" or "act"; causal connection within the spiritual order; results of actions; the law which governs the regrouping of the khandhas and rebirth in the Pali Canon and which weights the *jivas* down in Jaina thought.

Karmamarga (*Karmamārga* or *Karmayoga*). Lit. "the way through works"; the way through sacrifice in the Vedic period, and through disciplined action in the *Gita*.

Karuna (*Karuṇā*). Compassion, sympathy without attachment.

Kevalin. "Omniscient One"; a Jaina term for the individual whose influx of karma has stopped and whose permeating karma is worked out.

Khalsa (*Khālsā*). "Community of the Pure"; a Sikh term for those initiated into the community by drinking and being sprinkled with *amrit*, sweetened water.

Khandhas (Pali; Skt. **Skhandhas**). The components of phenomenal existence.

Krishna (*Kṛṣṇa*). Lit. "the Dark One"; a human hero in the *Mahabharata;* supreme deity in the *Bhagavad Gita;* avatar of Vishnu.

Kshatriyas (*Kṣatriyas*). A warrior, the second highest class.

Kusti. Parsi sacred thread.

Lakkhana (*Lakkhaṇa*). The three marks of existence in the Pali Canon: impermanence (*anicca*), no self (*anatta*), and suffering (*dukkha*).

Lokakasha (*Lokākaśa*). For the Jainas, the top of the universe, where purified *jivas* live in eternal bliss.

Linga (*Liṅga*). The male reproductive organ; symbol of Shiva.

Madhyamika (*Mādhyamika*). "The Middle Way" between realism and nihilism; a philosophical school associated with Nagarjuna; a system of logic which reduces ontological systems to absurdity.

Mahabharata (*Mahābhārata*). One of the two Indian epics; it contains the *Bhagavad Gita*.

Mahavira (*Mahāvīra*). "Great Hero," an epithet of Vardhamana, the Jaina saint.

Mahayana (*Mahāyāna*). "The Great Vehicle," the so-called Northern School of Buddhism.

Mahayogi (*Mahāyogī*). "Great ascetic," an epithet of Shiva.

Mandalas (*Maṇdalas*). Diagrams of mystic import.

Mantras. Short verses; mystic syllables often containing unintelligible sounds.

Math. Monastery.

Maya (*Māyā*). Occult, superhuman; in *advaita,* cosmic illusion.

Metta (*mettā*). Loving kindness, benevolent harmlessness.

Milindapanha (*Milindapañhā*). Lit. "Questions of King Milinda"; a Theravada text not actually in the Pali Canon.

Moksha (*Mokṣa*). Emancipation, release, enlightenment.

Mudita (*Muditā*). Sympathetic joy.

Mudras (*Mūdrās*). Ritual gestures with the fingers.

Nibbana (Pali; Skt. **Nirvāṇa**). The blowing out; state of enlightenment and bliss; the attainment of the Buddha.

Naojote. "One who offers prayers new"; initiation ceremony for the Parsi boy or girl.

Nataputta (*Nātaputta*). "Son of the Nath"; an epithet of Mahavira.

Nataraja (*Naṭarāja*). "Lord of dance"; an epithet of Shiva.

Nayanars (*Nāyanārs*). South Indian devotees to Shiva whose hymns form the *Devaram.*

Niganthas (*Niganṭhas*). Followers of Mahavira.

Nyasa (*Nyāsa*). Ritual movements of the hands.

Pabbajja. "Outgoing" from the world; a preparatory ordination for followers of the Buddha who sought to join the Sangha.

Panna (Pali *Paññā*) or **Prajna** (Skt. *Prajñā*). Insight or wisdom; for Nagarjuna, a non-dual intuition of the Real.

Parajikas (*Pārajikas*). The four offenses, any of which would cause expulsion of a bhikshu from the Sangha: sexual intercourse, theft, knowingly depriving a creature of life, boasting of some superhuman perfection.

Parinibbana (Pali; Skt. **Parinirvāṇa**). Complete escape from chain of causation; the release or liberation that occurs at death.

Patijnana (*Patijñāna*). Lit. "Knowledge of the father"; divine knowledge given by Shiva.

Patimokkha (Pali; Skt. **Prātimokṣa**). The 252 rules of the Sangha.

Pitris (*Pitṛs*). Distant and somewhat mythical male ancestors.

Prajapati (*Prajāpati*). "Lord of Beings"; originally a title of many Rigvedic deities, later used for the Rigvedic deity conceived to be above all others.

Prana (*Prāṇa*). Breath; the vital force in man that was considered for a time to be the unifying substance of the universe.

Prapatti. Surrender, absolute humility, a willingness to give up anything that is against God's will. *Prapatti* is an attitude that expresses itself in *bhakti.*

Prasada (*Prasāda*). Divine grace.

Pretas. Spirits of recently dead male ancestors.

Puja (*Pūjā*). Adoration and worship; rites of offerings and circumambulation of the temple or image.

Puranas (*Purāṇas*). A group of scriptures dating from the medieval period that emphasize bhakti.

Purdah. The Muslim practice of the veiling and seclusion of women.

Purusha (*Puruṣa*). Lit. "Man"; primordial sacrifice; the permanent and spiritual aspect of man in Samkhya and Yoga philosophies.

Radha (*Rādhā*). The consort of Krishna; one of the cowherd lasses.

Rakshas (*Rakṣas*). Demons.

Rama (*Rāma*). The great hero in the *Ramayana;* he is the incarnation of Vishnu, supreme deity of the Ramanandi or Ramawat sect.

Ramadan (*Ramadān*). The Muslim month of fasting.

Ramayana (*Rāmāyana*). One of the two great Indian epics, centering around Rama and Sita.

Rigveda (*Ṛgveda*); also **Riksamita**. The first of the four Vedic collections.

Rishis (*Ṛṣis*). Seers; those who apprehend eternal truth.

Rita (*Ṛta*). A cosmic and ethical order, the later extension of which is *dharma.*

Saddharmapundarika (*Saddharmapuṇḍarīka*). Lit. "Lotus of the True Law"; a Mahayana sutra with strong *bhakti* emphasis.

Sadhana (*Sādhanā*). Meditative exercises or discipline.

Samadhi (*Samādhi*). Concentration.

Samaveda (also *Samasaṁhitā*). A collection of melodies (*samans*) to be sung at the Soma sacrifice; the third of the four Vedic collections.

Samhitas (*Saṁhitās*). Collections of basic verses, including the *Rigveda.*

Samsara (*Saṁsāra*). Successive states of rebirth.

Samskaras. Life cycle of sacred events; ceremonies to secure divine favor from birth to death.

Sanatana Dharma (*Sanātana Dharma*). Lit. "Eternal religion"; a term used by Radhakrishnan and others to refer to Hinduism.

Sangha. The monastic order of the followers of the Buddha.

Sannyasin. Later term for the fourth stage of life, that of the "wanderer," or one who has renounced the world.

Sarasvati. The goddess of the river, one of the few female deities in the *Rigveda.*

Sati. Lit. "a virtuous or chaste woman"; the immolation of a widow on her husband's funeral pyre.

Satyagraha (*Sātyāgraha*). Lit. "holding on to truth"; the refusal, as by Gandhi, to participate in the working of an unjust system.

Savitri (*Savitr*). A Vedic solar deity.

Shakti (*Śakti*). Lit. "power"; a deity's power in form of his consort.

Shakyamuni (*Śakyamuni*). "Sage of the Shakyas"; an epithet of the Buddha.

Shiva (*Śiva*). An epithet of the Rigvedic Rudra, lit. "auspicious"; the destroyer; the great ascetic; lord of animals; and lord of the dance.

Shramanas (*Śramanas*). Ascetics.

Shravakas (*Śrāvakas*). Lit. "hearers"; Jaina lay followers.

Shruti (*Śruti*). Lit. "that which is heard"; hence, not of human origin, i.e., the Vedas.

Shuddhi (*Śuddhi*). The ceremony used by Arya Samaj to reclaim those who had left "Hinduism."

Shudras (*Śudras*). Members of the fourth class, who performed manual labors; not of the twice-born.

Shunyata (*Śūnyatā*). Void or emptiness.

Shvetambaras (*Śvetāmbaras*) Lit. "white-clothed"; a Jaina sect of monks who believed it possible to attain perfection even if one wore clothes.

Sikhs. Lit. "disciples"; followers of the True Name, a movement initiated by Nanak.

Sila (*Sīla*). Pali morality, as represented by the ten precepts for *bhikkhus* and the five precepts for laymen.

Sita (*Sītā*). In the *Ramayana,* the wife of Rama.

Smriti (*Smṛti*). Lit. "that which is remembered"; commentaries on *shruti* that are only authoritative for advaitins to the extent that they agree with *shruti.*

Soma. A plant and the exhilarating beverage made from it; the heavenly nectar of the gods; also, a Vedic deity.

Spenta Mainyu. Lit. "Holy or Bounteous Spirit"; a Parsi deity.

Sthanakavasis. A Jaina sect opposed to the use of images.

Sudrah. The sacred shirt used in the Parsi initiation ceremony.

Surya (*Sūrya*). The sun; a solar deity; an all-seeing deity.

Sutta Pitaka (*Sutta Piṭaka*). The second basket of the *Tipitaka,* containing collections of reputed sayings of the Buddha.

Sutra (*Sūtra;* Pali **Sutta**). Lit. "thread"; short statements; discourses of the Buddha.

Swadesi. Gandhi's term for the use of only those things produced in one's immediate neighborhood.

Swaraj. Gandhi's ideal of self-rule.

Syadvada (*Syādvāda*). The Jaina doctrine of maybe, a sevenfold logic of affirmation and denial.

Tanha (*Taṇha*). Grasping; desire.

Tantras. Texts connected with Saktism.

Tapas. Heat; austerities.

Tathagata (*Tathāgata*). "One who has thus come," an epithet of the Buddha; an enlightened being.

Tathata (*Tathatā*). Lit. "thatness" or "suchness"; the Real as void of all views.

Tattvas. The five forbidden things that are used in left-handed tantric ritual: wine, meat, fish, parched grain, and sexual intercourse.

Thags. Organized bands of devotees to Kali who murdered victims by strangulation; hence the English word "thugs."

Theravada (*Theravāda*). Lit. "Way of the Elders"; followers of Buddha who follow the Pali Canon.

Tilak. Symbolic marks on the body showing devotion to a particular deity.

Tipitaka (Pali; Skt. **Tripitaka**). Three baskets; the scriptures of the Theravadins (*Vinaya, Sutta,* and *Abhidhamma*).

Tirthankaras (*Tīrthaṅkaras*). "Fordfinders," a long line of great *jinas* who have achieved release; objects of worship of the Jainas.

Trikaya (*Trikāya*). The doctrine of the "three bodies" of the Buddha: the cosmic body (*Dharmakaya*), the body of bliss (*Sambhogakaya*), and the apparitional body (*Nirmanakaya*).

Trimurti (*Trimūrti*). The synthesis of Brahma, Vishnu, and Shiva into one deity.

Udgatri (*Udgatṛ*). A priest of the Samaveda ritual; a singer at Soma sacrifice.

Upanayana (*Upanāyana*). A rite of initiation that can only be performed by the three highest classes.

Upanishad (*Upaniṣad*). Lit. "to sit nearby devotedly"; mystical, philosophical texts and secret sayings; the texts that come at the end of the *Vedas* and are important for *Vedanta.*

Upasakas (*Upāsakas*). Male lay devotees of the Buddha; householders.

Upasikas (*Upāsikās*). Female lay devotees of the Buddha.

Upasampada (*Upasaṁpadā*). Lit. "the arrival"; ordination into full membership in the Sangha.

Upaya (*Upāya*). Device; skill in means.

Upekha (*Upakhā*). Equanimity, the quality of neutrality and non-attachment.

Uposatha. The fortnightly service of confession for *Bhikkhus.*

Vaishya (*Vaiṣya*). The commercial class, the third of the four classes.

Vajra. A thunderbolt, the weapon of Indra.

Vajrasattva. Lit. "being of diamond essence"; the fourth body whereby the Buddha embraced his Shakti, Tara, or Bhagavati.

Vanaprasthya (*Vānaprasthya*). A forest dweller, the third stage of life.

Vardhamana (*Vardhamāna*). A Kshatriya who became Mahavira and pointed the way to enlightenment for the Jainas.

Varna (*Varṇa*). Lit. "color"; the class system that evolved from the Aryan conquest of Dasyas, the fourfold division of society into Brahmans, Kshatriyas, Vaishyas, and Shudras.·

Varuna (*Varuṇa*). A Vedic deity, sovereign of the cosmic order, ruling with *Rita.*

Veda. Lit. "knowledge"; sacred knowledge. Also, a group of sacred texts considered *shruti* and hence not of human origination.

Vedi. The fire pit where Agni dwells.

Videhamukti. In Shankara's thought, a state of disembodied liberation following Jivanmukti.

Vijnanavada (*Vijñānavāda*). Yogacara (q.v.).

Vinaya Pitaka (*Vinaya Piṭaka*). The first basket of the *Tipiṭaka,* containing the rules for the Sangha.

Vishishtadvaita (*Viśiṣtadvaita*). A philosophical position of qualified non-dualism advocated by Ramanuja. The Absolute is qualified by diversity of interrelated elements.

Vishnu (*Viṣṇu*). A minor solar deity of the Rigveda who later became an important deity with numerous *avataras.*

Vishvakarman (*Viśvakarman*). Lit. "All Creator"; a late Rigvedic deity conceived to be above others.

Yajurveda (also *Yajursaṁhitā*). One of the four Vedas, a collection of sacrificial formulae.

Yasna. A liturgical book of the Parsis.

Yatis. Lit. "strivers"; Jaina monastic order comprised of those who give up the life of the householder.

Yogacara (*Yogācāra*). A philosophical school of the followers of the Buddha which held that only consciousness is Real; a method of withdrawal of the senses from supposed external objects until there is Thought only; the goal of pure subjectivity.

Yoni. Vulva, the symbol of female principle.

PART 3

Chinese Terms

Chen-jen. A Taoist immortal.

Ch'eng. Sincerity, truth, reality.

Ch'i. A Neo-Confucian term meaning ether or vacuous gas; the principle of individuation.

Ch'ien-ai. Universal love: in the philosophy of Mo ti, indiscriminant love.

Chih. Knowledge, wisdom.

Chung. Conscientiousness, loyalty.

Chun-tzu. Lit. "son of an aristocrat"; the true gentleman, superior person, or ideal man in Confucian thought.

Feng-shui. Wind and water: a term for geomancy.

Five Elements. The basic constituents of all things: metal, water, earth, fire, and wood.

Hou-chi. Lord Millet, the grain deity.

Hou-t'u. Lord Soil, the earth deity.

Hsiao. Filial piety.

Hsueh. Learning, study.

I. Righteousness.

Jen. A basic Confucian virtue: benevolence, love, humaneness.

Ju. Literati.

Ju-chiao. The teaching of the Literati: a traditional term for Confucius.

Kuei. The negative, demonic forces that are the basis of physical nature in man.

Li. Principle, reason.

Li. Propriety, courtesy, etiquette; principles of conduct.

Shang-ti. Supreme rule: Supreme Ancestor, the central deity of Shang people.

She-chi. The altar of earth and grain in ancient Chinese folk religion.

Shen. Positive, divine forces: good spirits; the superior aspect of human person: basis of intelligence and vital forces.

Shih. A knight, an ideal person similar to *chun-tzu* in Confucian thought.

Shu. Reciprocity, altruism.

Tao. The way, road, or path. In Taoism, the way of nature, the cosmic order or reality; in Confucianism, the way of society and human behavior.

Te. In Taoism, the manifestation of Tao in nature and affairs; in Confucian thought, moral force and influence.

T'ien. Heaven. This term has numerous meanings, extending from personalized divine force to the impersonal order of nature.

T'ien-ming. The mandate or decree of Heaven, implying a moral order running through the universe and human affairs.

Wen. Culture, decoration, bearing, poise.

Wu. Sorcerer, wizard, or shaman in Chinese popular religion.

Wu-wei. Non-action, by which all actions are completed. *Wu-wei* is a basic doctrine of Taoism.

Yin-yang. The contrasting cosmic forces making up the universe. Yin represents such negative features as dark, moist, cold, soft, female, etc., and yang the bright, dry, warm, hard, male characteristics in things.

Japanese Terms

Daimoku. The title of the *Lotus Sutra,* associated with the Nichiren Buddhist tradition.

Dōzoku. A group of related, nuclear families in a hierarchical arrangement involving status and obligations.

Gensō. The doctrine of the return of the Bodhisattva to this world to work for the salvation of beings, stressed in Shinran's Pure Land doctrine.

Hommon Kaidan. The ordination platform emphasized in Nichiren tradition.

Honji-suijaku. Fundamental-reality-trace-manifestation, basic terminology for the Buddhist philosophical theory developed in Japan, showing the gods as manifestations of the Buddha.

Hōza. Group meetings for mutual spiritual support in the Japanese Rissho-kosei-kai Buddhist organization.

Kami. In the Japanese Shinto tradition, divinity.

Kokugaku. National Learning, a term associated with the intellectual movement in Shinto tradition.

Kokutai. National Essence, National Polity, a term referring to the unique character and structure of the Japanese people in Shinto tradition.

Makoto. Sincerity, truth; a basic value in Shinto tradition.

Mappō. In Buddhist eschatology, the Last Age in the decline and disappearance of the *dharma.*

Matsuri. In Shinto tradition, a festival, service of a deity.

Musubi. In Shinto tradition, growth, creativity, productivity.

Norito. Shinto ritual prayers.

Oharae. Shinto prayer for purification.

On. Favor, goodness, kindness; to repay *on* is to be grateful and mindful of one's obligations.

Saisei-itchi. The union of religion and government in Japanese tradition.

Shakubuku. Forceful, aggressive efforts to convert someone, a term prominently associated with the Nichiren Buddhist tradition.

Sūkeisha. A voluntary member of a Shinto shrine because of belief or interest.

Ujiko. Lit. "son of the clan"; a member of a Shinto shrine because of birth or territorial relationship.

Zazen. In Zen Buddhism, the practice of sitting in meditation.

PART 5

Pronunciation of Arabic

Consonants:

b, d, f, h, j, k, l, m, n, r, s, t, z, and **sh** are pronounced roughly as in English.

w   This letter is either a consonant or a vowel according to its use. When it is a consonant it is transliterated as w and when a vowel as ū.

y   This letter is either a consonant or a vowel according to its use. When it is a consonant it is transliterated as y and when a vowel as ī.

'   Called hamzah, the Arabic sign rendered in this fashion represents a glottal stop or gentle closing of the throat. Such a throat closure is necessary, for example, in the pronunciation of any English word that begins with a vowel. In the middle of a word the hamzah is in effect a slight pause.

th   Like the th in *th*ink.

ḥ   A guttural h pronounced with a strong emission of breath from an open throat.

kh   A guttural fricative as in Scottish "lo*ch*" or German "a*ch*tung."

ṣ, ḍ, ṭ, ẓ Veliorized consonants corresponding with s, d, t, and z. These are all emphatic sounds achieved by pressing the tongue strongly against the upper teeth and releasing it suddenly. These letters also affect the following vowel, as may be seen in the contrast between sā (sa as in English *sag*) and ṣā (so as in English *solemn*).

dh   Like the th in *th*is.

'   Transliteration of the Arabic letter ayn, which has no equivalent in English. It is a strong guttural sound pronounced deep in the throat with a strong emission of breath.

gh   A sound like that made in gargling. It is very close in pronunciation to the r in Parisian French.

q   A hard k produced in the back of the throat.

Vowels (Arabic has three short vowels, three long vowels, and two dipthongs):

Short vowels (these are normally not written in an Arabic text):

a   Called fatḥah, it is pronounced like English a in *man,* English u in *nun,* or English e in *melody,* according to the consonant on which it is borne. The variety of sounds for all the short vowels is considerable.

i   Called kasrah, it is pronounced as in English d*i*m.

u   Called ḍammah, it is pronounced as in English p*u*ll.

Long vowels (these are always written by separate characters in an Arabic text. The long vowels are formed by drawing out the sound of the short vowels):

ā   Called 'alif, this letter is pronounced with

a lengthening of the English a sounds, as in saw or sag.

ī Called yā', this letter is pronounced like the English doubled e, as in eel.

ū Called waw, this letter is pronounced like the English doubled o as in booth.

Diphthongs:

ay Like English pay.

aw Like English ow, as in cow.

There are no rules for stress in Arabic; the length of syllables causes some to appear stronger than others.

In the Arabic definite article al-, the initial a is a connective that may be pronounced as a, i, or u, according to the conditions determined by the rules of grammar. A student who does not know Arabic should pronounce it simply a as in al-fresco. When the definite article is followed by any one of the following letters; the l assimilates to that letter and is given the same pronunciation: t, th, d, dh, r, z, s, sh, ḍ, ṣ, ṭ, ẓ, l, n. For example, the Arabic expression meaning "the man," al-rajūl, is pronounced ar-rajūl (ar-rajool). If the definite article is followed by any other letter, the l is pronounced as l.

'Abbasi (*'Abbāsī*). An adjectival form referring to the dynasty that succeeded the Ummawīs and that established its capital in Baghdad. The name is derived from that of Ibn 'Abbās, an uncle of the Prophet, who was the ancestor of the 'Abbāsī rulers.

'Abd al-'Aziz ibn Su'ud (*'Abd al-'Azīz ibn Su'ūd*). King of Arabia and founder of the Su'ūdī dynasty. His dates were 1880–1953.

'Abd al-Qadir al-Jilani (*'Abd al-Qādir al-Jīlānī*). A famous Ṣūfī and founder of the Qadarīyah order of mystics. His dates were A.D. 1077–1166.

Abu Bakr (*Abū Bakr*). A companion of Muḥammad, one of the first converts to Islām, and the first Khalīfah of the community.

Abu Hanifah (*Abū Ḥanīfah*). An 'Irāqī jurist of the second Islamic century and the founder of one of the four accepted Sunnī schools of law. He lived between A.D. 700 and 767.

Abu al-Hasan al-Ash'ari (*Abū al-Ḥasan al-Ash'arī*). An early Islamic theologian of great importance. He was the first to use Greek dialectic in the exposition and defense of traditionalist religious doctrines. He was, thus, the father of kalām among Sunnī Muslims. The great majority of Sunnī thinkers have considered themselves to belong to the school of al-Ash'arī. He died in A.D. 935.

Abu al-Husayn al-Nuri (*Abū al-Ḥusayn al-Nūrī*). A well known Islamic mystical poet and companion of al-Junayd. He died in A.D. 908.

Abu Talib (*Abū Ṭālib*). The uncle of Muḥammad

and the father of 'Alī. After Muḥammad was orphaned, he was raised in this uncle's home.

Abu Yazid al-Bistami (*Abū Yazīd al-Bisṭāmī*). A celebrated mystic of the third Islamic century who is well known for his preference of the doctrine of mystical intoxication over the doctrine of mystical sobriety and for his ecstatic utterances (shaṭaḥāt). He died in A.D. 874.

Adan (*'Adan*). The port city at the southwest tip of the Arabian peninsula.

Adl (*'adl*). Justice; in theology, the doctrine of God's justice.

Agha Khan (*Aghā Khān*). The title of the leader of one group of Ismā'īlī Muslims. The Aghā Khān's followers are concentrated principally in India, Pakistan, and East Africa. The present Aghā Khān is considered to be the forty-ninth imām of the group.

Ahl al-bayt. Lit. the people of the house, meaning the descendants of the Prophet. The political claim of the Shī'ah was that the khilāfah belonged exclusively to the ahl al-bayt.

Ahl al-sunnah wa al-jama'at (*ahl al-sunnah wa al-jamā'at*). Lit. the people of established custom and of the community. This is the self designation of the majority group of the Muslim community, those who are commonly called Sunnī.

Ahmad ibn Hanbal (*Aḥmad ibn Ḥanbal*). An early Islamic traditionalist famous for the strictness and conservatism of his views, also the founder of one of the four accepted Sunnī schools of law. He lived between A.D. 780 and 855.

Ahwal (*aḥwāl*). The spiritual states through which a Ṣūfī passes on the path to mystic union with God.

Aligarh (*'Alīgarh*). A town in Uttar Pradesh, India, which is the site of the 'Alīgarh Muslim University founded by Sir Sayyid Aḥmad Khān in 1875.

'Ali ibn Abi Talib (*'Alī ibn Abī Ṭālib*). The son of Muḥammad's uncle, Abū Ṭālib, and the husband of Muḥammad's daughter, Fāṭimah. 'Alī is the first of the imāms recognized by the Shī'ah.

Allah (*Allāh*). God. The word is composed of two elements, the Arabic article (al) and a contraction of the term meaning deity (ilāh). It is, thus, not a name for God but simply means "the God," the only God who exists.

Allahu akbar (*Allāhu akbar*). Lit. "God is greater," an expression of praise used in the call to prayer, in the prayer itself, and on many other occasions in the Muslim's life.

Ansar (*anṣār*). Lit. "helpers," the title bestowed on the followers of Muḥammad in Madīnah. It is contrasted with muhājirīn, or the followers who emigrated with Muḥammad from Makkah.

Arafat (*'Arafah*). A large plain near Makkah where pilgrims carry out the ceremony of wuqūf, or standing in the presence of God, which is the heart of the pilgrimage rites.

Ardabil (*Ardābīl*). A town in Azarbaijan, now in the northwestern section of Iran. The town was the headquarters of the Ṣūfī order, headed by Shaykh Ṣafiy al-Dīn, which gave rise to the Ṣafawī dynasty of Iran. The despoiled tomb of Shaykh Ṣafiy al-Dīn may still be seen there.

'Asabiyah (*'aṣabīyah*). The tie of solidarity among the members of an Arab tribe.

Al-Awza'i (*al-Awzā'ī*). An early Syrian jurist whose opinions are representative of the primitive stage of development of Islamic law. He died at approximately age 70 in A.D. 774.

Ayahs (*āyah*, pl. *āyāt*). Lit., "sign." In the *Qur'ān* the word means one of the evidences of God's existence and power. It is also used as the name for a Qur'anic verse which constitutes such an evidence.

Al-Azhar University. A famous center for Islamic learning established by the Fāṭimī rulers in Cairo in the tenth century. The school attached to the mosque of al-Azhar is perhaps the most famous and most respected such center in the entire Islamic world.

Badr. The site of the first and most important military engagement between Muḥammad and the Makkans.

Balakot (*Bālākōṭ*). A place in the foothills of the Himalaya where the Mujāhidīn suffered a decisive defeat in 1831 at the hands of the Sikhs.

Bani Hawazin (*Banī Hawāzin*). An Arab tribe against whom Muḥammad fought a major military engagement at the Battle of Ḥunayn.

Baqa' (*baqā'*). Lit. "remaining," the Ṣūfī expression for a state of mystical attainment beyond even extinction (fanā') in which the soul indwells continually in God.

Al-Baqillani (*al-Baqillānī*). A well known Muslim theologian adhering to the school of al-Ash'-arī. He is reputed as a foremost exponent of the doctrine of occasionalism, which characterized the Ash'arī school in its later phases. He died in A.D. 1013.

Barakah. Blessedness, or even holiness, a quality possessed by the mystic saints (awliyā') through which they exert their governance of the universe.

Batin (*bāṭin*). Lit. "hidden" or "concealed," the esoteric aspect of a doctrine or teaching that can be understood only through instruction from an authoritative teacher. The bāṭin is to be contrasted with the ẓāhir or the obvious, evident and, exoteric meaning of a doctrine or practice.

Batiniyah (*Bāṭinīyah*). Lit. "esotericists," the name given those of the Shī'ah who emphasize the importance of esoteric teaching in their doctrines. This designation implies extremism in the mouths of the opponents of the Bāṭinīyah. The name derives from the word bāṭin (q.v.).

Bismillah al-Rahman, al-Rahim (*Bismillāh al-Raḥmān, al-Raḥīm*). In the Name of God, the Compassionate, the Merciful. This formula occurs at the beginning of each chapter of the *Qur'ān* except one and is repeated for devotional purposes at many points in the Muslim's life.

Bourgiba (*Ḥabīb Bourgiba*). The president of the Republic of Tunisia. Prior to the independence of Tunisia he was a nationalist leader and head of the Destour Party. President Bourgiba was born in 1903.

Al-Bukhari (*Muḥammad ibn Ismā'īl al-Bukhārī*). Famous Arab traditionist whose ḥadīth collection is the most respected of the Six Sound Books. He lived between A.D. 810 and 880.

Caliphs. Khalīfahs (q.v.).

Dahr. Time; in the poetry of the pre-Islamic Arabs, considered to be the most powerful of the forces affecting human destiny.

Da'if (*ḍa'īf*). Weak. In the classification of traditions, this word refers to those which are least acceptable. In general it designates any tradition having a serious defect in the isnād.

Dar'iyah. A town in Arabia which was the headquarters of the Wahhābī Empire in the first phase of its existence. The town was captured by the Egyptians in 1818, and the Wahhābī power went into temporary eclipse.

Darwishes (*darwīsh*, pl. *darāwīsh*). A member of a Ṣūfī order, a Ṣūfī adept. The word is sometimes used in special reference to wandering Ṣūfī mendicants.

Dhikr. Lit "remembrance," the Ṣūfī ceremony of worship, of a different nature in each order. The principal element in such worship is the repetition of the name of God.

Druze (*Durūz*). A religious sect holding Ismā'īlī doctrines now to be found in the mountains of Lebanon and Israel. The group had its origin in religious controversies dating to the time of the Fāṭimīyah in Egypt.

Fana' (*fanā'*). Lit. "extinction," the Ṣūfī expression for the loss of personality and identity in the mystic's union with God.

Faqih (*faqīh*, pl. *fuqahā'*). An Islamic lawyer or one learned in the science of jurisprudence (fiqh).

Fard (*farḍ*). Under Islamic law that which is strictly obligatory, a religious duty whose performance is rewarded and whose neglect is punished. This is one of the five categories into which Islamic law divides all actions.

Fatimi (*Fāṭimī*). An adjectival form referring to the Fāṭimīyah, a North African Ismā'īlī dynasty with its capital in Cairo. The dynasty flourished between A.D. 909 and 1171; the period of its reign was one of the most brilliant in the history of Egypt.

Fatwa (*fatwā*, pl. *fatāwā*). The opinion of a juriconsult (Muftī) in response to a legal question (istiftā') referred to him. Such opinions do not constitute precedents, and the questions may be put by anyone whether part of the judicial system and the state machinery or not.

fiqh. Lit. "understanding." (1) In its oldest Islamic usage a word for theology. It is no longer used in this way. (2) Jurisprudence, the science of finding specific rules of law from the sources. This is the precise use of the word. (3) The body of law, written in books, resulting from the application of jurisprudential science. This is an imprecise and loose use of the word but a common one.

Fuqaha'. Pl. of faqīh (q.v.).

Ibn Furak (*ibn Fūrak*). Muslim theologian and author of a book entitled *Bayān Mushkil al-Aḥādīth,* which discusses problems in the ḥadīth, especially the problem of conflicting aḥādīth.

Futuwah (*futūwah*). (1) Fraternal corporations common in medieval Islām. The members of these corporations normally followed the same trade and lived together a communal existence. (2) The virtues of chivalry. The cultivation of these virtues played an important role in the Islamic guild organizations and in Ṣūfism.

Al-Ghazali (*al-Ghazālī;* sometimes *al-Ghazzālī*). An important Muslim philosopher, mystic, theologian, and jurist who died in 1111.

Ghulat (*ghulāt*). Lit. "extremists," an epithet applied to certain radical Shī'ah groups who believe that the imām is an incarnation of deity or in similar doctrines.

Hadith (*ḥadīth*, pl. *āḥādīth*). Something related or told, an oral report, something said; therefore, oral tradition. In religion ḥadīth refers especially to the reports of the sayings, actions, and approbations of the Prophet Muḥammad handed down from the earliest generations.

Hadramawt (*Ḥaḍramawt*). The southernmost section of the Arabian peninsula which borders the Indian Ocean.

Hafiz (*Ḥāfiẓ*). One who memorizes the text of the *Qur'ān.*

Hajj (*ḥajj*). The pilgrimage to Makkah.

Halal (*ḥalāl*). Lit. "untied" or "unbound," i.e., permissible. In Islamic law actions are broadly classified as either forbidden (ḥarām) or as permissible (ḥalāl).

Al-Hallaj (*al-Ḥallāj*). An important mystic, best remembered for the extremeness of his ecstatic utterances. He was executed in a particularly horrible way in Baghdād in A.D. 922 with the assent of some of the leading mystics of the day. In consequence he has become the great martyr of the Ṣūfī tradition. He is often referred to in mystical literature by the name Manṣūr. al-Ḥallāj lived between 858 and 922.

Hanbali madhhab (*Ḥanbalī madhhab*). The school of law founded by the famous traditionist, Aḥmad ibn Ḥanbal.

Hanafi (*Ḥanafī*). An adjectival form referring to the legal school founded by the Irāqī jurist, Abū Ḥanīfah.

Hanifs (*Ḥanīf,* pl. *Ḥunafā'*). A member of a group of religious seekers contemporary with Muḥammad. The Ḥunafā' appear to have been monotheists.

Haqa'iq (*ḥaqīqah,* pl. *ḥaqā'iq*). Lit. "realities." (1) Among Ṣūfīs a term for the attributes of God which are to be distinguished from his essence (dhāt or ḥaqq). (2) Among the Ismā'īlīs a term for the spiritual truths of their philosophical and religious system.

Haqq (*ḥaqq*). Lit. "truth" or "reality." This word is used as a designation of God or ultimate reality, especially by the Ṣūfīs.

Haram (*ḥarām*). Forbidden, one of the five categories into which all human actions are classified in Islamic law. Acts that are ḥarām are absolutely forbidden under pain of punishment.

Hasan (*Ḥasan*). The eldest son of 'Alī ibn Abī Ṭālib by Fāṭimah, the daughter of Muḥammad. He was, therefore, the elder brother of Imām Ḥusayn, the martyr of Karbalā'.

Hasan (*ḥasan*). Good or beautiful. In the classification of traditions from the prophet, this word refers to those of the middle category which are acceptable but not perfectly sound.

Al-Hasan al-Basri (*al-Ḥasan al-Baṣrī*). An important early Muslim ascetic, mystic, and theologian. His name is associated with the origins of taṣawwuf and with the sects known as the Qadarīyah and the Mu'tazilah. He lived between A.D. 642 and 728, largely in Baṣrah, where he was perhaps the best known religious figure of his day.

Hijrah. Flight, the name given to Muḥammad's emigration from Makkah to Madīnah. The Islamic calendar begins from this event.

Hubal. A pre-Islamic deity who was the principal god of the Ka'bah in Makkah before Muḥammad's conquest of the city.

Hud (*Hūd*). A pre-Islamic prophet mentioned in the *Qur'ān.*

Hudan. Guidance, one of the most important words in the Islamic religious vocabulary. The revelations in the *Qur'ān* claim themselves to be hudan for the God-fearing. See Sūrah II.1.

Al-Hujwiri (*Abū al-Ḥasan 'Alī al-Hujwīrī*). An Iranian mystic who wrote one of the earliest and most important descriptive works on Ṣūfism, *Kashf al-Maḥjūb* (*The Uncovering of That Which is Veiled*). He lived the latter part of his life in Lahore, where he is buried. He died sometime between 1072 and 1079.

Hunayn (*Ḥunayn*). A place near Makkah to the south where Muḥammad fought the greatest and most dangerous battle of his career against the Banī Hawāzin.

Husayn (*Ḥusayn*). The younger son of ʻAlī ibn Abī Ṭālib by Fāṭimah, the daughter of Muḥammad. When his elder brother renounced claims to the leadership of the community, Ḥusayn took up the cause. He was martyred with his family at Karbalāʼ by Ummawī troops.

ʻIbadat (*ʻibādāt*). Those religious duties which man owes to God, such as fasting and pilgrimage.

Ibrahim Pasha (*Ibrahīm Bāshā*). The son of Muḥammad ʻAlī Bāshā. Ibrahīm commanded the 1818 Egyptian military expedition to put down the Wahhābīs.

ʻId al-Adha (*ʻĪd al-Aḍḥā*). The festival of sacrifice, part of the concluding ceremonies in the rites of the pilgrimage. Pilgrims make their sacrifice at Minā while Muslims who have not made the pilgrimage sacrifice in their respective places. The sacrifice is made in commemoration of Ibrahīm's (Abraham's) willingness to offer his son.

ʻId al-Fitr (*ʻĪd al-Fiṭr*). The festival of the breaking of the fast which is celebrated on the first day of the month following Ramaḍān. The festival is an obligatory religious duty, just as the fast which precedes it is also obligatory.

Ihya' ʻUlum al-Din (*Iḥyāʼ ʻUlūm al-Dīn*). The Revivification of the Religious Sciences, the most important of the many writings of Abū Ḥāmid al-Ghazālī. The book is encyclopedic in scope and is notable especially for its attempt to weave Ṣūfī ideas and Sunnī doctrine into an integrated whole.

Ijma' (*ijmāʼ*). Consensus or agreement. In the science of jurisprudence ijmāʼ ranks as one of the roots of the law subordinate in importance to the Qurʼān and the sunnah.

Ijtihad (ijtihād). Exertion or effort, a legal term signifying personal intellectual endeavor toward the solution of a legal problem. The effort meant is that directed to the interpretation of the sources of the law and not free speculation.

Imam (*imām*, pl. *āʼimmah*). Leader. (1) The leader in prayer. (2) The khalīfah or head of the community. (3) A title given to learned and respected men such as the founders of the schools of law and certain theologians. (4) Among the Shīʻah the word refers to the group of descendants of ʻAlī through whom the spark of divine wisdom has been transmitted from father to son.

Imamah (*imāmah*). Lit. "leadership." Each of the major Islamic groups and sects has held a view of how and from what group the leader of the community should be chosen. Sunnī Muslims believe that the imām (leader) must be chosen from Quraysh while Shīʻah believe that he must be from the ahl al-bayt. The doctrine of imāmah acquired a special religious coloring among the Shīʻah, who believe the series of imāms to have been chosen by God and each of them to have been the locus of a divine spark of wisdom passed down through the chain of ʻAlī's descendants.

Imam Husayn ibn ʻAli (*Imām Ḥusayn ibn ʻAli*). The younger son of ʻAlī ibn Abī Ṭālib by Fāṭimah, the daughter of Muḥammad. It is he who was martyred by Ummawī troops at Karbalāʼ. He is given the title Imām as one in the series of persons in ʻAlī's line in whom the spark of divine wisdom has come to reside.

Imam Mahdi (*Imām Mahdī*). (1) Among the Shīʻah the title given to the hidden Imām whose return is expected. The Imām Mahdī will restore true religion as one of the events of the last days. (2) Among Sunnī Muslims the one who is expected as the restorer of religion in the last days is sometimes called the Mahdī, though not always. The belief in the Mahdī is not essential for Sunnī Muslims as it is for the Shīʻah.

Iman (*īmān*). Most often translated "faith," the word refers to the inner attitude of religious commitment and to the resulting certainty of heart.

Injil (*Injīl*). An Arabic transcription of the Greek word Gospel. The Islamic name for the Scripture that, according to Muslim belief, was revealed to Jesus.

Iqra (*Iqraʼ*). Read! or Recite! The angel's command to Muḥammad at the time of first revelation.

ʻIraqi (*ʻIrāqī*). Referring to the geographical region known as ʻIrāq.

Islam (*Islām*). (1) The name that Muslims give to their religious commitment as a whole. (2) In theology, the word means works as opposed to faith (īmān).

Isma'ili (*Ismāʻīlī*). An adjectival form referring to the Ismāʻīlīyah, one of the subgroups of Shīʻī Islām. They are in turn divided into several other subsects. They are famous for their belief that exoteric doctrine always has an esoteric counterpart (bāṭin).

Isnad (*isnād*). Lit. "foundation" or "support," the list of names of the transmitters of an ḥadīth which constitutes its authority.

Ithna ʻAshariyah (*Ithnā ʻAsharīyah*). Lit. "twelvers," the largest of the subgroups of Shīʻī Muslims, those who accept a series of twelve imāms.

Jabariyah (*Jabarīyah*). An early Islamic sect who believed that all things happen as the result of the direct exercise of the divine compulsive power (Jabr). They were, in other words, determinists.

Jalal al-Din al-Rumi (*Jalāl al-Dīn al-Rūmī*. Mystical poet and founder of the Mawlawīyah order, or the order of the Whirling Dervishes. He has been called the greatest of the Persian poets for the beauty of his numerous verses. Born in Balkh in Khūrasān, he lived most of his life in Konyā in Anatolia. His dates were A.D. 1207–1273.

Jamal al-Din al-Afghani (*Jamāl al-Dīn al-Afghā-*

nī). Muslim politician, agitator and reformer of the nineteenth century. Al-Afghānī played an important role in the contemporary Islamic renaissance. His name indicates that he was of Afghān origin, but the matter is disputed. His dates were 1839–1897.

Al-Jubba'i (*al-Jubbā'ī*). An early theologian of the Mu'tazilī school, the teacher of al-Ash'arī, against whom the latter revolted. He lived between A.H. 235 and 303.

Al-Juwayni (*al-Juwaynī*). A renowned Muslim jurist and theologian, most often known by the title, Imām al-Ḥaramayn (Imām of the Two Holy Places). He was born in A.D. 1028 and died in 1085.

Ka'bah (*Ka'bah*). The cubical stone building in the center of the sacred area of Makkah, called by Muslims the House of God. In pre-Islamic times the Ka'bah was a pagan shrine until Muḥammad cleansed it.

Kaba'ir (*kabā'ir*). Lit. "large ones." In Islamic theology the word refers to great sins whose consequences are the severance of the sinner's membership in the community.

Al-Kafi (*al-Kāfī*). The most important and respected book of traditions among the Shī'ah. Compiled by al-Kulaynī (d. A.D. 939), it is one of the "four books" that constitute the Shī'ī canon of ḥadīth literature.

Kalam (*Kalām*). Speech or word. Both the *Qur'ān* and Jesus are referred to as Kalām Allāh, the Word of God. In the expression 'ilm al-kalām, the science of discussion, the word refers to the activity of producing reasoned arguments for the elucidation and support of religious doctrines. In this sense it can best be translated as "theology." Whenever the word appears alone, it can normally be understood in the sense of "theology." Kalām may also often be translated as "dialectic."

Kalam Allah (*Kalām Allāh*). Lit. "the Word of God." Both the *Qur'ān* and Jesus are so designated.

Karamat (*karamāt*). The miracles of the Ṣūfī saints.

Karbala' (*Karbalā'*). A place in southwestern 'Irāq where Ḥusayn, the younger son of 'Alī ibn Abī Ṭālib and Fāṭimah, the daughter of Muḥammad, was martyred on the tenth day of the month of Muḥarram in A.H. 61 by Ummawī troops. The city is now a place of pilgrimage for Shī'ī Muslims.

Kasb. Lit. "acquisition," the doctrine taught by al-Ash'arī with regard to the problem of man's responsibility for his acts. Al-Ash'arī taught that all acts are performed by God's immediate initiative but once performed man acquires (kasb) them. Thus, men are responsible for their acts, and it is in accord with the justice of God that they should be punished or rewarded for what they do.

Kashf al-Mahjub (*Kashf al-Maḥjūb*). A treatise on Sufism by Al-Hujwiri (q.v.).

Khadijah (*Khadījah*). The widow whom Muḥammad married as his first wife.

Khalifahs (*Khalīfah,* pl. *Khulafā'*). Successor, the title of the men who succeeded Muḥammad in the rule of the Islamic community. The word is also used for the favorite disciple of a Ṣūfī shaykh, the one who will succeed to the shaykh's spiritual authority as head of the order upon the shaykh's death.

Khanqah (*khānqāh*). The Persian term for the headquarters of a Ṣūfī order. In Turkey and North Africa the corresponding terms are tekke and zāwiyah, respectively.

Khawarij (pl. *Khawārij*). Lit. "those who go out," an early Islamic sect with strict puritanical views. The Khawārij believed that the leadership of the community must be determined by the principle of unrestricted election, and the more extreme among them believed the commission of sin to be equivalent to apostasy.

Khutbah (*khuṭbah*). The address or sermon following Friday prayers in the mosque.

Kitab al-Muwatta' (*Kitāb al-Muwaṭṭa'*). The earliest surviving book of Islamic law, written by the Madīnah jurist, Mālik ibn Anas, who was the founder of one of the four accepted Sunnī schools of law. The book deals with matters of law and religion according to the practice of the people of Madīnah.

Al-Kulayni (*Muhammad ibn Ya'kūb al-Rāzī al-Kulaynī*). A highly respected Shī'ī scholar considered by many to be the renewer (mujaddid) of the fourth Islamic century. He was the compiler of the collection of traditions known as al-Kāfī (The Sufficient One).

Al-Lat (*al-Lāt*). A pagan goddess of pre-Islamic Arabia.

Madhhab (*madhhab,* pl. *madhāhib*). The generic term for the accepted Sunnī schools of law. Literally the word means "way," but it is usually translated as "school."

Madinah (*Madīnat-al-Nabī*). The City of the Prophet; the name given by Muslims to the oasis settlement on the Red Sea coastal plain of Arabia to which Muḥammad and his followers emigrated from Makkah. It was known as Yathrib prior to the emigration.

Makkah. The city on the Red Sea coastal plain of Arabia where the Prophet, Muḥammad was born and where Islām had its rise.

Makruh (*makrūh*). Lit. "hated, disapproved"; in Islamic law one of the five categories into which all human actions are classified. This category includes acts which should be avoided, though they are not subject to punishment.

Malik ibn Anas (*Mālik ibn Anas*). A famous traditionist and jurist of Madīnah and founder of one of the four accepted Sunnī schools of law. He lived between approximately 722 and 795 A.D.

Maliki (*Mālikī*). An adjectival form referring to

the legal school founded by Mālik ibn Anas, the Madīnah jurist.

Al-Manat (*al-Manāt*). A pagan goddess of pre-Islamic Arabia.

Al-Manar (*al-Manār*). An Egyptian journal published by Muhammad Rashīd Riḍā from 1897. This publication was the principal vehicle for the spread of the teachings of Muhammad 'Abduh. The name means "the minaret."

Mandub (*mandūb*). Recommended or approved, an action which is not strictly obligatory but which is worthy. This is one of the five categories into which Islamic law classifies human actions.

Maqamat (*maqamāt*). The stages or stations on the mystic path to unity with God.

Marwah (*al-Marwah*). A small hill or eminence of ground in Makkah which plays a role in the rites of the pilgrimage. Pilgrims run back and forth seven times between al-Marwah and al-Ṣafā, a second hill, to commemorate Hājar's (Haggar's) search for water for her thirsty son. Formerly the hill was the site of a pagan shrine.

Mashhad, sometimes **Meshed.** A city in Khurāsān, now included in the northeastern portion of modern Iran, and the capital of the Persian province of Khurāsān. In the year A.D. 818 'Alī al-Riḍā, the eighth imām of the Ithnā 'Asharīyah, died and was buried in this place. An enormous and impressively beautiful shrine has been erected about his grave, and it is the most revered place of pilgrimage for the Shī'ah of Iran.

Matn. The text or content of an hadīth or oral report about the Prophet. The matn is distinguished from the isnād, or list of supporting authorities.

Mawlawiyah (*Mawlawīyah*). The Ṣūfī order founded by Jalāl al-Dīn al-Rūmī with its headquarters at Konyā in Turkey. Members of the order are distinguished by a peculiar costume and a whirling dance to the accompaniment of music. The name derives from the title given to the founder Mawlānā (Our Master). The Turkish form of the word is Mevlevi.

Mihrab (*miḥrāb*). The niche in the wall of a mosque that indicates the direction of Makkah.

Mina (*Minā*). A town in a narrow valley east of Makkah where the concluding rites of the pilgrimage are performed. These include sacrificing an animal, throwing stones at three small pillars set at intervals in the main street of the town, and clipping the pilgrim's hair and nails.

Mount Hira' (Mount Hīrā'). A hill on the outskirts of Makkah where Muhammad retired for meditation and nocturnal vigils, also the site of the first revelation to Muhammad.

Mu'adhdhin. The one who calls to prayer, usually from the minaret of the mosque. This word is most often imprecisely transliterated as muezzin and is familiar in that form.

Mu'amalat (*mu'āmalāt*). The religious obligations which a man has toward other men.

Mu'awiyah (*Mu'āwiyah*). The first Ummawī khalīfah and the founder of the Ummawī dynasty.

mubah (mubāḥ). Permissible or allowed, in Islamic law one of the five categories into which all human actions are classified. This category includes a wide range of acts that are morally neutral.

Muhaddithun (*muḥaddithūn*). Persons learned in the science of hadīth, as the traditions of the Prophet are called.

Muhajirin (*muhājirīn*). Lit. "emigrants," the title by which are called the Makkan followers of Muhammad who emigrated with him to Madīnah.

Muhammad (*Muhammad ibn 'Abdullāh*). The prophet of Islam. Muhammad means "the praised one."

Muhammad Abduh (*Muhammad 'Abduh*). A modern Egyptian reformer, theologian, and jurist of enormous influence. 'Abduh may be considered the founder of Islamic modernism in the Arab world. He was an associate and disciple of Jamāl al-Dīn al Afghānī and held important posts in Egypt that allowed him to effect major reforms in education. The main thrust of his teaching was toward a purified Islam that would be in accord with reason and science. He was born in 1849 and died in 1905.

Muhammad Ali Jinnah (*Muhammad 'Alī Jinnāh*). A Muslim political leader in undivided India who lead the movement for Pākistān. After the partition of India and the creation of Pākistān, he became the first Governor General of Pākistān. His dates were 1876–1948.

Muhammad 'Ali Pasha (*Muhammad 'Alī Bāshā*). An Albanian Muslim who, as Khedive of Egypt under Turkish suzerainty, initiated in the first decades of the nineteenth century a series of educational, economic, and military reforms of far-reaching consequences. He lived between 1769 and 1849.

Muhammad ibn 'Abd al-Wahhab (*Muhammad ibn 'Abd al-Wahhāb*). An eighteenth century Islamic reformer who led a movement to restore and purify Islam. His principal concern was to purge Islām of all innovations (bid'āt), especially those introduced by the Ṣūfīs, such as the reverence for saints. The school of his followers is called Wahhābīyah, and the sect is prevalent today in Sa'ūdī Arabia where it has connection with the ruling house. His dates are 1703–1787.

Muhammad Ghori (*Muhammed Ghōrī*). The ruler of a kingdom in what is now Western Afghanistan. In the middle of the twelfth century this man conquered North India and founded the Sultanate of Delhi.

Muhammad Rashid Rida (*Muhammad Rashīd*

Riḍā). A Syrian disciple of Muḥammad 'Abduh and the publisher of the journal *Al-Manār*. Riḍā was largely responsible for the widespread dissemination of 'Abduh's ideas and for the interpretation of them that led to the Salafīyah movement.

Muharram (*Muḥarram*). The name of one of the months in the Islamic lunar calendar. It is of religious importance because the Shī'ah celebrate the passion and martyrdom of Imām Ḥusayn during the early part of the month, culminating on the tenth day, the anniversary of his tragic death.

Muhiy al-Din ibn al-'Arabi (*Muḥīy al-Dīn ibn al-'Arabī*). An Andalusian mystic whose teachings of pantheism have wielded an enormous influence on the history of later Sufism. He lived between A.D. 1165 and 1240, the first part of his life in Spain and the latter in the Eastern Islamic regions.

Mu'in al-Din Chishti (*Mu'īn al-Dīn Chishtī*). A famous mystic saint of the Chishti order who was a contemporary of the Emperor Akbar and through whose intercession a son was born to the Emperor. The Chishti order is among the most important in India where it is widely spread.

Mujahidin (*Mujāhidīn*). Lit. those who strive or make jihād, the holy war in the cause of Islām; a title adopted by the members of an Islamic revivalist movement in the Frontier region of India in the early nineteenth century.

Muqallad. One who accepts the opinions of a founder of one of the four accepted Sunnī schools of law as absolutely authoritative, or one who acts in obedience to blind authority in legal matters.

Murids (*murīd*, pl. *murīdūn*). Lit. "desirer," the Ṣūfī neophyte, seeker, or student who attaches himself to a shaykh in order to gain instruction and guidance in the Ṣūfī path (*ṭarīqah*).

Murji'ah. An early Islamic sect who held the position that commission of sin does not place one outside the community; rather, the decision is left to God.

Murshid. Lit. "guide," the title given to a Ṣūfī master, teacher, or shaykh by his disciples.

Muslim ibn al-Hajjaj (*Muslim ibn al-Ḥajjāj*). A famous collector of traditions from the Prophet. His ḥadīth collection along with that of al-Bukhārī are the two most respected of the Six Sound Books.

Mutasawwif (*mutaṣawwif*). A Muslim mystic or Ṣūfī, one who is an adept in taṣawwuf.

Mu'tazilah (*Mu'tazilah*). The name of the great theological school, also called the People of Unity and Justice, who were the true founders of Muslim dialectical theology. The school originated in Ummawī times and for some period enjoyed the patronage of the 'Abbāsī rulers before it disappeared.

Najaf (al-Najaf). A town in southwestern 'Irāq near Kūfah that is believed to be the burial place of 'Alī ibn Abī Ṭālib. It is, in consequence, a place of sanctity and pilgrimage for Shī'ī Muslims.

Najd. The high central plateau of the Arabian peninsula.

Al-Nazzam (*al-Naẓẓām*). An early Islamic thinker of the Mu'tazilī school. He was a poet and dialectician but above all a theologian. He died between A.D. 735 and 745 at an unknown date.

Nihavand (*Nihāvand*). A place near modern Hamadān in Iran where the Arab Muslim armies won a decisive victory over the Sassanians. The Battle of Nihāvand brought the Iranian plateau under Muslim control.

Nusayris (*Nuṣayrī*). An extreme Shī'ī sect of Syria.

Pir (*pīr*). The title given to a Ṣūfī master or shaykh, especially in the Indian subcontinent.

Qadariyah (*Qadarīyah*). (1) The name of an early Muslim sect which upheld the doctrine of free-will believing that man has the power (qadar) to control his own actions. (2) The name of a mystic order (ṭarīqah) founded by the saint 'Abd al-Qādir al-Jīlānī.

Qadi (al-qāḍī). The judge in one type of Islamic court.

Qiblah. The direction which the Muslim faces for prayer, i.e., the direction of Makkah.

Qiyas (*qiyās*). Analogy. In jurisprudence qiyās is considered one of the roots of the law, though it is subordinate to all of the remaining three.

Qum. A city in central Iran where is located the tomb and shrine of Fāṭimah al-Ma'ṣūmah, the sister of Imām 'Alī al-Riḍā, the eighth imām of the Ithnā 'Asharīyah. After Mashhad, it is the second most important place of pilgrimage for the Shī'ah of Iran.

Qur'an (*Qur'ān*). The Islamic Scripture.

Quraysh. The tribe into which Muḥammad was born.

Qusayy (*Quṣayy*). An ancestor of Muḥammad who was responsible for the Quraysh gaining possession of Makkah.

Qutb (*Quṭb*). The Pole or Axis, the great mystic saint who stands at the apex of the heirarchy of Ṣūfī saints that is always present in the world.

Rabi'ah al-'Adawiyah (*Rābi'ah al-'Adawīyah*). An early woman mystic of Baṣrah who was famous for her ascetic life and her teachings on mystic love. She lived between A.D. 714 and 801, chiefly in Baṣrah.

Rahbar. Leader, a title given to a Ṣūfī teacher, master, or saint.

Ramadan (*Ramaḍān*). The month of the Islamic lunar calendar in which fasting is obligatory during daylight hours.

Risalat al-Tawhid (*Risālat al-Tawḥīd*). *Treatise*

on the Unity of God, the title of the principal work on theology of Muḥammad 'Abduh.

Riyadh (*Riyāḍ*). A city in east central Arabia, the capital of the Kingdom of Sa'ūdī Arabia.

Saf (*ṣāf*). Pure, one of the words which scholars have cited as the possible origin of the term, Ṣūfī. Were this etymology accepted, which by and large it is not, then the word Ṣūfī would mean "seeker after purity."

Safa (*al-Ṣafā*). A small hill or eminence of ground in Makkah which plays a role in the rites of the pilgrimage. Pilgrims run back and forth seven times between al-Ṣafā and al-Marwah, a second hill, to commemorate Hājar's (Haggar's) search for water for her thirsty son. Formerly the hill was the site of a pagan shrine.

Safawi (*Safawī*). An adjectival form referring to the Persian dynasty of the sixteenth and seventeenth centuries. Under this dynasty Iran enjoyed one of the most brilliant periods of its cultural expression, especially under the greatest of Safawī rulers, Shāh 'Abbās.

Sagha'ir (*saghā'ir*). Lit. "little ones." In theology the word refers to minor sins that may be forgiven and which do not affect one's membership in the community.

Sahih (*ṣaḥīḥ*). Sound, healthy, right. In the classification of traditions from the Prophet the category "ṣaḥīḥ" designates the strongest and most reliable traditions. For this reason the word is applied to the six most respected collections of traditions known as the Six Sound Books. Ṣaḥīḥ is also frequently used as the title of each of the two collections of ḥadith by Muslim and al-Bukhārī. Together they are called by the dual form, Ṣaḥīḥayn.

Salat (*ṣalāt*). The ritual prayer which each believing Muslim is obligated to perform five times daily.

Salih (*Ṣāliḥ*). One of the pre-Islamic prophets mentioned in the Qur'ān.

Saljuq Turks (*Saljūq Turks*). A people of Central Asian origin who entered the 'Abbasī territories in the eleventh century and rapidly rose to become the ruling group in the 'Abbasī empire.

Sanusiyah (*Sanūsīyah*). One of the most important mystic orders of North Africa founded by Sīdī Muḥammad ibn 'Alī al-Sanūsī (born A.D. 1791). This widespread order was the spearhead of resistance to Italian imperialism in North Africa in the first part of the twentieth century.

Sawm (*ṣawm*). Fasting.

Sayyid Ahmad Khan (*Sayyid Aḥmad Khān*). An Indian Muslim thinker and leader of the nineteenth century. He was the founder of the college at 'Alīgarh in the United Provinces which later became the 'Alīgarh Muslim University. He was born in 1817 and died in 1898.

Sayyid Amir 'Ali (*Sayyid Amīr 'Alī*). Indian Muslim modernist and polemicist of the late nine-teenth and twentieth centuries. He was a member of the Ismā'īlī community and a judge in the Indian High Court. His book, *The Spirit of Islam,* is perhaps the most widely read of all Islamic modernist writings. He lived between 1849 and 1928.

Sayyid Jamal al-Din al-Afghani (*Sayyid Jamāl al-Dīn al-Afghānī*). A nineteenth century Muslim pamphleteer and politician who led a vigorous movement against European imperial domination of the Islamic world. He traveled widely, attracted many disciples, and had a part in important political events in several different Islamic countries. He was born in 1839 and died in 1897.

Shafi'i (*Shāfi'ī*). An adjectival form referring to the legal school founded by the jurist, al-Shā-fi'ī.

Al-Shafi'i (*Abū 'Abdullāh Muḥammad ibn Idrīs al-Shāfi'ī*). The famous jurist who was the founder of the Shāfi'ī school of law, one of the four accepted Sunnī schools. It is he who formulated and promulgated the theory of the four uṣūl al-fiqh. He lived between A.D. 767 and 820.

Shahadah (*shahādah*). Witness; the short testimony of faith that reads, "There is no God but the one God, and Muḥammad is His Prophet."

Shah 'Abd al-'Aziz (*Shāh 'Abd al-'Azīz*). One of the sons of Shāh Walīy Ullāh Dihlawī who promulgated the teachings of his father to others after him. He played a key role in the early nineteenth century in the development of Muslim consciousness, especially through his famous decision declaring India to be Dār al-Ḥarb, the Abode of War.

Shah Wali Ullah (*Shāh Walīy Ullāh*). Called the traditionist (muḥaddith) of Delhi (Dihlawī), an eighteenth century Indian Muslim reformer who led a movement for the restoration of Islam and the recouping of Muslim political fortunes in India during the time of decline of the Mughul Empire. His dates were A.D. 1703–1762/3.

Shari'ah (*sharī'ah*). Lit. "pathway," the normative pathway in which God wills that men should walk; therefore, a general name for the Islamic law.

Shaykh. Lit. "elder." (1) The title given to the man recognized as the leader of an Arab tribe. (2) A title of respect bestowed upon any learned or accomplished man. (3) A title given to a Ṣūfī master, teacher, or saint.

Shi'ah (*Shī'ah*). Lit. "party," one the major groups into which the Muslim community is divided. The original Shī'ah were distinguished by their view that leadership of the community after Muḥammad belonged by right to 'Alī. In later times the Shī'ah developed a distinctive religious point of view in which the principal element is the doctrine of the imamate.

Shirk. Polytheism, or the act of associating partners with God. Shirk is the most heinous sin in the Islamic catalogue.

Sifat (*ṣifah*, pl. *ṣifāt*). Qualities or attributes; in theology, the attributes of God.

Silsilah. Lit. "chain." (1) The chain of authorities making up the isnād of an ḥadīth. (2) The chain of spiritual authorities through whom the esoteric teaching of a Ṣūfī order has been transmitted.

Subhan Allāh (*subḥān Allāh*). "Praise be to God," an expression of adoration employed in Muslim worship and other times in Muslim life.

Sufi (*Ṣūfī*). A Muslim mystic. Originally the word referred to an ascetic practice of wearing rough robes of wool (ṣūf) but has come to be a designation of the Islamic mystical tradition altogether.

Sufism. The usual Western word for Islamic mysticism. Clearly, it is derived from Ṣūfī.

Sunnah. Established practice or custom; the recognized, accepted, and time-honored way of doing things. For all Muslims the word sunnah has a normative connotation, especially in matters of religion.

Sunni (*Sunnī*). A term applied to the majority group of Muslims, those who claim for themselves the title ahl al-sunnah wa al-jama-'at. It is sometimes translated orthodox, but this rendition is inaccurate. Sunnī is to be contrasted with Shī'ah.

Surah (*Sūrah*). A chapter in the *Qur'ān*.

Al-Tabari (*Abū Ja'far Muḥammad ibn Jarīr al-Ṭabarī*). Arab historian, jurist, and theologian. He is best known for two monumental works, his *History of Prophets and Kings* and his great commentary on the *Qur'ān*. He lived between A.D. 839 and 923.

Al-Taftazani (*Sa'd al-Dīn al-Taftāzānī*). An important Muslim thinker who lived between A.H. 722 and 791. Author of a well known commentary on the creed of al-Nasafi

Takhdhib (*takhdhīb*). Giving the lie to someone or accusing someone of being a liar. In the *Qur'ān* the act of giving the lie to God in the sense of considering His revealed words to be a lie is among the most reprehensible of sins.

Taqlid (*taqlīd*). Blind acceptance of authority; the doctrine that one must follow absolutely the teachings of one of the accepted four schools of law without resort to the roots of law and without exercising personal interpretation.

Tariqah (*tarīqah*). Lit. "pathway," the word used to designate one of the mystic orders or brotherhoods. The pathway is that leading to union with God, and it can be known only through the instruction given by a saint (walī) who has trod it.

Tasawwuf (*taṣawwuf*). Mysticism in its Islamic expression.

Tawhid (*tawḥīd*). Lit. "Unity," the doctrine of the unity of God which is the cardinal principle of Islamic theology.

Ta'ziyahs. (1) Popular dramatizations of the passion and martyrdom of the Shī'ī imāms. (2) Model buildings, often very elaborate, carried by Indian Shī'ī Muslims in processions on the tenth day of Muḥarram to symbolize the tomb of Imām Ḥusayn at Karbalā'. These models are destroyed at the conclusion of the procession and rebuilt the following year.

Tekke. The Turkish term for the headquarters of a Ṣūfī brotherhood. In North Africa and Iran the corresponding terms are zāwiyah and khānqāh, respectively.

Uhud (*Uḥud*). A hill on the outskirts of Madīnah where the Makkans won an indecisive victory over Muḥammad and his followers. The battle of Uḥud was potentially disastrous for Muḥammad, and though he was wounded, the Makkans did not follow up their advantage.

'Umar ibn al-Khattab (*'Umar ibn al-Khattāb*). A companion of Muḥammad, one of the first converts to Islām, and the second Khalīfah of the community. During the reign of 'Umar the first wave of the great conquests was carried out.

Ummah. Community or sometimes nation. The Islamic community is called an ummah in the *Qur'ān*, and the term is applied to other groups as well.

Ummawi (*Ummawī*). An adjectival form referring to the Banī Ummayah, a clan of Quraysh, from whom all the khalīfahs of the Ummawī dynasty were drawn.

Usul (*uṣūl*). Roots or principles. (1) The principles of any science or branch of learning. (2) In law, used in the phrase uṣūl al-fiqh, the reference is to the four roots or sources of the law.

Usul al-fiqh (*uṣūl al-fiqh*). The roots or sources of the law, a technical term in jurisprudence. The roots of the law are four: Qur'ān; sunnah; ijmā'; and qiyās.

'Uthman ibn 'Affan (*'Uthmān ibn 'Affān*). A companion of Muḥammad and third Khalīfah of the community. 'Uthmān was murdered by a group of dissidents.

Al-'Uzza (*al-'Uzzā*). A pagan goddess of pre-Islamic Arabia. She had a shrine not far from Makkah.

Wahhabi (*Wahhābī*). An adjectival form referring to the sect constituted by the followers of Muḥammad ibn 'Abd al-Wahhāb, the eighteenth century Arabian reformer; also, a member of that sect. The sect is noted for its puritanism and its zeal. The sect is now prevalent in Sa'ūdī Arabia because of its association with the ruling dynasty.

Walis (*Walī* pl. *awliyā'*). A mystic saint, one to whom the esoteric knowledge of the mystic path (ṭarīqah) is given and who possesses the power of miracles (karamāt) and of blessing (barakah). Muslims believe there to be a hierarchy of saints always living in the world and culminating in a principal saint called the Pole (Quṭb).

Waṣil ibn ʿAta (*Wāṣil ibn ʿAṭāʾ*). An early Muslim thinker, commonly said to be the originator of the Muʿtazilī school. He lived between A.D. 699 and 749.

Wuquf (*wuqūf*). Lit. "halt," the standing in the presence of God that is part of the pilgrimage. The wuqūf in the plain of ʿArafah is the heart of the pilgrimage, but there are other occasions of wuqūf in the pilgrimage, as well.

Yathrib. An oasis city on the Red Sea coastal plain of Arabia to which Muḥammad and his followers emigrated when their situation in Makkah became impossible. It was afterwards known as Madīnat al-Nabī, the City of the Prophet.

Zabur (*Zabūr*). The Islamic name for the Psalms of David.

Zakat (*zakāt*). The alms "in the way of God" which every believing Muslim is obligated to pay as part of his religious duty.

Zawiyah (*zāwiyah*). The name given at present in North Africa to the headquarters of a Ṣūfī brotherhood. In Turkey and Iran the corresponding terms are tekke and khānqāh, respectively.

Zayd ibn Thabit (*Zayd ibn Thābit*). One of the Prophet's secretaries who wrote down the revelations and, according to most accounts, was responsible for assembling the extant text of the *Qurʾān* in its present form.

Zaydi (*Zaydī*). An adjectival form referring to the Zaydīyah, one of the subgroups of Shīʿī Muslims. The sect recognizes Zayd, the son of Ḥasan, ʿAlī's oldest male offspring, as the carrier of the imāmah instead of Ḥusayn, ʿAlī's younger son. The sect is found today in Yemen and is noted for its adherence to Muʿtazilī views in theology.

Zuhada' (*zāhid*, pl. *zuhadāʾ*). Ascetics, practitioners of zuhd.

INDEX

71 72 73 7 6 5 4 3 2 1